Living Standards in the Past

Living Standards in the Past

New Perspectives on Well-Being in Asia and Europe

Edited by

ROBERT C. ALLEN
TOMMY BENGTSSON
and
MARTIN DRIBE

OXFORD
UNIVERSITY PRESS

OXFORD

UNIVERSITY PRESS

Great Clarendon Street, Oxford OX2 6DP

Oxford University Press is a department of the University of Oxford.
It furthers the University's objective of excellence in research, scholarship,
and education by publishing worldwide in

Oxford New York

Auckland Cape Town Dar es Salaam Hong Kong Karachi Kuala Lumpur
Madrid Melbourne Mexico City Nairobi New Delhi Shanghai Taipei
Toronto

With offices in

Argentina Austria Brazil Chile Czech Republic France Greece
Guatemala Hungary Italy Japan South Korea Poland Portugal
Singapore Switzerland Thailand Turkey Ukraine Vietnam

Oxford is a registered trade mark of Oxford University Press
in the UK and in certain other countries

Published in the United States
by Oxford University Press Inc., New York

British Library Cataloguing in Publication Data
Data available

Library of Congress Cataloging in Publication Data
Data available

ISBN 0–19–928068–1

1 3 5 7 9 10 8 6 4 2

Typeset by Newgen Imaging Systems (P) Ltd., Chennai, India
Printed in Great Britain
on acid-free paper by
Biddles Ltd., King's Lynn, Norfolk

Acknowledgements

This book brings together new evidence concerning living standards in pre-industrial Europe and Asia. Demographic events, health, stature, consumption, and wages are examined in terms of communities and individual households. Comparisons of living standards and well-being are made across social groups, countries, and continents. The diversity of experience within Europe and Asia is emphasized. The contributors include specialists in economics, history, and demography as well as Asian and European studies. The findings shed new light on the controversial question of when the West's lead in living standards over the rest of the world first emerged. This question has been the focus of a very lively debate involving scholars from economic history, history, and sociology. Some scholars in the tradition of Adam Smith and Robert Malthus argue that the gap in living standards was already large when industrialization started in the West, while others argue that standards of living were similar at that time, and thus, that the gap was a result of industrialization. It is only by providing new and more detailed evidence from many areas of human activity that the issue can be resolved, and this book is, we believe, an important step in this direction.

A workshop in Arild, Sweden, in August 2000, which brought together the necessary group of specialists, was organized within the activities of the European Science Foundation (ESF) network on 'Household and community dynamics: a Eurasian approach of mobility'. The European Science Foundation provided financial support for the workshop and the editors wish to express their gratitude to Dr John Smith, the ESF Scientific Secretary, for his interest and active support of the workshop. Thanks are also due to Mrs Geneviève Schauinger of ESF who helped the organizers with the administration of the workshop. The Bank of Sweden Tercentenary Foundation, the Crafoord Foundation, Lund, Sweden, the Research Programme in Economic Demography, Lund University, the Social Science and Humanities Research Council of Canada and its Team for Advanced Research on Globalization, Education, and Technology also gave generous financial support to the workshop and/or the volume, which we are grateful for.

Finally we would like to express our gratitude to B. A. Madeleine Jarl, Lund University, for her outstanding ability and patience in assisting us in editing this volume. Our sincere thanks also go to Cathy Douglas and Jessica Bean, who assisted us in editing several of the chapters.

Robert C. Allen, Tommy Bengtsson,
and Martin Dribe

Contents

List of Contributors   ix
List of Figures   xv
List of Maps   xviii
List of Tables   xix

Introduction   1
Robert C. Allen, Tommy Bengtsson, and Martin Dribe

1   Standards of Living in Eighteenth-Century China: Regional
    Differences, Temporal Trends, and Incomplete Evidence   23
    Kenneth Pomeranz

2   Farm Labour Productivity in Jiangnan, 1620–1850   55
    Bozhong Li

3   Wages, Inequality, and Pre-Industrial Growth
    in Japan, 1727–1894   77
    Osamu Saito

4   Agriculture, Labour, and the Standard of Living in
    Eighteenth-Century India   99
    Prasannan Parthasarathi

5   Real Wages in Europe and Asia: A First Look at the Long-Term
    Patterns   111
    Robert C. Allen

6   Sketching the Rise of Real Inequality in Early Modern Europe   131
    *Philip T. Hoffman, David S. Jacks, Patricia A. Levin,
    and Peter H. Lindert*

7   What Happened to the Standard of Living Before the
    Industrial Revolution? New Evidence from the Western
    Part of the Netherlands   173
    Jan Luiten van Zanden

8   Economic Growth, Human Capital Formation and Consumption in
    Western Europe Before 1800   195
    Jaime Reis

9   Health and Nutrition in the Pre-Industrial Era: Insights from
a Millennium of Average Heights in Northern Europe   227
Richard H. Steckel

10   The Burden of Grandeur: Physical and Economic Well-Being of
the Russian Population in the Eighteenth Century   255
Boris Mironov

11   Maternal Mortality as an Indicator of the Standard of Living
in Eighteenth- and Nineteenth-Century Slavonia   277
Eugene A. Hammel and Aaron Gullickson

12   The Standard of Living in Denmark in the Eighteenth
and Early Nineteenth Centuries   307
Hans Chr. Johansen

13   Short-term Demographic Changes in Relation to Economic
Fluctuations: The Case of Tuscany During the Pre-Transitional Period   319
Marco Breschi, Alessio Fornasin, and Giovanna Gonano

14   New Evidence on the Standard of Living in Sweden During the
Eighteenth and Nineteenth Centuries: Long-Term Development of
the Demographic Response to Short-Term Economic Stress   341
Tommy Bengtsson and Martin Dribe

15   Individuals and Communities Facing Economic Stress:
A Comparison of Two Rural Areas in Nineteenth-Century Belgium   373
Michel Oris, Muriel Neven, and George Alter

16   Living Standards in Liaoning, 1749–1909: Evidence from
Demographic Outcomes   403
James Z. Lee and Cameron D. Campbell

17   Demographic Responses to Short-Term Economic Stress in
Eighteenth- and Nineteenth-Century Rural Japan: Evidence from
Two Northeastern Villages   427
Noriko O. Tsuya and Satomi Kurosu

Index   461

List of Contributors

Robert C. Allen is Professor of Economic History at Oxford University and a Fellow of Nuffield College. He received his doctorate from Harvard University. He has written extensively on English agricultural history, international competition in the steel industry, the extinction of whales, the global history of wages and prices, and contemporary policies on education. His articles have won the Cole Prize, the Redlich Prize, and the Explorations Prize. His books include *Enclosure and the Yeoman: The Agricultural Development of the South Midlands, 1450–1850* (1992), which was awarded the Ranki Prize by the Economic History Association, and, most recently, *Farm to Factory: A Re-interpretation of the Soviet Industrial Revolution* (2003). Professor Allen is a Fellow of the British Academy and the Royal Society of Canada.

George Alter is Professor of History and Director of the Population Institute for Research and Training at Indiana University. In *Family and the Female Life Course* (1988) he applied event history methods to the demographic analysis of a historical population. 'Stature in Transition: A Micro-level Study from Nineteenth-century Belgium' (*Social Science History* 2004), co-authored with Neven and Oris, examines trends and differentials in height as an indicator of childhood experiences during the Industrial Revolution. Alter is co-editor of the second Eurasia Project volume, *Prudence and Pressure: Reproduction in Europe and Asia, 1700–1900* (in preparation).

Tommy Bengtsson is Professor of Demography and Economic History and Director of the Research Group in Economic Demography at Lund University. His historical studies include the analysis of demographic response to short-term economic stress as well as how conditions in early life influence social mobility, fertility, and longevity. His contemporary studies are on economic and social integration of the immigrant population in Sweden. Tommy Bengtsson is currently Chair of the IUSSP Committee on Historical Demography and Series co-editor of the MIT Press Eurasian Population and Family History Series. His latest books include *Life Under Pressure. Mortality and Living Standards in Europe and Asia, 1700–1900* (2004) (co-authored with C. Campbell and J. Z. Lee *et al.*), *Perspectives on Mortality Forecasting: Current Practices* (2003) (co-edited with Nico Keilman), and *Population and Economy. From Hunger to Modern Economic Growth.* (2000) (co-edited with O. Saito).

Marco Breschi is Professor of Demography at the University of Udine and the President of the Italian Society of Historical Demography. He has published widely on demographic history and on many related aspects of Italian populations.

Cameron D. Campbell is Associate Professor of Sociology, University of California at Los Angeles. He is the co-author with James Z. Lee of the book *Fate and Fortune in Rural China* (1997), and the co-author with Tommy Bengtsson, James Z. Lee, and other Eurasia project participants of the recently published *Life Under Pressure* (2004).

Martin Dribe is Associate Professor of Economic History at Lund University. He received his Ph.D. from Lund University in 2000 and has mainly been working on different aspects of the interaction between population and economy in preindustrial society, as well as on issues related to intergenerational land transmissions. His publications include the books *Leaving Home in a Peasant Society. Economic Fluctuations, Household Dynamics and Youth Migration in Southern Sweden, 1829–1866* (2000) and *Liv och rörelse. Familj och flyttningar i 1800-talets svenska bondesamhälle* (2003).

Alessio Fornasin is Research Fellow in Demography at the University of Udine and the Secretary of the Italian Society of Historical Demography. He has published extensively in the field of economic and demographic history, with a specific focus on Italian regional history.

Giovanna Gonano is Researcher of Applied Statistics at the University of Udine. She has focused her interest on the relationship between economy and demography in contemporary and historical societes.

Aaron Gullickson is Ph.D. in Sociology and Demography, University of California, Berkeley, and has a position as Assistant Professor of Sociology at Columbia University. He conducts research in historical demography, and on the biracial Black/White population in the United States. Recent publications include (with E. Hammel and A. Gullickson) 'Kinship Structures and Survival: Maternal Mortality on the Croatian-Bosnian Border 1750–1898', *Population Studies* (2004).

Eugene A. Hammel is Professor Emeritus of Demography and Anthropology at the University of California, Berkeley. He has done anthropological field work in Peru, Mexico, Serbia, Montenegro, Greece, California, and New Mexico, and is member of the National Academy of Sciences, and the American Academy of Arts and Sciences. Recent publications include (with E. Smith) *Population Dynamics and Political Stability* (2002); (with Mirjana Stevanovic) 'The Migration of Serbs and Albanians within and between Kosovo and Inner Serbia', in Brunet, Oris, and Bideau (eds.), *La demographie des minorites* (*The Demography of Minorities*) (2004); and (with A. Gullickson) 'Kinship Structures and Survival: Maternal Mortality on the Croatian–Bosnian Border 1750–1898' (2004). *Population Studies*.

Philip T. Hoffman is Richard and Barbara Rosenberg Professor of History and Social Science at the California Institute of Technology. He has worked on agricultural productivity, financial markets, and the political economy of institutions in Europe, and he is currently engaged in comparative studies of financial crises, military conquest, and long run growth. Recent publications include *Finance, Intermediaries, and Economic Development* (2003), co-edited with Stanley L. Engerman, Jean-Laurent Rosenthal, and Kenneth L. Sokoloff, and *Révolution et évolution: Les marchés du crédit notarié en France, 1780–1840*, Annales HSS 59 (March-April, 2004), co-authored with Gilles Postel-Vinay and Jean-Laurent Rosenthal.

David S. Jacks is currently an Assistant Professor of Economics at Simon Fraser University. His research focuses on global economic history in general and the process of market integration in particular. Works on the integration of commodity markets in early modern Northern Europe and in the nineteenth-century Atlantic economy are forthcoming in the *Journal of European Economic History* and *Explorations in Economic History*.

Hans Chr. Johansen is Professor of Economic and Social History at the University of Southern Denmark. Recent publications are 'Identifying People in the Danish Past', in *Pathways of the Past, Essays in Honour of Sølvi Sogner* (2002); 'Danish Coastal Shipping c.1750–1914', in *Coastal Shipping and the European Economy 1750–1980*, edited by John Armstrong and Andreas Kunz (2002); and *Danish Population History 1600–1939* (2002).

Satomi Kurosu is Associate Professor at Reitaku University in Chiba, Japan. She holds a Ph.D. in sociology from the University of Washington with a specialization in family studies. Her recent publications include: 'Who Leaves Home and Two Northeastern Villages 1716–1870', in F. van Poppel, M. Oris, and J. Z. Lee (eds.), *The Road to Independence: Leaving Home in Western and Eastern Societies: 16th–20th Centuries* (2004).

James Z. Lee is Professor of History and Sociology, Director of the Center for Chinese Studies, and Research Professor at the Population Studies Center and the Inter-University Consortium for Political and Social Research at the University of Michigan. Recent books include *Fate and Fortune in Rural China* (with Cameron Campbell) (1997), *One Quarter of Humanity* (with Wang Feng) (1999), and *Life Under Pressure* (with Tommy Bengtsson, Cameron Campbell *et al.*) (2004).

Patricia A. Levin has done postgraduate work in Economics and Mathematics at the University of California–Davis, and has a BA from Stanford University, a Masters Degree from the University of North Carolina, and is currently working as a Certificated Public Accountant.

Bozhong Li is Professor of History, as well as Chair of History Department and Director of the Center for Chinese Economy History Research at Tsinghua

University (Beijing, China). He is also a Visiting Professor at the University of Michigan (Ann Arbor, US). He has been working on imperial Chinese economic history for three decades and is the author of a body of work. Among his recent books are *Agricultural Development in Jiangnan, 1620–1850* (1998) and *Jiangnan de zaoqi gongyehua (The Early Industrialization in Jiangnan)* (2000).

Peter H. Lindert is Distinguished Professor of Economics at the University of California–Davis, where he also directs the Agricultural History Center. His books and journal articles have dealt with modern inequality trends, the welfare state, human fertility, international debt crisis, international trade competition, land quality, farm policy, soil history, and other topics. His latest book is *Growing Public: Social Spending and Economic Growth since the Eighteenth Century* (two volumes, 2004). He has served as the elected President of the Economic History Association.

Boris Mironov is Professor at St Petersburg State University and the Russian Academy of Sciences. Recent publications are *The Social History of Imperial Russia, 1700–1917* (two vols., 2000); 'New Approaches to Old Problems: The Well-Being of the Population of Russia from 1821 to 1910 as Measured by Physical Stature', *Slavic Review* (1999); and 'Russia: Modern Period', in *Oxford Encyclopedia of Economic History* (2003). He is currently preparing a book on the theme *Modernization and Well-Being of Russian Population in the Eighteenth through Twentieth Centuries: Anthropometric History.*

Muriel Neven is a Research Associate of the Belgian National Funds for Scientific Research attached to the University of Liège. In *Individus et familles: les dynamiques d'une société rurale. Le Pays de Herve dans la seconde moitié du XIXe siècle* (2003) she describes the challenges faced by rural families during the Industrial Revolution. She has also published in *The History of the Family* and *Continuity and Change*, and is currently working on the genetic, social, and economic dimensions of inheritance in nineteenth-century society, both in a vertical (intergenerational transfers) and horizontal (sibling effects) perspective.

Michel Oris is Professor of Economic History at the University of Geneva. His research is concerned with the economic and demographic history of industrialization in Eastern Belgium and the Canton of Geneva. He is co-editor of two recently published collections *When Dad Died. Individuals and Families Coping with Distress in Past Societies* (2002) and *The Road to Independence. Leaving Home in Western and Eastern Societies, 16th–20th Centuries* (2004). Those collections and the contribution in this volume developed from his participation in the *Eurasia Project for the Comparative History of Population and the Family* (EAP).

Prasannan Parthasarathi is Associate Professor of History at Boston College. He is the author of *The Transition to a Colonial Economy: Weavers, Merchants and*

Kings in South India (2001) and articles in *Past and Present* and the *Journal of Social History*.

Kenneth Pomeranz is Professor of History at the University of California, Irvine. Some of his major recent publications are *The Great Divergence: China, Europe and the Making of the Modern World Economy* (2000), 'Is there an East Asian Development Path?', *Journal of the Economic and Social History of the Orient* (2001), and 'Beyond the East-West Dichotomy: Resituating Development Paths in the Eighteenth Century World', *Journal of Asian Studies* (2002).

Jaime Reis has been Professor of Economic History at the European University Institute, Florence, and Professor and Dean at the Faculty of Economics at the New University of Lisbon. He is currently Senior Fellow of the Instituto de Ciências Sociais, Lisbon University. His latest publications include: 'How Poor was the Periphery before 1850? The Mediterranean versus Scandinavia', in Jeffrey Williamson and Sevket Pamuk (eds.), *The Mediterranean Response to Globalization before 1950* (2000) and 'Bank Structures, Gerschenkron and Portugal (pre-1914)', in Douglas J. Forsyth and Daniel Verdier (eds.), *The Origins of National Financial Systems: Alexander Gerschenkron Reconsidered* (2003).

Osamu Saito is Professor at the Institute of Economic Research (IER), Hitotsubashi University, Tokyo, and has been working in economic history and historical demography. He is currently Programme Leader of IER's Research Unit for Statistical Analysis in Social Sciences. His recent publications include *Population and Economy: From Hunger to Modern Economic Growth* (2000, co-editor with T. Bengtsson) and *Emergence of Economic Society in Japan, 1600–1859* (2004, co-editor with A. Hayami and R. P. Toby).

Richard H. Steckel is SBS distinguished Professor of Economics, Anthropology, and History at the Ohio State University. Since the mid-1970s, he has contributed to anthropometric history, an interdisciplinary field that blends subject matter from economics, history, human biology, and medical anthropology. His latest book (co-edited with Jerome Rose) on *The Backbone of History: Health and Nutrition in the Western Hemisphere* (2002) examines pre-Columbian health over the millennia. He has been the principal investigator on numerous projects funded by the National Science Foundation and is a Research Associate at the National Bureau of Economic Research.

Noriko O. Tsuya is Professor of Economics at Keio University in Tokyo. She holds a Ph.D. in sociology from the University of Chicago with a specialization in demography. Her recent publications include *Marriage, Work, and Family Life in Comparative Perspective: Japan, South Korea, and the United States* (with Larry L. Bumpass) (2004).

Jan Luiten van Zanden is Professor of Economic History at the University of Utrecht and Senior Researcher at the International Institute for Social History (Amsterdam). He has published on the economic history of the Netherlands—most recently with Arthur van Riel *The Structures in Inheritance. The Dutch Economy 1780–1914* (2004)—and is now working on Indonesian economic history and on economic growth in Europe before 1800.

List of Figures

1   Transformation of income to utility through goods, material
     characteristics, capabilities, and functionings   7
1.1 Supply and demand for hogs (reproduced from Perkins 1969: 72)   29
3.1 Labourers' real wages: the Kinai, 1727–1867 (1802–4 = 100)   81
3.2 Wage differentials: the Kinai, 1732–1865 (1802–4 = 100)   81
3.3 Two series of craftsmen's real wages: the Kanto, 1818–94
     (1840–4 = 100)   83
5.1 Real wages in Europe, 1500–1750 (silver wages deflated by CPI)   114
5.2 Masons' real wage, 1727–1913, England, Japan, and Italy   116
5.3 Building labourers' real wage, 1727–1913, England, Japan,
     and Italy   117
5.4 Farm labourers' real wage, 1727–1913, England, Japan,
     and Italy   117
5.5 Labourers' real wage, 1727–1913, England and Japan   118
6.1 Life expectancy at birth, 1500–1850   137
6.2 Selected prices relative to the price of bread or grain,
     1500–1900: (a) Panel A. England; (b) Panel B. Paris;
     (c) Panel C. Holland   148
6.3 Movements in the cost of living in top income groups, relative
     to the cost of living in the bottom 40% or in workers' households:
     (a) Panel A. England, 1500–1900; (b) Panel B. France, 1500–1900;
     (c) Panel C. Holland, 1540–1799   162
7.1 The price of 1,000 kcal in guilders (1763–1800)   182
7.2 The CPI for the western part of the Netherlands,
     1450–1800 (1450/74 = 100; polynomial trend added)   183
7.3 Real wages in the western part of the Netherlands,
     1450–1800 (1450/74 = 100; polynomial trend added)   184
9.1 Life expectancy and adult male height, late industrial period   232
9.2 Per cent urban and average male height   233
9.3 Average height of soldiers in Britain and of native born
     American soldiers   234
9.4 Average height of soldiers in Australia and Württemberg   235
9.5 Median height of conscripts in the Netherlands and France   237
9.6 Average height of conscripts in Sweden and Japan   238
10.1 Height of Russian recruits by birth year, 1700–99   260

11.1   Five-year lag sum elasticities of mortality for civil and military
       Croatian parishes, and Hungarian military heights centred on
       decade of birth   282
11.2   Historical maternal mortality rates   286
11.3   Risk per day of maternal death, by category   287
11.4   Maternal mortality by age and parity, Slavonian data   290
11.5   Gross maternal, background, and net maternal risk and
       probability of dying in childbirth, by year, five-year
       moving averages for all parities   292
11.6   Net maternal mortality at parities 1 and > 1, five-year
       moving averages   293
11.7   Net maternal mortality and infant mortality, five-year
       moving averages   293
12.1   Price indices 1700–1800   310
12.2   Number of deaths in Denmark 1700–1814   313
13.1   Taxable land rent for hectare, Grand Duchy of Tuscany (1834)   320
13.2   Percentages of mixed crop cultivation, Grand Duchy
       of Tuscany (1834)   321
13.3   Population density in km^2, Grand Duchy of
       Tuscany (1823–54)   322
13.4   Adult deaths (d_{20-60}). DLM, significance level—lag 0   332
13.5   Adult deaths (d_{20-60}). DLM significance level—lag 2   333
13.6   Child mortality rates (q_{1-4}). DLM, significance level—lag 2 334
14.1   Real wages (day-wage/rye price) in Malmöhus County
       and Sweden, 1766–1895   344
14.2   Life expectancy at birth (e_0) in Sweden, 1766/70–1891/95   346
14.3   (a) Age-specific death rates for male children (1–14 years)
       in Sweden, 1766/70–1891/95; (b) Age-specific death rates for
       female children (1–14 years) in Sweden, 1766/70–1891/95   347
14.4   Natural log local rye prices (actual values and HP-trend),
       1766/70–1891/95   356
15.1   Prices and trends in Sart, 1811–1910   387
15.2   Prices and trends in Land of Herve, 1846–1910   389
16.1   Estimated population size, 11 Liaoning state farm systems   408
16.2   Annual average of low sorghum prices   411
16.3   Cohort total marital fertility rate (16–50 *sui*) based
       on male births   414
16.4   Percentage of men married at different ages in Liaoning   416
16.5   Probability that a male aged 1 *sui* will die before reaching
       age 16 *sui* in Liaoning   419
16.6   Male and female period life expectancy at age 16 *sui*
       in Liaoning   419

17.1 Population size of the villages of Shimomoriya and Niita,
1716–1870   431
17.2 Raw rice prices (*ryo* per *koku*) in the market of Aizu,
1716–1863   434

List of Maps

11.1   Croatia, Slavonia, and the Military Border   279
17.1   Japan with Fukushima prefecture marked   430
17.2   Fukushima prefecture   431

List of Tables

1.1	Sugar and tea consumption in Europe and China (in pounds per capita)	37
1.2	Selected comparisons of cloth output and consumption (in pounds per capita)	37
3.1	Rates of change in real wages for skilled and unskilled occupations, 1727–1894 (in % per annum)	84
3.2	Rates of change in real wages for agricultural and non-agricultural occupations in eastern Japan, 1860–80 (in % per annum)	85
3.3	Comparisons between wage and output growth, 1700–1870	86
3.A1	The Kinai series: real wage and wage differential indices, 1727–1867 (1802–4 = 100)	90
3.A2	The Kanto series: nominal wage indices and real wage indices for Choshi and Edo/Tokyo, 1818–94 (1840–4 = 100)	94
4.1	Wages in the mid-eighteenth century	100
5.1	European and Asian baskets and nutrition	115
5.2	European wages relative to Indian in 1595	120
5.3	Indian standards of living, 1595 (in grams of silver) and 1961 (in rupees)	121
5.4	Real wages of farm workers, CPI deflator	122
5.5	Real wages of farm workers, calorie price deflator	123
5.A1	Base values for India in 1595	125
5.A2	Base values for China in late seventeenth century	126
5.A3	Base values for Japan in 1880–4	127
5.A4	Base values for England and Italy in 1750–9	128
6.1	Estimates of life expectancy at birth for various places and classes, 1500–1850	134
6.2	Selected household percentage shares of total expenditure, 1500–1832	140
6.3	The product pattern in price movements relative to the prices of bread or grains, European cities and region, 1500–1790	147
6.4	Movements in non-staple prices relative to staple food-grain prices, selected places and periods, 1500–1790	150
7.1	A comparison between the development of rent levels according to Lesger's data for Amsterdam (chain index and repeated rent index) and the average rents per house according to the registers of taxes on real estate, 1560/61–1806/08 (1806/08 = 100)	177

7.2	The development of the most important series (1550/74 = 100)	178
7.3	Stylized expenditure patterns	180
7.4	CPIs using four different weighting schemes, and the final index, 1450/74 = 100	181
7.A1	Relative and absolute prices of textiles, 1530/39–1790/99 (prices in guilders per el of 70 cm, and index 1530/9 = 100)	190
8.1	Long-term growth of per capita output (constant prices), seventeeth and eighteenth centuries	197
8.2	Literacy rates in Europe *c*.1800	202
9.1	Average heights of adult men, life expectancy, and percentage urban by stages of industrialization	231
9.2	Average heights in northern Europe estimated from adult male skeletons	241
9.3	Summary of adult male height trends in northern Europe	242
10.1	Variations of minimum height requirements (in cm) and age requirements (years) for recruits of the regular Russian army, 1730–1874	257
10.2	Stature of Russian recruits by birth year, 1700–99, by five-year cohorts	259
10.3	Size and distribution of land resources in eighteenth-century European Russia, crop capacity, and population	262
10.4	Output/seed ratios for the major grains in central Russia in the eighteenth century, by decades	263
10.5	Changes in the burden of taxes and dues on seigniorial serfs in eighteenth-century Russia	264
10.6	Changes in the burden of taxes and dues from state peasants (I), Appanage peasants (II), church (from 1764 Economicheskie) peasants (III), seignorial peasants (IV), and burgers (V) in eighteenth-century Russia (per capita)	265
10.7	Height by social groups, 1700–99	266
10.8	Losses to the state treasury from the gap between the increase in the poll tax and grain prices, 1725–1800	270
11.1	Data availability by parish and date	285
11.2	Stillbirth rates	288
11.3	Results of logistic regression	295
12.1	Occupational distribution of the Danish population in 1801	308
12.2	Influence of harvest results on the living standards of various segments of the population	312
12.3	Correlation coefficients between changes in rye prices, $(p_t - p_{t-1})/p_{t-1}$, and changes in mortality, $(m_t - m_{t-1})/m_{t-1}$	313
12.4	Covariation between fluctuations in demographic events and rye prices, 1669–1890	315
13.1	Grand Duchy of Tuscany. Principal socio-economic indicators (1832–4)	322

13.2 Estimated elasticity of wheat price fluctuations
on total adjusted deaths[a], Italy   328
13.3 Estimated elasticity of wheat price fluctuations on different
mortality indicators by age, Tuscany 1823–54   329
13.4 Estimated elasticity of wheat price fluctuations on
different mortality indicators by age, rural, and urban
Tuscany, 1823–54   331
14.1 Social structure of family heads in the four
parishes, 1766–1895   353
14.2 Effects of food prices on mortality in ages 25–55 for landless
and semi-landless in the four parishes, 1766–1895   359
14.3 Effects of food prices on mortality in ages 1–15 for landless
and semi-landless in the four parishes, 1766–1895   360
14.4 Effects of food prices on fertility for landless and semi-landless
in the four parishes, 1766–1895   363
15.1 Demographic regimes and family systems in the Land of Herve
and East Ardennes. A set of indicators, 1811–1900   380
15.2 Effects of grain prices on relative risks of demographic events
by sex and period, in Sart, Belgium   390
15.3 Demographic responses to price fluctuations in the Land of
Herve, 1846–1900. Estimated relative risks for a 10%
deviation from the trend   393
16.1 Available data   407
16.2 Levels of fertility, nuptiality, and mortality   413
16.3 Coefficients for year and logged low sorghum price from
Poisson regression of number of male births in the next year
for married females   415
16.4 Coefficients for year from the complementary log–log
regression of marriage in the next three years for
never-married males   417
16.5 Coefficients for logged low sorghum price from the
complementary log–log regression of death in the next
three years   420
17.1 Means of the covariates used for the discrete-time
event-history analysis of mortality responses to short-term
economic stress   442
17.2 Means of the covariates used for the discrete-time event-history
analysis of responses of marital fertility, first marriage, and
out-migration to short-term economic stress   442
17.3 Estimated effects of logged rice prices and household landholding
on the probability of dying in the next one year by sex   444
17.4 Estimated effects of logged rice price and household landholding
on the probability of having recorded marital birth in the
next one year   446

17.5 Estimated effects of logged rice prices and household landholding on the probability of first marriage in the next one year by sex and type of marriage   448

17.6 Estimated effects of logged rice prices and household landholding on the probability of out-migration in the next one year by sex and reason of migration   450

Introduction

ROBERT C. ALLEN, TOMMY BENGTSSON AND MARTIN DRIBE

Inequality in global living standards is a major challenge facing humanity in the new millennium. Real output per capita in Western Europe and North America is more than ten times that of many less developed countries. Differences are also substantial with respect to educational attainment, average length of life, and the general health of the population. Several dichotomies have been used to label this gap including rich and poor, developed–underdeveloped, developed–developing, North–South; the latter referring to its geographical boundaries. It also has, however, an East–West dimension—more obvious in the 1960s than today after some of the East-Asian countries have experienced rapid industrialization and tremendous economic growth.

The main concern of this book is to assess when the gap between the East and the West *emerged* and to not only take economic perspectives into consideration but social and demographic ones as well. The established view, stemming from the classical economists and still influential, is that the gap originated far back in history, perhaps thousands of years ago. This view has lately been challenged both by economists and demographers studying Asian history, stimulating an intense debate on the long-term economic development of Europe and Asia (especially China). Many of the arguments in this debate, however, have been based on fragmentary evidence collected from a few areas of a handful of countries. This book contributes to this debate by presenting a collection of historical analyses aiming to deepen and refine our knowledge of this important issue. The contributions cover major Asian and European countries and regions presenting new evidence and interpretations not only on income, health, and education but also on the ability to overcome short-term economic stress. In this way, we are able to provide a more substantial empirical foundation for debate on when the gap in living standards between the East and the West emerged.

1. The Established View Challenged

The established view that the gap emerged before the Industrial Revolution, perhaps thousands of years ago, was worked out in the eighteenth century in the context of trade between Europe and Asia. Since the Middle Ages, Europeans had imported tropical goods from Asia and found that they had to pay for them with silver since their manufactures were uncompetitive in Asian markets. This was partly a question of quality and partly a question of price—European goods were simply more expensive than their Asian counterparts. From the late seventeenth century onwards, the English East India Company took advantage of this differential and began to ship Indian cotton textiles to Europe. This trade was so successful that English woollen producers secured the prohibition of Indian calicoes in Britain. They continued to be re-exported, however, to other parts of Europe and to Africa and the Americas. The merchants engaged in these trades were well aware of the costs and prices of the goods they sold and observed that the cheapness of Indian cottons was a direct result of the lowness of Indian wages in comparison to those in England. This observation underlay the pessimistic view of Asian living standards.

The question was, were Asian wages even lower, on a percentage basis, than Asian prices? Adam Smith (1776/1937) thought so. 'Rice in China is much cheaper than wheat is any-where in Europe' (1776/1937: 189). Wages were still lower. 'The difference between the money price of labour in China and Europe, is still greater than that between the money price of subsistence; because the real recompense of labour is higher in Europe than in China, the greater part of Europe being in an improving state, while China seems to be standing still' (1776/1937: 189). As a result, 'the poverty of the lower ranks of people in China far surpasses that of the most beggarly nations in Europe' (1776/1937: 72). People living on fishing boats near Canton were so poor that 'any carrion, the carcass of a dead dog or cat, for example, though half putrid and stinking, is as welcome to them as the most wholesome food to the people of other countries' (1776/1937: 20). Smith had the same view of India (1776/1937: 206).

Why were real wages lower in Asia than in Europe? Adam Smith propounded the liberal view that stable and secure property rights, low taxation, limited government, and free trade were the bases of economic expansion, and expansion was the cause of high wages. 'The proportion between the real recompense of labour in different countries', he argued, 'is naturally regulated' by the 'advancing, stationary, or declining condition' of their economies (1776/1937: 189–90). While he objected to certain features of British policy—the Navigation Acts, which limited free trade, were objects of sustained attack—he regarded Britain's free labour, land, and product markets as particularly conducive to development. Asian wages were low because its economy was 'stationary'. This was due, in turn, to the lack of the broad markets, secure property, and limited government, which the English and the Dutch enjoyed.

China's economy was paradoxical because the country was both rich and stationary. The riches were due to its natural fertility and to a considerable division of labour based on internal commerce. China, like India and ancient Egypt, 'seem all to have derived their great opulence from inland navigation' (1776/1937: 20). The process was taken furthest in China. 'In the Eastern provinces of China . . . several great rivers form, by their different branches, a multitude of canals, and by communicating with one another afford an inland navigation much more extensive than that either of the Nile or the Ganges, or perhaps than both of them put together' (1776/1937: 20).

Rich as it was, however, Chinese institutions prevented the country from reaching its full potential. 'China seems to have been long stationary, and had probably long ago acquired that full complement of riches which is consistent with the nature of its laws and institutions. But this complement may be much inferior to what, with other laws and institutions, the nature of its soil, climate, and situation might admit of' (1776/1937: 95). Two institutions prevented China from developing further. One was restriction on foreign trade. 'A country which neglects or despises foreign commerce, and which admits the vessels of foreign nations into one or two of its ports only, cannot transact the same quantity of business which it might do with different laws and institutions' (1776/1937: 95). This was, perhaps, understandable, but was still regrettable. 'A great nation surrounded on all sides by wandering savages and poor barbarians might, no doubt, acquire riches by the cultivation of its own lands, and by its own interior commerce, but not by foreign trade. It seems to have been in this manner that the ancient Egyptians and the modern Chinese acquired their great wealth' (1776/1937: 462). Limiting foreign trade, however, limited the division of labour, and thereby limited the growth of income.

Insecure property rights also contributed to China's stationary state. 'In a country . . . where, though the rich or the owners of large capital enjoy a good deal of security, the poor or the owners of small capitals enjoy scarce any, but are liable, under the pretence of justice, to be pillaged and plundered at any time by the inferior mandarins', investment—hence, employment and output—will be less than they might be (1776/1937: 95). The proper function of the state, in Smith's view, was to establish clear and secure property rights, and the Chinese Empire failed that test. Smith, thus, explained the low standard of living in China with the same theory that explained the high standard of living in Europe.

Malthus (1803/1973) is famous for his population theories, and he marshalled them to explain Asian backwardness. Like Smith, he was impressed by the paradox of a highly productive agriculture and widespread poverty. He attributed the former to the fertility of the soil and the high standard of cultivation, which reflected state encouragement. This, in Malthus' view, induced a large population. 'The population which has arisen naturally from the fertility of the soil, and the encouragements to agriculture, may be considered as genuine and desirable' (1803/1973: 131). However, there were three 'encouragements to marriage' that increased the population beyond a reasonable level and 'which have caused the immense produce of the country to be divided into very small shares, and have consequently rendered China more populous, in proportion to its means of subsistence, than perhaps any other country in the world' (1803/1973: 128–9). These 'encourage-ments' included (1) ancestor worship, which led parents to have children to secure sacrifices to themselves after death, (2) 'prudence, because the children, particu-larly, the sons, are bound to maintain their parents', and (3) infanticide, which allowed parents to rid themselves of children they could not support (1803/1973: 129). Infanticide was regarded with such abhorrence that its practice was sufficient to conclude that the Chinese were desperately poor by European standards (Staunton 1797).

Malthus applied the same logic to India, where he also believed the standard of living to be very low. He entertained the prospect that Hindu asceticism would depress fertility (a preventive check) but concluded, 'from the prevailing habits and opinions of the people there is reason to believe that the tendency to early marriages was still always predominant' (1803/1973: 119). As a result 'the lower classes of people were reduced to extreme poverty... The population would thus be pressed hard against the limits of the means of subsistence, and the food of the country would be meted out to the major part of the people in the smallest shares that could support life'. Disaster was never far away. 'India, as might be expected, has in all ages been subject to the most dreadful famines' (1803/1973: 119).

Marx (1853/1983) was a third great classical economist, and he too, sought to explain Asian backwardness with his own brand of theory. In a series of newspaper articles, he propounded the highly controversial theory of the 'Oriental Mode of Production'. The West, in his view, had grown rapidly since its organization was capitalist. This system gave businesses maximum incentive to accumulate and innovate. In Asia, however, these incentives were lacking, and that lack can be traced to geography and the social institutions created to deal with it.

Marx saw 'irrigation' as 'the *sine qua non* of farming in the East' (1853/1983: 339) for two reasons. First, there were 'the vast tracts of desert, extending from the Sahara, through Arabia, Persia, India and Tartary, to the most elevated Asia highlands'. These dry lands could be made fertile if water was supplied, so 'artificial irrigation by canals and waterworks' became 'the basis of Oriental agriculture'. Second, in river valleys 'as in Egypt and India' as well as China, periodic 'inundations were used for fertilizing the soil'. Water was periodically released on the land, and for that 'advantage is taken of a high level for feeding irrigative canals' (1853/1983: 331). Thus, both the potentially fertile deserts and the rich river valleys required extensive and elaborate water control systems to achieve maximal fertility. In the West, the need for irrigation or water control 'drove private enterprise to voluntary association, as in Flanders and Italy'. However, in Asia, 'where civilization was too low and the territorial extent too vast to call into life voluntary association, the interference of the centralizing power of government' was called into play. The state in Asia took on the job of administering a vast system of public works, which required a class of civil servants, notably the mandarins in China.

The state administration of irrigation had two effects, both of which were detrimental to economic growth. First, the production of agriculture and thus the economy as a whole depended on the performance of the bureaucracy. 'In Asian empires we are quite accustomed to see agriculture deteriorating under one government and reviving again under some other government. There the harvests correspond to good or bad governments, as they change in Europe with good or bad seasons' (1853/1983: 332). In Asia, agriculture 'is not capable of being conducted on the British principle of free competition, of *laissez-faire* and *laisser-aller*' (1853/1983: 332). The result was a certain passivity since 'the Hindu... like all Oriental peoples' left 'to the central government the care of the great public works, the prime condition of his agriculture and commerce' (1853/1983: 333).

Marx saw Asian society as composed of atomistic villages under the sway of a despotic state that determined their prosperity by the quality of its administration. Each village combined agriculture with textile production through hand processes. 'Those family-communities were based on domestic industry in that peculiar combination of hand-weaving, hand-spinning and hand-tilling agriculture which gave them self-supporting power' (1853/1983: 335). These villages were the 'solid foundation of Oriental despotism', and they also stifled the rational acquisitiveness that propelled capitalism forward: 'they restrained the human mind within the smallest possible compass, making it the unresisting tool of superstition, enslaving it beneath traditional rules, depriving it of all grandeur and historical energies' (1853/1983: 335). But there was cause for hope: the 'old Asiatic society' would be destroyed by 'English steam and English free trade'. Modern capitalism would drive India forward (1853/1983: 335, 337).

These views remain influential. In his wide-ranging review of world economic history, *The Wealth and Poverty of Nations* (1998), David Landes has combined the ideas of Malthus and Marx into a sweeping account of Chinese stagnation that traces it back thousands of years. Landes' story begins when the Han, the ancestors of the modern Chinese, lived in the northern forests and subsisted on millet and barley. Landes sees the Han in a Darwinian competition with the other peoples of East Asia. The competitive advantage of the Han was early and universal marriage and maximal fertility. The Han bred faster than other Asians and gradually pushed south, displacing their competitors and occupying all of China. In this expansion, more people meant more soldiers and greater military power. 'In effect, this pattern of maximum reproduction enhanced political power, in terms both of combat fodder and of material for territorial expansion. In the last analysis, this was the story of Chinese aggrandizement over less prolific societies' (1998: 22, n. *).

As the Chinese occupied the great river valleys of central and southern China, they organized cultivation to maximize food production and population. Landes endorses Marx's hydraulic argument, as elaborated by Wittfogel (1957): 'the management of water called for supralocal power and promoted imperial authority' (1957: 27). Chinese history was like a 'treadmill' in which more people led to a bigger empire (in geographical terms), which led to more food, which led to more people. And then the cycle repeated (1957: 23). The capstone was the Celestial Empire's ideology that celebrated the superiority of Chinese culture, institutions, and imperial power. This rendered China peculiarly resistant to adopting western technology. By the nineteenth century, the Chinese Empire had fallen behind the West industrially and militarily. This backwardness was thousands of years in the making.

The postulate of backwardness, along with explanations for it, is the endowment that nineteenth-century social science bequeathed to modern Asian scholarship. Studies of these explanations not only called them into question but also raised the possibility that the postulate of backwardness itself was an error. Malthus' demographic explanation of Chinese backwardness has been severely attacked by Laveley and Wong (1998) and Lee and Wang (1999). Wong (1997) has questioned the use of

European models as templates for evaluating Chinese institutions, while Pomeranz (2000) has taken on Smith and Marx by arguing that Chinese property rights were as secure as those in Europe and markets as efficient. These findings led him to question the postulate of backwardness itself: 'It seems likely that average incomes in Japan, China, and parts of southeast Asia were comparable to (or higher than) those in western Europe even in the late eighteenth century' (Pomeranz 2000: 49). Parthasarathi (1998, 2001) has undertaken some eighteenth-century wage comparisons that point to the same conclusion for India.

While the postulate of backwardness has been called into question—and many of the explanations for it greatly undermined—the issue demands much more empirical research than has yet been undertaken. How did the standard of living in Europe and Asia compare in the seventeenth and eighteenth centuries? Grand issues like this have many dimensions, and all of them need to be investigated to establish sound conclusions.

2. Conceptualizing and Measuring Standard of Living

International comparisons of the standard of living raise three issues. The first is regional diversity. Both Europe and Asia contained leading and lagging provinces. Like must be compared with like before any judgement can be made as to which continent was most advanced. The second issue is the distribution of well-being within each continent. If inequality was greater at one end of Eurasia than the other, then equal average incomes would be consistent with the rich being richer while the poor were poorer. Distributionally sensitive indicators of the standard of living are needed, as are indicators of the average. The third issue concerns the definition of the standard of living. It is a complex concept, and it is far from obvious how it should be measured.

Though one could argue that the ideal way to define standard of living is by the total utility a person derives from consuming a set of goods as a result of labour, investments, or transfers, this approach is not operational. The reason is that the utility of various goods depends on personal characteristics and cannot be measured (Sen 1987: 14). Hence, most concepts of the standard of living focus on goods themselves, or the ability to access them; the latter often measured by production or income. Since the volume of goods accessible with a certain income depends on the prices of these goods, income is usually deflated by a cost-of-living index. Real income and real wages calculated in this way are widely used, not only for modern but also for historical comparisons. For modern societies, we have information about income both at individual and aggregate level, while historical data for individuals are rare. Instead we quite often have data on wages for various occupations. But the standard of living can be gauged in other ways as well.

Such a broader concept is reflected in the Basic Need Index, developed in the 1970s by the International Labour Organization (Ghai *et al.* 1977). This index includes food, clothing, shelter, health, education, water, and sanitation. The problem of how to weight these various items has been addressed repeatedly and different solutions proposed but a general consensus is still lacking. It also turns out that a ranking of countries, based on the Basic Need Index, is very similar to the one that uses real income per capita since the goods and services included in the index end up being a very large proportion of national income (World Bank 1984).

United Nation's Human Development Index (HDI), which is a composite of real income (GDP per capita), health (as measured by life expectancy), and knowledge (i.e. education), has replaced the Basic Need Index both in scientific and political circles. This new index correlates with the Basic Need Index as well as the gross domestic product (GDP) per capita (World Bank 1984), but the HDI places greater weight on education and health. In developing countries in the twentieth century, health and education have improved more rapidly than income with the result that the HDI has grown faster than GDP per head (Crafts 1996).[1] This is both a strength and a weakness. It is a strength because it emphasizes improvements in well-being that are not captured by GDP per head, but it is a weakness in that it imposes arbitrary weights on the constituent series and, in the process, double counts education and health: they enter the index in their own right but also as part of GDP (Bengtsson 2004).

The standard of living can also be defined in terms of Amartya Sen's (1992) concepts of 'functionings' and 'capabilities'. Since utility, which is the ultimate standard of well-being in this approach, is immeasurable, 'functionings' and 'capabilities' are introduced as measurable counterparts. Figure 1 illustrates the relationships. It is based on John Muellbauer's useful overview of standard of living concepts (1987: 40), as expanded by Bengtsson (2004), who added income and prices to the original figure.

Figure 1 illustrates how income is used to buy a certain amount of goods depending on prices. These goods have certain material characteristics, such as the amount of calories and proteins. Environmental factors, which also have an impact on these goods, include both individual liberty and common non-material conditions such as climate, clean air, and the absence of crime. Together with the personal characteristics, such as metabolism, they determine an individual's capabilities.

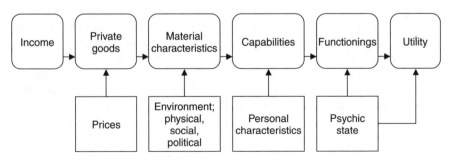

Figure 1 Transformation of income to utility through goods, material characteristics, capabilities, and functionings

Finally, capabilities in conjunction with the individual's psychic state, which includes personal characteristics as well as social constructs like religious faith or ideological beliefs, determine his or her functionings. These range from such elementary things as adequate nutrition, good health, physical robustness, and longevity to more complex ones such as self-respect (Sen 1992: 39).[2] Functionings are important since the utility an individual can realize depends on his or her functionings, and they are measurable, while utility is not. The upper boxes show transfers from income to utility, while the lower ones should be perceived as constraints or conditional factors.

As Figure 1 suggests, the standard of living can be measured at any point along the chain from income to functionings. The various measures are correlated, although imperfectly. Thus, they give us different views of the standard of living. We exploit that fact in this book. We avoid the weighted indices like the HDI, because they suppress information by aggregating the components. Instead, we examine the components separately. We consider economic concepts like income and consumption; demographic concepts related to functionings like height and life expectancy; and a recently developed indicator: the ability to overcome short-term economic stress.

These concepts can be applied to the 'average' person in society by applying aggregate data, to particular social groups, or to individuals when samples of individual level data are available. Whereas only limited details of the well-being of various groups can be obtained with highly aggregated measures, their strength lies in the fact that they cover large populations. While measures constructed for individual and family levels give details, they often cover small geographical areas and are therefore difficult to generalize from. In intermediate position, we have measures that show the situation for certain occupational or social groups. Thus, to obtain details and for generalization, the standard of living indicators at various levels of aggregation are needed.

All chapters in the book either compare one or a few measures across several countries or regions, or two or more measures within the same country or region. We use them coherently and simultaneously to get a better understanding of the historical well-being of various social groups in a number of countries in Europe and Asia. In doing so, we not only extend the means of comparison but also the objects of comparison, that is, we include more countries in the analysis than has been the case in earlier studies. And, by including standard of living indicators at micro, meso, and macro level, we obtain both details and generalization.

We start with the economic measures of living standards to illustrate our approach. Real GDP per head is the most commonly used economic measure of living standards. Maddison (1995) has projected global estimates of modern incomes back to the year nought, and his calculations support the classical economists, in that Europe has had the lead over China throughout the last two millennia. Like other researchers, however, we have serious doubts about the reliability of extrapolations that extend centuries into the past. Not only do they cumulate measurement errors, but they also impose modern price structures on historical economies, producing radically different types of commodities (Prados 2000). Instead, we explore real income measures that are based on early modern sources. The most practical indicator is the real wage. This measure is 'distributionally sensitive' in that it compares the standard of living of workers. This is both a strength and a weakness: a strength because it is targeted more closely to the masses of the population than GDP per head, and a weakness since it excludes incomes due to land and capital. Several chapters in the volume explore these complexities.

The next group of measurements are the demographic indicators. Health has received considerable attention from historians who have studied the history of heights, and we draw on that research for international comparisons, as we also do on more direct measures, such as life expectancy. Literacy has likewise been the subject of some research, and we discuss its determinants and consequences, but the information here is more limited than that for health and income.

Finally, at the end of this book, we study the standard of living with an indicator that has not been widely used, namely, the ability to overcome short-term economic stress; in particular, changes in the price of food.[3] In pre-industrial societies, food amounted to half or three quarters of expenditure (Myrdal 1933: 115; Scholliers 1960: 174; Abel 1966/1980: 142; Jörberg 1972: 182; Somogy 1973; see Livi-Bacci 1991: 87; Fang 1996: 93, 95; Pomeranz, Chapter 1, this volume). Consequently, an increase in the price of food sharply reduced the standard of living. The effect was particularly marked among the poor, who spent the biggest share of their income on food. Normal fluctuations in grain prices caused fluctuations of 10% to 20% in the calorie consumption of the poor, and the high grain prices following bad harvests had an even greater impact (Bengtsson 2004). The poor were less able than the rich to borrow money, and that inability compounded their difficulties. Poor labourers were even more vulnerable than poor cultivators; at least the latter grew some food, while the former had to purchase their consumption. Poor labourers, in particular, were forced to rely on charity or public assistance.

There were demographic responses—some intentional, some not—to high food prices. In the worst case, high prices caused death for those unable to buy enough to eat. In less extreme situations, people resorted to demographic strategies in response to high food prices. These included postponed marriages, migration, and delayed births. Studies of the correlation of death, migration, marriage, and childbearing with food prices, therefore, provide a new approach to the measurement of the standard of living. When aggregate data show that high food prices raised mortality or reduced fertility, one can conclude that the bulk of the population had a low standard of living. If disaggregate data show that only labourers exhibited such responses, then we know that average living standards were higher, but the poor were still vulnerable. With careful attention to the data, the study of the demographic response to price fluctuations tells much about the average standard of living in a society and about the situation of the least well-off.

In addition to the conceptual complexity, the scarcity of data also makes the intercontinental comparison of well-being a difficult quest. Previous efforts have often relied on fragmentary quantitative data or qualitative sources like travellers' accounts, anecdotes, etc. This is not said to depreciate the value of previous research efforts, but to stress the need for more research and new evidence. By broadening the concept of the standard of living, we also broaden the evidence that can be brought to bear on the issue. In this way, we can avoid the weaknesses of individual data sources and reach more robust conclusions.

The contributions have been grouped into three parts, each corresponding to an important dimension of standard of living. The first is economic: There are many indicators of economic well-being including the history of income, food production, wages, and prices. What do they tell us about the well-being in pre-industrial Europe and Asia? The second is demographic: Was Malthus right in claiming that mortality was high in most eighteenth-century populations due to population pressure on land? Did food shortage indirectly influence body height? Do demographic indicators of well-being show similar patterns as economic ones? The third combines the economic and demographic indicators into the new concept of standard of living previously discussed: Did pre-industrial populations in Asia respond to economic fluctuations by changes in mortality and fertility similar to Europe? How did the well-being of the poorest members and the better-off compare with regard to vulnerability to short-term economic stress?

3. Economic Indicators of Living Standards

The first part of the book is primarily concerned with economic indicators of well-being. Kenneth Pomeranz's contribution extends his path-breaking book *The Great Divergence* (2000) by considering more information on relative living standards in Europe and Asia. He argues that the Chinese consumed about 2,400 calories of food per adult equivalent in the eighteenth century—a figure comparable to those in Western Europe. Protein consumption was also on par with Europe in the seventeenth century, although Chinese consumption may have declined in the eighteenth. Scattered wage and price data point to a rough equality in food consumption between Europe and Asia. Moreover, at neither end of Eurasia did workers and peasants spend all of their income on basic food, and the share of income spent on other items were roughly equal, which, likewise, suggests a similar standard of living.

Eighteenth-century Chinese living standards can also be compared with living standards in the 1920s and 1930s, and those comparisons suggest a significant deterioration. Pomeranz proposes a Smithian explanation of the fall—intra-regional trade declined and with it consumption possibilities. Also, the decline in trade led to greater pressure on the land and resource base throughout the country. The result was deforestation and a greater variance in river levels that further reduced farm output. The poverty of China early in the twentieth century was not the result of centuries of backwardness but represented a decline from an eighteenth-century peak.

Li Bozhong's work on Chinese agriculture is an important beam in the revisionist reconstruction of Asian economic history. Smith's notion that the economy was 'stationary' is part of the bedrock of the traditional account. Li shows, instead, that productivity rose substantially in the seventeenth and eighteenth centuries. He has used farm handbooks to develop detailed descriptions of the size, labour requirements, and output (both food and textiles) across these centuries. Agricultural labour productivity rose by 30–40% (depending on the measure chosen) over this period. Li also argues that rising labour productivity translated into rising consumption per farm worker. The nineteenth-century vision of Chinese technology as static and unchanging must be replaced by one of progressive development, at least so far as agriculture in the Yangzi is concerned.

Prasannan Parthasarathi is well known for having argued that southern Indian living standards were on a par with England's in the eighteenth century. He extends these arguments in this volume in two ways. First, he offers additional mid-eighteenth-century evidence from Bengal that implies that the real incomes of its weavers, spinners, and farm workers were similar to those in South India and in Britain. Second, he offers a compelling explanation of high real wages and the competitiveness of Indian industry. Labour markets, he argues, were highly competitive. The various states of India competed among themselves for labour. They did this by investing in agricultural improvements including water control systems. As a result, the distribution of cultivation in eighteenth-century India had much less to do with soil characteristics than it did with the existence of well-organized states that could develop irrigation schemes. Abundant supplies of food meant that its price was low. Cheap food meant that wages (measured in silver) were low compared to Europe while real wages were similar. India's competitiveness in the manufacture of cotton textiles in the eighteenth century could be reconciled with the high standard of living of her population.

Robert Allen has studied the history of real wages across Europe from the late Middle Ages to the nineteenth century. These comparisons show that living standards were high and at about the same level around 1500 in all the cities studied. Thereafter, they diverged. In the next three centuries, living standards remained high in the leading commercial cities of northwestern Europe while falling by a half in the rest of the continent. How did Asian wages compare to this range of experience? Scattered evidence for Japan, India in 1595, and the Yangzi in the seventeenth and eighteenth centuries implies that the living standards of Asian labourers were similar to those in Italy, Germany, or France in the middle of the eighteenth century. These were the less successful parts of Europe. Skilled workers in India, however, did quite well. While the negative views of eighteenth- and nineteenth-century observers are rejected, much more wage and price data are needed before definitive conclusions can be reached on this issue.

The chapter by Philip Hoffman, David Jacks, Patricia Levin, and Peter Lindert as well as the chapter by Jan Luiten van Zanden concentrate on the measurement of economic well-being in Western Europe. Both chapters make improvements in the cost-of-living indices used to convert money incomes into purchasing power equivalents (real incomes). Van Zanden introduces house rents into the consumer price index (CPI) for Holland. This is important as rent increased very rapidly. Hoffman *et al.* argue that the spending patterns of the rich and the poor were very different, and that the prices of foods, which had great weight in the spending of the poor, inflated more rapidly than the prices of manufactures or the wages of servants, which had greater weight in the spending of the rich. Using social group-specific consumer price indices, therefore, shows that inequality increased even more than appears from the examination of nominal incomes. Hoffman *et al.* argue that house rents rose rapidly in France and England, as well as Holland, and that rise contributed to rising inequality by raising the real income of the rich relative to the poor. Both chapters suggest that the seventeenth and eighteenth centuries witnessed a sharp rise in inequality in northwestern Europe. Indeed, van Zanden finds that GDP per head rose significantly in the Netherlands, while the real wage grew little. A rise of rent, both of houses and of farmland, would reconcile the wage and GDP trends. Landowners were the immediate beneficiaries of early modern economic growth in Western Europe. This finding cautions us that sound comparisons of living standards in Europe and Asia must be broken down by social group and cannot be based simply on GDP per head or even real wages.

Japan was a key part of the global trading system, and its economy has been studied more systematically than that of other countries in Asia. Osamu Saito draws on that research and extends it with new data in his chapter on Japanese real wages between 1727 and 1894. He argues that Japanese growth in this period was qualitatively different from that in Europe, as exemplified by van Zanden's study of Holland, for instance. While GDP per head rose more rapidly than the wage rate in the Netherlands, the two economic indicators grew at the same rate in Tokugawa and early Meiji Japan. Saito argues that agricultural productivity growth in Japan meant that the marginal product of labour rose at the same rate as the average. The supply price of labour from the peasant sector thus increased over time, labour remained in agriculture, and wages rose in step with national income per head. Contrary to the usual revisionist view, it was differences in farm organization (not similarities) that explain the high Asian standard of living.

Jamie Reis expands the definition of the standard of living beyond the consumption of goods and services to include literacy. The ability to read and write increased dramatically in Europe between the Middle Ages and the Industrial Revolution. When Gutenberg invented the moveable type in 1453, perhaps 10% of the European population could read. By 1800, the proportion had risen everywhere and had reached about two-thirds in the leading economies of northern Europe. Some of this rise was related—as both cause and effect—to economic expansion, but, Reis argues, the increase in literacy went far beyond what was needed for economic development. In the Low Countries, Britain, and France, the 'overinvestment' in education was manifest as the acquisition of literacy by unskilled workers. For these people—and no doubt for many who were more prosperous—the ability to read was a consumer good that enriched life. Reis shows that the value of this ability, as measured by the cost of acquiring it, was a significant proportion of the wealth of working people.

4. Health and Height as Indicators of Well-being

The second part of the book is about health and height. These central dimensions of well-being are not only determined by the amount of calories and proteins we consume but also by environmental factors, such as access to water and sanitation systems, public health and medicine, as well as disease prevalence and work load. Thus, height and health are the outcomes of *net consumption of nutrients*—the amount we consume minus the body claims that stem from work and disease. Since nutritional consumption depends on income and the price of food, one would expect congruence between height and real incomes. The essays in this section investigate that question. Richard Steckel compares trends in heights with some economic indicators in several countries of Northern Europe and Japan. Boris Mironov, Eugene Hammel and Aaron Gullickson, and Hans-Christian Johansen explore the question with detailed studies of Russia, Slavonia, and Denmark respectively.

Steckel's essay places the debate over human welfare during industrialization in the context of the economic development since the Middle Ages. Steckel, one of the pioneers in analysing heights within an economic context (e.g. Sandberg and Steckel 1980; see also Steckel 1995), describes the height development in northern Europe as U-shaped. Combining skeleton data with records for military recruits, Steckel shows that average heights were impressive during the Middle Ages when men reached final heights of over 170 cm, on average, which was high even by late nineteenth-century standards. Heights started to decline at the end of the fifteenth century, plausibly due to climate change, growing inequality, urbanization, the global spread of diseases, and conflicts between states and churches. Stature increased again during the early nineteenth century, likely linked with dietary improvements, according to Steckel. Thus the long-term trends in heights in northern Europe fit quite well with the long-term changes in real wages outside the most prosperous cities shown by Allen (Chapter 5, this volume). Heights in Japan, Steckel's Asian example, start off at 155 cm in the period 1868–80 and improve with about 1 cm per decade to 160 cm in 1920–40. While Japan's growth rate is similar to other countries, they start off some 10 cm to 18 cm below pre-industrial north-European populations indicating low net nutritional consumption. The figures for Japan are also low compared to other Asian populations, like Koreans (Gill 1998) and Chinese (Morgan 1998), which are close to their European counterparts at the end of the nineteenth century.

Mironov shows that average height for recruits in Russia declined by 5 cm during the eighteenth century even as the country experienced one of its most brilliant periods militarily, politically, economically, and culturally. The decrease occurred as a consequence of a decline in consumption for ordinary people. The building of the empire demanded its contribution of the Russian people in terms of taxes. Inequality grew likewise and, as for the rest of Europe, Russia experienced increasing prices of food and a harsher climate. In the beginning of the eighteenth century, Russia was probably on par with the rest of Europe in terms of biological standard of living. Heights for recruits fell throughout Europe but more in Russia and by the end of that century, Russian soldiers were shorter.

Hammel and Gullickson show that living conditions in Slavonia deteriorated in the period 1750–1900. The authors not only use the standard indicators of the standard of living but also investigate in detail how institutional and market changes shaped the chances of survival of peasant women at childbirth. Malthusian pressure on resources links the demographic response to short-term changes in food prices. Hammel and Gullickson show that the stature of military recruits declined until 1850. They then show, by using a variety of indicators—including maternal mortality for first and higher order marriages, at first and higher order births, and infant mortality rate—how maternal mortality increased over time in parallel with increasing land shortage, diversion of labour to wage earning, and decay of the joint family system. Thus, the worsening of the conditions at childbirth reflected the general deterioration that took place. In contrast to the rest of Europe, conditions did not improve, either with respect to maternal mortality or living conditions in general, during the latter part of the nineteenth century.

Johansen undertakes a broad view of the standard of living in Denmark during the eighteenth and early nineteenth centuries. The traditional interpretation is that living conditions improved for the majority of the population in the last quarter of the eighteenth century as a result of a series of agricultural reforms and other measures taken to promote economic growth. Only the poorest part of the population remained close to the margins. This view has been based mainly on qualitative sources, but Johansen's chapter tests it with quantitative indicators. They do not entirely agree. Real wages declined at the end of the eighteenth century, but Johansen argues that this indicator applies only to a small part of the population, in particular day-labourers and cottagers without land who comprised about 10% of the population. The incomes of other groups, including tradesmen, farmers, and possibly their servants increased. Because the incomes of so many rose, Johansen finds no correlation between short-term changes in grain prices and the mortality rate after the agricultural reforms. These findings are corroborated by conscription records, which show a stable average height (165–167 cm) among army recruits from the end of the eighteenth century until the 1850s. By examining all of the quantitative indicators, Johansen constructs a more nuanced picture of living standards than any of the sources show on their own. While landless labourers suffered, Johansen reaffirms the traditional view that the standard of living of the majority increased from the start of the agricultural reforms in the 1780s to such an extent that the mortality crises of previous centuries disappeared.

The chapters in this section show the importance of examining a range of indicators of the standard of living. Generally speaking, all of them show improvement as economic development proceeds, but there are exceptions because not all groups share equally in the benefits of growth. Steckel's essay, which looks at the long sweep of history, shows how economic growth and improved health move together in the long run. Hammel and Gullickson, who concentrate on poor women in a backward region also find that all the indicators move together—in this case because they are concerned with only a part of society. In contrast, Johansen takes a broader view and shows that landless labourers failed to share in the growth process that improved the lot of the majority of Danes. Likewise, Mironov finds that height of the average Russian soldier fell despite the growth in the economy since the Imperial state siphoned off the benefits of growth, so they did not trickle down to the mass of the population. The possibility of divergent experience within a country must be kept in mind in making broad comparisons of well-being. Looking at a range of indicators is more likely to reveal contrasting experiences than while concentrating on a single one.

5. Demographic Response to Short-term Economic Stress

The final part of the book is devoted to demographic responses to short-term economic stress as an indicator of the standard of living. The most extreme case is when a rise in food prices raises mortality. The loss of life is itself an indicator of low living standards. In addition, the fact that rising price could cause death indicates that 'normal' food intake was precariously low. In less extreme situations, high food prices could lead to deferred marriage and family formation. The demographic response to food prices can be measured with longitudinal data for individuals including social status, access to land and other household characteristics as well as demographic events.

Marco Breschi, Alessio Fornasin, and Giovanna Gonano measure the mortality response to fluctuations in wheat prices in Tuscany during the period 1823–59. Their results show a positive correlation between mortality and price for all age groups except infants. This finding is in accordance with evidence from many other parts of Europe as well (Bengtsson and Reher 1998). These results indicate that a significant proportion of Tuscan society lived so close to the margin that their health and survival were affected by poor harvests. There were suggestive differences between different parts of Tuscany. It was, paradoxically, the wealthiest rural regions that showed the strongest mortality response to food price rises. In these areas, most work was done by wage labourers whose consumption was vulnerable to changes in the price of wheat. In contrast, sharecropping predominated in poorer regions, and sharecroppers had some protection against rising food prices since they raised food.

Tommy Bengtsson and Martin Dribe use data on individuals to study the impact of food price fluctuations on the fertility and mortality of landless people in the province of Scania in southern Sweden. Real wages and life expectancy both indicate that the standard of living of landless labourers did not start to rise until the second half of the nineteenth century. This result is corroborated by the demographic investigation. Landowning peasants took advantage of the new opportunities created by the transformation of agriculture in the first half of the nineteenth century to increase their incomes (Schön 1979). In contrast, the agricultural transformation and enclosure movement implied increased dependency on wage labour for the landless. The agricultural revolution also destroyed the village institutions that had previously provided income security to the poor. As a result of these changes, fluctuations in food prices had a greater impact on the mortality and fertility of landless labourers during the agricultural revolution than the years before or after.

Michel Oris, George Alter, and Muriel Neven undertook a longitudinal analysis of two rural areas in nineteenth-century Belgium—the Land of Herve and the East Ardennes. Both were poor and overpopulated, but they were also both adjacent to regions that were undergoing rapid economic development. One response in both regions was migration to the industrializing cities. Despite this opportunity, however, both regions showed evidence of endemic poverty: mortality and fertility in both communities were highly responsive to economic stress throughout the nineteenth century. Vulnerability remained high for women throughout the same period, indicating a relatively low standard of living well after the beginning of industrialization. In the East Ardennes, the poorest region, men were also vulnerable to economic stress during the first half of the nineteenth century, but this vulnerability diminished in the second half.

Cameron Campbell and James Lee compared the demographic responses to food price jumps in different regions of Liaoning in northeast China during the period 1749–1909 using micro level population registers. This province differs from the regions studied by Pomeranz and Li Bozhong in their contributions to this volume in terms of economic structure, population density, etc. In the northern and southern parts of Liaoning both the mortality and fertility response to changes in rice prices disappeared between the late eighteenth and early nineteenth centuries, indicating a rise in the standard of living and a level above that of some parts of Europe. In the central part of the province, however, conditions failed to improve, and the authors link the poor rural conditions to those in Shenyang. It was the leading city and experienced increasing economic difficulties in the nineteenth century. People in the adjacent countryside were also affected by this decline and tried to adjust both childbearing and marriage to the deteriorating economic conditions. In some districts, mortality remained sensitive to economic fluctuations throughout the nineteenth century. Thus, in the Shenyang region, rural living conditions remained poor, as they did in central China in Pomeranz's account. However, there was improvement in outlying country districts. The different trajectories highlight the need for regional analyses of the long-term economic and demographic development before drawing definitive conclusions about China as a whole.

According to Noriko Tsuya and Satomi Kurosu, Tokugawa Japan (1716–1870) differed in important ways from northeastern China. In Japan, marriage and migration were the demographic variables most sensitive to economic fluctuations. The economy had scarcely any effect on fertility, and the mortality response depended on age as well as sex. As for nuptiality, marriages in which the bride moved into the household of her husband were the most sensitive to economic fluctuations and responded with a lag of between two and four years: Japanese families were reluctant to take on additional household members following difficult economic times. Legally sanctioned migration declined when the economy was poor since there were few job openings, but unsanctioned migration increased as people desperately sought work. Women had low status in Japanese society, and the death rate among young girls rose when economic conditions were poor. More surprisingly, mortality also rose among elderly men in the same circumstances. The mortality patterns do parallel those found by Lee, Campbell and Tan (1992) for Liaoning, China, in the late eighteenth to late nineteenth century.

6. When the Gap between the East and the West Emerged

The contributions of this volume show the difficulties in comparing living standards across continents, and the gains to be had from combining different approaches. Regional disaggregation is important since some regions prospered while others declined at both ends of Eurasia. Likewise, disaggregation by class and status is important since some groups gained while others lost. The complexities involved in comparisons should not be overlooked. However, the findings in this book support the revisionist view that there were no systematic differences in living standards between Europe and Asia before the Industrial Revolution. The results can be summarized according to the three main dimensions discussed: economy, demography, and vulnerability to economic stress.

First turning to the economic dimension of living standards, income development varied a great deal across Europe in the 250-year period before the Industrial Revolution. While real wages were similar in fifteen European cities around 1500, a gap emerged in the seventeenth and early eighteenth centuries with the pre-industrial success of England and the Netherlands and the stagnation of Southern Europe (Allen 2001). Thus, the real wage gap within Europe in the mid-nineteenth century resulted from diverging economic trends in different countries slid back to the seventeenth century.

Income development also differed between different regions within countries. In England, for instance, it was only London that maintained high real wages, while provincial towns and the rural areas experienced the continental pattern of falling real wages in the sixteenth and early seventeenth centuries. Only in the late seventeenth and eighteenth centuries did the high wage economy spread to the rest of England (Allen 2001). Moreover, income development in Europe also differed between social groups between 1500 and 1800. Real income for the wealthier groups of society increased relative to the income of the poor, due to the different price histories of the goods consumed by these groups.

Thus, it appears that the economic development in Europe during the seventeenth and eighteenth century diverged not only between countries, but also between regions within countries and between social groups. Comparisons between the East and the West, therefore, depend on which areas and social groups are compared. Real wages for spinners and weavers in Southern India and Bengal seem to have been at least as high as English ones in the eighteenth century. Wages in India were lower than in Britain, but food prices were even lower due to higher productivity in agriculture. Also in Japan and parts of China, real wages in the eighteenth century seem to have compared fairly well with those in Italy, Germany, and France (cf. Hanley 1997; Kuznets 1971: Tables 1–2). In fact, China's richest regions—Yangzi and Lingnan—compared well even with England and Holland.

However, as several of the contributions of this book show, there were important regional differences within Asia during the pre-industrial period. While pre-industrial differences in well-being between the most developed parts of Europe and Asia were small, there were substantial differences between the most and least developed parts in each continent. The evidence for detailed comparisons across the full range of experience is not yet available. We can say, however, that the comparisons that have been made, which are generally for the most developed parts of Europe and China, fail to show the lead that Smith, Malthus, and Marx expected.

Comparisons of health indicators also point towards similar living standards at the two ends of Eurasia. In Europe, the height of adults declined from the late Middle Ages to *c*.1800 and thereafter rose steadily. This increased level of heights after 1800 has generally been seen as an indicator of an improving standard of living in Europe during this period. Unfortunately we do not have much Asian height data for comparison, but other demographic variables like life expectancy do not indicate substantial differences between Europe and Asia (see Bengtsson, Campbell, Lee *et al.* 2004). Quite the contrary, recent works by James Lee and Wang Feng (1999) and William Lavely and Bin Wong (1998) have challenged the classical view of the extreme population pressure in the East. These revisionists believe that Malthus was fundamentally incorrect and argue that deliberate infanticide was a more important check on population size than famines and other catastrophes. Early marriages, meanwhile, did not lead to a high birth rate because imbalances in the marriage market, created by female infanticide and restrictions on remarriage, meant that many men could never marry. Furthermore, the fertility of married couples was lower than in Europe because intervals between marriage and first birth were long by intention, as were subsequent birth intervals. Thus, family institutions differed greatly between China and Western Europe but the outcome in terms of life expectancy and population growth was about the same.

Finally we turn to the demographic response to economic fluctuations. The three European populations studied—southern Sweden, eastern Belgium, and Tuscany—showed marked demographic responses to economic stress. In Italy, the overall mortality rate rose in step with rising food prices. The poorer segments of Swedish and Belgian society exhibited the same response, although not the better-offs who were prosperous enough to avoid this fate. Johansen discovered the same pattern in Denmark. These results show that the standard of living of the least well-off people in Europe—and the majority in Tuscany—was at such a low level in the early nineteenth century that high food prices pushed up mortality. In both eastern Belgium and southern Sweden, conditions improved in the second half of the nineteenth century, indicating a rising standard of living. The developments of real wages and life expectancy are in accord with this finding.

In the two Asian populations—Liaoning in northern China and northeastern Japan—similar demographic responses to economic stress were also present. However, in these cases, the main differences in response were between different members of the household. In general, people with low status in the household, like female infants and children in the case of Japan, were the ones hardest hit by economic hardship, but in some cases groups with higher status, for example elderly males, were also severely affected in Asia (see also Bengtsson, Campbell, Lee *et al.* 2004). Over time the demographic response to economic stress generally declined, indicating improved living standards in these Asian communities in the nineteenth century. Indeed, even at an early date, some districts in Liaoning were more prosperous than many parts of Europe when the mortality response to high food prices is the indicator.

The contributions of this book show the highly complex and diverse pattern of the standard of living in the pre-industrial period. The general picture emerging from these studies is not one of a great divergence between East and West during this period, but instead one of considerable similarities. These similarities not only pertain to economic aspects of standard of living but also to demography and the sensitivity to economic fluctuations. In addition to these similarities, there were also pronounced differences within the East and within the West—differences that in many cases were larger than the differences between Europe and Asia. This clearly highlights the importance of analysing several dimensions of the standard of living, as well as the danger of neglecting regional, social, and household specific differences when assessing the level of well-being in the past.

Notes

1. Dasgupta and Weale (1992: 120) have extended it to also include political and civil liberties. The new index is highly correlated with HDI and thus with income per capita.
2. One such functioning that Sen discusses is not being 'ashamed to appear in public', referring to Adam Smith (Sen 1987: 17). Smith exemplified this with the person who, in order not to be ashamed to appear in public, needed to wear a white linen shirt.
3. For a more detailed discussion of this concept, see Bengtsson (2004). The idea of analysing the demographic response to short-term economic stress within different social groups, combining longitudinal micro-demographic data with macro-economic data, was first developed by Bengtsson (1989, 1993) and has been refined within the Eurasia Project on Population and Family History, in particular when it comes to the importance of household characteristics and transfers within the household in conditioning the response to stress (see Bengtsson, Campbell, Lee *et al.* 2004).

References

Abel, W. (1966/1980) 'Nonparametric Inference for a Family of Counting Processes'. *Annals of Statistics*, 6: 534–45.

Allen, R. C. (2001) 'The Great Divergence in European Wages and Prices from the Middle Ages to the First World War'. *Explorations in Economic History*, 38: 411–47.

Bengtsson, T. (1989) 'Real Wage Variation and Adult Mortality: Life Events in Västanfors, 1750–1859'. Paper presented at the IUSSP General Conference, New Dehli.

—— (1993) 'Combined Time-Series and Life Event Analysis: The Impact of Economic Fluctuations and Air Temperature on Adult Mortality by Sex and Occupation in a Swedish Mining Parish, 1757–1850', in D. Reher and R. Schofield (eds.), *Old and New Methods in Historical Demography*. Oxford: Clarendon Press.

—— (2004) 'Living Standards and Economic Stress', in T. Bengtsson, C. Campbell, J. Z Lee *et al.* (eds.), *Life Under Pressure: Mortality and Living Standards in Europe and Asia, 1700–1900*. Cambridge, MA: MIT Press, chapter 2.

—— and Reher, D. (1998) 'Short and Medium Term Relations between Population and Economy', in C.-E. Nuñez (ed.), *Debates and Controversies in Economic History. Proceedings of the Twelfth International Economic History Congress*. Madrid: Fundación Ramón Areces.

—— Campbell, C., Lee, J. Z. *et al.* (2004) *Life Under Pressure: Mortality and Living Standards in Europe and Asia, 1700–1900*. Cambridge MA: MIT Press.

Crafts, N. (1996) 'The Human Development Index: Some Historical Comparisons'. Working Papers in Economic History, No. 33/96. London: School of Economics.

Dasgupta, P. and Weale, M. (1992) 'On Measuring the Quality of Life'. *World Development*, 20(1): 119–31.

Fang Xing (1996) 'Qingdai Jiangnan shi zhen tanwei (Cities and Towns in Qing Jiangnan)'. *Zhongguo jingji shi yanjiu* (Research in Chinese economic history), 11(3): 91–8.

Ghai, Dharam P. *et al.* (1977) *The Basic-Needs Approach to Development: Some Issues Regarding Concepts and Methodology*. Geneva: International Labour Office.

Gill, I. (1998) 'Stature, Consumption, and the Standard of Living in Colonial Korea', in J. Komlos and J. Baten (eds.), *The Biological Standard of Living in Comparative Perspective*. Stuttgart: Franz Steiner Verlag, 122–38.

Jörberg, L. (1972) *A History of Prices in Sweden, 1732–1914*, Vols. 1–2. Lund: Gleerups.

Kuznets, S. (1971) *Modern Economic Growth: Rate, Structure, and Spread*. New Haven/ London: Yale University Press.

Landes, D. S. (1998) *The Wealth and Poverty of Nations: Why Some are So Rich and Some So Poor*. New York: W.W. Norton and Co.

Laveley, W. and Wong, R. B. (1998) 'Revising the Malthusian Narrative: The Comparative Study of Population Dynamics in Late Imperial China'. *Journal of Asian Studies*, 57: 714–48.

Lee, J., Campbell, C., and Tan, G. (1992) 'Infanticide and Family Planning in Late Imperial China: The Price and Population History of Rural Liaoning, 1774–1873', in T. G. Rawski and L. Li (eds.), *Chinese History in Economic Perspective*. Berkeley, CA: University of California Press.

Lee, J. Z. and Wang, F. (1999) *One Quarter of Humanity: Malthusian Mythology and Chinese Realities, 1700–2000*. Cambridge, MA: Harvard University Press.

Livi-Bacci, M. (1991) *Population and Nutrition*. Cambridge: Cambridge University Press.

Maddison, A. (1995) *Explaining the Economic Performance of Nations: Essays in Time and Space*. Aldershot: Elgar.

Malthus, T. R. (1803/1973) *An Essay on the Principle of Population*, introduction by T. H. Hollingsworth. London: J. M. Dent and Sons Ltd.

Marx, K. (1853/1983) 'The British Rule in India' and 'The Future Results of British Rule in India', in E. Kamenka (ed.), *The Portable Karl Marx*. New York: Penguin Books USA, pp. 329–41.

Morgan, S. L. (1998) 'Biological Indicators of Change in the Standard of Living in China during the 20th Century', in J. Komlos and J. Baten (eds.), *The Biological Standard of Living in Comparative Perspective*. Stuttgart: Franz Steiner Verlag, 7–34.

Muellbauer, J. (1987) 'Professor Sen and the Standard of Living', in G. Hawthorn (ed.), *The Standard of Living*. Cambridge: Cambridge University Press, 39–58.

Myrdal, G. (1933) *The Cost of Living in Sweden, 1830–1930*. London: P. S. King and Sons.

Parthasarathi, P. (1998) 'Rethinking Wages and Competitiveness in the Eighteenth Century: Britain and South India'. *Past and Present*, 158: 79–109.

——(2001) *The Transition to a Colonial Economy. Weavers, Merchants and Kings in South India, 1720–1800*. Cambridge: Cambridge University Press.

Pomeranz, K. (2000) *The Great Divergence: China, Europe, and the Making of the Modern World*. Princeton, NJ: Princeton University Press.

Prados de la Escosura, Leandro (2000) 'International Comparisons of Real Product, 1820–1990: An Alternative Data Set'. *Explorations in Economic History*, 37: 1–41.

Sandberg, L. G. and Steckel, R. H. (1980) 'Soldier, Soldier, What Made You Grow so Tall?'. *Economy and History*, 23: 91–105.

Scholliers, E. (1960) *De levenstandaard in de XVe en XVIe eeuw te Antwerpen; loonarbeid en honger*. Antwerp: De Sikkel.

Schön, L. (1979) *Från hantverk till fabriksindustri*. Kristianstad: Arkiv.

Sen, A. (1987) 'The Standard of Living', Lecture I and II in G. Hawthorn (ed.), *The Standard of Living*. Cambridge: Cambridge University Press.

——(1992) *Inequality Reexamined*. New York: Russell Sage Foundation.

Smith, A. (1776/1937) *An Inquiry into the Nature and Causes of the Wealth of Nations*, edited by E. Cannan. New York: The Modern Library.

Somogy, S. (1973) 'L'alimentatione dell'Italia'. In *Storia d'Italia*, vol. 5. Turin: Einaudi.

Staunton, G. L. (1797) *An Authentic Account of an Embassy from the King of Great Britain to the Emperor of China*, 2 Vols.

Steckel, R. H. (1995) 'Stature and the Standard of Living'. *Journal of Economic Literature*, 33: 1903–40.

Wittfogel, K. A. (1957) *Oriental Despotism: A Comparative Study of Total Power*. New Haven: Yale University Press.

Wong, R. B. (1997) *China Transformed: Historical Change and the Limits of European Experience*. Ithaca, NY: Cornell University Press.

World Bank (1984) *World Development Report 1984*. New York: Oxford University Press.

1 Standards of Living in Eighteenth-Century China: Regional Differences, Temporal Trends, and Incomplete Evidence

KENNETH POMERANZ

1. Introduction

Any evaluation of either the standard of living or subsistence security in eighteenth-century China will have many gaps. Even for China's richest and best documented region—the Yangzi Delta, with roughly 31,000,000 people (using a narrow definition) in the late eighteenth century—there is a great deal we do not know. Nonetheless, as I have argued in more detail elsewhere, what we do know suggests a rough comparability between China and Europe, and between the most advanced areas within each of those two large and varied regions. Most of the additional material that I introduce below tends to confirm this; it also helps us say with somewhat more precision what we still do not know, and where we may still find relatively large differences.

Also at issue, of course, is the relationship between 'standard of living' and subsistence security—a relationship that was becoming increasingly indirect in early modern Europe, as average real incomes rose while the distribution of income became more unequal. Indeed, the chapters by Hoffman *et al.* (Chapter 6, this volume) and Allen (Chapter 5, this volume) strongly suggest that both these trends were more pronounced than we realized, in part because rich and poor consumed different market baskets, whose relative prices underwent very significant shifts. When we add the cost of housing to the standard Phelps Brown price index—which is largely focused on the commodities purchased by the poor—trends in their real income become even more unfavourable in most of Europe's early modern cities. On the other hand, once we add some of the goods and services purchased by wealthier people (in ever-increasing amounts) during the early modern era, it becomes likely that for a significant minority of the population, the standard of living was improving considerably more rapidly than we had realized, raising the overall European average. My own Sino-European comparisons have been centred largely on the poor majority in both societies; and while there were groups of 'middling' and wealthy Chinese who also enjoyed rising fortunes in the eighteenth century, we are nowhere near being able to estimate their numbers. They may have been a smaller percentage of the general population than in at least northwestern Europe; in that case, there would be more difference than I had seen between average standards of living in eighteenth-century China and Europe, even if my comparisons of the relative well-being of the majority in each society are roughly accurate. In what follows, I hope to at least make clear what we do and do not know about subsistence security, average living standards, and the living standards of the poor, and to point to places where East–West comparisons along these multiple axes may differ from each other. Finally, I discuss a number of reasons why both average standards of living and subsistence security may have declined sharply in some parts of China during the nineteenth and early twentieth centuries. This is important both in its own right and to reinforce the plausibility of relatively high eighteenth-century estimates.

2. Food

Basic caloric intake is one of the areas where we can be most confident that Chinese were no worse off than their European counterparts. Using data on the diets of landless agricultural labourers contained in seventeenth-century agricultural treatises—which refer mostly to conditions in the advanced Yangzi Delta—Ming-te Pan calculates that they represent a daily diet of 4,700 calories during the working months.[1] Overall figures are of course lower, but estimates of *per capita* grain consumption in the eighteenth century average about 2.2 *shi* of rice equivalent per person (including both sexes and all ages).[2] If the estimate of Chinese grain output *c*.1753 by Guo Songyi is even close to accurate, this is a very substantial underestimate,[3] and the large rations and heavy labour of Pan's farm workers were actually closer to the mark. Meanwhile, one of the assumptions behind the 2.2 *shi* estimate is that per capita grain consumption in the eighteenth century was somewhere in between our figures for the 1930s (which are very low) and those for 1953, when circumstances had begun to improve after years of war and civil war. I will argue below, that there are reasons to doubt this and would myself be inclined to use at least the 2.5 *shi* per person estimate used by Pierre-Etienne Will and R. Bin Wong in their work (Will and Wong 1991: 465). However, I will ignore all these possibilities for now, and work with the 2.2 *shi* estimate.

This converts to 1,837 calories per person from rice alone. If the age structure of the population was about the same as in the 1930s,[4] this would work out to 2,386 calories per adult equivalent of grain alone. This would compare favourably with the various estimates for workers in late eighteenth- and nineteenth-century England (the richest part of Europe) cited by Clark, Huberman and Lindert, which range from 1,500 to 2,400 calories per person from all foods, and would be close to most of the figures they later cite for more prosperous periods (Clark, Huberman, and Lindert 1995: 223–6). It matches almost precisely Carole Shammas' estimate for England as a whole (including all classes) in the late eighteenth century: 2,349 per adult equivalent (Shammas 1990: 134). It compares very well with figures often given for various parts of continental Europe: most figures I have found for eighteenth-century France, for instance, are between 1,800 and 2,500 calories per day. In the southern Netherlands (Belgium) *c*.1800, the average food intake is estimated at between 2,180 and 2,440 calories per capita per day; the poor fared worse (Lis and Soly 1979: 182). J. C. Toutain estimated average caloric intake in France at only 1,800 calories per capita per day in the eighteenth century.[5] R. J. Bernard collected twelve 'food pensions' from one region, which were supposed to provide for all the food needs of the recipient: only two of the twelve diets in question reached the Chinese average of caloric intake from rice alone, and eight out of twelve were below 2,000 calories per day (Bernard 1975: 35, 39).

Estimates of per capita grain consumption, relief rations, and so on, do not seem to vary much between richer and poorer parts of China, though these figures are admittedly sparse and not always reliable. The daily ration for convicts in prison or on their way to exile in central Asia was roughly 2,800 calories per day of grain (plus a small allowance for other food) before 1775, with the same ration being given (oddly enough) to men, women, and children. After 1775, it was reduced to roughly 2,333 calories per adult (Waley Cohen 1991: 118–19) which still compares favourably with the diet of the English poor at the end of the century. The famine relief ration distributed in kind *c*.1740 was much less than this—a mere 1,400 calories worth, which would barely support survival—but since 'the usual rule' was to distribute half of the relief in kind and the other half in cash, these rations too probably averaged around 2,800 calories for adults in the eighteenth century (Will 1990: 132–3).

The *stability* of the basic grain supply, however, did vary enormously by region. Except for a period of flooding in the 1830s and 1840s (of which more later), the Yangzi Delta suffered relatively few natural catastrophes, and its position on the coast and at the mouth of a river system which drained close to one-third of China meant that though the area always relied on imports for some of its food, widespread famine was virtually unknown there, between the catastrophes at the end of the Ming (1644) and during the Taiping Rebellion (1851–64). Famine also appears to have been rare in the rice bowls of the middle and upper Yangzi, the southern Manchurian frontier, and Taiwan. These were areas that generally produced large surpluses, and both merchants and the state regularly moved grain out of these regions. However, there was nothing quite comparable to the absolute priority accorded to Paris, Madrid, and other early modern European capitals, which forced continued exports even during harvest shortfalls, and thus made what were normally grain-surplus regions among the places most at risk of famine.[6] Much of north and northwest China, on the other hand, suffered from China's least reliable rainfall, its most disaster-prone rivers, and relatively poor transport facilities; in north China these conditions were complicated by dense population. Though it was in these areas that the state mounted its most impressive efforts at food supply stabilization and famine relief, they never achieved the same degree of food security as either the Yangzi Delta or some of the grain-exporting areas; and, as we shall see, the state's efforts to alleviate this problem became far less reliable in the nineteenth century.

Europe, of course, also had a wide range of famine vulnerability by region. England (though not all of Britain) was essentially free from widespread famine from mid-seventeenth century onwards, much like the Yangzi Delta, and some other parts of north and northwest Europe were not far behind. Most of the Continent, however, remained vulnerable until well into the nineteenth century. This included not only notoriously poor areas (e.g. the Balkans) but also some relatively rich ones (e.g. the German Rhineland).[7] A systematic comparison of how much of the Chinese and European populations had what degrees of risk is far beyond the scope of this chapter, but as long as we avoid comparing all of China to a few much smaller nations in Europe, it still seems likely that we would find rough comparability through the eighteenth century.

2.1   Beyond basic calories

For non-grain foods, comparisons are harder to make, but when we can do so, eighteenth-century China fares reasonably well. Chinese meat and (especially) dairy consumption levels were surely lower overall than European ones, given far lower ratios of livestock to population. But protein intake was nonetheless probably adequate for most people, and in some cases probably exceeded what was available to ordinary Europeans: any overall European edge is probably accounted for by very high protein consumption among a relatively small group of well-to-do people. It also seems likely that Chinese protein consumption was higher in the mid-eighteenth century than it was in the early twentieth century according to the data compiled by J. L. Buck. Unfortunately, Chinese sources consistently refer to 'a piece' of meat, fish, or beancurd without specifying its size. However, Pan Ming-te has made plausible (and probably conservative) estimates of the size of portions referred to in the discussion of workers' diets in the *Shenshi nongshu*, a widely used and often reprinted seventeenth-century agricultural manual. Using Pan's estimates and the data in the manual itself (read in the most cautious way possible) I arrive at an estimate of roughly 22 g of animal protein per day (over the course of the year) and 7 g of protein from beancurd/day, to give a total of 29 g per day of actual protein from these relatively protein-rich foods. For purposes of comparing Chinese diets to standard contemporary nutritional guidelines, this is the figure that should be added to the protein content of the rest of the diet (mostly cereals): I will refer to it below as 'actual protein intake'. However, some studies of pre-industrial European populations, plus the classic study of early twentieth-century China by John L. Buck, for some reason omit the step of estimating how much protein there actually is in a given serving of meat, fish, or eggs: they simply record the portion size of protein-rich foods, as if they were 100% protein, and later add this number to the protein content of cereals to get a total protein intake. This approach greatly inflates the amount of protein in the diet, and so should not be compared to nutritional standards to judge a population as probably free from deficiencies; however, it is useful to have this number for early Qing China for purposes of comparability with the other studies. I will refer to it as the 'protein portion', rather than 'actual protein intake' to keep the two distinct. Using the data and calculations described above, the 'protein portion' would be 124 g per day for seventeenth-century Yangzi Delta farm workers, even before we add any protein content in the rice they ate.

These figures are higher than one might expect and, as we shall see, they compare rather well with both eighteenth-century European and twentieth-century Chinese data. It is also worth noting that while rice provides very little protein per pound or calorie of consumption, what protein there is, is of high quality. Thus in a very high-calorie diet, such as that of the farm labourers described above, rice protein alone might meet the person's needs, at least according to some authorities; it would have added about 44 g of protein per day to the diet of somebody consuming the conservatively estimated 'average adult rice ration' for China as a whole, and an impressive 85 g per day for labourers eating the diet in *Shenshi nongshu*.[8] Thus actual protein intake would range between 73–114 g per day, and the less accurate 'protein portion' might be estimated as 168–209 g per day, depending on which estimate of rice consumption one uses.

Consequently, the situation would seem to compare quite favourably with John L. Buck's estimates of anywhere from 57 to 148 g of 'protein portions' from all sources per adult male equivalent in six mostly poor counties in the 1920s (Buck 1930/1971: 374) with averages ranging from 82 to 117 g per adult male equivalent (again including all sources) in each of the eight regions into which he divided his large 1937 study of China (Buck 1937/1964: 419). The actual protein intake would of course be smaller than the 'protein portion', but once the protein content of grain consumed was added in (giving us the 73–114 g band), the result would meet the US government's recommended daily allowance of 66 g per day of actual protein for an adult male, or the international minimum standard of an equivalent of 37 g per day of actual egg or milk protein for a 143 pound adult male.[9] As a percentage of total calories, protein intake would be somewhere below the recommended 10–15% if the person in question was consuming the enormous quantities of grain cited in *Shenshi nongshu* for agricultural labourers in summer and fall, and within or slightly above that band if they were eating something closer to 2,500 or even 3,000 calories of grain.

Moreover, this was not the extent of protein consumption, even for these very poor workers. This is made clear by the absence of poultry and eggs from the diets in the agricultural manuals. Even agricultural labourers typically had access to a small plot for raising vegetables and chickens; in fact, in many parts of the country it was still customary for farm labourers to make ceremonial presents of eggs to their employers on certain holidays. (The agricultural manuals probably omit them because they are concerned with telling landowners what they need to provide for their labourers.) Interestingly, Buck found in the twentieth century that though large numbers of eggs were produced on Chinese farms, only a very small percentage of them were consumed on the farm. His 1930 survey suggested that the average farm family had about 4 chickens, but his 1937 study suggested that they consumed only 40 eggs (per 5-member person family) per year, out of perhaps 200 produced (Buck 1930/1971: 218, 1937/1964: 258 n. 12, 411). The vast majority of eggs, Buck argued, were too valuable as a source of cash to be eaten by the producers; more and more were being exported to raise cash (Buck 1937/1964: 430). In the seventeenth and eighteenth centuries, exports of eggs were clearly not a factor, and it seems likely that most farm families had less of a need to raise cash than their warlord-era descendants: taxes were lower, fuel that one could gather was more plentiful, and probably more household goods were self-produced. Under the circumstances, it seems likely that a much larger share of eggs produced were actually consumed on the farm in earlier days, though for now this must remain speculative.

There seems little doubt, then, that, on average, actual protein intake was quantitatively sufficient—as was even the generally lower intake noted by Buck in most regions of China in the 1930s. It should be remembered, though, that such averages do not reflect various scenarios that would have had important health implications: for instance, the substantial possibility that children or pregnant women may have been deprived of adequate protein while all the meat in the diet went to men working in the fields. Moreover, it is harder to be sure of the quality than the quantity. In Buck's twentieth-century survey, most of the protein came from cereal and vegetable sources, as all animal products (including eggs) provided an average of only 77 calories per adult male equivalent per day— much less than the estimate for seventeenth-century farm labourers derived here (Buck 1937/1964: 407, 411). And while, as noted above, rice protein is of fairly high quality (but limited quantity, unless one eats a lot), this is not true for wheat or for some of the other grains consumed by poorer people, especially in the north. Under these circumstances—and using ideas about the low quality of vegetable protein that are now questioned, especially of rice—Buck and other observers had doubts about whether the quality of the protein in the average Chinese diet was sufficient for certain groups, such as growing children (Buck 1937/1964: 418). If the figures adapted from *Shenshi nongshu* are even close to being representative, and if recent science that has upgraded our impression of the adequacy of vegetable proteins is accurate, this had probably not been a widespread problem in the Yangzi Delta over the last 200 years. Unfortunately, we lack the data to make even these rough estimates for other parts of seventeenth- or eighteenth-century China.

Is it plausible that protein consumption was a good deal higher in the seventeenth and eighteenth centuries than in the early twentieth century? In his famous work on Chinese agriculture 1368–1968, Dwight Perkins argues that the ratio of hogs (by far the most important meat source) to human population had been roughly constant from the 1360s to 1957—though he admitted that he had very little evidence for this crucial assumption (Perkins 1969: 71–3). However, Perkins' own supply and demand schedule for hogs suggests that (1) once hogs become sufficiently numerous that they cannot be fed entirely on chaff and garbage, the cost of raising them rises rapidly, so that more hogs can be raised only if demand is strong enough to sustain

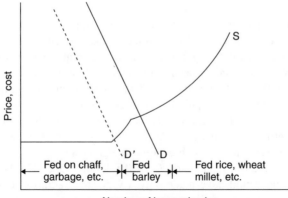

Figure 1.1 Supply and demand for hogs (reproduced from Perkins 1969: 72)

S: Supply schedule for hogs—the cost of raising hogs rises steeply when farmers switch from feeding hogs chaff to feeding them grain. The cost of grain rises more and more rapidly as farmers cut increasingly into their own (or the nation's) grain consumption (solid line).
D′: Demand schedule for hogs where hogs are only used as the source of pork (dashed line).
D: Demand schedule for hogs where hogs supply both pork and fertilizer (solid line).

sharply rising prices, (2) the demand schedule for hogs shifts sharply to the right insofar as hogs are an important source of fertilizer as well as meat. Thus, the number of hogs in an area such as the lower Yangzi (in which cultivated acreage in the late Ming was already close to its twentieth-century maximum) should be very sensitive to the demand for pig manure (Figure 1.1).

Further, beginning in the late seventeenth century, more and more Yangzi Delta farmers began to apply large amounts of imported soybean cake to their fields—a fertilizer that to a great extent replaced, rather than supplemented night soil.[10] It thus seems likely that the amount of hog-derived fertilizer being used by each farmer would have declined over time as soybean cake fertilizer spread, and with it the number of (and demand for) pigs relative to farmers: a reasonable proxy, in this economy, for the availability of pork per capita. By the 1930s, the middle and lower Yangzi (grouped together in Buck's 'Yangzi Rice/Wheat' area) used less than two-thirds the quantity of animal manure and night soil per acre as did China as a whole (even though they had far more humans per acre), and more than double the amount of other fertilizers per acre.[11] Perkins himself also notes that a late Ming source gives an estimate of manure use per acre in Jiaxing prefecture (in the Yangzi Delta) that is roughly equal to Buck's estimate for south China as a whole in the 1930s (Perkins 1969: 73). This figure is, in turn, 87% higher than the 1930s figures for Buck's 'Yangzi Rice/Wheat' region—the region which includes Jiaxing, though it is far larger, including most of the lower and middle Yangzi (Buck 1937/1964: 259). This would seem to confirm the guess that this area had had far more pigs per crop acre in the late Ming than it had by the 1930s: a period when it also had considerably fewer humans than it would have had by the mid-eighteenth century, or the early twentieth century.[12] It thus seems more likely that our relatively high estimates for seventeenth-century protein intake estimates are roughly accurate and that Perkins was right to guess that meat consumption was unchanged over centuries—though we certainly need more evidence to prove either case.[13] It would then seem likely that protein availability had already declined significantly by the late eighteenth century—as population grew and easier access to soybean cake cut into demand for hog wastes—but was probably not yet down to the levels observed in early twentieth-century Jiangnan. Li Bozhong has also provided evidence that cows and oxen, rare in twentieth-century Jiangnan agriculture, were somewhat more plentiful in the Ming and early Qing (Li 2000: 275–6, 278–80). These were work animals and would have made only a very small additional contribution to protein intake, but the dynamics causing their numbers to decline may have been similar.

If per capita meat consumption in particular was indeed declining in late imperial China, this would fit the long-term trend in early modern Europe as well: though in relatively land-rich, livestock-using Europe this decline began from a much higher base. Braudel estimates that meat consumption in Germany fell by 80% between the late Middle Ages and 1800 (Braudel 1981: 196). In Toulouse, the average consumption of beef fell from 15 k per capita in 1655–9, to 7 kg in 1750 (though there was also some consumption of other meats).[14] The latter figure would work out to 20 g per day of meat, or barely 4 g per day of actual protein from this source—considerably less than our figures, though missing data make any systematic comparison impossible.

Indeed, the general picture of protein supply in late eighteenth-century western Europe seems no better, and often worse, than these Chinese figures—though the way that some historians calculate it complicates comparisons. Lis and Soly's estimate of total protein intake per capita in the 'average' southern Netherlands diet *c*.1800—73.2 g per person per day, of which only 22.5 g was a 'protein portion' from animal sources (Lis and Soly 1979: 182)—is near the bottom of Buck's above-cited range of figures for twentieth-century rural China, and much lower than the estimates we have made for the seventeenth and eighteenth centuries. Actual protein intake in such a diet would be under 60 g per day. Of course, 1800—in the midst of the Napoleonic Wars—was a particularly bad year, but the comparison is nonetheless suggestive. Toutain's figures for Napoleonic France, which suggest about 200 kcal/day of protein—only about 50 kcal of it came from animal protein[15]—would convert to different amounts of protein in grams depending on precisely what foods were involved. The weight of the protein-rich food however, that is, the 'protein portion', is unlikely to have been above 50 g per day, and the quantity of protein actually obtained at the most was 10 g/day. Even if we add protein from the rest of the diet, we would have a total protein intake of perhaps 70 g—matching the very bottom of our range of Chinese estimates.[16] Bernard's figures from Gévaudan range, with one exception, from 32 to 75 g of actual protein per day, including protein obtained from cereals; the one exception is 89 g

(Bernard 1975: 37 n. 1, 38). For Britain, D. J. Oddy estimates 49 g of protein per capita per day for 1787–93, using family budgets for rural labourers—a figure which appears to be for actual intake, not 'protein portions'. (Working backwards from his data to get an estimated 'protein portion' for purposes of comparability, I got about 75 g per person per day for those years.) This rises to 62 g in a 1796 sample, but does not exceed 66 g until a 1937 sample.[17]

For vegetables (and thus many vitamins), it seems very likely that comparisons would favour China, since early modern Europeans tended to eat very few vegetables. Chinese cooking methods also preserved the vitamins in vegetables better than European ones. Again working from *Shenshi nongshu*, Pan estimates that the average daily ration of vegetables (again, excepting anything grown in one's own garden) would be about 200 g/day (Pan 1998: 17). By contrast, Buck's figures for the 1920s (in this case from one county in Anhui) comes to 190.3 k/year of various vegetables for families with an average of 4.88 adult male equivalents.[18] This works out to only 107 g/day per person—barely half of the estimated seventeenth-century level. But consumption estimates for fruits and vegetables are likely to be particularly unreliable, both in China and in Europe, because much of this consumption did not pass through the market: even today, such estimates are almost always lower than reality (Aymard 1979: 2).

Overall, then, the food component of the standard of living seems generally comparable in eighteenth-century China and Europe, and in the most advanced regions of each. Admittedly, for the poorer and more poorly documented parts of China we must rely in part on the assumption that non-grain food consumption was no lower in the late eighteenth century than in the early twentieth century. Nevertheless, as I will try to show near the end of this chapter, it is precisely those regions for which such a claim is most compelling. Of course, a great deal of information is still missing but from what we do know, there are as many reasons to give China an edge over Europe as vice versa.

At least comparable nutritional levels are also suggested by the fact that eighteenth-century rural Chinese life expectancies—between thirty and forty in most available studies—are quite comparable to those for eighteenth-century England, and higher than those found in most studies of continental European populations.[19] Moreover, since recent studies suggest that Chinese birth rates were below European ones throughout the 1550–1850 period,[20] while the overall rate of population growth was first faster (1550–1750) and then similar (1750–1850),[21] we have a further indication that Chinese death rates could not have been significantly higher than those for even the wealthier countries of Europe in the late eighteenth century.

Moreover, Chinese appear to have reached these nutritional standards without spending any more of their incomes on basic foodstuffs than did their European counterparts. Fang Xing's study of Yangzi Delta farm labourers suggests that they spent 55% of their cash and kind earnings on basic grain supplies in the seventeenth century, and almost the same amount (54%) in the early nineteenth century (Fang 1996: 93, 95). This is almost exactly the same as the figure for rural poor in the 1790s cited by Phelps Brown and Hopkins, and since agricultural labourers were the poorest non-beggars in China, the comparison seems apt (Phelps Brown and Hopkins 1981: 14). Moreover, Fang's method of calculation seems more likely to understate than overstate the consumption of these labourers (Pomeranz 2000a: 137, n. 110). Data compiled by Carole Shammas suggests that in comparison with at least southern England the results may have remained quite close until much later. She estimates that agricultural labourers spent 72% of their incomes on food in 1837–8, and finds figures fluctuating between 50% and 70% for various samples (not all of them from such poor people) until 1900 (Shammas 1990: 124–6). She also estimates that 66% of food expenditures went for cereals in south England.[22] Assuming that farm labourers were able to spend as much of their food budget on non-cereals as other labourers in south England (which seems optimistic, since they generally earned much less), they would have been spending 48% of their income on grain: just very slightly below Fang's lower Yangzi estimate.

Moreover, Fang does not calculate peasant incomes directly. Instead he relies on accounts of the minimum expenditures needed for clothing, firewood, and so on (again, mostly in agricultural manuals). Thus he excludes various other kinds of expenditures: for example, *occasional* very large expenditures for life-cycle rituals; jewellery, which even poor women seem to have had some of (Pan 1994: 85); clothes for special occasions;[23] entertainment, and so on. Overall, then, it is much more likely that Fang has underestimated what even farm labourers could spend on things beyond basic calories than that he has overestimated it: and yet his estimates seem comparable to those for the English poor.

For the early twentieth century, we again have data from J. L. Buck, which suggests that peasants in six counties of 'East Central China' spent 53.8% of their income on food (Buck 1937/1964: 386)—and therefore presumably less than that on basic cereals. But these were farm families of all sorts, not just landless labourers, and Buck's sample has been criticized for being skewed towards more prosperous families. It thus seems likely that by this indicator, too, the Chinese poor of the eighteenth century were somewhat better off than their early twentieth-century counterparts.

3. Income Distribution

The very poor in China, then, were quite likely doing as well or better than the very poor of western Europe, but that was not very well in either case. When we try to estimate how many people were *not* very poor, and what their standards of living looked like, we run into massive difficulties. We can make rough estimates for a couple of groups, which suggest that they had plenty to spend—matching the accounts in literary sources of booming consumption. But far too much remains unknown for us to put forward the sorts of hypotheses for China that Hoffman *et al.* (Chapter 6, this volume) advance for Europe. And while most of the evidence we have still argues for rough comparability in both elite and 'middle class' consumption, this must remain conjectural.

At the top of the society (not counting a relatively small group of privileged Manchus), there is no question that many members of a loosely defined 'gentry' class had plenty of money. Chang Chung-li's famous estimates of the income of the Chinese gentry have many problems, but are still the best we have. He estimates that in the late nineteenth century, a group of gentry and their immediate families, totalling perhaps 7.5 million people, had an income of about 645,000,000 *taels*, or 24% of national income (Chang 1962: 327, 329). At roughly 430 *taels* per family of five, such people would have had to spend only a tiny fraction of their income (under 4%) on cereals; even a luxurious diet could hardly have taken up much of their total spending. A century earlier, the numbers would have been different, of course; but the percentage of gentry in the population would not have been much different (around 2%), and most of their spending would certainly have been on things other than basic subsistence.

As I have noted elsewhere, Chang's figure of 24% of income going to something like the top 2% of the population[24] is not much different from figures we can derive for England and Wales, drawing on the work of Peter Lindert and Jeffrey Williamson. (Europe as a whole would be a better comparison, but no such figures are available that I know of.) Leaving out the royal family, their numbers suggest that the top 2% of the population received 19% of national income in 1688; 22% in 1759, and 23% in 1801–3.[25] This rough coincidence is certainly no substitute for a more general comparison of income distribution at all levels of the society, but it is some indication that the disparity between the poor and the very rich was not very large.

The big problem, of course, is estimating the numbers and standards of living of those who were neither at the top nor at the bottom of the society. Some recent work on the clerks and runners who occupied the bottom of the hierarchy in local government offices—and were probably the least prestigious literate occupational group in late Imperial China—provides some interesting information. Bradly Reed has estimated that yamen runners in late nineteenth-century Baxian (Sichuan) made perhaps 35–65 *taels* per year and head runners 2–3 times that much; he puts the income of yamen clerks considerably higher, at 100–150 *taels* per year, and head clerks at 300–400 *taels*. He cites other scholars who have suggested higher figures.[26] We know little about the consumption habits of such people—despite, or perhaps partly because of, stereotypical complaints from their social superiors that they spent huge amounts on alcohol and prostitutes—but it would appear that they had substantial amounts of money to spend. And while the numbers of such people are not known, Reed has made an estimate of 100 clerks for his county (before it was opened to foreign trade and residence in 1890, leading to a huge boom in legal and administrative business and in the number of clerks), and anywhere from 250 to 450 runners.[27] While Baxian probably had more personnel than the average of China's roughly 1,500 counties, and all counties had presumably less personnel a century earlier, it seems conservative to guess that there would have been 250,000 clerks and runners in mid- to late-eighteenth-century China—representing, with their families, perhaps 1.25 million people. Many of them also had other financial interests in their families—landowning, small businesses, etc.—which would have raised their incomes further. Reed suggests that a clerk's income would have been roughly on par with that of a shop manager, while that of a runner (some of whom did not even need minimal literacy) would have been better than that of 'most manual labourers' in the towns and cities (Reed 2000: 207). This is not much to go on, though it suggests that these people were probably not far above or below a large class of so-called 'petty-urbanites' (*xiao shimin*) making up about 5% of the total population: teachers, artisans, clerks, small merchants, and so on.[28] (Other scholars and contemporary officials have suggested numbers of clerks and runners which are more than double these, but Reed's more conservative figure will do for our purposes, since the intent is to have these yamen underlings stand for a broad stratum of *xiao shimin*.)

Beyond these groups, there is even less to go on. We have some wage figures for urban workers, but most are of very limited use: they are, for instance, often unclear about the extent of in-kind supplements to the cash wage. One of the few examples we have that includes an estimate of cash wages, the value of in-kind supplements, and an estimate of the cost of living for a working-class family comes from a salt works in late nineteenth-century Sichuan.[29] If the numbers are accurate, a family of four needed 3,600 *wen* in cash to live on, of which it spent roughly 600 *wen* for grain; it received grain worth 900 *wen* as part of the humblest worker's wages (brine carriers and hammermen received a bit more), plus a very small amount of other food, which we will discount. If this 4,500 in-cash and in-kind represented the family's total budget, then grain would be roughly one-third of total living expenses for these workers. It appears that this would have given the family an annual grain supply of 8.4 *shi* of husked grain: almost exactly the average figure we have used for China as a whole.[30] (It is not clear, however, how the poorest workers would have raised the 3,600 *wen* in cash, since their pay ranged from 1,000 to 2,200 *wen*, unless either their wives and/or children contributed to much of the family budget. Many, of course, may not have had families, but anyone who was trying to support four people on such a wage would have been far below the 'minimum' cited above, and spending almost everything on grain.)

Other workers in this salt works must have had considerably more to spend on things beyond the bare necessities. The best-paid salt makers earned four times the cash wage of the poorest workers, the cashier three times, foremen five to six times, assistant accountants seven to eight times, and the head accountant twenty times. Throughout the scattered wage data we have, we find very large differentials between unskilled workers on the one hand and skilled workers, supervisors, and clerks on the other; this might suggest that the latter groups were relatively prosperous, as I have suggested, but there are also good reasons not to leap to this inference.[31]

Zhao Gang's historical survey of wage data provides details on monthly cash wages for various kinds of textile workers which, when converted into unhusked rice, range from 0.29 to 4.19 *shi* of grain per month (3.5–50.4 per year). For less-skilled workers, about 5 *shi* (which equalled 2.75 *shi* of husked grain) a year seems typical. If we assume that such a worker also received roughly 5 *shi* of husked grain per year in kind (slightly higher than the grain allowance for the poorest salt workers in the nineteenth-century example),[32] had a wife and two children and no other income, he would have come up slightly short of even providing his family with an all-cereals diet meeting the caloric average. But a single unskilled (or in some cases even skilled) worker could not feed a whole family elsewhere in the eighteenth-century world either and, as I have argued elsewhere, there may have been less of a gap in earning power between poor Chinese men and women in the eighteenth century than was the case in Europe.[33] If the wife in this example added to the budget half as much as the husband's cash and in-kind earnings, 75% of their combined earnings would provide an average caloric intake, making them roughly as poor as the English agricultural workers in the 1830s mentioned above. And if many of the poorest wage workers were single, they would actually have had a substantial portion of their income to spend on things other than food. This is quite likely since (1) many workers who were in the poorest pay classifications would have moved up with time and married then; and (2) many of those who did not, probably joined the estimated 10–15% of Chinese males who never married.

The much larger and more important problem of estimating the numbers and incomes of the rural majority—those that were neither gentry-landlords, nor the landless labourers we have discussed above—is not even this far advanced. All we can say is that (1) agricultural yields were sufficient to feed everyone, and (as we shall see below) to produce more cloth per capita than Europeans wore—leaving aside the crucial issue of income distribution; (2) the relatively widespread own-ership of land, dispersion of by-employments, and generally light tax rates may have made for a more equal distribution of income than in most commercialized agrarian societies; (3) tenants and small farm owners must have generally been better off than the landless labourers discussed above; and (4) such people were not leaving the land at rates sufficient to change the urban/rural distribution of population very much.[34] Income differentials do not, of course, automatically trigger large migra-tions, so we cannot infer much from their absence: but if even those with some property or secure tenancies in the countryside had been vastly poorer than petty urbanites, one would probably expect more movement than the record suggests. While there obviously were huge numbers of poor people in the countryside, general living standards, employment opportunities, and subsistence security seem to have been adequate to keep the overwhelming majority of them in place in the eighteenth century. As we shall see, at least subsistence security probably declined in the nineteenth and early twentieth centuries in most regions. The general standard of living may have as well, but more through the growing weight of poor regions in China-wide aggregates than through declining consumption in particular places. Before we return to this contention, we need to look at what the consumption levels of things besides basic foodstuffs were in the eighteenth century.

4. 'Non-essential' Consumption

If most Chinese ate fairly well by pre-industrial standards, and even the poor had some money left over, what did they spend it on? Unfortunately, we have nothing for China that is comparable to the inventories of possessions held at death for many places in Europe, but we do have other information. Literary evidence includes lots of material from domestic travellers describing (and usually decrying) increases in popular consumption; fiction that aspired to realism describes a vast range of goods for sale in even some rather small and remote towns. Lists of 'products sold' included in local histories are also suggestive, though these must be treated with caution, as such histories might mechanically repeat the list from an earlier edition, or list items that were only occasionally available. We also have a few direct descriptions of the food, clothing, and home furnishings of families at various levels in the social hierarchy.[35] We also have the accounts of various European visitors, most of whom, before 1800, compare levels of consumption favourably with those back home. For instance, two English emissaries who travelled from Beijing to Canton in 1793, were very struck by how much the people they saw smoked (Staunton 1799: II, 48; Macartney (1793) in Cranmer-Byng 1963: 225)—a comment lent additional support by a source claiming that even toddlers smoked in Zhejiang.[36] Also interesting is Gaspar Da Cruz's admiring account of the construction and furnishing of the homes of China's more successful farmers. The latter, though earlier than would be ideal for our purposes, is interesting because Da Cruz (a Portuguese ship captain arrested for smuggling at Canton, who was eventually exiled to the southwest and left the country overland into Burma) saw areas far off the beaten track. It is also suggestive because Da Cruz said he was describing the homes of what he called 'successful husbandmen' rather than the officials and great merchants who made up China's real upper class;[37] and also because, given China's severe timber shortages and the surprisingly limited use of stone in domestic construction, one would expect housing to be among the areas in which Chinese consumption would most lag behind the European.

I have also taken steps towards measuring some part of this consumption quantitatively. Usually this had to be done by working backwards from estimates of the amount of land under various crops, multiplying by contemporary yield estimates, and subtracting exports where they are relevant. This introduces various uncertainties, but I have also taken various steps to ensure that these estimates are conservative.[38] Even so, they are quite surprising. It may be no shock to see that *per capita* tea and silk consumption were higher in China than in Europe, but consider the following data for sugar and for ordinary cloth (Tables 1.1 and 1.2).

Despite the uncertainties that surround these numbers, they are quite instructive: perhaps especially those for cloth. They suggest that in Jiangnan, the richest part of China, cloth production per capita in 1750 was comparable to that in England fifty years later. We cannot easily move to an estimate of cloth consumption, since much of this cloth was shipped to other parts of China; but England, of course, also

Table 1.1 Sugar and tea consumption in Europe and China (in pounds per capita)

	Europe	Europe, except Britain	Britain	England	Non-Russian Europe[a]	China
Sugar						
1680	1.0	0.85	4.0	—	—	—
1750	2.2	1.9	10.0	—	—	3.8–5.0[b]
1800	2.6	1.98	18.0	—	—	—
Tea						
1780	—	—	—	1.0	0.12	—
1840	—	—	—	1.4	0.25	0.7

[a] Includes England.
[b] Consumption per capita for country as a whole with heavy concentration to the Lower Yangzi, southeast coast, and Lingnan, where consumption may have been as high as 10 pounds per capita.

Sources: Production figures from Philipps (1990: 58–61), for Portuguese and Spanish colonies, Steensgaard (1990: 140), for French, Dutch, and English colonies, Braudel (1981: 251–2), Gardella (1994: 6, 38), Xu and Wu (1985: 99). European population figures from McEvedy and Jones (1978: 28), British consumption figures from Mintz (1985: 67, 73), substituting year 1700 figures for 1680 in this table. For Chinese calculations, see Pomeranz (2003: ch. 3).

Table 1.2 Selected comparisons of cloth output and consumption (in pounds per capita)

	Yangzi Delta[a]	China	United Kingdom	France	Germany
Cotton cloth, *c.*1750	11.2–14.5[b]	6.2–8.3[c]	—	—	—
Silk cloth, *c.*1750	2.0[b]	—	—	—	—
Ramie, *c.*1750	—	3.5[d]	—	—	—
Mixed cloth, *c.*1800[e]	—	—	12.9[f]	8.4	5.0

[a] Population app. 31 million in 1750, omitting salt-producing prefectures from the large definition in Wang (1989).
[b] Amount consumed locally unknown. For an adjustment of Yangzi Delta textile output downward from the figures in Pomeranz (2000a) see also Pomeranz (2002).
[c] Probably nearer lower end of range.
[d] Ramie was not included in estimates of cloth in Pomeranz (2000a). It does appear, however, that it was still quite significant though it is usually agreed that it was steadily losing ground to cotton. In the early twentieth century, production was still about 1.5 billion pounds, or roughly 3.5 pounds per capita. Whether per capita was higher than that was 150 years earlier (either because of a smaller population or because many people had not yet fully switched to cotton) or lower (because the highland areas in which much ramie was raised were not yet as fully exploited) remains conjectural.
[e] Combination of cotton, linen, and wool.
[f] About 8.7 pounds per capita consumed within the United Kingdom.

Sources: See Pomeranz (2000a: appendix F) and idem for discussion of data problems.

exported a large portion of the cloth it produced. For China as a whole, it suggests per capita cloth consumption that was probably lower than that of France, but comparable to that of Germany—which would presumably be a good deal above that of Europe as a whole. This is suggestive not only because clothing is an important category of expenditure, but because, according to Engel's Law, it is one of the first areas in which one would expect expenditures to increase once basic food needs have been met. Thus, while it is no substitute for an overall 'market basket' of goods, it is a good preliminary indicator of comparative living standards for the general populations of China and Europe.

It is also interesting that these numbers are, once again, higher than those derived in various estimates for early twentieth-century China. I have explained at length elsewhere why I believe that China's total cotton output quite likely declined between 1750 and 1900 or, at best, did not increase much, while population roughly doubled (Pomeranz 2000*a*: 139–42, 334–8). If that assertion is correct, then there is no conflict between my figures and the later ones, either for cotton, or for sugar and tea. And an analysis of regional trends—to which we will turn shortly—leads to similar conclusions.

First, though, a few more things should be said about eighteenth-century consumption levels both of necessities and non-necessities. Per capita fuel supply, as I have argued elsewhere, was probably as adequate as it was in most of Europe in the eighteenth century, despite an increasingly unfavourable ratio of people to wooded acreage in both places (Pomeranz 2000*a*: 222–36). That China, in particular, was able to sustain adequate supplies of fuel was in part due to various labour-intensive expedients that were much less necessary in Europe—in particular, the burning of crop residues and the gathering of small wood—as well as to a different kind of cooking, more efficient stoves, and, in the case of south China, a generally warmer climate. The extra labour probably fell mostly on women and children. With cooking fires going for less time each day, Chinese homes may have been, on average, less warm, but also less smoky. And the general pattern of fuel gathering—relying more on small groves, often within the family's own courtyard, and less on consolidated blocks of forest owned by nobles—may have made for more even distribution and greater security of fuel supply, and less conflict over it, even if average levels were no better. At present, though, there is little chance of quantifying anything beyond those average levels—and even that is speculative.

Housing was one area in which Chinese living standards may well have been falling behind European ones by the late eighteenth century. In part, this would have been the result of the increasing pressure on wood supply mentioned above, and the fact that China did not replace wood with stone in residential construction on anything like the scale of at least England. Some other housing amenities that were becoming more common in Europe, such as glass windows, remained quite rare in China. We should be careful not to paint these as universal patterns—recent research suggest that England's 'Great Rebuilding' reached only a minority of the population, and that a majority of the eighteenth-century poor still lived in one to three rooms, made largely of wood and clay; brick, even for the chimney, appears to have been quite exceptional among at least the rural poor (Shammas 1990: 159–65). Workers' houses in early industrial Leeds, Liverpool, and Nottingham usually had one room on each of two or three floors, so there was no more differentiation than in the homes of the Chinese poor; privies and water supply were still shared with neighbours (Daunton 1990: 203). For the most part, housing in continental Europe was worse. The first quantitative figures we have for Chinese housing quality comes from J. L. Buck's early twentieth-century rural surveys. While they far exceed what is cited for the seventeenth-century English rural poor in floor space per capita, and 39% of buildings even on 'small farms' featured tile roofs,[39] the comparison is hardly a well-controlled one. And though I have pointed out elsewhere that Buck's figures on average furniture ownership throughout China seem to compare quite well with those for two seventeenth-century samples for the rural Netherlands (a much richer-than-average part of Europe) examined by Jan de Vries, there are many problems with comparing those figures. The best guess, I would say, is that this is an area in which the majority of Chinese may well have been keeping up with their European poor, or even continuing to outdo them, but in which a minority of better-off western Europeans may well have been improving their circumstances faster than their Chinese counterparts.

Consumption, of course, includes services as well as goods, and here comparisons become even more difficult. Mid-Qing literati and officials wrote an enormous amount (usually with a censorious tone) about the growing numbers of ordinary people frequenting tea houses, travelling (especially, but not exclusively, for pilgrimages), hiring religious specialists to perform rituals, patronizing travelling entertainers of various sorts, and so on. Few used numbers that are useful to us, but we know that some of the most popular pilgrimage sites for instance, welcomed as many as 1,000,000 people per year (Pomeranz 1997: 188). In the Yangzi Delta, Fan Shuzhi has identified a number of towns, each with only a few thousand people that had anywhere from 40 to 100 recorded tea houses in the early nineteenth century (Fan 1990: 279). For so many of these establishments to survive, a significant number of people from the surrounding villages must also have been partaking of the food, entertainment, and gambling that they offered. The boom in the number of itinerant religious specialists in the eighteenth century—which some have taken as a sign that increasing numbers of people were economically desperate[40]—can just as well be read as a sign that the society in general was able to support an increased number of such people. (They received no support from any religious establishment, and survived by being paid for services and/or begging.)

Of course, people everywhere spend some of their incomes on rituals, celebrations, and entertainment. Early modern European texts are also full of complaints about the 'wasteful' activities of the poor, and their frequency and stridency may say more about elite attitudes than about the numbers of people or levels of spending involved. Still, there may be some grounds for speculating that such activities would have comprised a larger share of plebeian consumption in eighteenth-century China than Europe. Looking at the comparison from one side, the relatively lesser importance and complexity of kinship in Europe (speaking in gross, general terms) may well have contributed to a stronger need to mark statuses by consumption of goods, and a greater penetration of fashion (which, among other things, raises the share of goods in the budget by making them socially obsolete before they are physically so).[41] That, in turn, would tend to direct spending away from services. At the same time, the more complex and prominent kinship relations in which Chinese were embedded did not simply reproduce themselves—people were taught whom they had important ties with, and how to act towards them, through ritual con-vocations in which one incorporated as many of the people with whom one could claim such ties as one could afford.[42] And since neither a state nor an established church registered marriages in Qing China, the burden fell on each family to mount an event capable of showing the relevant neighbours that what they were entering into was a legitimate marriage, rather than the purchase of a concubine or an illicit cohabitation. Various social and cultural historians have made the point that the combination of rapid commercialization and the erasure of almost all formal legal status distinctions by 1730—including those which had isolated entertainers and commercial sex workers from ordinary commoners—greatly increased pressure at all social levels to perform marriages in a way that clearly showed that the bride's parents were not 'selling' her.[43] While we should not put too much credence in twentieth-century complaints by self-styled 'modernizers' (both foreign and Chinese) that the Chinese 'wasted' an unusual amount of their resources on such events—much less read them back into the eighteenth century—it seems to me quite likely that there was, indeed, a difference in the relative shares of goods and services in the discretionary spending of ordinary Chinese and Europeans. If so, that would make the rough comparability in those goods we can measure all the more impressive a testament to the relatively high standard of living (for a pre-industrial society) of eighteenth-century China.

5. How Plausible is a Nineteenth-Century Decline in Living Standards?

As I have noted repeatedly above, the standard of living I am sketching for eighteenth-century China would not only compare well to Europe's, but would exceed in many ways what investigators found in early twentieth-century China. A generation ago, this would have raised few eyebrows: it was widely agreed that the nineteenth century had been a long series of catastrophes for China, so that there would have been little reason to doubt that the eighteenth century had been better than the early twentieth century. In general, however, scholars of this period also saw early twentieth-century China in such bleak terms that imagining a nineteenth-century decline did not require eighteenth-century Chinese, except a small elite group, to have had much beyond bare subsistence. The nineteenth-century decline was usually seen in terms of violent fluctuations around what had always been a very low average (i.e. lesser security against natural and man-made disasters), not in terms of lower levels of consumption in disaster-free years.[44] Moreover, a good deal of scholarship since the mid-1980s has suggested that the early twentieth century was marked by at least some economic improvement, meaning that any argument that eighteenth-century living standards were higher must lean even more heavily on a negative view of nineteenth-century trends. Finally, the older view of a catastrophic nineteenth century generally had in the background a picture of eighteenth-century China already beset by inexorably mounting 'overpopulation' and/or an inability to innovate (whether due to politics or culture) which, of course, is very different from the story I have been telling here. Thus, though it goes beyond the eighteenth century, a brief account is in order of how the relatively prosperous China I described fell upon harder times, and where we should and should not expect to see that reflected in the standard of living.

Eighteenth-century China did indeed show serious signs of ecological strain, though simple overpopulation will not explain them. I have emphasized in my recent book that these strains were by no means unique. Europe, though far more sparsely populated, also faced serious pressures, which were already creating serious problems in some areas, and might have created far more had not vastly increased flows of resources from overseas and underground (especially coal mines) been brought into play. For present purposes, what matters is that though serious, these problems did not amount to a 'Malthusian' crisis, in which areas were no longer able to sustain the standards of living previously achieved. In the Yangzi Delta, where locally produced supplies of food, fuel, fibre, and building materials were inadequate, a set of quite effective strategies for dealing with the problem were in place: (1) preventive checks which stopped further population growth;[45] (2) various labour-intensive techniques to economize on the use of land and fuel; (3) enormous amounts of extra-regional trade, which brought in about one-sixth of the region's rice, huge quantities of timber, all of its sugar, huge amounts of raw cotton, and soybeans which, though they were largely used for beancake fertilizer, would have been enough to feed 3–4,000,000 people per year.[46] This made the beancake trade alone larger than all of Europe's long-distance grain trade put together.[47]

By the late eighteenth century, however, one crucial part of this triad—long-distance trade—was becoming less effective. Many peripheral regions—unlike the Yangzi Delta—were experiencing very rapid population growth, and might well have had less surplus of land-intensive commodities to 'vent' in any case. But at least equally important, these regions were diversifying their economies. The middle Yangzi, for instance—the Delta's principal 'rice bowl'—was increasingly growing its own cotton and making its own cloth rather than putting all of the additional labour that its increased population represented into double-cropping grain and trading for cloth (Li Bozhong 1998: 108). As late as the 1930s (despite steamships, telegraphs, and other new technologies conducive to further market integration), long-distance rice shipments along the Yangzi were *much* less than they had been in the mid-eighteenth century.[48] During the 1600s, people in north China cotton country had figured out how to spin their cotton despite the seasonal aridity that used to cause the thread to break. Spinning and weaving there boomed, quality slowly caught up with that of the middle-grade cloth previously imported from the Yangzi Delta, and raw cotton exports became very small by the early nineteenth century.[49] Timber exports from various interior regions to the Delta declined in the late eighteenth and early nineteenth century for a variety of reasons: over-cutting and land clearance for farms along the Han River, the growth of local demand (both due to population increase and to the development of timber-using industries such as paper-making and charcoal iron making, particularly in Sichuan), and problems with transportation (both along the Yangzi and on smaller rivers).[50] Only the Manchurian frontier trade continued to grow apace.

This pattern of development had a number of consequences that matter to our story. The simplest and most benign is that the regional distribution of population growth tended to depress China-wide consumption averages. The Yangzi Delta, for instance, with the country's highest living standards, had probably about 18% of China's population in 1750, 9% in 1850, and 6% in 1950; thus, even if it maintained fairly high levels of consumption, these would do less and less to raise 'national' averages. Throughout the empire, the pattern was that less prosperous macro-regions had the fastest population growth (with the exception of Manchuria), and that within each macro-region, the fastest growth tended to be in the peripheries.[51]

In the case of some goods, where consumption had been heavily concentrated in a few regions, the effects could be dramatic. Three relatively prosperous macro-regions—the lower Yangzi, Lingnan, and the southeast coast—accounted for most of eighteenth-century sugar consumption. They may have had 40% of China's people in 1750, but only 25% in 1850. This alone would depress China-wide averages enough to account for most of the difference between my low-end estimate for 1750 and J. L. Buck's much lower figures for the 1920s.[52]

For kinds of consumption that were not as geographically concentrated, the changing regional distribution of population and proto-industry explains less, but it is nonetheless crucial to our overall story. First, since shifting demographic weights would produce an apparent decline in standard of living even if the standard of living within each region was completely unchanged, they help reconcile the decline hypothesis with the relative paucity of sources noting a decline in living standards in particular areas prior to the great mid-nineteenth-century catastrophes. In the places from which the most texts are preserved, there probably was little or no decline to observe. Second, while many factors contributed to this pattern of development— state subsidies to migration, gender norms which favoured a 'man ploughs, woman weaves' division of labour where possible (rather than having all family members in the fields), high transport costs as settlement moved further away from principal rivers, and simple Smithian dynamics (which made an increasingly complex division of labour within interior regions profitable as their population grew)—none of them require us to find unusual 'blockages' or pathologies in eighteenth-century China to explain at least this part of its nineteenth-century problems.

But this decline in inter-regional trade had other dimensions, which depressed living standards in other ways. In some cases, shortages of particular commodities were probably serious enough to have a significant inhibiting effect on further development. Li Bozhong, for instance, has argued that soaring wood prices (especially for construction timber, and also for fuel) had a serious inhibiting effect on proto-industrial expansion in the Yangzi Delta (Li Bozhong 1994a: 86–9, 94, 2000: 337–42).

Robert Marks and others also have shown the effects of timber shortage on ship-building in Guangdong and Fujian (Marks 1997: 168). The loss of external markets for the Delta's middle-grade cloth and the decline in inland rice surpluses also meant that the cloth it continued to produce was worth less: a given piece may have bought 50% less rice in 1840 than in 1750 (Pomeranz 2000a: 323–36). This presumably affected labour allocation decisions.

In areas where growing population combined with stagnant or declining trade, there was increasing pressure on the ability of the land to feed the local population. In areas with relatively warm climates and lots of water, such as southern paddy-rice country, there were still various ways to approach this problem through labour-intensification that raised per-acre yields; this was also true where it was possible to import rising quantities of off-farm fertilizer. But in huge areas where none of this applied, it seems very unlikely that per-acre yields could have kept up with popu-lation, and there was often not much land left to clear. In those cases, it seems likely that food crops retook some land that had been allocated to cash crops in the eighteenth century, shrinking the total amount of the crop available. I have argued elsewhere that this was probably true for cotton in north China (one of the country's two principal growing areas) between 1750 and 1900 (Pomeranz 2000a: 139, 334–8). Even if the acreage under cotton, tobacco, indigo, etc., did not actually shrink, it seems very likely that it declined in per capita terms. (Cotton yields per acre, for instance, do not seem to have changed at all until twentieth-century hybrids, irrigation methods, and chemicals came along.) Lillian Li has shown that the grain markets of north China were less integrated across space in the nineteenth century than in the eighteenth century (Li 2000: 678, 682, 688–9, 696). Perhaps this was due to transport problems; perhaps it was because, as areas increasingly con-centrated on food production, there was less trade; or perhaps it was because, as the whole region had less of a margin above subsistence than before, local harvest shocks of a given size produced larger price spikes.

Attempting to reconstruct budgets for a 'typical' north China farm family in the eighteenth and early twentieth centuries, Pan Ming-te comes up with a much smaller surplus above subsistence in the twentieth century—even though he did not factor in disasters of any sort.[53] There is some indirect evidence of improving nutritional and living levels (based on anthropometric, nuptiality, and fertility data) for southern Manchuria and for Beijing, but we have yet to see much evidence to support an optimistic scenario for many other parts of the country (Campbell and Lee, Chapter 16, this volume). Thomas Rawski's book, the most thorough of the works arguing for an improvement in the Chinese economy in the early twentieth century, shows convincing evidence of impressive growth in the lower Yangzi and Manchuria and makes a reasonable case that this powered the entire country to a more impressive aggregate performance than other scholars have realized. Nevertheless, Rawski too acknowledges that we cannot show with certainty any improvement for the rest of the country, and that his aggregate figures could even be consistent with an overall decline in other regions (Rawski 1989: 271). Moreover, Rawski's work only examines the period from roughly 1914 to 1937; even if an optimistic scenario could be supported for most places during this period, it would say nothing about the century before that.

Equally important for our purposes, increased regional self-reliance often led to the over-exploitation of local resources as people attempted to replace land-intensive imports—and thus to ecological crises that became subsistence crises. An early and historically important example is the deforestation of the steep hillsides of western Zhejiang and Anhui, just west of the Yangzi Delta, from the late eighteenth century on. (Other, gentler, hills nearby had been cleared beginning in the fifteenth century, but this had far less environmental impact.) While this was once seen as a Malthusian story—in which it was presumed that people cleared these hillsides in order to plant them with newly available corn that they could eat—this story no longer fits the available evidence. (This evidence shows, for instance, no food supply shortage in the region, the strong commercial orientation of the groups who cleared the hillsides, and their lack of interest in terracing the hillsides, which would have allowed them to farm them for much longer.) It seems likely, instead, that this deforestation was driven by the desire for the lumber itself to supply a still buoyant Yangzi Delta market, which was having trouble with some of its traditional sources of imports; the corn-planting was a temporary measure, which helped feed the loggers cheaply and with minimal investment of labour.[54]

The results of deforesting these steep slopes were catastrophic for the Delta counties downstream. The 1830s and 1840s brought the worst flooding the Delta had seen in at least two centuries—flooding which contemporaries understood quite clearly was linked to hillside clearance. From 1840 onwards, incidents of resistance to both rents and taxes (which were conventionally supposed to be decreased in years of disaster) likewise became more frequent than at any other point in the Qing dynasty (Bernhardt 1992: 55–83). Gentry in the region also began making the unprecedented claim that the region needed to be permanently relieved of some of its special grain tribute responsibilities (Polachek 1975: 226–7). Since the Yangzi Delta was by far the most heavily taxed part of the country, and these were years of mounting challenges for the state—due to problems with the Yellow River further north (Dodgen 1991: 53–9), the Opium War, and increased social unrest (some of which fed into the massive rebellions that began in 1851)—this was a particularly inopportune time for these problems to occur and may well have had very long-lasting political and economic consequence. As we shall see shortly, after the great rebellions, the state was both weakened and reoriented in ways that greatly exacerbated ecological strains, and were not easily repaired.

Ecologically though, this particular episode of over-exploitation was not one of the worst—in part because once the great rebellions were over, the lower Yangzi was plugged in to new sources of land-intensive imports (from Southeast Asia to the Pacific Northwest), which made a return to such measures unnecessary. After the war, large portions of these hills were successfully reforested—and enough of them stayed that way that the region never again faced comparable flooding. Neither the property rights regime in the area nor the effectiveness with which it could be enforced (often cited as contributing factors in the deforestation, and with good reason) had improved, but access to imports had. Other regions, which had a harder time reversing the trend towards regional self-sufficiency, were not so lucky; the roughly contemporaneous over-cutting of trees in Shaanxi's Bashan range, for instance, was never repaired (Vermeer 1991: 311–15, 325–9).

The situation was often worst of all in those relatively poor regions which during the high-Qing had received some sort of central government support that helped underwrite continued stable subsistence in increasingly fragile ecologies. A particularly severe case was the inland portion of the north China plain—particularly the area near the Yellow River and the northern sections of the Grand Canal. Here a combination of slowly mounting ecological problems, the state's fiscal difficulties, and a shift in the state's priorities under pressure from abroad (to military modernization, indemnities for lost wars, attempts to jump-start mechanized industry in coastal areas, and public services for areas that might be threatened with foreign takeovers if they were too disease-ridden or disorderly) led to the abandonment, first of the Grand Canal, and subsequently of much of the central government role in flood control. The results were a massive increase in flooding, loss of access to badly needed supplies of wood and stone (for dike construction), far greater problems with banditry and other forms of disorder, and—in a vicious cycle—further withdrawal of both public and private resources. Though it is not possible to calculate precisely how much these problems may have lowered the region's standard of living, I estimated in an earlier work that by the 1920s and 1930s the annual costs of these interlinked ecological and political problems were equal to at least 10% of the region's agricultural output, and possibly over 20% (Pomeranz 1993: 218–20, 287–93).

Probably very few other areas suffered this badly, but many had lesser problems of a similar sort. Funds that had once subsidized well-digging in various poor and semi-arid regions dried up at roughly the same time that larger populations were pushing down the water table, growing local industries destroyed hillside forests, and so on.[55] And increased economic and ecological stress often meant a decline in public safety, further pushing the downward spiral. Last but by no means least, the state's efforts to promote subsistence security became far less effective in the nineteenth century. The state-supervised (though not always state-run) granary system was already on the decline by the end of the eighteenth century, and was essentially irrelevant after 1850 (Will and Wong 1991: 75–98). It appears that this system had been best developed and had had its greatest effects in areas that were not well positioned to rely on trade to cushion harvest shocks (Shiue 1998: ch. 2). Thus, its decline once again hit hardest at those places that were relatively autarkic (and perhaps getting more so, especially as transportation infrastructure decayed).

Meanwhile, forces beyond anybody's control may have been creating more crises to deal with. The nineteenth and early twentieth century was a bad time for China meteorologically. This was both a matter of background conditions (a prolonged cool period in the first half of the nineteenth century, which would have been particularly damaging for areas that were trying to squeeze in an extra crop to deal with growing pressures on the land), and in terms of sudden shocks, such as the unusually severe El Niños that produced horrific north China droughts in 1876–9 (1877 was the driest in the previous 200 years) and 1897–9, and the unusually severe La Niñas that produced massive floods in other years.[56] That weather became much less significant in the North Atlantic as its margin above subsistence grew after 1800 (and weather fluctuations were generally more benign than in monsoon areas, anyway), does not mean it should drop out of our narratives for other areas.

Overall, then, there seem to be a good many reasons to think that both the standard of living in 'average' years, and security against fluctuations in exceptional years, declined in much of China (though not everywhere) between the late eighteenth and early twentieth century. This serves to buttress our estimates of a relatively high standard of living in eighteenth-century China. The political and ecological dynamics of this decline, and their interconnections, also serve to remind us that there is no reason for regional trends to be the same across China, but also that no part of China was fully immune from changes in the others—even, or perhaps especially, as inter-regional trade declined and fragile political mechanisms for maintaining the conditions for relative prosperity became correspondingly more important. That large systemic problems caused Chinese living standards to stagnate—at best—while the West's rose with unprecedented speed in the nineteenth century need not imply that we should already find pernicious effects of these problems a century earlier, causing China to fall steadily and inexorably behind. There are a number of new issues to consider—particularly with respect to the numbers and living standards of 'middling' Chinese whose fortunes might (or might not) parallel those of the Europeans emphasized by Hoffman *et al.* (Chapter 6, this volume)—but in the meantime, a picture of general comparability still seems warranted.

Notes

1. Pan (1998: 10–11). Lest this seems absurdly high, Pan also provides a plausible recon-struction of daily labour effort during busy months that shows how these labourers could have consumed that much.
2. See Marks (1991: 77–8) for a justification of this figure.
3. Guo (1994: 46–7) estimates grain production in that year as 275,737,216,000 *jin* of unhusked rice and its equivalent, which (converting at an average of 55% to edible grain) becomes 151,655,468,800 *jin,* or just over 1,000,000,000 *shi* of edible rice equivalent. Subtracting perhaps 15% for next year's seed would give us 850,000,000 unhusked *shi* for people to eat. If the population was roughly 225,000,000 at the time (Guo uses the official figure of 184,000,000, but that is generally considered too low), we would have about 3.77 *shi* per person per year: about 70% above the 2.2 *shi* 'average' suggested by Marks and adopted here. This would convert to about 300 k of rice per person per year: enough to support 3,200 calories per day for everyone, or well over 4,000 calories per day per adult equivalent. It should be noted, however, that Guo's estimating techniques are quite rough, and no more precise calculation is possible with the materials known to be available.
4. See Perkins (1969: 301).

5. Cited in Aymard (1979: 6).
6. See, for example, Wong (1982, 1997), Will (1990: 298–9, 302–10), Tilly (1975), Grantham (1989), Shiue (1998).
7. See, for example, Post (1977: 44–6) for famine conditions in various portions of Germany, and especially in the Habsburg lands; and Post (1977: 40, 108) for a comparison with the less extensive, but still regionally devastating famines of 1845–7.
8. Guthrie (1971: 71) cites a biological value (BV) of 86 for rice protein (egg = 100, fish and beef = 75, and wheat gluten = 44), with a BV of 70 considered capable of supporting growth as long as quantities are adequate. Guthrie (1971: 69) tells us that it takes 1,186 kcal of rice to provide 22 g of protein (versus fewer than 200 of most meats and fish). At this rate, it would take 3,500 calories of rice alone to meet the US RDA for an adult male from rice alone (Guthrie 1971: 68)—more than the average Chinese intake, but less than that of the farm labourers cited above, who would take in almost 85 g of this high-quality protein. It has been more conventional to argue that rice protein, like most other vegetable proteins, is an incomplete protein, which needs to be supplemented by others, which have large amounts of the amino acids it has relatively little of. This argument, however, is based on rat studies, which are not conclusive, and the biological value scale for protein is based, to the extent possible, on human studies. The point is still disputed, but the trend in opinion seems to favour a more generous valuation of at least some vegetable proteins. See especially D. J. Milt-Ward *et al.* (1992) who say older methods 'overestimate the value of some animal proteins for human needs while underestimating the value of some vegetable proteins'.
9. FAO (1974: 19), Guthrie (1971: 65, 68). See also Buck (1937/1964: 420) for a slightly lower figure.
10. Much of the reason for the switch was that soybean cake was far more concentrated—providing perhaps twenty times as much nutrient per pound applied—so that making the switch saved vast amounts of labour, see Pan (1994: 36–8, 110–13). That advantage would obviously be lost if each farm owner or labourer continued to apply just as much night soil while also adding the new work of applying soybean cake.
11. Buck (1937/1964: 259). Given Buck's estimate of the relative fertilizer output of humans and large livestock (1930/1971: 224), this would suggest that the 'Yangzi Rice/Wheat' area should have had considerably less than half the number of large animals per person as the rest of the country. Buck's figures however, suggest that the number of large animals per farm, per person, and per crop acre in this region varied from a bit under 0.6 to a bit over 0.6 for China as a whole (1937/1964: tables: 246, 255). Either way, the basic point being made here would hold.
12. Early twentieth-century population in the Yangzi Delta was not much above mid-eighteenth-century figures, but those figures were already 75–100% above those for the late Ming, see Li (1994*b*: 30–3).
13. Note also Perkins' comment (1969: 301–3) that even some of Buck's grain availability data seem implausible unless China was converting much more grain than he finds plausible to either meat or alcohol. While Buck's figures may indeed be too high in many cases, the possibility of at least some additional indirect consumption cannot be ruled out, even for a period conventionally considered one of agrarian crisis.
14. Lis and Soly (1979: 113). For conversion of beef into grams of protein, see Watt and Merrill (1963: 12–13).
15. Cited in Aymard (1979: 6–7, 14).

16. I assume here that most of the starch in the diet described by Toutain (making up roughly 70% of its calories) was in the form of relatively nutritious whole wheat bread, and estimate protein content based on Watt and Merrill (1963: 18–19).

17. Oddy (1990: 274). This figure appears to be a conversion of the estimate on p. 269 of the amount of meat in the diet.

18. Buck (1930/1971: 371) combining his categories of legumes and vegetables, with almost 90% coming from the latter category, and cabbage alone making up one-third of the total.

19. Compare Lavely and Wong (1998), especially table II and figure III, and Lee and Campbell (1997: 79) with Wrigley and Schofield (1981: 230, 708–13) and see Razzell (1993: 757–63) for a suggestion that these figures are too high. (Razzell's suggested adjustment for infant mortality alone would bring life expectancy at birth of 37.0 down to somewhere between 31.6 and 34.0.) For continental examples, see Knodel (1988: 68–9) and Blayo (1975) (showing a much lower life expectancy in France).

20. See Li Zhongqing (1994: 3).

21. Li Bozhong (1994*b*: 32–4); compare with McEvedy and Jones (1978: 28–9).

22. Shammas (1990: 136). Here she relies on late eighteenth-century figures, though there is little reason to assume that consumption of other foods rose for the poor until after 1840, see Mokyr (1988: 90–1).

23. See the complaint about peasants' 'gaudy' clothing at religious festivals by the official Chen Hongmou in Chen (1820/1962: 4a–6b).

24. His 'gentry' is sufficiently loosely defined that it would include many of the richest merchants, though only if they purchased honorary degrees—a more common phenomenon in the nineteenth than the eighteenth century.

25. See Pomeranz (2000*a*: 136–7); Lindert and Williamson (1982: 393, 396–7, 400–1).

26. Reed (2000: 206–7). He adds a casual estimate (the point is not important for his argument) that it would have cost about 10 *taels* to feed an adult for a year at this time and place, but I suspect the actual number would be significantly lower. See note 29 for a much lower estimate of the cost of eating at roughly the same time and not very far away.

27. Reed (2000: 45–51, 146–8). My figure for runners averages Reed's estimates of statutory runners and extrastatutory runners for 1848 and 1876, omitting the abnormally low one for 1855 (a year of civil war).

28. In Pomeranz (2000*a*: 249–50) I discuss some (among many) possible reasons for Chinese families of this period not to automatically head for areas with higher per capita incomes. Sommer (2000) is a book that puts great emphasis on the increased number of people on the move in eighteenth-century China, and shows that the Qing were quite worried about what these movements suggested, but there is no clear evidence to show that their numbers grew faster than one would expect given the general population rise and on-going commercialization.

29. Cited in Xu and Wu (2000: 344–5).

30. This assumes that we can use both the retail grain prices reported by another worker in the salt works, which refer to an unusually large local *dou* (a volume measure), as cited in Xu and Wu (2000: 345).

31. Much of the data was collected in the 1950s and 1960s projects aimed at demonstrating the importance of proletarian class struggle over the centuries in China, and thus may have selected examples showing the largest disparities. This would be particularly true for late Qing data, which sometimes was based on the recollections of elderly workers. Also, to the extent that there were uncounted in-kind supplements to cash wages, there is

no reason to assume that they rose proportionately with cash wages, since no worker would need eight times (much less twenty times) as much grain as he could eat. On the other hand, in-kind wages may have increased in step with cash wages after all. The government paid certain workers with grain allowances that far exceeded their needs and that they then sold on the market, and the practice might have been copied elsewhere. The salt works material also tells us of certain kinds of in-kind payments and extra allowances (e.g. for tobacco) that were only granted to those higher up the ladder.

32. Again, assuming the use of local measures—see note 31.
33. Pomeranz (2003). See also Pomeranz (2000*a*: 319) and compare Horrell and Humphries (1995: 102–3).
34. The Qing were intensely concerned about people leaving the land, and complained about what was undoubtedly a rising number of people doing so—but China remained, in comparative perspective, a remarkably rural society, and the share of urban population was probably flat or falling slightly in the eighteenth century.
35. Particularly striking accounts may be found in the novels *Jin ping mei* and *Xingshi yinyuan zhuan*—striking in part because they deal with a medium-sized city and a small town, respectively, in north China rather than with any of the country's great metropolises. For some reflections on consumption in China by a leading historian of early modern European consumption, see Burke (1993: 148–61). I deal with this at much greater length in Pomeranz (2000*a*: ch. 3).
36. Cited in Dermigny (1964: III, 1253).
37. DaCruz in Boxer (1953: 106, see also 99).
38. By starting with the quantity of land reported on the tax rolls, we build in a big conservative bias, since under-reporting was chronic throughout China. I have used the highest estimates I could plausibly defend of the amount of land that was under basic grain crops, and where estimating cash-crop production for an area was particularly tricky, I have simply omitted it from national totals, even though contemporaries may have remarked often that it produced the good in question. In the case of sugar, for instance, I have counted only output in Guangdong and Taiwan plus known imports, though we know that mainland Fujian was also a major producer, and production scattered through the rest of China was estimated by a contemporary to be about one-ninth of the total of Guangdong, Taiwan and that uncounted mainland Fujian output (cited in Daniels 1996: 97, 105). And within Guangdong itself I have used a figure for cash-cropping area more than 20% below that generated in Robert Marks' study of that province, and assigned only one-tenth of this cash-cropping area to sugarcane: a figure that Marks suggests is almost certainly too low. For further discussion, see Pomeranz (2000*a*: ch. 3).
39. Buck (1937/1964: 442 on floor space, 443 table 5, on building materials).
40. See, for example, Kuhn (1990: 43–7, 111–12), Sommer (2000: 12–14, 99–101).
41. I analyse fashion, partly along these lines, in Pomeranz (2000*a*: 152–62).
42. This remains the pattern even today in much of rural China—much to the state's dismay—a high priority for many families as they have become more prosperous since 1978 has been to extend and strengthen their web of social ties through hosting more ritual events, and greatly expanding the guest lists at them, see Yan (1996: 225–6).
43. See, for example Rowe (1992), Mann (1997), Sommer (2000).
44. A classic statement of the stagnation thesis is Fairbank, Reischauer, and Craig (1973: 435–44, 643–6). Eastman (1988: 80–1, 92), representing a later generation of scholars,

nonetheless sees the choice as one between two different explanations of why Chinese peasants (in Tawney's famous phrase) were in water up to their necks, and then, as I do, emphasizes the role of politics in explaining the increased frequency of 'ripples' that could drown such a person.

45. See Lee and Wang (1999: 84–92, 97–9), Li (1994*b*: 41–2, 46–52).
46. Y. C. Wang (1989: 423–30, on rice), Lu (1992: 493, on raw cotton), Marks (1997: 172–6, on sugar), Li Bozhong (2000: 321–7, on timber), Adachi (1978, on soybeans).
47. Compare Braudel (1981: 127).
48. Skinner (1977: 234–5, 713, n. 30–2), Ch'uan and Kraus (1975: 77). If Ch'uan and Kraus are right, and Perkins is right about the 1930s, these shipments had declined by some-where between 73% and 82%. A decline of this magnitude seems hard to believe, but it is also not necessary to my argument.
49. Lu (1992: 482–3), Bray (1997: 217). Bray quotes a source saying raw cotton exports from the North had already become trivial in the eighteenth century, but this seems an exaggeration.
50. See Menzies (1996: 562) and Xu and Wu (2000: 240–6); on transport problems, see Osborne (1989: 52–6, 71, 81–5); on how these problems were complicated by increased exactions by officials and local strongmen, see Lu and Chen (1986: 31–2).
51. See Lee and Wang (1999: 116) for a useful map showing this pattern (but using provinces as the unit of analysis), and Pomeranz (2000*b*: 45) for a table producing some salient examples.
52. See Pomeranz (2000*a*: 123–4).
53. Pan (1994: 115–23, 344–83, see 382–3 for a summary statement).
54. See Pomeranz (2000*b*: 50–3) for a brief account; Pomeranz (2000*c*) makes the case in more detail.
55. See for example Pomeranz (2000*a*: 237–8), Pan (1994: 116–18), Xu and Wu (2000: 231–3, 257–9, 287), Vermeer (1991: 311, 325–8).
56. On temperatures, see Marks (1997: 217–19). On the unusually severe El Niños and their effects, see Davis (2001: 64–79, 248–51, 271, 341–75).

References

Adachi, K. (1978) 'Daizu kasu ryûtsû to shindai no shôgyôteki nôgyô'. *Tôyôshi Kenkyû*, 37(3): 35–63.
Aymard, M. (1979) 'Toward the History of Nutrition: Some Methodological Remarks', in R. Forster and O. Ranum (eds.), *Food and Drink in History: Selections from the Annales Economies, Sociétés, Civilisations*, Vol. 5. Baltimore/London: Johns Hopkins University Press, pp. 1–16.
Bernard, R. J. (1975) 'Peasant Diet in Eighteenth-Century Gévaudan', in E. Forster and R. Forster (eds.), *European Diet from Pre-Industrial to Modern Times*. New York: Harper Torchbooks.
Bernhardt, K. (1992) *Rents, Taxes and Peasant Resistance: The Lower Yangzi Region, 1840–1950*. Stanford: Stanford University Press.
Blayo, Y. (1975) 'La mortalité en France de 1740 à 1829'. *Population* (November/December): 138–9.
Boxer, C. (ed.) (1953) *South China in the 16th Century*. London: Hakluyt Society.

Braudel, F. (1981) *The Structures of Everyday Life*, translation by Sian Reynolds. New York: Harper and Row.

Bray, F. (1997) *Technology and Gender: Fabrics of Power in Late Imperial China*. Berkeley, CA: University of California Press.

Buck, J. L. (1930/1971) *Chinese Farm Economy: A Study of 2866 Farms in Seven Localities and Seven Provinces in China*. Chicago, IL: University of Chicago Press. Reprinted Ann Arbor, MI: University Microfilms International.

—— (1937/1964) *Land Utilization in China*. New York: Paragon Book Reprint Corp.

Burke, P. (1993) '*Res et Verba*: Conspicuous Comsumption in the Early Modern World', in J. Brewer and R. Porter (eds.), *Consumption and the World of Goods*. New York: Routledge, pp. 148–61.

Chang, C.-L. (1962) *The Income of the Chinese Gentry*. Seattle, WA: University of Washington Press.

Chen, H. (1820/1962) 'Fengsu tiaoyue', in C. He and Y. Wei (eds.), *Huang chao jingshi wenbian*, 68: 4a–6b. Reprinted Taibei: Guofeng chubanshe.

Ch'uan, H-S. and Kraus, R. (1975) *Mid-Ch'ing Rice Markets and Trade: An Essay in Price History*. Cambridge, MA: Harvard University Press.

Clark, G., Huberman, M., and Lindert, P. H. (1995) 'A British Food Puzzle, 1770–1850'. *Economic History Review*, 48(1): 215–37.

Daniels, C. (1996) 'Agro-Industries: Sugarcane Technology', in J. Needham (ed.), *Science and Civilization in China*, Vol. 6, part III, section 42a. Cambridge: Cambridge University Press, pp. 5–39.

Daunton, M. J. (1990) 'Housing', in F. M. L. Thompson (ed.), *The Cambridge Social History of Britain 1750–1950*, Vol. II. New York: Cambridge University Press, pp. 195–250.

Davis, M. (2001) *Late Victorian Holocausts: El Niño Famines and the Making of the Third World*. New York: Verso.

Dermigny, L. (1964) *La Chine et L'Occident: Le Commerce a Canton au XVIIIe Siècle 1719–1833*. Paris: S.E.V.P.E.N.

Dodgen, R. (1991) 'Hydraulic Evolution and Dynastic Decline: The Yellow River Conservancy, 1796–1855'. *Late Imperial China*, 12(2): 36–63.

Eastman, L. (1988) *Family, Fields, and Ancestors: Constancy and Change in China's Social and Economic History, 1550–1949*. New York: Oxford University Press.

Fairbank, J. K., Reischauer, E. O., and Craig, A. M. (1973) *East Asia: Tradition and Transformation*. Boston, MA: Houghton Mifflin.

Fan, S. (1990) *Ming Qing Jiangnan shi zhen tanwei*. Shanghai: Fudan daxue chubanshe.

Fang, X. (1996) 'Qingdai Jiangnan nongmin de xiaofei'. *Zhongguo jingji shi yanjiu*, 11(3): 91–8.

Food and Agriculture Organization (FAO) (1974) *Handbook of Human Nutritional Requirements*. Geneva: World Health Organization.

Gardella, R. (1994) *Harvesting Mountains: Fujina and the China Tea Trade 1757–1937*. Berkeley, CA: University of California Press.

Grantham, G. (1989) 'Jean Meuvret and the Subsistence Problem in Early Modern France'. *Journal of Economic History*, 49(1): 184–200.

Guo, S. (1994) 'Qingdai liangshi shichang he shangpin liang shuliang de guce'. *Zhongguo shi yanjiu*, 64(4): 40–9.

Guthrie, H. Andrews (1971) *Introductory Nutrition*, 2nd edn. St. Louis: C.V. Mosby.

Horrell, S. and Humphries, J. (1995) 'Women's Labour Force Participation and the Transition to the Male-Breadwinner Family, 1790–1865'. *Economic History Review*, 48(1): 89–117.

Knodel, J. (1988) *Demographic Behavior in the Past: A Study of Fourteen German Village Populations in the Eighteenth and Nineteenth Centuries*. New York: Cambridge University Press.

Kuhn, P. (1990) *Soulstealers: The Chinese Sorcery Scare of 1768*. Cambridge, MA: Harvard University Press.

Lavely, W. and Wong, R. B. (1998) 'Revising the Malthusian Narrative: The Comparative Study of Population Dynamics in Late Imperial China'. *Journal of Asian Studies*, 57(3): 714–48.

Lee, J. and Campbell, C. (1997) *Fate and Fortune in Rural China: Social Organization and Population Behavior in Liaoning, 1774–1873*. Cambridge: Cambridge University Press.

—— and Wang, F. (1999) *One Quarter of Humanity: Malthusian Mythologies and Chinese Realities*. Cambridge, MA: Harvard University Press.

Li, B. (1994a) 'Ming Qing shiqi Jiangnan de mucai wenti'. *Zhongguo shehui jingji shi yanjiu*, 1: 86–96.

—— (1994b) 'Kongzhi zengchang yi bao fuyu—Qingdai qian, zhongqi Jiangnan de renkou xingwei'. *Xin shixue*, 5(3): 25–71.

—— (1998) *Agricultural Development in Jiangnan 1620–1850*. New York: St. Martin's Press.

—— (2000) *Jiangnan de zaoqi gongyehua*. Beijing: Shehui kexue wenxian chubanshe.

Li, L. (2000) 'Integration and Disintegration in North China's Grain Markets, 1738–1911'. *Journal of Economic History*, 60(3): 665–99.

Li, Z. (James Lee) (1994) 'Zhongguo lishi renkou zhidu: Qingdai renkou xingwei ji qi yiyi', in Z. Li and S. Guo (eds.), *Qingdai huangzu renkou xingwei de shehui huanjing*. Beijing: Peking University Press, pp. 1–17.

Lindert, P. H. and Williamson, J. (1982) 'Revising England's Social Tables 1688–1812'. *Explorations in Economic History*, 19: 385–408.

Lis, H. and Soly, C. (1979) *Poverty and Capitalism in Pre-Industrial Europe*. Hassocks. Sussex: Harvester Press.

Lu, H. (1992) 'Arrested Development: Cotton and Cotton Markets in Shanghai, 1350–1843'. *Modern China*, 18(4): 468–99.

Lu, J. and Chen, B. (1986) *Changzhou shi mucai zhi 1800–1985*. Changzhou: Changzhou mucai gongsi.

Macartney, G. (1793/1962) In J. L. Cranmer-Byng (ed.), *An Embassy to China: Being the Journal Kept by Lord Macartney During his Embassy to the Emperor Ch'ien-lung, 1793–1794*. London: Longmans Publications.

Mann, S. (1997) *Precious Records: Women in China's Long Eighteenth Century*. Stanford: Stanford University Press.

Marks, R. (1991) 'Rice Prices, Food Supply, and Market Structure in 18th Century China'. *Late Imperial China*, 12(2): 64–116.

—— (1997) *Tigers, Rice, Silk, and Silt: Environment and Economy in Guangdong, 1250–1850*. New York: Cambridge University Press.

McEvedy, C. and Jones, R. (1978) *Atlas of World Population History*. New York: Penguin.

Menzies, N. (1996) 'Forestry', in J. Needham (ed.), *Science and Civilization in China*, Vol. 27. Cambridge: Cambridge University Press, pp. 541–690.

Milt-Ward, D. J., Newsholme, E. A, Pellett, P. L., and Uauy, R. (1992) 'Amino Acid Scoring in Health and Disease', in N. S. Scrimshaw and B. Schürch (eds.), *Protein-Energy Inter-actions*. United Nations ACC Subcommittee on Nutrition. International Dietary Energy Consultancy Group. Lausanne: United Nations University. Available online at www.unu.edu/unupress/food2/UID07E/uid07e1k.htm.

Mintz, S. (1985) *Sweetness and Power: The Place of Sugar in Modern History*. New York: Penguin.

Mokyr, J. (1988) 'Is there Life in the Pessimist Case? Consumption during the Industrial Revolution, 1790–1850'. *Journal of Economic History*, 48(1): 69–92.

Oddy, D. J. (1990) 'Food, Drink, and Nutrition', in F. M. L. Thompson (ed.), *The Cambridge Social History of Britain, 1750–1950*, Vol. II. New York: Cambridge University Press.

Osborne, A. (1989) 'Barren Mountains, Raging Rivers: The Ecological and Social Effects of Changing Land-use on the Lower Yangzi Periphery in Late Imperial China', unpublished Ph.D. dissertation, History, Columbia University.

Pan, M-T. (1994) 'Rural Credit Market and the Peasant Economy (1600–1949)—The State, Elite, Peasant, and "Usury"', unpublished Ph.D. dissertation, History, University of California, Irvine.

——(1998) 'Who Was Worse Off?' unpublished paper delivered at 1998 meeting of Chinese Historians in the United States, Seattle.

Perkins, D. H. (1969) *Agricultural Development in China, 1368–1968*. Chicago, IL: Aldine Publishing.

Phelps Brown, E. H. and Hopkins, S. (1981) *A Perspective of Wages and Prices*. London: Methuen.

Philipps, C. R. (1990) 'The Growth and Composition of Trade in the Iberian Empires', in J. Tracy (ed.), *The Rise of Merchant Empires*. New York: Cambridge University Press, pp. 34–101.

Polachek, J. (1975) 'Gentry Hegemony in Soochow', in F. Wakeman and C. Grant (eds.), *Conflict and Control in Late Imperial China*. Berkeley, CA: University of California Press, pp. 211–56.

Pomeranz, K. (1993) *The Making of a Hinterland: State, Society, and Economy in Inland North China, 1853–1937*. Berkeley, CA: University of California Press.

——(1997) 'Power, Gender and Pluralism in the Cult of the Goddess of Taishan', in R. B. Wong, T. Hunters, and P. Yu (eds.), *Culture and State in Chinese History*. Stanford: Stanford University Press, pp. 182–204.

——(2000a) *The Great Divergence: China, Europe, and the Making of the Modern World Economy*. Princeton: Princeton University Press.

——(2000b) 'Re-thinking the Late Imperial Chinese Economy: Development, Disaggrega-tion and Decline, circa 1730–1930'. *Itinerario*, 24(3/4): 29–74.

——(2000c) 'More "Malthusian Mythologies?" Rethinking Living Standards, Environ-ment, and "Population Pressure" in the 19th Century Lower Yangzi'. Paper presented at Conference on Standards of Living and Population in Pre-Industrial Societies, Arild, Sweden, August.

——(2002) 'Beyond the East–West Dichotomy: Resituating Development Paths in the Eighteenth-Century World'. *Journal of Asian Studies*, 61(2): 539–90.

——(2003) 'Women's Work, Family, and Economic Development in Europe and East Asia: Long-term Trajectories and Contemporary Comparisons', in G. Arrighi, H. Takeshi, and M. Selden (eds.), *The Rise of East Asia: Perspectives of 50, 150, and 500 Years*. London and New York: Routledge, pp. 124–72.

Post, J. (1977) *The Last Great Subsistence Crisis in the Western World*. Baltimore, MD: Johns Hopkins University Press.

Rawski, T. (1989) *Economic Growth in Prewar China*. Berkeley, CA: University of California Press.

Razzell, P. (1993) 'The Growth of Population in Eighteenth Century England: A Critical Reappraisal'. *Journal of Economic History*, 53(4): 743–71.

Reed, B. (2000) *Talons and Teeth: County Clerks and Runners in the Qing Dynasty*. Stanford: Stanford University Press.

Rowe, W. (1992) 'Women and the Family in Mid-Qing Thought: The Case of Chen Hongmou'. *Late Imperial China*, 13(2): 1–41.

Shammas, C. (1990) *The Pre-Industrial Consumer in England and America*. Oxford: Clarendon.

Shenshi nongshu (1639/1962) In Y.-P. Yun (general ed.), *Xue hai lei bien, baibu congshu jicheng*, Vol. 256. Taibei: Yiwen shuguan.

Shiue, C. (1998) 'Trade, Storage and the Qing Granary System', unpublished Ph.D. dissertation, Yale University.

Skinner, G. W. (1977) 'Regional Urbanization in Nineteenth Century China', in G. W. Skinner (ed.), *The City in Late Imperial China*. Stanford: Stanford University Press, pp. 211–49.

Sommer, M. (2000) *Sex, Law, and Society, in 18th Century China*. Stanford: Stanford University Press.

Staunton, G. (1799) George Staunton, *An Authentic Account of an Embassy from the King of Great Britain to the Emperor of China*. Philadelphia, PA: R. Campbell.

Steensgaard, N. (1990) 'Trade of England and the Dutch before 1750', in J. Tracy (ed.), *The Rise of Merchant Empire*. New York: Cambridge University Press, pp. 102–52.

Tilly, C. (1975) 'Food Supply and Public Order in Modern Europe', in C. Tilly (ed.), *The Formation of National States in Western Europe*. Princeton, NJ: Princeton University Press, pp. 380–455.

Vermeer, E. (1991) 'The Mountain Frontier in Late Imperial China: Economic and Social Developments in the Bashan'. *T'oung Pao*, 77: 306–35.

Waley Cohen, J. (1991) *Exile in Mid-Qing China: Banishment to Xinjiang, 1758–1820*. New Haven, CT: Yale University Press.

Wang, Y-C. (1989) 'Food Supply and Grain Prices in the Yangtze Delta in the Eighteenth Century', in *The Second Conference on Modern Chinese History*. Taibei: Academia Sinica, 2: 423–62.

Watt, B. K. and Merrill, A. L. (1963) *Composition of Foods: Raw, Processed, Cooked*. Washington: US Department of Agriculture Handbook No. 8, revised.

Will, P-E. (1990) *Bureaucracy and Famine in Eighteenth Century China*. Stanford: Stanford University Press.

—— and Wong, R. B. (1991) *Nourish the People: The State Civilian Granary System in China, 1650–1850*. Ann Arbor, MI: University of Michigan Press.

Wong, R. B. (1982) 'Food Riots in the Qing Dynasty'. *Journal of Asian Studies*, 41(4): 767–88.

—— (1997) *China Transformed: Historical Change and the Limits of European Experience*. Ithaca, NY: Cornell University Press.

Wrigley, E. A. and Schofield, R. S. (1981) *The Population History of England, 1540–1871*. Cambridge: Cambridge University Press.

Xu, D. and Wu, C. (1985) *Zhongguo zibenzhuyi de meng ya*. Beijing: Renmin chubanshe.

—— —— (2000) *Chinese Capitalism 1522–1840*. New York: St. Martin's.

Yan, Y. (1996) *The Flow of Gifts: Reciprocity and Social Networks in a Chinese Village*. Stanford: Stanford University Press.

2 Farm Labour Productivity in Jiangnan, 1620–1850

BOZHONG LI

1. Introduction

How did people really live in late Imperial China? With one-third of the Eurasian population living in China at this time, an answer to this question is important for gaining an understanding of life in this region in the pre-industrial period. It has been generally thought that the standard of living in China declined from relative prosperity to severe poverty by the end of the nineteenth century.[1] In the last two decades, this traditional view has been challenged by a small but growing number of scholars who claim that the standard of living was rising, not falling, in late Imperial China.[2] Since a long-term rise in the standard of living would be unthinkable in a society in which labour productivity declined among the overwhelming majority of producers, these scholars must demonstrate that labour productivity did rise during this period. In late Imperial China, agriculture continued to take up the bulk of the Chinese economy. The majority of the Chinese people still earned their living from farming, although commerce and industry were growing at the time. It is clear, therefore, that the standard of living could not increase if farm labour productivity declined. A study of farm labour productivity, therefore, is crucial to assessing the new view that the standard of living improved in late Imperial China.

The central theme of this chapter is that labour productivity on farms did improve in Jiangnan between 1620 and 1850. The region of Jiangnan, located in east China and consisting of eight late Imperial Chinese prefectures in the Yangzi Delta,[3] has been the most economically and culturally advanced area in China for centuries. The years 1620–1850 form the last period before China 'opened' to the industrial West in the mid-nineteenth century. In some sense, this region is the best 'window' through which we can clearly see economic changes in China before the arrival of the modern west. It is no wonder that the economic history of Jiangnan from 1620 to 1850 has attracted so much attention from scholars in China, Japan, and the United States.

The analysis in this chapter focuses on farm labour productivity in Jiangnan, and is based on two decades' research on the economic history of the region during the two centuries prior to 1850. The chapter begins with a critical analysis of the principal arguments presented by those who hold to the conventional viewpoint.

A discussion of the major changes in the peasant economy will follow, focusing on those changes that have been crucial to growth in farm labour productivity. I will then describe the process through which farm labour productivity changed in the region. In the last part of the chapter, I will deal briefly with the standard of living issue: did it really improve in Jiangnan during the period under study or not?

2. Changes in the Factors of Production in Jiangnan Farming

One of the most commonly accepted notions in studies of Chinese history is that farm labour productivity declined in the late Imperial period. Even for those who reject the stereotype clichés of a 'stagnant and unchangeable China', who see economic changes in late Imperial China resembling those of early modern western Europe, the fundamental picture has changed little.[4] Jiangnan has drawn the most attention, partly because of its special position in Chinese economic history. It is generally argued, whether explicitly or implicitly, that farm labour productivity in Jiangnan had been declining from long before even the early seventeenth century.[5]

If one examines the conventional story more closely, however, it becomes clear that it is based upon several frequently made assertions. First, it is thought that Jiangnan witnessed a rapid population growth during the eighteenth and early nineteenth centuries, even though it had been the most populated area of China well before the seventeenth century. Second, because almost all arable land had been opened up as early as the late fourteenth century, land increased little, if not at all, in Jiangnan during the following centuries. Consequently, the acreage per capita of cultivated land shrank rapidly. Third, yields per mu[6] of the major crops are believed to have reached a ceiling in the context of traditional technology by the late sixteenth century or even earlier. Since no major technological breakthroughs appeared during the following centuries, there was a centuries-long stagnation of yields per mu of major crops. When yields were constant, increased labour inputs would make the returns on labour diminish at an accelerating rate. These arguments lead to an unavoidable and indisputable conclusion; farm labour productivity would fall. It is on the basis of these claims that some celebrated theories, such as Mark Elvin's 'high-level equilibrium trap' and Philip Huang's 'involutionary growth', have been put forth. Unfortunately, the evidence to support these claims is inadequate for pre-1850 Jiangnan history. Therefore, any theory based on these arguments is quite likely to be discredited since they rest on fragile ground.

2.1 Labour supply

In the old story, the chief culprit behind the decrease in farm labour productivity is rapid population growth. But this Malthusian explanation does not square with the reality of Jiangnan at all. There was no such 'population explosion' in Jiangnan during the period we are concerned with. According to my estimates, Jiangnan's population increased from about 20 million in 1620 to 36 million in 1850: an increase of 80% over 230 years (Bozhong Li 1994*b*, 1998: 19–20). In other words, the average growth rate of the Jiangnan population was only about 0.3% a year. By the standards of the 'early modern' world, this rate is quite low.[7] More surprisingly, and contrary to the prevailing view, this slow growth cannot be attributed to such Malthusian 'positive checks' as wars, civil wars, natural disasters, or epidemic diseases, but to effective birth control. This is what kept the rate of population growth below that of economic growth.[8]

Accelerated urbanization also had an important influence on demographic change in Jiangnan. The region's urbanization rate increased from 15% to 20% between 1620 and 1850, which means that the population grew one quarter less rapidly in rural areas than in urban areas. Even though the total population in Jiangnan increased by 80%, the number of adults able to work, both male and female, increased by only 70% in rural areas during these two centuries. Moreover, general descriptions by contemporary observers give an impression of a situation in which a considerable proportion of the able rural adult population were not engaged in agricultural or industrial activities, and that this proportion was increasing during the period. Without accurate statistics, I could only make a conservative estimate of 10% as the proportion of non-working, able adults in that period (Bozhong Li 1998: 20–1, 2000*a*: ch. 9). If these people were excluded, the increase in the total rural labour force would be smaller still.

Rural industrialization contributed greatly to the slow growth of the labour supply in Jiangnan agriculture. The rapid development of rural industry, especially textiles, created a large and increasing number of jobs for the rural labour force. More and more peasants, mainly female, were drawn from farming to rural industry. Their departure created a shortage of labour in Jiangnan agriculture, not a surplus of labour as is commonly believed.[9] From the sixteenth century on, seasonal labour was increasingly used in farming[10] since insufficient labour could be found from within the family. When all of these changes are taken into consideration, we can see that during the period under study the farm labour force grew much more slowly in Jiangnan than previously believed.

2.2 Cultivated land

Buck has provided definitions for 'crop area' and 'crop *mu*' that are very helpful for the study of changes in cultivated land in Jiangnan. 'Crop area' represents the land area devoted to crops, while 'crop *mu*' refers to the number of *mu* of different crops raised in one year (Buck 1930: 18). Because multi-cropping is practised, one *mu* of 'crop area' may be equivalent to two or even more 'crop *mu*'. Total 'crop area' in Jiangnan did not change much during the period, totalling roughly 45 million *mu*. But 'crop *mu*' increased remarkably, thanks to the spread of double-cropp double-cropping index rose from about 140% to about 170% between seventeenth and the mid-nineteenth century. This represents an increase of 13.5 million *mu* of sown area, corresponding to 30% of the total cultivated land of Jiangnan (Bozhong Li 1998: 33).

Another significant change to cultivated land in Jiangnan is the improvement of land quality. These improvements were focused on the transformation of water-logged land in eastern Jiangnan, the most important agricultural area in the region. This land improvement is called 'drying the land' (Hamashima 1989). The process took centuries and was completed in the mid-nineteenth century (Kitada 1988: 40–2; Bozhong Li 1998: 28–9). This improvement resulted in a substantial increase in the productivity of land in Jiangnan. For example, in the mid-nineteenth century, one *mu* of paddy could support a person in the core areas of Jiangnan, but the ratio for the whole country was 4 *mu*/person (Guo Songyi 1994). In this sense, 1 *mu* of well improved land may equal several *mu* of less improved land in terms of productivity. These improvements also facilitated regional specialization of agriculture. Different crops were planted in the respective areas most suited for their cultivation. Consequently, three major crop areas appeared and expanded in Jiangnan in this period; cotton in the east, mulberry in the south, and rice in the remaining areas. In the cotton and mulberry areas, income per *mu* from these crops was obviously better than incomes from rice. An average year's cotton harvest is equivalent to a very good year's rice harvest in cotton areas, while mulberry produced twice the net income of rice in mulberry areas (Bozhong Li 1995).

2.3   Farm technology

If we consider technological advance to be the first appearance of a new technology, then almost all of Jiangnan's most important advances did come before 1620. These advances led to the emergence, in the Ming period, of the 'new double-cropping system' of double-cropping rice and winter crops (wheat, beans, and rapeseed).[11] Mulberry and cotton farming technology also developed early, though was limited to particular areas. Advances in cotton technology came later because cotton was introduced later. Generally speaking, however, the major improvements in the region's agricultural technology were complete by the late Ming period.

But as a historical process, technological advance has a double character: first, techniques continue to improve after their initial appearance; and second, the new techniques are applied widely after some time has passed, especially in the pre-modern period.[12] Only after the use of a new technique has become widespread, can it have a major influence on economic change. If we view agricultural technological change in Jiangnan in this way, we find that although most of the major techno-logical improvements were completed before 1620, these technological advances did not spread and come into common usage in the whole region until the Qing period. Moreover, although there were fewer new techniques invented, Jiangnan still witnessed some important technological progress in the period under study. Fertilizer technology is a particular case. The widespread use of bean cakes represents one of the most significant technological advances in Jiangnan agricultural history and can be called a 'fertilizer revolution'.[13] In addition, there were many other technological improvements which may not have been very conspicuous, nor very expensive, but all of them very useful.

2.4   Capital investment

Agriculture benefited from both rural industrialization and commercialization because they led to the creation of new and important sources for agricultural investment. First, vigorously developing rural industries absorbed a great deal of the rural labour force, mostly female, away from farming. The returns from female labour were higher in spinning, weaving, or silkworm raising than in farming. Second, rapidly growing rural commerce facilitated the expansion of cash crops. The returns from planting cash crops were generally higher than that from planting grain, especially since rice imports were increasing remarkably during the two centuries under study. Both rural industrialization and commercialization increased peasants' income substantially, making it possible for peasants to invest more in their farms. Compared to their predecessors in the Ming period and earlier, Jiangnan peasants in the Qing period could afford more fertilizers and other materials of production such as improved varieties of silk cocoon and mulberry seedlings, charcoal for silkworm raising and silk reeling, and so on. They could also invest more in water control, in land improvement, or in transforming paddies into mulberry groves. The development of rural banking and credit also enabled peasants to get loans or other financial support more easily (Fang Xing 1994; Min-te Pan 1996; Bozhong Li 1999: 491), especially since the real interest rates of rural loans declined in most of the period under study (Fang Xing 1999: 2138–74). It is not surprising that there was a substantial increase in farm investment at this time (Bozhong Li 1984). In mid-nineteenth-century Jiangnan, a common peasant family working 10 *mu* of land usually owned a property worth 184 thousand copper coins (140 *taels* of silver). Of that, 118 thousand coins were 'productive goods' (land, seeds, farm instruments, fertilizer, fodder, etc.) and the rest were 'consuming goods' (food, housing, etc.) (Fang Xing 1999: 2125–9). That is, production expenses were much more than consumption expenses, an indication that farm capital investment was greater than in the past.

The improvement of land, advances in farm technology, and increased agricultural investment together ushered in a rise in yields per *mu* of major crops during the two centuries under study. Although increased yields of wheat and mulberries were insubstantial, yields of other crops increased significantly. For example, cotton yields per *mu* increased by one fifth, from about 80 to around 100 catties.[14] However, this increase was dwarfed by what happened in rice. Earlier studies conclude that there was no increase in rice yields during the period. However, my macro analysis of demand and supply[15] leads to quite a contrary conclusion that rice yields rose by nearly a half (47%), from 1.7 *shi*[16] to 2.5 *shi* in the period. This is the greatest increase for any two-century period in pre-modern Jiangnan history (Bozhong Li 1998: 130–1, 1999: 500–1).

3. Changes in the Jiangnan Peasant Economy

Generally speaking, changes in the production factors themselves do not necessarily affect labour productivity. They do so only when they interact with each other and with a particular unit of production. Since the basic unit of production is a single peasant family in pre-industrial Jiangnan, these changes will influence farm labour productivity only through the peasant family economy. The changes discussed above suggest a new pattern of peasant economy, which appeared at the turn of the seventeenth century and spread during the subsequent centuries. I call this pattern 'the trinity pattern', because three of the most important advances in the Jiangnan peasant economy are combined within it. These advances include 'one year double-cropping', 'one man works 10 *mu*', and 'man ploughs and woman weaves'. More specifically, these expressions mean that a man works 10 *mu* of fields with double-cropping, while the woman raises silkworms and reels silk, or spins and weaves cotton. I will now discuss each of these aspects in greater detail.

3.1   One year double-cropping

The system of 'one year double-cropping' is the same as the 'new double-cropping' introduced earlier in the chapter. This technique appeared in the mid-Ming period and spread during the following centuries. By the mid-nineteenth century, it had become the dominant crop pattern in Jiangnan. From an agronomic viewpoint, the system is undoubtedly superior to any alternate crop regimes. First, this new system is very well suited to the ecological environment of Jiangnan, making it possible for the system to spread everywhere in the region.[17] Second, an important feature of the new system is that it entails rotating dry- and wet-field crop cultivation. Because the rotation of different crops can reduce the depletion of soil nutrients and even raise the soil's fertility, the new system improves land when it is used.[18] The resulting improvement of the land means that comparatively small quantities of fertilizer and labour were needed to achieve a good yield. In addition, with a greater variety of second crops, the new system gave farmers more freedom to choose the crop best suited to the various local conditions, therefore allowing them to maximize their income.

Economically, the major advantage of this new system is that it reduced the number of non-working days in the slack seasons, making farm work more continuous and more like industrial production. More importantly, under this regime the amount of labour inputs did not necessarily increase at the same rate as the growth in output. This was because winter crops (especially certain beans and rapeseed) need comparatively less labour and investment. In absolute terms though, the new system needed more fertilizer than the single-cropping system, or double-cropping of rice and green manure plants.[19] The spread of the new system caused a remarkable increase in yield per *mu* of rice.

During the two centuries under study, fertilizer use increased greatly for major crops, while labour inputs changed little. In fact, increasing labour input per *mu* of major crops ceased by the late sixteenth century. In this sense, Jiangnan agriculture clearly became more capital intensive. This new crop regime, therefore, represents a new kind of agricultural intensification—capital intensification (mainly fertilizer), not labour intensification (Bozhong Li 1984, 1998: ch. 5). Because labour inputs increased more slowly than output, Jiangnan agriculture could escape from a 'high-level equilibrium trap' or 'involutionary growth'.[20]

The benefits of the 'one year double-crops' can only be maximized when a particular set of conditions are met. Of these conditions, farm size is one of the most important.

3.2   One man works 10 mu

In the context of a particular technology, farm size plays a crucial role in determining farm labour productivity. Inappropriate farm size, whether too big or too small, will aggravate the imbalance between labour requirements and labour supply for the different farming tasks. Labour requirements are different from job to job, but labour supply usually comes from within a family and is quite rigidly fixed.[21] The gaps between supply and demand will increase under a multi-cropping system because busy seasons become shorter.[22] This imbalance reduces labour productivity because a considerable amount of labour is wasted in some jobs, while production suffers from an insufficient labour supply for other tasks. Only when each of the various skill groups within the labour pool is allocated in such a way as to meet labour requirements efficiently, can farm labour productivity be maximized. This can only be achieved when farm size is optimized so as to make the most efficient use of family labour.

Finding the optimal farm size is crucial to an increase in farm labour productivity, but 'optimal' does not necessarily mean 'large' as is often thought. For a given circumstance (especially technological), an increase in labour productivity is not necessarily associated with an expansion of farm size. Though farm size is related closely to the man–land ratio, it is not only determined by that ratio.[23] In many cases, other factors may be more determinative. The old cliché that a falling man–land ratio results in the shrinking of farm size, and that the shrinking in turn drives farm labour productivity down is simplistic and superficial. From this perspective, the man–land ratio is considered to be the only relevant factor. All other factors are assumed to be non-existent. Yet, these factors do exist and play a significant role in the formation of farm size. A simple calculation of the ratio of cultivated land to total population shows that Jiangnan's average farm size did shrink remarkably in the period under discussion: cultivated land (*crop area*) per capita dropped 45% between the early seventeenth and mid-nineteenth centuries. But that provides only a superficial picture. If the urban population and non-agricultural families in the countryside are excluded, crop area worked by a peasant family still dropped, but only by 40%, from 15 to 9 *mu*.[24] If we take into account double-cropping with an index of 140% in the early seventeenth century and 170% in the mid-nineteenth century, we will find that farm size decreased by only 30%, from 21 to 15 *mu*. Moreover, if rural women are excluded, there was no drop, but rather, a rise, in terms of *crop mu* per worker.

Under the new double-cropping system, a farmer will use his labour most efficiently when he works about 10 *mu* of cultivated land (Bozhong Li 1986, 1998: 68–79). In fact, the pattern of 'one man works 10 *mu*' came to predominate in Jiangnan, not only because it saves labour, but also because it involves many major advances. These include more skilful management, greater use of fertilizer, rational land use, specialized or professional farming, and so on.[25] Moreover, in a farm of about 10 *mu*, a farmer can do almost all the farm work by himself and does not need to ask for his wife's help. This makes it possible for the female labour force to shift from farming to rural industry. With women employed elsewhere, the numbers of people working on the family farm were greatly reduced. Consequently, farms went from being a two-worker farm to a one-worker farm. The change had a great impact on farm labour productivity.

The pattern of 'one man works 10 *mu*' first appeared in the late sixteenth century and was widely adopted during the following centuries. By the mid-nineteenth century, it had become the norm determining farm size in Jiangnan. Even though Jiangnan lost half of its population during the Taiping Rebellion, and the man–land ratio improved significantly after 1850, farm size did not change much. While there are many reasons why peasants did not expand their farms, relatively high labour productivity from this 'optimal' size is unquestionably an important factor.

3.3   Man ploughs and woman weaves

The expression 'man ploughs and woman weaves' (*nan geng nu zhi*) represents a pre-industrial pattern of gender-based division of labour within peasant families. Though the pattern is thought to have been universal in pre-modern Chinese history,[26] it should be noted that even in the late Ming period, the vast majority of rural women in Jiangnan still worked with men in the field, while men also worked on spinning and weaving with women. It is in the period under study that division of labour between the sexes became clear, reaching its highest point in the mid-Qing period (Bozhong Li 1996*b*, 1996*c*). Consequently, there was a significant increase in the number of women who shifted from farming activities to spinning and weaving. In Songjiang Prefecture (the centre of the cotton industry of Jiangnan) during the mid-nineteenth century, 90% of the female rural labour force spun and wove for 60 hours a week.[27] Such was the case in other places in eastern Jiangnan, but to a lesser degree. In western Jiangnan, a similar phenomenon happened even earlier. Women in this region were drawn to silkworm raising and silk spinning as early as the late sixteenth century and did not work in the fields (Bozhong Li 1996*b*, 1996*c*). Since the return to female labour was considerably higher in textile handicrafts and silkworm raising than in farming, the incomes of peasant families increased substantially.[28] Therefore, the development of this pattern of 'man ploughs and woman weaves', not only reduced the supply of labour in farming, but also led to an increase in incomes, the source of agricultural investment.

On the basis of the three major advances of peasant economy discussed here— 'one year double-cropping', 'one man works 10 *mu*', and 'man ploughs and woman weaves'—a new pattern of peasant economy, the 'trinity pattern', was formed in Jiangnan. This combination of advances underpins the tremendous gains in efficiency in the peasant economy of pre-modern Jiangnan. In the next section, I will examine whether this pattern did in fact increase farm labour productivity.

4. Increased Farm Labour Productivity in Jiangnan

One of the problems with the previous studies has been their tendency to account for labour productivity using modern standards. Though labour productivity can generally be defined as the amount of output or income produced per unit of labour,[29] the standards for calculating labour productivity will vary across different societies. Previously I have pointed out that the methods used in calculating labour productivity in pre-modern Chinese agriculture differ in four ways from those used in modern industrial societies.[30] For the discussion in this chapter, farm labour productivity will be calculated using the peasant family as the unit of labour and a year as the standard for time. Male and female labour productivity will be discussed separately, since a division of labour between the sexes became much clearer during this period.

The 'trinity pattern' is the optimal pattern in the Jiangnan peasant economy because under this pattern higher yields per *mu* can be achieved with lower inputs. As I point out above, in the early seventeenth century, a farm ran, on average, 15 *mu* of cultivated land with a multi-cropping index of 140%, the second crop being wheat. The yield per *mu* was 1.7 *shi* for rice and 1 *shi* for wheat. If all the 15 *mu* of land were planted in rice, this farm would harvest 26 *shi* of rice and 6 *shi* of wheat, together equivalent to 30 *shi* of rice.[31] In contrast, in the mid-nineteenth century, the average farm size was 9 *mu* with a multi-cropping index of 170%. Per *mu* yield was 2.5 *shi* of rice and 1 *shi* of wheat. Farm output was 23 *shi* of rice and 6 *shi* of wheat, totalling 27 *shi* of rice, 10% below the early seventeenth-century figures. However, if we calculate labour productivity according to the number of workers, output per worker would be 15 *shi* of rice in the early seventeenth century and 27 *shi* of rice in the mid-nineteenth century respectively. That is, the figure for the late Ming period is only 55% of the mid-Qing figure.

If this macroanalysis is insufficient, a concrete example may be helpful. Western Songjiang will be used for this purpose. This area is located in eastern Jiangnan and is a typical agricultural region, with rice as its staple product. But before the discussion begins, I will remind the reader: the Songjiang case is very exceptional, since most peasant families never farmed as much land nor had as high yields in late Ming Jiangnan.

In western Songjiang, a peasant family could plant 25 *mu* of rice and harvest 2.5 *shi/mu*, for a total of 62.5 *shi* of rice in the late sixteenth century in which period one-year-one-crop pattern was dominant (He Liangjun 1959: 115). In contrast, an early nineteenth-century peasant family planted 10 *mu* with rice at 3 *shi/mu* and wheat at 1 *shi/mu*, for a combined total of 37 *shi* of rice (Jiang Gao 1963: 3b–10a). We can see that the mid-Qing's total is only 60% of the late Ming example. Moreover, production costs per *mu* of rice were equivalent to about 1 *shi* of rice in both cases. Costs for wheat were about one-fourth of those of rice, or 0.25 *shi* of rice/*mu*, in the mid-Qing case.[32] Subtracting production costs, the late Ming family had a net income of 37.5 *shi* and the Qing family 24.5 *shi*, about 65% of the figure for the earlier period. Thus, labour productivity for the mid-Qing would seem to be one-third lower than for the late Ming. However, if we subject our example to further scrutiny, we come to quite a different conclusion.

First, in the term of output per worker, the late Ming farm is quite different from the mid-Qing farm. It has already been shown that there is a great difference between the numbers of farm workers in the two cases. In the late Ming case, farming was done by both the husband and wife, while in the mid-Qing period it was done just by the husband. If we calculate productivity according to an individual worker, a late Ming worker produced 31 *shi*, but a mid-Qing produced 37 *shi*, about 20% higher. After subtracting costs of production, the net output per worker is 18.8 *shi* in the Ming case and 24.5 *shi* in the Qing case. That is, net output per worker is 30% higher in mid-Qing than in the late Ming.

Second, outputs per workday in the two cases quite clearly differ from each other. During the period under study, labour inputs per *mu* did not change much. A *mu* of rice took ordinarily about fifteen workdays (including irrigation),[33] while a *mu* of wheat took three workdays.[34] For the late Ming farm, 375 workdays were required to work its 25 *mu* of paddy. On the mid-Qing farm, 10 *mu* of rice needed only 150 workdays, and 10 *mu* of wheat required about 30 workdays. The 10 *mu* of rice and wheat together required 180 workdays. Labour inputs were less than half of those of the late Ming period, the total harvest being about 60% of the example from the earlier period. This implies that production per workday is one quarter higher for the Qing case than for the Ming. More specifically, a Ming workday produces 1.7 *dou*[35] of rice and a Qing workday produces 2.1 *dou*. Subtracting costs of production, net daily production in the Ming is 1 *dou* of rice and 1.4 *dou* in the Qing, or 40% higher. This example from western Songjiang shows that, whether calculated on an annual or daily basis, farm labour productivity was increasing during the period under study.

Finally, I will make a brief analysis of rural female labour productivity. As 'another half of the men', or 'another half of the sky' as a modern Chinese proverb says, women's labour has important influences on men's farm productivity. Taking a western Songjiang peasant family as an example, I will make a comparison of family labour productivity under different patterns of peasant economy.

In the case of western Songjiang, as we have just seen, a late sixteenth-century peasant family had two workers—a man and a woman—and cultivated 25 *mu* of rice, with a yield per *mu* of 2.5 *shi*. Labour requirements for 25 *mu* of rice were about 375 days. All farm work was shared by the man and the woman, except land preparation, which customarily was men's work and accounted for 50 workdays.[36] Each of them, therefore, worked for 163 days. After the field practice was finished, rice needed to be husked, which was also commonly 'man's work' and took the man 63 days.[37] Altogether, the man worked for 275 days a year and the woman worked for 163 days. Since 300 days are the maximum number of workdays of a peasant for all kinds of productive work (farming and handicrafts), the man had only 25 days to work at other jobs.[38] As for the woman, her maximum workdays were only about 200 days a year (Bozhong Li 1996*b*, 1996*c*). Since she had already worked in the fields for 163 days, she had only 37 days to do other productive work. Here we assume that the peasant and his wife devoted all their non-farming workdays to cotton spinning and weaving, to a total of 62 days. In pre-eighteenth-century Jiangnan, it usually took about seven days to produce one bolt of cotton cloth.[39] Therefore, the man and woman could produce about 9 bolts of cotton cloth within 62 workdays, which could only meet the annual cloth consumption of the family itself. The total output from 25 *mu* of rice was 62.5 *shi* of rice. If both the rent of 31.3 *shi* and production costs (excluding 'wages') of 12.5 *shi* are taken away, the net income (including 'wages') was 18.7 *shi*. The net income (including 'wages') from a bolt of cloth is worth, on average, 1.5 *dou* of rice in the early and mid-Qing. Using this ratio as the standard, 9 bolts were worth 1.4 *shi*. Together, their total net income was 20 *shi*.

In contrast, during the mid-Qing, the family worked only 10 *mu* with a total output of 37 *shi*. Since labour requirements were 18 workdays a *mu*, the total labour inputs were 180 days. Adding in 37 days for husking and branning, the total becomes 217 workdays, all of which were worked by men only. This would leave the typical farmer 83 days to do other work (assuming cotton handicrafts).[40] Since the wife was not required to work in the fields, she could devote all her 200 workdays to cotton spinning and weaving. Altogether, the farmer and his wife could work 283 days in cotton handicrafts. With one bolt of cotton cloth taking six days to make during the eighteenth and nineteenth centuries, 283 workdays would result in 47 bolts of cloth. Accordingly, the income from this quantity of cloth was equivalent to 7.1 *shi* of rice. After subtracting rents of 15 *shi* and production costs (excluding 'wages') of 6.3 *shi*, they could receive a net income (including 'wages') of 15.7 *shi* from the output of the 10 *mu*. Together, the total net income was 23 *shi*.

The difference in total incomes between the two families is 15%. Moreover, we should note that a high per *mu* yield of 2.5 *shi* of rice on a big family farm of 25 *mu* is very seldom seen in sources relating to Ming–Qing Jiangnan.[41] In contrast, in the mid-Qing there is plenty of evidence referring to per *mu* yields of 3 *shi* of rice with 1 *shi* of wheat (which can be converted to 0.7 *shi* of rice) on a small family farm of 10 *mu* or less.[42] Therefore, for most areas in Jiangnan, the difference in labour productivity between farms in the late Ming and those in the mid-Qing will be even greater than those seen in Songjiang. If we use a lower yield figure for the late Ming Songjiang family farm, say 2 *shi*,[43] the net farm income of the family would fall to 12.5 *shi*. Together with income from cotton handicrafts, the total would be 14 *shi*, 40% lower than that of the Songjiang family during the mid-Qing.[44] All of the results in the preceding analysis indicate that farm productivity did increase in Jiangnan during the period concerned. In this sense, the region did experience real economic growth.[45]

5. Rise in the Standard of Living of Jiangnan Peasants

Since labour productivity and the standard of living are inseparably linked, the rise in farm labour productivity in Jiangnan implies an increase in the peasants' standard of living. Earlier studies, like those examining labour productivity, have claimed that the standard of living of Jiangnan peasants continued to drop to a 'minimum subsistence level' throughout the period under study.[46] However, as I argued in relation to the previous studies of labour productivity, this conventional wisdom is undocumented and does not withstand further scrutiny. The concern here then is to determine whether the standard of living of peasants in Jiangnan did improve during the relevant two centuries.

First, wage changes for farm workers indicate that standards of living improved among Jiangnan peasants. There was a steady increase in the wages of farm workers. It is no wonder that complaints could be heard repeatedly from employers about farm labour becoming more and more expensive during the two centuries. The increase is related to the 'Chinese price revolution' which was the result of a large-scale and continuous influx of silver. However, the movement of prices was generally favourable to Jiangnan peasants during most of the period.[47] Consequently, as Wei Jinyu has documented, real wages in farming rose sharply in cash, and moderately in kind, between the early seventeenth and the mid-nineteenth centuries. The increase in the real wage meant that it took four or five farm workers to support an adult in the late Ming, but by the mid-Qing only one or two hired labourers were needed to maintain the same standard of living (Wei Jinyu 1983).

E. A. Wrigley has developed a method to gauge the development of labour productivity in agriculture (Wrigley 1987) which I think is very helpful. From this perspective, Wei's results suggest that the number of mouths fed by every one hundred people working on the land would increase remarkably. It can be concluded, therefore, that farm labour productivity did increase in Jiangnan during the two centuries under study. In addition, this period also saw a decline of real rental rates (Fang Xing 1992), though no evidence suggests that the tax burden became heavier in this period. On the contrary, it seems to have become lighter.[48] There is little doubt, therefore, that real incomes of peasants did improve considerably in Jiangnan at this time.

Second, the quality of the peasants' diet also improved in Jiangnan during the period. Fang Xing suggested that ordinary Jiangnan peasants ate more fish, meat, and tofu, drank more tea and wine, and consumed more sugar than ever before (Fang Xing 1996, 1999: 2175–92). Farm labourers were clearly better fed in the mid-nineteenth century than in the seventeenth century, whether in terms of the quantity or quality of meat, fish, and wine, all of which they consumed in substantial quantities (James Lee and Wang Feng 1999: 29–31).

Third, the improved standard of living can also be seen in the increase in consumption, not only of 'ordinary goods' like cotton cloth, but also of 'luxury goods' such as silk, wine, tobacco, and opium. Bao Shichen, an early nineteenth-century Jiangnan scholar, provides us with a description of the consumption of wine, tobacco, and opium in Suzhou Prefecture. This description indicates that the consumption of these items increased remarkably in the early nineteenth century (Bao Shichen 2001: 56–9). According to John Barrow, a contemporary western observer in China at the turn of the nineteenth century, most of the people in northern Zhejiang (a part of Jiangnan) wore silk (Barrow 1806: 572). But such accounts are rare in the literature before the late eighteenth century.

The Jiangnan peasants' choice of food also supports the argument that living standards rose in the eighteenth and nineteenth centuries. During these two centuries, an increasing number of Jiangnan peasants lived on rice that was imported from the middle and upper Yangzi. Rather than planting sweet potatoes in their fields and then consuming them as food, they preferred to purchase the expensive rice from far away. Sweet potatoes were much cheaper than rice, but there was a major social barrier to its consumption: eating them was usually considered to be a symbol of abysmal poverty. This barrier could have been overcome if the standard of living in Jiangnan really fell, as was the case in Fujian during the same period. The increasing consumption of imported rice, rather than sweet potatoes, is thus inconsistent with any thesis that the standard of living had plummeted following a long decline of more than two centuries.

Fourth, the pattern of migration during the period under study also suggests improved living conditions in Jiangnan. In the Qing times, there were large-scale migrations from highly populated east China to rich and less populated regions like northeast China, Taiwan, and southeast Asia. However, there is little evidence to suggest that such emigration took place from Jiangnan, even though it had been the most crowded region in China and enjoyed a central position in the development of water transportation. On the contrary, Jiangnan witnessed continuous in-migration. Most immigrants rushed into prosperous cities and towns located in east Jiangnan to work in industry. It is perhaps surprising that the majority of these immigrant workers did not come from neighbouring villages, but from peripheral areas of Jiangnan, or even from outside Jiangnan. Why did the local rural labour force not prefer to work outside their villages? One main reason seems to be economic: they could have a better income when they worked in the villages.[49]

Finally, I will examine the standard of living in Jiangnan in the mid-nineteenth century from a broader perspective. As Jacque Gernet, Ping-ti Ho, and others have suggested, the Chinese peasant lived quite well in late Imperial times when compared with their counterparts in the major countries of early modern western Europe or in Tokugawa Japan.[50] Being residents of the most prosperous area of China at that time, peasants in Jiangnan enjoyed the highest standard of living of their counterparts in the rest of the country. These peasants were well fed and clothed whether by late Imperial Chinese standards or by early modern European standards. It would be wrong to argue that they must have lived at 'minimum subsistence level'.

As was the case for farm labour productivity, the conventional wisdom that the standard of living declined in late Imperial China is principally based on an old and misleading Malthusian conception. Neither does the conventional wisdom on the standard of living square with what we know from Jiangnan history. Therefore, a new perspective is called for, even in the relatively well-trodden field of the pre-industrial Jiangnan rural economy.

Notes

1. For recent evidence of this decline, see Maddison (1998: ch. I, II). Using his PPP method, Maddison estimated that in China the GDP per capita was US $450 (in 1990 US$) in 960, rose to US $600 in 1280, stagnated during the following centuries until 1820, then declined to US $537 in 1952. In contrast, in Europe (excluding Turkey and ex-USSR) the GDP per capita was US $400 in 960, increased to US $500 in 1280, and US $870 in 1700, jumped to US $1,129 in 1820 and US $4,374 in 1952 (Maddison 1998: 25, 40).
2. See Wang Jiafan (1988), Bozhong Li (1996a), Fang Xing (1996, 1999: 2175–92), and especially James Lee and Wang Feng (1999: 29–31).
3. The prefectures include Jiangning (Yingtian), Zhenjiang, Suzhou (including the department of Taicang), Songjiang, Jiaxing, Huzhou and Hangzhou, see Bozhong Li (1990).
4. From the nation-wide discussions of the 'Sprouts of Chinese Capitalism' in the 1950s, 1960s, and 1980s and of the 'Long Persistence of Feudalism' in the early 1980s, it is apparent that the majority of mainland Chinese scholars have tended to agree that farm labour productivity declined in late Imperial China. Outside the mainland, some scholars have suggested that farm labour productivity remained constant in late Imperial China on the whole, or even rose a bit in some areas within 'developing' and 'undeveloped' parts of China (Perkins 1969: 18–19; Wang Yejian and Huang Guoshu 1989). But nobody has so far explicitly claimed that such was the case in 'developed' parts of China, which was the homeland of the majority of the Chinese people.
5. For example, Mark Elvin's theory of 'high-level equilibrium trap', which is apparently based on the experience of Ming–Qing Jiangnan, is roughly identical with the view that farm labour productivity declined in late Imperial China (Elvin 1973: ch. 16). Chen Hengli made it clear that in Huzhou and Jiaxing of central Jiangnan, the level of farm labour productivity achieved in the late seventeenth century is obviously higher than in the 1930s and 1950s (Chen Hengli 1961: ch. 2). Philip Huang also pointed out that farm labour productivity declined over time during the period of 1350–1979 (Huang 1990: ch. 1). On the other hand, although Perkins argued that per capita output, or farm labour productivity, remained constant in China on the whole between 1368 and the 1950s, he attributed it to both the expansion of cultivated land and the increase in yields per unit of

cultivated land. In the case of Jiangnan, however, according to Perkins as well as most scholars of Ming–Qing Jiangnan history, no new land was available and yields increased little during the period, while population grew considerably and most of that growing population still depended on farming for their livelihood. One would have to infer that farm labour productivity must have been falling.

6. A *mu* is 0.0667 hectares.

7. For demographic changes in major parts of the world—China, India, Europe, Japan, and so on—in 'early modern times', see Maddison (1998: 20) and Frank (1998: 167–9). From their updated works, we can see that the Jiangnan population grew even more slowly than Europe during the period between 1700 and 1820 (Maddison) or between 1650 and 1850 (Frank). The annual growth rate of Jiangnan population is also much lower than that of the Chinese national rate which is estimated 0.6% a year between 1650 and 1850, and far less than the 3% or more in many developing countries since World War II (Perkins 1969: 24).

8. A wide range of methods to control population growth was employed, including infanticide, delayed marriage, lower proportion of ever married, abortion, contraception, sterilization, and the like. See Bozhong Li (1994*b*, 2000*a*).

9. It is the shortage that was a principal barrier to double-cropping of rice (two crops of rice within a year) and some farming methods of rice such as the pit cultivation (*quzhong fa*). All of these cropping methods are more labour-intensive than double-cropping of rice and winter crops. In addition, from the late Ming period on, more and more Jiangnan peasants had to hire labour to help them in farming in peak seasons, because their wives had to concentrate on silk or cotton handicraft. See Bozhong Li (1999: 488–90).

10. The increase in short-term hired labour after the mid-Ming period is one of the main research topics within the 'sprouts of capitalism' literature of mainland Chinese historians. A representative discussion can be found in Li Wenzhi (1983: especially part 3).

11. Though double-cropping of rice and wheat appeared much earlier (I dated its first appearance back to the Tang times, see Bozhong Li 1982), great differences can be found between pre-Ming and Ming double-cropping. That is why Kitada has referred to them as the old and the new double-cropping (Kitada 1988: ch. 2, 3). For further discussions, see Bozhong Li (1994*a*, 1998: 50–1).

12. Mark Elvin has argued that when studying technological progress one must distinguish between invention (the earliest appearance), innovation (the application of invention to production), and dissemination (the spread of an innovation), see Bozhong Li (1994*a*). These distinctions are important for evaluating Qing Jiangnan agricultural technology.

13. Perkins called the discovery of the fertilizer potential of bean cakes a significant exception to the more general picture of a stagnant technology in late Imperial China (Perkins 1969: 71). As has already been pointed out above, however, for economic growth, the widespread use of a new technique may be even more important than the discovery of it. It is during the early and mid-Qing that the use of bean cakes became widespread in Jiangnan, because of a sharply expanding import of beans and bean cakes (Bozhong Li 1998: ch. 6). Therefore, considering the importance of it in the agricultural history of Jiangnan, it is not an exaggeration to call the widespread use of bean cakes a 'fertilizer revolution'.

14. A catty is equal to around 0.5 kg.

15. The method I use is as follows: first, I seek the total rice output of Jiangnan by subtracting import from total consumption, then find the yield per *mu* by dividing the output by acreage under rice cultivation, and finally examine the result against yield records available from different sources.

16. A *shi* is 100 litres.

17. In contrast, the old double-cropping can be applied only in limited places, mainly in 'high fields' in western Jiangnan, but not in 'low fields' in eastern Jiangnan which is much more important agriculturally, see Bozhong Li (1994*a*, 1998: 50–1). As for double-cropping of rice, it has never spread widely. In the mid-Qing, in spite of encouragement from local officials such as Governor Lin Zexu and free instruction from local gentry-agriculturists like Pan Zenyi, few Jiangnan peasants responded. In the 1960s and 1970s, to increase grain production from each piece of land, great efforts were made to advocate double-cropping rice by the state. But it caused a series of problems. Thus after 1978 double-cropping rice was given up and there was a return to a rotation regime of rice and winter crops.

18. In an agronomic analysis of modern Zhejiang cropping systems, Fang Zaihui has pointed out that double-cropping of rice with wheat, barley, rapeseed, and broad beans is the best cropping regime for most of Zhejiang. Because the soil can be turned over and sun dried after the rice is harvested and will not be waterlogged when these winter crops are planted after rice, they are especially good for the soil of paddy fields. In contrast, alternative cropping regimes (single-cropping or double-cropping rice or combining rice with green manure crops) reduce the physical and chemical degradation of soil that results from long-term waterlogging of the paddy fields. If waterlogged for a long period of time, the structure and properties of the soil are degraded (Fang Zaihui *et al.* 1984: 40, 161–7, 309–10). For this reason, as early as in the late seventeenth century, Zhang Luxiang said that planting wheat on rice fields could dry and loosen the soil, 'benefiting future planting of rice' (Zhang Luxiang 1983: 106).

19. It is, of course, much less than double-cropping of rice. But as is pointed out above, double-cropping of rice has not spread in Jiangnan.

20. In contrast, as Guo Songyi has also pointed out, double-cropping of rice alone was not as worthwhile as double-cropping of rice and wheat (Guo Songyi 1994). But either labour input or capital input is much more in double-cropping of rice than in double-cropping of rice and wheat. As for the double-cropping of rice and beans or rapeseed, the inputs are even less.

21. Taking rice cultivation as an example, labour supply may be too much for some jobs (weeding in rice cultivation for instance), while it may be highly inefficient for other works (land preparation and seedling transplanting, for instance). See Bozhong Li (1986, 1998: 68–75).

22. That is one of the major reasons why double-cropping of rice cannot spread in Jiangnan. Perkins has suggested that in China, even into the 1950s, there was no labour surplus, but a shortage of labour during agricultural peak seasons (Perkins 1969: 59–60). The shortage was the major barrier of the spread of double-cropping of rice, because the labour requirements of double-cropping of rice are much heavier than in double-cropping of rice and wheat and the requirements are highly uneven for different seasons. For Jiangnan, Kenneth Walker has suggested that in the present-day province of Jiangsu where most of Jiangnan is located, the labour supply has been estimated to have been on average less than half that necessary for ideal double-cropping rice conditions (Walker 1968: Table III).

23. To raise labour productivity in a farm, at least four methods can be adopted: (1) the acreage of cultivated land increases, but the number of the workers does not; (2) the number of the workers decreases, but the acreage of the farmland does not; (3) both the number of the workers and the acreage of farmland do not change, but the farmland

is more intensively cultivated; and (4) both the number of the workers and the acreage of farmland are unchanged, but land is multi-cropped (Bray 1986: 2–3). It is clear that only the first method is related with the expansion of farm size.

24. Since the late Ming, total crop area in Jiangnan has not changed much; it has been roughly 45 million *mu*, while Jiangnan had about 3 million agricultural families in 1620 and 5 million in 1850, see Bozhong Li (1998: 19–23, 26–7, 2000*b*: ch. 9).

25. It is no wonder Zhang Luxiang, a late-seventeenth-century Jiangnan scholar and agriculturist, said that 'a good peasant farmed no more than ten *mu*' (Zhang Luxiang 1983: 148). Almost two centuries later, Tao Xi, a Jiangnan scholar and high-ranking official, noticed that a man cultivating 10 *mu* was still the norm; if a family had more than 10 *mu*, it needed to hire labour (Tao Xi 1927: 6a, 17a–b).

26. In mainland Chinese scholarship, 'man ploughs and woman weaves' has been seen as the normal division of labour for thousands of years. It has also been considered a major characteristic of the economic structure of Chinese 'feudal' society (Bai Gang 1984: ch. 3.4, 3.5, 3.12–3.15, and 4.8). But as I argued in my 1996 article, in Jiangnan, the pattern did not prevail until the seventeenth century and it became predominant just in the eighteenth century.

27. Xu Xinwu (1992: 215), cf. Bozhong Li (2000*b*: ch. 8).

28. Philip Huang has argued that labour productivity was lower in non-grain cash cropping than in grain production. (Huang 1990: 78–84) We should note that this viewpoint relies mainly on studies of the cotton industry in Jiangnan during the nineteenth century and the first part of the twentieth century. As we know, however, economic conditions in China worsened in the nineteenth century. In the case of Jiangnan, the cotton handicraft industry suffered not only from the general economic contraction, but also from exposure to competition from cotton textile producers in the industrialized West. Therefore, conclusions drawn from this later period are not helpful to the discussion here.

29. For the definition see Perkins (1986: 87) and Crafts (1989).

30. The differences are: (1) modern industrial labour productivity is calculated on the basis of a day or hour, but traditional agricultural labour productivity is calculated mainly according to the year; (2) modern industrial labour productivity is per worker, but traditional agricultural labour usually takes the family as the unit; (3) modern industrial labour is basically of one kind, while peasant labour has more types; (4) modern labour's results are usually expressed in money, but in traditional agricultural societies we must use real goods in many cases, because a commercial economy is not sufficiently developed. In general, the four points apply to Jiangnan agriculture in the period under discussion, see Bozhong Li (1998: 134–5, 1999: 492–3).

31. The wheat is converted into 4.2 *shi* of rice according to the common rate of conversion in Ming–Qing Jiangnan which is 1:0.7, see Bozhong Li (1998: 208).

32. On production costs of rice and wheat, see Bozhong Li (1998: 139–40, 1999: 502).

33. Rice cultivation in Ming–Qing Jiangnan, from preparing the soil through harvesting, required about 10 workdays/*mu*. If we add the labour for pumping water and collecting and transporting fertilizer the total is 15 workdays/*mu* (Bozhong Li 1984, 1998: 139, 1999: 504).

34. According to the calculations on labour expenses in *Pumao nongzi* each *mu* of wheat, barley, or rye required 3 workdays (Jiang Gao 1963: 9b).

35. One *dou* is 10 litres.

36. It takes 2 workdays to prepare 1 *mu* of rice (Jiang Gao 1963: 11a). In a single-cropping regime, a peasant can prepare 25 *mu* during the period of land preparation. Preparing the land is very hard; normally it is only a man's responsibility.

37. A family plants 25 *mu*; each *mu* produced 2.5 *shi* for 62.5 *shi*. Men do the job of husking the rice at the rate of 1 *shi*/day (Jiang Gao 1963: 11a). When speaking of wheat, because it is not clear how much labour it takes to bran, I have to use the rate for rice.

38. In rural societies, peasants do not work every day. This maximum number of workdays of a Jiangnan peasant within a year is derived from modern field investigations, see Xu Xinwu (1992: 469) and Bozhong Li (1999: 504). This number does not contradict the calculation of wages of a long-term farm hand on the basis of 360 days a year, because he still had to eat and be clothed even if he did not have work to do in the slack seasons.

39. A bolt of cloth was 3.63 square yards.

40. As pointed out earlier, the maximum number of workdays per year is 300 days.

41. In fact, the example given by He Liangjun is the only record I have ever seen.

42. For example, Zhang Haishan (1992) says, 'Now [1804] the land is limited and the people are many in Suzhou and Songjiang. A man cannot work 10 *mu*'. Paddy productivity in this period reached 3 *shi*/*mu* in both Suzhou and Songjiang (Bao Shichen 2001: 58; Jiang Gao 1963: 3b). For more evidence, see Bozhong Li (1996a, 1999).

43. According to Gu Yanwu, a mid-seventeenth-century Jiangnan scholar. See Bozhong Li (1998: 126–7).

44. On the output in western Songjiang, see Li Bozhong (1998: 139–40, 1999: 506–8).

45. If we consider labour productivity the key factor in deciding whether growth is 'extensive' or 'intensive', then this would be a case of intensive growth. For a more detailed discussion, see Feuerwerker (1992).

46. It is a common opinion that peasants' living standards declined over time in late Imperial China. Most mainland Chinese historians of the older generation believe that the 'feudal exploitation' (rents, taxes, usury, and the like) became so severe that most peasant families could not have survived if they had relied only on farming. Even when they found new sources of income from sericulture and textile handicrafts, it is thought that they still lived at a minimum level of living (Chen Zhenhan 1955; Fu Zhufu and Gu Shutang 1956; Xu Xinwu 1981: 40–4, 105–6; Bai Gang 1984: 221; Fu Yiling 1991: 91, 95; Wang Tingyuan 1993). In the west, some scholars see 'population pressure' as the chief culprit behind the pauperization of peasants. They argue that the pressure created a growing surplus of labour and drove peasants' living standards to a 'minimum subsistence' level, for example, Quan Hansheng (1958) and Philip Huang (1990: ch. 5). This view has been accepted since the 1980s by many mainland Chinese historians such as Hong Huanchun (1988: 91–2). Most of their attention, Chinese and western, has concentrated on Jiangnan.

47. During this period, silk and cotton cloth, Jiangnan's major exports, and rice, Jiangnan's major import and most important food, all rose in price. But generally, before the early nineteenth century, Jiangnan peasants benefited from the price markup (Bozhong Li 1998: ch. 6).

48. After the Qing dynasty was established, the tax burdens of the late Ming were equalized to a large degree so that the burdens for most peasants were reduced, at least in per capita terms.

49. The fact that Jiangnan peasants were unwilling to work in cities and towns cannot be attributed to their conservatism or their 'home-attaching' complex. As residents of the most commercialized area of China, they were unwilling to miss any chance to make money. Qi Yanhuai, an early nineteenth-century scholar and official, figuratively said: 'Shanghai people see the inland travel to Nanjing or Qingjiang as long-distance trips, but they travel by boat between Shanghai and Guandong four or five times a year and never

mind the distance' (Qi Yanhuai 1826). In fact, Nanjing or Qingjiang are hundreds of miles from Shanghai, but Guandong (southern Manchuria) is thousands of miles away. The only reason why they preferred to risk the sea voyage is that they could make more money from the flourishing sea trade that existed between Shanghai and Guandong in the mid-Qing period.

50. Jacque Gernet has confidently asserted that 'the Chinese peasant of the Yongzheng (1723–35) and of the first half of Qianlong (1736–65) era was in general better nourished and more comfortable than his French counterpart in the reign of Louis XV' (cited by R. Bin Wong 1998: 25). Ping-ti Ho has also suggested that the peasants of eighteenth-century China lived better than their counterparts of eighteenth-century France, of early nineteenth-century Prussia, or of Tokugawa Japan (Ping-ti Ho 1959: 194). Even in the mid-nineteenth century, which is usually seen as a period of emerging general social crisis, Robert Fortune, a careful first-hand observer, wrote that the diet of tea-picking labourers in East China was clearly better than that of harvest labourers in Scotland, his motherland: 'A Chinaman would starve upon such food (that Scotch labourers had)' (Fortune 1847/1987: 12).

References

Bai, G. (1984) *Zhongguo fengjian shehui changqi yanxu wenti lunzhan de youlai yu fazhan.* Beijing: Zhongguo shehui kexue chubanshe.

Bao, S. (2001/1851) *Qimin sishu.* Beijing: Zhonghua shuju.

Barrow, Sir J. (1806) *Travels in China.* London: T. Cadell and W. Davies in the Strand.

Bray, F. (1986) *The Rice Economics: Technology and Development in Asian Societies.* Oxford: Basil Blackwell.

Buck, J. L. (1930) *Chinese Farm Economy.* Nanjing: The University of Nanking and the China Council of the Institute of Pacific Relations.

Chen, H. (1961) *Bunongshu yanjiu.* Beijing: Nongye chubanshe.

Chen, Z. (1955) 'Mingmo Qingchu (1620–1720) Zhongguo de nongye laodong shengchanlu, dizu he tudi jizhong', originally in *Jingji yanjiu* (Beijing), 3: 24–39, reprinted in Zhongguo renmin daxue zhongguo lishi jiaoyanshi (ed.), *Zhongguo zibenzhuyi mengya taolunji.* Bejing: Sanlian shudian (1957), pp. 272–94.

Crafts, N. (1989) 'The Industrial Revolution: Economic Growth in Britain, 1700–1860', in A. Digby and C. Feinistein (eds.), *New Directions in Economic and Social History*, Vol. 1. London: Macmillan Press.

Elvin, M. (1973) *The Pattern of the Chinese Past.* Stanford: Stanford University Press.

Fang, X. (1987) 'Lun Qingdai qianqi mianfangzhi de shehui fengong'. *Zhongguo jingjishi yanjiu* (Beijing), 1: 79–94.

——(1992) 'Qingdai qianqi Zhongguo de fengjian dizulu'. *Zhongguo jingjishi yanjiu* (Beijing) 2: 61–9.

——(1994) 'Qingdai qianqi nongcun de gaolidai ziben'. *Qingshi yanjiu* (Beijing), 3: 11–26.

——(1996) 'Qingdai Jiangnan nongmin de xiaofei'. *Zhongguo jingjishi yanjiu* (Beijing), 3: 91–8.

——(1999) 'Nongmin jingji pian', in X. Fang, J. Wei and J. Jing (eds.), *Zhongguo jingji tongshi (Qingai juan).* Beijing: Jingji ribao chubanshe pp. 1911–2192.

Fang, Z., Tang, Q., and Chen, M. (1984) *Zhejiang de gengzuo zhidu.* Hangzhou: Zhejiang kexue jishu chubanshe.

Feuerwerker, A. (1992) 'Presidential Address: Questions about China's Early Modern Economic History that I Wish I Could Answer'. *Journal of Asian Studies*, 51(4): 757–69.

Fortune, R. (1847/1987) *A Journey to the Tea Countries of China and India*. London: Midmay.

Frank, A. G. (1998) *ReOrient: Global Economy in the Asian Age*. Berkeley, CA: University of California Press.

Fu, Y. (1991) *Ming Qing fengjian tudi suoyouzhi lungang*. Shanghai: Shanghai renmin chubanshe.

Fu, Z. and Gu, S. (1956) 'Zhongguo yuanshi ziben jilei fasheng chihuan de yuanyin'. *Tianjin ribao* (Tianjin), 7, Column on History.

Guo, S. (1994) 'Qing qianqi nanfang daozuo diqu de liangshi shengchan'. *Zhongguo jingjishi yanjiu* (Beijing), 1: 1–30.

Hamashima, A. (1989) 'Tudi kafa yu keshang huodong: Mingdai zhongqi Jiangnan dizhu zhi touzi huodong', in *Zhongyang yanjiuyuan di er jie guoji hanxue huiyi lunwenji*. Taipei: Zhongyang yanjiuyuan.

He, L. (1959/late sixteenth century) *Siyouzhai congshuo*, reprinted by Zhonghua shuju, Beijing.

Ho, P. (1959) *Studies on the Population of China, 1368–1953*. Cambridge, MA: Harvard University Press.

Hong, H. (ed.) (1988) *Ming Qing Suzhou nongcun jingji ziliao*. Nanjing: Jiangsu guji chubanshe.

Huang, P. (1990) *The Peasant Family and Rural Development in the Yangzi Delta, 1350–1988*. Stanford, CA: Stanford University Press.

Jiang, G. (1963/1834) *Pumao nongzi*, reprinted by Shanghai tushuguan, Shanghai.

Kitada, H. (1988) *So-Gen-Min-Shin ki Chugoku Konan sankakushu no nogyo no shinka to noson shokugyo no hattatsu ni kansuru kenkyu* (1986–7 nendo kagaku kenkyuhi hojokin—ippan kenkyu C kenkyu hokokusho) (mimeographed by Star shokai).

Lee, J. Z. and Wang, F. (1999) *One Quarter of Humanity: Malthusian Mythology and Chinese Realities*. Cambridge, MA: Harvard University Press.

Li, B. (1982) 'Woguo daomai fuzhongzhi chansheng yu Tangdai changjiang liuyu kao'. *Nongye Kaogu* (Nangchang), 2: 65–72.

—— (1984) 'Ming Qing shiqi Jiangnan shuidao shenchan jiyue chengdu de tigao'. *Zhongguo Nongshi* (Nanjing), 1: 4–37.

—— (1986) 'Ming Qing Jiangnan zhong dao nonghu shengchan nengli chutan'. *Zhongguo nongshi* (Nanjing), 2: 1–18.

—— (1990) 'Jianlun "Jiangnan diqu" de jieding'. *Zhongguo shehui jingjishi yanjiu* (Xiamen), 4: 100–7.

—— (1994a) 'Tian, Di, Ren de bianhua jiqi dui Ming–Qing Jiangnan shuidao shengchang de yingxiang'. *Zhongguo jingjishi yanjiu* (Beijing), 4: 103–21. English translation: 'Changes in Climate, Land and Human Efforts: The Production of Wet-Rice in Jiangnan during the Ming and Qing Dynasties' (by M. Elvin), in M. Elvin and T. Liu (eds.) (1988), *Sediments of Time: Environment and Society in Chinese History*. New York, NY: Cambridge University Press, pp. 447–86.

—— (1994b) 'Kongzhi zengzhang, yi bao fuyu: Qingdai qianqi Jiangnan de rekou xingwei'. *Xin Shixue* (Taipei), 5(3): 25–71.

—— (1995) 'Ming–Qing Jiangnan cansang muchan kao'. *Nongye kaogu* (Nanchang), 3: 196–200, 4: 239–49.

——(1996a) ' "Zui di shenghuo shuizhun" yu "renkou yali" zhiyi'. *Zhongguo shehui jingjishi yanjiu* (Xiamen), 1: 31–7.

——(1996b) 'Cong *"fufu bing zuo"* dao *"nan geng nu zhi"*—Ming–Qing Jiangnan nongjia funu laodong wenti tantao zhi yi'. *Zhongguo jingjishi yanjiu* (Beijing), 1: 99–107.

——(1996c) ' "*Banbiantian*" jiaose de xingcheng—Ming–Qing Jiangnan nongjia funu laodong wenti tantao zhi er'. *Zhongguo jingjishi yanjiu* (Beijing), 3: 10–22.

——(1998) *Agricultural Development in Jiangnan, 1644–1850.* Houndmills, England: Macmillan Press/New York: St. Martin Co.

——(1999) 'Nongmin laodong shengchanlu de tigao', in X. Fang, J. Jing, and J. Wei (eds.), *Zhongguo jingji tongshi Qingai juan.* Beijing: Jingji ribao chubanshe, pp. 485–532.

——(2000a) 'Duotai, biyun yu jueyu: song, yuan, ming, qing shiqi jiangzhe diqu de jieyu fangfa jiqi yunyong'. *Zhongguo xueshu* (Beijing), 1: 71–99.

——(2000b) *Jiangnan de zaoqi gongyehua.* Beijing: Zhongguo shehui kexue chubanshe.

Li, W. (1983) 'Ming Qing shidai Zhongguo nongye zibenzhuyi mengya wenti', in W. Li, J. Wei, and J. Jing (co-authors), *Ming Qing shidai Zhongguo nongye zibenzhui mengya wenti.* Beijing: Zhongguo shehui kexue chubanshe.

Maddison, A. (1998) *Chinese Economic Performance in the Long Run.* Paris: Development Centre of the Organization for Economic Co-operation and Development.

Pan, M. (1996) 'Rural Credit in Ming–Qing Jiangnan and the Concept of Peasant Petty Commodity Production'. *Journal of Asian Studies,* 55(1): 94–117.

Perkins, D. (1969) *Agricultural Development in China, 1368–1968.* Chicago, IL: Aldine Publishing Company.

——(1986) *China: Asia's Next Economic Giant?* Seattle and London: University of Washington Press.

Qi, Y. (1826/1992) 'Haiyun nan cao yi', in C. He (ed.), *Huangchao jingshi wenbian,* reprinted by Zhonggua shuju. Beijing.

Quan, H. (1958) 'Yapian zhanzheng qian Jiangsu de mian fangzhi ye'. *Qinghua xuebao* (new series) (Taipei), 1:3.

Tao, X. (1864–84/1927) *Zu he,* no publication place given.

Walker, K. R. (1968) 'Organization for Agricultural Production', in A. Eckstein, W. Galenson, and T. Liu (eds.), *Economic Trends in Communist China.* Edinburgh: Edinburgh University Press.

Wang, J. (1988) 'Ming–Qing Jiangnan xiaofei fengqi yu xiaofei jiegou miaoshu'. *Huadong shifan daxue xuebao* (Shanghai), 2: 22–32.

Wang, T. (1993) 'Lun Ming Qing shiqi Jiangnan mianfangzhi ye de laodong shouyi jiqi jingying xingtai'. *Zhongguo jingji shi yanjiu* (Beijing), 3: 91–8.

Wang, Y. (Yeh-chien Wang) and Huang, G. (1989) 'Shi ba shiji Zhongguo liangshi gongxu de kaocha'. *Jindai Zhongguo nongcun jingjishi lunwenji.* Taipei: Zhongyang yanjiuyuan jindaishi yanjiusuo.

Wei, J. (1983) 'Ming–Qing shidai nongye zhong dengjixing guyong laodong xiang feidengjixin guyong laodong de guodu', in W. Li, J. Wei, and J. Jing (co-authors), *Ming Qing shidai Zhongguo nongye zibenzhui mengya wenti.* Beijing: Zhongguo shehui kexue chubanshe, pp. 318–516.

Wong, R. B. (1998) *China Transformed—Historical Change and the Limits of European Experience.* Ithaca: Cornell University Press.

Wrigley, E. A. (1987) 'Urban Growth and Agricultural Change: England and the Continent in the Early Modern Period', cited in J. L. van Zanden (1999) 'The development of agricultural productivity in Europe, 1500–1800', in B. J. P. van Bavel and E. Thoen (eds.), *Land Productivity and Agro-system in the North Sea (Middle Ages–20th Century) Elements for Comparison*. Turnhout: Brepols, pp. 357–75.

Xu, X. (1981) *Yapian zhanzheng qian Zhongguo mianfangzhi shougongye de shangpin shengchan yu zibenzhuyi mengya wenti*. Nanjing: Jiangsu renmin chubanshe.

—— (1992) *Jiangnan tubu shi*. Shanghai: Shanghai shehui kexue chubanshe.

Zhang, H. (1992/ early-nineteenth century) 'Ji gu hui yi', in C. He (ed.), *Huangchao jingshi wenbian* (reprinted by Zhonggua shuju, Beijing), juan.39. huzheng 14 cangchu shang.

Zhang, L. (late seventeenth century/1983) *Bu nongshu*, annotated by H. Chen and D. Wang, published as *Bunongshu jiaoshi*. Beijing: Nongye chubanshe.

3 Wages, Inequality, and Pre-Industrial Growth in Japan, 1727–1894

OSAMU SAITO

1. Introduction

The early modern European paradox—a divergence between the slow but unmistakably rising trend in per capita gross domestic product (GDP) and the long decline in real wages—has invited scholarly speculations on how to best 'model' an economy exhibiting such seemingly conflicting tendencies. No consensus has emerged so far. What does seem certain at this stage of research, however, is that these contrasting trends were the results of market-led, 'Smithian' growth, associated with the rise of metropolitan cities, overseas and long-distance trade, proto-industrialization, the increasing pace of proletarianization and, in the case of England and the Low Countries, agricultural investments made by enterprising landlords. All this, as Jan Luiten van Zanden (Chapter 7) and Philip Hoffman *et al.* (Chapter 6) hint in their contributions to this volume, seems to suggest that the growth of the European economy was accompanied by widening income differentials during the early modern period, as has been observed for many countries in later periods and as the Kuznetz curve indicates for modern growth. According to this interpretation, therefore, *pre-industrial* growth also bred inequality.

Should we expect that East Asian peasant economies experienced similar changes in the level of real wages and wage differentials during the period before the onset of industrialization? In his recent article on Asia, Jeffrey Williamson (2000) found that real wages lagged behind per capita GDP in all Asian countries before the First World War, which suggests that inequality increased generally during the first globalization boom. Japan's wage–GDP ratio too, according to his estimates, underwent a sharp decline from the 1870s onwards before flattening out in the interwar period. But, apart from the estimation problem concerning the Japanese case, what about trends *before* the impact of world trade was felt? Did growth in pre-globalization Asia also breed inequality?

The present chapter will address this question by looking at wage data in Japan for 1727–1894, linking the latter half of the Tokugawa to the early Meiji era. In Japan, as in many other countries, this period saw the growth of commerce and

The author is grateful to Bob Allen, Debin Ma, and Kaoru Sugihara for their comments and suggestions on an earlier version of this chapter.

industry. During the late Tokugawa years, it was primarily in the countryside where trade and industry proliferated and grew steadily, if at a modest pace. After the opening of the country to world trade in 1859,[1] the sudden emergence of export markets enabled the rural economy, especially of silk-producing eastern Japan, to grow further. In short, growth in eighteenth- and nineteenth-century Japan was market-led and rural-centred (Smith 1973; Saito 1983; Shimbo and Saito 2004).

However, since there were long swings in the series of wages and prices over the 170-year period, and since there is no single time-series covering the entire period, I should like to examine the evidence I have marshalled so far (in Saito 1998), phase by phase. The focus is not simply on the trend in the general level of real wages, but more on its relationship with the trend in wage differentials within the working population, in the context of the changing phases of the eighteenth- and nineteenth-century economy. Wage labour in that period was supplied in most cases from peasant households. In such a society, it is true that wage earnings were not synonymous with the family income of the poor peasant household. Most data are of wage rates, not of total earnings that workers actually received, since wage work was often undertaken to supplement the peasant household's meagre earnings from farming; thus it is not a straightforward matter to translate the evidence on wage differentials into income inequality. However, given the paucity of pre-modern data on income differentials, the first step is to explore wage data thoroughly, and then to examine their relationship to macro measures of output growth.

The first phase, 1727–1820, was a period in which the Kinai economy grew. The Kinai was Tokugawa Japan's most advanced core region. But its growth slowed towards the end of the eighteenth century. Productivity growth in agriculture tapered off, and some of the region's manufacturing activities died back as a result of competition from remote regions that started 'exporting' labour-intensive products of cottage industries to the core region. In the Kinai during this period, a contraction in occupational wage differentials took place with the real wage level for unskilled farm workers rising. This was the conclusion from my own observations based on nominal and real wage series for the Kinai area, more specifically for a village near Osaka and for Kyoto (Saito 1978). Section 2 of the present chapter will confirm this conclusion with a slightly different set of real wage series.

Regarding the trends in the 1820–94 period, there is no agreement among the specialists. The general price level changed course around 1820 as the shogunate debased the currencies and the nation entered an inflationary phase. Scholars working on contemporary sources such as the Mitsui House's wage books find that the real wage level for builders declined sharply towards the end of the last decade of the Tokugawa regime, that is, the late 1860s (Umemura 1961; Kusano 1996), while those using data for carpenters and other building craftsmen in Edo (later renamed Tokyo) compiled retrospectively by Meiji trade associations tend to emphasize that real wages did rise between 1830 and 1894 despite erratic movements due to short-term monetary shocks and external disturbances such as famines and earthquakes. In particular, the Sano series of carpenters' wages has often been referred to as evidence of a growing economy in the late Tokugawa period (Sano 1962; Hanley and Yamamura 1977; Hanley 1997). It was also chosen by Williamson (1998) for his database of Asian wages and relative factor prices, which in turn has been used by Robert Allen (Chapter 5, this volume) to bridge a gap between the earlier series and the modern, government statistics-based series. Undoubtedly there are data problems with all of these materials. Data from Tokugawa merchant houses tend to show nominal wage rates as fixed for long periods, suggesting that adjustments to price changes were made, at least in part, with allowances and other extra payments. On the other hand, a close look at the retrospective surveys reveals irregular fluctuations in the individual nominal wage-rate series, which casts doubt upon their consistency as time-series data. In Section 2, I present a revised series of builders' real wages in Edo/Tokyo plus another comparable series of soy-sauce makers' real wages in Choshi, a town in the same Kanto area. The two series, together with some additional sets of evidence for eastern Japan, suggest that the period should be divided into two, that is, the phase between 1820–70 in which the general level of real wages was declining while wage differentials seem to have widened, and the phase after 1870 when the trends were clearly reversed.

Then in Section 3, attention will be turned to the relationship between trends in real wages and output growth in the longer-run. I shall argue that traditional Japan did not exhibit the drastic divergence between wage change and output growth that was experienced in early modern western Europe. In the final section I shall briefly explore the factors that could account for the differences between the two pre-modern growth processes.

2. Real Wages and Wage Differentials

The Tokugawa economy was composed of two separate currency zones, that is, Osaka and the silver-using western provinces (where *monme* was the standard unit of currency) and Edo and the gold-using eastern half (where *ryo* was the standard unit).[2] It is convenient, therefore, to discuss the wage data using an east–west regional framework. Generally, agricultural productivity in the western provinces, particularly in the areas around Osaka and along the Inland Sea coasts, was high and commercialization advanced. This, together with the financial power generated by Osaka's wholesale merchants who dominated the Edo–Osaka trade and other transactions between the two currency zones, pushed Kinai's position well above the eastern regions, including the Kanto, an area surrounding the capital city of Edo. It is no coincidence, therefore, that we have more data for the Kinai region, especially in earlier periods. In the course of the latter half of the Tokugawa regime, however, the central government made explicit their preference that gold should become the standard of money in the national economy. This new policy was first implemented in the 1770s when silver coins began to be denominated in a gold unit. The following period witnessed an irreversible decline of the Osaka merchants' control over both credit and commodity markets and, hence, a decline in the economy in the silver zone (Shimbo and Saito 2004). The monetary crisis occasioned by the opening of the country and the influx of Mexican dollars that followed was a further blow to the silver-using Kinai economy. The value of silver dropped dramatically against that of gold during the 1860s, and the Meiji government that replaced the old shogunate set the new *yen* on parity with the *ryo*, the basic unit of gold under the Tokugawa shogunate (Ohkura and Shimbo 1978). In order to link the late Tokugawa to the Meiji series accurately, therefore, price and wage data in Edo/Tokyo and other locations in the east should be chosen. For earlier periods, on the other hand, we have no choice but to use the Kinai series.

2.1   The Kinai

Here we review four series of real wage indices: for agricultural day labourers and for carpenters, both of whom were employed by a wealthy farmer in Kami-Kawarabayashi, a village near Osaka, for day labourers in Kyoto, and for carpenters in Osaka. As far as the Kami-Kawarabayashi and Kyoto indices for the 1727–1830 period are concerned, they are only slightly different from those I presented in the 1978 article. The difference is in the deflator. The previous ones were deflated by cost-of-living indices estimated by Mataji Umemura (1961), in which rice was given a weight of 46%. This was probably too high a weight in the Tokugawa consumption basket. There is another series of consumer price indices calculated by Hiroshi Shimbo based on much the same data but with a different rice weight of 30%, which may be a little too low (Shimbo 1978: 31–5). Given the fact that the rice price fluctuated more wildly than the prices of other consumer goods, it is expected that the use of the latter weight would produce a slightly less volatile series of real wages. For this reason, I decided to use the Shimbo series to deflate nominal wages in the Kinai. As for the period after 1830, I extend the Kyoto series of day labourers to 1867 and introduce a new real wage series for skilled urban workers that begins in 1830. For these post-1830 series, too, the Shimbo estimates are used to deflate the nominal wage rates. The results are shown in Appendix Table 3.A1.

To take a long view, Figure 3.1 charts movements of real wage indices for both rural and urban unskilled workers in the Kinai. A close look at the overlapping period 1791–1830 reveals that, although the urban indices are more volatile than the rural ones, the direction of movement in the two series does not disagree. Indeed, actual wage data show that in the early eighteenth century the wage rate for day labourers in the city of Kyoto was substantially higher than that in Kami-Kawarabayashi, a village a little more than 40 km away from the city. However, during the 1750s and 1760s Kyoto's market rate caught up to the village's (Saito 1978: 92). Thereafter, the wage rate for the city's unskilled workers was equilibrated with that for agricultural work. In the base period of 1802–4, for example, the wage rate for spring tasks performed by Kami-Kawarabayashi farm workers was 1.0 *monme* while the corresponding spring rate in Kyoto's casual labour market was on average 0.92 *monme*. Turning to

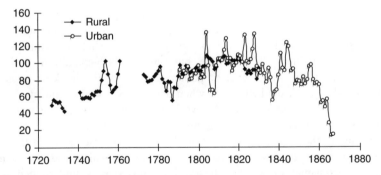

Figure 3.1 Labourers' real wages: the Kinai, 1727–1867 (1802–4 = 100)
Source: Appendix Table 3.A1.

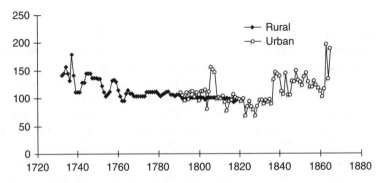

Figure 3.2 Wage differentials: the Kinai, 1732–1865 (1802–4 = 100)
Source: Appendix Table 3.A1.

the long-run trend, it is evident that, up to about 1820, the real wage level rose. After 1820 the trend was reversed. The next two decades saw extremely volatile movements caused by the shogunate's debasement of currencies between 1818 and 1829 and by the so-called Tempo famine of 1833–8. From 1820 to 1870 real wages were on the decline, and the decline was particularly steep after 1840. This fall reflected a higher rate of price increase in the Kinai than in eastern Japan, due chiefly to changes in the money market during the late Tokugawa period.

The corresponding graphs of occupational wage differentials are shown in Figure 3.2. The graph for earlier periods represents ratios of carpenters' to agricultural day labourers' wage rates in the village of Kami-Kawarabayashi, while the latter shows urban differentials, that is, the ratio of Osaka carpenters' wages to Kyoto day labourers'. In the base years of 1802–4, the village carpenters' wage rate was 2.6 times higher than the spring rate for agricultural labourers while the urban carpenters earned 4.7 times more than the unskilled did, suggesting that urban craftsmen enjoyed a higher skill premium than their rural counterparts. However, such urban–rural differentials changed over time, as Figure 3.2 (in which the ratios in 1802–4 are set at 100) demonstrates. Clearly there is an inverse relationship between Figures 3.1 and 3.2, which not only confirms what was said about the period up to 1830 in my 1978 article, but can also be generalized: during the Tokugawa period, the wage level of poorer sections of the working population caught up with that for the better paid when real wages rose. In contrast, the wage gap between the two sections of the workforce widened when the wage level declined in real terms. What remains uncertain, however, is to what extent the sharp decline in the real wage level of the Kinai was representative of the whole economy since the macroeconomic weight of silver, which was the standard medium of exchange in western Japan, was substantially undermined in the course of the late Tokugawa period. We should, therefore, turn to wage data in the gold-using east.

2.2   *Eastern Japan*

There is a set of Edo builders' real wage series covering the 1830–94 period. These series, probably the most widely quoted wage series for Japan, were estimated by Yoko Sano more than forty years ago. The data source she utilized was a table of daily money wage rates for six occupations in Edo/Tokyo's building trades, that is, carpenters, masons, *tatami* makers, joiners, thatchers, and sawyers. The dataset was compiled in the Meiji period by the Chamber of Commerce, who asked guild officers and old men in the trade to collect data retrospectively. Probably because of this method of data collection, there are sudden jumps and drops in the wage series of individual trades and the number of jumps exceeds that of drops, thus producing a possible upward bias. Sano, however, made no adjustments to the data. Some of the upward spikes in the carpenter series in the 1850s and the early 1870s were spotted by Williamson (1998: 39). He replaced them with figures derived by interpolation but failed to purge other aberrations, so that the series still shows a slightly upward trend from 1830 to the early 1860s. In fact, more serious than single-year spikes are cases where the overall level jumped upward or downward abruptly. A check on the six nominal wage series reveals that there was no synchronization of such abrupt changes from one occupation to another. In order to remove these aberrations, I therefore took the following steps: first, all the six rates of nominal wage change were calculated from year one to year two; second, the highest and the lowest ones were removed; third, the remaining four were averaged; finally, the average was linked to the similarly calculated rate of change from year two to year three, and so on, producing a series of average nominal wage rates for the building trade from 1830 to 1894. This nominal series with the base year of 1840–4 was deflated by the new consumer price indices for Edo/Tokyo derived from Saito (1998: 189–92). The results are reported in Appendix Table 3.A2.

Figure 3.3 shows this graph. Note that it no longer exhibits an upward trend during the period up to the early 1860s, which was a feature of both the Sano and Williamson series, and that the series trends upwards, though feebly, after the

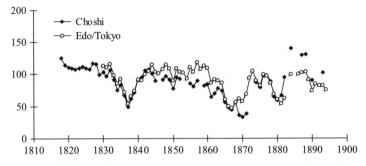

Figure 3.3   Two series of craftsmen's real wages: the Kanto, 1818–94 (1840–4 = 100)
Source: Appendix Table 3.A2.

late 1860s. While this is an improvement over previous indices, errors may still remain. Fortunately, the pattern in Figure 3.3 can be verified with another new series for Choshi, a town some 90 km east of Edo, covering the period from 1818 to 1893. The town was famous for its soy-sauce manufacturing and one Choshi manufacturer's wage books allow us to construct a composite series of annual wage payments weighted by the number of workers in various skill grades. The standard composition of the workforce was one master (*tōji*), two head workers (*kashira*), and eighteen 'lads' (*wakamono*). The weighted average of their wages, therefore, should be regarded as representing the wage level of those near the middle of the traditional work pyramid or, more generally, that of the semi-skilled. The nominal wages thus calculated are deflated by the same Edo/Tokyo consumer price series, set out in Appendix Table 3.A2 and shown, together with the graph for Edo/Tokyo builders' real wages, in Figure 3.3. The trends in the Choshi series are even more pronounced than in the Edo/Tokyo series: real wages declined almost continuously in the period before 1870, then turned strongly upwards.

2.3   The overall pattern

Table 3.1 summarizes the foregoing observations in a different manner. Each entry in the table indicates an average annual rate of change in the real wage level calculated from the 'slope' of a regression line fitted for the period specified. According to figures for the Kinai (printed in italics), agricultural labourers' real wages increased faster than did carpenters' during the first phase of 1727–1820, while the next phase, 1820–67, saw an opposite phenomenon. The first observation refers to rural and the second to urban trends. Yet since the Kinai had developed well-integrated regional labour markets by the late eighteenth century, both can be linked together so as to represent longer-run trends over the entire 1727–1867 period.

However, it is worth noting that the rate at which real wages declined was slower in the Kanto town of Choshi than in the Kinai, and that the contrast becomes more

Table 3.1 Rates of change in real wages for skilled and unskilled occupations, 1727–1894 (in % per annum)

	Rural		Urban	
	Skilled/semi-skilled	Unskilled	Skilled	Unskilled
1727–1820	*0.2*	*0.7*	—	—
1820–67	−1.1	—	−0.2[a]	− 2.1
(1840–67)	(−1.6)	—	(−2.5)	(− 5.0)
1867–94	4.5	—	1.1	—

Notes: The rates of change are 'slopes' of least-square regression lines calculated from the observations in the period specified. The slopes are all statistically significant except the one with [a]. The figures in italic type are for Kinai rates. The rural skilled and unskilled are for carpenters and agricultural day labourers in Kami-Kawarabayashi while the urban skilled is for carpenters in Osaka and the urban unskilled for day labourers in Kyoto. The figures in upright type are for Kanto rates. The rural skilled is for soy-sauce makers in Choshi and the urban skilled for building craftsmen in Edo/Tokyo.

Source: Appendix Tables 3.A1–3.A2.

pronounced if the inflationary period of 1840–67 is singled out. Since the pace of decline was also slower in Edo, this should be taken to imply that the Kinai rates overstated the extent to which real wages declined in the 1820–67 phase.

What is not obvious from Table 3.1 is whether real wages for the rural unskilled lagged behind the Choshi semi-skilled workers. Unfortunately, there are no records for villages around Choshi of quality comparable to the Kami-Kawarabayashi wage data. It is documented that in a village near Edo 'rice wages' for farm servants decreased, but in a rather inconclusive manner since the Choshi series reflected the weighted average wages of both skilled and less-skilled workers rather than skilled only (Saito 1998: 31).[3] However, the Choshi case draws our attention to an important aspect of the question. According to evidence unearthed by Suzuki (1990) and summarized in Saito (1998: 38), allowances for food and bonus payments were on the increase over the period concerned. The amount of those extra payments fluctuated, but the trend was for them to increase more than compensating for the losses caused by high prices. In the years before 1830 the standard yearly pay was on average 5.3 *ryo* and the total earnings with all extra payments included amounted to 12 *ryo* in 1840–4 prices, but by the 1845–71 period the average standard pay declined to 3.4 *ryo* in real terms, whereas the total amount the soy-sauce makers received increased to 15.6 *ryo*. This particular instance may not have been typical. However, if such extra allowances were not uncommon for other skilled workers at the time of high prices but inaccessible to the unskilled who were employed on a day-to-day basis, then it follows that the actual occupational differentials measured by total wage earnings were somewhat greater than the recorded wage rates implied. Thus, it is likely that in the developing Kanto economy too, wage differentials did widen as the level of real wages slumped until about 1870. After that, the trend was reversed and, as Table 3.1 shows, wage growth in the country town was much stronger than in the capital city of Tokyo.

Table 3.2 Rates of change in real wages for agricultural and non-agricultural occupations in eastern Japan, 1860–80 (in % per annum)

	Male		Female	
	Agricultural	Craft	Agricultural	Silk reeling
1860–70	−4.4	−3.5	− 3.9	−3.4
1870–80	4.9	3.7	5.0	3.8

Notes: Rates are deflated by the Edo/Tokyo cost-of-living index series (three-year averages). Calculation is based on the arithmetic means of reported wage rates. The number of provinces reporting rates varied from occupation to occupation as well as from benchmark year to year. Male: agricultural, 21, 21, and 28; craft, 14, 15, and 23. Female: agricultural, 21, 21, and 27; silk reeling, 12, 13, and 19.

Source: Calculated from Saito (1998: 43, 190).

It is possible to substantiate these points with more comprehensive evidence on wage changes in eastern Japan, though for the shorter period of 1860–80. Statistics compiled by the new Meiji government's agricultural bureau in 1881 show rural wage levels for the benchmark years of 1860, 1870, and 1880, by sex and occupation as well as by province. It seems that the way in which past information was collected was much the same as for the Edo/Tokyo builders' wages and, probably for that reason, the number of provinces reporting evidence for non-agricultural occupations tended to be fewer in earlier years, especially in 1860. However, the information on agricultural day labourers, both male and female, craftsmen, and female reelers, is considered reasonably usable. The silk industry was, thanks to strong overseas demands for Japanese raw silk, booming in that period and reeling was a job requiring women's dexterity and hand skills. Thus, reeling wages may be regarded as for skilled female labour just as craftsmen's are for male labour. By using the same Edo/Tokyo cost-of-living indices as for the Choshi series, therefore, annual rates of change in real wages are calculated for these four cases in rural eastern Japan.

The results are set out in Table 3.2. All the four columns confirm that the downward trend was reversed in the 1870s. More importantly, in the 1860s, when the real wage level was in sharp decline, the real wage of unskilled farm workers declined even more sharply, whereas in the next decade when strong wage growth occurred it was their wages that grew fastest. This relationship between trends in the level and in differentials holds for both male and female workers. This relationship was the usual pattern during the age of rural development in Japan.

3. Real Wages and Output Growth

Having established that in pre-industrial Japan wage growth was *not* associated with widening wage differentials, we now ask how changes in output were related to trends in real wages.

Only two attempts have so far been made to estimate overall growth of output in Tokugawa Japan. One is for the farm sector only, and was derived from Tokugawa data on taxed land. Under the Tokugawa system every piece of taxable land was assessed in terms of its productive capacity and expressed in *koku* of rice equivalent (called *kokudaka*). Thus the *kokudaka* was a measure of farm output covering all agricultural products, and the national aggregates exist for 1598, 1645, 1697, 1721, 1830, and 1872. But it is believed that from the 1697 compilation onwards the gap between the officially assessed and the actual production capacity tended to widen, due to productivity growth that undoubtedly took place from the mid-seventeenth century. Satoru Nakamura compared the 1872 *kokudaka* figure with total farm output from early Meiji government statistics. By assuming that the productive capacity of the land was enhanced by land-improvement investments made by *samurai* admin-istrations, he allocated the difference between these output measures over the entire period in question according to the period-by-period numbers of land-improvement projects recorded during the Tokugawa era (Nakamura 1968: 168–74).[4] The estim-ates thus derived for two benchmarks of 1700 and 1872 are set out in the second column of Table 3.3. In view of a notion widely held in the Tokugawa period that 1 *koku* of rice was enough to feed one person for one year, it is worth noting that the availability of farm products in the benchmark year of 1700 was above the level of 150 kg (1 *koku*)/person and increased over time. Judging from several case studies of agricultural land productivity in the Tokugawa period, it is not inconsistent with a similarly gradual rise in the level of rice yields (Yasuba 1987: 299; Yagi 1990).

On the basis of these Nakamura estimates, Angus Maddison (2001) recently put forward hypothetical GDP figures by topping up non-farm products which were simply assumed to have grown somewhat faster than farm output (column 3 of Table 3.3, expressed in 1990 international dollars: Maddison 2001: 254–8, 264). Given the fact that most industrial crops, cocoons, and even raw silk were covered by the early Meiji 'farm' statistics and hence included in Nakamura's calculation,

Table 3.3 Comparisons between wage and output growth, 1700–1870

	Wage growth (1700 = 100)	Growth of per capita output	
		Farm sector (kg)	GDP (1990 dollars)
1700	100	169	570
1870	118	201[a]	737
1700–1870 (% per annum)	0.10	0.10	0.15

[a] Figure is for year 1872.

Notes: Wage growth is calculated from Table 3.1, on the assumption that from 1700 to 1820 real wages increased at 0.6% annually, the same pace as for the weighted average of Kami-Kawarabayashi's carpenters and agricultural labourers (weights are taken from the Choshi case, that is, 0.14 for the skilled and 0.84 for the unskilled), then from 1820 onwards at the same pace as for the Choshi series of soy-sauce makers, that is, at −1.1% until 1870.

Sources: Table 3.1 and Maddison (2001: 255, 264).

it is debatable if growth in the non-farm sector was appreciably higher than that of the farm sector. It is true, however, that textiles expanded substantially. According to a recent survey of non-agricultural activities in Tokugawa times (Odaka 2001), for example, the output of cotton cloth in three rural districts exhibited a fourfold increase from the late eighteenth century to 1840, stagnated for three decades, then started growing again from the 1870s onwards. But in other sectors growth was far less spectacular. In the brewing of *saké*, *miso* paste, and soy sauce, undoubtedly the largest single manufacturing sector of the day, output growth seems to have been modest. It is of course extremely difficult to quantify how modest it was, but judging from recent studies in other research areas, such as works on consumption and the world of commodities (Hanley 1997; Koizumi 1999), the overall impression is that industrial output must have increased marginally faster than farm output. In that case, the degree of overestimation by Maddison was not significant.

It is not easy to give comparable evidence concerning wage growth because there is no single real wage series running through the entire period. Given the nature of the quantitative information set out in Table 3.1, my judgement is that the linked series of Kami-Kawarabayashi and Choshi real wages probably represent the general pattern of change better than other combinations. Since the Choshi series is a composite of skilled and less skilled workers' real wages, the Kami-Kawarabayashi series should also be a composite of carpenters' and agricultural day labourers'. Using the Choshi weights (0.86 for the skilled and 0.14 for the less skilled) implies that real wages in Kami-Kawarabayashi rose at the average annual rate of 0.6% from the first benchmark of 1700 to 1820, then declined at 1.1% in real terms until 1870—a decline like that experienced by Choshi's workers from 1818 to 1867. It is likely that rural wages in other regions rose at a slower rate than the Kami-Kawarabayashi wages in the eighteenth century and peaked much later in the early nineteenth century (Saito 1998: 31, 45–6). In this respect, the Kami-Kawarabayashi data probably overstates the degree of wage increase in the eighteenth century. However, the decline exhibited by the Choshi series after 1818 may also have overstated the degree of decline. The errors offset each other, so it is probably safe to say that this calculation is not off the mark when the start is compared with the end point. The results of this exercise are shown in column (1) of the table.

This table tells us that the growth rate of real wages during Japan's age of rural development was between 0.1% and 0.15% per annum. If the end point were set at 1890 or 1900, the growth rates would become slightly higher. Whatever the end point, growth of that magnitude was neither very impressive nor was it a miserable achievement. More important, however, is that real wages rose at exactly the same pace as farm output grew. This cannot be a coincidence. As we have already seen, rice yields exhibited a tendency to increase. There were regional differences too. The rise in the productivity of agriculture in the Kinai started early and appeared to taper off, or even to dip, sometime in the early nineteenth century, whereas that in the eastern provinces started late but continued until about 1850, which is a pattern almost identical to the one for real wages as suggested above. That said, however, the secular trend was unmistakably upward, and it is demonstrated that the long-term movement of rents in kind per unit of land was very much similar to that of rice yields. In other words, the proportion of rents to yields remained stable at the level of 60–70% during the latter half of the Tokugawa period (Tomobe 1996). The *samurai* government's tax rate on land was high but remained static in relation to the official *kokudaka* assessment (Smith 1968), which meant that after-tax rent earnings of landlords increased slightly. The wage–rent ratio, by implication, would have increased in the first phase and declined in the second, but it is probable that the ratio showed a marginally downward trend over the long-run.

The tempo of the wage increase was not so different from that of per capita GDP growth, either.[5] Clearly there was thus no *divergence* between wage growth and output growth. As mentioned earlier, we may not be able to equate this evidence with that on the income gap between the peasantry near the bottom and the population group near the middle of the income distribution. But given the unambiguous evidence in Table 3.3, it is probably safe to suggest that income inequality did not increase during the period concerned. This is a conclusion which is consistent with what we have seen in Section 2.

4. Discussion

Robert Allen (Chapter 5, this volume) suggests that Japan's history of real wages was characterized by 'both close integration of the [labour] markets and the absence of the dynamic urban economy' of the northwest European type, the latter of which echoes the point made by Thomas Smith in his classic essay on 'pre-modern economic growth' (Smith 1973). He contrasted Tokugawa Japan's *rural-centred* development with western Europe's *urban-centred* growth, noting that the lack of overseas trade and virtually static population in late Tokugawa Japan induced the decline of towns, especially of large towns, which meant that losses were imposed on the merchant class. With the Tokugawa shogunate's imposition of tight restrictions on foreign intercourse in the mid-1730s, the days of merchant-adventurers had gone. Instead, large-scale mercantile enterprises that concentrated on domestic, inter-regional trade emerged and merchant houses based in Osaka came to dominate the nation's economy. Organizationally they were big businesses with a multi-unit, complex managerial structure. Their profit rates were no longer very high but they traded extensively and efficiently. This type of merchant became a casualty of the growth of rural commerce and industry in the eighteenth and nineteenth centuries. The age of rural development saw the decline of large cities such as Edo and Osaka, on the one hand, and the rise of small country towns, on the other. After the opening up of trade with foreign countries in 1859 the large cities re-emerged as dynamic centres of growth. Yet, as the available evidence indicates with respect to wage differentials between agriculture and industry, those between large and small firms within industry and trends in income distribution (Minami 1998; Saito 1998), and contrary to the remark made by Williamson (2000: 34–5), it was not until after the 1910s that the growth in earnings of the urban rich and middle classes started to outstrip that of the labouring public. Pre-First World War Japan had not yet broken away from the traditional growth regime.

That said, however, another set of factors should also be commented on. Elsewhere, based on the observation that in 1840s Chōshū, a province in western Japan, the average wage rate for unskilled workers in salt farms was equal to the marginal labour productivity in farming derived from production function estimates (Nishikawa 1978), I suggested that it was agricultural productivity that determined the supply price of unskilled labour from the peasant farm household and, hence, that wage differentials contracted in the phase up to 1820 due to the rising productivity level in the farm sector (Saito 1978). As long as a peasant farm household was an independent decision-making unit of production, this is the mechanism which enabled the market wage rate for the non-farm unskilled labour force to keep pace with output growth. Given the evidence we now have for the second and third phases, and given the regional pattern of change in real wages and rice yields that we have established for the entire period, this mechanism must have been working throughout the period in question. In other words, rising productivity in farming acted as one factor that prevented the widening of the real wage–GDP gap in eighteenth- and nineteenth-century Japan.

This consideration has an important implication for the discussion of pre-modern growth. Agricultural progress of this type acted as a brake on the process of proletarianization, which is believed to have taken place across early modern European countries. The proposition that peasants' asking price of labour was determined by the marginal productivity of labour on their own farm implies that if the market wage rate was low in comparison with their farms' productive capacities, then labour would not be supplied. They would stay on the land. Hence, there would be no proletarianization. Here, by 'productivity' I do not mean just rice and other food crops. Any item the farm household produced should be included in our consideration. Indeed, as I demonstrated elsewhere by using early Meiji household returns in the sericultural province of Kai and district statistics in the cotton-growing prefecture of Osaka, the introduction by peasant cultivators of cash crops such as cotton and mulberry trees had an effective countervailing effect opposing the oft-assumed tendency for rural commercialization to create a landless labour force (Saito 1986). Throughout the Tokugawa–Meiji years, and even in the period between the two World Wars, contemporaries were concerned with tenancy problems but never mentioned the emergence of a rural landless class as a social problem. To quote Ronald Dore writing on the post-war land reform:

Tenancy increased while the number of hired labourers was never, before the last war, higher than some 300,000 (out of a total of 14 million agricultural workers) and most of these were either young men and girls, half labourers and half family servants, living in and supplementing the labour of the family on a bigger-than-average peasant holding, or else casual labourers with no permanent employer. (Dore 1959: 17)

As noted earlier, the emergence of a well-integrated labour market between the peasant farm household and urban sectors was one feature of the economic history of late Tokugawa Japan. The situation prior to the onset of industrialization, on the face of it, resembled what the Lewisian model of unlimited supply of labour postulated. In such a setting, the peasant sector would certainly appear as a pool of cheap labour if marginal productivity in farming were low and static. With a slow but steady rise in productivity in a period of static population, however, the farm sector could determine the direction and pattern of 'pre-modern economic growth'. This too was a variant of 'Smithian' growth. It was this pattern that characterized eighteenth- and nineteenth-century Japan and distinguished it from early modern western Europe.

Appendix

Table 3.A1 The Kinai series: real wage and wage differential indices, 1727–1867 (1802–4 = 100)

Year	Day labourers' real wages		Skilled–unskilled differentials	
	Agricultural (1)	Kyoto (2)	Rural (3)	Urban (4)
1727	49.9	—	—	—
1728	56.1	—	—	—
1729	55.0	—	—	—
1730	53.0	—	—	—
1731	53.7	—	—	—
1732	46.9	—	141.5	—
1733	42.2	—	145.0	—
1734	—	—	156.8	—
1735	—	—	145.0	—
1736	—	—	132.1	—
1737	—	—	179.0	—
1738	—	—	141.9	—
1739	—	—	111.4	—
1740	—	—	111.4	—
1741	65.5	72.1	111.4	—
1742	58.2	83.7	127.9	—
1743	58.3	77.3	127.9	—
1744	59.4	84.1	145.5	—
1745	59.0	80.7	145.5	—
1746	57.9	94.5	145.5	—
1747	63.1	77.5	137.1	—
1748	61.9	91.3	137.1	—
1749	65.5	91.6	137.1	—
1750	66.4	125.0	135.2	—
1751	66.8	134.0	135.2	—
1752	79.9	88.0	121.5	—

Table 3.A1 (*Continued*)

Year	Day labourers' real wages		Skilled–unskilled differentials	
	Agricultural (1)	Kyoto (2)	Rural (3)	Urban (4)
1753	90.5	99.7	111.4	—
1754	102.2	106.1	103.4	—
1755	86.8	84.9	107.9	—
1756	74.4	72.7	112.4	—
1757	65.5	77.7	131.6	—
1758	68.3	81.1	133.3	—
1759	71.4	84.7	129.9	—
1760	87.2	87.2	114.9	—
1761	101.9	92.4	104.2	—
1762	—	—	95.2	—
1763	—	—	95.2	—
1764	—	—	108.7	—
1765	—	—	114.9	—
1766	—	—	108.7	—
1767	—	—	108.7	—
1768	—	—	104.2	—
1769	—	—	104.2	—
1770	—	—	104.2	—
1771	—	—	104.2	—
1772	—	—	104.2	—
1773	85.8	—	104.2	—
1774	83.7	—	111.1	—
1775	78.2	—	111.1	—
1776	78.6	—	111.1	—
1777	79.9	—	111.1	—
1778	84.6	—	111.1	—
1779	87.0	—	112.4	—
1780	90.5	—	107.5	—
1781	95.8	—	104.2	—
1782	81.2	—	106.4	—
1783	76.7	—	108.7	—
1784	66.8	—	111.1	—
1785	77.9	—	112.4	—
1786	77.5	—	106.4	—
1787	55.3	—	106.4	—
1788	71.0	—	103.1	—
1789	70.2	—	106.4	—
1790	84.2	—	106.4	—
1791	97.6	91.9	103.1	109.5
1792	87.1	82.5	99.0	104.5
1793	86.5	90.2	99.0	94.9

Table 3.A1   (*Continued*)

Year	Day labourers' real wages		Skilled–unskilled differentials	
	Agricultural (1)	Kyoto (2)	Rural (3)	Urban (4)
1794	96.8	87.5	99.0	109.5
1795	94.3	95.4	99.0	97.8
1796	88.1	80.2	101.0	110.9
1797	90.0	81.0	101.0	112.2
1798	91.9	90.8	101.0	102.2
1799	93.8	86.5	101.0	109.5
1800	91.0	96.9	101.0	94.9
1801	90.9	81.8	101.0	112.2
1802	95.7	86.2	101.0	112.2
1803	96.9	82.6	98.0	114.9
1804	108.6	135.9	101.0	80.7
1805	106.2	96.8	101.0	110.9
1806	104.7	67.8	101.0	156.0
1807	101.1	67.7	101.0	150.8
1808	92.2	63.8	101.0	146.0
1809	94.6	96.6	101.0	98.9
1810	104.4	104.3	101.0	101.1
1811	102.1	104.2	101.0	98.9
1812	106.4	102.9	100.0	103.4
1813	107.6	114.6	99.0	92.9
1814	98.5	128.5	100.0	76.7
1815	100.1	105.6	99.0	93.9
1816	104.9	105.2	97.1	96.8
1817	103.3	90.4	92.6	105.7
1818	102.0	96.1	95.2	101.1
1819	102.8	99.9	—	98.9
1820	109.2	109.4	—	97.8
1821	102.4	108.0	—	93.9
1822	100.4	100.5	—	98.9
1823	92.8	132.6	—	68.6
1824	87.0	101.0	—	84.4
1825	90.6	99.4	—	93.9
1826	87.0	104.0	—	83.6
1827	91.7	115.6	—	79.3
1828	91.3	134.0	—	68.2
1829	80.4	95.4	—	85.2
1830	93.2	90.9	—	96.8
1831	—	87.3	—	95.9
1832	—	97.7	—	89.3
1833	—	87.0	—	95.9
1834	—	77.0	—	92.9

Table 3.A1 *(Continued)*

Year	Day labourers' real wages		Skilled–unskilled differentials	
	Agricultural (1)	Kyoto (2)	Rural (3)	Urban (4)
1835	—	93.1	—	97.8
1836	—	81.8	—	89.3
1837	—	55.1	—	133.0
1838	—	65.3	—	146.8
1839	—	67.3	—	142.3
1840	—	85.3	—	139.4
1841	—	111.3	—	112.2
1842	—	93.0	—	106.0
1843	—	91.1	—	143.8
1844	—	124.0	—	105.3
1845	—	119.4	—	105.3
1846	—	90.4	—	130.2
1847	—	92.6	—	129.0
1848	—	74.7	—	148.4
1849	—	78.7	—	131.5
1850	—	78.0	—	127.8
1851	—	74.3	—	122.1
1852	—	83.1	—	138.0
1853	—	74.6	—	145.2
1854	—	79.9	—	129.0
1855	—	95.4	—	120.0
1856	—	97.3	—	119.0
1857	—	79.3	—	130.2
1858	—	74.5	—	123.3
1859	—	76.6	—	116.9
1860	—	73.7	—	112.2
1861	—	52.6	—	102.2
1862	—	55.1	—	116.0
1863	—	47.7	—	196.5
1864	—	56.6	—	134.5
1865	—	27.9	—	188.5
1866	—	13.7	—	—
1867	—	14.9	—	—

Notes: Column (1) is for agricultural day labourers in Kami-Kawarabayashi and column (2) for day labourers in Kyoto. The former is a composite of wage rates for various farm tasks, whereas the latter is the spring rate. The deflator is for Kyoto (1802–4 = 100). Column (3) is the ratio of carpenters' to day labourers' wage rate in Kami-Kawarabayashi while column (4) is the ratio of carpenters' wage rate in Osaka to labourers' wage rate in Kyoto (the average of 1802–4 is set at 100). In the base period of 1802–4, the mean money wage rate for spring tasks that Kami-Kawarabayashi agricultural day labourers received was 1.0 *monme* and that for Kyoto day labourers 0.92 *monme* per person-day. The mean money wage rate for Kami-Kawarabayashi carpenters in the same period was 2.6 *monme* and that for Osaka carpenters 4.3 *monme* per person-day.

Source: Saito (1998: 181–8).

Table 3.A2 The Kanto series: nominal wage indices and real wage indices for Choshi and Edo/Tokyo, 1818–94 (1840–4 = 100)

Year	Nominal wage indices		Real wage indices	
	Choshi (1)	Edo/Tokyo (2)	Choshi (1)	Edo/Tokyo (2)
1818	91.2	—	125.1	—
1819	84.7	—	113.5	—
1820	83.8	—	110.4	—
1821	84.9	—	109.5	—
1822	83.1	—	107.2	—
1823	81.9	—	109.6	—
1824	82.5	—	112.1	—
1825	84.2	—	109.9	—
1826	86.8	—	107.2	—
1827	87.4	—	117.0	—
1828	90.6	—	115.3	—
1829	86.4	—	99.1	—
1830	88.3	96.2	103.5	112.8
1831	84.4	96.2	96.8	110.3
1832	87.8	96.2	106.0	116.2
1833	89.5	96.2	91.4	98.3
1834	84.0	96.2	74.7	85.5
1835	85.5	96.2	82.8	93.1
1836	88.7	96.2	66.2	71.8
1837	86.8	96.2	48.7	54.0
1838	90.6	96.2	61.3	65.1
1839	93.6	96.2	72.0	74.0
1840	96.6	96.2	91.8	91.4
1841	101.0	96.2	95.2	90.7
1842	101.4	96.2	105.7	100.3
1843	99.8	96.2	107.8	103.9
1844	101.2	115.4	100.8	114.9
1845	100.4	115.4	90.0	103.5
1846	—	115.4	—	101.2
1847	98.5	115.4	91.8	107.5
1848	98.7	117.7	96.4	114.9
1849	100.0	117.7	91.7	108.0
1850	101.5	117.7	76.8	89.0
1851	102.3	117.7	94.5	108.7
1852	104.9	117.7	92.3	103.6
1853	—	117.7	—	102.5
1854	—	120.0	—	93.1
1855	101.4	130.9	85.7	110.7
1856	102.9	130.9	80.7	102.7
1857	99.7	130.9	89.6	117.6
1858	—	130.9	—	107.6
1859	95.3	130.9	82.1	112.7

Table 3.A2 (*Continued*)

Year	Nominal wage indices		Real wage indices	
	Choshi (1)	Edo/Tokyo (2)	Choshi (1)	Edo/Tokyo (2)
1860	100.2	130.9	84.1	109.9
1861	99.3	133.5	63.9	85.9
1862	101.4	133.5	69.4	91.3
1863	115.9	133.5	77.4	89.2
1864	119.3	138.8	73.9	85.9
1865	128.9	138.8	55.8	60.1
1866	151.0	158.2	46.9	49.2
1867	154.2	158.2	44.6	45.8
1868	156.9	158.2	55.7	56.1
1869	160.2	276.9	35.5	61.3
1870	169.1	299.1	32.3	57.2
1871	165.3	299.1	37.7	68.2
1872	—	299.1	—	93.3
1873	—	338.0	—	103.9
1874	329.7	338.0	87.2	89.4
1875	327.7	344.7	78.6	82.6
1876	341.8	344.7	97.9	98.7
1877	351.6	348.2	97.6	96.6
1878	354.7	348.2	87.9	86.3
1879	347.3	369.0	64.5	68.6
1880	384.1	387.5	59.4	60.0
1881	484.7	391.4	66.8	53.9
1882	599.5	391.4	95.0	62.0
1883	—	—	—	—
1884	544.2	383.5	140.5	99.0
1885	—	—	—	—
1886	—	383.5	—	99.8
1887	484.9	383.5	129.0	102.0
1888	483.0	383.5	130.4	103.6
1889	—	383.5	—	91.8
1890	473.4	383.5	90.3	73.2
1891	—	383.5	—	84.3
1892	—	383.5	—	81.7
1893	477.9	383.5	102.4	82.2
1894	—	383.5	—	74.5

Notes: Column (1) is for soy-sauce makers' yearly pay in Choshi while column (2) is for building craftsmen's wage rates in Edo/Tokyo. The deflator for both columns is the Edo/Tokyo cost-of-living index series (1840–4 = 100). In the base period of 1840–4, the mean money wage earnings in Choshi's soy-sauce making are 12.0 *ryo* for the master, 6.4 *ryo* for head workers, and 4.8 *ryo* for lads per person-year, the weighted average being 5.32 *ryo*. In Edo, the mean money wage rate in the same period was 0.084 *ryo* for masons, 0.1174 *ryo* for *tatami* makers, 0.062 *ryo* for thatchers, and 0.0948 *ryo* for sawyers. The average, both weighted and unweighted, happens to be 0.09 *ryo* per person-day.

Source: Saito (1998: 189–92).

Notes

1. Japan was under the Tokugawa shogunate's 'seclusion' policy from the 1630s to 1859. For one thing, the term 'seclusion' may be a misnomer because, as a trade policy, the point of the regulations was to bring overseas trade under strict control by confining foreign merchants to one port, Nagasaki. There were two other trade channels as well, that is, the Tsushima and Satsuma routes. On the other hand, it is true that the volume of overseas trade did decline during the long 'seclusion' period.
2. More precisely, three different currencies were issued by the shogunate: gold coin, silver by weight, and copper coin or penny cash which was circulated in both gold and silver zones. Silver was never circulated as coin, only by weight. In Osaka, therefore, as transactions grew merchant-issued bills, expressed in silver as a unit of account, came to be used widely.
3. Other rice wage series are summarized in Yasuba (1987: 299), based on which he suggested that the sharp reduction of real wages in the Kinai was a rather exceptional result of the 'socio-economic disruption' in the late Tokugawa period.
4. The *koku* is a measure of volume or capacity. As a rice equivalent, however, the *kokudaka* can be converted into a weight measure (with 1 *koku* being 150 kg of rice). Here I adopted Angus Maddison's conversion results (2001: 255).
5. One could make a fine tuning to the calculation of wage growth by distinguishing the last three years of upturn from the previous phase of decline. In that case, of course, the re-calculated rate of increase in real wages would get closer to that for GDP growth in Table 3.3.

References

Dore, R. P. (1959) *Land Reform in Japan*. London: Oxford University Press.

Hanley, S. B. (1997) *Everyday Things in Premodern Japan: The Hidden Legacy of Material Culture*. Berkeley, CA: University of California Press.

—— and Yamamura, K. (1977) *Economic and Demographic Change in Preindustrial Japan, 1600–1868*. Princeton, NJ: Princeton University Press.

Koizumi Kazuko (1999) *Dōgu to kurashi no Edo jidai*. Tokyo: Yoshikawa Kobunkan.

Kusano Masahiro (1996) *Kinsei no shijō keizai to chiikisa*. Kyoto: Kyoto Daigaku Gakujutsu Shuppankai.

Maddison, A. (2001) *The World Economy: A Millennium Perspective*. Paris: OECD Development Centre.

Minami, R. (1998) 'Economic Development and Income Distribution in Japan: An Assessment of the Kuznets Hypothesis'. *Cambridge Journal of Economics*, 22: 39–58.

Nakamura Satoru (1968) *Meiji ishin no kiso kōzō*. Tokyo: Miraisha.

Nishikawa, S. (1978) 'Productivity, Subsistence, and By-employment in the Mid-nineteenth Century Chōshū'. *Explorations in Economic History*, 15: 69–83.

—— Odaka Konosuke, and Saito Osamu (eds.) (1996) *Nihon keizai no 200-nen*. Tokyo: Nihon Hyoronsha.

Odaka, K. (2001) 'Non-agrarian Production and Capital Formation in Pre-modern Japan'. *Journal of International Economic Studies*, 15: 119–30.

Ohkura, T. and Shimbo, H. (1978) 'The Tokugawa Monetary Policy in the Eighteenth and Nineteenth Centuries'. *Explorations in Economic History*, 15: 101–24.

Saito, O. (1978) 'The Labor Market in Tokugawa Japan: Wage Differentials and the Real Wage Level, 1727–1830'. *Explorations in Economic History*, 15: 84–100.

—— (1983) 'Population and the Peasant Family Economy in Proto-industrial Japan'. *Journal of Family History*, 8: 30–45.

—— (1986) 'The Rural Economy: Commercial Agriculture, By-employment, and Wage Work', in M. B. Jansen and G. Rozman (eds.), *Japan in Transition: From Tokugawa to Meiji*. Princeton, NJ: Princeton University Press, pp. 400–20.

—— (1998) *Chingin to rōdō to seikatsu suijun: Nihon keizaishi ni okeru 18–20 seiki*. Tokyo: Iwanami Shoten.

Sano Yoko (1962) 'Kenchiku rōdōsha no jisshitsu chingin: 1830–1894 nen'. *Mita gakkai zasshi*, 55: 1009–36.

Shimbo Hiroshi (1978) *Kinsei no bukka to keizai hatten*. Tokyo: Toyo Keizai Shimposha.

—— and Saito, O. (2004) 'The Economy on the Eve of Industrialization', in A. Hayami, O. Saito, and R. P. Toby (eds.), *Emergence of Economic Society in Japan 1600–1859*. Oxford: Oxford University Press, pp. 337–68.

Smith, T. C. (1968) 'The Land Tax in the Tokugawa Period', in J. Hall and M. B. Jansen (eds.), *Studies in the Institutional History of Early Modern Japan*. Princeton, NJ: Princeton University Press, pp. 263–83; reprinted in Smith (1988) 50–70.

—— (1973) 'Pre-modern Economic Growth: Japan and the West'. *Past and Present*, 60: 127–60; reprinted in Smith (1988) 15–49.

—— (1988) *Native Sources of Japanese Industrialization, 1750–1920*. Berkeley, CA: University of California Press.

Suzuki Yuriko (1990) 'Shōyu seizōgyō ni okeru koyō rōdō', in Hayashi Reiko (ed.), *Shōyu seizōgyō-shi no kenkyū*. Tokyo: Yoshikawa Kobunkan, pp. 131–96.

Tomobe Ken'ichi (1996) 'Tochi seido', in Nishikawa Shunsaku, Odaka Konosuke, and Saito Osamu (eds.), *Nihon keizai no 200-nen*. Tokyo: Nihon Hyoronsha, pp. 135–51.

Umemura Mataji (1961) 'Kenchiku rōdōsha no jisshitsu chingin 1726–1958 nen'. *Keizai kenkyū*, 12: 172–6.

Williamson, J. G. (1998) 'Real Wages and Relative Factor Prices in the Third World 1820–1940: Asia', Harvard Institute of Economic Research Discussion Paper No. 1844.

—— (2000) 'Globalization, Factor Prices and Living Standards in Asia Before 1940', in A. J. H. Latham and H. Kawakatsu (eds.), *Asia Pacific Dynamism 1550–2000*. London: Routledge, pp. 13–45.

Yagi Hironori (1990) 'Nōgyō', in Nishikawa Shunsaku and Abe Takeshi (eds.), *Sangyōka no jidai, jō*. Tokyo: Iwanami Shoten, pp. 113–62.

Yasuba, Y. (1987) 'The Tokugawa Legacy: A Survey'. *Economic Studies Quarterly*, 38: 290–308.

4 Agriculture, Labour, and the Standard of Living in Eighteenth-Century India

PRASANNAN PARTHASARATHI

1. Introduction

It has been widely believed that standards of living in Europe have been superior to those of India at least since 1500. This opinion may be found in the writings of European travellers who, after Vasco da Gama's discovery of the sea route to India, visited the subcontinent in growing numbers and returned home with accounts of the endemic poverty and misery to be found in the Indian subcontinent.[1] From the late seventeenth century there was increased interest in Indian poverty as Europeans cited it to explain the low prices of Indian products, in particular the cotton textiles that quickly developed a large-scale following in the markets of western, central, and eastern Europe. Scores of writers attributed the cheapness of these cloths to the oppression of labour that was characteristic of despotic rulers in India.

In recent years, however, these arguments for the greater prosperity of Europeans have begun to be questioned. Kenneth Pomeranz, on the basis of evidence drawn largely from China, but also from South and Southeast Asia, has argued that life expectancies and consumption of cloth—two measures of the standard of living— were comparable across the Eurasian land mass. I have shown that wages calculated in terms of grain were roughly equal in Britain and South India in the mid-eighteenth century and that Indian labourers were not the victims of unrelenting exploitation and oppression. These calculations are summarized in Table 4.1 (Parthasarathi 1998; Pomeranz 2000).

South India, the region my earlier wage figures were drawn from, had long been a major centre of cotton textile manufacturing. By the eighteenth century, however, Bengal had become the largest textile producing and exporting centre in the Indian subcontinent. Table 4.1 also contains data on the wages of weavers and spinners in Bengal. The returns for both groups fall within the range for those occupations in both Britain and South India. Therefore, the evidence for Bengal confirms my earlier arguments for comparability of real wages in South Asia and Britain in the mid-eighteenth century.

Household budget data also suggest similar economic conditions for artisans in Britain and Bengal. In 1807 a Bengal artisan in 'comfortable circumstances' devoted 49% of his expenditures on food to rice while the figure for a 'common'

Table 4.1   Wages in the mid-eighteenth century

	Britain	South India	Bengal
Weaving (lbs/week)	40–140	65–160	55–135
Spinning (/lb)	4d.–2s.	7d.–2s.	5d.–2s.
Agricultural labour (lbs/week)	30–35	26–30	—

Notes: The wages for weaving and agricultural labour are given in terms of pounds of grain per week, wheat for Britain and rice for South India and Bengal. For spinning they are given in terms of earnings per pound of yarn spun but with correction for differences in grain prices. For further details see Parthasarathi (1998).

Sources: For Britain and South India see Parthasarathi (1998); for Bengal weavers' incomes were taken from Sinha (1961: Vol. 1, 176), Mitra (1978: 113), and Hossain (1988: 62) and spinners' incomes from Mitra (1978: 128–9). Rice prices for Bengal are from Mitra (1978: 123), Marshall (1987: 28), and Datta (2000: 255).

artisan was 85% (Datta 2000: 193). In late eighteenth-century Britain, according to a recent study, 'bread was overwhelmingly the chief food, generally accounting for 40–80% or even more of the weekly income, according to family circumstances and the prevailing price of the loaf' (Petersen 1995: 4). Note that the British figures of 40–80% represent bread as a proportion of *total* income, while the Bengal figures of 49% and 85% are for expenditures on food only.

The comfortable economic position of weavers in India is suggested in other ways as well. For instance, there is substantial data that skilled weavers, but by no means the most highly skilled, in various parts of South India owned cattle. These animals were an important source of wealth, as the offspring could be sold in the thriving market for cattle in South India. They also represented a form of insurance as they could be sold in times of economic distress. In addition, the cows would have provided dairy products for the weaver family, which would have represented an important source of protein and fat. A Bengali man who accompanied Francis Buchanan on his tour of South India in 1812 remarked that, although most goods were far more expensive than in Bengal, the price of yoghurt was far lower. This is a sign of the abundant cattle population of southern India. Other suggestions for adequate economic resources come from the fact that weavers in South India paid taxes on their looms to political authorities. In Britain, by contrast, weavers, even in urban areas, were deemed too poor to pay taxes.

2. The Labour Market and the Standard of Living

The high standard of living of weavers as well as other labouring groups in South India (and more generally in the Indian subcontinent) was rooted in the traditions and practices of the labour market. These traditions gave labouring groups enormous bargaining power in their relations with merchants, 'employers', and even political authorities. Perhaps the most critical was the freedom that weavers and other producers possessed to pick up and move, which gave them enormous flexibility and power.

The mobility of producers has been best documented for South India. Perhaps most famously, several writers have remarked upon the peripatetic habits of South Indian weavers, who were known to leave whole villages deserted in a night, to the dismay of merchants and political officials. Weavers were also well aware of the power their 'freedom to migrate' gave to them in dealings with merchants. As an East India Company official put it in the late eighteenth century: '[The weavers] know how necessary they are to the Company and think if they become turbulent they need fear no severe treatment for their insolence lest they should desert, which they are ever ready to threaten if not dealt with according to their pleasures.'[2]

The ability to move was no less true for South Indian producers in agriculture. The mobility of these labourers is perhaps most apparent in the dry zones where in several areas of South India a period was set aside every year during which peasants could migrate. In the area around Bellary this period lasted from early April to mid-July and was known as the 'kalawedi' season. At this time, producers moved to new villages, and sometimes even to new revenue divisions (taluks), and took up land for cultivation. The same practice was found in the Baramahal where according to a description from Alexander Read, an early British revenue official, producers 'are commonly hired for the year or the season only, [and] are at liberty to move where they please, in quest of new services, during the "Calliwaddies", or "spring months."'[3] Similar movement was reported in North Arcot and Chingleput. In the latter, Lionel Place estimated that around 13% of the population shifted villages annually.[4]

Mobility of the producer may be less apparent in the areas of rice cultivation, where the group involved in much of the activity of cultivation, *adimai* in Tamil, has typically been portrayed as tied to the land or to an agricultural superior, either as slave, serf, bonded labourer, or in other unfree relationships. Gyan Prakash (1990) has shown in the context of northern India that these are profound misreadings of this relationship (see also Washbrook 1993). In the south, even late eighteenth- and early nineteenth-century observers who operated within the discourse of slavery noted some features of the relation which could not be contained within that discourse:

A pariah, the slave of his landlord, may with his permission, enlist in the army, or in the service of a European gentleman, as a servant (and many have done so without their permission), exercising all the rights of free men. Indeed, even if he remains with his master as a slave, I apprehend that as regards all acts between him and strangers, he possesses the same rights as free men.[5]

The other major category of cultivators in the wet areas was 'porragoodies' or 'pycarries'. These were a mobile class of cultivators who entered into annual sharecropping contracts with holders of superior rights. According to F. W. Ellis, an early nineteenth-century revenue official, these contracts could be renewed, but if the two parties reached no agreement, the pycarries were free to enter into others in the same or different village. Pycarries were especially critical for the restoration of rice cultivation after political turmoil or devastating droughts, when labour was in very short supply. In the late eighteenth century, an influx of pycarries allowed Tanjore to recover quickly from the loss of labourers due to out-migration during the Mysore Wars.[6]

3. The State, Agriculture, and the Labour Market

If standards of living in India and Britain were at least comparable in the eighteenth century, why were Indian cotton textiles so cheap? I have argued elsewhere that although wages calculated in terms of grain were more or less equal, in India money wages were far lower because the price of grain, the single most important item in the consumption of labouring households, was far lower in India. In South India, for instance, the price of grain was half that of Britain. Bengal was long reputed to have cheap provisions, and when that province is included in the comparison, the results are even more striking. Grain prices in Bengal were a quarter of those in Britain, and about half those in South India! Given the low prices for food, it is no surprise that manufactures could be obtained for far less in the Indian subcontinent. Adam Smith recognized this fundamental difference between Asia and Europe and he observed that:

[I]n rice countries, which generally yield two, sometimes three crops in the year, each of them more plentiful than any common crop of corn, the abundance of food must be much greater than in any corn country of equal extent...The same super-abundance of food...enables them to give a greater quantity of it for all those singular and rare productions which nature furnishes but in very small quantities; such as the precious metals and the precious stones. (Smith 1976: 228)

In this passage, Smith implicitly attributed the superior productivity of Indian agriculture to the climatic and geographic conditions that permitted double- and triple-cropping. While not wanting to ignore the importance of these conditions, the limitations of such an explanation become evident if one examines agricultural productivity data for the nineteenth century. By the end of the century, as a consequence of major technical advances wheat output per acre in England had equalled or surpassed that of rice in South India, where paddy productivity had stagnated or even declined. This nineteenth-century divergence suggests that eighteenth-century differences were due not simply to geography. Rather technological, institutional, and political factors were also critical.

Of course, the institutional and political context has not been lost in writings on Asian agriculture, but constructions such as Oriental despotism and agrarian bureaucratic empires continue to loom over these issues. David Landes, for instance, has recently revived the despotism of Asia, and made it central to rice cultivation in China:

the management of water called for supralocal power and promoted imperial authority. This link between water and power was early noted by European observers, going back to

Montesquieu and reappearing in Hegel, later copied by Marx. The most detailed analysis, though, is the more recent one of Karl Wittfogel, who gave to water-based rule the name of Oriental despotism, with all the dominance and servitude that implies. (Landes 1998: 27)

Writings on agriculture in medieval South India have provided important correctives to the Wittfogel thesis and have pointed to the local institutions, most importantly the temple and councils of local notables (the *nadu* and *mahanadu*) that constructed and maintained irrigation works and oversaw the sharing of water (Stein 1984*a*, *b*; Ludden 1985; see also Bray 1986: 63–8). Evidence from the late eighteenth century continues to highlight the importance of local institutions for agricultural development in South India. In the 1790s, Lionel Place noted that a fraction of the harvest in each village was set aside as 'tank morrah' for the maintenance and improvement of irrigation works.[7]

Nevertheless, the following account of repairs conducted on a major dam on the Cauvery River shows that regional political authorities, in this case the king of Tanjore, also were pivotal for the construction and maintenance of irrigation systems:

When I arrived at the annacathy [annicut or dam] I found the Rajah's people employed in repairing the damage from the bank and masonry sustained last year. There were at work at this time about 700 coolies and 200 bricklayers or masons, including their assistants and chunam beaters at the works in and connected with the annacathy are entrusted to the direction of a Bramin, the Rajah's Head Hircar.[8]

Admittedly the annicut was the largest and most important structure in the vast South Indian system of water control, but state activities shaped the agrarian landscape in countless, less dramatic ways as well. This is suggested by the location of agrarian activity in eighteenth-century South India, which cannot be explained solely by local initiative.

The distribution of zones of highly productive agriculture indicates a close correspondence between political authority and agricultural improvement and investment. This was in part a result of medieval activity in agriculture at which time political authority legitimated itself through presentations of land and cash to temples. These institutions then funnelled these gifts into agriculture, especially for rice cultivation, as this was a sure way to receive a high and reliable rate of return on these funds. Less is known on the institutional and political arrangements that promoted agricultural development in post-medieval centuries (after 1600) when temples declined in importance, but this link between political power and agricultural improvement continued to exist, albeit on a different institutional basis. The distribution and location of cotton cultivation in late eighteenth-century South India clearly illustrates the continued importance of political authority in the shaping of the agrarian landscape.

Cropping patterns in South India have most commonly been attributed to geographical and ecological factors such as the location of soils and the availability of water (Baker 1984: ch. 1; Ludden 1985: 51–67). These factors, however, are not sufficient to explain the pattern of cotton cultivation. Cotton in South India was cultivated under two very different regimes, intensive and extensive, and each form of cultivation was found on very different soils. Intensive cultivation was carried out on heavy, black soils, while extensive was found on thin, red soils. In many parts of South India red and black soils were often found in close proximity, and there was abundant red and black soil throughout South India. Before the nineteenth century, however, intensive cultivation was largely concentrated in two areas, Madurai and the area of the southern Deccan around Bellary. The limited distribution of intensive cultivation becomes even more puzzling given that it was far more profitable than extensive cultivation as it yielded at least twice as much cotton per acre.

This pattern becomes explicable when political power is incorporated into the picture. Extensive cultivation required very little capital. Red soils were easily ploughed and the peasant-cultivator put up his supply of seed. Although intensive cultivation was far more lucrative, it depended upon the availability of abundant supplies of capital. Funds were needed to clear and plough the heavy black soils and to hire the labourers who carried out essential tasks such as ploughing and picking. According to Thomas Munro, who served as the revenue officer in Bellary in the early nineteenth century, political and revenue authorities provided a significant fraction of the capital necessary for cultivation on black soils. This took the form of taccavi, or advances for the financing of production:

These lands, after having lain waste eight or ten years, cannot be broken up without a large plough drawn by six yokes of bullocks, and they must afterwards be cleared of the roots of the long grass with which they are overrun, by a machine drawn by seven or eight yokes. The expense of setting a single plough in motion is about 150 pagodas, so that it can only be done by substantial ryots, or by the union of two or three of those whose means are less. A considerable portion of the bullocks employed are from Nellore, and it is absolutely necessary that the yoke next to the plough be of that breed. It is for the purchase of that yoke, which usually costs from 20 to 24 pagods that the ryots require tuckavi.[9]

The areas where intensive cultivation was concentrated, Madurai and Bellary, formed the cores of major political formations. Being politically important, they were the focus of state activities to improve agriculture, with the goal of increasing the revenue potential of territories. Outside these two areas, mainly in Coimbatore and Tirunelveli, although black soils were plentiful, they were not brought under the plough until the nineteenth century and the new cotton economy that emerged, which linked South Indian peasants with China, Bombay, and eventually local cotton mills. Coimbatore and Tirunelveli lay outside major South Indian political centres. Coimbatore was a frontier region from its initial settlement in the medieval period. Its status was to change only from the late nineteenth century when it became a dynamic and booming agricultural, and later industrial, centre (Arokiaswami 1956; Baker 1984: 93–5). The black soils in Tirunelveli were similarly a frontier zone and until the nineteenth century investment in the Tirunelveli region was directed towards paddy cultivation in the valley of the Tambraparni River (Ludden 1985: ch. 1–3).

The connection between political authority and high agriculture was not unique to South India, but was found also in other areas of the subcontinent. Perhaps most strikingly, in the case of Mughal North India even by 1600 much of the land in the heartland of the empire, around Agra for instance, had been brought under cultivation. As one moved to the peripheries of Mughal power, far less of the arable land had been cleared and brought under the plough (Moosvi 1987: 39–73). Similar connections between political authority and agricultural development have been identified for North India, western India, and Bengal in the eighteenth century (Gordon 1978; Bayly 1983: ch. 2; Eaton 1993: ch. 8).

Why did political authorities in South Asia engage in agricultural improvement? First, it was essential for the successful pursuit of political power and statecraft, and even came to be seen as an obligation of political power. The granting of taccavi and other forms of assistance for agricultural production came to be seen as a necessary part of the right to collect revenue. Cultivators also demanded such participation by their political superiors as it forced these authorities to bear some of the risks associated with the agricultural enterprise. Second, the structure of the labour market propelled investment in agriculture. Agricultural improvement was the means by which village leaders, little kings, and even maharajahs competed for labour in the conditions of extreme labour shortage that prevailed in the eighteenth century.

Compelling evidence for the importance of agriculture for kingship comes from texts produced in South India between the sixteenth and eighteenth centuries. The *Amuktamalyada,* a Telugu work attributed to the Vijayanagar Emperor Krishnadeva Raya (reign from 1509 to 1529), imparted the following advice to a sovereign: 'The extent of a state is the root cause of its prosperity. When a state is small in extent then both virtue (*dharma*) and prosperity (*artha*) will increase only when tanks and irrigation canals are constructed'. Similar sentiments on the importance of agriculture were contained in the *Rayavacakamu,* a Telugu text on statecraft that is dated to the late sixteenth or early seventeenth century. It instructed the king to 'beget the sevenfold progeny, which are a son, a treasure, a temple, a garden, an irrigation tank, a literary work, and a village established for Brahmins'. Elsewhere the *Rayavackamu* states:

A broken family, damaged tanks and wells,
a fallen kingdom, one who comes seeking refuge,
cows and Brahman, and temples of the gods—
supporting these is four times as meritorious.

Similar ideas persisted until the late eighteenth century, and under Islamic rule in South India. In particular, very much in the spirit of earlier writings on statecraft, Mysore under Tipu Sultan sought to promote agricultural improvement and expansion. Inducements to invest in agriculture, including reductions in revenue and privileged forms of land tenure such as exemptions from taxation, were offered. In addition, the Mysore state itself supplied capital in the form of taccavi. The granting of taccavi was widespread in late eighteenth-century South India. In Tanjore, English East India Company officials reported that 'advances for cultivation are made in grain and occasionally in money, and when it does not suit the convenience of the circar to make any, the inhabitants are allowed to borrow money, and to charge in their final settlement with the Circar at the rate of 1% monthly on the amount of the customary advance'.[10] John Gurney's work (Gurney 1968) on the Nawab of Arcot abundantly shows the importance of taccavi for the functioning of the agrarian and revenue order within his territories.

Taccavi and state participation in agricultural improvement was found in northern India as well. In the case of the Mughal state Irfan Habib has identified both fiscal measures to promote agriculture as well as direct administrative undertakings for the construction of irrigation works, including the digging of wells and the building of dams and canals (Habib 1999: 296–7; see also Chandra 1958: 35–51).

Customs of statecraft was not the only factor propelling political participation in agriculture. These activities were also propelled by the structure of the labour market in eighteenth-century South India. As we have already seen, agricultural producers in South India, and elsewhere on the subcontinent, were highly mobile and this mobility translated into competition for them. Thomas Munro witnessed this competition in the Ceded Districts during 'kalawedi' season when village headmen offered low revenue rates to attract cultivators. The political competition for labour was intensified by South Indian political traditions, which did not extend to kings' coercive power to limit the mobility or right to migrate of labouring groups. The exercise of political power in this way was not considered a legitimate exercise of sovereign power.[11] In this political order, incentives such as reduced revenue and the financing of improvements in production systems were the means by which political authorities could attract cultivators and labourers. Agricultural improvements were especially important as they made it possible to offer the favourable conditions, in particular higher and more secure incomes, which could draw in hands for the business of cultivation. The importance of agricultural improvement for access to supplies of labour is suggested by Lionel Place, who observed the following after the repair of a tank in a village near Madras:

Previous to the repair of the tank—it is not know how long—the lands had been uncultivated, but so soon as this work was completed, the descendants of many families who had formerly been the hereditary servants of the Brahmins claimed, and were admitted to their inheritance, although in the intermediate time they had taken up other occupations, and might be supposed to have forgot it. (Bayley and Huddleston 1862: 47–8)

4. Conclusion

This chapter has shown that in the eighteenth century standards of living, calculated in terms of grain wages, were comparable between Britain and South India and Bengal, which were both major centres of population and economic activity in the Indian subcontinent. This is a surprising finding given the enormous weight of received wisdom, and also in light of the fact that the demands on this grain bundle would have been far greater in Britain than in Bengal or South India. The colder British climate would have meant greater expenditures on housing, fuel, and clothing. Therefore, it is quite plausible to conclude that the *real* standard of living was higher in South Asia.

The chaper has argued that the key to the high standards of living on the Indian subcontinent was the structure of the labour market. Labour market institutions directly contributed to the well-being of labourers by giving them enormous bargaining power. For this the mobility of producers, artisanal as well as agricultural, was crucial. The easy option to exit the 'employment relation', which was further enhanced by the labour shortages of the eighteenth century, meant that labourers were able to lay claim to a secure share of the social product.

The structure of the labour market also indirectly contributed to the standard of living in India. As the use of coercive powers to limit labour mobility was not a legitimate exercise of state power, holders of political power were forced to undertake agricultural improvements in order to attract and fix labour. This translated into higher productivity in agriculture as higher quality land could be brought under the plough, systems of water control could be constructed and more valuable crops could be cultivated. All of these made possible high standards of living for those engaged in agricultural production. A highly productive agriculture also benefited artisans as cheap food meant cheap prices for their manufactures on global markets, and high demand for their services. Therefore, the standard of living in eighteenth-century India was very much a product of the political institutions that were characteristic of the Indian subcontinent.

Notes

1. A summary of these accounts may be found in Moreland (1920: 265–70).
2. *South Arcot Collectorate Records* (1778: Vol. 79, 11–15).
3. *Board's Collections*, No. 752, F/4/17, 22–3.
4. *North Arcot District Records* (1801: Vol. 23, 5–76); Washbrook (1993).
5. *Minutes of Evidence Taken Before the Select Committee on the Affairs of the East India Company* (1832: Vol. 1, 575).
6. Bayley and Huddleston (1862: 716–17); *Report of the Tanjore Commissioners*, *A.D. 1799* (1905: 23).
7. *Board of Revenue Proceedings* (1796: Vol. 144, 559–60).
8. Mackenzie General (1777: Vol. 59, 15).
9. Munro made these observations in 1806. The passage may be found in Gribble (1875: 201–2).
10. *Report of the Tanjore Commissioners, A.D. 1799* (1905: 24).
11. For further details, see Parthasarathi (2001: ch. 5).

References

Arokiaswami, M. (1956) *The Kongu Country; Being the History of the Modern Districts of Coimbatore and Salem from the Earliest Times to the Coming of the British.* Madras: University of Madras.

Baker, C. J. (1984) *An Indian Rural Economy: The Tamilnad Countryside, 1880–1955*. Delhi: Oxford University Press.

Bayley, W. H. and Huddleston, W. (1862) *Papers on Mirasi Right Selected from the Records of the Madras Government*. Madras: Pharoah & Co.

Bayly, C. A. (1983) *Rulers, Townsmen and Bazaars: North Indian Society in the Age of British Expansion, 1770–1870*. Cambridge: Cambridge University Press.

Board of Revenue Proceedings (1796), Tamil Nadu Archives, Chennai (Madras).

Board's Collections, Oriental and Indian Office Collections, British Library, London.

Bray, F. (1986) *The Rice Economies: Technology and Development in Asian Societies*. Oxford: Basil Blackwell.

Chandra, S. (1958) 'Some Institutional Factors in Providing Capital Inputs for the Improvement and Expansion of Cultivation in Medieval India'. *Indian Historical Review*, 11: 35–51.

Datta, R. (2000) *Society, Economy and the Market: Commercialisation in Rural Bengal, c.1760–1800*. Delhi: Manohar.

Eaton, R. (1993) *The Rise of Islam and the Bengal Frontier, 1204–1760*. Berkeley, CA: University of California Press.

Gordon, S. (1978) 'The Slow Conquest: Administrative Integration of Malwa into the Maratha Empire'. *Modern Asian Studies*, 11(1): 1–40.

Gribble, J. D. B. (1875) *A Manual of the District of Cuddapah*. Madras: Government Press.

Gurney, J. D. (1968) 'The Debts of the Nawab of Arcot, 1763–1776', unpublished Ph.D. dissertation, Oxford University.

Habib, I. (1999) *The Agrarian System of Mughal India*, 2nd edn. Delhi: Oxford University Press.

Hossain, H. (1988) *The Company Weavers of Bengal: The East India Company and the Organization of Textile Production in Bengal 1750–1813*. Delhi: Oxford University Press.

Landes, D. (1998) *The Wealth and Poverty of Nations: Why Some Are So Rich and Some So Poor*. New York, NY: W. W. Norton and Company.

Ludden, D. (1985) *Peasant History in South India*. Princeton, NJ: Princeton University Press.

Mackenzie General (1777) *Some Enquiries into and Account of the State of the Annacathy, May 1777*. Oriental and India Office Collections, British Library, London, Vol. 59.

Marshall, P. J. (1987) 'The Company and the Coolies: Labour in Early Calcutta', in P. Sinha (ed.), *The Urban Experience, Calcutta: Essays in Honour of Professor Nisith R. Ray*. Calcutta: Riddhi–India.

Minutes of Evidence Taken Before the Select Committee on the Affairs of the East India Company (1832), Vol. 1. London: Public, 575.

Mitra, D. B. (1978) *The Cotton Weavers of Bengal, 1757–1833*. Calcutta: KLM.

Moosvi, S. (1987) *The Economy of the Mughal Empire c.1595: A Statistical Study*. Delhi: Oxford University Press.

Moreland, W. H. (1920) *India at the Death of Akbar*. London: MacMillan and Co.

North Arcot District Records (1801) Tamil Nadu Archives (TNA), Chennai (Madras).

Parthasarathi, P. (1998) 'Rethinking Wages and Competitiveness in the Eighteenth Century: Britain and South India'. *Past and Present*, 158: 79–109.

—— (2001) *The Transition to a Colonial Economy: Weavers, Merchants and Kings in South India, 1720–1800*. Cambridge: Cambridge University Press.

Petersen, C. (1995) *Bread and the British Economy, c.1770–1870*, edited by A. Jenkins. Aldershot, England: Scholar Press.

Pomeranz, K. (2000) *The Great Divergence: China, Europe and the Eighteenth-Century World Economy*. Princeton, NJ: Princeton University Press.

Prakash, G. (1990) *Bonded Histories: Genealogies of Labour Servitude in Colonial India*. Cambridge: Cambridge University Press.

Report of the Tanjore Commissioners, A.D. 1799 (1905). Tanjore: Government Press.

Sinha, N. K. (1961) *The Economic History of Bengal: From Plassey to the Permanent Settlement*, 2nd edn. Calcutta: KLM.

Smith, A. (1976) *The Wealth of Nations*, Canaan edition. Chicago, IL: University of Chicago Press.

South Arcot Collectorate Records (1778), Cuddalore Consultations. Tamil Nadu Archives, Chennai (Madras).

Stein, B. (1984a) 'The Economic Functions of a Medieval South Indian Temple', in B. Stein (ed.), *All the Kings' Mana: Papers on Medieval South Indian History*. Madras: New Era Publications.

—— (1984b) 'The State, the Temple and Agricultural Development: A Study in Medieval South India', in B. Stein (ed.), *All the Kings' Mana: Papers on Medieval South Indian History*. Madras: New Era Publications.

Washbrook, D. (1993) 'Land and Labour in the Late Eighteenth-Century India: The Golden Age of the Pariah?' in P. Robb (ed.), *Dalit Movements and the Meanings of Labour in India*. Delhi: Oxford University Press.

5 Real Wages in Europe and Asia: A First Look at the Long-Term Patterns

ROBERT C. ALLEN

1. Introduction

Understanding the causes of economic development and underdevelopment has been a central concern of social science since its inception. A paradigm case is the contrast between Europe, which has had a growing economy since before the Industrial Revolution, and China and India, seemingly trapped in backwardness until recent decades. Elaborate theories have been spun to explain the divergence. Possible causes include differences in modes of production (capitalist or Asiatic), the efficiency of property rights, world empire, religion, political fragmentation or centralization, and the presence or absence of the scientific spirit. Revisionist historians have called much of this speculation into question. In a thoroughgoing reassessment, Pomeranz (2000), for instance, has shown that land, labour, capital, and product markets were as efficient in China as in Europe. Theories emphasizing differences in property rights and modes of production are contradicted by these findings. While the theories have been sweeping, their factual basis has been weak. The working hypothesis in the standard literature is that Europe was ahead of Asia well before the Industrial Revolution. In contrast, to Pomeranz 'it seems likely that average incomes in Japan, China, and parts of southeast Asia were comparable to (or higher than) those in western Europe even in the late eighteenth century'.[1] The evidence offered is important, but indirect, as it does not include comparisons of income and its purchasing power. In his discussion of parallel issues for India, Parthasarathi (1998) quotes numerous eighteenth-century English observers who claimed that living standards were higher in Europe. Many of them cite the low level of wages in India as support for their conclusions. Parthasarathi disputes this evidence and offers some comparisons of his own that show the real earnings of weavers in India were higher than those of their counterparts in eighteenth-century England. This comparison is important evidence but needs to be replicated for other times and places if it is to be accepted as generally true.

What incomes should be compared? Gross Domestic Product (GDP) per head is the most common measure of living standards. While estimates are being pushed back into the nineteenth century and even earlier, the difficulties are immense and reliability will always be a concern. Moreover, the early modern states of Europe and Asia were often non-egalitarian, so average income may be a poor guide to the standard of living of the majority of the population. To address both issues, this chapter explores the implications of real wages for the history of living standards.

Wages played two roles that must be distinguished. First, they represented the cost of labour to manufacturers. To compare wages, we need the market exchange rate to convert wages from one currency to another. However, in many cases, we lack those exchange rates. This is particularly true for the intercontinental comparisons that most interest us. There is a solution, however. Silver coins were the principal medium of exchange in most countries in the early modern period. Consequently, the exchange rates can be approximated by the relative amount of silver represented by their units of account. To make these comparisons, we convert English *pence* and Chinese *tael*, for instance, into the weight of silver they could buy. Expressed in grams of silver, Indian and Chinese wages were, indeed, much less than European wages, as noted by the commentators cited by Parthasarathi. English observers were well aware of this fact, as it explained the low price of the Indian cloth they shipped to Europe, Africa, and the Americas. Whether low silver wages imply a low standard of living is another matter, however.

Second, wages reveal the standard of living if they are compared to the price of consumer goods. This is the interpretation that matters in assessing the prosperity of Asia vis-à-vis Europe. Provided low Asian wages were matched by low consumer goods prices, the standard of living of workers could have been the same at both ends of Eurasia even though Asian manufacturers had a competitive advantage in the textile industry. In other words, the wage observations of Parthasarathi's eighteenth-century commentators are—possibly—compatible with his revisionism.

The European side of the comparison is reasonably well documented due to the long-standing tradition of writing price histories. These provide time series of prices and wages that extended as far back as the thirteenth century. For many important European cities, one can construct real wage indices back to 1500, and the levels of real wages can be compared across cities as well as over time. The deflators in these indices are based on important consumer goods like food, fuel, and cloth.

The history of prices and wages in Asia remains highly fragmentary since comprehensive price histories have not yet been written. Japan is something of an exception to this generalization, as to so many others, since there have been studies of prices in leading cities running back into the Tokugawa period. These series stop in the 1720s, however, so the seventeenth century, which is of great historical interest, remains a statistical Dark Age.

If they can be executed, real wage comparisons will throw much light on relative living standards in the seventeenth and eighteenth centuries. There is a second issue they can address as well. The early modern period needs to be brought into rapport with the nineteenth and twentieth centuries. If the revisionists are right and Asia was as prosperous as Europe before the Industrial Revolution, how are we to understand the great difference in incomes in the twentieth century? Did China and India stand still as Europe advanced or was there immiseration in Asia as well? To answer this question, early modern Asian wages must be compared to wages in the same region in the twentieth century.

Definitive conclusions on both questions await the writing of comprehensive price histories for Asia. What can be done at present is to marshal the existing evidence to see what generalizations it suggests. I begin by reviewing the history of real wages in Europe, and then consider the published information for Japan, China, and India. The aim is, first, to compare real wages in Europe and Asia in the seventeenth and eighteenth centuries, and, second, to see whether low Asian living standards in the twentieth century represent a descent from earlier prosperity or whether Asia was simply marking time while Europe progressed.

2. Trends and Levels of Real Wages in Europe

In the case of Europe, I rely on my own investigation of real wages in major cities of Europe from the late Middle Ages to the First World War (Allen 2001). The cities include London, Oxford,[2] Antwerp, Amsterdam, Paris, Strasbourg, Madrid, Valencia, Naples, Milan, Florence, Vienna, Leipzig, Krakow, Gdansk, Lwow, and Warsaw. These are cities for which price histories—with their many tables of prices and wages—have been written. Building craftsmen and labourers and, occasionally, male agricultural workers are the groups whose living standards can be studied. The wages and prices were entered into computer files. The local weights and measures were translated into metric equivalents. The local units of account were converted into grams of silver. The conversion to silver was not made because silver has any transcendent significance. Instead, the procedure approximates the market exchange rate between the units of account since silver coins were the medium of exchange. This material makes it possible to compare wages across Europe, to compute consumer price indices[3] over time and across space, and, finally, to calculate real wage levels by dividing silver wages by their purchasing power.

This inquiry establishes three important generalizations about living standards in Europe:

First, there was growing divergence in living standards between 1500 and 1750 (see Figure 5.1). At the end of the Middle Ages, real wages were remarkably similar across Europe. In the next two centuries, real wages collapsed in southern and central Europe. The drop was much less in London and the Low Countries. These were the growth poles of the early modern economy, and their living standards returned to the high level of the late fifteenth century. A large gap had

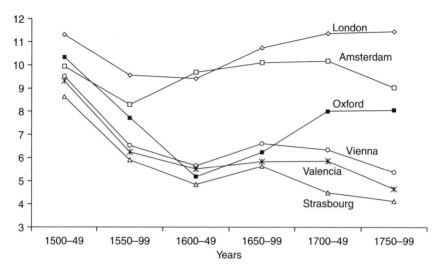

Figure 5.1   Real wages in Europe, 1500–1750 (silver wages deflated by CPI)

Source: See text.

emerged between these centres of international commerce and the rest of the continent by 1750.

Second, the sixteenth-century drop in the real wage in English provincial towns was as steep as on the continent and much greater than the decline in London. However, the dynamism of London spread to the rest of England in the eighteenth century. Real wages in places like Oxford rose sharply after 1700 when they surpassed wages in southern and central Europe and began to close the gap with London. These gains were confined to the urban economy. There had been little difference in the wage of Oxfordshire agricultural and building workers before 1700, but a gap emerged in the eighteenth century and continued to grow in the nineteenth century as Oxford building workers shared in the benefits of economic development, while farm workers were left behind.

Third, there was some fluctuation in the real wage series in England between 1500 and 1850, but no general advance was realized before the last third of the nineteenth century. It was only after 1870 that real wages finally began to rise in many cities in Europe and only then that the levels of the late fifteenth century were surpassed. The Industrial Revolution raised GDP per head, but it took a century before it raised the standard of living of building workers.

3. Real Wages in Asia

Ideally, real wages in Asia and Europe should be compared by specifying a basket of consumer goods that could be priced in both continents. The cost of that basket would be the deflator that converted nominal into real wages. This was the procedure used to compare living standards across Europe in Allen (2001), but it must be modified to deal with differences in diet between Europe and Asia. Bread was the major source of calories in Europe and accounted for about one-third of spending in the European consumer price index. Rice was the counterpart in Asia. Calculations for India, where bread was also consumed, show that rice was the cheapest source of calories. This was generally true in China, although in Yangzi wheat gruel was cheaper in the summer and eaten by the poorest people (Li 1998).

I have dealt with the issue of bread and rice by specifying different baskets for Europe and Asia (Table 5.1). 143 kg of rice/year was included in the Asian basket versus 208 kg of bread in the European basket. Rice has more calories per kilogram than bread, and these weights correspond to the same calorie intake per day (1950). (The European diet, however, was richer in protein.) The budgets also include peas (or beans), meat, and fat (*ghi*, butter, or oil depending on the locale). Non-foods include oil for illumination and cotton cloth in Asia and linen in Europe. 'When in Rome, do as the Romans' was the philosophy that defined the basket of goods, subject to the requirement that it yield the same number of calories. Weights and nutritional composition are shown in Table 5.1.

This scheme can be applied to India, but not all of the prices are available for Japan and China. Two methods have been adopted to solve this problem. One is to estimate the missing prices by using Indian price relatives. The resulting prices, the costs of the baskets, and the implied real wages are set out in the Appendix, Tables 5.A1–5.A4. These calculations are extended, or other indices are linked to them, as will be explained. The second approach is to simplify the calculations radically by using the cost of a calorie implied by the prices of rice and bread as the deflator. Both procedures lead to similar results.

Table 5.1   European and Asian baskets and nutrition

	India			Europe		
	Quantity	Daily calories	Daily protein	Quantity	Daily calories	Daily protein
Foods						
Rice	143.0 kg	1403	39	—	—	—
Bread	—	—	—	208.0 kg	1400	57
Peas	52.0 l	161	10	52.0 l	161	10
Meat	26.0 kg	179	14	26.0 kg	179	14
Fat	10.4 kg	208	0	10.4 kg	208	0
Total	—	1951	63	—	1948	81
Non-foods						
Oil	2.6 l	—	—	2.6 l	—	—
Cloth	5.0 m	—	—	5.0 m	—	—

Source: Appendix, Tables 5.A1–5.A4.

3.1   Japan

I begin with Japan since it has the most elaborated statistical history. Prices and wages for Kyoto, Osaka, and Edo and some villages have been collected. These allow the calculation of real wages from 1726 to the twentieth century. Ohkawa *et al.* (1967: 153–5, 245) include the prices of many consumer goods from 1879 onwards as well as series of wage rates for building craftsmen, building labourers, and agricultural workers. These have been used to link the Japanese wage and price series with Europe. Five-year averages (1880–4) of the prices of the commodities shown in Table 5.1 were used to calculate the cost of the consumption basket shown there. The cost of that basket relative to the cost of the same basket in Europe was used to convert the average Japanese wages of building craftsmen, building labourers, and male day-labourers in agriculture for 1880–4 into 'real' terms. Indices of real wages in Japan[4] were, then, rebased to equal this average value. These real wage series can be compared to European ones to measure the growth and level of living standards of the population in the two ends of Eurasia.

The comparisons are carried out in Figures 5.2–5.5. Figure 5.2 shows the real wage of skilled building craftsmen (carpenters and masons) in London, Oxford, northern Italy, and Kyoto from 1727 to 1913. The real wage was similar in Kyoto and northern Italy, and there is little evidence of any increase before the First World War. Oxford wages were not much higher in the eighteenth century. London wages were highest throughout, and after about 1800, the Oxford wage rose above the Japanese wage approaching the London wage. After 1850, the

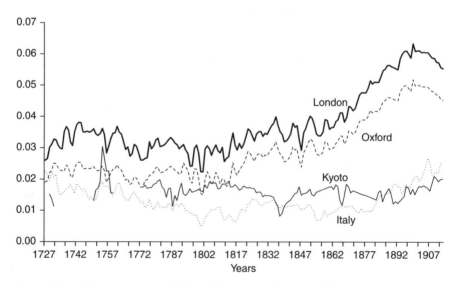

Figure 5.2   Masons' real wage, 1727–1913, England, Japan, and Italy
Source: See text.

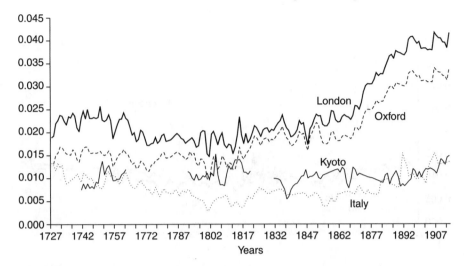

Figure 5.3 Building labourers' real wage, 1727–1913, England, Japan, and Italy
Source: See text.

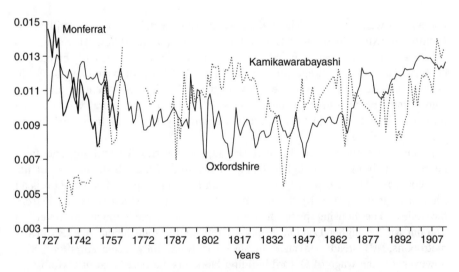

Figure 5.4 Farm labourers' real wage, 1727–1913, England, Japan, and Italy
Source: See text.

wage in both London and Oxford rose decisively above the real wage in southern Europe and Japan. The wages of building labourers showed the same pattern (Figure 5.3).

Figure 5.4 summarizes the evidence respecting the wage of farm labourers. The Oxford series, which represented the earnings of male agricultural labourers in the

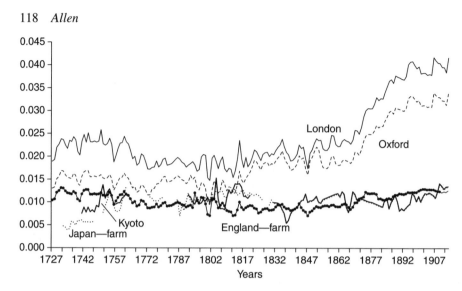

Figure 5.5   Labourers' real wage, 1727–1913, England and Japan
Source: See text.

county, showed no trend. The Italian wage data are taken from the village of
Montferrat (Montaldeo) near Genoa for 1727–65 (Doria 1968). There was no
significant difference between Oxfordshire and Italian wages in the early eighteenth
century. The Japanese wage series is for the small town of Kamikawarabayashi
near Kyoto. Real wages were very low in the early eighteenth century and were
significantly below European farm wages. The rise in agricultural wages in the
mid-eighteenth century in Japan, an increase noted by Tokugawa historians, closed
the gap with Europe.

Figure 5.5 combines the English and Japanese series for building and farm
labourers. This figure highlights important features of the labour markets of the
two countries. (1) Real wages were highest in London. In part, this premium is an
illusion as it was offset by the higher cost of housing, which is excluded from
the index. The housing price differential was not large enough, however, to
account for the higher London wages—it reflects the tight labour markets of the
metropolis; (2) steady advance in the real wage only occurred after 1870,
however; (3) the wage of Oxford building labourers exceeded that of Oxfordshire
farm labourers in the early eighteenth century. This was a new development,
for their wages were very similar in earlier centuries, and it represents the spread of
a strong economy outward from London, throughout the Home Counties; (4) by the
early nineteenth century, Oxford wages were following those of London, breaking
away from Oxfordshire farm wages. Those remained constant throughout the period
as labour left agriculture.

The situation in Japan was very different. The real wages of labourers in Kyoto
and Kamikawarabayashi were identical—or virtually so—for the whole period.

This indicates both close integration of the markets and the absence of the dynamic urban economy that disequilibrated English labour markets and led to higher wages in English cities than in Japanese. Japanese labourers' wages were similar to those of English farm workers throughout and close to those of Oxford labourers in the eighteenth century.

Figures 5.2–5.5 have important bearing on the assessment of Japanese economic performance. Japanese living standards in the late Tokugawa were on a par with those in provincial England. Japanese wages were not as high as those in the western European growth poles, but they were similar to those on most of the continent. The figures also indicate that living standards began to diverge for most people after 1870. This was not because Japanese wages fell but because wages in England rose for many people. Should we regard pre-industrial Japanese economic performance as a success? It was in the sense that Japanese living standards were similar to those in many parts of Europe, but Japan lacked the high-wage economy of the dynamic cities of northwestern Europe. That economy was the leading edge of general prosperity. As more of England became incorporated into that economy, the advance in wages became more general. Japan did not achieve the same break-through until after First World War, perhaps even until after Second World War (Minami 1986: 296–396).

3.2   India

For the study of real wages in India, I rely on evidence and sources used in the debate on long-run living standards that appeared in the *Indian Economic and Social History Review* in the 1970s.[5] The discussion ranged from real incomes to agricultural productivity to demographic indicators. Here I am concerned only with the real wage evidence. Comparisons were drawn between 1595 and *c*.1960 (in most cases). The latter was chosen to establish long-run trends. The former was dictated by a unique document—Abul Fazl's *Ain-i Akbari*—which recorded wages and prices paid (presumably) in Agra amidst much other information on the Mughal Empire.

The *Ain-i Akbari* reports the prices of all of the commodities shown in Table 5.1, so it is straightforward to compare the price levels in India in 1595 to Europe at various dates. The chosen years are 1500–9, 1600–19, and 1750–9; that is, wages and prices in each European city in those years are compared to Indian wages and prices in 1595. Obviously, it would be desirable to have Indian prices for the same dates, but that evidence is not available. The values for 1500–9 show the European situation before the price revolution and at the real wage peak of the fifteenth century for most places. Averages for 1600–19 show European wages at the end of the price revolution, while values for 1750–9 do the same for the eve of the Industrial Revolution. Table 5.2 shows comparisons between London, Oxford, Amsterdam, Valencia, Vienna, and northern Italy.

Even before the price revolution, wages and prices in Europe exceeded those in India. The Italian price level in 1500, for instance, was triple that of India in 1595.

Table 5.2 European wages relative to Indian in 1595

	London	Oxford	Amsterdam	Valencia	Vienna	Northern Italy
Unskilled						
1500–9	1.88	1.50	2.29	1.42	1.76	0.88
1600–19	1.38	0.83	1.83	1.02	1.18	0.91
1750–9	2.00	1.32	1.86	1.00	1.00	1.10
Skilled						
1500–9	1.29	0.97	1.48	0.97	1.13	0.70
1600–19	0.86	0.54	1.13	0.53	0.65	0.80
1750–9	1.27	0.85	1.05	0.51	0.69	0.78

Source: Appendix, Tables 5.A1–5.A4.

In 1600–19, after the European inflation, the differential widened to almost 6 to 1. It is no wonder that European explorers found many good buys in the Indies or that commodities flowed from East to West with the trade being balanced by silver flows from Europe to Asia.

It was a similar story with wages. Indian wages in 1595 were a third or a half of European wages in 1500 when both are expressed in grams of silver per day. Comparisons around 1600 show even larger differences. The low silver wages noted in the eighteenth century were long-standing.

Table 5.2 compares European real wages in the years shown to Indian real wages in 1595. In the table, the Indian real wage is set equal to 1.00. Real wages were high and reasonably uniform across Europe in 1500–9 and fell everywhere except Italy in the sixteenth century. The Italian decline happened in the fifteenth century. The drop was least in London and Amsterdam. In the seventeenth and eighteenth centuries, there was little change in real wages in Valencia, Vienna, or Strasbourg. In England and the Low Countries, on the other hand, wages rebounded. Table 5.2 shows the same divergence in living standards as was shown by Figure 5.1.

Since the wages in Table 5.2 are indexed with respect to Indian wages in 1595, it also shows European living standards relative to Indian living standards at the end of the sixteenth century. The high water mark of European wages in the fifteenth century exceeded the Indian level in 1595. Population growth in Europe in the sixteenth century pushed European wages below Indian wages except for the few booming cities of the northwest. Skilled workers did particularly well in India since skilled wages there were twice that of unskilled wages, while the premium was only about 50% in Europe and Japan. Unskilled workers in south and central Europe earned about the same real income as their counterparts in India, while skilled workers did better in India than in south or central Europe. In northwestern Europe, unskilled workers did better than in

Table 5.3   Indian standards of living, 1595 (in grams of silver) and 1961 (in rupees)

Item in basket	Quantity in basket	1595		1961	
		Price	Expense	Price	Expense
Rice	142.2 kg	0.22	31.5	0.57	86.9
Peas	52.0 l	0.09	4.5	0.38	19.9
Mutton	26.0 kg	0.72	18.6	0.37	95.9
Ghi	10.4 kg	1.16	12.0	5.94	61.8
Oil	2.6 l	0.88	2.3	2.30	6.0
Cloth	5.0 m	0.91	4.5	2.46	12.3
Total	—	—	73.5	—	277.3
Unskilled wage	—	—	0.83	—	2.40
Real wage	—	—	0.011294	—	0.008656

Source: Appendix, Tables 5.A1–5.A4.

India, while the earnings of skilled workers were a toss-up. These results confirm that Parthasarathi's findings for English weavers were not limited to that group.

What happened to Indian living standards in the next four centuries? The contributors to the standard of living debate did not compute conventional real wage indices. Instead, they calculated how much of each good could be purchased if all of the wage were spent on it. Results for 1595 were compared to those for *c*.1960. The conclusion was that workers' living standards declined over these four centuries.

This pessimistic conclusion is confirmed with the real wage framework utilized here (Table 5.3). The basket of goods cost 73.5 g of silver in 1595 and 277.3 rupees in 1961. The relative difference is 3.77 (= 277.3/73.5). Over the same period, the wage of an unskilled worker changed from 0.83 g of silver to 2.4 rupees, that is, by a factor of 2.89 (= 2.4/0.83). The implication is that the real wage fell by 23.3% (1.028 = 2.89/3.77) in almost four centuries. This finding confirms Desai's pessimism.

3.3   China

The data for China are the most limited. Li (1998) provides a detailed, quantitative account of farm productivity in the Yangzi valley in the seventeenth and eighteenth centuries. Agricultural handbooks are the main source of his information, and they report 'typical' prices of rice, wheat, and cotton cloth as well as farm wages. By extrapolating the missing prices with Indian relative prices, the cost of living and the real wage of farm workers in the Yangzi can be compared to their counterparts in England, Italy, and Japan. These are the pertinent comparisons since we have no information about wages in Chinese cities. One thing India and China had in common was low wages and prices in the early modern period: the Chinese price and wage levels were only about one-third of the English levels when expressed in grams of silver. This is the immediate reason that China was so competitive in the production of manufactured goods.

Since prices as well as wages were lower in China than in Europe, low Chinese silver wages do not imply that the standard of living was lower in China. This is confirmed by Table 5.4, which shows the real wage of farm labour *c*.1500, *c*.1600, and *c*.1750. The Chinese value shown for 1750 really applies to the late seventeenth century. The real wage of unskilled labour in India *c*.1595 is also shown. It is not certain that this refers to farm labour; however, the similarity of the wage of farm and non-farm labour in pre-industrial Japan and in seventeenth-century Oxfordshire increases the interest in the Indian comparison, whatever the exact nature of the work being done.

Table 5.4 shows the well-established fall in English real wages after 1500. The level of wages in 1600 and in 1750 can be compared to the Asian economies. By this reckoning, European farm wages were slightly higher than Asian wages in the early modern period, but the difference is small.

Farm workers were poor and devoted large fractions of their income to bread or rice. In view of the weaknesses of the Asian price data for other commodities, it might be better to relate wages to the cost of a calorie implied by bread and rice rather than to the broader cost of living index. Table 5.5 does this. It shows the number of calories that could be purchased with a day's wage if all of the money was spent on rice or bread. The real wage was generally of the order of 10,000 calories per day. In interpreting this figure, allowance must be made for non-working days and for the other family members supported by the wage earner. Allowing a 300-day work year would reduce family calorie consumption to 8,219 ($= 10,000 * 300/365$), which would support a wife and several children. Of course, if any of them generated income, as they often did, the situation would be eased further. The family could then buy items besides food and expand their consumption of animal products that cost more per calorie. Using the price of a calorie as a deflator indicates that there was little difference in the standard of living of English, Chinese, and Japanese farm workers. Italian farm workers, by these figures, were in a particularly difficult situation: their earnings

Table 5.4 Real wages of farm workers, CPI deflator

	England	Northern Italy	Japan	China	India
1500	0.017	0.012	—	—	—
1600	0.010	0.014	—	—	0.011
1750	0.011	0.010	0.009	0.009	—

Source: Appendix, Tables 5.A1–5.A4.

Table 5.5 Real wages of farm workers, calorie price deflator

	England	Northern Italy	Japan	China	India
1500	15,339	10,746	—	—	—
1600	9,160	5,742	—	—	13,441
1750	9,961	5,654	10,552	9,996	—

Notes: Figures in the table show the number of calories that can be purchased with a day's earnings if all of the money is spent on bread (in Europe) or rice (in Asia). A kilogram of rice is assumed to contain 3,570 calories and a kilogram of bread 2,450 calories.

were not enough to support a family. Asia did not lag behind Europe according to Table 5.5.

If China was not far behind Europe prior to the Industrial Revolution, did the large difference in living standards in the twentieth century result from European advance or Chinese decline or a combination of the two? Buck's (1937: 306) famous survey of Chinese farms in the 1920s throws some light on the matter. He reports that the average full-time farm labourer in the Yangzi could buy 1,187 kg of rice if he spent his full yearly earnings (including the value of payments in kind) on that commodity. Assuming he worked 300 days per year, this corresponds to a daily 'real' wage of 14,125 calories in the 1920s. This is the 'real' wage using the rice price as the deflator and is, therefore, directly comparable to the figures in Table 5.5. By these figures, the standard of living in the Yangzi rose by over 40% between the early eighteenth and early twentieth centuries. This assessment of living standards is consistent with Brandt's (1989) interpretation of Chinese agricultural development in the late nineteenth and early twentieth centuries. Chinese poverty in the early twentieth century, by these figures, was not the result of Chinese decline but rather of growth that was slower than Europe's.

4. Conclusion

The wage comparisons undertaken in this chapter support several important conclusions about living standards in pre-industrial Europe and Asia.

First, wages expressed in grams of silver were lower in China and India than in Europe. The views of the eighteenth-century observers cited by Parthasarathi are confirmed. This is important since it was the proximate cause of Asia's competitive advantage in textiles and luxury manufactures and was, thus, the basis for Asian–European trade in the early modern period. Why these differentials persisted for hundreds of years is an important question in international and monetary economics that must be addressed to explain the dynamics of the world economy in this period.

Second, low Asian silver wages were matched by low Asian prices with the result that living standards in Asia were similar to those in many parts of Europe.

Farm workers in Europe and urban workers in central and southern Europe did not enjoy higher living standards than their counterparts in Asia.

Third, some parts of Europe did generate higher real wages than we find in Asia. When real wages were at their peak following the Black Death, most Europeans had a higher standard of living. But this was a transitory condition for most of the continent. High wages persisted only in the commercial centres of the northwest—London and the Low Countries generally. During the eighteenth century, the provincial towns of England were drawn into the same high-wage orbit, but agriculture was left behind. This dynamic, urban economy was the engine of growth in early modern Europe, and Asia appears to have had no counterpart. It is possible, of course, that a more extensive Asian database would reveal a parallel: the absence of information on urban Chinese wages is particularly troubling in this regard. However, neither the Japanese cities nor the capital of the Mughal Empire had particularly high wages. The evidence at hand suggests that Asia lacked Europe's engine of growth.

This point may be put differently. The revisionist literature on Asia argues that it exhibited Smithian growth, just like Europe. This may be, but Smithian growth can be intense or moderate; it can lead to an industrial revolution, but it need not. The issues here were rehearsed in the debate about proto-industrialization, and Coleman's (1983) scepticism about its importance applies equally to Smithian growth.

Fourth, the wage data lend support to the classical notion of a 'subsistence' wage. Leaving aside Europe's transitory fifteenth-century real wage peak and the high wages generated by the commercial success of the northwest, most of the continent settled down to wage levels like those in Asia. Was this coincidence or were there demographic or other equilibrating processes that kept incomes at a similar level across Eurasia? Alternatively, were wages destined to be the same from Portugal to Japan unless the labour market was disrupted by a major demographic shock or by continuous growth in demand due to capital accumulation and technological advance?

Fifth, only in India was there evidence of falling real wages between the early modern period and the twentieth century. In China and Japan, they were constant or rising. There was a difference in living standards between Europe and Asia in the twentieth century because Europe pushed ahead, while growth in Asia was moderate in the extreme.

These conclusions are only as good as the wage and price data that underlie them, and for Asia they are weak, indeed. The International Price History Commission emphasized the importance of long series of wages and prices as the basis for sound economic history. One hundred years of research have blessed European historians with price histories that allow the measurement of market integration, inflation, and productivity, as well as the reconstruction of living standards across the continent. Global comparisons show the necessity of extending this research worldwide. Who will write the price histories of Delhi and Beijing, of Shanghai and Bombay?[6]

Appendix

Table 5.A1   Base values for India in 1595

	Indian units	Grams of silver per metric unit
Commodity prices		
Rice	20 dam/man	0.221 g/kg
Peas	6 dam/man	0.087 g/l
Meat	65 dam/man	0.717 g/kg
Fat[a]	105 dam/man	1.158 g/kg
Oil	80 dam/man	0.882 g/kg
Cloth	3 dam/yard	0.908 g/m
Cost of basket[b]	101.058 g of silver	
Wages		
Unskilled	3 dam/day	0.830463 grams of silver/day
Skilled	7 dam/day	1.937747 grams of silver/day
Real wage[c]		
Unskilled	0.011294	
Skilled	0.026352	

[a] Fat was ghi.
[b] Cost of basket obtained by multiplying quantities by silver prices shown here.
[c] Real wage is wage divided by cost of basket.

Notes: Assumptions about weights, measures, and money: one rupee of 40 dam weighed 11.07284 g of pure silver, one man equals 25.1 kg, and 1 l of peas weighs 0.76 kg.

Table 5.A2 Base values for China in late seventeenth century

	Chinese units	Grams of silver per metric unit
Commodity prices		
Rice	1 *tael/shi*	0.555 g/kg
Peas	—	[0.219g]/l[c]
Meat	—	[1.803g]/kg[c]
Fat[a]	—	[2.219g]/kg[c]
Oil	—	[2.219g]/l[c]
Cloth[b]	0.31 *tael/bolt*	2.355 g/m
Cost of basket[d]	247.3088 g of silver	
Wage		
Farm	0.05 *tael*/day	1.553333 g of silver/day
Real wage[e]		
Farm	0.008527	

[a] Fat was oil.
[b] Cloth price is Li's (1998: 149) figure for the net income that producers received from making cloth inflated by Pomeranz's (2000: 319) ratio of output to labour costs.
[c] Silver prices in brackets calculated as price of rice multiplied by the ratio of the Indian price of the commodity to the Indian price of rice as given in Appendix, Table 5.A1.
[d] Cost of basket obtained by multiplying quantities in Table 5.1 by silver prices shown here.
[e] Real wage is wage divided by cost of basket.

Notes: Assumptions about weights, measures (Li 1998: xvi–xvii), and money: one *shi* of paddy rice weighs 65 kg (1.3 dan or picul each weighing 50 kg), one bolt of cloth equals 3.63 sq. yards or 3.03 sq. m, and one *tael* weight 31.06667 g of pure silver.

Table 5.A3 Base values for Japan in 1880–4

	Japanese units	Grams of silver per metric unit
Commodity prices		
Rice	0.09476 yen/sho	1.662 g/kg
Peas	0.06000 yen/sho	1.163 g/L
Meat	—	[5.403]g/kg[b]
Fat[a]	—	[6.650]g/kg[b]
Oil	—	[6.650]g/kg[b]
Cloth	0.502 yen/tan	3.7530 g/m
Cost of basket[c]	540.3853 g of silver	
Wage		
Unskilled	0.2 yen/day	5.00 g of silver/day
Skilled	0.2975 yen/day	7.44 g of silver/day
Farm	0.1975 yen/day	4.94 g of silver/day
Real wage[d]		
Unskilled	0.009200	
Skilled	0.013685	
Farm	0.009085	

[a] Fat was oil.
[b] Silver prices in brackets calculated as price of rice multiplied by the ratio of the Indian price of the commodity to the Indian price of rice as given in Appendix, Table 5.A1.
[c] Cost of basket obtained by multiplying quantities in Table 5.A1 by silver prices shown here.
[d] Real wage is wage divided by cost of basket.

Notes: Assumptions about weights, measures, and money: one yen equalled 25 g of silver. Ohkawa *et al.* (1967: 153) state that one sho of rice weighed 1.425 kg, while one sho of soy beans weighed 1.29 kg. Li (1998: 205, n. 4) reports that one tan of cloth equalled 4.1 sq. yards (3.43 sq.m²).

Table 5.A4 Base values for England and Italy in 1750–9

	England[a]	Northern Italy
Commodity prices		
(grams of silver per metric units)		
Bread	1.37 g/kg	0.91 g/kg
Peas	0.42 g/kg	0.58 g/kg
Meat	3.33 g/kg	2.32 g/kg
Fat[b]	6.89 g/kg	2.32 g/kg
Oil	3.19 g/kg	2.32 g/kg
Cloth	4.87 g/m	8.63 g/m
Cost of basket[c]	579.736 g	381.982 g
Wage		
Unskilled	7.42 g/day	3.44 g/day
Skilled	11.14 g/day	5.73 g/day
Farm	5.57 g/day	2.10 g/day
Real wage[d]		
Unskilled	0.014909	0.009737
Skilled	0.022383	0.016229
Farm	0.011191	0.009752

[a] Wages shown for England are for Oxford. London wages were 16.70 g/day for skilled and 11.14 for unskilled.
[b] Fat was butter in England and oil in Italy.
[c] Cost of basket obtained by multiplying quantities in Table 5.A1 by silver prices shown here.
[d] Real wage is wage divided by cost of basket.

Notes: See Allen (2001) for discussion of underlying data.

Notes

1. Pomeranz (2000: 49). See Pomeranz (op. cit. 31) for his summary of the standard literature.
2. Really the small towns in southern England whose wages were collected by Phelps Brown and Hopkins (1955). Oxford is among them.
3. While house rents have been included in the consumer price indices of some cities, no systematic attempt has yet been made to compare house rents across countries as well as over time. While that is a major limitation of the existing estimates, rent accounted for only 5–10% of consumer spending, so its importance should not be overstated.
4. For 1727–1831, Saito's (1978: 89–91) nominal wage series for carpenters and day labourers in Kyoto and day labourers in Kamikawarabayashi were deflated by Crawcour and Yamamura's (1970) 'Sauerbeck' and Kyoto consumer price indices. (Saito's wage series, which end in 1830, were extended to 1831 on the assumption that they equalled 100 in that year.) These series were extended to 1880–4 using Williamson's (1998: 39) real wage series for Japanese workers. The resulting three series were linked to the real wages of building craftsmen, labourers, and farm labourers computed from Ohkawa (1967) as explained in the text.
5. Desai (1972, 1978), Heston (1977), Moosvi (1973, 1977). Mukerjee (1976) produced a parallel set of calculations that made their way into the debate.
6. Work has been done on this question for India—for example, Habib (1963, 1982), Hasan (1969), Chaudhuri, S. (1977), Chaudhuri, K. N. (1978), Attman (1981), van Santen (1982), and Prakash (1985)—but the range and completeness of the wage and price series are far less than for Europe.

References

Ain-i-Akbari of Abul Fazl-i-Allami (1949) translated by H. S. Jarrett. Calcutta: Royal Asiatic Society of Bengal.

Allen, R. C. (2001) 'The Great Divergence: Wages and Prices from the Middle Ages to the First World War'. *Explorations in Economic History*, 38(4): 411–47.

Attman, A. (1981) 'The Bullion Flow Between Europe and the East, 1000–1750'. *Actae Regiae Societatis Scientiarum et Litterarum Gothoburgensis, Humanoria*, 20, Gothenburg.

Brenner, J. (1986) 'Textile Producers and Production in Late Seventeenth-Century Coromandel'. *Indian Economic and Social History Review*, 23.

Brandt, L. (1989) *Commercialization and Agricultural Development: Central and Eastern China, 1870–1937*. Cambridge: Cambridge University Press.

Buck, J. L. (1937) *Land Utilization in China*. Nanking: University of Nanking.

Chaudhuri, K. N. (1978) *The Trading World of Asia and the English East India Company, 1660–1760*. Cambridge: Cambridge University Press.

Chaudhuri, S. (1977) *Trade and Commercial Organization in Bengal, 1650–1720*. Calcutta: Firma K. L. Mukhapadhyay.

Coleman, D. C. (1983) 'Proto-industrialization: A Concept Too Many'. *Economic History Review*, 2nd series, 36(3): 435–48.

Crawcour, E. S. and Yamamura, K. (1970) 'Tokugawa Monetary System: 1789–1868'. *Economic Development and Cultural Change*, 18(4), part 1: 489–518.

Desai, A. V. (1972) 'Population and Standards of Living in Akbar's Time'. *Indian Economic and Social History Review*, 9: 43–62.

——(1978) 'Population and Standards of Living in Akbar's Time—A Second Look'. *Indian Economic and Social History Review*, 14: 53–80.

Doria, G. (1968) *Uomini e terre di un borgo collinare dal XVI al XVIII secola*. Milan: Dott. A. Giuffrè editore.

Habib, I. (1963) *Agrarian System of Mughal India*. Bombay: Asia Publishing House.

——(1982) 'Monetary Systems and Prices', in T. Raychaudhuri and I. Habib (eds.), *Cambridge Economic History of India*, Vol. I, c.1200–c.1750. Cambridge: Cambridge University Press, pp. 360–81.

Hasan, A. (1969) 'The Silver Currency Output of the Mughal Empire and Prices in India during the 16th and 17th Centuries'. *Indian Economic and Social History Review*, 4: 85–116.

Heston, A. W. (1977) 'The Standard of Living in Akbar's Time—A Comment'. *Indian Economic and Social History Review*, 14: 391–6.

Li, Bozhong (1998) *Agricultural Development in Lianging, 1620–1850*. Houndmills, Basingstoke, Hampshire: Macmillan Press.

Minami, R. (1986) *The Economic Development of Japan: A Quantitative Study*. New York: St. Martin's Press, Inc.

Moosvi, S. (1973) 'Production, Consumption, and Population in Akbar's Time'. *Indian Economic and Social History Review*, 10: 181–95.

——(1977) 'Note on Professor Alan Heston's "Standard of Living in Akbar's Time—A Comment"'. *Indian Economic and Social History Review*, 14: 397–401.

Moreland, W. H. (1962) *India at the Death of Akbar*. Delhi: Atma Ram and Sons.

Mukerjee, R. (1976) *The Economic History of India, 1600–1800*. Allalabad: Kitab Mahal.

Ohkawa, K. *et al.* (1967) *Estimates of Long-Term Economic Statistics of Japan since 1868, Prices*, Vol. 8. Tokyo: Toyo Keizai Shinposha.

Phelps Brown, E. H. and Hopkins, S. V. (1955) 'Seven Centuries of Building Wages'. *Economica*, 22: 195–206.

Pomeranz, K. (2000) *The Great Divergence: Europe, China, and the Making of the Modern World Economy*. Princeton, NJ: Princeton University Press.

Parthasarathi, P. (1998) 'Rethinking Wages and Competitiveness in the Eighteenth Century: Britain and South India'. *Past and Present*, 158: 79–109.

Prakash, O. (1985) *The Dutch East India Company and the Economy of Bengal, 1630–1720*. Princeton, NJ: Princeton University Press.

Saito, O. (1978) 'The Labor Market in Tokugawa Japan: Wage Differentials and the Real Wage Level, 1727–1830'. *Explorations in Economic History*, 15: 84–100.

van Santen, H. (1982) *De Verenigde Oost Indishe Compagnie in Gujarat en Hindustan, 1620–1660*. Leiden: Meppel.

Williamson, J. G. (1998) 'Appendix to Real Wages and Relative Factor Prices in the Third World, 1820–1940'. *Harvard Institute for Economics Research*, 1844. Available on the website at http://post.economics.harvard.edu/faculty/jwilliam/papers/1844text.pdf (June 2004).

6 Sketching the Rise of Real Inequality in Early Modern Europe

PHILIP T. HOFFMAN, DAVID S. JACKS, PATRICIA A. LEVIN, AND PETER H. LINDERT

1. Introduction

The life styles of the rich, the poor, and the middle-income ranks involve consuming very different bundles of goods and services. By definition, staples (necessities) are a large share of what the poor consume, and luxuries are a higher share of what the rich consume, generation after generation. Any strong historical trend towards making staples more expensive relative to luxuries should widen the inequalities in real living standards.

Yet our explorations of inequality trends in the past have missed this point. We have been content to trace the history of economic inequality around trends in the conventional shares of income or wealth in current prices, without noticing what the movements of relative prices implied about inequality.[1] This chapter uses tentative estimates to support these conjectural conclusions:

1. Before 1914, and especially before 1815, movements in inequality within and between European nations were more pronounced than have been appreciated. Introducing the concept of real, as opposed to nominal or conventional, income inequality reveals these pronounced inequality movements because relative prices happened to move very differently for the poor and the rich before 1914.
2. Between 1500 and 1790–1815 the prices of staple foods rose much more than the prices of what the rich consumed. This greatly magnified the rise in real-income inequality because in those days the poor and the rich depended more heavily on buying factor services from each other than is true today. The poor needed land-intensive food and housing, and land was owned and rented out by the rich. The rich, in turn, hired servants much more than today, so that the fall in workers' real wages became a fall in the cost of living an affluent lifestyle.
3. The opposite happened between 1815 and 1914, for two main reasons. One is that real wages rose, and servants became more expensive and less common. The other is that globalization cut Europe's price of food relative to other goods and services.

We begin with some basic issues of early modern historiography, emphasizing some contradictions and puzzles that a concept of real-income inequality can help to resolve.

2. Rethinking Early Modern Inequality

Two promising but difficult paths are leading towards a new appreciation of the rise of global inequality in living standards from the early sixteenth through the early nineteenth centuries. One path explores the great global divergence in the average living standards of countries and continents, while the other explores economic inequality within societies. Global divergence between countries appears to have emerged within Europe in this era, and much of western Europe began to pull ahead of Asia in the late eighteenth and early nineteenth centuries. Inequality within the nations of Europe may also have been rising (van Zanden 1995; Pomeranz 2000; Allen 2001).

Neither path is easy to clear in a pre-statistical era, but both are leading towards a new history of inequality. In this new history, the highly unequal world of the early nineteenth century was neither inherited from an ancient feudal order nor created by the Industrial Revolution. Rather, both paths are leading us towards the suspicion that humans were not yet as starkly unequal when Vasco de Gama and Columbus set sail as their descendants were to become in the early nineteenth century.

A concept of real, as opposed to nominal or conventional, inequality in human living standards will help us make progress along both paths. Using such a concept suggests that on balance, the long era from about 1500 to the 1820s was indeed an era of rising global inequality, like the era since the 1820s.[2] To clear the way for this suggestion, a first step is to overhaul the conventional measurements of the gaps between nations' average real incomes.

Measures of early income inequality between nations may have been particularly distorted by the working-class bias in our comparative studies. Driven by social concerns and a partial data base, we have concentrated too much on comparing the abilities of ordinary workers to buy ordinary food. This leads to an anomaly: in the very era where we suspect that western Europe is starting to pull ahead of eastern Europe and Asia, our only measures—those conventional food-wage measures— imply that western Europe was actually *declining*, except in Amsterdam and southern England for certain periods. If so, it must have been the rise of western Europe's middle and upper classes that pulled the region's product per capita far ahead of the rest of the world before the 1820s.

As this conjecture implies, inequality *within* the nations of western Europe has risen greatly. In fact, the real gaps have widened even more greatly than the widening of nominal income gaps can reveal. The magnified swings in real inequality were caused by the interaction of population growth with concentrated land ownership and Engel's law. Concentrated land ownership and Engel's law together meant that the poor and the rich depended greatly on each other's factor services. Population growth, by supplying more labour, tipped the terms of inter-class trade against workers, who needed more land-intensive food. This combination was broken up by the French Revolution and by globalization in the nineteenth century.

3. First Things First: Differences in Early Modern Life Expectancy

The concept of living standards that most scholars will rightly favour is the broad one of lifetime resources, not resources per hour or per year. Even if one's view were confined to a monetized measure of a person's free time plus consumption of goods and services, an inquiry into living standards must start from the length of life itself—especially for early settings, in which food scarcity meant shorter life.[3]

What little we know about inequalities in the length of life before the early nineteenth century serves to preview what we will find about inequalities in real incomes. On the one hand, comparing national average life expectancies across Europe or around the globe is extremely difficult, and we cannot say much about systematic inequalities. The available estimates signal a possible global rise in life expectancies dating from the seventeenth century, but with no clear change between national average lengths of life. On the other, looking within nations, we can detect a widening of inequalities, in this case within western European countries in the eighteenth century.

Direct estimates of national average life expectancy before the mid-nineteenth century are concentrated in the seven countries whose experience is summarized in Table 6.1 and Figure 6.1. The advance of English life expectancy as mapped by the Cambridge Group for the History of Population and Social Structure makes the best baseline for comparison with other groups and nations. That English series showed some improvement in life expectancy from the mid-sixteenth century to the early seventeenth, then a century of retreat to the old mortality, and finally a sustained rise after the mid-eighteenth century. The improvement after the mid-eighteenth century looks stronger and certain in writings since the original estimates were presented in the path-breaking Wrigley–Schofield volume in 1981. The Cambridge Group's new reconstitution volume seems to show a stronger rise after 1750, in line with the suggestions raised by Razzell and others (Razzell 1994, 1998, 1999, forthcoming; Wrigley *et al.* 1997).

No other national population represented in Table 6.1 and Figure 6.1 seems to have lived longer than the English did. Even around 1750, at the start of the great lengthening of English life, only the estimates for Sweden seemed to match the English,[4] and Sweden fell behind thereafter. As for China, a central interest in this volume, we have two straws in the wind. On the one hand, the available quantitative estimates like those for Beijing men in Table 6.1 and Figure 6.1 show shorter life spans in a few Chinese localities. On the other, Pomeranz has argued that we really cannot tell that Chinese populations died younger than Europeans (Pomeranz 2000: chapter 1).

Table 6.1 Estimates of life expectancy at birth for various places and classes, 1500–1850

Nation	Place	Socio-economic classes	Time period or approx. year	Life expectancy at birth (E_0)[a]			Source and comments
				Males	Females	Both	
Belgium	Sart	All	1811–45	—	—	39.4	Oris, Alter, and Neven (in this volume Chapter 15)
China	Anhui	All	1300–1800	31.0	26.0	28.6	Lee and Wang (1999: 54–5)
China	Beijing	All, urban	1644–1739	27.2	24.6	25.9	Lee and Wang (1999: 54–5)
China	Beijing	All, urban	1740–1839	33.6	—	—	Lee and Wang (1999: 54–5)
China	Beijing	All, urban	1840–99	34.7	—	—	Lee and Wang (1999: 54–5)
Denmark	Nation	All	1780–9	34.0	35.9	34.9	Andersen (1984: 125)
Denmark	Nation	All	1790–9	39.4	41.5	40.4	Andersen (1984: 125)
Denmark	Nation	All	1800–9	40.4	43.3	41.8	Andersen (1984: 125)
Denmark	Nation	All	1810–19	40.8	43.6	42.1	Andersen (1984: 125)
Denmark	Nation	All	1820–9	40.0	41.9	40.9	Andersen (1984: 125)
Denmark	Nation	All	1830–9	36.4	38.3	37.3	Andersen (1984: 125)
Denmark	Nation	All	1840–9	43.0	45.2	44.1	Andersen (1984: 125)
France	Nation	All	1740–9	23.8	25.7	24.7	Bideau et al. (1988: 236)
France	Nation	All	1750–9	27.1	28.7	27.9	Bideau et al. (1988: 236)
France	Nation	All	1760–9	26.4	29.0	27.7	Bideau et al. (1988: 236)
France	Nation	All	1770–9	28.2	29.6	28.9	Bideau et al. (1988: 236)
France	Nation	All	1780–9	27.5	28.1	27.8	Bideau et al. (1988: 236)
France	Nation	All	1790–9	—	32.1	—	Blayo, as cited in Bengtsson et al. (1984: 49)
France	Nation	All	1800–9	—	34.9	—	Blayo, as cited in Bengtsson et al. (1984: 49)
France	Nation	All	1810–19	—	37.5	—	Blayo, as cited in Bengtsson et al. (1984: 49)
France	Nation	All	1820–9	—	39.3	—	Blayo, as cited in Bengtsson et al. (1984: 49)
France	Nation	All	1831–40	—	39.9	—	Van de Walle, as cited in Bengtsson et al. (1984: 49)

Country	Region	Category	Period				Source
France	Nation	All	1841–50	—	41.6	—	Van de Walle, as cited in Bengtsson et al. (1984: 49)
Germany	(?)		1750–9	—	—	36.4	Perrenoud (1997)
Prussia	Blüthen	All	1765–1800	28.4	36.7	32.6	Hagen (2002: chap. 4)
Sweden	Nation	All	1751–60	—	38.3	—	Perrenoud (1997)
Sweden	Nation	All	1761–70	—	44.3	—	Perrenoud, in Bengtsson et al. (1984: 49)
Sweden	Nation	All	1771–80	—	35.0	—	Perrenoud, in Bengtsson et al. (1984: 49)
Sweden	Nation	All	1781–90	—	36.8	—	Perrenoud, in Bengtsson et al. (1984: 49)
Sweden	Nation	All	1791–1800	—	40.1	—	Perrenoud, in Bengtsson et al. (1984: 49)
Sweden	Nation	All	1801–10	—	37.5	—	Perrenoud, in Bengtsson et al. (1984: 49)
Sweden	Nation	All	1811–20	—	40.1	—	Perrenoud, in Bengtsson et al. (1984: 49)
Sweden	Nation	All	1821–30	—	43.8	—	Perrenoud, in Bengtsson et al. (1984: 49)
Sweden	Nation	All	1831–40	—	43.7	—	Perrenoud, in Bengtsson et al. (1984: 49)
Sweden	Nation	All	1841–50	—	46.0	—	Perrenoud, in Bengtsson et al. (1984: 49)
Sweden, Scania	4 parishes	All	1765–1815	36.2	35.1	35.7	Bengtsson and Dribe (1997: Table 2.1)
Sweden, Scania	4 parishes	All	1815–65	40.2	41.2	40.7	Bengtsson and Dribe (1997: Table 2.1)
Switzerland	Glaris	All	1751–60	—	—	32.6	Perrenoud (1997)
Switzerland	Geneva	All, urban	1625–49	—	—	23.6	Perrenoud, in Bengtsson et al. (1984: 49)
Switzerland	Geneva	All, urban	1650–74	—	—	25.7	Perrenoud, in Bengtsson et al. (1984: 49)
Switzerland	Geneva	All, urban	1675–99	—	—	27.1	Perrenoud, in Bengtsson et al. (1984: 49)
Switzerland	Geneva	All, urban	1700–24	—	—	28.3	Perrenoud, in Bengtsson et al. (1984: 49)
Switzerland	Geneva	All, urban	1725–44	—	—	33.8	Perrenoud, in Bengtsson et al. (1984: 49)
Switzerland	Geneva	All, urban	1745–69	—	—	34.0	Perrenoud, in Bengtsson et al. (1984: 49)
Switzerland	Geneva	All, urban	1770–90	—	—	33.2	Perrenoud, in Bengtsson et al. (1984: 49)
Switzerland	Geneva	All, urban	1800–25	—	—	39.7	Perrenoud, in Bengtsson et al. (1984: 49)
UK	England	All	1550–74	—	—	34.5	Wrigley and Schofield (1981: table A3.1)
UK	England	All	1575–99	—	—	38.7	Wrigley and Schofield (1981: table A3.1)
UK	England	All	1600–24	—	—	39.1	Wrigley et al. (1997: 295)
UK	England	All	1625–49	38.7	37.6	38.2	Wrigley et al. (1997: 295)
UK	England	All	1650–74	38.1	36.3	37.2	Wrigley et al. (1997: 295)

Table 6.1 (Continued)

Nation	Place	Socio-economic classes	Time period or approx. year	Life expectancy at birth (E_0)[a]			Source and comments
				Males	Females	Both	
UK	England	All	1675–99	35.4	35.4	35.4	Wrigley et al. (1997: 295)
UK	England	All	1700–24	36.6	36.8	36.7	Wrigley et al. (1997: 295)
UK	England	All	1725–49	35.8	37.4	36.6	Wrigley et al. (1997: 295)
UK	England	All	1750–74	40.7	40.0	40.4	Wrigley et al. (1997: 295)
UK	England	All	1775–99	40.8	39.5	40.2	Wrigley et al. (1997: 295)
UK	England	All	1800–9	—	—	44.8	Wrigley et al. (1997: 295)
UK	Britain	Peers	1550–74	37.8	38.2	38.0	Hollingsworth (1977: birth cohorts)
UK	Britain	Peers	1575–99	36.0	38.3	37.1	Hollingsworth (1977: birth cohorts)
UK	Britain	Peers	1600–24	33.6	35.9	34.7	Hollingsworth (1977: birth cohorts)
UK	Britain	Peers	1625–49	31.7	34.2	32.9	Hollingsworth (1977: birth cohorts)
UK	Britain	Peers	1650–74	30.0	33.7	31.8	Hollingsworth (1977: birth cohorts)
UK	Britain	Peers	1675–99	33.2	35.3	34.2	Hollingsworth (1977: birth cohorts)
UK	Britain	Peers	1700–24	34.9	37.5	36.2	Hollingsworth (1977: birth cohorts)
UK	Britain	Peers	1725–49	38.8	37.4	38.1	Hollingsworth (1977: birth cohorts)
UK	Britain	Peers	1750–74	44.6	45.9	45.2	Hollingsworth (1977: birth cohorts)
UK	Britain	Peers	1775–99	46.9	49.2	48.0	Hollingsworth (1977: birth cohorts)
UK	Britain	Peers	1800–24	49.3	51.9	50.5	Hollingsworth (1977: birth cohorts)
UK	Britain	Peers	1825–49	52.2	58.4	55.2	Hollingsworth (1977: birth cohorts)
Europe		Ruling families	1500–99	32.1	36.0	34.0	Peller (1965: 98)
Europe		Ruling families	1600–99	28.1	33.7	30.8	Peller (1965: 98)
Europe		Ruling families	1700–99	36.1	38.2	37.1	Peller (1965: 98)
Europe		Ruling families	1800–49	45.9	48.1	47.0	Peller (1965: 98)

[a] The expectancy for both sexes is calculated as $(0.516$ male $E_0) + (0.484$ female $E_0)$ in most cases here.

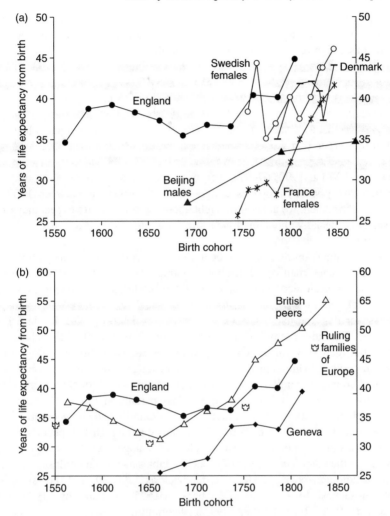

Figure 6.1 Life expectancy at birth, 1500–1850

Any comparisons beyond the few countries in Table 6.1 and Figure 6.1 are covered in statistical darkness. For any country outside of western Europe, and for many within western Europe, we still do not know how mortality changed. Thus, Pomeranz's valid doubt about shorter life spans in China rests on the scarcity of data.

To get an indirect sense of how mortality compared across countries and regions, some have tried to supplement direct estimates of national average life expectancy with indirect reasoning based on the rate of population growth. That rate must equal the crude birth rate plus the immigration rate minus the crude death rate. If we know that some other regions had faster population growth than western Europe without having higher birth rates or more net immigration, then they must have had lower death rates. If this contrast continued for a century or longer, one could use the lower death rate as a sign of lower age-adjusted mortality.

As it happens, some areas did have faster population growth than England or western Europe as a whole between 1500 and 1800. China's population grew as fast as England's, and faster than that of western Europe (McEvedy and Jones 1978; Wrigley *et al.* 1997; Lee and Wang 1999). So did the population of Russia. Asia as a whole grew as fast as western Europe as a whole. In the case of China, at least, one could further argue that the total fertility rate was not higher than in Europe, suggesting that its faster population growth must have owed something to a lower death rate (Lee and Wang 1999: 67–99). Yet, even this inference requires assumptions about how many west Europeans emigrated to the Americas between 1500 and 1800. In general, then, we are still in doubt about the superior life expectancy of the English, and especially about any longer life for western Europe as a whole, for any time before 1800.

Looking within countries, one can be a little more certain about inequality trends in life expectancies than one can about contrasts between national averages. In general, the top socio-economic classes and their children lived longer after 1750. Genealogical studies show us that the British peers' family members began surviving longer than the national average by 1750 or a little earlier (Table 6.1 and Figure 6.1). The ruling families of Europe did not fare as well as British peerage families, but their survival did catch up with the English national average in the eighteenth century, which apparently gave them longer life than the averages for continental countries. Similarly, the eighteenth century also brought better survival chances for infants of middle- and upper-class parents in England, France, and Geneva. Before *c.*1750, being born into a top-class family had an uncertain average effect on longevity. A child born to a high family among British peers, or in the ruling families of Europe, did not have a clear advantage over the average English newborn. On the other hand, wives of French notables had better adult survival rates than local commoners had, at least as far back as 1700–39, and the families of notables in Geneva lived longer as far back as 1625–44 (Perrenoud 1975, 1997; Bideau *et al.* 1988; Razzell 1998, 1999, forthcoming).

Thus within the nations of western Europe, the reigning suggestion—or guess—is that life spans were correlated with socio-economic class after 1750, or perhaps earlier.[5] This correlation suggests that inequality was at least as great across the major income classes over their whole lifetimes as it was in annual income terms, starting around 1750 or earlier.

4. Whose Real Income? Whose Cost of Living? What Prices?

The rise in income inequality in the latter half of the eighteenth century was probably the second of two great widenings of intra-national income inequality in the early modern era, the earlier one coming between 1500 and the 1640s (or 1650).

To see the likelihood of these two great widenings, we need to start with differences in consumption styles and how they interacted with the remarkable swings in relative prices between 1500 and the 1820s.

The fact that the rich and the poor consume very different things means that movements in relative prices can affect them very differently. The same may be true of rich versus poor nations. Historians of the sixteenth through eighteenth centuries have misinterpreted differences in early modern living standards by overlooking the effects of income–class contrasts in lifestyles on real-income differences between regions and on inequality trends within nations.

A first step towards giving this point its due is taken in Table 6.2's overview of class differences in expenditure patterns. Note how much more familiar are the working-class contexts at the top of each panel than the middle- and upper-class contexts that follow. In expenditure studies, as in studies of income and prices, scholars have fixed their attention on the working class and the poor. We are accustomed to historical household budgets that are spent mostly on food. Even as late as the eve of World War I, Britain's cost of living was still tracked by an index giving 60% weight to food, when food was actually just 27% of consumer expenditures (Bowley 1921: 67; Feinstein 1972: T61). The food share of working-class budgets has always exceeded the national average, which in turn exceeded food's share of consumption by the middle- and upper-income groups, who spend more on servants, clothing, and miscellaneous luxuries. That income-class contrast gave rise to Engel's law in the nineteenth century.[6]

Engel's law works over time and across nations as well. Over time, any improvements in national income per capita cut the share spent on food. Our early mostly-food household budgets, like those from England's poor in 1787–96, come from a setting where food had already dropped below half of national expenditure. Across nations, too, the higher the average income, the lower the share spent on food.

The contrasts in what people consumed mean that any comparisons in real purchasing power depend on which prices are used. The choice matters greatly. The early modern world had greater spatial and temporal variations in relative prices than any seen in the twentieth century, at least until the two oil shocks of 1973 and later. Yet the received price history of the early modern era uses a biased set of prices, following a few series out of proportion to their shares of expenditures. Specifically, that history has these biases

Overusing the prices of	Underusing the prices of
staple products, especially food	luxuries
standardized older products	new products
international traded goods	non-traded products
wholesale products	retail products
physical goods	services
products intensively using land, natural resources, and capital	products intensive in labour, both unskilled and skilled

Table 6.2 Selected household percentage shares of total expenditure, 1500–1832

	Bread	Other grain	Meat, fish, etc.	Dairy	Drink & sugar	All food & drink	Fuel & light	Clothing	Rent	Servants	Other	Total
Panel A: England-Wales												
Workers and the poor												
Bottom 40%, 1688 (King-Stone 1988)	8.5	21.3	6.7	11.2	5.2	59.7	6.3	15.9	13.8	0.0	4.3	100.0
Phelps Brown and Hopkins (1981)	5.7	14.3	25.0	12.5	22.5	80.0	7.5	12.5	—	0.0	—	100.0
Poor in 1787/96 (Davies 1795; Eden 1797)	14.2	35.3	12.7	5.0	5.0	72.1	7.3	6.4	14.2	0.0	—	100.0
Workers 1788/92 (Feinstein 1998)	13.8	31.1	9.0	8.3	16.9	79.0	5.0	6.0	10.0	0.0	—	100.0
Workers 1828/32 (Feinstein 1998)	16.3	22.8	10.4	9.1	17.5	76.0	5.0	8.0	11.0	0.0	—	100.0
Middle and upper classes												
Sarah Fell, 1675–6	—	—	—	—	—	29.3	8.8	8.0	14.2	10.6	29.1	100.0
Rachael Pengelly, 1694–9	—	'staples' = 23.7		—	14.6	39.9	13.6	9.8	12.6	7.0	17.1	100.0
Gregory King, Esq. c.1695	—	—	—	—	—	39.0	3.4	19.5	11.5	8.6	18.1	100.0
In 1688 (King-Stone 1988)												
Middle income household	4.8	11.9	7.6	6.9	6.9	43.4	5.7	19.3	21.6	0.0	10.0	100.0
Households; top 20%	1.6	4.0	8.3	4.1	8.5	31.5	3.4	20.6	9.7	10.1	24.7	100.0
Households; top 10%	1.3	3.3	7.8	3.8	7.8	28.9	3.3	19.6	9.6	12.9	25.7	100.0
Households; top 5%	1.0	2.4	7.4	3.5	7.0	25.9	3.2	19.0	10.4	13.5	27.9	100.0
National expenditures, 1688	4.5	11.4	10.2	7.5	9.8	50.4	—	23.5	—	—	26.1	100.0

Panel B: France

	Bread	Other grain	Salt & spices	Meat, fish, etc.	Dairy	Drink & sugar	All food & drink	Fuel & light	Rent	Clothing	Servants	Other
Workers and the poor												
Rural worker 1832	49.0	—	—	14.7	—	5.9	69.6	1.6	6.5	16.1	0.0	6.2
Urban worker 1832	34.5	—	—	21.2	—	10.6	66.4	4.7	5.8	16.3	0.0	6.9
Urban artisan c.1700	23.3	—	—	20.9	11.6	27.9	83.7	—	—	—	0.0	—
Rural worker 1763	30.8	—	—	15.4	—	15.4	61.6	11.0	8.4	14.9	0.0	4.1
Urban worker, Abbeville 1764	23.1	5.4	8.0	7.4	13.0	—	56.8	12.8	7.2	16.8	0.0	6.4
Strasbourg 1745/54 (Allen 2001)	21.9	6.0	—	14.0	9.3	20.8	72.0	20.9	—	5.3	—	1.8
Duc de Saulx-Tavanes, 1788	0.7	1.0	—	5.3	1.8	4.1	13.3	6.7	13.7	36.9	21.1	8.3
Rural noble 1410, (i)	7.7	—	0.4	9.0	3.1	14.8	35.0	—	—	—	—	—
Rural noble 1410, (ii)	2.9	—	0.1	3.4	1.2	5.6	13.3	—	—	—	—	—
Parisian bourgeois family, 1880–1919	5.0	2.9	—	22.8	14.1	16.1	12.7	1.1	2.9	3.8	1.8	16.8
Parisian bourgeois family, 1920–39	4.2	2.7	—	25.6	15.1	12.5	17.9	0.9	2.2	3.1	1.5	14.3
Parisian bourgeois family, 1938–54	3.0	2.5	—	27.0	14.9	8.7	20.0	0.9	1.9	3.2	1.0	16.7

Composition of gross national product (PIB)

	Food and agriculture	Industry, excl. food	Services
France, 1781–90 (Toutain 1987: 56, 61)	49.1	28.8	22.2

Table 6.2 (Continued)

	Bread	Other grain	Meat, fish, etc.	Dairy	Drink & sugar	All food & drink	Fuel & light	Clothing	Rent	Consumer services	Other	Total
Panel C: The Netherlands												
Holland labourer, 15th century	40.0	—	15.0	5.0	10.0	75.0	7.0	9.0	7.0	0.0	2.0	100.0
Holland labourer, 18th century	30.0	—	5.0	5.0	5.0	60.0	11.0	15.0	11.0	0.0	3.0	100.0
The Netherlands elite, 1800/52	22.1	—	5.2	5.9	4.1	60.8	8.9	15.4	11.4	0.0	3.5	100.0
The Netherlands elite, 1806/62	16.0	—	12.0	9.0	9.0	56.0	1.0	10.0	7.0	8.0	18.0	100.0

	Bread	Other grain	Meat, fish, etc.	Dairy	Drink & sugar	All food & drink	Fuel & light	Clothing	Rent	Servants	Other	Total
Panel D: Other nations												
Antwerp, mason's family, 1596–1600	49.4	—	—	22.6	—	78.5	6.0	10.1	5.4	—	—	100.0
Berlin, mason's family, c.1800	44.2	—	—	14.9	2.1	72.7	6.8	6.1	14.4	—	—	100.0
Germany (Palatinate) 1500–1700	—	36.0	11.0	9.0	6.0	68.0	8.0	12.0	8.0	—	4.0	100.0
Milan, typical family, 1801	13.9	10.4	—	16.3	—	70.1	3.8	12.0	4.1	—	10.0	100.0
Spain, 16th century	—	20.0	23.5	—	10.0	60.5	5.0	4.5	—	—	30.0	100.0

Notes and sources: Here 0.0 is believed to be zero, and — implies the sum is either excluded or implicit in some other category. All estimates appear to exclude tax payments.

Panel A: England-Wales
The 1675–6 expenditures of Sarah Fell, widow of Swarthmore Hall, are based on the summary in Wetherill (1988: 128–36). We have adjusted Wetherill's summary of Fell's expenditures to exclude farm and livestock production, and to include the equivalent rental cost of occupied housing. The rental value of housing should have

been more than she paid in rent, since she owned her main residence. To estimate the full value of housing she and her family occupied, we have used a 14.2% share close to the share of all housing in Gregory King's version of GDP. (Her annual expenditures were nearly twice the national average income of £39.18 per family in 1688, putting her in the 'middle-class' range.)

Rachael Pengelly of Finchley, 1694–9: We start again from Wetherill (1988: 123–8, 133), preferring the period of rapid turnover in the composition of Rachael's household up through 1699, instead of the period of apparently incomplete records (1700–9). We make the same adjustments as in Sarah Fell's case, but accept the sizeable rent payments as the full value of the occupied housing. Her annual household expenditures of £89 were more than twice the national average per family in 1688 (£39.18).

Gregory King's own household accounts for himself, wife, clerk, servant maid, and boy, London 1695, are from Laslett (1973: introduction and p. 250). Like Laslett, we trusted King's detail by person rather than his faulty addition to get totals. We added £24.51 rent, based on his London residence and Esquire status (Laslett 1973: 201, 246). We get a non-tax expenditure of £174.575 for him. We interpret the maid's pay as only her stated wage of £15, not this plus her £13.375 part of the household's itemized expenses.

The weights for the bottom 40%, middle-income, top 20%, top 10%, and top 5% income groups' average consumption patterns, start from Gregory King's notebooks, with extensions by R. Stone (1988). They have been modified further here, first by separating bread from other farinaceous, then by adding rents and servant pay, and by deducting an estimate of fuel and light expenditures from the all-other category. Then, the overall grains category was divided into 2/7 bread and 5/7 other grains, a division suggested by the Davies (1795) and Eden (1797) samples of 1787–96. This division applies to all indices shown in this table. The total expenditures used in the underlying estimates here are the King-Stone expenditure sums for each income class plus our separate estimate of rents and servant pay. These differ from the total expenditures in King's famous social table, with the Lindert-Williamson revisions, largely because King's expenditure detail differed from the total expenditures in his main table.

The domestic service expenditures in England-Wales in 1688 are estimated as described in the working paper version of this chapter, see Hoffman et al. (2000: Appendix A, Part C).

Following the established convention, all these consumer price index estimates exclude taxes and savings. The total for all food and drink includes expenditures not detailed here, especially for fruits and vegetables and spices.

Panel B: France

Urban artisan (and family), c.1700 is from Morineau (1985: 236).

Rural worker 1763 = colon aunisien 1763, from Morineau (1985: 214–17).

Urban worker, Abbeville, 1764, from Morineau (1985: 218–19). Since budget leaves family with a surplus but no expenditures for clothing, the present calculations assume that half of the surplus is saved and the rest spent on clothing.

Duc de Saulx-Tavanes 1788: The calculations, (i) add 12 times January 1784 expenditures for speciality foods to a 5000 livre annual budget for basic foods (Forster 1971: 121), and (ii) assume that basic food is broken down as for top 5% in England.

Rural noble 1410, (i) = Guillaume de Murol, noble in Auvergne, from Charbonnier (1980: Vol. 1, 128–33). The accounts give food expense only; the present calculation assumes a 35% total food expenditure share.

Rural noble 1410, (ii) is the same as with (i), but assuming 13.3% total food expenditure.

Paris bourgeois family shares are from Singer-Kérel (1961).

Table 6.2   (*footnote continued*)

Panel C: The Netherlands

The total for food and drink includes expenditures for potatoes, peas, and other vegetables not listed separately.

The 'other' category includes soap and 'other (industrial)'.

The source is van Zanden (2000).

Panel D: Other nations

The Antwerp mason's family-of-five expenditures are the Scholliers estimates cited in Abel (1973: 199). Clothing includes miscellaneous (divers) expenditures. The total for food and drink includes dried beans, but no drink. Abel (1973: 342) also supplied the estimates for the Berlin mason's family of five, for which clothing again includes miscellaneous, and the total for food and drink includes 11.5% for other products of vegetable origin.

The source for the Palatinate is Phelps Brown and Hopkins (1959: 28) and that for 16th-century Spain is Hamilton (1934: 276).

The source for Milan 1801 is De Maddalena (1974: 253–4, 330).

There are two good reasons for our biased choices. One reason is that we care more about some categories in the first group, particularly life-sustaining staples and the traded goods over which nations went to war. The other reason is that the prices listed on the left are more available. The price series that are most available for constant product definitions over many decades are those for standardized staples in wholesale trade. Yet the more elusive prices listed on the right must get a larger share of our attention if our historical numbers are to reflect the realities of early modern inequality.

5. Revising the International Divergence of Real Incomes, 1500–1820s

The usual biases in our scholarly search have distorted our view of international differences in average income in three ways. First, using common wage rates as proxies for national income per person has hidden the contribution of property-income growth to the overall rise of national income. Second, focusing on food prices has probably hidden part of the west European rise of real income per person for the long periods 1500–1640s and 1740s–1800s, since food prices rose dramatically relative to other prices. Third, perhaps a PPP (Purchasing Power Parity) bias in international price comparisons has overstated the levels, rather than the trends, of international real-income differences, as has happened consistently in the second half of the twentieth century.

Recent work by Jan Luiten van Zanden and Robert Allen has already supported this third point about PPP bias in the sixteenth through eighteenth centuries (van Zanden 1999; Allen 2001, 2003). Comparing the prices of grain and a few other products across regions and nations, they find that prices are higher where wages are higher, when both are measured in silver. Here is an initial sense in which international comparisons of incomes, in this case the daily wage in grams of silver, may overstate early modern differences in real purchasing power. A deeper exploration of PPP bias in comparing levels of income or consumption will require gathering data on more goods and services, including many non-tradables, and converting them into grams of silver per modern metric unit. Pursuing this third kind of bias must await a laborious comparison of archaic units of measurement from across Europe and around the world. Here we can only make the first two points, those relating to the overemphasis on ordinary workers' wages and on food prices.

5.1 Workers versus nations

It is a simple point. As long as we continue to draw our living-standards data from the poor and from ordinary workers, we are unlikely to find any real-income advantage of living in western Europe before the 1820s. The food consumption and clothing and availability of warmth will look no greater than in Poland or in China. Such an impression is reinforced by the apparent decline in real wages in western

Europe from the sixteenth through the eighteenth centuries.[7] There is the danger of thinking that the global divergence of real incomes dating from the 1820s[8] was something new in world economic history, when it is more likely that western Europe began pulling away in the mid-eighteenth century or even earlier. What most international comparisons have missed is the unmistakable rise of property incomes from the mid-eighteenth century on, and in some cases from 1500 on. When prosperity in the upper part of society is combined with the stagnation or decline in real wages, the net result will be a greater apparent rise in real national income per person in western Europe than elsewhere before the nineteenth century. The possible magnitude of this adjustment will be sketched when we come to the real inequality trends within England, France, and Holland.

5.2   Cheaper luxuries, greater divergence between nations

A second point about income–class differences in spending patterns also suggests that we may have understated the rise in global inequality before the 1820s. It is very likely that luxury goods became cheaper relative to staple foods over most of the period from 1500 to 1820. Part of the cheapening took the form of consumer gains from new luxury goods. This early modern phenomenon is well known (van der Woude and Schuurman 1980; Wetherill 1988; Shammas 1990; Brewer and Porter 1993; Jardine 1996). Yet its importance for real incomes is as hard to quantify for that period as it is for officials trying to introduce new goods and services into today's cost-of-living indices.[9] In fact, for fashion goods, luxuries are *intended* to change constantly, frustrating our search for consistent time series.

How can the role of new goods be quantified? There is much that can be done by working from both ends of this stretch of the path. Quantitative social historians can continue estimating the values of new consumer durables from probate inventories and other archival documents. Economists can apply new developments in index-number theory that allow us to put bounds on the consumer welfare gains from the arrival of new goods.[10] While the ultimate magnitudes of the welfare gains from new goods are unknown, they presumably helped the rich more than they helped the poor.

New goods aside, the available time series on the prices of a few older goods and services show that the prices of necessities generally rose faster than the prices of other goods and services between the early sixteenth and the late eighteenth centuries. Drawing on the International Price History Project of the interwar years, one can follow the price trends of a dozen major non-staple products of consumption from 1500 or earlier through 1790 or later in a few dozen European cities and regions. We have summarized the trends in relative or 'real' prices of non-staples, relative to a food grain or bread, in Table 6.3 and Figure 6.2, with fuller detail in Table 6.4. The common denominator in all these relative-price series is a staple food-grain item. The price of bread, a true consumer good, is available to play this role for regions in three leading countries, but in most cases one must use a grain price as if it were a food price.

Table 6.3 The product pattern in price movements relative to the prices of bread or grains, European cities and regions, 1500–1790

	Product	Cities or regions	Median real-price change relative to bread or grains, c.1500–c.1790
The greatest real-price rises	Cinnamon	S. England, Holland, New Castile	+70% (1600–1790)
	Housing rents	England, Paris, Holland	+40%
Possibly rising slightly relative to breads and grains	Fuels	16 Cities or regions	+14%
About the same trend as bread and grains	Soap	5 Cities or regions	−1%
	Wines	7 Cities or regions	−3%
	Candles	W. Brabant, Edinburgh	−6%
	Meats	7 Cities or regions	−11%
Definite real-price drops relative to bread and grains	Unskilled labour	13 Cities or regions	−37%
	Paper	8 Cities or regions	−53%
	Textiles	9 Cities or regions	−56%
	Beer	4 Cities or regions	−61%
	Sealing wax	S. England (1500–1700)	−65%
	Silver	13 Cities or regions	−69%
	Sugar	Barcelona, Gdansk, New Castile	−85%

Notes and sources: The cities or regions involved are: Southern England, London, Edinburgh, West Brabant, Holland, The Netherlands, Paris, Barcelona, New Castile, Valencia, Andalucia, Naples, Milan, Modena, Florence, Vienna, Augsburg, Frankfurt, Krakow, Lvov, Warsaw, Gdansk, and Copenhagen. For the numerous sources, some dating back to the International Price History Commission publications, see Hoffman *et al.* 2000. The Hoffman real-price series for Paris are summarized in Table 6.3. For textiles, the 9 cities or regions exclude Italian cities for which the real price rose slightly.

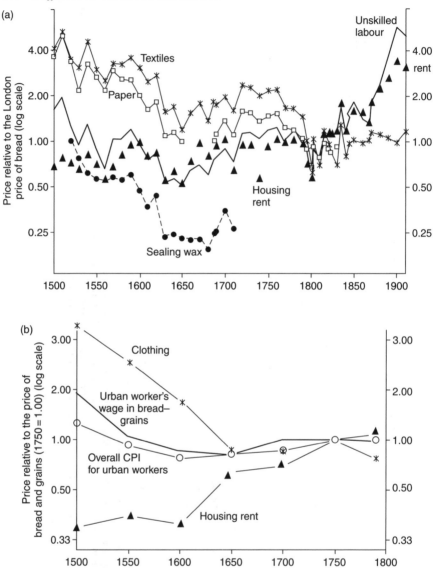

Figure 6.2   Selected prices relative to the price of bread or grain, 1500–1900: (a) Panel A., England; (b) Panel B. Paris; (c) Panel C. Holland

The general pattern in relative-price trends over the whole 1500–1790 period is fairly clear, despite the variations by place and by era. As sketched in Table 6.3, unskilled labour definitely fell in price (wage) relative to the cost of grains and bread. The overall three-century drop in this food wage varied between a modest 9% (Krakow) and drastic drops of more than 60% (Gdansk, Warsaw, and Spain).

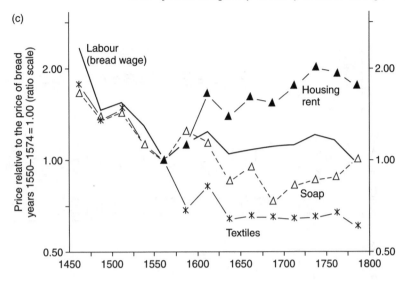

(c)

Figure 6.2 *Continued*

The declines were concentrated in the inflationary sixteenth and the late eighteenth centuries.

So great was the rise in food scarcity that few items rose in price faster than basic food grains. The prices of meats, wine, soap, and candles moved in proportion to food-grain prices, neither faster nor slower. One category that clearly rose in price faster than food was rent, either on housing or on the land that produced that food. Another might be the set of luxury spices from the distant tropics. Like the cinnamon price featured here, the prices of pepper, nutmeg, and cloves also rose faster than grain prices in many settings, two exceptions being pepper in sixteenth-century Augsburg and ginger and saffron in eighteenth-century Warsaw. Yet spices made up only a tiny share of household expenditures, even for the rich.[11] More relevant, the cost of such fuels as firewood, charcoal, coal, and peat rose at least as fast as the food price. While the food crisis may have been greater than the fuel crisis in the sixteenth and the late eighteenth centuries, fuel scarcity was more evident than food scarcity in the trends between 1600 and 1750.

While succeeding generations of unskilled workers found it increasingly hard to afford rent, food, and fuel, other product prices rose more slowly than their wage rates. That was generally true of beer, textiles and clothing, writing paper, some miscellaneous luxuries, and sugar, as sketched towards the bottom of Table 6.3. At the very bottom of the price-trend ranks were silver and national moneys of account, since these centuries brought considerable price inflation. Setting aside the two forms of money, the products falling in price relative to food had two salient features: (1) their production made intensive use of factors that were getting cheaper across these centuries and (2) they tended to be luxuries.

Table 6.4 Movements in non-staple prices relative to staple food-grain prices, selected places and periods, 1500–1790

Place	Non-staple price numerator	Food-grain price denominator	Rate of relative-price movement, % per decade					Total net % change in periods covered here	Notes
			c.1500–1600	c.1600–1650	c.1650–1700	c.1700–1750	c.1750–1790		
Unskilled labour									
S. England	Labour	/Bread, London	−5.04	−11.69	11.90	5.89	−4.52	−37.86	(a)
Paris	Labour	/Bread	−7.67	−2.71	5.93	1.43	0.47	−42.75	(b)
Holland	Labour	/Bread	−2.38	−1.65	1.08	1.70	−4.20	−33.00	(c)
Barcelona	Labour	/Wheat	−9.09	10.31	−5.37	−3.17	−15.34	−64.11	(e)
New Castile	Labour	/Wheat	—	—	—	—	−16.17	—	(e)
Valencia	Labour	/Wheat	−4.88	—	—	3.25	−18.11	−68.02	(e)
Andalucia	Labour	/Wheat	—	−8.32	1.98	−10.37	3.35	−52.86	(e)
Vienna	Labour	/Wheat	—	7.17	−9.18	−0.43	−7.19	−24.34	(f)
West Brabant	Labour	/Rye	−4.84	−4.65	5.45	4.08	−4.32	−35.32	(g)
Frankfurt	Labour	/Rye	−8.65	9.99	—	—	—	—	(i)
Naples	Labour	/Barley	—	—	—	—	−3.87	—	(j)
Milan	Labour	/Bread	—	−10.79	11.51	−3.74	−3.80	−21.94	(k)
Florence	Labour	/Food grain	−1.90	—	—	—	—	—	(l)
Modena	Labour	/Wheat	−7.44	−0.80	6.70	—	—	—	1552–1700, (m)
Edinburgh	Labour	/Bread	−8.32	3.58	6.89	−5.28	10.13	−7.71	1530–1780, (n)
Gdansk (Danzig)	Labour	/Rye	−11.09	10.27	−4.04	−5.13	−11.60	−67.39	(p)
Warsaw	Labour	/Rye	—	1.19	−22.79	−9.69	6.12	−61.49	(q)
Krakow	Labour	/Rye	—	1.38	3.38	4.81	−13.21	−9.30	(r)
	Labour	Medians =	−7.44	0.20	3.38	−0.43	−4.32	−37.86	

Housing rent

Region	Commodity	Ratio							Note
S. England	Housing rent	/Bread, London	3.78	−11.68	14.31	−2.14	1.01	42.06	(a)
Paris	Housing rent	/Bread	0.43	13.24	3.55	8.70	2.99	295.24	(b)
Holland	Housing rent	/Bread	—	4.53	1.94	5.51	−2.69	56.73	(c)

Fuel

Region	Commodity	Ratio							Note
S. England	Coal	/Bread, London	−2.17	16.19	3.55	−2.63	103.06	—	(a)
Paris	Firewood	/Bread	−6.90	15.56	0.74	5.32	2.48	49.48	(b)
Holland	Peat	/Bread	−1.33	−2.77	−4.19	7.53	−0.35	−13.35	(c)
Barcelona	Firewood	/Wheat	—	2.37	5.05	−4.50	—	14.25	(e)
Barcelona	Charcoal	/Wheat	−6.27	1.94	6.57	−3.18	6.19	−14.24	(e)
New Castile	Firewood	/Wheat	—	−14.77	0.42	−1.47	−3.43	−62.91	(e)
New Castile	Charcoal	/Wheat	—	0.82	7.03	−8.66	0.05	−6.76	(e)
Valencia	Firewood	/Wheat	−3.43	2.95	—	—	—	—	(e)
Valencia	Charcoal	/Wheat	−10.65	1.66	—	—	—	—	(e)
Andalucia	Firewood	/Wheat	−18.54	−5.51	—	—	—	—	1553–1648, (e)
Andalucia	Charcoal	/Wheat	−2.16	−0.89	—	—	—	—	1553–1648, (e)
Vienna	Firewood	/Wheat	—	−0.73	2.08	2.16	−3.62	1.99	(f)
West Brabant	Charcoal	/Rye	−8.46	9.10	1.39	15.24	−2.21	29.48	(g)
Augsburg	Beef	/Rye	2.75	0.34	0.73	9.38	−5.86	69.19	(h)
Frankfurt	Charcoal	/Rye	3.34	−3.35	−0.58	14.64	4.32	162.41	(i)
Naples	Firewood	/Barley	—	—	—	—	−1.89	—	(j)
Milan	Charcoal	/Bread	—	−0.59	1.20	1.15	3.41	25.31	(k)
Florence	Firewood	/Food grain	−2.77	—	—	—	—	—	(l)
Copenhagen	Firewood	/Wheat	—	—	—	−11.93	−7.35	—	(o)
Gdansk (Danzig)	Firewood	/Rye	—	—	—	2.13	−3.26	—	(p)
Krakow	Firewood	/Rye	−5.30	0.15	0.90	−17.26	—	−72.50	(r)
Fuels		Medians =	−4.37	0.15	1.20	2.13	−2.05	14.25	

Meats

Region	Commodity	Ratio							Note
S. England	Meat	/Bread, London	4.93	−11.58	8.88	−1.43	4.77	49.96	(a)

Table 6.4 (*Continued*)

Place	Non-staple price numerator	Food-grain price denominator	Rate of relative-price movement, % per decade: c.1500–1600	c.1600–1650	c.1650–1700	c.1700–1750	c.1750–1790	Total net % change in periods covered here	Notes
Paris	Beef	/Bread	−13.96	−7.11	0.77	−1.31	3.97	−82.53	(b)
Holland	Meat	/Bread	−1.72	1.09	−0.32	2.44	−2.04	−11.15	(c)
Barcelona	Meat	/Wheat	−0.13	1.88	1.72	−2.90	−6.27	−21.40	(e)
New Castile	Meat	/Wheat	−1.78	−3.33	15.58	−10.55	−2.40	−24.38	(e)
Valencia	Meat	/Wheat	−1.01	2.05	—	—	—	—	(e)
Andalucia	Meat	/Wheat	−3.53	4.34	—	—	—	—	1553–1648, (e)
West Brabant	Beef	/Rye	−2.20	0.78	6.21	4.08	1.54	46.62	(g)
Frankfurt	Beef	/Rye	—	7.64	−4.12	0.58	0.46	22.70	(i)
Naples	Veal	/Barley	—	—	—	—	5.18	—	(j)
Milan	Veal	/Bread	—	—	—	−3.30	6.01	—	(k)
Florence	Meat	/Food grain	−2.51	—	—	—	—	—	(l)
Modena	Veal	/Wheat	−7.29	—	—	—	—	—	1510–1600, (m)
Gdansk (Danzig)	Beef	/Rye	—	—	—	−0.46	−9.37	—	(p)
Meats		Medians =	−1.99	1.09	1.72	−1.31	1.00	−11.15	
Beer									
Augsburg	Beer	/Rye	—	—	−2.11	3.80	−5.09	−12.12	(h)
Gdansk (Danzig)	Beer	/Rye	0.10	−1.08	−2.69	−7.14	−6.38	−55.91	(p)
Warsaw	Beer	/Rye	—	2.34	−26.23	−17.56	−5.11	−85.24	(q)
Krakow	Beer	/Rye	−6.47	−3.03	−3.80	17.58	−19.53	−65.86	(r)
Wine									
Barcelona	Wine	/Wheat	6.56	5.66	−7.08	−6.88	−2.56	8.61	(e)
New Castile	Wine	/Wheat	2.11	−5.06	13.02	−2.65	−11.55	−6.27	(e)
Valencia	Wine	/Wheat	−0.09	−4.82	—	—	—	—	(e)

Andalucia	Wine	/Wheat	−15.15	9.00	5.42	10.24	−8.73	−0.47	1553–1798, (e)
Frankfurt	Wine	/Rye	3.38	4.76	—	—	—	—	(i)
Milan	Wine	/Bread	—	−1.61	7.80	2.39	−11.10	−3.09	(k)
Modena	Wine, red	/Wheat	−10.37	2.88	12.18	—	—	−31.49	1552–1700, (m)
Copenhagen	Wine	/Wheat	—	—	—	—	−6.40	—	(o)
Gdansk (Danzig)	Wine (Rhine)	/Rye	—	—	—	−0.24	−13.19	—	(p)
Warsaw	Wine	/Rye	−16.05	−12.26	−0.47	−12.15	−5.10	−94.01	(q)
Krakow	Wine	/Rye	−3.01	−6.47	19.49	14.38	−16.12	24.54	(r)
	Wine	Medians =	−1.55	−1.61	7.80	−0.24	−9.92	−3.09	

Sugar

S. England	Sugar	/Bread, London	—	—	5.68	0.17	−4.13	6.25	1660–1790, (a)
Barcelona	Sugar	/Wheat	5.24	−3.34	−20.81	−11.67	−4.42	−82.85	1558–1798, (e)
New Castile	Sugar	/Wheat	−3.30	−2.95	−13.73	−8.11	−7.75	−84.53	1553–1798, (e)
Valencia	Sugar	/Wheat	3.23	−0.89	—	—	—	—	(e)
Andalucia	Sugar	/Wheat	4.18	−3.04	−14.62	—	—	—	1553–1648, (e)
Augsburg	Sugar	/Rye	—	−3.64	—	—	—	—	(h)
Naples	Sugar	/Barley	—	—	—	—	1.80	—	(j)
Milan	Sugar	/Bread	—	—	—	−9.10	2.79	—	(k)
Florence	Sugar	/Food grain	−6.45	—	—	—	—	—	(l)
Florence	Wine	/Food grain	1.36	—	—	—	—	—	(l)
Modena	Sugar	/Wheat	−4.32	7.29	—	—	—	—	1552–1650, (m)
Gdansk (Danzig)	Sugar	/Rye	—	—	—	−7.91	−24.12	—	(p)
Warsaw	Sugar	/Rye	—	—	−26.58	−10.56	−15.04	−88.11	(q)
	Sugar	Medians =	1.36	−3.00	−14.62	−8.61	−4.42	−83.69	

Cinnamon

S. England	Cinnamon	/Bread, London	—	—	2.64	0.10	12.47	78.48	1660–1790, (a)
Holland	Cinnamon	/Bread	—	14.65	5.78	−1.68	17.01	275.50	(d)
New Castile	Cinnamon	/Wheat	—	12.50	11.17	−8.95	3.60	120.59	(e)
Krakow	Cinnamon	/Rye	−6.65	—	—	—	—	—	(r)

Table 6.4 (*Continued*)

Place	Non-staple price numerator	Food-grain price denominator	Rate of relative-price movement, % per decade:					Total net % change in periods covered here	Notes
			c.1500–1600	c.1600–1650	c.1650–1700	c.1700–1750	c.1750–1790		
Soap									
S. England	Soap	/Bread, London	—	-16.63	16.65	-0.07	7.06	-0.65	1600–1770, (a)
Holland	Soap	/Bread	-1.28	-7.27	-3.05	3.26	3.35	-28.52	(c)
Barcelona	Soap	/Wheat	—	5.05	2.33	-6.75	0.52	3.31	(e)
New Castile	Soap	/Wheat	—	—	-10.44	-4.82	2.71	-49.89	(e)
Valencia	Soap	/Wheat	-3.07	-5.34	—	—	—	—	(e)
Andalucia	Soap	/Wheat	1.89	-1.85	—	—	—	—	1553–1648, (e)
Vienna	Soap	/Wheat	—	-0.12	-3.17	6.51	-3.72	-0.74	(f)
Copenhagen	Soap	/Wheat	—	—	—	—	-12.85	—	(o)
Soap		Medians =	-1.28	-3.59	-3.05	-0.07	1.62	-0.74	
Candles									
West Brabant	Candles	/Rye	-3.19	-7.56	2.65	5.67	10.18	8.74	(g)
Frankfurt	Candle wax	/Rye	-3.71	-5.02	—	—	—	—	(i)
Naples	Candles	/Barley	—	—	—	—	-3.21	—	(j)
Milan	Candles	/Bread	—	—	—	-5.05	-1.62	—	(k)
Florence	Tallow candles	/Food grain	-0.62	—	—	—	—	—	(l)
Modena	Candle (sego)	/Wheat	1.07	-4.54	—	—	—	—	(l)
Edinburgh	Candles	/Bread	-6.22	0.17	6.84	-2.45	—	-20.88	1552–1700, (m)
Gdansk (Danzig)	Candles	/Rye	—	—	—	-0.06	-8.53	—	1530–1750, (n)
Candles		Medians =	-3.19	-4.78	4.75	-1.26	-2.41	-6.07	(p)
Textiles									
S. England	Textiles	/Bread, London	-2.91	-17.02	10.51	2.02	-9.65	-56.47	(a)
S. England	Velvet	/Bread, London	—	—	—	-3.85	-13.36	-53.70	(a)

Location	Product							Note
Paris	Wool socks	/Bread	−9.75	−13.64	1.01	4.84	−5.15	−81.43	(b)
Holland	Textiles	/Bread	−6.63	−1.30	0.07	0.21	−1.53	−55.75	(c)
New Castile	Linen	/Wheat	—	1.50	−3.18	−4.91	−1.13	−21.26	(e)
West Brabant	Linen	/Rye	−14.19	−7.69	4.12	10.71	−11.04	−80.94	(g)
Augsburg	Canvas	/Rye	−5.40	0.50	−8.88	8.63	−5.61	−55.12	(h)
Frankfurt	Linen	/Rye	−6.27	0.06	−13.92	—	—	—	(i)
Naples	Cotton cloth	/Barley	—	—	—	—	7.22	—	(j)
Milan	Cloth/linen	/Bread	—	−6.78	8.59	−3.33	4.00	14.18	(k)
Florence	Cloth	/Food grain	−8.55	—	—	—	—	—	(l)
Modena	Cloth (alto)	/Wheat	—	0.99	9.33	—	—	—	1552–1700, (m)
Gdansk (Danzig)	Woollen (gray)	/Rye	—	—	—	−0.55	−0.38	—	(p)
Warsaw	Linen	/Rye	—	—	—	−29.45	16.85	—	(q)
Krakow	Linen	/Rye	−15.74	−15.75	10.56	8.67	−7.50	−85.97	(r)
Textiles		Medians =	−7.59	−4.04	2.56	0.21	−3.34	−55.75	

Paper

Location	Product							Note
S. England	Paper	/Bread, London	−5.46	−12.90	—	1.58	−8.89	−76.39	ends in 1777/81, (a)
Paris	Paper	/Bread	−6.80	−21.52	−12.29	—	—	−85.27	1500–1650 (b)
Barcelona	Paper	/Wheat	−3.75	8.88	−6.46	3.12	−7.34	−53.42	(e)
New Castile	Paper	/Wheat	—	—	−0.21	0.05	−6.04	−44.04	(e)
Vienna	Paper	/Wheat	—	−1.98	−7.20	−10.01	−7.19	−55.97	(f)
Augsburg	Paper	/Rye	−6.84	−4.35	−6.20	10.64	2.74	−49.14	(h)
Frankfurt	Paper	/Rye	0.82	1.47	—	1.57	—	−16.06	(i)
Gdansk (Danzig)	Paper	/Rye	—	—	—	14.12	−11.78	—	(p)
Warsaw	Paper	/Rye	—	—	—	−16.96	2.40	—	(q)
Krakow	Paper	/Rye	−12.53	0.12	3.65	7.11	—	−52.56	(r)
Paper		Medians =	−6.13	−1.98	−6.33	1.58	−7.19	−52.99	

Table 6.4 (*Continued*)

Place	Non-staple price numerator	Food-grain price denominator	Rate of relative-price movement, % per decade:					Total net % change in periods covered here	Notes
			c.1500–1600	c.1600–1650	c.1650–1700	c.1700–1750	c.1750–1790		
Silver									
England	Silver	/Bread, London	−10.28	−11.80	6.44	1.58	−6.89	−79.97	(a)
Paris	Silver	/Bread	−13.89	−3.97	7.06	6.85	−5.34	−71.22	(b)
The Netherlands	Silver	/Rye	−10.56	−0.66	−2.05	8.25	−7.66	−69.11	(s)
Barcelona	Silver	/Wheat	−8.94	−4.48	8.75	6.83	−13.61	−63.27	(e)
Andalucia	Silver	/Wheat	—	−2.08	12.45	8.92	−15.16	28.61	(e)
New Castile	Silver	/Wheat	−14.70	−3.02	14.42	1.93	−16.74	−81.87	(e)
Valencia	Silver	/Wheat	−9.67	−4.30	7.05	3.46	−11.46	−70.28	(e)
Belgium	Silver	/Wheat	−11.79	−5.12	0.89	11.65	−5.34	−68.08	(s)
Northern Italy	Silver	/Wheat	−11.72	8.30	10.66	−1.61	−7.33	−45.25	(s)
Frankfurt	Silver	/Rye	−11.54	−3.19	−8.13	5.23	−2.98	−81.34	(s)
Augsburg	Silver	/Rye	−8.60	−1.85	0.21	−6.34	6.97	−64.62	(s)
Austria	Silver	/Rye	−7.69	−4.28	−1.26	2.99	0.17	−60.47	(s)
Poland	Silver	/Rye	−20.70	−6.24	3.90	4.49	−3.84	−90.81	(s)
	Silver	Medians =	−11.05	−3.97	6.44	4.49	−6.89	−69.11	
Miscellaneous products									
S. England	Chocolate	/Bread, London	—	—	—	5.34	−17.35	−39.46	(a)
S. England	Pewter	/Bread, London	−3.92	−11.97	—	—	—	—	(a)
S. England	Sealing wax	/Bread, London	−7.96	−13.47	8.86	—	—	−64.84	1510–1700, (a)

Notes and sources: 'Labour' here means unskilled non-agricultural labour hired by institutions, usually for building, but also for menial tasks.

(a) England: Centred five-year averages through 1700, then annual figures. Prices for London bread are from Mitchell (1988) spliced to Boulton's (2000) flour series for 1580–1700, and to the Phelps Brown and Hopkins (1957, 1981) farinaceous series for 1500–40. Housing rents are from Clark (2002). The series for soap, velvet, chocolate, cinnamon, pewter, and sealing wax are from Beveridge (1939). The prices of silver are taken from Feaveayear (1963).

(b) Paris: Centred nine-year averages. The figures for wool socks include quotes from Orléans as well as from Paris. The bread series is extended back before 1750 using a wheat series. The sources are Baulant (1968, 1971, 1976), d'Avenel (1894–1926), and Hauser (1936).

(c) Holland: The source is van Zanden (2000). The actual time periods are the quarter centuries just prior to the years shown. Thus, *c.*1500 is really 1475–99; *c.*1600 is 1575–99, and so on, except that 1790 is really 1775–99. The overall-period change for house rents covers only the period since 1575–99.

(d) Posthumus, cinnamon: The source is Posthumus (1946: Table 66).

(e) Spain: The sources are Feliu i Montfort (1991) for most series, and Hamilton (1934, 1947) for linen and cinnamon. Most of the five-year averages are centred on 1503, 1550, 1600 (nine-year averages), 1648, 1700, 1750, and 1798.

(f) Vienna: The source is Pribram *et al.* (1938). The time periods are bounded by the averages for 1593–7, 1653–7, 1698–1702, 1738–47, and 1773–7.

(g) West Brabant: The main source is Verlinden *et al.* (1959–65) with some pre-1600 data from van der Wee (1963). The rates are based on five-year averages, except that '1500' is centred on 1502.

(h) Augsburg: The source is Elsas (1936–49). The estimates are rates of change between five-year averages.

(i) Frankfurt: The source is Elsas (1936–49). The estimates are rates of change between five-year averages, with some use of nearby dates necessary.

(j) Naples: The source is Romano (1965).

(k) Milan: The sources are De Maddalena (1950) and Sella (1968) for 1605/09–1648/52 and 1648/52–1701/05, and De Maddalena (1974) for 1701/05–1748/52 and 1748/52–1788/92. Wheat bread (pano) is the deflator to the *c.*1700 dates, then wheat. Each commodity changes definition slightly between the seventeenth-century periods and the eighteenth-century periods. Labour changes from 'lavorante o garzone' to a mason's assistant or boy. The fuel item changes from charcoal (carbone de legno) to firewood (legna). Wine becomes specifically white wine in the eighteenth-century series. The cloth item changes from woollen cloth 'alto' to linen cloth.

(l) Florence: The source is Parenti (1942, 1967). The changes are from 1520/22 to 1608/12. The rate of price change for meat is a simple average of the rates of change in the grain prices of veal, beef, and mutton.

(m) Modena: The source is Basini (1974). The initial and final quinquennia are 1550–4 and 1696–1700.

(n) Edinburgh: The source is Gibson and Smout (1995).

(o) Copenhagen: The source is Friis and Glamann (1958). The initial date is 1712, and the interim benchmark for firewood is 1739–42.

(p) Gdansk (Danzig): The sources are Pelc (1937) and Furtak (1935). The benchmark dates are 1543–7, 1598–1602, 1648–52, and 1696–1700 for the first three columns, and 1701–5, 1748–52, 1788–92 for the next two columns. *Caution:* The period 1647–53 was one of extraordinarily high grain prices, lowering all the real prices deflated by the 1648–52 rye price here.

(q) Warsaw: The sources are Adamcyk (1938) for prices and unskilled wages 1558–1700, and Siegel (1936, 1949) for prices and unskilled wages 1701–1815.

(r) Krakow: The sources are Pelc (1935) for prices through 1600, and Tomaszewski (1934) for prices and wages from 1601 on.

(s) Silver prices, in terms of food grains: Abel (1973: Tables I, II). The averages refer to the decades ending in the rounded year: 1491–1500 for 1500, etc. up to 1781–90 for 1790. The only exception is that the 1500 benchmark for Northern Italy is represented by 1501–10.

The falling-real-price products in the lower half of Table 6.3 tended to make relatively more use of labour and capital, which were falling in relative price.[12] By contrast, the main rising-real-price products—housing, fuel, and food—called for more intensive use of land (farmland, forests, and mineral reserves); the factor that was rising in price. The pattern does not fit perfectly, of course. Spices were not land intensive in a sense that is meaningful for western Europe, and increasingly cheap sugar did use land. Yet as a general rule, land intensity is lower in the lower half of Table 6.3's list of products. This factor–price pattern suggests a cost-side explanation for some of the price trends.

The other salient feature of the falling-real-price products in the lower half of Table 6.3 is that they tended to be luxuries, or at least not staples. The tendency was rough, and had its exceptions. Beer was a luxury in the working-class end of the spectrum, though sugar was not (Clark *et al.* 1995: 224) and luxury wines did not fall in price relative to food grains. Most studies find that clothing was slightly a luxury good, which should imply the same for the textiles that were fashioned into clothing. Writing paper, chocolate, pewter, and sealing wax were surely luxury goods, and they fell considerably in price relative to food grains.[13] And as we shall note in Section 6, labour itself was a luxury, in the sense that the rich spent a greater share of their income buying labour.

This inter-product pattern in real prices before 1820 brought greater real-income gains for richer regions, just as it did for richer classes within each region. Developing truly national cost-of-living indices, with luxuries taking a greater share of expenditure in the richer regions, would probably show that the global inequality of real purchasing power rose faster than the global inequality of income measured in units of any one good such as silver or wheat.

6. Trends in the Class-Specific Cost of Living, 1500–1820s

How has the traditional focus on wage rates and on grain or bread prices biased our view of real-wage trends and inequality trends *within* countries?

If one just expanded the cost-of-living deflator to include such familiar non-food goods as beverages, clothing, fuel, and light, then the traditional real-wage studies would not need a massive adjustment. We could end up seeing only that average real incomes declined a bit less in this era than past studies of the food wage have implied.

Yet, the partial expansion of the cost-of-living bundle should not stop there. It should also explore how the cheapening of luxuries relative to staples interacts with those differences in expenditure shares illustrated back in Table 6.2. By omitting these interactions, past studies have missed the inegalitarian feature of cost-of-living trends before the early nineteenth century. That is, difficulties in both concepts and data have caused us to underestimate the widening of the economic gaps within nations. This is true not only of the real-wage literature but also of the literature that has followed nominal income inequality.[14] It is time to probe more deeply into real-income inequality.

The next step is to supplement the introduction of a few luxury goods in Table 6.3, Figure 6.2, and Table 6.4 with further discussion of two particular differences in lifestyle between top and bottom income classes. With these in view, we will be able to construct class-specific cost-of-living indices and measures of trends in real-income inequality.

6.1 The declining real cost of servants

The real-wage rate itself has a further implication about real inequality. High-income families hired labour directly as household servants and day servants. So the lower the real-wage rates sank before 1820, the cheaper the cost of living the high-income lifestyle. This key point needs to be quantified as best the data permit. Conversely, the rise in real wages after the 1820s meant that the cost of living of the rich advanced faster than the cost of living for workers. Who hired servants, and in what numbers, can be roughly gauged from a variety of sources. Since servants' nominal wages apparently followed the wage rates for the unskilled agricultural workers (Snell 1985: 25–47, 411–17), which in turn moved similarly with unskilled building wages before 1820, one can use an unskilled wage rate as a rough index for servants' wages.

To the extent that upper-class employers paid their servants in kind, one could say that expenditures on servants are already built into the data on other expenditures of the household. That is the case for the English data in Table 6.2, though not for the Duc de Saulx-Tavanes. Yet even for the English data, it makes sense that the pay in kind for servants varied in its nominal value with the nominal wage of servants, more directly than with the prices of the goods and services purchased for them. Accordingly, we have inferred the shares of food and other items implicitly paid to servants by applying low-income consumption weights to total expenditures on servants, and have deducted these from the rich-household expenditures on these other categories in Table 6.2. To the estimated full servant bill—both for those paid in kind and for those paid in cash—we use the unskilled wage rate as the barometer of their unit cost. The unskilled wage rate itself thus becomes a luxury-service price, one that greatly affects our estimates of the trend in living costs for the rich.

6.2 Selling food or housing to themselves

The meaning of price movements depends critically, of course, on whether one is a buyer or a seller. Past measurements of the cost of living and real wages have assumed that households sell everything they make and buy everything they consume. That is often not the case, of course. Many households consume what they produce. Others sell more of a consumer good or service than they use, making them beneficiaries of higher prices of that good or service.

The first place where the consumption of non-purchases intrudes into the traditional discussion is in the consumption by lower-income rural households of food and clothing they produce themselves. As Witold Kula and William Hagen have rightly warned, ordinary peasants do not experience anything like a 30% loss of real income when food prices rise 30% relative to the wage rate (Kula 1976; Hagen 1986). In many cases, their real income is wholly unaffected. This clearly important point is hard to quantify. In England, the socio-occupational categories in the social tables of 1688–1803 imply that among families with below-average income the share of home food consumption that was home produced was probably between 4% and 30% of total income.[15] The importance of home production will have been greater in less market-integrated settings. In early modern Europe, this kind of protection against price movements was probably greater in the countryside and to the east. All subsequent discussions of real wages as measures of the real purchasing power of 'the masses' should acknowledge that real-wage measures overstate the real-income importance of movements in those measured real wages.

Yet the likely magnitude of home production as a share of workers' incomes would not have been as great as the share of a different kind of home production, one that affected the top income groups. The fact that high-income groups bought housing mainly from themselves needs particular attention here.

For all the narratives about the cost and condition of workers' housing, very few historical cost-of-living indices have been able to include housing rents. This is not surprising, since housing is more varied and changing in its quality than bread or coal. For housing, as for fashionable luxuries, the variety and change frustrate our attempts to build long-run time series. Yet in a few cases it has proven possible to produce long time series of the rental prices of housing of given quality. We now have fair housing rent series for Holland and Belgium. Philip Hoffman has assembled another index for pre-Revolutionary Paris. In addition, Gregory Clark has now assembled credible housing rent series extending from the mid-seventeenth to the mid-nineteenth centuries for London, for the rest of England, and for England as a whole.[16]

Housing rents, as we saw in Table 6.4, rose at least as fast as the cost-of-living index in general up to the early nineteenth century, and they rose even faster across the rest of that century. Over the last five centuries as a whole, housing is probably the one major consumer price that might have kept pace with the wages of labour, when quality is held constant.

If everybody spent the same share of their budget on rented housing then the movements in the relative price of housing would play little role in class differences in cost-of-living trends. Housing's share of a broad concept of total income or expenditures is indeed roughly constant across the income classes in any given year. Economists have noted that the income elasticity of housing is near enough to unity that one could use the value of occupied housing as an index of permanent income.[17] So as far as the use of housing is concerned, its rough proportionality to income might suggest that movements in the real price of housing should not have caused any difference in cost-of-living trends between the rich and the poor.

Yet, the impact of house-rent movements on the different income classes was probably far from neutral, since the rich owned housing and the poor typically did not. It would clearly be wrong to imagine that a jump in rents would impoverish an affluent household that owned its own home. And if that affluent household owned housing that it rented out to others, the jump in market rents would raise, and not lower, its real income. Many affluent households were in fact exporters, not importers, of residential housing. A rise in real rents would therefore favour the rich.

The fact that housing owners were higher in the income ranks than housing occupants would still not have complicated our accounting for relative real incomes *if* the historical record of nominal incomes had correctly included all the incomes that owners received from their residential properties, including their own (owned) home. Had that been the case, then any jump in real rents would be recorded correctly as a jump in their nominal income, partly offset by the fact that some of the housing they own was consumed by themselves rather than rented out for income.

That is apparently not the case, however. None of the scholarly estimates of early high incomes makes any explicit reference to an imputation for owner-occupied housing. Typically someone like Gregory King would show awareness of owner-occupied housing only in separate discussion of the nation's housing stock, and would not carry its value over to any tabulation of income by class. Nor, as far as we can tell, did the official returns on income taxation in England and France give this point its due. Our views of the real-income movements of high-income groups are in danger of implicitly assuming that they had to rent all their housing from landlords. We will have stepped into that trap if we take nominal incomes, excluding imputations for owner-occupied housing, and deflate them by a cost-of-living index that implies that these affluent families had to rent all their lodging.

Any era in which rents rose faster than the composite price index on the rest of a lower-class consumer bundle was likely to have been an era in which the cost of living rose even less for the most propertied classes than even the present estimates show.[18]

6.3   Tentative cost-of-living indices by income class

Armed with the expenditure shares in Table 6.2 and price series like those illustrated in Tables 6.3 and 6.4, one can put together cost-of-living indices that apply to the expenditure patterns of the different income ranks. Figure 6.3 summarizes the contrasts in the cost-of-living trends for the top and bottom groups. In Figure 6.3, a rise is egalitarian in that it means that the cost of living rose more for the rich than for the poor. A decline is inegalitarian.

The cost-of-living deflators for different income classes moved very differently before the early nineteenth century. For England (Panel A in Figure 6.3), the movements reveal historical eras that seem to match those delineated by other inequality indicators. First, during the famous but gradual price revolution between 1500 and 1650, the top income groups enjoyed a relative decline of about 20% in their cost of living, in the form of less price inflation, relative to the prices faced by workers and the poor. Then, between *c.*1650 and *c.*1750, the common people had

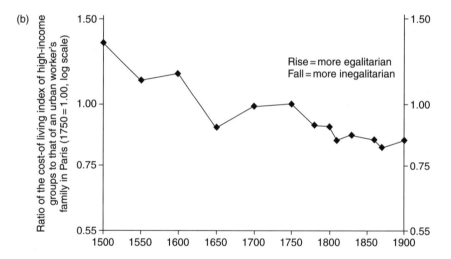

Figure 6.3 Movements in the cost of living in top income groups, relative to the cost of living in the bottom 40% or in workers' households: (a) Panel A. England, 1500–1900; (b) Panel B. France, 1500–1900; (c) Panel C. Holland, 1540–1799

the better of it, with a reversal of that previous 20% movement. That is, by 1750 the cost-of-living bundles of the rich and the poor stood in the same relative-price ratio as they had 250 years earlier. In the second half of the eighteenth century, this swing was itself reversed again, so that in 1800 the relative cost-of-living hardship of being poor was as bad as back in 1650. In the late nineteenth century, the pendulum swung back in favour of workers and the poor. In fact, it swung further their way than at any time over the previous three centuries. The early modern English swings,

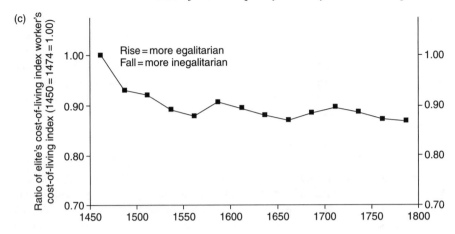

Figure 6.3   *Continued*

those before the early nineteenth century, were dominated by swings in the relative price of staple foods.

In pre-Revolutionary France, the broad class differences in cost-of-living trends looked similar. Relative to an urban working-class household, a wealthy noble family had a declining cost-of-living up to the 1650 benchmark, especially if homeownership shielded them from the rapid rise in housing rents. In this respect, nobles and wealthy merchants differed. Some rented their high-class housing, just as the Duc de Saulx-Tavanes rented his Paris residence. Others owned their own housing, just as the Duc owned his country estate. There is again an egalitarian drift between 1650 and 1750 and a reversal between 1750 and 1790 though these movements were smaller than those in England were.

In Holland, as in France and England, the cost of a high-income lifestyle declined relative to the cost-of-living in a working-class household, as shown in Panel C of Figure 6.3. In both Holland and France, the real movement in relative living costs came in the era before 1650. We see only a slight imitation of England's late eighteenth-century inegalitarian trend.

7. Rough Estimates of 'Real Inequality' Trends for Early Modern England, France, and Holland

Real-income inequality is an important index-number concept that could be fully formalized with an explicit overall welfare function that combines different people's individual well-being. Even though the poor and the rich have the same tastes in the abstract, having very different resources means that the same price movements affect their welfare very differently. A formal model of social welfare in this spirit has been developed by Dale Jorgenson, Erwin Diewert, and Daniel Slesnick (Jorgenson and Slesnick 1983; Diewert 1990; Slesnick 1998). It allows one to combine welfare changes for the poor and the rich into the same overall welfare metric. Here we follow a similar approach, but to avoid the troublesome index-number concept of overall real well-being we will illustrate real inequality movements only in ratios of the real income of higher income ranks to the real-income movements of lower ranks.[19] The ratios of real purchasing power can help answer such questions as 'What happened to the relative abilities of higher and lower income ranks to buy things in the proportions typical of their lifestyles?' or 'How did the real incomes of higher and lower income ranks compare with those of their counterparts in earlier generations?'.

The history of real-income movements seems more volatile than that suggested by more conventional measures of nominal income inequality. In England and Wales, both the egalitarian change between Gregory King's 1688 and Joseph Massie's 1759 and the subsequent inegalitarian change from 1759 to Patrick Colquhoun's 1802 (1801–3) were apparently greater in real terms than in nominal terms. This can be illustrated by looking at what happened to the ratio of top-decile income to the income of the bottom two fifths between 1759 and 1802. In nominal terms this ratio rose by 50% (from 14.4 to 21.8). But in real terms, it rose by 76% (from 13.0 to 21.8). That is, the movement of real inequality proves to have been a magnification of the movement in nominal inequality.

In the case of eighteenth-century France, too, the price movements amplified the movements in nominal income inequality. The trends were modest in this case, however, and they seemed to reverse at mid-century. The income ratios dividing the rich and the poor may have narrowed a bit between 1700 and 1750, and re-widened between 1750 and 1790. These modest movements are subject to wide ranges of possible error, as Morrisson and Snyder warn us (Morrison and Snyder 2000). For what it is worth, the same shift from a possibly egalitarian trend before 1750 to an inegalitarian trend between 1750 and the Revolution was magnified by the movement of relative prices.

For Holland, price movements seem to have magnified a greater and more prolonged rise in inequality. The current price estimates of van Zanden accentuate the inegalitarian drift in his earlier estimates of Holland's nominal income distribution (van Zanden 1995, 2000). Over the entire three centuries from 1500 to 1808, say his estimates, the rich got richer and the poor got poorer, with the gaps widening even more in real terms than in nominal terms.

Would a closer look at other countries and regions also show that relative-price movements accentuated the widening of gaps between the rich and the poor before the early nineteenth century, as they seem to have done when incomes widened in England, France, and Holland?

8. Conclusion

The greatest divergence of the early modern era was probably the rise of the upper-income groups of northwest Europe relative to everybody else. The privileged ranks of the West gained in material well-being relative to the rest of their own societies and to national averages. In terms of life expectancy, the gains for Europe's upper classes at least kept pace with those for other documented groups after 1650, if we may judge from contrasts between ruling families' experiences and national averages.

In terms of what they could purchase in a given year of their life span, the upper-income ranks of northwest Europe were pulling away from others even more clearly than previous estimates have revealed, thanks to trends in relative prices. The eras that stood out as eras in which price trends favoured the rich were also eras in which a rise in nominal inequality also favoured the rich.

The era with the clearest inegalitarian trends seems to have come long before any Industrial Revolution or globalization. It was between 1500 and 1650 that the rich benefited most from the relative cheapening of new luxury goods and of old luxury goods such as domestic servants, while soaring land rents probably also enhanced their nominal incomes. In the same period, the poor faced a trend towards scarcity of food, housing, and land. As far as we can tell, this shift toward dear food and cheap luxuries was experienced throughout most of Europe before 1650.

Inegalitarian trends revisited at different times between 1650 and the turbulent 1790–1815 era. For England and France, at least, one might argue for a second inegalitarian era across the second half of the eighteenth century. For England, this second inegalitarian age probably came between 1740 and 1795–1815. It might have had a similar dating for France, but data limitations allow us to see only a slightly inegalitarian trend change between 1750 and 1790. For Holland, the timing was quite different. The three centuries of rising inequality traced by van Zanden were slightly augmented by inegalitarian price movements. Yet of the whole three-century pre-industrial era, the time when relative-price movements contributed the most to purchasing power at the top and misery for the masses was the period before 1650.

The divergence in early modern price trends also carries an implication for trends in international inequality, at least within Europe. To the extent that all countries shared a drift toward scarce grain and cheaper luxuries between 1500 and 1800, the real purchasing power of the richest nations, especially England and Holland, must have risen above other nations' purchasing power even faster than the silver-price or constant-price comparisons could reveal. Real purchasing power must have risen faster, other things equal, in countries where consumption patterns favoured the goods that were falling in relative price. Over most of the sixteenth through eighteenth centuries, those falling-price goods tended to be luxuries, giving an extra relative bargain to England and Holland.

Notes

1. Two laudable exceptions should be noted. The first is Witold Kula (1976: 119–31). In Kula's pioneering exercise, we see the first good sketch of the importance of differences in cost-of-living movements, though without any link-up with income measures and with

some limitations of commodity and geographic coverages. Kula offered stylized 'terms of trade' measures. His stylized nobility sold only rye, divided by a useful price series for a 'basket of goods', consisting of good quality cloth, good quality paper, French wine, pepper, coffee, and sugar. Absent from this list are any meat, drink other than wine, or labour services, a luxury purchase we have emphasized. His stylized peasants sold a mixture of rye, oats, butter, and eggs in exchange for cloth, nails, and salt. The second exception is Williamson (1976), who explored movements in real income based on different cost-of-living indices for the different US income classes since 1820. Williamson's study, like the present, found that movements in relative prices typically accentuated the movements in nominal income inequality. The US relative-price effects he studied were, however, less dramatic than those revealed here. Besides these two exceptions, the closest approach to some of our present points was made by Wilhelm Abel (1973) but he mentioned only food versus other goods, and left the price effects unquantified.

2. 'The 1820s' here represent a compromise post-war benchmark. In some cases, the phrase means the initial post-war era of recovery on the Continent and agricultural depression in England, 1815–20. It also serves as a link to Angus Maddison's (2001) estimates for 1820 in his study of the world economy and to the argument by O'Rourke and Williamson (2000) that international price convergence may not have progressed between the 16th century and the 1820s. In other cases, it refers to the 1831 output benchmark date for the United Kingdom or to the Morrisson and Snyder (2000) benchmark estimates of French inequality in 1836. And for some continental countries the disruption of the French war era 1790–1815 will require stopping the evidence at 1790 instead of the 1820s. Similarly, we will at times equate the 1640s or even the early seventeenth century with 1650 and the 1740s with 1750 as turning points. The dating of turning points has to be flexible, since different series changed trends at different times.

3. The sensitivity of mortality to food scarcity is confirmed by several studies in this volume.

4. So say not only Table 6.1's estimates for Swedish females 1750–9 but also the reconstitution experiments of Bengtsson and Oeppen on population data from Scandia in southern Sweden 1650–1750 (Bengtsson and Oeppen 1993). Apart from mortality crises around 1675 and 1705, Scandia's mortality seemed no worse than English over this century.

5. This way of summarizing the inequality of life spans is the conventional way which tends to focus on class and to view the survival of infants as something experienced by their parents' class. A more logical approach would be to view all persons as separate individuals, and to follow the inequality in life spans and in consumption per lifetime. On this more logical approach, inequality of life spans in western Europe has been dropping ever since 1750, thanks mainly to the elimination of infant mortality. It has not been dropping for the world as a whole, however (Bourguignon and Morrisson 2002).

6. Table 6.1's distinctions between the full-rent and no-rent expenditures for the upper classes will be discussed in Section 6.

7. For the strong conclusion that workers' abilities to purchase food were declining in most European settings across the second half of the eighteenth century or longer, see Phelps Brown and Hopkins (1957, 1959, 1981); Braudel and Spooner (1966); van Zanden (1999); and Allen (2001, 2003).

8. The monotonic rise of global income inequality since 1820 is documented by Bourguignon and Morrisson (2002).

9. This is not to imply that all new goods were luxuries. The New World introduced the potato and other new foods that were to become staples. Yet, the introduction of these was not sufficient in its impact to prevent the rise in the real price of staple foods relative to luxuries before 1820. Two other likely exceptions were health related: cotton clothing and other aids to sanitation might have helped the poor as much as the middle- and upper-income groups. Even these new goods had a not-so-egalitarian side, to the extent that they raised the labour supply, bidding wages down and rents up.

10. For example, see Feenstra (1994, 1995) and Hausman (2003).

11. For example, in 1784–6, spice imports were less than 1% of the value of imports into Great Britain (Davis 1979: 110). They would have taken an even smaller share of income in the top 20% of families.

12. That labour was increasingly cheap relative to most products and the overall cost of living is evident in Table 6.4 and in the real-wage studies of van Zanden (1999), Allen (2001, 2003), and earlier authors. The cheapening of capital inputs follows mainly from the drop in interest rates (Allen 1988; Homer and Sylla 1991; Clark 1998).

13. On a musical note, another luxury that became cheaper relative to bread or the overall cost of living was a London opera ticket. While other nominal prices rose between the 1720s and 1786–1878, opera tickets stayed fixed at 10s 6d for boxes and the pit, and at 3–5s for the gallery (Hunter 2000: 35).

14. For example, see Lindert and Williamson (1982, 1983) and van Zanden (1995).

15. This statement uses the social tables in Lindert and Williamson (1982) and assumes that home production could have been 100% of income for lesser freeholders and husband- men, and 10% for labourers, vagrants, paupers, and cottagers.

16. On housing rents in Holland from the mid-sixteenth century on, see van Zanden (2000) and the sources cited there. A series for Bruges from 1500 on is given by Verlinden (1959–65). Clark (2002) presents new series for England and Wales 1550–1909.

17. For an application of the unit-elastic assumption about housing to the economic history of inequality, see Williamson (1985).

18. Our more detailed treatment in the working paper version (Hoffman *et al.* 2000: Tables 4–6) sets extreme bounds on the importance of this residence–ownership effect. As warned in the text here, the bounded estimates that give maximum impact to this effect suggest that it may have heightened the rise of real inequality in rising-rent periods like the sixteenth century.

19. This chapter confines itself to sketching movements in early modern inequality in income *before, rather than after, taxes and transfers*. The pre-tax, pre-transfer focus avoids the difficult task of exploring fiscal incidence, a topic too vast to undertake here. So for the time being, we must perpetuate an inconsistency shared by most of the literature presenting real-income time series. We use a price deflator appropriate to disposable income—that is, after-tax and after-transfer income—as a denominator for original income, from which taxes and transfers have not been netted out.

References

Abel, W. (1973) *Crises agraires en Europe, XIIIe—XXe siècle*, a translation of the 1966 edition of *Agrarkrisen und Agrarkonjunktur*. Paris: Flammarion.

Adamcyk, W. (1938) *Ceny w Warszawie w XVI i XVII wieku*. Lwow: Sklad Główny.

Allen, R. C. (1988) 'The Price of Freehold Land and the Interest Rate in the Seventeenth and Eighteenth Centuries'. *Economic History Review*, 41(1): 33–50.

——(2001) 'The Great Divergence: Wages and Prices from the Middle Ages to the First World War'. *Explorations in Economic History*, 38(4): 411–47.

——(2003) 'Progress and Poverty in Early Modern Europe'. *Economic History Review*, 46 (3): 403–43.

Andersen, O. (1984) 'The Decline of Danish Mortality before 1850 and its Economic and Social Background', in T. Bengtsson, G. Fridlizius, and R. Ohlsson (eds.), *Pre-Industrial Population Change*. Stockholm: Almqvist and Wicksell.

Basini, G. L. (1974) *Sul Mercato di Modena Tra Cinque e Seicento: Prezzi e Salari*. Milano: Dott. A Giuffré.

Baulant, M. (1968) 'Le prix des grains à Paris de 1431 à 1788'. *Annales ESC*, 23: 520–40.

——(1971) 'Le salaire des ouvriers du bâtiment à Paris de 1400 à 1726'. *Annales ESC*, 26: 463–83.

——(1976) 'Prix et salaires à Paris aux XVIe siècle: Sources et résultats'. *Annales ESC*, 31: 954–95.

Bengtsson, T. and Dribe, D. (1997) 'Economy and Demography in Western Scandia, Sweden, 1650–1900'. Area report presented at the Europe–Asia Project meeting in Kyoto, Japan, January 11–14. www.ekh.lu.se/ekhmdr/eapwp.pdf.

——Fridlizius, G., and Ohlsson, R. (eds.) (1984) *Pre-Industrial Population Change*. Stockholm: Almqvist and Wicksell.

——and Oeppen, J. (1993) 'A Reconstruction of the Population of Scandia 1650–1760'. *Lund Papers in Economic History* 32. Lund University, Department of Economic History.

Beveridge, W. H. (1939) *Prices and Wages in England from the Twelfth to the Nineteenth Century*, reprinted 1966. London: Frank Cass.

Bideau, A. *et al.* (1988) 'La mortalité', in J. Dupâquier *et al.* (eds.), *Histoire de la Population Française, De la Renaissance à 1789*, Vol. 2. Paris: Presses Universitaires de France, pp. 221–91.

Boulton, J. (2000) 'Food Prices and the Standard of Living in London in the "Century of Revolution", 1580–1700'. *Economic History Review*, 53(3): 455–92.

Bourguignon, F. and Morrisson, C. (2002) 'Inequality among World Citizens: 1820–1992'. *American Economic Review*, 92(4): 727–44.

Bowley, A. L. (1921) *Prices in the United Kingdom, 1914–1920*. Oxford: Clarendon Press.

Braudel, F. P. and Spooner, F. (1966) 'Prices in Europe from 1450 to 1750', in E. E. Rich and C. H. Wilson (eds.), *Cambridge Economic History of Europe, Volume IV: The Economy of Expanding Europe in the Sixteenth and Seventeenth Centuries*. Cambridge: Cambridge University Press, pp. 374–486.

Brewer, J. and Porter, R. (1993) *Consumption and the World of Goods*. London: Routledge.

Charbonnier, P. (1980) *Une autre France: La seigneurie rurale en basse auvergne du XIVe au XVI siècle*, 2 vols. Clermont-Ferrand: Institut d''études du Massif Central.

Clark, G. (1998) 'Land Hunger: Land as a Commodity and as a Status Good, England, 1500–1910'. *Explorations in Economic History*, 35(1): 31–58.

——(2002) 'Shelter from the Storm: Housing and the Industrial Revolution, 1550–1909'. *Journal of Economic History*, 62(2): 489–511.

——Huberman, M., and Lindert, P. (1995) 'A British Food Puzzle, 1770–1850'. *Economic History Review*, 48(2): 215–37.

Avenel, G. Viccomte d' (1894–1926) *Histoire économique de la propriété, des salaires, des denrées et do tous les prix en général, depuis l'an 1200 jusqu'à l'an 1800*, 7 vols. Paris: Impr. Nationale.

Davies, Rev. David (1795) *Case of Labourers in Husbandry Stated and Considered*. Bath: R. Cruttwell.

Davis, R. (1979) *The Industrial Revolution and British Overseas Trade*. Leicester: Leicester University Press.

De Maddalena, A. (1950) *Prezzi e aspetti di mercato in Milano durante il secolo XVII*. Milano: Malfasi.

——(1974) *Prezzi e mercedi a Milano dal 1701 al 1860*. Milano: Banca Commerciale Italiana.

Diewert, W. E. (ed.) (1990) 'The Theory of the Cost-of-Living Index and the Measurement of Welfare Change', *Price Level Measurement*. Amsterdam: North-Holland, pp. 79–147.

Eden, Sir Frederic Morton (1797) *The State of the Poor*, 3 vols. London: J. Davis.

Elsas, M. J. (1936–49) *Umriss einer Geschichte der Preise und Löhne in Deutschland vom ausgehenden mittelalter bis zum beginn des neunzehnten jahrhunderts*, 2 vols. in 3 parts. Leiden: Sijthoff.

Feavearyear, A. E. (1963) *The Pound Sterling*, 2nd edn. Oxford: Clarendon.

Feenstra, R. C. (1994) 'New Product Varieties and the Measurement of International Prices'. *American Economic Review*, 84(1): 157–77.

——(1995) 'Exact Hedonic Price Indexes'. *Review of Economics and Statistics*, 78(4): 634–53.

Feinstein, C. H. (1972) *National Income, Expenditure and Output of the United Kingdom, 1855–1965*. Cambridge: Cambridge University Press.

——(1998) 'Pessimism Perpetuated: Real Wages and the Standard of Living in Britain during and after the Industrial Revolution'. *Journal of Economic History*, 58(3): 625–58.

Feliu i Montfort, G. (1991) *Precios y Salarios en la Cataluña Moderna*, 2 vols. Madrid: Banco de España.

Forster, R. (1971) *The House of Saulx-Tavanes—Versailles and Burgundy, 1700–1830*. Baltimore, MD: Johns Hopkins University Press.

Friis, A. and Glamann, K. (1958) *A History of Prices and Wages in Denmark, 1660–1800*. London: Longmans Green.

Furtak, T. (1935) *Ceny w Gdansku w latach 1701–1815*. Lwow: Sklad Główny.

Gibson, A. J. S. and Smout, T. C (1995) *Prices, Food, and Wages in Scotland 1550–1780*. Cambridge: Cambridge University Press.

Hagen, W. W. (1986) 'Working for the Junker: The Standard of Living of Manorial Laborers in Brandenburg, 1584–1810'. *Journal of Modern History*, 58 (March): 143–58.

——(2002) *Ordinary Prussians: Brandenburg Junkers and Villagers, 1500–1840*. Cambridge: Cambridge University Press.

Hamilton, E. J. (1934) *American Treasure and the Price Revolution in Spain, 1501–1650*. Cambridge: Harvard University Press.

——(1947) *War and Prices in Spain, 1651–1800*. Cambridge: Harvard University Press.

Hauser, H. (1936) *Recherches et documents sur l'histoire des prix en France de 1500 à 1800*. Paris: Commité scientifique pour l'histoire des prix.

Hausman, J. (2003) 'Sources of Bias and Solutions to Bias in the Consumer Price Index'. *Journal of Economic Perspectives*, 17(1): 23–44.

Hoffman, P. T., Jacks, D. S, Levin, P. A., and Lindert, P. H. (2000) 'Sketching the Rise of Real Inequality in Early Modern Europe', Working Paper 102. Agricultural History Center. University of California–Davis.

Hollingsworth, T. H. (1977) 'Mortality in the British Peerage Families since 1600'. *Population*, numéro spécial (in English).

Homer, S. and Sylla, R. (1991) *A History of Interest Rates*, 3rd edn. New Brunswick, NJ: Rutgers University Press.

Hunter, D. (2000) 'Patronizing Handel, Inventing Audiences'. *Early Music* (February): 32–49.

Jardine, L. (1996) *Worldly Goods: A New History of the Renaissance*. New York, NY: Doubleday.

Jorgenson, D. and Slesnick, D. T. (1983) 'Individual and Social Cost of Living Indexes', in W. E. Diewert and C. Montmarquette (eds.), *Price Level Measurement*. Ottawa: Statistics Canada, pp. 241–323.

Kula, W. (1976) *An Economic Theory of the Feudal System: Toward a Model of the Polish Economy 1500–1800*. London: New Left Books.

Laslett, P. (ed.) (1973) *The Early Classics: John Graunt . . . Gregory King*. London: Gregg.

Lee, J. Z. and Wang Feng (1999) *One Quarter of Humanity*. Cambridge: Harvard University Press.

Lindert, P. H. and Williamson, J. G. (1982) 'Revising England's Social Tables, 1688–1812'. *Explorations in Economic History*, 19(4): 385–408.

——and——(1983) 'Reinterpreting Britain's Social Tables, 1688–1913'. *Explorations in Economic History*, 20(1): 94–109.

Maddison, A. (2001) *The World Economy: A Millennial Perspective*. Paris: OECD.

McEvedy, C. and Jones, R. (1978) *Atlas of World Population History*. London: Allen Lane.

Mitchell, B. R. (1988) *British Historical Statistics*. Cambridge: Cambridge University Press.

Morineau, M. (1985) *Pour une histoire économique vraie*. Paris: Presses Universitaires de Lille.

Morrisson, C. and Snyder, W. (2000) 'The Income Inequality of France in Historical Perspective'. *European Review of Economic History*, 4(1): 59–84.

O'Rourke, K. H. and Williamson, J. G. (2000) 'When Did Globalization Begin?' NBER Working Paper 7632 (April).

Parenti, G. (1942) *Prezzi e mercato del grano a Siena (1546–1765)*. Florence: Carlo Cya.

——(1967) 'Prezzi e Salari a Firenze dal 1520 al 1620', in R. Romano (ed.), *I Prezzi in Europa dal XIII secolo a oggi*. Turin: Giulio Einaudi.

Pelc, J. (1935) *Ceny w Krakowie w latach 1396–1600*. Lwow: Sklad Glówny.

——(1937) *Ceny w Gdansku w XVI I XVII wieku*. Lwow: Sklad Glówny.

Peller, S. (1965) 'Births and Deaths among Europe's Ruling Families since 1500', in D. V. Glass and D. E. Eversley (eds.), *Population in History*. London: Arnold.

Perrenoud, A. (1975) 'L'inégalité sociale devant la mort à Genéve au XVIIIéme siècle'. *Population*, 30, special number.

——(1984) 'The Mortality Decline in a Long-term Perspective', in T. Bengtsson, G. Fridlizius, and R. Ohlsson (eds.), *Pre-Industrial Population Change*. Stockholm: Almqvist and Wicksell, 41–70.

——(1997) 'La mortalité', in J.-P. Bardet and J. Dupaquier (eds.), *Histoire des populations de l'Europe'*, Vol. 1. Paris: Fayard, pp. 289–316.

Phelps Brown, E. H. and Hopkins, S. V. (1957) 'Wage-rates and Prices: Evidence for Population Pressure in the Sixteenth Century'. *Economica*, 24(96): 289–306.

——and——(1959) 'Builders' Wage-rates, Prices and Population: Some Further Evidence'. *Economica*, 26(101): 18–37.

—————(1981) *A Perspective of Wages and Prices.* London: Methuen.

Pomeranz, K. (2000) *The Great Divergence: China, Europe, and the Making of the Modern World Economy.* Princeton: Princeton University Press.

Posthumus, N. W. (1946) *Inquiry into the History of Prices in Holland.* Leiden: E. J. Brill.

Pribram, A. F., Geyer, R., and Koran, F. (1938) *Materialen zur Geschichte der Preise und Löhne in österreich.* Wein: Ueberreuter.

Razzell, P. E. (1994) *Essays in English Population History.* London: Caliban Books.

——(1998) 'The Conundrum of Eighteenth-Century English Population Growth'. *Social History of Medicine,* 11(3): 469–500.

——(1999) 'Demography, Economics, and the Changing Social Structure of England during the Industrial Revolution'. Manuscript.

——(forthcoming) 'Wealth, Socio-economic Status, and Mortality in England, 1500–1899'. *Economic History Review.*

Romano, R. (1965) *Prezzi, salari e servizi a Napoli nel secolo XVIII (1734–1806).* Milan: Banca Commerciale Italiana.

Sella, D. (1968) *Salari e Lavoro Nelledilizia Lombarda durante il secolo XVII.* Pavia: Succ. Fusi.

Shammas, C. (1990) *The Pre-industrial Consumer in England and America.* Oxford: Clarendon Press.

Siegel, S. (1936) *Ceny w Warszawie w latach 1701–1815.* Lwow: Sklad Glówny.

——(1949) *Ceny w Warsawie w Latach 1816–1914.* Poznan: Sklad Glowny.

Singer-Kérel, J. (1961) *Le coût de la vie a Paris 1840–1954.* Paris: A. Colin.

Slesnick, D. T. (1998) 'Empirical Approaches to the Measurement of Welfare'. *Journal of Economic Literature,* 36(4): 2108–65.

Snell, K. D. M. (1985) *Annals of the Labouring Poor: Social and Agrarian Change in England, 1660–1900.* Cambridge: Cambridge University Press.

Stone, R. (1988) 'Some Seventeenth Century Econometrics: Consumer Behaviour'. *Revue Européene des Sciences Sociales,* 26: 19–41.

Tomaszewski, E. (1934) *Ceny w Krokowie w latach 1601–1795.* Lwow: Sklad Glówny.

Toutain, J.-C. (1987) *Le produit intérieur brut de la France de 1789 a 1982. Economies et Sociétés.* Cahiers de l'I.S.M.E.A., Série Histoire quantitative de l'économie française, no. 15.

Verlinden, C. (ed.) (1959–65) *Dokumenten voor de Geschiedenis van Prijzen en Lonen in Vlaanderen en Brabant.* Brugge: De Tempel.

Wee, H. van der (1963) *The Growth of the Antwerp Market and the European Economy.* The Hague: Nijhoff.

Wetherill, L. (1988) *Consumer Behavior and Material Culture in Britain, 1660–1760.* London: Routledge.

Williamson, J. G. (1976) 'American Prices and Urban Inequality since 1820'. *Journal of Economic History,* 36(2): 303–33.

——(1985) *Did British Capitalism Breed Inequality?* Winchester, MA: Allen and Unwin.

Woude, A. van der and Schuurman, A. (eds.) (1980) *Probate Inventories: A New Source for the Historical Study of Wealth, Material Culture, and Agricultural Development.* Wageningen: Afdeling Agrarische Geschiedenis.

Wrigley, E. A., Davies, R. S., Oeppen, J. E., and Schofield, R. S. (1997) *English Population History from Family Reconstitution 1580–1837.* Cambridge: Cambridge University Press.

——and Schofield, R. S. (1981) *The Population History of England, 1541–1871.* Cambridge: Harvard University Press.

Zanden, J. L. van (1995) 'Tracing the Beginning of the Kuznets Curve: Western Europe during the Early Modern Period'. *Economic History Review*, 48(4): 643–64.

—— (1999) 'Wages and the Standard of Living in Europe, 1500–1800'. *European Review of Economic History*, 3(2): 175–98.

—— (2000) 'Towards a Second Generation of Consumer Price Indices for the Early Modern Period: Experiments with New Data for the Western Part of the Netherlands', Paper presented at the Arild Conference on 'New Evidence on the Standard of Living in Pre-industrial Europe and Asia', 1–5 August.

7 What Happened to the Standard of Living Before the Industrial Revolution? New Evidence from the Western Part of the Netherlands

JAN LUITEN VAN ZANDEN

1. Introduction

In the second half of the 1990s, several important studies were published which showed that the standard of living in the most developed parts of Asia (China and India in particular) in the early modern period was on par with those in the most advanced regions of Europe (see especially Parthasarathi 1998; Pomeranz 2000: 36–42; Allen (Chapter 5, this volume); and Parthasarathi Chapter 4, this volume). This is based on new evidence concerning various indicators such as life expectancy, levels of consumption, and in particular, real wages, especially in the eighteenth century. Implicitly, and at times also explicitly, it is assumed that this also implies that levels of economic development as measured by gross domestic product (GDP) per capita in those different parts of the Eurasian continent must have been similar as well. This contrasts sharply with the estimates of GDP made from attempts to reconstruct historical national accounts, which have shown that at the beginning of the nineteenth century there was a big gap in GDP per capita between western Europe on the one hand and China, India, Indonesia, and Japan on the other hand.[1]

One of the problems with the new comparative studies is that the relationship between GDP per capita and the standard of living is very complex. This is evident from the large body of literature that addresses what happened to the standard of living during (early) industrialization. The debate on this issue relating to Britain seems to have converged to the view that early industrialization did not result in major gains in living standards; for example, the conclusions of the synthetic study by Feinstein on real incomes during industrialization were highly pessimistic (Feinstein 1998). The literature on the 'biological standard of living' has produced a comparable 'height paradox', the finding that in a number of countries (the United States, the Netherlands, Great Britain) early industrialization went together with stagnation or even decline in the average stature of the population (Floud, Wachter, and Gregory 1990; Komlos 1996; Tassenaar 2000). The reasons for this are still unclear, but probably include a worsening of the disease environment as a result of urbanization and a possible decline in the consumption of certain food products.[2] It may well be that the 'costs of modernization' were such that (large) parts of the population did not profit from the first phases of industrialization.

In another chapter I have argued that a similar 'growth paradox' can probably be found in Europe during the early modern period (van Zanden 1999). In short, the argument is that real wages declined between the fifteenth and the (end of the) eighteenth century, in spite of the ongoing process of economic development, which resulted in moderate growth of GDP per capita, especially in the North Sea region (the Low Countries and Britain).

However, this study, and independent estimates made by de Vries (1994*a*) and Allen (1998) concerning the development of real wages in this area, also suggest that the Netherlands may have been an exception to this rule. During the period in which its economy was very dynamic (between the 1580s and the 1670s) nominal wages increased considerably, and this may have led to an improvement in the real wage (and may perhaps also have affected other dimensions of the standard of living). The problem that is at the core of this chapter is what happened to the standard of living of the inhabitants of the western part of the Netherlands during this period. Specifically, did they profit from the 'Golden Age', the period of dynamic economic development between the 1580s and the 1670s?

First, I concentrate on one of the weaknesses of previous studies (including my own), measuring price changes. I hope to show that a more careful estimation of the consumer price index (CPI) of workers can dramatically change our view of what happened to real wages. A database is constructed to analyse price changes between 1450 and 1800, which also makes it possible to examine changes in the prices of goods that were consumed by other social groups, particularly the elite. The main body of this chapter therefore presents new evidence about changes in the cost of living in Holland (or more accurately, the western part of the Netherlands, because data from the adjacent province of Utrecht are also included) between 1450 and 1800, and discusses the importance of this new CPI for measuring changes in real incomes.

Next, I give an overview of other evidence related to changes in the standard of living between the fifteenth and the eighteenth centuries, and discuss briefly what these results mean for our understanding of the process of economic growth before industrialization. In the concluding section, I return to the original problem: what happened to the relationship between income per capita and real wages in the early modern period? Does the fact that, within western Europe, real wages and GDP per capita diverged help to explain the different outcomes of the historical national accounts, in which large disparities in GDP per capita between Asia and western Europe at about 1800 are found, and the results from the recent work on standards of living in both regions which point towards much smaller differences?

2. The Need for a Second Generation of Consumer Price Indices

Current interpretations of the long-term development of the real wage in Europe between the late Middle Ages and the early nineteenth century are still largely based on the pioneering work of a generation of scholars who worked on this issue between the 1930s and 1960s. The massive research effort was undertaken foremost by the members of the International Scientific Committee on Price History, set up in 1929, who published an impressive series of histories of prices and wages focusing on this period.[3] A number of these studies (Hamilton, Hoszowski) included indices for the development of prices (cost of living) and wages in their cities or regions, and scholars such as Abel (1966) and Slicher van Bath (1960) used this material to map the long-term changes in wages and prices between 1000 and 1850. The most elaborate work on the reconstruction of long series of wages and the cost of living was undertaken by Phelps Brown and Hopkins in the 1950s.[4] Not only did they construct such series for England between 1264 and 1954, but they also analysed the consequences of the price revolution of the sixteenth century by using the data from Hamilton (1934), Elsas (1936/1940), Pribram (1938) and others in constructing similar indices for continental cities and regions. Comparable indices of prices and wages were constructed for Spain (1500–present; Reher and Ballasteros 1993), Antwerp (1400–1700; van der Wee 1975), the western part of the Netherlands (de Vries 1994*a*; see also de Vries and van der Woude 1997), and other cities and regions.[5]

These authors were interested in changes in the level of prices and wages in the long-run and, perhaps foremost, in the calculation of real wages as an indicator of the standard of living. Their conclusions were in general pessimistic: real wages declined strongly between the fifteenth and the beginning of the nineteenth century, a decline that was especially sharp during the price revolution of the sixteenth century and again after about 1750. Only in a few cases—Antwerp in the sixteenth century (van der Wee 1975), and Holland in the first half of the seventeenth century (de Vries and van der Woude 1997)—did nominal wages increase more rapidly than prices and did economic expansion result in an increase in real wages.

The quality of the series of this 'first generation' of historical consumer price indices has only been tested in one case: the debate on the standard of living during the English Industrial Revolution. The pioneering chapter by Lindert and Williamson (1983) and new research by Feinstein (1998) brought clearly to light the weaknesses of the Phelps Brown and Hopkins (PBH) indices—both of wages and of prices—and the subsequent discussion has made clear the many problems involved in measuring long-term changes in the real wage, even for a period and a country which is relatively well documented. Whereas the first-generation studies concentrated on the wages of a small section of the labour force—basically the wages of certain labourers in the construction industry—Lindert and Williamson set out to construct a representative income series for all members of the labour force.

Moreover, the more recent work on price indices has also shown how sensitive these are to the use of different weights and the inclusion of other categories of expenditure (e.g. rents) in the CPI.[6]

In this chapter I focus on the second issue: the construction of a 'second-generation' CPI for the western part of the Netherlands. The reasons for doing this are that the first-generation CPIs have not always included the right price series (for example, no rents or rye prices instead of bread prices) and have used fixed weights for very long periods of time. An additional reason is to find out how important the introduction of a new item of consumption—potatoes—was for the cost of living. I hope to show what the consequences of these weaknesses are, and how an attempt to improve the CPI may affect our view of the development of the standard of living in the early modern period.

3. The Database

For the most important articles of consumption, long series of institutional prices were collected mainly from two sources: Posthumus' *Nederlandsche Prijs-geschiendenis* (1943/64), and a recently published database of prices paid by the cloister of Leeuwenhorst between 1410 and 1570 (de Moor 2000), which fills some of the gaps left by Posthumus' work. All prices refer to prices paid by institutions (hospitals, chapters, and orphanages), except for two special series: rye bread, based on the assize, and rents (see Appendix for details about the sources).

In the first-generation CPIs, the price with the largest weight was wheat or rye (or malt, oatmeal, etc.). In Holland, especially in the cities, the making of bread was already concentrated in specialized bakeries during the fifteenth and sixteenth centuries, which meant that consumers did not buy grains but bread, of which the price was set by the city. During the seventeenth century, indirect taxation on milling increased sharply, which meant that the margin between the price of rye and the price of rye bread became much larger than it had been in the early sixteenth century.[7] During the seventeenth and eighteenth centuries, bread prices increased much more than the price of rye (see Table 7.2), and measuring real wages in terms of rye clearly gives a biased impression of their development.

Another major change is the inclusion of a series on rents, an item of expenditure that is missing in all first-generation CPIs. On the basis of a vast database of houses owned by institutions and by the city, Lesger (1986) has constructed chain indices for the development of rents of houses in Amsterdam between 1550 and 1850. His method of constructing the indices has been criticized by Eichholtz and Theebe (1998, 1999). They state that a chain index does not reflect the housing market correctly, because rental contracts were often for periods longer than one year, and only in the years that a contract was renewed did a new market valuation of the property occur (whereas a chain index 'assumes' that in the intervening years the rent and therefore the market value remains the same). They applied a more sophisticated method to construct what they called a repeated-rent index; from

Lesger's database of 48,620 yearly rent figures, they used only the information which related to the renewal of contract periods, that is, to actual changes in the observed rents. Using regression analysis they estimated on an annual basis the average change of these rents, and in this way created a repeated-rent index for the 1550–1850 period, which is also by its nature corrected for changes in the quality of the houses. It is possible to compare the long-term changes in these series with the average rents of all houses in Holland in different periods (Table 7.1). The comparison shows that in the very long run the different series developed in a similar way: a very strong increase in rents between the 1560s and 1630s, followed by a much more moderate increase in the next century, then stagnation during the eighteenth century, and even some decline between 1806–8 and 1816–26. The average rent per house rose, however, more than the repeated-rent index, which may be an indication of changes in the quality of the housing stock. The differences between Lesger's chain index and Eichholtz and Theebe's repeated-rent index appear to be rather small, but are nevertheless significant, especially for the early period.

The very rapid increase in rent levels in the period after 1560 is confirmed by other data. In Alkmaar, for which we have a complete and consistent set of data for 1561 and 1632, average rents went up by 428% (van den Berg and van Zanden 1993). The decline of rents during the second half of the eighteenth century is corroborated by Pot's (1994) research into house rents in Leiden. He found a fall of about 5–10% between 1750 and 1808, which is consistent with Lesger's data. These data and the comparison made in Table 7.1 also justify, in my view, the use of the Amsterdam repeated-rent series to estimate the development of rents in Holland.

The other series were directly derived from the two price histories mentioned, although some problems did occur. There were many gaps in the series of beer prices, which were filled by using price data from beer–vinegar and vinegar, which were produced by the same breweries (the long-run development of beer–vinegar

Table 7.1 A comparison between the development of rent levels according to Lesger's data for Amsterdam (chain index and repeated rent index) and the average rents per house according to the registers of taxes on real estate, 1560/61–1806/08 (1806/08 = 100)

	Lesger's data		Rents per house (Holland)	
	Chain indices[a]	Repeated rent index	Absolute (fl)	Index
1560/61	15	18	9.38	11
1630/32	65	68	55	62
1730/32	108	110	100	112
1806/08	100	100	89	100
1816/26	90	95	94	106

[a] unweighted average of the series A, B, and C.

Sources: Lesger (1986), Eichholtz and Theebe (1998), data on average rents per house: Soltow and van Zanden (1998: 28, 136; van Zanden 1987: 576).

prices and beer prices seem to have been almost identical). After 1740, the institutions did not buy beer any more; it had been replaced by coffee and tea and to some extent by *jenever* (Dutch gin). Therefore, after 1740 beer prices were linked to an unweighted index of the prices of coffee, tea, and *jenever*. Finally, prices of textiles after 1550 are rather scarce. We were unable to make annual estimates of their development and had to rely on different series of the prices of cloth and of linen—both with many gaps—to construct the long-term development of textile prices as a series of average prices for ten year periods (1550–9, 1560–9, etc).[8] Table 7.2 shows the development of the individual series.

The reconstructed series of the long-term development of prices are in themselves interesting. It appears, for example, that rents increased more rapidly than all other prices, which is what one would expect in a region of rapid demographic growth and urbanization. But beer prices increased almost as rapidly (and even more rapidly than rents between 1550–74 and 1575–99); the heavy indirect taxation of beer helps to explain the strong increase in its relative price. Rye prices increased almost tenfold during the three and a half centuries covered by these data, but the prices of other agricultural products—butter, meat, and peas—went up even more, especially during the century after 1575 when the Dutch economy went through its Golden Age. The relative increase in the prices of butter and meat testifies to a strong growth in the demand for these luxury goods. The growing disparity after 1550–74 between the prices of rye (which is representative of all grains) on the one hand, and beer and bread on the other hand, is probably caused by increased taxation and perhaps by the stagnation of productivity growth in these industries. It is striking that the prices of other industrial commodities and of fish increased less than the

Table 7.2 The development of the most important series (1550/74 = 100)

	Rent	Bread	Rye	Butter	Drink	Peas	Meat	Fish	Text	Peat
1450–74	—	27	27	29	43	31	42	57	48	43
1475–99	—	41	41	40	63	57	50	61	56	46
1500–24	—	42	42	46	64	55	49	59	62	61
1525–49	—	57	57	58	66	63	63	72	64	75
1550–74	100	100	100	100	100	100	100	100	100	100
1575–99	180	160	160	169	244	169	164	122	110	157
1600–24	344	208	175	240	241	243	227	156	171	183
1625–49	410	292	240	319	316	301	316	158	188	249
1650–74	499	310	225	325	337	417	350	195	203	249
1675–99	476	308	196	307	427	409	328	227	199	212
1700–24	536	306	188	294	512	335	353	235	196	230
1725–49	582	288	167	302	461	292	346	235	188	285
1750–74	589	303	196	311	508	370	346	249	202	329
1775–99	633	359	239	337	623	438	389	379	217	349

Sources: See Appendix.

prices of agricultural commodities; especially textiles (and paper, not shown in the table) became much less expensive in the long run.

4. The Weights and New Products

The inclusion of rents and the price of bread is a major step forward in comparison with the first-generation CPIs. The selection of different weighting schemes is another potential area of improvement. Phelps Brown and Hopkins, for example, assumed that the weighting scheme remained unchanged between the thirteenth and the twentieth centuries, which is a strong assumption. Theoretically, one would expect consumers to adapt to changes in relative prices in such a way as to increase the consumption of goods, which were becoming cheaper. Shammas (1990) has documented such a process for England, showing that the share of foodstuffs in the budget was already falling and the share of industrial goods was rising during the early modern period. De Vries and van der Woude (1997) have summarized comparable evidence related to the changes in consumption patterns in the Netherlands; their main sources were the accounts of institutions for which it has been possible to reconstruct their pattern of expenditure on consumption goods. Ongoing research by Arthur van Riel on expenditure patterns in the nineteenth century are another source of information (see van Zanden and van Riel 2000: 409). On the basis of these studies two sets of weights for labouring families have been constructed: one for the eighteenth century (linked to indices 1720–44 = 100) and one for the fifteenth century (1450–74 = 100). The latter weights are rather similar to the ones applied by Phelps Brown and Hopkins, whereas the eighteenth-century weights are modelled after the nineteenth-century expenditure pattern found in van Riel's work. I have also added the estimated expenditure pattern of the Dutch elite during the first half of the nineteenth century, which was reconstructed by Arthur van Riel. This elite weighting scheme was estimated on the basis of a comparison between the expenditure pattern of the labourers from budget studies and the structure of expenditure of the total population from the reconstructed national accounts (see Smits, Horlings, and van Zanden 2000); the elite was the difference between the two, taking into consideration their share in total income. The 'other industrial goods' which appear in the latter budgets have been allocated to the other items of non-food expenditure. (See Table 7.3.)

These four expenditure patterns were applied to the price series, which eventually were converted into indices 1450–74 = 100. To find out how important the use of different weighting schemes is, I calculated four CPIs on this basis (1450–74 = 100) (see Table 7.4). The index of wages was used as the price index of consumer services in the elite CPI, which represents the 'consumption' of the labour of servants.

The similarities between the different series are perhaps more striking than the differences. The two indices based on the estimated expenditure patterns of labourers in Holland show a remarkable degree of similarity. This is an important result as it shows that, in spite of the fact that the labourers tried to adapt to changes

Table 7.3 Stylized expenditure patterns

	Labourer			Elite	
	England c. 13–20th	Holland c. 15th	Holland c. 18th	Netherlands 1806/62	Netherlands 1800/52
Foodstuff					
Bread (Rye)	20.0	40.0	30.0	22.1	16.0
Dairy product					
Butter	12.5	5.0	5.0	5.9	9.0
Meat	25.0	10.0	3.0	4.4	9.0
Fish	—	5.0	2.0	0.8	3.0
Vegetables					
Peas etc.	—	5.0	15.0	5.0	5.0
Potatoes	—	—	—	11.8	—
Drink	22.5	10.0	5.0	4.1	4.0
Other					
Groceries	—	—	—	6.7	10.0[a]
Foodstuff, total	80.0	75.0	60.0	60.8	56.0
Textiles	12.5	9.0	15.0	15.4	10.0
Fuel (Peat)	7.5	7.0	11.0	8.9	1.0
Soap	—	2.0	3.0	3.5	5.0
Rent	—	7.0	11.0	11.4	7.0
Consumer services	—	—	—	—	15.0
Other (Industrial)	—	—	—	—	6.0[b]
Total	100.0	100.0	100.0	100.0	100.0

[a] In the elite index this was estimated as sugar 5% and pepper 5%.
[b] Estimated by the price of paper.
Based on: nineteenth-century budgets: van Zanden and van Riel (2000: 409), other budgets: de Vries and van der Woude (1997: 708–9), Phelps Brown and Hopkins (1981).

in relative prices by adjusting their demand patterns (i.e. by consuming less expensive bread, meat, and butter, and more cheap textiles), they were unable to do much about the enormous increase in the general price level. An important reason for this was that they were 'forced' to spend more on housing, due to the fact that rents were going up relative to all other prices.

The absence of this rent squeeze, which has been ignored in much of the literature on the price revolution of the early modern period, largely explains the difference between the England price index (i.e. the price index using the PBH weights) and the Holland indices, although the substitution of bread prices for rye also played a role. The elite CPI also shows a much less rapid increase, which is mainly due to three developments: (1) bread had a much smaller weight in the basket of the elite; (2) the elite profited from the relative decline of the price of consumer services (wages); and (3) they also profited from the decline of the prices of industrial and colonial products, which they consumed in much larger quantities than the

Table 7.4 CPIs using four different weighting schemes, and the final index, 1450/74 = 100

	England	Holland fifteenth century	Netherlands eighteenth century	Elite	Final index
1450–74	100	100	100	100	100
1475–99	133	140	142	123	140
1500–24	141	146	150	133	146
1525–49	170	182	183	158	182
1550–74	275	299	296	254	299
1575–99	476	494	480	433	494
1600–24	575	658	668	567	658
1625–49	767	873	863	716	873
1650–74	794	958	982	778	973
1675–99	791	955	960	754	955
1700–24	841	980	957	764	945
1725–49	805	950	936	752	923
1750–74	866	1,011	1,018	796	1,006
1775–99	1,004	1,177	1,168	910	1,113

Sources: Tables 7.2, 7.3, and Appendix.

labourers. This experiment suggests that in the early modern period, relative prices moved in general in a direction which was unfavourable for the lower classes (i.e. sharp increases in the prices of bread, beer, and of rents) and favourable for the elite (i.e. a relative decline of wages—and therefore of household services—and of industrial prices).[9]

Changes in the patterns of consumption of the labourers did not affect their CPI very much, however. The strong decline in meat consumption and the increased demand for industrial products that can be observed in early modern Europe were rather weak attempts to stem the tide of the almost continuous rise of prices (only after 1675 did inflation come to a halt). Similar results were obtained by Phelps Brown and Hopkins (1981: 89), who in one of their papers also referred to an experiment with different weights for their CPI, but which did not have a big impact on its long-term development. This is a striking result, because one would expect a rather different outcome, that is, that changes in relative prices and demand patterns combined would have moderated the price increases to some extent. Labourers were, however, 'trapped' because they really needed basic foodstuffs and shelter and could not switch out of them to an extent which would seriously have changed their 'terms of trade' (i.e. the relationship between nominal wages and the CPI).

There may have been one exception to this. In the literature on changes in patterns of food consumption in this period much attention has been paid to the rise of the potato, a crop which replaced bread and vegetables (peas and beans) on the tables of labourers in the second half of the eighteenth century. This occurred in a period of renewed inflation when Dutch nominal wages remained more or less the same (and therefore real wages seem to have declined substantially). Noordegraaf and others have suggested that labourers may have stabilized their real incomes by switching to potatoes, which provided many more calories per guilder.

There are different ways to change the CPI in order to take this process into account. The standard procedure is to create new indices on the basis of the new expenditure patterns which come into existence, in this case, as a result of the introduction of the potato; on the basis of the qualitative literature on this topic and the nineteenth-century budgets it can be estimated that the share of potatoes in the budget increased from 3% in the 1770s to 6% in the 1780s and 9% in the 1790s.

A 'quasi-hedonic' price index can also be estimated: assuming that the aim of consumption (of bread and potatoes) is the intake of calories, one can calculate the relative prices of the calories contained in these products, and introduce the price of potatoes accordingly. The welfare effect of getting more calories per guilder from potatoes is then taken into account (the weights are again identical to the ones used in the first approach; 3% for the 1770s etc.). Figure 7.1 gives an indication of the kilo-calories that one guilder represented, which clearly shows the big difference in price per calorie between potatoes on the one hand and bread and peas on the other hand.

Both adaptations of the CPI show a more moderate rate of inflation after 1763 when the series of potato prices begins. If we accordingly recalculate the CPI based on the eighteenth-century weights, and set 1763 = 100 for convenience, the index for 1790–9 is 122.9 for the unchanged CPI, 119.5 for the CPI with a conventional introduction of the potato, and 115.9 for the recalculated CPI with a 'hedonic' introduction of the new crop. It appears that the potato did make a difference, but it only lowered the rate of inflation after 1763 by about a third.

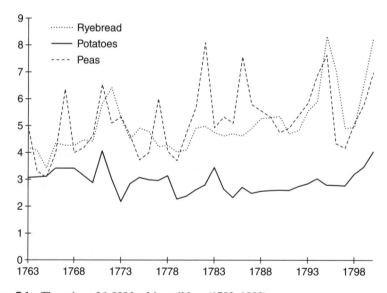

Figure 7.1   The price of 1,000 kcal in guilders (1783–1800)

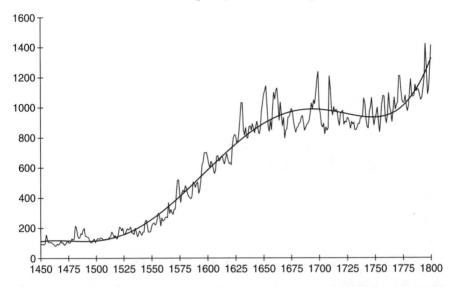

Figure 7.2 The CPI for the western part of the Netherlands, 1450–1800 (1450/74 = 100; polynomial trend added)

The final CPI was calculated on the basis of the fifteenth-century weights for the period 1450–1656 (1450–74 = 100) and on the basis of the eighteenth-century weights for the period 1656–1800 (1720–44 = 100).[10] The final index (recalculated 1450/74 = 100) is shown in Figure 7.2. It shows a pattern which is to some extent well known: a huge increase in the price level during the sixteenth century and the first half of the seventeenth century, followed by much more stable development between about 1650 and 1750, and a second strong increase after about 1750 (though compared with the sixteenth-century price revolution this increase was rather moderate). Comparable first-generation calculations by de Vries and van der Woude showed a decline after about 1660, which is not present in this series. The difference is largely due to bread prices—instead of rye prices—and the role of rents.

5. Real Wages

To find out what happened with real wages, I used the data on nominal wages collected by de Vries for the period 1500–1815, which refer almost exclusively to the wages of building labourers,[11] and which were also extended backwards to include the 1450–1500 period using data from Noordegraaf and Schoenmakers (1984). The wage series used is very 'traditional' and needs modification as a result of future research, which is, however, beyond the scope of this chapter.[12]

The real wage index that is presented in Figure 7.3 shows a very strong decline in the period between the 1460s and the 1570s. The decline was characterized

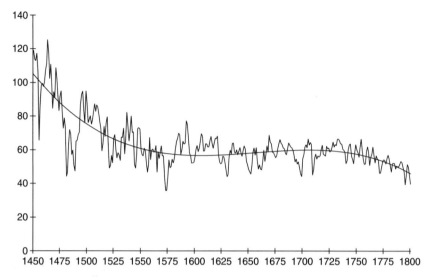

Figure 7.3   Real wages in the western part of the Netherlands, 1450–1800 (1450/74 = 100; polynomial trend added)

by a huge fall in real wages during the 1480s (the result of very high prices during years of war and harvest failure), a stabilization during the decades surrounding 1500, followed again by deep troughs in the 1520s and a renewed decline after 1560, which leads to the 'years of hunger' after the Revolt of 1572. After the disastrous decade following the Revolt, real wages returned to the level of the 1540s and 1550s, and remained at that level for more than a century and a half, from the 1580s to 1760s. I do not find strong evidence for an increase in real wages during the Golden Age of the first half of the seventeenth century, nor does the decline in cereal prices which set in after about 1660 have much of an effect on the real wage. Long-run stability (though not without fluctuations, of course) seems to have been normal during the greater part of the seventeenth and eighteenth centuries; only after about 1760–70 did real wages begin to decline again.

A number of changes have not, however, been taken into account. Noordegraaf (1985) and de Vries (1994a) assumed an increase in employment in the years after the Revolt because many holidays were abolished during the Reformation and the booming economy created a strong demand for labour. However, it is unclear whether an increase in working hours should be interpreted as a gain or as a loss in welfare. Leisure is a consumption good, and there probably existed a positive relationship between the demand for leisure and real income. Increased working hours can also be interpreted as an adaptation to the decline in the real wage that occurred after the 1460s. If we want to estimate the development of real family income, changes in the working hours of men as well as changes in the participation of women and children must be taken into account, along with changes in non-wage incomes such as work in proto-industry and changes in household production.

In general, we lack sufficient sources to reconstruct family income in any detail. I have, therefore, attempted in another chapter to interpret the real wage as an important input in the decision-making process of households which determines the choices the members of a household can make. If the crucial 'terms of trade' are declining (or are in absolute terms, low) a household cannot afford leisure and luxury consumption goods, and will have to substitute inferior goods for goods of a higher quality—that is, its standard of living so defined would have declined (see van Zanden 1999). The standard of living in this view can be interpreted as the degree of freedom a household has in its decision-making process: low real wages certainly limit its choices, whereas high real wages increase them.[13] Therefore, in my view, we should not make corrections for changes in working hours, participation ratios, etc., when we analyse real wages as an indicator of the level and development of the standard of living.

Another aspect which needs to be mentioned is the decline in the amplitude of fluctuations around the trend value of the real wage. Visual inspection of the series suggests that after about 1600 these fluctuations become less sharp, which would certainly imply a positive welfare effect. This is valid assuming that the welfare loss of a sharp decline in real wages is higher than the welfare gain of a comparably large increase and that households are unable to save the extra real income of good years to finance the deficit of the bad years. This may, however, be the result of changes in the CPI itself (the introduction of rents after 1550 and of bread prices after 1596). More research into this topic is necessary to understand these dynamics.[14]

6. Other Evidence Concerning the Development of the Standard of Living

The decline of the real wage during the early modern period is confirmed by other evidence concerning the standard of living. A team of archaeologists led by Maat has in a number of studies documented the decline in the stature of men and women buried in the western part of the Netherlands. The combined result of three studies of the average heights of men during the Middle Ages has shown that they were probably over 170 cm tall. A group of canons ($n = 23$) was found to be 174 cm on average, whereas the inhabitants of a Delft infirmary ($n = 25$) averaged 'only' 170.5 cm; in the following period (between 1433 and 1652), however, a study of the cemetery of the same infirmary showed that average height had declined to 168.9 cm. In a number of studies related to seventeenth- and eighteenth-century males, average heights were found to be about 166 cm, a decrease of about 4 cm compared to the situation in the fourteenth and early fifteenth centuries.[15] During the first half of the nineteenth century, when the real wage remained at the low level it had settled to at the end of the eighteenth century, the average stature of conscripts also showed strong fluctuations consistent with the changes in the real wage (displaying troughs in the mid-1840s and mid-1850s). Only after about 1860, at the same time the heights of Dutch men started to rise, did real wages begin to increase sharply but it took until the beginning of the twentieth century before the stature that was probably normal in the Middle Ages was attained once again.[16]

The long-term correlation between real wages and stature strongly supports the conclusions about standards of living drawn from the study of real wages. Cross-sectional analysis points in the same direction. One of the striking results of the analysis of heights of conscripts in the Netherlands at the beginning of the nine-teenth century is that there appears to be an inverse relationship between the level of economic development (in terms of urbanization ratio and income) and the biolo-gical standard of living. The contrast especially between 'backward' Drenthe, which had the tallest recruits, and highly developed Holland and Zeeland, with the shortest recruits, is very striking (see Noordegraaf and van Zanden 1995: 419; Tassenaar 2000). This evidence is consistent with a study of the regional variation in the distribution of income in the same period, which documented huge differences between the west, where inequality was very high, and the rest, where the income distribution was much less skewed (and which showed that Drenthe had by far the lowest inequality, see Soltow and van Zanden 1998: 135–41).

The decline in real wages and stature was probably related to changes in con-sumption patterns. The consumption of meat and fish probably declined in the long run, especially in the cities. In the city of Leiden, meat consumption per capita fell by more than 50% between the 1470s and 1801–4. Herring, which was a staple diet during the fifteenth and sixteenth centuries, became a luxury during the eighteenth and nineteenth centuries. Part of the explanation is offered by the changes in relative prices, the prices of food products increased much more than those of industrial products, which may have induced consumers to switch towards the latter (see Table 7.2). As a result, the per capita consumption of industrial products may have increased sub-stantially, in spite of the decline of real wages. A few studies into the long-term development of material wealth have tended to show such an increase.[17] In a previous section it was argued that the quality of housing probably improved a lot between 1500 and 1800, although this does not necessarily mean that the per capita consumption of housing increased, because the population probably grew faster than the supply of housing space. Finally, there is much evidence that literacy rates of both men and women went up substantially between 1500 and 1800. This may have been the largest item of capital formation during this period and it must have resulted in major increases in the welfare of the population (Kuijpers 1997; see Reis, Chapter 8, this volume).

Demographic indicators of the development of the standard of living for the Netherlands have not been studied much. There is some evidence that the mean age of marriage rose substantially during the sixteenth century.[18] This rise is consistent with the decline of the standard of living and fits into the Hajnal hypothesis that the two were intimately connected. A further, but less dramatic, rise in the mean age of marriage is documented for the period after about 1650 (de Vries 1985: 665).

Faber (1976) has formulated the hypothesis that during the seventeenth century subsistence crises were thanks to the booming economy, almost absent from the Netherlands whereas during the eighteenth century, as a result of economic stagnation, they returned. This hypothesis was tested by Noordegraaf and van Zanden (1995), who used series on the number of deaths in three cities (Rotterdam, Amsterdam, and Alkmaar) to study the relationship between prices (of grains, and the cost-of-living index constructed by de Vries) and mortality. Applying the method developed by Weir (1984), they found no effect of grain prices or the cost of living on fluctuations in the number of deaths in seventeenth-century Rotterdam, but significant effects were noticed in eighteenth-century Amsterdam and Rotterdam, which appears to confirm the Faber hypothesis. However, closer inspection of the series shows that until the 1670s the pattern was dominated by the cyclical occurrence of the plague.[19] The variation in the number of deaths around the trend—which may be considered to be an indicator of the effects of exogenous shocks on the demographic system—did not increase after 1700, but remained at the same level (for Rotterdam, the standard deviation was about 0.20). Therefore, it is questionable whether this analysis of the changing relationship between grain prices and the number of deaths can be used to infer a decline in the standard of living in the eighteenth century. For the nineteenth century (in fact, 1811–70), Galloway (1988) has demonstrated a rather weak relationship between grain prices and the death rate; his analysis showed a much stronger influence of grain prices on birth rates and marriage rates.

7. Conclusions and Discussion

The second-generation CPI presented in this chapter, in combination with wage data collected by de Vries, has shown that even in the relatively dynamic economy of the western part of the Netherlands real wages declined during the early modern period. The decline was fastest between 1450/75 and the middle of the sixteenth century, after which a long period of stability followed, ending in the second half of the eighteenth century. Previous estimates, which indicated some increase in purchasing power during the Golden Age, are probably (much) too optimistic: this period of brilliant economic performance, traditionally dated from the 1580s to the 1670s, did not lead to real-wage growth. The stabilization of real wages after the middle of the sixteenth century was, however, an important achievement—in other parts of (northern) Europe this probably did not occur and real wages continued to decline. England may, however, be another exception (see Allen 1998).

At the same time, GDP per capita increased by perhaps 35–55% between 1510/14 and the 1820s (van Zanden 1987, 1992, 2002). There appears to have been a 'great divergence' between wage growth and output growth. An increase in the number of days and hours worked can only help to explain a small part of this divergence.[20] New estimates of the size and composition of the GDP of Holland at the beginning of the sixteenth century suggest that the share of wages in income (including the imputed wage income of the self-employed) was much higher than during the nineteenth century.[21] This shift was related to fundamental changes in income distribution (see also the chapter by Hoffman *et al.*, Chapter 6, this volume).

This does not, however, necessarily mean that there was a sharp polarization in the income distribution. There is no doubt that the rich (i.e. the merchants) became much wealthier in real terms, certainly compared to labourers, whose real income fell. But certain parts of the middle classes grew too, because economic development resulted in increased demands for salaried employees (whose relative incomes rose as well) and in the growth of a 'middle class' of shopkeepers, middlemen, and specialized craftsmen. The absolute gap between the top and the bottom widened markedly, but at the same time the social layers in between grew in size and complexity. The possibilities for upward social mobility remained intact, whereas the rewards to rises in status increased as income disparities went up. This combination of processes also helps to explain why investment in human capital continued to rise and literacy increased substantially. It became increasingly profitable to invest in one's children in order to enhance their chances at social mobility.

Finally, this divergence between the real wage and the development of GDP per capita may also help to explain the paradox that was mentioned at the beginning of this chapter: that at about 1800 the standard of living in the most advanced parts of Asia was perhaps as high as in western Europe, whereas GDP per capita in Asia was probably less than 70% of the European level.

Appendix

Sources of Data Information

General

Series of prices are mainly derived from the second volume of Posthumus (1964), and are generally prices paid by institutions in Utrecht, Leiden, and Amsterdam. Additional sources are the registers of the *broodzetting* of Leiden (which was followed by the rest of Holland) and, for the period 1450–1550, prices paid by the Abbey of Leeuwenhorst (near Leiden), collected by Trudy de Moor (2000). Before 1530 the Utrecht prices, which were set in Utrecht *stuferi* and *albi*, were converted in Holland ponden/guilders on the basis of the 'exchange rates' published by Posthumus (1964: 28). After this conversion it can be shown that in the long-run prices of wheat, rye, herrings, and beer in Leiden and Utrecht moved quite closely together, which suggests that already after 1450 regional markets in the western part of the Netherlands were integrated rather well.

Individual series

• Rye bread
Between 1596 and 1800 prices are derived from Posthumus' *History of the Leiden Textile Industry* (1936/39), which gives the prices of rye bread (of 12 lbs) according to the Leiden *broodzetting*. For the years before 1596, only price data from outside the western part of the country are available (Kuppers and Van Schaik 1981). This material could not be used for this study; therefore I assumed that before 1596 (that is before taxation on milling became very severe) bread prices developed in the same way as rye prices.

● Drink

For 1450–1740, this is the price of one vat of beer, on the basis of Posthumus (1964: no. 70, 172, 283, 368). These series have large gaps, especially during the 15th and 16th century and for interpolation, use was made of two series of 'beer–vinegar' (no. 124) and 'vinegar' (no. 223), since these products were often also made in breweries in which more or less the same inputs were used. Regressions showed a rather strong correlation between the development of prices of beer and of (beer) vinegar, which made it possible to use the vinegar series for interpolation.

After 1740, the wholesale prices of Surinam coffee, Buoy Tea, and Corn–Brandy (Posthumus 1943: no. 78, 80, 100) were substituted for the prices of beer (as a result of the declining consumption of beer no beer prices are available after 1740 because institutions apparently stopped buying the drink).

● Butter

(one vat) based on Posthumus (1964: 104, 180, 250) and De Moor (2000).

● Meat

(100 lbs) Posthumus (1964: 101, 203 (beef), 376), and De Moor (2000).

● Legumes

(Yellow) peas (last): Posthumus (1964: 98a, 99, 165, 265) and De Moor (2000).

● Fish

1450–1580: Herrings (one vat): Posthumus (1964: 36, 112, 208) and De Moor (2000); 1580–1800: Stockfish (100 lbs): Posthumus (1964: 113, 365).

● Potatoes

After *c*.1770, potato consumption grew rapidly in Holland, probably mostly at the expense of the consumption of vegetables/peas and beans. Potato prices for Leiden were published by Pot (1994: note, however, that in table 5 and table 6, p. 310, for the years 1792–1812 he has confounded prices of potatoes and of rye bread with each other).

● Textiles

1450–1540: Based on series of relative prices of linen and cloth compiled by Posthumus from Utrecht data, Posthumus (1964: LXX–LXXIII, no. 5 and 40). Especially for the period *c*.1570–1700, textile prices are rare and the series published by Posthumus show many large gaps. However, the available series show that textile prices were relatively stable; it therefore seems warranted to concentrate on the long-term changes and calculate ten year averages. The index for 1530–1800 is based on the series, which are presented in a table below. All data are from Posthumus (1964) and it concerns: (a) black cloth: no. 5 and fragmentary data on pp. 694–5; (b) red cloth: no. 8 and fragmentary data on pp. 694–5; (c) coloured cloth: no. 9, 291 and fragmentary data on pp. 694–5 and; (d) linen: no. 40, 292 and data from pp. 696–7. Those series have only one decade—1530/9—in common, which is taken as the basis of the textiles-index. The data for the index are presented in the table below; it was calculated as the unweighted average of the available data of cloth and linen prices per decade, after the elimination of a few extreme values (in 1600/09 and 1620/29) which were replaced by interpolated values. Because the prices of cloth and of linen show a similar development, which is confirmed for the period 1630–1800 by the evolution

Table 7.A1   Relative and absolute prices of textiles, 1530/39–1790/99 (prices in guilders per el of 70 cm, and index 1530/9 = 100)

Period	Cloth	Cloth: black	Cloth: red	Linen: coloured	Linen	Index
1530/9	1.18	1.30	1.05	0.13	0.13	100
1540/9	1.40	1.36	1.50	0.13	0.15	116
1550/9	—	—	1.58	0.15	0.18	135
1560/9	—	—	2.16	0.22	0.25	189
1570/9	—	—	2.38	0.24	—	206
1580/9	2.40	1.50	—	—	—	160
1590/9	3.35	1.69	—	—	—	208
1600/9	—	—	—	0.59	—	454(258)
1610/9	5.75	2.18	—	0.35	—	309
1620/9	—	1.20	—	0.46	—	223(328)
1630/9	3.59	—	—	0.50	—	346
1640/9	—	1.89	—	0.57	—	292
1650/9	4.82	1.56	—	0.60	—	331
1660/9	6.14	—	—	0.64	—	383
1670/9	—	1.85	—	0.61	—	306
1680/9	—	3.42	—	0.56	—	347
1690/9	—	3.56	3.50	0.58	—	351
1700/9	—	—	3.60	—	—	343
1710/9	—	—	3.58	—	—	341
1720/9	—	—	3.60	0.35	—	306
1730/9	—	—	3.75	0.36	—	317
1740/9	—	—	3.75	0.40	—	332
1750/9	—	—	4.00	0.33	—	333
1760/9	—	—	4.24	0.38	—	348
1770/9	—	—	4.19	0.42	—	361
1780/9	—	—	4.00	0.49	—	379
1790/9	—	—	4.25	0.43	—	368

of textile prices according to the prices on the Amsterdam exchange (see Posthumus 1943), the long-term evolution of textiles prices seems to be rather robust—short-term changes are however not captured by this series.

• Fuel

Price of peat (per scow/ton) from Posthumus (1964: no. 18, 44, 125, 266, 348).

• Soap

Price of quarter ton of soap from Posthumus (1964: no. 134, 228).

• Sugar

De Moor 2000 (until 1560); Posthumus (1964: no. 177, 263).

• Paper

Posthumus (1964: no. 19, 273 and 389).

• Pepper

De Moor (2000); Posthumus (1964 no. 43, 133, 330).

- Rent

No series of rent was available for the period 1450–1550; it was assumed that the price of rent moved with the rest of the cost of living. After 1550, the repeated rent index of Eichholtz and Theebe (1998) was adopted.

Notes

1. A survey is presented by Maddison (1995).
2. Especially relative luxuries such as meat and milk, see Komlos (1996).
3. The classic studies are Beveridge (1939), Hamilton (1934), Pribram (1938), Posthumus (1943/1964), and Elsas (1936/1940) and the related studies of Hoszowski (1954) for Poland and of Verlinden *et al.* (1959/1965) for Flanders.
4. See the collection of papers published in 1981.
5. An overview is presented in van Zanden (1999).
6. See also the contribution on prices and real wages in sixteenth-century London in Rappaport (1989).
7. Before 1596 no good data on bread prices were available, unfortunately, but it may be assumed that both prices moved in a more or less identical way before that date, see van Schaïk (1999).
8. For more details, see Appendix.
9. See Lindert (1998) for a similar discussion of the development of British relative prices between 1740 and 1910.
10. The year 1656 was selected to link the two indices because the experiment in comparing the two indices on the basis of 1450/74 = 100, showed that they had an identical level in that year.
11. My index is the unweighted average of the data for hodmen and for helpers of masons; see de Vries and van der Woude (1997: 610–11).
12. The inclusion of other groups of labourers would perhaps lead to a stronger increase in nominal incomes, because the incomes of salaried personnel grew more rapidly than nominal wages in construction and their share of the labour force must have gone up too, but there are no accurate data to estimate these changes; see Soltow and van Zanden (1998: 43–4).
13. See Sen (2000) for the link between freedom and economic welfare.
14. See Persson (1999: 106–13) for evidence on the decline in price fluctuations during the early modern period.
15. See Onisto, Maat, and Bult (1998: 15–16) for a summary of these findings.
16. The long-term trend during the nineteenth and early twentieth centuries has been analysed by de Meere (1982).
17. More precisely, they showed that the number of (industrial) durable consumer goods probably went up, which does not necessarily mean that per capita real expenditure grew at the same rate, see de Vries (1994*b*).
18. For women this increase was from about twenty during the late fifteenth and early sixteenth centuries, to about twenty-five during the 1590s, see van Zanden (1993: 27–8).
19. See Noordegraaf and Valk (1988) for their chronology.
20. This increase reached levels of perhaps 25% on a per capita basis between 1500 and 1800, see Noordegraaf (1985) and Scholliers (1983).

21. 65–70% in 1510/14 versus *c.* 40–45% between 1807/24, respectively, see van Zanden (2002).

References

Abel, W. (1966) *Agrarkrisen und Agrarkonjunktur.* Hamburg/Berlin: Parey.
——(1998) 'The Great Divergence: Wages and Prices from the Middle Ages to the First World War'. Paper presented at the annual meeting of the EHA, Durham.
Berg, W. J. van den and Zanden, J. L. van (1993) 'Vier eeuwen welstandsongelijkheid in Alkmaar, ca 1530–1930'. *Tijdschrift voor sociale geschiedenis,* 19: 193–216.
Beveridge, W. H. (1939) *Prices and Wages in England from the Twelfh to the Nineteenth Century.* London: Longmans, Green.
Eichholtz, P. M. A. and Theebe, M. A. J. (1998) 'A Long-Run Repeated-Rent Index for Residential Property'. Research memorandum, University of Amsterdam.
——————(1999) 'Zo vast als een huis'. *Economisch Statistische Berichten,* 84: 132–4.
Elsas, M. J. (1936/1940) *Umriss einer Geschichte der Preise und Löhne in Deutschland.* Leiden: Sijthoff.
Faber, J. A. (1976) *Dure Tijden en Hongersnoden in preindustrieel Nederland.* Amsterdam: Rodopi.
Feinstein, C. H. (1998) 'Pessimism Perpetuated: Real Wages and the Standard of Living in Britain During and After the Industrial Revolution'. *Journal of Economic History,* 58: 625–58.
Floud, R., Wachter, K. W., and Gregory, A. (1990) *Height, Health and History: Nutritional Status in the United Kingdom, 1750–1990.* Cambridge: Cambridge University Press.
Galloway, P. R. (1988) 'Basic Patterns of Annual Variation in Fertility, Nuptiality, Mortality, and Prices in Pre-industrial Europe'. *Population Studies,* 42: 275–303.
Hamilton, E. J. (1934) *American Treasure and the Price Revolution in Spain, 1501–1650.* Cambridge, MA: Harvard University Press.
Hoszowski, S. (1954) *Les Prix à Lwow XVIe–XVIIe siècles.* Paris: S.E.V.P.E.N.
Komlos, J. (1996) 'Anomalies in Economic History: Toward a Resolution of the "Antebellum Puzzle"'. *Journal of Economic History,* 56: 202–14.
Kuijpers, E. (1997) 'Lezen en schrijven. Onderzoek naar dhet alfabetiseringsniveau in zeventiende eeuws Amsterdam'. *Tijdschrift voor sociale geschiedenis,* 23: 490–522.
Lesger, C. (1986) *Huur en conjunctuur in Amsterdam 1550–1850.* Amsterdam: Historisch Seminarium.
Lindert, P. (1998) 'When did Inequality Rise in Britain and America?' in L. Borodkin and P. Lindert (eds.), *Trends in Income Inequality During Industrialization.* Madrid: Fundacion Fomento de la Historia Economica, pp. 21–39.
—— and Williamson, J. (1983) 'English Workers' Living Standards during the Industrial Revolution: A New Look'. *Economic History Review,* 36: 1–25.
Maddison, A. (1995) *Monitoring the World Economy 1820–1992.* Paris: OECD Development Center.
Meere, J. M. M. de (1982) *Economische ontwikkeling en levensstandaard in Nederland gedurende de eerste helft van de negentiende eeuw.* s-Gravenhage: Nijhoff.
Moor, T. de (2000) *Prijzen en lonen in het cistercienzerinnenklooster Leeuwenhorts bij Noordwijkerhout tussen 1410/11 en 1570/71.* Amsterdam: Historisch Seminarium.

Noordegraaf, L. and Schoenmakers, J. T. (1984) *Daglonen in Holland 1450–1600*. Amsterdam: Historisch Seminarium.

——(1985) *Hollands welvaren?* Bergen: Octavo.

——and Valk, G. (1988) *De Gave Gods: de pest in Holland vanaf de late Middeleeuwen*. Bergen: Octavo.

——and Zanden, J. L. van (1995) 'Early Modern Economic Growth and the Standard of Living: Did Labour Benefit from Holland's Golden Age?' in C. A. Davids and J. Lucassen (eds.), *A Miracle Mirrored. The Dutch Republic in European Perspective*. Cambridge: Cambridge University Press, pp. 410–38.

Onisto, N., Maat, G. J. R., and Bult, E. J. (1998) 'Human Remains from the Infirmary "Oude en nieuwe gasthuis" of the City of Delft in the Netherlands 1265–1652 AD'. *Barge's Anthoprologica*, 2.

——(1998) 'Rethinking Wages and Competitiveness in the Eighteenth Century: Britain and South India'. *Past and Present*, 158: 79–109.

Persson, K. G. (1999) *Grain Markets in Europe 1500–1900*. Cambridge: Cambridge University Press.

Phelps Brown, E. H. and Hopkins, S. V. (1981) *A Perspective of Wages and Prices*. London: Methuen.

Pomeranz, K. (2000) *The Great Divergence. China, Europe, and the Making of the Modern World Economy*. Princeton, NJ: Princeton University Press.

Posthumus, N. W. (1936/1939) *De geschiedenis van de Leidsche lakenindustrie*. 's Gravenhage: Nijhoff.

——(1943/1964) *Nederlandsche prijsgeschiedenis*. Leiden: Brill.

Pot, G. P. M. (1994) *Arm Leiden. Levensstandaard, bedeling en bedeelden, 1750–1854*. Hilversum: Historische Vereniging Holland.

Pribram, A. F. (1938) *Materialien zur Geschichte der Preise und Löhne in Österreich*. Wien: [s.n.].

Rappaport, S. (1989) *Worlds Within Worlds: Structures of Life in Sixteenth-century London*. Cambridge: Cambridge University Press.

Reher, D. and Ballasteros, E. (1993) 'Precios y salarios en Castile la Nueva, 1501–1991'. *Revista de Historia Economica*, 11: 101–51.

Schaïk, R. van (1999) 'Marktbeheersing: overheidsbemoeienis met de levensmiddelenvoorziening in de Nederlanden (14de–19de eeuw)', in C. Lesger and L. Noordegraaf (eds.), *Ondernemers en bestuurders*. Amsterdam: Neha, pp. 465–90.

Scholliers, E. (1983) 'Werktijden en arbeidsomstandigheden in de pre-industriele periode', in E. Scholliers and P. Scholliers (eds.), *Werktijd en werktijdverkorting*. Brussel: Centrum voor Hedendaagse Sociale Geschiedenis, pp. 11–18.

Sen, A. (2000) *Development as Freedom*. New York: Anchor Books.

Shammas, C. (1990) *The Pre-industrial Consumer in England and America*. Oxford: Clarendon Press.

Slicher van Bath, B. H. (1960) *De Agrarische geschiedenis van West-Europa*. Utrecht/ Antwerpen: Aulaboeken.

Smits, J. P., Horlings, E., and Zanden, J. L. van (2000) *Dutch GDP and its Components, 1800–1913*. Groningen: Groningen Growth and Development Center.

Soltow, L. and Zanden, J. L. van (1998) *Income and Wealth Inequality in the Netherlands 16th–20th century*. Amsterdam: Het Spinhuis.

Tassenaar, P. G.(2000) *Het verloren Arcadia*. Groningen: Labyrinth.

Verlinden, C. *et al.* (1959/1965) *Dokumenten voor de geschiedenis van prijzen en lonen in Vlaanderen en Brabant.* Brugge: Rijksuniversiteit Gent.

Vries, J. de (1985) 'The Population and Economy of the Preindustrial Netherlands'. *Journal of Interdisciplinary History*, 15: 661–82.

——(1994*a*) 'How did Pre-Industrial Labour Markets Function?' in G. Grantham and M. MacKinnon (eds.), *Labour Market Evolution.* London: Routledge, pp. 39–63.

——(1994*b*) 'The Industrial Revolution and the Industrious Revolution'. *Journal of Economic History*, 54: 249–70.

——and Woude, A. van der (1997) *The First Modern Economy.* Cambridge: Cambridge University Press.

Wee, H. van der (1975) 'Prijzen en lonen als ontwikkelingsvariabelen'. *Album offert à Charles Verlinden.* Gent: Universiteit Gent, pp. 413–47.

Weir, D. R. (1984) 'Life under Pressure: France and England, 1670–1870'. *Journal of Economic History*, 44: 27–47.

Zanden, J. L. van (1987) 'De economie van Holland in de periode 1650–1805: groei of achteruitgang?' *Bijdragen en mededelingen betreffende de geschiedenis der Nederlanden.* 102: 562–609.

——(1992) 'Economic Growth in the Golden Age'. *Economic and Social History in the Netherlands*, 4: 5–26.

——(1993) *The Rise and Decline of Holland's Economy.* Manchester: Manchester University Press.

——(1999) 'Wages and the Standard of Living in Europe, 1500–1800'. *European Review of Economic History*, 3: 175–98.

——(2002) 'Taking the Measure of the Early Modern Economy: Historical National Accounts for Holland in 1510/14'. *European Review of Economic History*, 6: 131–63.

——and Riel, A. van (2000) *Nederland 1780–1913.* Amsterdam: Balans.

8 Economic Growth, Human Capital Formation and Consumption in Western Europe Before 1800

JAIME REIS

1. Introduction

This chapter focuses on three aspects of pre-industrial European economic history and the possible relationships between them. The first, based on a growing body of recent studies, concerns the long-term growth experienced by the European economy over the two and a half centuries prior to the Industrial Revolution, or, at least, by important parts of it. It was an unequal process, in terms of time and space, which had as one of its consequences the emergence, by the eighteenth century, of significant differences of income per capita that may have helped to shape the course of industrialization over the next century or so. The second is a correlate of the first and refers to the probable rise in the standard of living over the same period. Once again, it was an uneven evolution, with a very diverse impact on social groups, gender, and the rural/urban divide, as well as on nations and the regions within them. The third aspect has to do with the remarkable increase in human capital that accompanied these other two processes and, especially, the unprecedented rise in literacy that was a part of it. This too was hardly a homogeneous or linear development, either spatially or temporally, and its causes and consequences have yet to be clearly understood.

The maps of these three histories reveal similarities that suggest some interactions between these variables. In particular, they raise two interesting possibilities. One is that human capital may have provided an important contribution to economic growth, in a similar fashion to what has been claimed so often for the nineteenth and twentieth centuries. The other is that human capital in turn may have been causally determined by income and may have come to represent a relevant item in the growing consumption evidenced by Europeans, along with such 'new' goods as better and fancier textiles, house furnishings, exotic foodstuffs, and personal adornments. The second of these issues is the one on which we concentrate here. We do this first of all by asking whether the meaning and purpose of literacy do

The author wishes to thank Gerben Bakker, Hans Boedeker, and Laurence Fontaine for their help.

indeed allow us to regard it as a part of the bundle of items that define the standard of living of Europeans in the pre-industrial era. In the second place, we explore the extent to which this acquisition may serve as a guide in assessing the presumable improvement in welfare in the event that the resources available for consumption should have been growing over time relative to the population.

The chapter, which is entirely based on secondary sources, consists of four parts. The first presents evidence in support of a growth in income per capita in Europe from the sixteenth to the eighteenth centuries, and discusses the standard of living debate that goes with it. The next section maps the rise of human capital during the same period and discusses its principal determinants. It also shows that to an important degree human capital functioned as an investment good, the acquisition of which served to enhance the productivity of those who possessed it. The third considers the other uses to which reading and writing could be put in this historical context, with special attention to book ownership and reading for pleasure and edification. The aim is to try and separate that part of human capital which could be viewed as an investment good, because of its economic functionality, from that which might be seen as an end in itself. Only the second can be deemed a direct source of utility and can therefore be included in the basket of consumable goods that income could buy. The fourth part discusses the implications of this for the standard of living question prior to modern industrialization. It tries to show that the contribution of human capital as an immaterial good was in fact significant and justifies a revision of current views regarding the levels of well-being achieved before 1800. This is followed by a conclusion.

2. Long-Term Growth and Standard of Living in Pre-Industrial Europe

The quantification of Europe's macroeconomic performance between the sixteenth and the eighteenth centuries has attracted considerable interest over the last decade or so. Essentially this can be divided into three types of exercises. In an initial stage, attempts were made to estimate gross domestic product (GDP) per capita at constant prices over long periods, by both direct and indirect methods. Despite the not unexpected problems with data, assumptions, and index numbers, interesting and challenging results for several countries and for periods of two or more centuries have become available as a result. The picture that has emerged from this is not only one of stagnation or even slight regression over some areas of western Europe (Iberia, Italy, and Poland) but also of fairly sustained growth in the Netherlands, Belgium, France, and England (Table 8.1). Rates were far from constant over time and even in the economically more dynamic regions they averaged no more than a couple of decimals of a percentage point over the entire period. It has been tentatively suggested that, between 1600 and 1800, the economy of western Europe grew per capita at about 0.1% a year or about 22% *in toto* (Malanima 1995), a conclusion that, although modest, nevertheless contradicts a 'stagnationist'

Table 8.1 Long-term growth of per capita output (constant prices), seventeenth and eighteenth centuries

	Period	Overall growth (%)	Annual rate (%)
Belgium (Flanders/Brabant)	1610–1812	32	0.14
Italy (north and centre)	1600–1800	0	0
Spain (Castile)	1590–1800	7	0.03
Holland	1580–1795	38	0.15
England	1570–1750	69	0.30
Poland	1580–1820	−10	−0.04
France	1600–1800	32	0.20

Notes: The one for France is a lower bound estimate. The same source also proposes a growth rate of 0.6% per annum.

Sources: Blomme, Buyst, and van der Wee (1994); Malanima (1994); Yun (1994); van Zanden (1993); Snooks (1994); Topolski and Wyszczenki cited by van Zanden (Chapter 7, this volume); Marczewski (1961).

perspective on the Early Modern period and hints at quite a different 'pre-Industrial Revolution growth model' for the continent.[1]

A second type of research has focused instead on the evolution of real wages (PPP—purchasing power parity—deflated)[2] for both skilled and unskilled urban labour. This follows a tradition of evaluating the movement of GDP per capita or of productivity using these indicators when direct information is unavailable. The claim is that over the long run a fairly good match can be obtained between proxy and proxied variables (Williamson 1995). The data gathered recently for seventeen major cities reveal noticeable parallels with the findings above (Allen 1998; Ozmucur and Pamuk 2002). A gentle upward trend is displayed for the London–Amsterdam region between the late sixteenth and late eighteenth centuries,[3] and confirms its strong performance as revealed in Table 8.1. Stagnation or slow decline characterizes the situation in Naples, Antwerp, Florence, Milan, Madrid, Paris, and Strasbourg to the west and south. This reveals some discrepancies with the picture presented earlier, for example, Paris and Strasbourg, but otherwise strong parallels with it too. To the east, in a region that has received less attention in this field, the picture of stagnation/decline is similarly visible, in Leipzig, Vienna, Krakow, Warsaw, and Istanbul. The exceptions are Augsburg and Gdansk. The conclusion points again to a probably slight long-run increase in GDP per capita in the aggregate, encompassing both dynamic and stagnant/regressive situations across Europe, as well as periods of growth alternating with stagnation or even with contraction.

A third approach corroborates to some extent the outline of the long-term evolution of per capita GDP shown above by providing a league table for this variable around 1810. This macroeconomic outcome at the end of the Ancien Régime brings to light again the contrast between the most dynamic economies portrayed in Table 8.1—England, the Netherlands, Belgium, and France—and, at quite a distance, a by now clearly peripheral group composed of Iberia, Italy, and Poland, with roughly half the income level of the Anglo–Dutch 'economic core' (van Zanden 1998).[4]

This revision of the long-run economic evolution of pre-industrial Europe, which allows for some measure of growth, is far from implausible, on both theoretical and empirical grounds. The former rests on the severe critique to which the previously and widely accepted 'stagnationist' approach to this question has been subjected (Persson 1988; Grantham 1999). According to these authors, the economies of this period were not locked into a stationary equilibrium from which escape was possible only in the case of some strong exogenous shock. Technological progress was indeed available in most fields of production if the right conditions were met. Perhaps the most important of these was demographic growth, which led to market broadening and to incentives for a greater degree of division of labour and regional specialization. This laid the foundations of slow but steady processes of learning-by-doing as the increase in the repetition of productive operations increased the probability of finding better ways of operating. Technical knowledge was thus increased and, given the right institutions, became cumulative, irreversible, and transferable to future generations.

Recent data on productivity and structural change reinforce this point of view and come from three different areas of research. The most important, given the primordial role of agriculture at the time, is the way in which the productivity of labour in this sector mirrored the path of GDP per capita. From the early sixteenth to the middle of the eighteenth centuries it rose in England by 100% and in the Netherlands by 40%, whereas elsewhere it was more or less constant (Allen 2000). In the case of France and using a different measure of productivity—TFP—a slow improvement in overall agricultural efficiency in the long run can also be shown (Hoffman 1996). This is punctuated by periods of regression and strong regional contrasts, but reveals a variation that is very similar to the 10% rise for labour productivity between 1600 and 1750 established by Allen (2000).

The rising trend of urbanization and its particular intensity in the more dynamic northwest is a second reason for endorsing the growth scenario we are considering, particularly as regards the Netherlands, which achieved a remarkable degree of city development by the seventeenth century (de Vries 1984). This conclusion is founded on the widely recognized fact that productivity at this time was considerably higher and more apt to increase in manufacturing and the services, the two pillars of the urban economy, than in agriculture (van Zanden 1998). It is also borne out by the generally higher per capita incomes associated with life in the towns and the cities, a fact which in turn was responsible, at least in part, for the rising inequality of income distribution in the areas of high urbanization (van Zanden 1995).

A third factor that is likely to have contributed to an upward income trend is the expansion of the labour input relative to the population that was characteristic of this period. This could have originated in several ways. One was the decline of real wages that van Zanden (1999) has pinpointed and which could have driven workers to make a compensatory larger effort in terms of days and hours in employment.

An alternative and not contradictory interpretation links this increased collective exertion to the occurrence of an 'Industrious Revolution' in Europe. According to de Vries (1994), what drove households to engage to a greater extent in wage employment, and to a lesser one in domestic duties, was the appearance of new consumption opportunities offered by the market for goods.[5] This stimulated new levels of consumerism that could only be achieved by means of these greater workloads. At the same time, in some better-off regions infrastructural development improved year round transport to such a degree that it reduced seasonality in certain types of activity, with the consequence that the labour force found itself occupied for longer periods in the year than used to happen before (de Vries and van der Woude 1997).

Although the study of the pre-industrial standard of living is still in its early days, at first sight, an evaluation of its movement should not present great difficulties, given the evidence on real wages and GDP per capita adduced above. In fact, agreement on this subject seems somewhat elusive. On the one hand, the evidence marshalled by van Zanden (1999) points in the direction of steadily declining real wages in most parts of Europe, with two negative effects on welfare. The first was a reduction in per capita consumption of better quality foodstuffs, such as animal products. The second was a loss of utility caused by the poorer segments of the community having to work more, as noted above, in order to make up for the shortfall in real income. A contrary, 'optimistic' perspective is based on several arguments. To begin with, the alternative PPP real wage estimate by Allen (1998) brings to light a more ambiguous portrayal of the situation. In some places, wages rose, in others they fell, and in still others they stagnated. In the second place, one may want to question how different the marginal utility of leisure was from zero for the mass of the lowly paid, underemployed, and/or seasonally employed workers, as the 'pessimist' case requires, and therefore whether working more brought a net loss of utility to them. Finally, there is the claim of a 'consumption revolution', which appears to have swept through eighteenth-century Europe and was probably present in some places already in the seventeenth. The improvement and enlargement of living quarters, the growing acquisition of higher quality durables, and the consumption of large amounts of exotic foodstuffs in such diverse places as England, France, Spain, Tuscany, and the Netherlands, all signal a picture of broad material improvement, across all classes and in both city and country, that goes very much against the idea of stagnation or regression in the standard of living.[6]

The 'material consumption' approach to this emerging standard of living controversy is not the only methodological possibility but it is probably the most frequently used. This does not mean, however, that it is exempt from serious technical shortcomings.[7] Some of these are common to any attempt to handle the problem. Scarce and unreliable data and ambiguous results that do not lend themselves to unequivocal interpretation are the chief ones here although they are perhaps less problematic in this instance than in the case of the other methodologies at our disposal.[8] Other difficulties are more specific and have to do with its focus on post mortem inventories as the principal source of information.

One distortion this causes is that it leaves out that sizeable fraction of the population that was too poor to be worth recording in this way because they possessed so few durable articles of consumption. Another is that it fails completely to take into account current consumption, thus ignoring the bulk of acquisitions made in the course of a person's lifetime. As a result, questions pertaining to the life cycle of individuals receive no attention either. Any conclusion drawn therefore can only reflect their welfare status at a very special moment of their existence and yields little knowledge concerning the population as a whole.

From the point of view of this chapter, the main defect of the 'material consumption' approach, however, is its exclusive focus on material articles. Although the latter were indisputably the principal source of utility of the pre-industrial population, it is argued below that during this period there was a significant shift in personal expenditure away from material and towards immaterial goods. The centrepiece of this exercise is human capital formation, an indicator that is not usually included in standard of living studies and can be used in two ways. As an item of personal expenditure, it can serve to gauge the economic capacity to acquire, in the same manner in which the presence of mirrors, textiles, or sugar and coffee can. Alternatively, human capital generates a stream of utility of a kind that is not commonly taken into consideration, probably because of the problems of measurement it raises. During the period in question, like some material assets it conferred status and rank on its possessor and it could enhance the productive capacity of its bearer. But it was also a means to the fruition of individual non-material satisfaction such as comes from a greater knowledge and a better understanding of one's self, an enlarged ability to communicate with others, a richer religious experience, or the possibility of participation in public or community life. The present study is directed at the second of these perspectives. It constitutes therefore a response to the call to widen the discussion on living standards in the past by adding to the conventional purchasing power of private income approach broader aspects such as are proposed by the Human Development Index (HDI) methodology (Crafts 1997).

3. The Rise of Human Capital

The history of human capital in Ancien Régime Europe is a difficult and immense undertaking. In order to render the subject somewhat less unmanageable this chapter takes a restricted view of the concept, in the form of literacy, and uses the capacity of individuals to sign their names on documents such as marriage registers, wills, or other public declarations as its measure. It therefore ignores that vast part of the stock of human capital the acquisition of which did not involve schooling, whether formal or informal, and concerned mastering directly productive skills, for example, apprenticeship to crafts or learning on the job.[9] It also means that it leaves out those aspects of human capital, which are often referred to in the specialized literature and pertain to health and physical vigour.

Historically, this notion of literacy can have many meanings. It can go all the way from being barely able to read a printed text (often helped by previous memorization) to a capacity to read handwriting and to write one's own thoughts in a coherent manner. Distinguishing between these gradations is a complex task, which for earlier times is often rendered unviable by a lack of suitable data. The choice here of signatures as a proxy, although heavily criticized in the literature is nevertheless widely endorsed and can be justified on several grounds (Schofield 1973; Hoyler 1998). It is objective, it can be expressed quantitatively and it is fairly homogeneous across space and time, a vital condition for comparative analysis. It has the further merit of reflecting not only an ability to read, which by itself would otherwise be practically impossible to test for, but also a certain manual ability to handle writing materials, even if not necessarily to write in the fullest meaning of the term.[10] The acquisition of this level of literacy therefore presupposed a relatively sustained and prolonged effort of learning, particularly as during these centuries reading and writing were distinct forms of know-how which, unlike nowadays, were achieved in separate and successive periods, typically of three years at a time. The consensus is that before 1850, that is before the rise of officially promoted mass education in Europe, the proportion of those able to sign their names was higher than of those merely able to read but not write, and was lower than those able both to read and to write sentences.[11]

If it is perhaps exaggerated to say that between 1500 and 1800, Europe experienced an 'educational revolution', one cannot deny that during these centuries a profound transformation took place nevertheless in this field. According to Étienne François (1989), it was 'one of the most important mutations in the European history of the early modern period'. Although the rhythm of change varied over time and final outcomes were hardly the same everywhere, there was a striking alteration throughout the continent. From a minute familiarity with reading and writing at the beginning of the sixteenth century, for example, in England 10% of males and close to 0% of females (Cressy 1981), levels were reached three hundred years later that were several times higher in all countries, and in some regions were not far from the 100% mark.

Table 8.2 presents a literacy map of Europe at the end of the eighteenth century which renders evident the remarkable progress in educational attainment made since the sixteenth century. Admittedly, the use of national literacy rates as measured by the ability to sign, at a time of so much intra-national heterogeneity, is a perilous undertaking. The picture that emerges for the end of the Ancien Régime is, however, a clear one.[12] The essential facts have been known for some time although fresh research keeps on filling it in with new facts. Around 1800, there was a high literacy core occupying roughly a broad swathe of northwest Europe, where already 60–80% of the male population could read and write, the same being true for somewhat above 40% of the female one. These figures cover the rural and the urban sectors and they refer to present day Belgium, the Netherlands, England and Scotland, Germany, west of the Stralsund–Dresden line, and France, north of the Geneva–St Malo line. Beyond the northern, eastern, and southern edges of this region,

Table 8.2   Literacy rates in Europe *c*.1800 (% of adults who could sign their name)

	Males	Females	All
England	60	40	—
Scotland	65	15	—
France	48	27	—
N. France	71	44	—
S. France	44	17	—
Belgium	60	37	—
Netherlands[a]	73	51	—
Germany			
Saxony	80	44	—
Hesse	91	43	—
Norway	—	—	21
Sweden	—	—	20–25
Portugal[b]	—	—	< 20
Italy			
Piedmonte[c]	—	—	25
Duchy of Parma	45	23	—
Marche	17	6	—
Hungary[b]	—	—	6

[a] Available for 1700
[b] For rural population
[c] For 1848

Sources: Mainly Chartier (1985–7), and also Ruwet and Wellemans (1978), Kuijpers (1997), Hofmeister *et al.* (1998), Markussen (1990), Nilsson (1997), Magalhães (1994), Marchesini (1983), Brambilla (1991), and Toth (1998).

literacy rates fell to significantly lower levels: for males, between 10% and 45% and for females from less than 10% to 20%.[13] This refers to Scandinavia and East Germany and Hungary, on the one hand, and to Spain, Italy, Portugal, and France, south of the Geneva–St Malo line, on the other.

For earlier periods, the data is patchier and less reliable and therefore the long-run trends are hard to identify except for in a few countries. The sixteenth century was apparently a time of rapid growth, with male literacy doubling in England and increasing rapidly also in France and Spain. By the second half of the seventeenth century, these countries had reached similar levels of literacy and had been joined and then overtaken by the Netherlands. The large urban population of the latter had experienced a fast increase in reading and writing skills from the late sixteenth century, thereby achieving unrivalled heights in Europe. Growth in England during the 1600s was also among the fastest—it doubled between 1600 and 1700 (Stephens 1990). By the eighteenth century, the paths of these four better known countries were clearly parting. The pace of change in reading and writing skills was slowing down to stagnation in Spain and in France, there was a pronounced deceleration.

In England, there was still a growth of 50% over the period 1700–1800 while in the Netherlands, the 1700 level was already so high—at 70%—that further expansion had to be slow.[14] In terms of national literacy levels, there had been a major shift during these three centuries. Southern Europe, which had led the way in the sixteenth-century expansion, lost its dynamism during the second half of the period. In the meantime, the economically and socially more vigorous regions of the seventeenth and eighteenth centuries accelerated and overtook the South, to constitute the core of *c.*1800 alluded to above. Beneath these national level indicators, enormous differences were present, however, which only become apparent when we narrow our perspective to the level of the region, the town, the village, or the hamlet. A suggestive example comes from Provence, where during the late seventeenth century good literacy scores were attained in the villages of the right bank of the river Durance, while the communities across the water were sunk in illiteracy (Vovelle 1975).

When considered in the very long run, it is no less impressive that this rise in human capital was also very much the result of a spontaneous process, not of one that was exogenously imposed on society by the state or the church. Indeed, most states neither wished nor felt capable of centralizing, uniformizing, regulating, and financing a universal educational system, as was to happen subsequently, during the nineteenth and twentieth centuries. Even less were they inclined to use coercion in order to reduce illiteracy in the sense we are using here, and few that tried succeeded convincingly.[15] Indeed, to speak of a 'system' would be nothing but a misdescription of the educational situation of most of pre-industrial Europe.[16] A not insignificant proportion of children learned to read and write in contexts other than the school. The well to do had private tuition in the home, children who were apprenticed to a craftsman were taught by him as a rule (van Deursen 1991) and a small but unknown number were autodidacts.[17] Schools, in one form or another, were thus the principal but by no means the exclusive vehicle for the spread of literacy—for instance, in sixteenth-century Castile, one third of a sample of 800 defendants tried by the Inquisition were literate but had never attended school (Nalle 1989).

In the formal sector, the means to learn to read and write (and also count, a technique that is not considered here) were provided by a large variety of sources in anything but a coherent manner. The state, the church, the lords temporal and spiritual, town and city authorities, pious institutions, such as orphanages and confraternities, local communities, or simply private enterprise, all catered for this need. Equally diverse was the spread across territory and across time of this collective but chaotic effort, with the resulting enormous disparity in the availability of educational resources relative to population. Even at short distances, from one parish to the next, an abyss could separate two neighbouring experiences in this field.

For the arguments advanced by this chapter two features of early modern educational practice deserve to be stressed. As mentioned earlier, the decision to impart reading and writing skills to oneself or to one's progeny was essentially a private, household affair. In most of the major cities and towns of Europe, orphans, the offspring of prisoners, or children who were felt to have escaped parental control might be compelled to attend a school and be submitted to education as a 'civilizing process', but they were far from the majority (van Deursen 1991).[18] Typical was what happened in late seventeenth-century France where, despite various royal edicts to the contrary 'there was never any likelihood of children being forced to go to school' (Houdaille 1977). The second feature lies in the fact that the exercise of this choice faced important constraints. These included the uneven distribution of schools, the poor quality of many teachers (teacher training only became a reality in the nineteenth century), the disfavour of the higher spheres of society vis-à-vis the education of the lower classes, and popular prejudice against the replacement of oral tradition by written forms of expression. The most important one, however, was clearly the cost that education entailed for the individual or the family.

Apart from the opportunity cost of keeping a child out of work for several years, in the majority of cases schooling had to be paid for by its recipients to an extent that depended on the degree of other support received from the Church, the local authorities, or private benefactors (Schofield 1973). In the second half of the eighteenth century in Paris, 166 schools were for profit while only eighty were charitable but even the latter required some payment from most students, to cover the teacher's salary (Saugnieux 1986). Fees were extremely varied but rarely insignificant, particularly for that large part of the working population who earned a miserable wage and only had an insecure and/or seasonal occupation; or who were independent producers in the primary sector and highly vulnerable to the contingencies of the weather, prices, or of personal health.[19] Indeed, insofar as this can be discussed with any precision, the consensus of the literature is that it was a heavy burden and for many an economic impossibility.[20]

The preceding remarks strongly suggest that human capital at this time had two features that likened it to an investment good. Its acquisition had a cost, which meant forsaking some present consumption for the sake of future benefit, and, once acquired, it could perform over a lengthy period, in this case probably a lifetime. Besides this, the decisive question is whether it also served to generate a stream of utility over the duration of the investment and for this there is abundant evidence that indeed it did. This comes from three main areas of human endeavour where it is clear that pragmatic reasons were instrumental in driving many men and women across early modern Europe to invest in the capacities that human capital bestowed upon them.

The first of these was the role of literacy in acquiring, consolidating, and signalling social status. From early on, in the upper classes everywhere in Europe, that is, excluding all those in trade or manual occupations, reading and writing skills were virtually universal. Yet how 'necessary', in practice, was this to the English gentry or to the members of the 'three robes' in France? For some it would have been very important for the exercise of their occupations, but for many others—all those who were not actively engaged in administering estates, participating in politics, public administration, military activity, or justice—it was hardly imperative. On the other hand, not to receive an education, probably at a higher level than the simple three Rs, would have been unthinkable, so much had it become a mark of social distinction, apart from the fact that anyone in these strata was liable to be called upon to undertake such tasks at any moment (Quéniart 1977). The mass of the population was not alien, however, to such considerations either. Further down the social ladder, for anyone seeking upward mobility, literacy could be a powerful and indispensable tool. In late seventeenth-century rural Catalonia, for example, rich peasants who sought to rise socially, left the traditional hearth to go and live in the town and had their children educated.[21] The same goes for Griete Pietersdochter, a poor widow with four illiterate children in seventeenth-century Amsterdam. Her second husband was also of humble origin but was able to become rich and rose to high officialdom in the city. The offspring of this later marriage were sent to school and became literate (de Vries and van der Woude 1997). The counter-proof is constituted by that great majority of Europeans who had no realistic hope of ever changing their position in life. According to Houston (1988), this was one of the main reasons that strongly limited their interest in education and therefore the spread of literacy during pre-industrial times.

A second motivation for acquiring literacy is illustrated by a recent article by Nilsson, Pettersson, and Svensson (1999), who have identified the need for a more powerful 'transactions technology' among farmers in southern Sweden. Around the turn of the eighteenth to the nineteenth centuries, it became increasingly important for them to be able not only to sign their names clearly but also to be able to apprehend the meaning of legal charters, leases, titles of ownership, and so on. On this depended their successful participation in the then on-going process of land redistribution and enclosure, the legal intricacies of which were hardly minor.[22] As a result, during the 1780–1820 period, in freeholding parishes, the literacy of peasants rose from around 40% to over 80% and the highest rate was to be found among those who applied for enclosure.[23] Obviously, situations of this kind were not so common in earlier periods but the concept of a 'transactions technology' finds a useful application in the far more numerous cases of participation in local government by members of the 'popular classes'. Thus, it is interesting to note that in several well-known instances of low-income mountainous regions, where literacy was unexpectedly high for a rural milieu, an active involvement in a very open and democratic conduct of local affairs was prevalent. This was so, for instance, in the Alps near Briançon during the eighteenth century, where at assemblies of heads of households, more than 90% of them signed legal documents, the same happening contemporaneously in Hesse (Granet–Abisset 1996; Hofmeister *et al.* 1998).

The preceding examples illustrate some of the ways in which the self-interest of individuals and even of communities might be served by raising literacy standards. Human capital in this form found its most powerful motivation, however, in its day-to-day usefulness for the exercise of professional occupations and in this sense was strongly determined by development and economic growth. Both points have been forcefully made in a variety of national and chronological contexts and the evidence that sustains this is nothing less than abundant. For the macroeconomic perspective, what has been asserted by de Vries and van der Woude (1997) about seventeenth-century Netherlands can be claimed for almost anywhere in early modern Europe.[24] The importance of education to industrialization remains unclear and contested but its importance to the development of a differentiated, complex commercial economy needs no further rehearsal here. From a micro point of view, the conclusion is the same. Already in the sixteenth century, in early Reformation Germany, many towns were promulgating ordinances to foster education, not on religious grounds, but because it was deemed important that both artisans and tradesmen learn to read, write, and count (Gawthrop and Strauss 1984). The same functionality was present in seventeenth-century England where the literacy of craftsmen was deemed 'roughly commensurate' with occupational requirements (Cressy 1981) and in France it was the same. Besides a rise over time in the proportion of the labour force engaged in occupations that called for reading and writing skills, an upward drift in literacy was also occurring driven by the increased requirement in this respect within many occupations themselves. This could arise in a variety of ways. One of them was the expanding recourse, in retail activities, to customer credit, particularly during the eighteenth century, and the consequent need among small traders and shopkeepers to administer effectively an increasingly complex system of 'accounts books' in which the appropriate tallies were kept (Chartier *et al.* 1976). Another was the rise in the cultural level of the clientele itself which created a greater demand for sophistication on the part of suppliers too, a phenomenon that was particularly visible in the 'higher trades', such as cabinet makers, barbers, and tailors (Quéniart 1977). Finally, the educational needs associated with the greater complexity of certain tasks themselves have been suggested as being on the rise (Houston 1988). The strength of the link between literacy and productivity finds support in the large literature that describes the socio-economic stratification of literacy among males during the period. The picture varies little from country to country or even from region to region. At the top of the pyramid, where one encounters the nobility, the high administration and professionals such as doctors, pharmacists, and lawyers, the ability to sign (and probably much else as well) was practically universal by the seventeenth century. In the towns, they were closely followed by large merchants, financiers, contractors, and the like, also with high attainments from early on, and at a distance by people in trade and in the 'better' crafts. In London, of the last two categories the first one was already in the 60% range by the late sixteenth century, rose to 70–80% during the next 100 years and was almost universally literate by the middle of the eighteenth century. Meanwhile, in provincial England they progressed at a more gradual pace: 40%, 50–60%, and 70% respectively. The lower crafts followed a parallel path but further down the scale (Cressy 1980). In a rural setting, the better-off farmers, whether landed or tenant and in whichever country, also formed a cultural elite endowed with reasonably higher and rising educational achievement. On the other hand, unskilled manual workers occupied the lowest positions, both in rural and in urban settings, usually with very low rates, which over time climbed slowly, if at all, and then only in the more 'advanced' countries of the European core. At one extreme of this spectrum, we find that 66% of Amsterdam's 'proletarians' could sign their names already by 1700, while in the twenty-three English parishes studied by Schofield (1973) the figure was 65% for labourers and servants in 1785–1814. At the other end, peasants and farm workers in Hungary and around Parma reached no higher than a 6% rate around 1800 (Marchesini 1983; Toth 1998).

A further demonstration of the importance of the practical benefits of human capital in determining whether to acquire it lies in the role played by gender in its distribution throughout society. Everywhere in Europe and at all times until well into the nineteenth century, women were considerably less literate than men and only rarely did this gap close much. Moreover, when literate their ability in reading and writing tended to be of a lower standard than that of men in the same socio-economic stratum (Grevet 1985). One reason was that in a situation of scarcity of resources, it made sense to undereducate girls and favour boys instead because the latter were the future heads of households and holders of the jobs where this know-how was required. This is confirmed by the fact that women tended to be relatively more literate where they were business associates of their husbands or were in business for their own account, as was frequently the case of widows. It was thus not enough that they were their wives, a situation in which their ignorance would be freely allowed to reflect their lowly social status (Quéniart 1977). But this outcome was also a non-economic response to the prevalent code of values. For as long as women, in early modern society, occupied a subordinate position within the family and the community it would have to be so since 'the overriding aim was to offer an education appropriate to a person's established place in society' (Houston 1988). Like the poor, whom many feared might want to leave their lowly station and aspire to something better if they were sent to school (Larquié 1987), a greater extent of female literacy was viewed by many as unsettling for the natural order of things.[25]

Finally, it must be noted that although demand side factors played the major role in determining the pattern of the spread of literacy, supply side elements also shaped this outcome, and some of them clearly associated with the evolution of real income per capita too. Location was one of them. The unequal density of the population and better or worse communications made an enormous difference to the provision and cost of schooling and therefore to the chances of escaping illiteracy. In northern Castile, for instance, the famous Catasto de Ensenada (1754) reveals that only 22% of localities had a teacher and about as many again were within reach of a school. In other words, in the other half, the possibility to learn to read and write was virtually nil, whatever the other circumstances (Amalric 1987). From this point of view, the urban environment was the most favourable of all. As a rule it had not only a higher number of schools per capita and an easier access to them, but it was where there were better teachers and where the authorities inspected them more regularly and thoroughly (Compère 1995). But this was not the only reason why towns and cities had literacy rates that tended to be at least 20% higher than in the countryside. The daily life of early modern towns was permeated by the written word to an extent undreamed of in rural parts, as a result of the more frequent contact with the law, the authorities and the frequency of the circulation of printed information.[26]

They contained the highest proportion of individuals engaged in occupations—crafts, trade, and other services—for which at least an elementary education was essential, not to mention the fact that they concentrated the majority of the highly educated who served in the Church, the administration, and the professions. On average, their inhabitants were more prosperous when compared with the rural population and could therefore more easily afford the acquisition of this know-how. And those who were not well off were eligible for the many charitable opportunities that were available in the cities and towns, where their wealthy founders tended to live. Finally, it was among urban dwellers that the small degree of upward mobility that was possible in pre-industrial times had its principal locus.[27] Taking the upper classes as a role model entailed copying their cultural traits and the first step was schooling and the achievement of literacy. Being physically and socially closer to them in the cities made this still more likely to happen (Furet and Ozouf 1977).

4. Human Capital as an Article of Consumption

A Mincerian approach (Mincer 1974) thus appears to provide quite a satisfactory way of analysing the growth and distribution of human capital in early modern Europe. To a great extent, human capital gave individuals a positive return on the resources expended to achieve it and they responded by acquiring it when the conditions warranted it. As the economy developed—and in particular underwent extensive urbanization and the expansion of the services and manufacturing—opportunities for making literacy economically advantageous rose too, and reading and writing skills spread throughout society at the appropriate levels. A similar effect was brought on by the growth of the state and the gradual replacement of traditional norms by the written law, both of which raised the premium on this 'transactions technology'.

A second implication of the situation depicted in the preceding section is that if this had been the whole story, then human capital would have no place in an enquiry into the standard of living, particularly one that was based on examining the stock of wealth of individuals over time. If it were found to be essentially like a producer good, such as tools, animals, or land, from which a stream of future earnings could be derived, and nothing else, it would no longer be an end in itself and therefore not an object of consumption, whether durable or not. In this case, it would be unsuitable as an indicator of consumption standards since the reason for which it was acquired was to produce more efficiently and/or to produce more. The question this poses is whether human capital could indeed have had any other functions besides. In other words, could it be considered in fact as an article of consumption to be included in the basket of standard of living goods? In this part of the chapter, we try to make a case for this possibility.

In fact, there is every reason to accept that reading and writing skills, for our purposes, can also be likened to a consumer durable that would be appropriate for inclusion in this basket. On the one hand, they were obtained by means of a market-related activity—education—that had a cost, and in order to enjoy a stream of gratification over a more or less prolonged period. Their acquisition was practically free of non-market restrictions and was therefore part of the standard mechanism whereby consumers allocate scarce resources to different ends in order to maximize their utility, an essential premise of the standard of living discussion. Although in itself not a form of direct satisfaction, except insofar as it could have had some kind of social symbolism that could be enjoyable in itself, human capital gave access to other forms of gratification which could be enjoyed as long as this asset was present and usable.[28] These forms belonged to 'the non-material side of life, such as reading, religion, family life, friends, gossip, and games [which] were deeply valued and thus, in some sense, necessary' (Weatherill 1993). Reading, either for amusement or edification and spiritual uplift, was probably the most common way of using literacy in this way.[29] For a smaller number, literacy was also the indispensable vehicle whereby personal correspondence could take place and thus the barrier of distance, to which all oral communication is subject, could be overcome. According to Jacques-Louis Ménétra, a Parisian artisan of the late eighteenth century, writing was 'a way of keeping up contacts, giving news of himself, receiving money, and announcing his return when he was away from home' (Roche 1982). A third and still more restricted, but also more sophisticated field of application was the composition of autobiographic registers. This exercise became widespread in higher circles mostly from the seventeenth century but was not unknown to the humbler strata of society (Spufford 1979; Foisil 1986; Markussen 1990).

Potentially, the same literary skills could serve these 'consumption' ends as much as they could have 'functional' uses, and thus to analyse their respective importance it is necessary to find a way of separating them in their effects.[30] Obviously, it is extremely difficult to say what part of an individual's human capital was a consumer durable and what part was a producer good. Even if this could be achieved, however, the problem still would remain of creating a proxy that would help gauge the extent of the personal, non-occupational benefits of being literate. Of the three aspects of immediate satisfaction made possible by literacy, which were mentioned above, the consumption of reading matter is not only the easiest to deal with, but also probably the one with the greatest impact on people's lives. This renders it an attractive approach through which to establish how those who were literate could make use of this capacity and what its value was to them, apart from other uses it might have. Since reading became closely connected during the period considered with the printed word, it is to the latter that we now turn our attention.

A great deal has been written on the history of the book in early modern Europe, and as a result a lot is known about its production, sale, possession, and diffusion, not to mention the types of literature encompassed by this activity. Estimates of the output of such a dispersed and complex industry are naturally less than reliable but all sources concur in that the number of copies produced reached remarkably high figures early on and expanded at a notable pace throughout the period considered. For the entire sixteenth century, a total of some 150 to 200 million copies is likely and for the eighteenth century, it may have reached ten times that amount (Chartier 1987; Houston 1988).[31] Since the population rose in the meantime by 80%, this affords an unmistakable sign of a strong upward movement in individual book-ownership during these centuries. This was naturally accompanied by a tremendous intensification in the respective trade, both fixed and itinerant. Not only a strong specialization developed but also a myriad of networks of a regional, national, and international scope which, by the eighteenth century, spread from Geneva, Troyes, Venice, Avignon, and Amsterdam into the deepest recesses of the countryside (Dooley 1996; Mellot 2000). The average consumption of books went from two per capita and per century in the 1500s to ten in the 1700s, an evolution one should expect to see reflected in the statistics regarding book ownership derived from post-mortem inventories. This is indeed what happens, whether it is among Friesland farmers, where the proportion of the deceased with books increased from 10% to more than 50% of the families between the sixteenth and the eighteenth centuries (de Vries 1974); Madrid, where it went from 26% to 36% (Cruz and Corbacho 1999); Alsace, an essentially peasant society, where the rise was from 8% to 20–30% in the course of the 1700s (Boehler 1995); or England, 'where circumstantial evidence points to an increase in the reading public from the Civil War onward' (Stephens 1990).

Books were never cheap during these centuries and it should come as no surprise that their possession could not have been distributed at all evenly throughout society. Here we encounter again patterns that resemble those we considered while discussing literacy in conjunction with income and occupation. During the sixteenth century, libraries were mainly owned by the upper strata and the clergy, while in the popular classes book-owning families would not have exceeded 10% of the total and the number of items belonging to each one was tiny. But like the 'consumption revolution', there was a 'book revolution' in Europe too, which translated into a 'trickle down effect' through society that is reminiscent of what happened during the seventeenth and eighteenth centuries with respect to other consumer durables. In Paris, for example, the percentage of artisans and trades people possessing books rose to 16.5% in 1700 and to 35% in 1780, and a similar movement is reported for the nine cities of western France where post-mortem inventories have been analysed (Chartier 1987; Fairchilds 1993). Although a desire to emulate one's betters and rise above one's equals may have been at the root of such a trend, as has been claimed for material consumption in general, there is evidence that increases in real income were also responsible. The very high rank order correlation between classes of income and of book-holding families in England between 1675 and 1725 suggests this possibility strongly (Weatherill 1988; Shammas 1993). In Kimpenerwaard, a rich rural district of the Netherlands, overall book-holding rose from 45% to 76% of families between the seventeenth and the eighteenth centuries but the 'middle class' always had more than the peasants and within each class the better-off always owned more than the poorer elements (Kamermans 1999). These and other similar findings make it tempting to conclude that book ownership may have mirrored the use of literacy for non-functional purposes and would therefore enable us to determine the extent to which human capital served as a vehicle for immaterial consumption, independently of the other uses it might have. Unfortunately, there are several reasons why this link cannot be established.

The first point to make in this connection is that little solid evidence has been adduced to show what the direct correspondence between literacy and book ownership may have been in the early modern period. On the other hand, it is clear that not all who read books owned them, and not all books were read at all or were read for mere gratification. Many seventeenth- and eighteenth-century library inventories reveal the presence of 'technical books', on law, pharmacy, medicine, agronomy, and other practical subjects which would hardly qualify them for the 'spiritual' uses that we are looking for here (Chartier 1985–7). Indeed, it has been claimed that 'the private ownership of books was clearly oriented towards the practical needs of men, their profession, and the interests to which the latter gave rise' (Bödeker 1995). Books of this kind were really like producer goods, acquired to enhance their owners' productivity or gain, and generally not for reading for pleasure. They should not form part of any standard of living assessment exercise. Another aspect is that having a library for many also had a token value that contributed to status, this being as true for the humble as it was for the great. Among the former, it was not uncommon to have a Bible in the house that was probably never used but was held as a symbol of respectability and religiosity, and sometimes even for curative purposes. Lastly, books might not be consumed only or even at all by their owners but by somebody else and indeed by several readers successively. At a time when they were expensive items, it should come as no surprise that they were often borrowed informally but also from libraries or obtained by hire, two practices which proliferated in eighteenth-century towns and cities (François 1989; Braida 1995).

A more serious preoccupation arises out of the fact that reading was not confined to books alone. An enormous amount of it and a steadily growing one too, focused on 'chap books', 'street literature', 'romances de cordel', or 'livres bleus', as they were variously designated across Europe, as well as newspapers, fly sheets, and other ephemeral publications. The first of these categories is particularly important for the present context given their abundance and widespread dissemination throughout society. They were unbound, poorly printed volumes, made out of the cheapest paper and varying in length from a few to as many as 200 pages. Although often 'sensational, scurrilous and pornographic' (Stephens 1990), the majority were serious and often devoted to religious, technical, and educational themes (Mandrou 1974; Hébrard 1996). They were traded over vast distances and handled through complex networks of wholesalers and chapmen. Their numbers cannot be assessed with any precision given that they were distributed to a large extent by peddlers and that they were rarely if ever mentioned in post-mortem inventories.[32] Being very cheap, they were probably deemed to be worthless second hand and therefore not to be registered, but their frailty also ensured that they left little trace amongst the possessions of the deceased.[33] Nonetheless, historians agree that they were a major source of reading satisfaction. In early eighteenth-century London, for example, just one of the fourteen London dealers who dealt in them had 400,000 copies in stock on the occasion of his death (Chartier 1987). In Turin, the print run in almanacks alone for one year came to 230,000, at a time (1783) when the population of the city and its territory was slightly over 300,000 (Braida 1995). In Lisbon, meanwhile, it was commented that the circulation of 'cordel' literature was 'abundant' (Lisboa 1998).

While we may assume that for the many who had books, literacy was important because it was an indispensable means to deriving enjoyment through their consumption for its own sake, an even greater number were going to the trouble and expense of acquiring the means to read and yet owned none. What makes this even more of a paradox, however, is the fact this second group also lacked any clear functional reason, of the kind we examined in the preceding section, for making an investment in this capacity. Indeed, as literacy rates rose in Europe, particularly during the eighteenth century, a growing share of this seems to have been unrelated to any practical purpose for those involved. Many who did not need it for their productive activities came to participate in the process. This is particularly obvious with unskilled labourers but also applies to a lesser degree to the 'lower crafts', to artisans who engaged in a very limited amount of direct commercialization, and even to small traders and shopkeepers some of whom would not have been literate before. This evolution is particularly striking as regards the first of these categories given that they could not have required this acquisition for any practical use at all. Yet in England, for example, the literacy rate in this stratum rose from about 10%, at the end of the sixteenth century, to 20–30%, one hundred years later (Cressy 1980) and to 41% by the middle of the eighteenth century (Schofield 1973). During the same period, in Amsterdam, it went from 40% to 66% (in the case of 'proletarians') (Kuijpers 1997) and, in Lyon, it rose from 20% to 37% for day workers and from 20% to 41% for gardeners during the eighteenth century, while in Provence the share of the literate among unskilled rural labour rose from 4% to 8% in the course of the eighteenth century (Vovelle 1975; Chartier *et al.* 1976).[34] Interestingly, in Paris, among arrested petty criminals—who mainly stole food—60% were illiterate in 1730 but by 1785 this was down, impressively, to 40% (Roche 1987).

The issue this raises is whether this expanded willingness to invest in human capital on the part of the poorer layers of society can be taken as a part of the consumer revolution and therefore reinforces the message of the latter as regards the pre-industrial standard of living debate. Since human capital was necessarily formed at the expense of material consumption, such a conclusion seems unavoidable. The question which remains is to grasp what can have motivated the shift in the allocation of resources towards more widespread literacy among the many who stood to gain so little or even nothing from it in purely practical terms. Several factors may have shaped this situation. Furet and Ozouf (1977) have argued that emulation of the higher orders provided some of the motivation, just as it did with the consumption revolution in general, and that the lower strata pushed their offspring towards literacy as part of an imitative process. Houston (1988) has added that 'higher wages for labourers might encourage investment not only in consumer durables but also in education', suggesting a high income-elasticity of demand for this group. At the same time, it is tempting to think that the growing availability and increasing penetration of rural markets, during the 1700s, by the 'blue book' business, the only reading matter that was affordable to such people, had something to do with this 'downward percolation' effect. From originally having had an urban and more affluent readership in the sixteenth and seventeenth centuries, in the eighteenth century blue books became rural, 'plebeian', and truly popular, thanks to the thrust of 'colportage' and rising literacy (Botrel 1996). By 1730, they were said to have invaded the provinces in France and were known by heart throughout the countryside. By the first half of the nineteenth century, their readership in this country had become entirely rural (Lyons 1997), a spread that strengthens our argument that the poorer classes were using their new-found literacy to read, even though their inventories show far fewer families with books than families where literacy was present.

All in all, it seems difficult to go against the notion that the analysis of the standard of living must be incomplete if proper attention is not paid to the place of human capital in it. This does not mean that the level of human capital can simply serve, by retropolation, as an indicator of the level of real income, although the latter clearly influenced the rate at which the former was formed.[35] Indeed, the relationship between them is too complex to be modelled in such a manner. On the other hand, in the case of the unskilled and the barely skilled, human capital as an end in itself can be clearly distinguished, since it had no other purpose. This allows us to take an important step towards rendering it measurable so that it can meaningfully be included among the stock of durables used in order to evaluate how well-off people were in early modern Europe. The following section presents an exploratory effort in this direction.

5. Implications for the Standard of Living

In a controversial study, David Mitch (1992) has argued that, during the nineteenth century, England was grossly over-educated. The stock of human capital was well in excess of what was called for by the jobs performed, and its contribution to the epoch's rapid economic growth was therefore small. This enormous literacy surplus was due to two circumstances: a steady expansion of educational facilities and a rising demand for reading and writing skills as a form of consumption by an increasing well-off society. Put in other words, the average product of human capital investment was positive and quite significant but at the margin, it may have been much smaller as a result of the complementary, non-investment role it had in society.

The present study detects a similar though not identical pattern in Europe during the latter half of the early modern period. At this time too, there was a surplus of human capital in the sense that certain segments of the population were educated without correspondence to their professional needs. In contrast, as we saw above, the total stock of human capital varied to quite a large extent in consonance with the evolving requirements of the economy. This suggests two inferences. One is that the contribution of human capital to any growth there may have been will, in all likelihood, have been significant. The other is that, in this case, the literacy surplus was probably still quite small although it was on a long-term upward trend. Our interest lies in the second of these issues, that is, the extent of the acquisition of human capital as a form of immaterial wealth that individuals procured in order to enhance their spiritual well-being in particular and their welfare in general. The next question is whether this can be quantified and, if so, with what result.

To achieve this, we begin by treating the capacity to read and write (proxied by the ability to sign) as a costly asset in the portfolio of consumption durables that individuals accumulated and enjoyed during their lifetimes—furniture, clothing, ornaments, etc. The assessment of this portfolio and its components corresponds, somewhat arbitrarily, to the end of their lives because that is when they were usually inventoried. As is common in the literature, the total value thus obtained is employed, after suitable deflation, as a yardstick for gauging the standard of living and the relative weight of the items contained in this basket of more or less durable goods (Schuurman and Walsh 1994). In the present case, it serves for appraising the relative importance that human capital had in the overall picture. The first problem then is to put a monetary figure on human capital and this can be done in one of three ways.

Unlike most consumer durables, which would have had some sort of second-hand use and therefore a potential market price, human capital disappears with its possessor. In this perspective, the correct approach would be to attribute a value of zero to it. Since, however, what we seek to capture with this exercise is the value of the asset's fruition during its owner's lifetime, this solution appears unhelpful. A second way is to value the stream of utility over a given period by a conventional measure such as the asset's rental value, using normal depreciation and discount rates. Given that human capital can be assumed to suffer no depreciation—it might indeed appreciate with use—this should constitute a relatively simple operation once we have its capital cost. The difficulty this time lies in estimating the equivalent stream of satisfaction generated by all the other assets in the inventory, an elusive target given that in many cases we would not know, either their current age or their depreciation schedules. The third option is a stock, rather than a flow solution, and it is this we follow here. It consists in taking the historic cost of human capital and confronting it with the current market value of the material assets in the portfolio. The disadvantage of doing this is that we shall be comparing articles valued by different methods. This is mitigated, however, by the fact that human capital, in principle, does not depreciate and so it matters little when it is appraised. Furthermore, once it is acquired, it cannot be transacted, which means in effect that there is no other practical way of pricing it.

The present estimate refers to early eighteenth-century England and France, two cases for which reasonable data exist with respect to all the required parameters and where a consumption revolution is supposed to have been in full swing. The historic cost in question aggregates two items: the cost of education and the opportunity cost incurred by withdrawing the learner from the labour market. As regards the former, contemporary observers noted that normally it took three years to learn to read and, following that, another three years to learn to write (van Deursen 1991), though there are numerous instances on record of gifted individuals who required only a few months for either (Spufford 1979). Since we are considering only those who could sign their names but could not necessarily write any more than that, we assume that the second part of their education was limited to an additional year. This gives us a lower bound estimate. At mid-century, in Birmingham, a low cost elementary school charged pupils 3–5 shillings each per quarter (Money 1993), that is, taking the lower value, a total of £2.4 for the four year education of our premise and very close to Mitch's (1999) figure of £2.0 for the early nineteenth century.[36] In France, monthly fees varied between 3 and 4 *sols* for tuition in reading and between 4 and 6 *sols* for learning to write (Houdaille 1977; Grevet 1987). On an assumption of ten months a year of schooling, this would entail a global cost of elementary literacy of an order of 6.5 to 9 *livres tournois*. Since Chartier *et al.* (1976) put a figure of 13 livres on this, we adopt for the present exercise an intermediate estimate of 9 livres.[37]

Putting a value on the labour time lost in the process is a good deal more hazardous and depends on several not easily specifiable factors. To begin with, there was a wide range of possible ages over which education could be acquired. We assume here, again for the sake of a lower bound estimate, an early, low opportunity cost range, from 6 or 7 to 10 or 11 years. In the second place, there is the vexed question of the role of child labour in the pre-industrial European economy, on which views are divergent while little hard evidence is available to help sort them out. In proto-industrial areas, children were far more sought after for paid employment but in the majority of situations, which were agrarian based, occupational opportunities for them were scarce. Boys and girls became farm servants usually at thirteen or fourteen years of age but smaller children helped in the family and were unlikely to be hired for any significant task or length of time. Around 1800 in England, Horrell and Humphries (1995) have established a participation rate in agriculture for the under tens of only 15%, a state of affairs which is confirmed by Cunningham (1990).

The problem is compounded by a dearth of information on wage rates, which are available only for adults. As an upper bound limit, we take a child's wage to have been one-fifth of that of an adult (Spufford 1985; van Deursen 1991) and assume an average annual occupation rate for them of 15%, in other words, 45 days of employment. The lower bound limit is given by a situation of full unemployment and hence zero income. Between 1700 and 1750, an unskilled male rural worker in early eighteenth-century England earned about £20 a year (Mitchell 1988), and therefore the opportunity cost of achieving proficiency in reading and writing would have been something like £2.4 at the most and, at the least, nothing. The full historic cost of being literate in this context thus amounted altogether to between £2.4 and £4.8. A similar exercise for France adopts the same assumptions regarding time of work and child/adult wage ratios. In the early eighteenth century, the remuneration for unskilled labour in the countryside varied between 10 and 15 *sols* per day (Morineau 1972; Chartier *et al.* 1976; Baehrel 1988) and if we take 12.5 *sols* as representative, the opportunity cost of a child acquiring literacy would come to 22.5 livres and the full cost, including schooling, to between 9 and 31.5 livres.

Having quantified the value of human capital, the next step is to place this in context, the most appropriate one being naturally the stock of wealth owned by the people under consideration. In early eighteenth-century England, rural labourers left estates worth on average £16, while slightly up the social ladder, for husbandmen and small farmers, the figure was double this amount (Weatherill 1988). This included all goods and chattels but the average value of household goods alone, the reality on which the standard of living discussion focuses, was far lower—respectively £5 and £8.[38] The implication is that even at the lowest end of the estimated range the cost of acquiring the most basic sort of literacy was substantial in terms of the domestic economy of the social strata in question—somewhere in the region of 50% of the accumulated material wealth of individuals at the end of their lives. For France, the contrast between household wealth and the capital cost of literacy is less sharp but still implies a recasting of the standard of living evaluation based exclusively on material goods. The inventories of rural labourers that have been examined for this period were characteristically below 500 livres, and their household possessions did not exceed 100 livres in total so that here too it can be said that human capital represented a valuable asset in the lives of a great many of the humblest people who acquired it (Baulant 1975; Waro–Desjardins 1993; Boehler 1995).

The results of our estimations are of the roughest kind and the only claim that can be safely made on their behalf is that they provide us with an order of magnitude for the importance of a critical and increasingly significant immaterial good in people's lives. One finding this points to is that if human capital is treated on par with material consumer durables then the level of welfare in the eighteenth century for the mass of the population has to be revised upward relative to earlier centuries. A second is that the spread of literacy during the 1700s, in particular for those on the lowest rungs of the social ladder, clearly indicates an improvement in terms of the broadly defined standard of living that has been proposed above. Not only is the notion of a consumer revolution hereby reinforced but also it becomes clear that, in fact, this process reached much further down, into the realm of the poor and 'un-inventoried', whose welfare status on the whole has escaped the scrutiny of the historian. Finally, it should be noted that human capital also enriched men and women in other reaches of society, and, among the better-off, it seems likely that this immaterial good would have had a higher value for the inventory since their schooling was better. It seems likely, however, that in the case of the humble, the weight this represented in total wealth would have been greater, a fact that suggests a further possible revision—the gap between the rich and the poor may have been less than has been thought until now.

What is more remarkable, though, is that this numerous group of poor literates spent their resources to obtain this capacity, knowing full well that they were not investing in a producer good. For them, this human capital could serve practically only as an end in itself to generate a stream of welfare of a wholly immaterial nature. Although our assumptions may be faulted to some extent and our quantification, albeit a lower bound result, stands to be corrected, arguably the substance of our inference is not affected. The fact remains that taking human capital into consideration in this way is advisable and liable to affect the traditional calculation of standard of living levels to a substantial degree.

6. Conclusions

In economic history, human capital is usually treated as an enhancement of the capacity to produce. In this chapter, we explore ways of perceiving it also as a capacity to enjoy. As a result, it is argued that human capital should be integrated into the standard of living debate, in this case in the framework of pre-industrial Europe. In order to make this a manageable exercise, human capital is limited here to formal cognitive skills—reading and writing—and attention is focused on its two basic uses. On the one hand, it is like a producer good, which is invested in so as to increase productivity, and thus is irrelevant to any evaluation of the standard of living that employs levels of durable material consumption as the yardstick. On the other hand, it is the immaterial means to various forms of non-physical gratification, one of which—exemplified here by book reading for its own sake—is examined in some detail. The picture that emerges shows that between the sixteenth and the eighteenth centuries an enormous rise in literacy took place and represented a deliberate allocation of resources by individuals who in this way sought to augment this form of satisfaction. To this extent, there was an increase in welfare and this has to be factored into the traditional modes of assessing the long-term movement in the standard of living. In a short and more technical section, we propose a way of quantifying such increments, at least for certain social strata. Although this is a very tentative approach, the result suggests that the welfare gains obtained from human capital could be relatively large and may contribute to a needed clarification of the standard of living debate in pre-industrial times.

Notes

1. Maddison (2001) describes per capita growth between 1000 and 1820 in western Europe as a fairly steady process but 'a slow crawl', at a rate of 0.14% a year.
2. There are two ways of deflating the nominal wage series of the different regions/countries available in order to render them comparable in real terms. Exchange rates is one of them but has been considered by most of the current literature as apt to produce distortions given that they do not reflect differences in prices of non-tradable goods and are affected by capital movements. The alternative is to use purchasing power parity adjustment (PPP). This involves establishing the cost at local prices in these places of a common basket of consumer goods and using the resulting indices to deflate nominal wages. The intuition is

that this exercise shows how much the nominal wage will buy in a given place compared to what it does in another taken as the reference.

3. A picture confirmed by de Vries (1994) for the sixteenth and seventeenth centuries.

4. We have added Portugal and Italy to van Zanden's collection of countries by extrapolating back to 1810 their relative position of 1850, as given in Reis (2000). This exercise, if extended to Scandinavia, would place Sweden and Denmark on a par with France and Belgium.

5. Clark and Van Der Werf (1998) cast doubt on this argument by claiming that work loads were already so high in the Middle Ages that they could not have increased much in the seventeenth or eighteenth centuries.

6. Brewer and Porter (1993), Weatherill (1988), Torras and Yun (eds.) (1999), Malanima (1994), Boehler (1995), Baulant (1975), Kamermans (1999), and Fairchilds (1993) provide many examples.

7. For a full critique, see the Introduction in Torras and Yun (1999).

8. All of them are illustrated in the present volume. Anthropometric history has proved valuable for later periods but as yet very little information on heights is available for the early modern period. The demographic approach is similarly helpful but is better at bringing to light major shifts in welfare than at portraying the gradual evolution over time that the 'material consumption' approach can offer. Real wages are best in this respect but as they are used to estimate GDP per capita too, they do not allow us to contrast this result with its impact on the standard of living. The first two have the advantage of extending the concept of the standard of living beyond the narrow field of real wages, food, and durables consumption to include health, physical vigour, leisure, and general amenity.

9. This does not mean that professional skills and literacy could not be learned at the same time and indeed often were. For examples of this, see Spufford (1979).

10. There is a large discussion about the meaning and usefulness of signatures for the history of literacy. For some references, see Houston (1988), Parker (1980), Stephens (1990), Quéniart (1977), and Saugnieux (1986).

11. Notwithstanding, the correlation between signing and being able to copy a phrase was low in nineteenth-century Denmark, according to Markussen (1990). Grevet (1987) notes that, in the Pas-de-Calais, towards 1800 there was a 20 percentage point difference between the proportion of males who could sign the marriage register and males who were considered 'literate' by official enquirers.

12. There are few reliable national estimates, the most famous being the French one by Maggiolo (Furet and Ozouf 1977). Most of the data used here are culled from more or less local studies and extrapolated, at some risk, to national levels.

13. For an early identification of these historical literacy regions, see Chartier (1985–7). It revises Cipolla's (1969) classic analysis thanks to the enormous flow of new information produced during the 1970s and 1980s.

14. There is a vast range of literature on these countries. The most useful proved to be Gelabert (1987), Benassar (1983), and Viñao Fraga (1990) for Spain; Houdaille (1977) and Furet and Ozouf (1977) for France; Hart (1976) and Kuijppers (1997) for the Netherlands; Gouveia (1998), Magalhães (1994), and Marquilhas (2000) for Portugal; Marchesini (1983) for Italy; and Sanderson (1991) and Schofield (1973) for England.

15. For a general warning to avoid transposing educational models from the nineteenth century to earlier times, see Compère (1995).

16. The exception occurred in parts of Prussia and in Sweden during the eighteenth century, where the Pietist movement was taken over by the state and a centralized system of

education was organized. The aim was religious—the universal acquisition of a reading ability that would permit a direct reasonable knowledge of some of the Bible and of the Catechism, but always under supervision.

17. In the Alpes, near Briançon, where autodidactic arrangements were common, by 1800 93% of males could sign. See Granet–Abisset (1996), and Vovelle (1975).

18. On the other hand, in some Dutch provinces, parents were penalized if they failed to send their children to school (Spufford 1995).

19. In the Netherlands, de Vries and van der Woude (1997) estimate that half the seventeenth-century population of Amsterdam was under these conditions but in other places it was probably more. See the scenarios outlined for French eighteenth-century workers and the vulnerability induced in them by price changes in Morineau (1972).

20. See Houston (1985 and 1988), van Deursen (1991), Larquié (1987), Nilsson and Svärd (1994), Amalric (1987), and Grevet (1987).

21. Moreno Claverías (1999). I am grateful to the author of this text for allowing me to use this chapter of her Ph.D. thesis on 'Pautas de consumo en la Cataluña de los siglos XVII y XVIII'. The same point is made for Provence by Vovelle (1975), who notes that the *ménagers* concerned themselves with becoming literate when they entered the ranks of the *propriétaires*.

22. Literacy was also becoming instrumental for them by allowing easier access to credit and to the burgeoning market for their produce.

23. At the other end of Europe, Magalhães (1994) has noted that the increase in the volume of legal documents pertaining to land and wealth in Portuguese rural society was having a similar effect.

24. See also Magalhães (1994), Stephens (1990), Spufford (1995), Benassar (1983), Cressy (1981), and many others.

25. Cases are cited of women who, owing to early widowhood, ran craft shops and businesses or farms, although this was not the norm. Artisans, liberal professionals, shopkeepers, and the like were supposed to be men. In 1742, only 14% of taxable households in Amsterdam were headed by women (de Vries and van der Woude 1997).

26. Amsterdam, one of the most literate cities of seventeenth-century Europe, owed much of its prosperity to its role as an 'information exchange' where widespread literacy was obviously crucial (Smith 1984).

27. But in rural society, opportunities existed too, as David Cressy (1980) has noted, and literacy was a component of it.

28. People can learn to read and write but later, for lack of use, may forget these skills, a not unusual occurrence in this period, as related by several authors.

29. Religious purposes, in particular, have long been associated with literacy in the early modern period, a link that has been the subject of a vast outpouring of publications. Works with a spiritual content of whatever persuasion certainly were the most common form of book until the late eighteenth century both in terms of production and in libraries, but a considerable body of recent writing has cast doubts on religious factionalism as a long-term force driving the spread of literacy or of book reading. See Parker (1980), Cressy (1981), Gawthorp and Strauss (1984), François (1989), van Deursen (1991), and Spufford (1995).

30. According to Nicolas and Nicolas (1992), 'although literacy is considered a consumption good today, during the early industrial revolution literacy was an investment good, the attainment of which was an investment decision by the family household'. Our view, on the contrary, is that at this time and earlier both forms co-existed, often in the same person.

31. The number of different titles published in Europe during the eighteenth century was 3 million. In Germany alone, output was between 2 and 5 million copies a year (Houston 1988).

32. According to Braida (1995), the distribution circuit is the best way of understanding at what sort of public a particular type of publication was directed. In Italy, for example, agricultural almanacs might appear to be suited to a peasant readership but could not have been so, in fact, as they were sold in bookshops and not by peddlers.

33. In eighteenth-century France typically they cost one *sol*, about one-twentieth of the price of an inexpensive book (Chartier 1987). In England and the Netherlands, their price was around a fourth or a fifth of the daily wage of an unskilled labourer (Spufford 1985).

34. These figures are confirmed by several regional studies in the second volume of Furet and Ozouf (1977).

35. Several authors have noted, for instance, the coincidence between periods of prosperity or poverty, on the one hand, and the acceleration or retardation of the spread of literacy, on the other. See Grevet (1985), Houston (1985), Nicolas and Nicolas (1992).

36. In late eighteenth-century Kilmarnock fees for instruction in reading and writing were three shillings per quarter (Houston 1985).

37. One *livre tournois* was the equivalent of 20 *sous* or *sols*.

38. This is less though not a great deal less than what is indicated by Shammas (1993), who puts the ratio of durables to total wealth at around 50%.

References

Allen, R. C. (2000) 'Economic Structure and Agricultural Productivity in Europe, 1300–1800'. *European Economic History Review,* 4: 1–26.

—— (1998) 'The Great Divergence: Wages and Prices in Europe from the Middle Ages to the First World War', University of British Columbia, Department of Economics Discussion Paper No. 98–12.

Amalric, J. P. (1987) 'Un Réseau d'Enseignement Élémentaire au XVIIIème Siècle: Les Maîtres d'Écoles dans les Campagnes de Burgos et de Santander', in *De l'Alphabétisation aux Circuits du Livre en Espagne XVIè-XIXè Siècles.* Paris: Éditions du Centre National de la Recherche Scientifique.

Baehrel, R. (1988) *Une Croissance. La Basse-Provence Rurale de la Fin du Seizième Siècle à 1789. Essai d'Économie Historique Statistique.* Paris: École des Hautes Études en Sciences Sociales.

Baulant, M. (1975) 'Niveaux de Vie Paysans autour de Meaux en 1700 et 1750'. *Annales E.S.C.,* 30: 505–18.

Benassar, B. (1983) 'Les Résistances Mentales', in J. P. Amalric *et al.* (eds.), *Aux Origines du Retard Économique de l'Espagne XVIè-XIXè Siècles.* Paris: Éditions du Centre National de la Recherche Scientifique.

Blomme, J., Buyst, E., and van der Wee, H. (1994) 'The Belgian Economy in a Long Term Historical Perspective: Economic Development in Flanders and Brabant, 1500–1812', in A. Maddison and H. van der Wee (eds.), *Economic Growth and Structural Change. Comparative Approaches over the Long Run.* Milan: Bocconi University.

Bödeker, H. E. (1995) 'D'une "Historie Litéraire du Lecteur" à l'Histoire du Lecteur. Bilan et Perspectives de l'Histoire de la Lecture en Allemagne', in R. Chartier (ed.), *Histoires de la Lecture: Un Bilan des Recherches.* Paris: IMEC.

Boehler, J. M. (1995) *Une Société Rurale en Milieu Rhénan: La Paysannerie de la Plaine d'Alsace (1648–1789)*. Strasbourg: Presses Universitaires de Strasbourg.

Botrel, J. F. (1996) 'Les Recherches sur le Livre et la Lecture en Espagne XVIIIè-XIXè Siècles', in R. Chartier and H.-J. Lüsebrink (eds.), *Colportage et Lecture Populaire. Imprimés de Large Circulation en Europe XVIè-XIXè Siècles*. Paris: IMEC.

Braida, L. (1995) 'Quelques Considérations sur l'Histoire de la Lecture en Italie. Usages et Pratiques du Livre sous l'Ancien Régime', in R. Chartier (ed.), *Histoires de la Lecture: Un Bilan des Recherches*. Paris: IMEC.

Brambilla, E. (1991) 'Alfabetismo e Società nelle Marche in Età Napoleonica', in A. Bartoli Langeli and X. Toscani (eds.), *Istruzione, Alfabetismo, Scritura. Saggi di Storia dell' Alfabetizzazione in Italia (Sec. XV–XIX)*. Milano: Franco Angeli.

Brewer, J. and Porter, R. (eds.) (1993) *Consumption and the World of Goods*. London: Routledge.

Chartier, R. (1987) *Lectures et Lecteurs dans la France de l'Ancien Régime*. Paris: Seuil.

——(1985-7) 'Les Pratiques de l'Écrit', in P. Ariès and G. Duby (eds.), *Histoire de la Vie Privée*. Paris: Seuil.

——Compère, M. M., and Julia, D. (1976) *L' Éducation en France du XVIe au XVIIIe Siècle*. Paris: Société d'Édition d'Enseignement Supérieur.

Cipolla, C. M. (1969) *Literacy and Development in the West*. Harmondsworth: Penguin.

Clark, G. and Van Der Werf, Y. (1998) 'Work in Progress? The Industrious Revolution'. *Journal of Economic History*, 58: 830–43.

Compère, M. M. (1995) *L'Histoire de l'Éducation en Europe: Essai Comparatif sur la Façon dont elle s'Écrit*. Paris: Institut National de Recherche Pédagogique.

Crafts, N. R. F. (1997) 'The Human Development Index and Changes in the Standards of Living: Some Historical Comparisons'. *European Economic History Review*, 1: 299–322.

Cressy, D. (1980) *Literacy and the Social Order. Reading and Writing in Tudor and Stuart England*. Cambridge: Cambridge University Press.

——(1981) 'Levels of Illiteracy in England, 1530–1730', in H. J. Graff (ed.), *Literacy and Social Development in the West: A Reader*. Cambridge: Cambridge University Press.

Cruz, J. and Corbacho, J.C. Sola (1999) 'El Mercado Madrileño y la Industrialisacion en España durante los Siglos XVIII–XIX', in J. Torras and B. Yun (eds.), *Consumo, Condiciones de Vida y Comercialización. Cataluña y Castilla, Siglos XVII–XIX*. Avila: Junta de Castilla y Leon.

Cunningham, H. (1990) 'The Employment and Unemployment of Children in England c.1680–1815'. *Past and Present*, 126: 115–50.

Dooley, B. (1996) 'Printing and Entrepreneurialism in Seventeenth-Century Italy'. *Journal of European Economic History*, 25: 569–97.

Fairchilds, C. (1993) 'Consumption in Early Modern Europe. A Review Article'. *Comparative Studies in Society and History*, 35: 850–8.

Foisil, M. (1986) 'L'Écriture du For Privé' in P. Ariès and G. Duby (eds.), *Histoire de la Vie Privée*. Paris: Seuil.

François, É. (1989) 'Lire et Écrire en France et en Allemagne au temps de la Révolution', in H. Berding, É. François, and H.-P. Ullmann (eds.), *La Révolution, la France et l'Allemagne: Deux Modèles Opposés de Changement Social?* Paris: Maison des Sciences de l'Homme.

Furet, F. and Ouzouf, M. (1977) *Lire et Écrire: L'Alphabétisation des Français de Calvin à Jules Ferry*. Paris: Éditions de Minuit.

Gawthrop, R. and Strauss, G. (1984) 'Protestantism and Literacy in Early Modern Germany'. *Past and Present*, 104: 11–55.

Gelabert, J. E. (1987) 'Niveaux d'Alphabétisation en Galice (1635–1900)', in *De l'Alphabétisation aux Circuits du Livre en Espagne XVIè–XIXè Siècles*. Paris: Éditions du Centre National de la Recherche Scientifique.

Gouveia, A. Camões (1998) 'Educação e Aprendizagens. Formas de Poder na Paideia do Portugal Moderno'. *Ler História*, 35: 11–44.

Granet-Abisset, A-M. (1996) 'Entre Auto-Didaxie et Scolarisation. Les Alpes Briançonnaises'. *Histoire de l'Éducation*, 81: 111–41.

Grantham, G. (1999) 'Contra Ricardo: On the Macroeconomics of Pre-Industrial Economies'. *European Review of Economic History*, 3: 199–232.

Grevet, R. (1985) L'Alphabétisation Urbaine sous l'Ancien Régime: L'Exemple de Saint-Omer (fin XVIIè–début XIXè siècle)'. *Revue du Nord*, 67: 609–32.

——(1987) 'L'Instruction des Ruraux dans le Pas-de-Calais au Début de la Révolution Française'. *Revue du Nord*, 69: 309–22.

Hart, S. (1976) *Geschrift en Getal: Een Keuze Uit de Demografisch-, Economisch-en Sociaal-Historische Studiën Opgrond van Amsterdamse en Zaanse Archivalia 1600–1800*. Dordrecht: Historische Vereniging Holland, Hollandse Studiën, 9.

Hébrard, J. (1996) 'Les Livres Scolaires de la Bibliothèque Bleue: Archaïsme ou Modernité?' in R. Chartier and H. J. Lüsebrink (eds.), *Colportage et Lecture Populaire. Imprimés de Large Circulation en Europe XVIè–XIXè Siècles*. Paris: IMEC.

Hoffman, P. T. (1996) *Growth in a Traditional Society: The French Countryside 1450–1815*. Princeton, NJ: Princeton University Press.

Hofmeister, A. *et al.* (1998) 'Elementary Education, Schools and the Demands of Everyday Life: North West Germany in 1800'. *Central European History*, 31: 329–84.

Horrell, S. and Humphries, J. (1995) ' "The Exploitation of Little Children": Child Labour and the Family Economy in the Industrial Revolution'. *Explorations in Economic History*, 32: 485–516.

Houdaille, J. (1977) 'Les Signatures au Mariage de 1740 à 1829'. *Population*, 32: 65–90.

Houston, R. A. (1985) *Scottish Literacy and the Scottish Identity. Illiteracy and Society in Scotland and Northern England, 1600–1800*. Cambridge: Cambridge University Press.

——(1988) *Literacy in Early Modern Europe: Culture and Education, 1500–1800*. London: Longman.

Hoyler, M. (1998) 'Small Town Development and Urban Literacy: Comparative Evidence from Leicestershire Marriage Registers 1754–1890'. *Historical Social Research*, 23: 202–30.

Kamermans, J. A. (1999) *Materiele Cultuur in de Krimpenerwaard in de Zeventiende en Achttiende Eeuw. Ontwikkeling en Diversiteit*.Wageningen: A.A.G Bijdragen.

Kuijpers, E. (1997) 'Lezen en schrijven. Onderzoek naar het Alfabetiseringsniveau inb zeventiendeeeuws Amsterdam'. *Tijdschrift voor Sociale Geschiedenis*, 23: 490–522.

Larquié, C. (1987) 'L'Alphabétisation des Madrileños dans la Seconde Moitié du XVIIème Siècle: Stagnation ou Évolution?', in *De l' Alphabétisation aux Circuits du Livre en Espagne, XVIè–XIXè Siècles*. Paris: Éditions du Centre National de la Recherche Scientifique.

Lisboa, J. L. (1998) 'Mots (dits) Ecrits: Formes et Valeurs de la Diffusion des Idées au 18ème Siècle au Portugal', Ph.D. dissertation, European University Institute, Florence.

Lyons, M. (1997) 'What Did Peasants Read? Written and Printed Culture in Rural France, 1815–1914'. *European History Quarterly*, 27: 165–97.

Maddison, A. (2001) *The World Economy. A Millenial Perspective*, Paris: OECD.

de Magalhães, J. P. (1994) *Ler e Escrever no Mundo Rural do Antigo Regime: Um Contributo para a História da Alfabetização e da Escolarização em Portugal*. Braga: Universidade do Minho.

Malanima, P. (1994) 'Italian Economic Experience: Output and Income, 1600–1800', in A. Maddison and H. van der Wee (eds.), *Economic Growth and Structural Change. Comparative Approaches over the Long Run*. Milan: Bocconi University.

——(1995) *Economia Preindustriale. Mille Anni: Dal IX al XVIII Secolo*. Milan: Mondadori.

Mandrou, R. (1974) *De la Culture Populaire au 17è et 18è Siècles: La Bibliothèque Bleue de Troyes*. Paris: Stock.

Marchesini, D. (1983) 'Sposi e Scolari. Sottoscrizioni Matrimoniali e Alfabetismo tra Sette Ottocento'. *Quaderni Storici*, 18: 601–23.

Marczewski, J. (1961) 'Some Aspects of the Economic Growth of France, 1660–1958'. *Economic Development and Cultural Change*, 10: 369–86.

Markussen, I. (1990) 'The Development of Writing Ability in the Nordic Countries in the Eighteenth and Nineteenth Centuries'. *Scandinavian Journal of History*, 15: 37–63.

Marquilhas, R. (2000) *A Faculdade das Letras. Leitura e Escrita em Portugal no Século XVII*. Lisabon: Imprensa Nacional-Casa da Moeda.

Mellot, J. D. (2000) 'Libraires en Campagne: Les Forains Normands du Livre à la Fin du XVIIIe Siècle', in *Le Livre Voyageur (1450–1830). Actes du Colloque Internationale*. Paris: Klincksieck.

Mincer, J. (1974) *Schooling, Experience and Earnings*. New York: National Bureau of Economic Research.

Mitch, D. F. (1992) *The Rise of Popular Literacy in Victorian England: The Influence of Private Choice and Public Policy*. Philadelphia, PA: University of Pennsylvania Press.

——(1999) 'The Role of Education and Skill in the British Industrial Revolution', in J. Mokyr (ed.), *The British Industrial Revolution: An Economic Perspective*. Boulder, CO: Westview Press.

Mitchell, B. R. (1988) *British Historical Statistics*. Cambridge: Cambridge University Press.

Money, J. (1993) 'Teaching in the Market Place', in J. Brewer and R. Porter (eds.), *Consumption and the World of Goods*. London: Routledge.

Moreno Claverias, B. (1999) 'La Formación de Categorías en Función de la Posesión: Cuatro Estrategias de Consumo y Representación, 1670–1690'. Unpublished paper, European University Institute, Florence.

Morineau, M. (1972) 'Budgets Populaires en France au XVIIIe Siècle'. *Revue d'Histoire Économique et Sociale*, 50: 203–37, 449–81.

Nalle, S. T. (1989) 'Literacy and Culture in Early Modern Castille'. *Past and Present*, 125: 65–96.

Nicholas, S. J. and Nicholas, J. M. (1992) 'Male Literacy, "Deskilling" and the Industrial Revolution'. *Journal of Interdisciplinary History*, 23: 1–18.

Nilsson, A. (1997) 'What do Literacy Rates in the 19th Century Really Signify? New Light on an Old Problem from Unique Swedish Data', unpublished paper presented at the XXII Meeting of the Social Science History Association, Washington DC.

——Pettersson, L., and Svensson, P. (1999) 'Agrarian Transition and Literacy: The Case of Nineteenth Century Sweden'. *European Review of Economic History*, 3: 79–96.

—— and Svärd, B. (1994) 'Writing Ability and Agrarian Change in Early 19th Century Rural Scandia'. *Scandinavian Journal of History*, 19: 251–74.

Ozmucur, S. and Pamuk, S. (2002) 'Real Wages in the Ottoman Empire, 1469–1914'. *Journal of Economic History*, 62: 293–321.

Parker, G. (1980) 'An Educational Revolution? The Growth of Literacy and Schooling in Early Modern Europe'. *Tijdschrift voor Geschiedenis*, 93: 210–22.

Persson, K. G. (1988) *Pre-Industrial Economic Growth: Social Organization and Technological Progress in Europe*. Oxford: Basil Blackwell.

Quéniart, J. (1977) 'Les Apprentissages Scolaires au XVIIIè Siècle: Faut-il Réformer Maggiolo?'. *Revue d'Histoire Moderne et Contemporaine*, 24: 3–27.

Reis, J. (2000) 'How Poor was the Periphery before 1850? The Mediterranean vs. Scandinavia', in S. Pamuk and J. G. Williamson (eds.), *The Mediterranean Response to Globalization before 1950*. London: Routledge.

Roche, D. (1982) *Journal de ma Vie: Jacques-Louis Ménétra, Compagnon Vitrier au 18è Siècle*. Paris: Montalba.

——(1987) *The People of Paris. An Essay in Popular Culture in the Eighteenth Century*. Leamington Spa: Berg.

Ruwet, J. and Wellemans, Y. (1978) *L'Analphabétisme en Belgique (XVIIIème–XIXème Siècles)*. Louvain: Bibliothèque de l'Université.

Sanderson, M. (1991) *Education, Economic Change and Society in England 1780–1870*. London: Macmillan.

Saugnieux, J. (1986) *Les Mots et les Livres. Études d'Histoire Culturelle*. Lyon: Presses Universitaires de Lyon.

Schofield, R. S. (1973) 'Dimensions of Illiteracy, 1750–1850'. *Explorations in Economic History*, 10: 437–54.

Schuurman, A. J. and Walsh, L. S. (eds.) (1994) *Material Culture: Consumption, Life-style, Standard of Living, 1500–1900*. Milan: Bocconi University.

Shammas, C. (1993) 'Changes in English and Anglo-American Consumption from 1550 to 1800', in J. Brewer and R. Porter (eds.), *Consumption and the World of Goods*. London: Routledge.

Smith, W. D. (1984) 'The Function of Commercial Centers in the Modernization of European Capitalism: Amsterdam as an Information Exchange in the Seventeenth Century'. *Journal of Economic History*, 44: 985–1005.

Snooks, G. D. (1994) *Was the Industrial Revolution Necessary?* London: Routledge.

Spufford, M. (1979) 'First Steps in Literacy: The Reading and Writing Experiences of the Humblest Seventeenth Century Spiritual Autobiographies'. *Social History*, 4: 407–35.

——(1985) *Small Books and Pleasant Stories: Popular Fiction and its Readership in Seventeenth Century England*. Cambridge: Cambridge University Press.

——(1995) 'Literacy, Trade and Religion in the Commercial Centres of Europe', in K. Davids and J. Lucassen (eds.), *A Miracle Mirrored: The Dutch Republic in European Perspective*. Cambridge: Cambridge University Press.

Stephens, W. B. (1990) 'Literacy in England, Scotland, and Wales, 1500–1900'. *History of Education Quarterly*, 30: 545–72.

Torras, J. and Yun, B. (eds.) (1999) *Consumo, Condiciones de Vida y Comercialización. Cataluña y Castilla, Siglos XVII–XIX*. Avila: Junta de Castilla y Leon.

Toth, G. (1998) 'Peasant Literacy in Hungary in the Seventeenth-Nineteenth Centuries', unpublished paper presented at the International Economic History Congress, Madrid.

Viñao Fraga, A. (1990) 'The History of Literacy in Spain: Evolution, Traits and Questions'. *History of Education Quarterly*, 30: 573–99.

Vovelle, M. (1975) 'Y-a-il eu une Révolution Culturelle au XVIIIè Siècle? L'Éducation Populaire en Provence'. *Revue d'Histoire Moderne et Contemporaine*, 22: 89–141.

de Vries, J. (1974) *The Dutch Rural Economy in the Golden Age, 1500–1700*. New Haven, CT: Yale University Press.

——(1984) *European Urbanization, 1500–1800*. Cambridge, MA: Harvard University Press.

——(1994) 'The Industrial Revolution and the Industrious Revolution'. *Journal of Economic History*, 54: 249–70.

——and van der Woude, A. (1997) *The First Modern Economy. Success, Failure and Perseverance of the Dutch Economy, 1500–1815*. Cambridge: Cambridge University Press.

Waro-Desjardins, F. (1993) 'Permanences et Mutations de la Vie Domestique au XVIIIè Siècle: Un Village du Vexin Français'. *Revue d'Histoire Moderne et Contemporaine*, 40: 3–29.

Weatherill, L. (1988) *Consumer Behaviour and Material Culture in Britain, 1660–1760*. London: Routledge.

——(1993) 'The Meaning of Consumer Behaviour in Late Seventeenth and Early Eighteenth Century England', in J. Brewer and R. Porter (eds.), *Consumption and the World of Goods*. London: Routledge.

Williamson, J. G. (1995) 'The Evolution of Global Labour Markets since 1830: Background, Evidence and Hypotheses'. *Explorations in Economic History*, 32: 141–97.

Yun, B. (1994) 'Proposals to Quantify Long Term Performance in the Kingdom of Castille, 1550–1800', in A. Maddison and H. van der Wee (eds.), *Economic Growth and Structural Change. Comparative Approaches over the Long Run*. Milan: Bocconi University.

van Deursen, A. T. (1991) *Plain Lives in a Golden Age. Popular Culture, Religion and Society in Seventeenth Century Holland*. Cambridge: Cambridge University Press.

van Zanden, J. L. (1993) *The Rise and Decline of Holland's Economy*. Manchester: Manchester University Press.

——(1995) 'The Beginning of the Kuznets Curve: Western Europe during the Early Modern Period'. *Economic History Review*, 48: 643–64.

——(1998) 'An Experiment in Measurement of the Wealth of Nations. International Disparities in Agricultural and GDP per Capita at about 1810', in B. van Ark, E. Buyst, and J. L. van Zanden, *Historical Benchmark Comparisons of Output and Productivity*. Seville: Fundación Fomento de la Historia Económica.

——(1999) 'Wages and the Standard of Living in Europe, 1500–1800'. *European Economic History Review*, 3: 175–98.

9 Health and Nutrition in the Pre-Industrial Era: Insights from a Millennium of Average Heights in Northern Europe

RICHARD H. STECKEL

1. Introduction

For over half a century, quantitative economic historians have pondered the fates of workers and other segments in the population during the industrial revolutions of the nineteenth and early twentieth centuries. While everyone agrees that the standard of living eventually improved, much discussion has focused on how various groups fared during the decades that industrialization actually unfolded. Scholars of the subject have asked who gained and who lost in the process (and why), and whether industrialization was accompanied by events that adversely affected health and human welfare. In the case of England, debate has been particularly lively and factions have coalesced into camps of optimists and pessimists. Controversy persists because evidence about the past is often meagre and, in any event, health and human welfare are complex and difficult to assess under the best circumstances of data availability (for a discussion of issues, see Engerman 1997).

This chapter places the debate over human welfare during industrialization in the context of very long-term economic developments by examining an important aspect of living standards—health and nutrition—since the early Middle Ages. I use average stature determined from military records along with average heights estimated from a neglected source, skeletal data.[1] Average height measures a population's history of *net* nutrition—diet minus claims on the diet made by work and by disease.[2] Considering the industrial period as a backdrop for comparative study, I describe the U-shape that average heights took over the past millennium in northern Europe and suggest a research agenda for analysing this remarkable time trend in health and nutrition.

A revised version of a paper prepared for the conference on 'New Evidence on the Standard of Living in Preindustrial Europe and Asia', which was held in Arild, Sweden, 1–5 August 2000. The author thanks Robert Allen, Tommy Bengtsson, Mike Haines, John Komlos, conference participants, members of the Chicago Area Economic History Seminar, and participants at the 2001 Social Science History Association meetings for comments and suggestions.

2. Background

Although lacking survey results on the subject, I suspect that few scholars would challenge whether the substantial resources allocated to the standard of living debate have been worthwhile investments as a whole. No doubt, many would object to some books or papers, but all would recognize that industrialization has been the biggest news of the past two centuries on the economic front. Unquestionably, industrialization transformed social and economic life, and even poor groups within modern industrial countries have greater access to most types of material goods and live longer lives than the upper classes in the pre-industrial era. Study of industrialization is also warranted for insights that may help guide developing countries now undergoing the process.

Considerable devotion to the subject of welfare during industrialization is justified, but the neglect of the pre-industrial era is curious. The lack of attention cannot be explained by a supposition that industrialization was the only major dynamic feature of social and economic life over the past several millennia. Earlier transformations were arguably on par if not more significant, including the shift from foraging to farming, the rise of cities, and European expansion and colonization that began in the 1400s.

The neglect might be explained by temporal distance from the present, a forceful point among those scholars who believe that modern policy implications should flow from the work of most if not all economists, including economic historians. People of this persuasion may ask what could possibly be learned about problems in the modern world by studying the pre-industrial era. In reply, one might observe that the pre-industrial world of the past is relevant because parts of today's developing regions approximate pre-industrial conditions of the eighteenth or nineteenth centuries. More importantly, study of pre-industrial economies is justifiable as a form of basic research. All social scientists understand the value of large, diverse samples for generalizing about human behaviour, and the past is certainly diverse. In any event, economic historians, and historians, are seldom beholden to arguments that research must demonstrate immediate applications. Many are content in viewing research purely as consumption, or satisfying desires of intellectual curiosity.

On a practical level, data availability is a problem, at least for the type of monetary measures that economists are accustomed to using, such as real GDP, real wages, or wealth. While it is certainly not true that abundant data exist for the taking, it is also not true that evidence is completely lacking. Over the years I have been impressed by the ingenuity of historians and economists in developing new data resources, a record that leads one to doubt whether most useful sources have been exploited. Recently, the frontiers of research were extended backward in time and over space, at least in the dimension of wages and prices (Allen 2001).

Finally, new data sources and methods have been developed for assessing human welfare. Speaking metaphorically, one may think of the history of human welfare in a country or region as a long sausage or salami; each slice represents a year (or other time unit) of social performance that can be divided into broad categories of health, material goods, and psychological elements, which may have spiritual or metaphysical components. The example of the new anthropometric history shows that a significant portion of the health component is measurable from military records and other sources of height data (Steckel 1998). Skeletal evidence greatly extends backward in time the portion of the salami that is visible, broadens it to include women and children, and unlike stature alone, includes information on degenerative health processes associated with hard work and ageing. This chapter makes a small down-payment on the larger research agenda of integrating the analysis of pre-industrial height data from skeletal records and military sources into the literature of economic history.

3. Height Patterns during Industrialization

Before attempting to study human health and nutrition in pre-industrial times, it is necessary to determine when the industrial period began. Although some scholars debate whether 'revolution' should be appended to 'industrial' in describing the process, the changes were revolutionary from the perspective of several centuries of history. Because it was a complex phenomenon involving many dimensions of change that occurred at different rates in various countries, its chronological dates and its nature are inevitably ambiguous. Most economic historians view Rostow's stages of economic growth as inordinately rigid, and they are sceptical of its implications for an inevitable sequence of well-defined steps that each country experienced. But most economic historians do agree that the process had a significant chronological structure: at a minimum, England was the first industrial country and the phenomenon spread from west to east across Europe.[3]

In order to fold heights into the debate over socio-economic performance during industrialization, it is useful to divide the process of change within each country into three chronological parts (early, middle, and late) based on an intuitive rather than a formulistic mix with an emphasis on dates of achieving modern economic growth. Also considered were the extent of mechanization, urbanization, per cent of the labour force involved in agriculture, and the amount of technological change, which have in varying degrees been part of the process of industrialization or modernization in all countries that underwent the experience. Assigning dates and phases is inevitably a matter of judgement, but the contributors to *Health and Welfare during Industrialization* were comfortable with three rough categories. In the early industrial period, the transition to a modern industrial economy began. Industrialization and modernization spread geographically and diversified in the middle period, and became widespread and dominant in the late industrial phase. Notably, a few countries do not fit well with this conception of industrialization. Because they retained large agricultural sectors or experienced little mechanization and developed few factories, the term 'modernization' may be more appropriate in describing their experiences. Australia, for example, relied extensively on agriculture and mining, while the Netherlands (lacking coal and waterpower) developed banking, shipping, and services.

3.1   Height and economic growth

Table 9.1 depicts average heights and other information during the early, middle, and late stages of industrialization in eight countries whose adult male heights were studied in Steckel and Floud (1997).

In examining the table, one is struck by the diversity of experience across countries in heights, and in life expectancy and the per cent urban. Average heights varied by over 15 cm within each phase, while the per cent urban differed by as much as 30 percentage points in the early phase (the Netherlands versus the United States) and nearly 50 points in the late phase (Japan versus Sweden). While all life expectancies were somewhat compressed in the pre-industrial phase, differing by less than 13 years (Australia versus the United Kingdom), by the late phase Australia had leaped ahead of the pack (65.4 years) while Japan lagged nearly 20 years behind (47 years).

3.2   Height and life expectancy

In arguing for average height as a general welfare measure, it is useful to consider its relationship to a more widely employed measure of health—life expectancy at birth. Understanding of average height as a population's history of net nutrition implies that a positive correlation should exist. Biological deprivation that retards human growth also increases the risk of death, a relationship that is magnified by the synergy between diet and disease (Scrimshaw *et al.* 1968). Several studies on modern data confirm that average height declines as mortality rates increase (Waaler 1984; Fogel 1993; Steckel 2001).

Some critics of anthropometric history base their doubts on a selective effect of height on survival. Because studies on individual data have found that short people are less likely to survive (Friedman 1982; Waaler 1984), high mortality erodes the left tail of the height distribution. If this was the only effect of higher mortality, then taller heights would indicate poorer health. But it is not the only effect: survivors also grow less because they endured the biological stress causing higher mortality. The former effect is small because under conditions of increasing biological stress, many tall people also fail to survive. Empirically the second effect far outweighs the former. At the national level, heights and life expectancy are highly and positively correlated in the late twentieth century (Steckel 2001).

Data for estimating the relationship between average height and life expectancy in a historical setting are meagre, but available for all countries in the late industrial periods. Figure 9.1 shows the scatter diagram for the United States, the United Kingdom, the Netherlands, France, Sweden, Germany, Japan, and Australia, which

Table 9.1 Average heights of adult men, life expectancy, and percentage urban by stages of industrialization

Country	Dates	Height (cm)	Life expectancy	% Urban
Pre-industrial phase				
UK	1720–60	165.1	33.7	22.6
US	1800–20	173.0	45.3	6.9
France	1800–20	164.1	36.0	19.0
The Netherlands	1830–50	164.0	35.0	38.0
Sweden	1830–50	168.0	42.1	9.7
Germany	1830–50	—	36.9	30.5
Australia	1840–60	172.5	46.0	30.0
Japan	1868–80	155.3	36.0	34.5
Early industrial phase				
UK	1760–1800	168.2	36.0	29.4
US	1820–50	172.4	41.7	10.5
France	1820–50	164.4	39.3	22.0
The Netherlands	1850–70	165.9	40.0	44.0
Sweden	1850–70	169.1	43.9	11.2
Germany	1850–70	166.2	37.6	34.4
Australia	1860–90	172.0	48.0	42.0
Japan	1880–1900	157.0	38.0	50.0
Middle industrial phase				
UK	1800–30	170.7	38.6	38.7
US	1850–80	170.6	40.9	22.3
France	1850–80	165.4	41.0	31.0
The Netherlands	1879–1900	168.6	45.0	46.0
Sweden	1870–1900	171.4	49.3	17.2
Germany	1870–90	167.5	38.9	43.6
Australia	1890–1920	172.0	59.2	53.0
Japan	1900–20	158.8	44.0	60.0
Late industrial phase				
UK	1830–70	166.9	39.5	54.1
US	1880–1910	170.2	45.6	37.2
France	1880–1910	166.7	45.5	39.0
Germany	1890–1913	169.7	46.8	56.1
The Netherlands	1900–25	172.0	55.2	56.0
Sweden	1900–25	173.5	57.4	25.7
Australia	1920–40	173.2	65.4	60.0
Japan	1920–40	160.0	47.0	75.5

Source: Steckel and Floud (1997: 425, table 11.2).

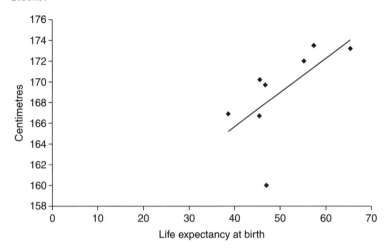

Figure 9.1   Life expectancy and adult male height, late industrial period
Source: Estimated from data in Steckel and Floud (1997: table 11.2).

incorporates data taken from Table 9.1. The estimated regression line is (*t*-values in parentheses):

$$\text{Height} = 152.48 + 0.330 \text{ (Life expectancy)}, \quad N = 8, \quad R^2 = 0.40$$
$$\qquad\qquad (18.03) \qquad\quad (1.98)$$

The average height of adult men increased by 0.33 cm for every year by which life expectancy increased. The scatter diagram reveals that Japan is a substantial outlier, and if this country is omitted, the R^2 rises to 0.79 and the regression coefficient is statistically significant at 0.01. Japan's stature was much too low, given its life expectancy, probably because the time frames of the two measures are different. Conditions in the 1930s and early 1940s, when the young adults of mid-century were growing children, were likely worse than those forming the basis for life expectancy in 1950, a few years following the end of the Second World War. It is also possible that the height–life expectancy relationship is somewhat non-linear at low levels of health.

3.3   Height and urbanization

Historical demographers have long observed the adverse effect of urban areas on health prior to the early twentieth century (see, for example, United Nations 1973: 131–2; Preston and Haines 1991: chs 4–5). Numerous factors explain the connection, including congestion in factories and places of living, which promoted the spread of communicable diseases. Accumulation of waste, impure water supplies, and inflows of people bearing pathogens increased the urban population's exposure to pathogens. High poverty levels and high prices for food (relative to rural areas) also acted to increase mortality rates.

Table 9.1 shows that average male height and per cent urban (towns or cities of 2,500 population or more) varied widely across the countries during the middle phase of industrialization, a period of intense change. The extremes in stature were established by the heights of Australians (172 cm) and by those of the Japanese, which fell more than 13 cm below. In urban development, the Swedes had the smallest share living in towns or cities (only 17.2%) while the Japanese were the most urban (60%).

It was not accidental that the Japanese were both the shortest and the most urban. In an era before widespread, effective investments in public health and personal hygiene, the congestion and turnover associated with urban living increased the chances of exposure to pathogens. Other features detrimental to health are often found in cities, such as a large number of poor people who lacked access to food, clothing, and shelter that would have reduced resistance to disease.

The scatter diagram in Figure 9.2 confirms the adverse effect of urbanization on health. The estimated regression equation is (*t*-values in parentheses):

$$\text{Height} = 174.07 - 0.153 \ (\text{Per cent urban}), \quad N = 8, \quad R^2 = 0.27$$
$$(40.69) \qquad\qquad (-1.47)$$

For every percentage point increase in the degree of urbanization, average male height fell by about 0.15 cm. This magnitude is significant in a practical sense because the transition from a low (say, 20%) level of urbanization to a moderately high level (say 50%) would have decreased average height by 4.5 cm. The notable outlier to the inverse relationship was Australia, which had the tallest population and the second highest level of urbanization. If Australia is dropped from the

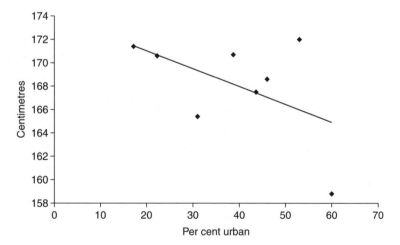

Figure 9.2   Per cent urban and average male height

Source: Estimated from data in Steckel and Flood (1997: table 11.2).

regression, the *t*-value rises to −2.60, R^2 increases to 0.57, and the regression coefficient increases (in absolute value) by 50%.

What factors explain the exceptional nature of health and urbanization in Australia? One was the relative geographic isolation of the country from major disease currents that affected cities in Europe and in North America. Another is the remoteness of the major cities within Australia from each other, which helped to reduce the spread of infectious disease. Moreover, Australia's industrialization (or modernization) occurred late enough to benefit from significant investments in public health. This last feature distinguishes Australia from Japan, which was also a country late to industrialize within this group.

3.4   Temporal patterns

Additional factors that influenced heights during industrialization, and possibly in the pre-industrial period, can be discerned from study of temporal patterns within countries. Although the various series might be arranged on a continuum in terms of depth and duration of cycles, the patterns are readily grouped into three categories: (a) significant and prolonged declines in health during a large phase of industrialization; (b) a mixture that included a short and modest downturn during industrialization; and (c) sustained, but not necessarily monotonic, gains in stature.

The United States and the United Kingdom fit the first pattern, which is given in Figure 9.3. Americans were very tall by global standards in the early nineteenth century as a result of their rich and varied diets, low population density, and relative equality of wealth. Between 1830 and roughly 1890, however, the average height of American men fell by 4.4 cm, a reversal that was not offset until the 1920s. Consistent with this height decline, life expectancies tabulated from genealogies

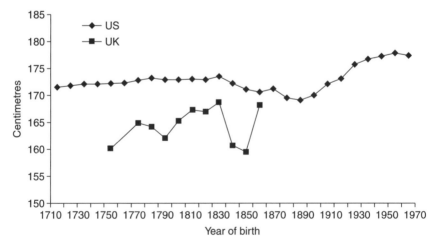

Figure 9.3   Average height of soldiers in Britain and of native born American soldiers
Sources: Steckel (forthcoming 2005: figure 12) and Floud, Wachter, and Gregory (1990: table 4.8).

also show deterioration near the middle of the century (Pope 1992). Researchers in the field have suggested numerous possible causal factors for the decline, including the spread of disease affiliated with the development of railroads, canals, and steamboats (for discussions, see Steckel 1995; Komlos 1998). Also mentioned are higher food prices; growing inequality; increasing market integration; the emergence of business cycles that led to malnutrition during contractions, urbanization, and the rise of public schools that exposed children to major diseases. Unfortunately, research has not advanced to the point of assigning plausible weights to these factors, but some progress is being made by examining the relationship between local (county) agricultural, socioeconomic, and demographic conditions and the height of recruits from the county (Haines, Craig, and Weiss 2003).

Although health deterioration of about 9 cm in average height among soldiers also occurred in Britain during the early mid-nineteenth century, the timing is probably more coincidental than emblematic of linkage among similar causal factors across the two countries.[4] While it is possible that growing trade and commerce spread disease, as in the United States, it is more likely that a major culprit was rapid urbanization and its associated increase in exposure to diseases (Floud and Harris 1997). This conclusion is reached by noting that urban born men were substantially shorter than the rural born, and between the periods of 1800–30 and 1830–70 the share of the British population living in urban areas leaped from 38.7% to 54.1%.

Australia and Württemberg illustrate pattern (b) of short, modest cycles shown in Figure 9.4. Both realized gains in health during industrialization, but progress was choppy or otherwise interrupted by relatively brief cycles in height. Adult males reached about 162.8 cm (average of rural and urban) in the province of Württemberg

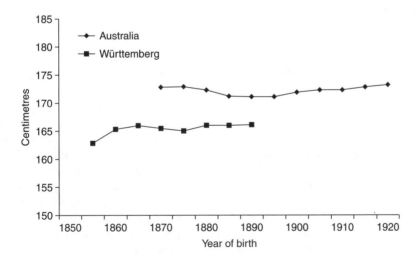

Figure 9.4   Average height of soldiers in Australia and Württemberg

Sources: Whitwell, de Souza, and Nicholas (1997: figure 10.3; raw data provided by authors) and interpolated as a weighted average of rural and urban from Twarog (1997: table 7.29).

for cohorts born on the eve of industrialization, which began in the 1860s (Twarog 1997). A small spurt in average height to 166 cm occurred during the early 1860s which was followed by a decline of 1 cm over the next decade. Recovery but stagnation at 166 cm occurred in the 1880s and 1890s. This temporal pattern was related to the financial crash of 1873 and the subsequent depression, that lasted into the early 1890s. Occupational differences in stature indicate that the professional classes were protected during the early phases of the economic depression, and the loss in health was concentrated among the middle and lower classes. Thus, growing inequality played an important role in Germany's health trends during industrialization.

Two features distinguish the Australian experience: the tall stature (about 172.5 cm) on the eve of modernization that was followed by a large cycle in heights whereby the average height of the mid-1870s was not attained again until the second decade of the twentieth century (Whitwell *et al.* 1997). The tall stature is undoubtedly related to an inexpensive but diverse diet that was also rich in protein, a phenomenon supporting the view that Australia was a workingman's paradise. Even though the share living in urban areas was relatively high (about 50%), overall population density was low and the country and its major cities were relatively isolated from globalization, which hampered the spread of communicable diseases.

But some troubles occurred even in these relatively idyllic circumstances. The height downturn of 1.8 cm in the 1880s and 1890s was the result of a double whammy. The share living in urban areas was already high (43% in 1881) and then jumped 8 percentage points in the decade following. A sanitary crisis ensued and typhoid fever, which disproportionately affected the young, was epidemic in the cities. Although the pace of urbanization fell considerably during the 1890s, GDP declined and remained relatively low for a decade, thereby dampening any hopes for quick recovery in heights and health.

The Netherlands, France, Sweden, and Japan fall into the last category: sustained increases in stature, interrupted at most by brief, tiny declines or modest stagnation. Prominent in the Dutch experience was a twenty-year pre-industrial height decline of 1.9 cm that began in 1815, which was caused in part by rising food prices and stagnating nominal wages (i.e. a decline in purchasing power). Thereafter, average heights increased more or less continuously into the twentieth century with the exception of small reversals in the early 1840s and in the early 1870s. The former was probably affected by harvest failures (the 'hungry forties') and the latter was associated with the economic depression of the 1870s (Drukker and Tassenaar 1997).

Similarities and contrasts in the Dutch and the French experiences are shown in Figure 9.5. The French did not have the small and brief cycles of the Dutch before mid-century, but they did experience considerably less height gain thereafter. While the Dutch gained 3.8 cm between birth cohorts of 1850 and 1890, the French increase was slightly less than one-third as much. In France, the modest advance in heights was accompanied by progress in performance measures such as GDP per capita and life expectancy. France also experienced a decline in economic conditions that contributed to slow growth in average heights. In the 1860s, a downturn in real wages was followed by fifteen years of economic stagnation (Weir 1997).

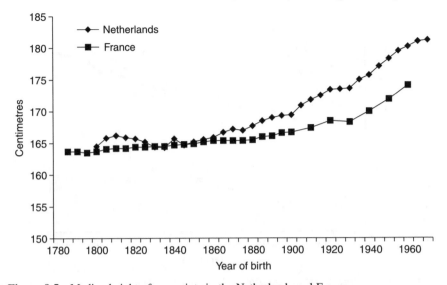

Figure 9.5 Median height of conscripts in the Netherlands and France

Sources: Drukker and Tassenaar (1997: table 9A.1); personal correspondence from J.W. Drukker on 28 February 1999, Weir (1997: table 5B.1), and van Meerten (1990: 775–6).

Japan opened the industrial era at the end of the nineteenth century with the smallest stature (about 157 cm) of any industrializing country (see Figure 9.6). Hampered by a low protein diet, thereafter progress was slow and significantly correlated with per capita GDP but adversely affected by economic policy that diverted resources to the military (Honda 1997). Its high level of urbanization and modest investments in public health were an obstacle to human health and physical growth. Economic stagnation in the 1920s and the depression of the 1930s (which was rather mild in Japan) brought the modest gains in height to a halt in the mid-1930s.

Sweden realized the most sustained increase in health during the most intense period of industrialization (late nineteenth century). Figure 9.6 shows that average adult male heights rose from 168 to 172.5 cm between 1860 and 1900. The only downturn was the small reversal that occurred during the crop failures of the late 1860s, which had little to do with industrialization (Sandberg and Steckel 1997). Paralleling the growth in stature were declines in childhood mortality rates of roughly 50%. It is notable that Sweden had the least urbanized population among the eight countries studied, and it also benefited from public health measures such as vaccination, and from relatively low food prices created by the spread of potato cultivation and imports of food from America.

3.5 Generalizations

Study of height and mortality patterns in counties, diverse by time period of industrialization and by environmental factors, indicates that a combination of

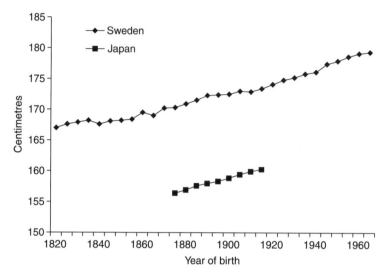

Figure 9.6   Average height of conscripts in Sweden and Japan
Sources: Sandberg and Steckel (1997: table 4.1) and Shay (1994: table 10.A6).

general tendencies and idiosyncratic factors affected health during the industrial revolutions of the nineteenth and early twentieth centuries. In an era when public health policies were often lacking or meagrely enlightened by theories of disease causation, urbanization was a widespread culprit in ill health within countries studied in Europe and in the Pacific, and within the United States. Height was inversely correlated with degree of urbanization across countries, and rising urbanization led to health deterioration, especially in England, Australia, and Japan.

Major business cycles also affected heights and health. France, the Netherlands, Germany, and Australia were victims of major downturns. Changing economic opportunities, in the form of growing inequality, adversely affected heights in Germany and the United States.

Diets were important for health and human growth. Countries with the tallest men (Australia and the United States) had excellent access to a variety of foods, including several rich sources of protein. Food was expensive and the diet was low in protein in the country with the smallest stature (Japan).

Lastly, public health policy (or lack thereof) was also important for heights. Countries that industrialized early, such as the United States and the United Kingdom suffered the most, in part because the adverse effects of trade and population concentrations on health could not be offset by health policies informed by reliable theories of disease causation. Merely arriving late on the scene was no guarantee of protection against the by-products of industrialization, however, as shown by the Japanese case where resources that could have been used for public health and human growth were diverted to the military.

4. Pre-industrial Heights

Among the eight countries studied in *Health and Welfare During Industrialization*, all but Germany have some military height data that cover small portions of the pre-industrial era. In the absence of detailed information, economic historians may tend to view the pre-industrial world as a vague but homogeneous lump defined by its heavy reliance on agriculture, the preponderance of home manufacturing, and antiquated methods of production. Table 9.1 shows, however, that on the eve of industrialization, average heights ranged widely from 155 cm in Japan to approximately 173 cm in the United States and Australia. Most European countries clustered near 164 or 165 cm, but the Swedes reached 168 cm.

In all but the United States, the pre-industrial populations were also smaller, often by several centimetres depending upon the exact years of the comparisons. Considering the pre-industrial and middle phases, for example, the height differences shown in Table 9.1 were about 2 cm in France, roughly 4 cm in Japan, the Netherlands and Sweden, and about 5 cm in Britain (but note that average heights declined significantly in Britain for cohorts born in the 1840s and early 1850s). Average heights in the United States were about 3 cm lower in the middle compared with pre-industrial times.

What were the important socio-economic conditions affecting pre-industrial heights? It would seem appropriate to begin with mechanisms that were powerful in explaining height differences during industrialization—urbanization and abundant access to land. The two countries with the tallest people (Australia and the United States) score well on the latter category and Sweden was the tallest and least congested of the European countries. Access to land tended to ameliorate poverty, helped promote dietary diversity and reduced the spread of disease by lowering population density. Countries with the shortest populations were relatively urban, a feature long known to have impaired health. Australians were tall despite a large (30%) urban population, likely because the cities were isolated from each other and from much of the rest of the world.

If low urbanization and low population density were good for health, it is a fair question to ask why so many of the pre-industrial populations were so short, compared with their industrial counterparts. After all, the adverse factors of urbanization and population density tended to increase with industrialization. With the exception of the United States and Britain in the late industrial phase, there must have been something good for health about industrialization that more than offset the features that were bad.

4.1 Extending the record

Before attempting to generalize, or even begin to formulate a research agenda on the possible causes of small stature in the pre-industrial era, it is essential to inspect additional evidence. Figures 9.3–9.6 make clear that the time span available for study of pre-industrial heights from military records is rather short (or non-existent) in all countries.[5] Skeletal data, in which stature is inferred from long bone (femur) lengths, provide information on the more distant past. Before examining the results, however, it is worth discussing the methodology of using skeletons to estimate heights.

Valid use of skeletons requires knowledge of sex and age at death.[6] For all parts of the skeleton, the female elements typically have smaller size and lighter construction. These differences become pronounced in the skull and the pelvis beginning in late adolescence, but before these ages, sex cannot be accurately determined. The skeletal features of robust adult females may resemble those of small and light adult males, but using multivariate analysis, it is possible to estimate sex of adults with a high degree of accuracy in well-preserved remains.

Over a person's lifetime, the skeleton undergoes sequential chronological change. The changes are pronounced in dentition among children and in fusion of the epiphyses (or 'growth plates') in various bones of children and in young adults. Among older adults, there are systematic changes in the shape of the pubic symphysis that are used as a guide to age. Above age 50, however, these techniques (and others) become increasingly unreliable, and for this reason, older adults are often grouped together for analytical purposes. In estimating the height of adults, it is the fusion of epiphyses in the long bones that is the key for estimating adult height. Once fusion has occurred, growth ceases and length does not change even with increasing age. On average, approximately 26% per cent of an adult person's height is contained in the femur. Trotter and Gleser (1952) developed the most widely used formula for converting femur length into height.

Excavated burials may not reflect the once-living population if burials were geographically dispersed, excavation was incomplete or quality of preservation of the bones was poor. Therefore, in this line of work it is useful to compare results from a particular site with those from sites where these problems are thought to be minimal.

Table 9.2 gives details from individual studies found in a search of the literature in physical anthropology from sources easily accessible in the United States. Although some results were available for other parts of Europe, only northern Europe had studies that span the entire period from the early Middle Ages to the present. My first effort leaves a gap for the fifteenth and sixteenth centuries, which additional search may fill.

Table 9.3 summarizes results by era for those studies that give evidence for time periods as small as two or three centuries. Studies reporting results for burials during 'Medieval Era' or the 'Middle Ages' are lumped together in the middle of the table. It is remarkable if not stunning that the average heights during the early and late Middle Ages exceeded those observed for the eve of industrialization by several centimetres. While one should always devote some attention to the issues of representativeness and sampling in skeletal data, the large number of studies covering several northern countries suggests that the results cannot be dismissed as a statistical fluke or aberration. It is conceivable that all of the estimated heights for

Table 9.2 Average heights in northern Europe estimated from adult male skeletons

Era	Place	Average height (cm)	Sample size	Source
9–11th cent.	Iceland	172.3	22	Steffensen (1958)
9–17th cent.	Iceland	172.2	71	Steffensen (1958)
10–11th cent.	Sweden	176.0	8	Gilberg (1976)
11–12th cent.	Iceland	172.0	27	Steffensen (1958)
11–17th cent.	Iceland	171.0	16	Steffensen (1958)
12th cent.	Norway	170.2	42	Hanson (1992)
12th cent.	Britain	168.4	233	Munter (1928)
12–13th cent.	Norway	172.2	—[*]	Huber (1968)
12–16th cent.	Iceland	175.2	6	Steffensen (1958)
13th cent.	Denmark	172.2	31	Boldsen (1984)
13th cent.	Sweden	174.3	66	Gejvall (1960)
13–14th cent.	England	171.8	—[*]	Huber (1968)
Middle Ages	Sweden	170.4	457	Steffensen (1958)
Middle Ages	Denmark	172.0	190	Bennike (1985)
Middle Ages	Denmark	172.6	43	Bennike (1985)
Middle Ages	Norway	172.1	314	Holck & Kvaal (2000)
Middle Ages	Denmark	175.2	27	Holck (1997)
Middle Ages	Norway	167.2	1,792	Holck (1997)
Middle Ages	Sweden	170.4	457	Werdelin (1985)
13–16th cent.	Holland	172.5	87	Maat *et al.* (1998)
11–16th cent.	Holland	176.2	23	Janssen & Maat (1999)
11–16th cent.	Sweden	172.8[a]	499	Arcini (1999)
17–18th cent.	Iceland	169.7	17	Steffensen (1958)
17–18th cent.	Holland	166.0	41	Maat (1984)
17–18th cent.	Holland	166.7[b]	102	Maat (1984)
18th cent.	Iceland	167.0	4	Steffensen (1958)
18th cent.	Norway	165.3	1,956	Holck (1997)
17–19th cent.	Iceland	169.2	21	Steffensen (1958)
18–19th cent.	Britain	170.3	211	Molleson & Cox (1993)

[a] Simple average across seven combinations of sites and dates.
[b] Sex of the 102 skeletons was unknown but based on written evidence, a sex ratio of 50–50 was assumed. Since men are on average 10 cm taller than women, the overall average height for the sample was adjusted upward by half this amount (5 cm) to estimate equivalent average height for men.
[*] Not available or missing information.

the Middle Ages were biased upward by some as yet undiscovered process of selection, but one would then wonder why that selection process ceased to be a factor in the centuries immediately prior to industrialization.

Generalizing about pre-industrial height trends will be difficult without more evidence from the fifteenth through the eighteenth centuries. It seems reasonable to suggest, at least tentatively, that net nutritional conditions of the past millennium reached a low point in Europe prior to the onset of industrialization. Between the Middle Ages and the twentieth century, heights were U-shaped with a minimum

Table 9.3 Summary of adult male height trends in northern Europe

Era	Place	Simple average of average heights (cm)	Source
9–11th cent.	N. Europe	173.4	Table 2, rows 1, 3, 4
12–14th cent.	N. Europe	171.5	Table 2, rows 6–8, 10–12
Middle Ages	N. Europe	171.4	Table 2, rows 13–19
17–18th cent.	N. Europe	167.5	Table 2, rows 23–5
18th cent.	N. Europe	166.2	Table 2, rows 26–7
17–19th cent.	N. Europe	169.8	Table 2, rows 28–9
Late 19th cent.	Sweden, The Netherlands, Britain	169.7	Sandberg and Steckel (1997: 129); Drukker and Tassenaar (1997: 341); Floud and Harris (1997: 102);
1930	Sweden, The Netherlands	172.5	Sandberg and Steckel (1997: 129); Drukker and Tassenaar (1997: 341)

attained sometime between 1450 and 1750, when historical heights become widely available from military records. The onset of the decline (and ultimately its causes) can be established only by a search for more evidence from published or unpublished sources.[7]

Taking the evidence at face value indicates that average heights fell from an average of 173.4 cm in the early Middle Ages to a low of 165.8 cm during the seventeenth and eighteenth centuries. This decline of 7.6 cm exceeds by a factor of two any fluctuations observed during industrialization. Recovery to levels achieved a millennium ago was not attained until the early twentieth century. Both the extraordinary level relative to recent times and the U-shaped time trend are remarkable phenomena worthy of considerable study.

Some people may claim that genetic factors are responsible for the tall statures observed during the Middle Ages, pointing to the fact that northern Europeans are taller, even today, than those from more southern European countries (Schmidt, Jorgensen, and Michaelsen 1995). But the southern Europeans of the modern period, who tend to be poorer, are catching up, and in any event, studies of children around the globe indicate that children who grow up under similarly good environmental conditions have about the same heights (Malcolm 1974; Martorell and Habicht 1986). If genetic factors were relevant, presumably they had little or no effect on the trend within areas surrounded by the North Sea and the Baltic. Thus, I seek environmental explanations for northern Europe's U-shaped trend in stature.

In suggesting candidates for further study, it is relevant to recall that average height measures a population's history of *net* nutrition—diet minus claims on the diet, made by work and by disease. Urbanization and growing population density, which occurred during industrialization, increased exposure to disease. Could the diet have been poorer and work more arduous in pre-industrial times, by enough to offset the benefits of lower population density? And if the diet was poorer and the work was more arduous, why was net nutrition so good before the sixteenth century?

The data at hand confront conventional wisdom about changes in living standards since the Middle Ages, and lead one to ask: Why did net nutrition decline sometime between the Middle Ages and the pre-industrial period? Why did heights generally improve during the nineteenth century, albeit with interruptions in some countries, when some factors adverse to heights (urbanization, inequality, and business cycles) were getting worse?

As I do not have convincing answers to these questions, I look forward to additional research. It seems to me, however, that the millennium long U-shape of average stature in northern Europe might have been connected with seven major phenomena: climate change; growing inequality in real incomes after 1500; urbanization and growth of trade that spread diseases; wars of state building; religious conflicts; the global spread of new varieties of disease associated with European expansion and colonization; and population cycles. We are faced, then, not with a dearth of plausible explanations but rather measuring their impacts on health and weeding out influences among those that were unimportant.

4.2 Possible causes of good net nutrition during the Middle Ages

At the outset, it is useful to consider why average heights were surprisingly large during the Middle Ages. One might debate the representativeness of the results, something that is useful more generally of findings so at odds with preconceptions. Because numerous skeletal studies are essentially uniform in reporting statures in the Middle Ages that were tall by standards of the late nineteenth century, it seems prudent to accept them at face value (at least provisionally) and move to possible explanations.[8]

According to the data at hand, northern European heights did not consistently exceed those of 800–1300 until the early twentieth century. One important factor in this remarkable pattern may have been climate. Agriculture during the period from about AD 900–1300 benefited from what climate historians call the 'Medieval Warm Period.' Based on ice cores, tree rings, and other sources, climate historians believe that temperatures during this era were as much as 2–3°C warmer than a few centuries later, and 0.7–1.0°C above the twentieth-century averages (see Fagan 2000). At the beginning of this era, the Vikings settled in Iceland and later in Greenland. This temperature change may not appear to be significant, but it was enough to extend the growing season by 3–4 weeks in many settled regions of northern Europe. The weather was sufficiently warm that commercial vineyards were viable 300–500 km north of their range in the twentieth century. Moreover, it allowed cultivation of previously unavailable land at higher elevations. Therefore, a population that was probably smaller relative to later eras, quite possibly had a portfolio of better land from which to choose in producing crops. A result would have been more agricultural output (at the same or less work effort) compared with the centuries immediately following the Middle Ages.

It is well known that economic isolation, in the form of little trade beyond local interaction, also characterized life during the Middle Ages, at least relative to later centuries when regional commodity markets developed significantly. Anthropometric historians have noted the benefits to health and average heights of geographic isolation, low population density, or lack of commercial development for outlying areas within Sweden, Austria Hungary, Japan, Ireland, and the United States (Margo and Steckel 1982, 1992; Sandberg and Steckel 1987; Komlos 1989; Shay 1994; Nicholas and Steckel 1997; Cuff 1998). The protective effect of isolation, in the era before effective public health, probably operated through insulation from communicable diseases. In this regard, it is notable that the bubonic plague made its dramatic appearance in the significant revival of trade during the late Middle Ages.

Urban areas were bad for health, as established from their high mortality rates and the small statures of those who resided in such places for a significant portion of their childhood growing years. To my knowledge, this demographic phenomenon was found in all areas of the world until the late nineteenth or early twentieth centuries, when public health measures and improvements in personal hygiene significantly reduced exposure to pathogens. Moderately large cities were absent from northern Europe until the late Middle Ages (for discussions of urban growth see de Vries 1984; Hohenberg and Lees 1985). As late as the end of the thirteenth century, significant urbanization was confined mainly to southern Europe, in northern Italian towns such as Milan, Florence, Venice, and Genoa, each of which probably exceeded 100,000 in population. At this time, Paris was the only city in northern Europe that may have fallen into this category. The southern Low Countries were moderately urbanized by the late Middle Ages (the fourteenth century), but the largest city, Ghent, probably had no more than 50,000 inhabitants, while London and Cologne held fewer than 40,000 people at this time. Therefore, the overwhelmingly rural distribution of the population was an asset for health.

4.3   Possible factors in the health decline

A cooling trend began around 1200 and by the fourteenth century, weather related events began to cause havoc in northern Europe (Fagan 2000). By the late fourteenth century, the Vikings had abandoned Greenland and in the next century, England no longer cultivated wine. By 1600, when the coldest two centuries of the Little Ice Age began, pack ice surrounded Iceland for much of the year, the Thames River often froze during the winter, glaciers advanced significantly in the Alps, and vast schools of cod had long since left European waters for warmer temperatures of the western Atlantic. The climate change was likely to have imposed greater economic and health costs on northern Europe where food production existed under weather conditions that were closer to the margin.

Important for agricultural production and health, the climate change was irregular. Imbedded within the general cooling period of 500–600 years were numerous seesaws of 15–40 years' duration. The changing weather patterns made it difficult for individuals alive at the time to identify true long-term trends, which were noticeable only with intergenerational perspective. The lack of knowledge about actual trends postponed adaptations to the cooling climate, and during temporary reversals of cooling, encouraged investments in ways of farming and living that later proved unsuccessful.

Urbanization and growth of trade that began in the late Middle Ages gathered steam in the sixteenth and seventeenth centuries. In northern Europe, there was only one city of 100,000 or more people in 1500 (de Vries 1976). By 1600, the number of people living in such places had quadrupled, and within another century it had tripled again. As height studies for the late eighteenth and early nineteenth centuries show, large cities were particularly hazardous for health, acting as reservoirs for the spread of communicable diseases (Steckel and Floud 1997: ch. 11). Therefore, it would not be surprising if urbanization following the Middle Ages contributed to an overall decline in health.

The spread of disease that began with revival of trade and urbanization was reinforced by another source of pathogens that began in the late 1400s, and later intensified: global exploration and trade. The voyages of Columbus and Vasco da Gama were merely the first of thousands by which Europeans acquired global information that was used to build and maintain colonial empires. Within 300 years, Europeans had mapped most of the globe and established numerous colonies or trading centres on all continents or islands significant for producing saleable products. Syphilis is only one of numerous diseases that spread during this era. It is well known that the early stages of globalization began in the late 1400s and eventually led to the worldwide diffusion of many diseases into previously isolated regions or continents (Crosby 1972, 1986).

As a measure of net nutrition, average height is adept at measuring a population's consumption of basic necessities such as food, clothing, shelter, and medical care. In countries with high levels of per capita GDP, most people have enough of these to satisfy basic needs. But in poor countries or among the poor in moderate-income countries, large numbers of people are biologically stressed or deprived, which leads to stunting. In addition to income, average height is therefore sensitive to the degree of inequality (Steckel 1983, 1995). It is difficult to acquire information about income or wealth inequality in the distant past, but Hoffman *et al.* (2002) have been ingenious in assembling related information by using information on the prices of products heavily consumed by the rich or by the poor. In their study of price patterns for staple foods and fuels relative to the prices of luxury goods, such as servants, they find that real inequality rose considerably during the sixteenth century and remained high until the twentieth century. It was during the era from 1500 to 1650, however, that the rich benefited most from soaring land rents (a source of income for many of the well-off) while the poor faced higher prices for food, housing, and land. As far as Hoffman *et al.* can tell, this trend persisted throughout most of Europe.

Since the poor comprised a large segment of the population, it is plausible to believe that growing inequality could have increased biological stress in ways that reduced average heights in the centuries immediately following the Middle Ages.

Although state building could be credited, in many cases, with eventually improving economic efficiency, the early stages of the process also absorbed resources, cost human lives in conflict, and may have increased inequality. Someone might be able to argue that religious wars and conflicts improved health when or shortly after they occurred, but I find it difficult to imagine a mechanism. From the War of the Roses in the late fifteenth century and the Reformation in the early sixteenth century, many parts of Europe were in sporadic and sometimes protracted conflict or turmoil until the conclusion of the Napoleonic wars in 1815.

Economists and historians have long discussed Malthusian processes affecting population health and growth. Positive checks on growth, in the form of higher mortality rates created by growing pressure of population on resources, would have led likely to diminished stature. John Komlos (2000) has argued that industrialization was an adaptive response to such pressures, but presumably they existed (without or with less adaptive success) in earlier centuries. The course of population over the past millennium is reasonably well chronicled (see McEvedy and Jones 1978) and plausibly periods of rapid growth that pressed on available resources and given technologies could have been a factor in height trends. The rapid growth of population from the eleventh through the early fourteenth centuries, for example, might have been a factor contributing to height declines of the late Middle Ages.

It would be premature to attempt to identify an era that was the worst in the last millennium for European health and nutrition, but historical evidence suggests that the seventeenth century is a leading candidate (de Vries 1976). Contributors to *The General Crisis of the Seventeenth Century* (Parker and Smith (eds.) 1997), focus on Europe but argue that the hardship probably spread well beyond this region. During this century numerous adverse forces acted together. It was part of the coldest period of the Little Ice Age, and subsistence crises were numerous. Religious turmoil was raging as signified by the Thirty Years War, and political instability was marked by the English Civil War and by numerous peasant uprisings. Economic inequality was intense as indicated by the rise in the price of necessities relative to luxuries. Global colonization and the associated spread of diseases were in full swing, as was a rapid increase in the number of large cities. It remains, however, to connect these events to changes in average stature.

4.4　Height recovery

The forces that led to increasing average heights are difficult to pinpoint without additional evidence on the times and places where increases occurred. It is hard to see how industrialization could have reduced exposure to pathogens. Growing population congestion, migration, and trade associated with the process were likely to have spread communicable diseases. If correct, one must look to other factors, such as the retreat of the Little Ice Age that could have contributed to higher yields in agriculture. There were also other sources of improving productivity in agriculture that began in the eighteenth century, such as new crops for forage and food, new crop rotations, enclosures, better drainage systems, and mechanical equipment. McKeown (1983) has been the strongest advocate for better diets in improving health in the nineteenth century, and Fogel (1985) has used data on average heights and agricultural production to buttress and quantify this point of view. Razzell (1993) and Livi-Bacci (1983) have downplayed the contribution of nutritional inputs to improving health over the long term, citing factors such as the independence of many diseases from nutrition, human adaptability to food availability, smallpox inoculation, and changing virulence of diseases.

While more research should be done, connections have been made between rising heights and improving diets in specific countries. Weir (1997) argues that growing meat consumption contributed significantly to rising heights in nineteenth-century France. Sandberg and Steckel (1980) suggest that diffusion of potatoes was important to improvements in stature in Sweden in the early nineteenth century. More generally, dietary improvement in nineteenth-century Europe was made possible by technical improvements, such as light iron ploughs, steam threshers, mechanical harvesters, and commercial fertilizers, as well as by agrarian reforms such as enclosures or emancipation of serfs (Tracy 1964; Trow-Smith 1967; Jones 1968). In the middle of the nineteenth century, diets also received a boost from the free trade movement. This and greater speed and lower transportation costs on long ocean voyages made it feasible to import foodstuffs from Australia and from the land-rich countries in the western hemisphere, principally the United States, Canada, and Argentina (O'Rourke and Williamson 1999). There is also evidence that public health measures, though based on an inaccurate theory of disease causation, were somewhat effective in reducing mortality rates in cities (Szreter 1988).

An increase in average height may have been assisted by gains in consumption per person that followed from reductions in conflicts that absorbed resources. Although there were some revolutions and assorted small wars in Europe during the nineteenth century, the Napoleonic Wars, which ended in 1815, were the last major conflict until the First World War. Some religious strife persisted, but in fewer places and at lower levels than existed during the Reformation.

5. Concluding Remarks

While there are certainly qualifications to be noted, the major empirical finding reported in this chapter is the U-shaped pattern in average heights from the early Middle Ages through the late nineteenth century in northern Europe. After a long period of approximate stability at levels that were impressive even by standards of the late nineteenth century, heights declined sometime after the end of the Middle Ages. Plausibly, the height decline might be linked with climate change that accompanied the onset of the Little Ice Age; growing inequality; urbanization; the global spread of diseases after the late 1400s; and conflicts associated with state building and religion. Because it is reasonable to believe that greater exposure to pathogens accompanied industrialization, and there is evidence of growing effi- ciency in agriculture and greater trade in foodstuffs, it is reasonable to link height gains during the early and mid-nineteenth century with dietary improvements.

Much research remains to be done on the exact time-path of average heights, and substantially more information from skeletal evidence is available. A large research programme is now in the planning stages to gather this evidence and analyse it in light of related information on climate and of socio-economic information from historical sources and from the archaeological record.

For over half a century economic historians have focused on the question of whether there was immiserisation during industrialization, a debate that has split researchers into camps of optimists and pessimists. This is and continues to be an interesting topic for research. But with the perspective of 1,000 years of history, whatever happened with regard to downturns in welfare during this era, they were likely small compared to the vast changes that probably occurred since the early Middle Ages. Therefore, economic historians who are inspired by variation and diversity in the historical record would do well to consider this much broader time span of evidence.

Notes

1. Average heights calculated from skeletal data have long been used by physical anthro- pologists but little used by other social scientists. For a study of England oriented towards medical historians, see Stephen Kunitz (1987).
2. Readers unfamiliar with the methodology of anthropometric history may want to consult the discussion and references in Steckel (1995).
3. For a contrary view of European industrialization see Komlos (2000).
4. The height estimates are from Floud, Wachter, and Gregory (1990) but there has been a lively exchange over the timing and extent of the height decline in Britain (Floud, Wachter, and Gregory 1993a,b; Komlos 1993a,b). Komlos agrees a decline occurred near mid-century, but places it at a lower level and within the context of his estimates of an overall decline after 1760.
5. Some seventeenth-century military records in France contain measurements of soldiers, which are useful for studying pre-industrial trends in heights. Komlos, Hau, and Bourguinat (2001) report an upward trend (with moderate fluctuations) in average height for birth cohorts of the late seventeenth to the mid-eighteenth centuries. Further search efforts might reveal additional pre-industrial height records for other countries.
6. For discussions of these issues see White (1991: 308–20) and Buikstra and Ubelaker (1994: chs 3–4).
7. The National Science Foundation recently funded an extensive project that will collect and analyse data from skeletons covering the last 10 millennia in Europe. The effort will obtain not just heights (from femur lengths) but also information on degenerative joint disease, dental decay, anaemia, and other skeletal indicators of chronic biological stress. A module in a larger project envisioned on a global history of health, I will work with three

co-investigators and numerous collaborators in Europe in gathering and analysing skeletal data that will be matched with socio-economic and climate information (Steckel 2003).

8. This is not the first time that anthropometric historians have found surprising if not startling results. The very small statures of slave children followed by remarkable catch-up growth, the American height decline during the mid-nineteenth century, and the very tall statures of the Equestrian Plains tribes in the United States are three additional examples.

References

Allen, R. C. (2001) 'The Great Divergence in European Wages and Prices from the Middle Ages to the First World War'. *Explorations in Economic History*, 38: 411–47.

Arcini, C. (1999) 'Health and Disease in Early Lund: Osteo-Pathologic Studies of 3,305 Individuals Buried in the First Cemetery Area of Lund, 990–1536'. *Archaeologica Lundensia*, 8.

Bennike, P. (1985) *Palaeopathology of Danish Skeletons*. Denmark: Akademisk Forlag.

Boldsen, J. (1984) 'A Statistical Evaluation of the Basis for Predicting Stature from Lengths of Long Bones in European Populations'. *American Journal of Physical Anthropology*, 65: 305–11.

Buikstra, J. E. and Ubelaker, D. H. (1994) *Standards for Data Collection from Human Skeletal Remains*. Fayetteville: Arkansas Archeological Survey.

Crosby, A. W. Jr. (1972) *The Columbian Exchange: Biological and Cultural Consequences of 1492*. Westport, CT: Greenwood Press.

——(1986) *Ecological Imperialism: The Biological Expansion of Europe, 900–1900*. Cambridge: Cambridge University Press.

Cuff, T. (1998) 'The Effects of Economic Development on the Biological Standard of Living: Market Integration and Human Stature in Antebellum Pennsylvania'. Ph.D. dissertation, University of Pittsburgh.

de Vries, J. (1976) *The Economy of Europe in an Age of Crisis, 1600–1750*. New York: Cambridge University Press.

——(1984) *European Urbanization, 1500–1800*. Cambridge, MA: Harvard University Press.

Drukker, J. W. and Tassenaar, V. (1997) 'Paradoxes of Modernization and Material Well-Being in the Netherlands during the Nineteenth Century', in R. H. Steckel and R. Floud (eds.), *Health and Welfare During Industrialization*. Chicago: University of Chicago Press, pp. 331–77.

Engerman, S. L. (1997) 'The Standard of Living Debate in International Perspective: Measures and Indicators', in R. H. Steckel and R. Floud (eds.), *Health and Welfare During Industrialization*. Chicago: University of Chicago Press, pp. 17–45.

Fagan, B. (2000) *The Little Ice Age: How Climate Made History, 1300–1850*. New York: Basic Books.

Floud, R., Wachter, K. W., and Gregory, A. S. (1990) *Height, Health, and History: Nutritional Status in the United Kingdom, 1750–1980*. Cambridge: Cambridge University Press.

—— —— and ——(1993a) 'Measuring Historical Heights—Short Cuts or the Long Way Around: A Reply to Komlos'. *Economic History Review*, 46: 145–54.

—— —— and ——(1993b) 'Further Thoughts on the Nutritional Status of the British Population'. *Economic History Review*, 46: 367–78.

Floud, R and Harris, B. (1997) 'Health, Height, and Welfare: Britain, 1700–1980', in R. H. Steckel and R. Floud (eds.), *Health and Welfare During Industrialization*. Chicago: University of Chicago Press, pp. 91–126.

Fogel, R. W (1985) 'Nutrition and the Decline in Mortality since 1700: Some Preliminary Findings', in S. L. Engerman and R. E. Gallman (eds.), *Long-Term Factors in American Economic Growth*. Chicago: University of Chicago Press, pp. 439–555.

—— (1993) 'New Sources and New Techniques for the Study of Secular Trends in Nutritional Status, Health, Mortality, and the Process of Aging'. *Historical Methods*, 26: 5–43.

Friedman, G. C. (1982) 'The Heights of Slaves in Trinidad'. *Social Science History*, 6: 482–515.

Gejvall, N. G. (1960) *Westerhus; Medieval Population and Church in the Light of Skeletal Remains*. Lund: H. Ohlssons boktr.

Gilberg, R. (1976) 'Stengade-vikingernes skeletter', in J. Skaarup (ed.), *Stengade II: en langelandsk Gravplads med grave fra romerskjernalder og vikingetid*. Rudkobing: Langelands Museum, pp. 220–7.

Haines, M. R., Craig, L. A., and Weiss, T. (2003) 'The Short and the Dead: Nutrition, Mortality, and the "Antebellum Puzzle" in the United States'. *Journal of Economic History*, 63: 382–413.

Hanson, C. (1992) 'Population-Specific Stature Reconstruction for Medieval Trondheim, Norway'. *International Journal of Osteoarchaeology*, 2: 289–95.

Hoffman, P. T., Jacks, D., Levin, P. A., and Lindert, P. H. (2002) 'Real Inequality in Europe Since 1500'. *Journal of Economic History*, 62: 322–55.

Hohenberg, P. M. and Lees, L. H. (1985) *The Making of Urban Europe, 1000–1950*. Cambridge: Harvard University Press.

Holck, P. (1997) *Cremated Bones. A Medical-Anthropological Study of an Archaeological Material on Cremation Burials. Antropologiske Skrifter* no. 1c. Oslo: Anatomical Institute, University of Oslo.

—— and Kvaal, S. (2000) *Skjelettene Fra Clemengkirken i Oslo. Antropologiske skrifter* no. 5. Oslo: Anatomisk institutt, Universitetet i Oslo.

Honda, G. (1997) 'Differential Structure, Differential Health: Industrialization in Japan, 1868–1940', in R. H. Steckel and R. Floud (eds.), *Health and Welfare During Industrialization*. Chicago: University of Chicago Press, pp. 251–84.

Huber, N. M. (1968) 'The Problem of Stature Increase: Looking from the Past to the Present', in D. R. Brothwell (ed.), *The Skeletal Biology of Earlier Human Populations*. Oxford: Pergamon Press, pp. 67–102.

Janssen, H. A. M. and Maat, G. J. R. (1999) 'Canons Buried in the "Stiftskapel" of the Saint Servaas Basilica at Maastricht, A.D. 1070–1521: A Paleopathological Study'. *Barge's Anthropologica*, 5, 2nd edn., Leiden.

Jones, E. L. (1968) *The Development of English Agriculture, 1815–1873*. London: Macmillan.

Komlos, J. (1989) *Nutrition and Economic Development in the Eighteenth-Century Habsburg Monarchy*. Princeton, NJ: Princeton University Press.

—— (1993a) 'The Secular Trend in the Biological Standard of Living in the United Kingdom, 1730–1860'. *Economic History Review*, 46: 115–44.

—— (1993b) 'Further Thoughts on the Nutritional Status of the British Population'. *Economic History Review*, 46: 363–6.

—— (1998) 'Shrinking in a Growing Economy? The Mystery of Physical Stature During the Industrial Revolution'. *Journal of Economic History*, 58: 779–802.

—— (2000) 'The Industrial Revolution as the Escape from the Malthusian Trap'. *Journal of European Economic History*, 29: 307–31.

Komlos, J., Hau, M., and Bourguinat, N. (2001) 'The Anthropometric History of Early-Modern France', unpublished manuscript, University of Munich.

Kunitz, S. J. (1987) 'Making A Long Story Short: A Note on Men's Height and Mortality in England from the First through the Nineteenth Centuries'. *Medical History*, 31: 269–80.

Livi-Bacci, M. (1983) 'The Nutrition-Mortality Link in Past Times: A Comment'. *Journal of Interdisciplinary History*, 14: 293–8.

Maat, G. J. R. (1984) 'A Search for Secular Growth Changes in the Netherlands Preceding 1850', in J. Borms, R. Hauspie, A. Sand, C. Susanne, and M. Hebbelinck (eds.), *Human Growth and Development*. New York: Plenum Press, pp. 185–91.

Maat, G. J. R., Mastwijk, R. W., and Sarfatij, H. (1998) *Een Fysisch Anthropologisch Onderzoek van Begravenen bij het Minderbroedersklooster te Dordrecht, circa 1275–1572 AD*. Amersfoort: Riijksdienst voor her Oudheidkundig Bodemonderzoek.

McEvedy, C. and Jones, R. (1978) *Atlas of World Population History*. New York: Facts on File.

Malcolm, L. A. (1974) 'Ecological Factors Relating to Child Growth and Nutritional Status', in A. F. Roche and F. Falkner (eds.), *Nutrition and Malnutrition: Identification and Measurement*. New York: Plenum Press, pp. 329–52.

Margo, R. A., and Steckel, R. H. (1982) 'The Heights of American Slaves: New Evidence on Slave Nutrition and Health'. *Social Science History*, 6: 516–38.

—— and —— (1992) 'The Nutrition and Health of Slaves and Antebellum Southern Whites', in R. W. Fogel and S. L. Engerman (eds.),*Without Consent or Contract: Conditions of Slave Life and the Transition to Freedom*. New York: W.W. Norton, pp. 508–21.

Martorell, R. and Habicht, J. P. (1986) 'Growth in Early Childhood in Developing Countries', in F. Falkner and J. M. Tanner (eds.), *Human Growth: A Comprehensive Treatise*, Vol. 3. New York: Plenum Press, pp. 241–62.

McKeown, T. (1983) 'Food, Infection, and Population'. *Journal of Interdisciplinary History*, 14: 227–47.

Molleson, T. and Cox, M. (1993) *The Spitalfields Project: Volume 2—The Anthropology*. Council for British Archaeology Research Report 86. York: Council for British Archaeology.

Munter, A. H. (1928) 'A Study of the Lengths of the Long Bones of the Arms and Legs in Man, with Special Reference to Anglo-Saxon Skeletons'. *Biometrika*, 28: 258–94.

Nicholas, S. and Steckel, R. H. (1997) 'Tall But Poor: Living Standards of Men and Women in Pre-Famine Ireland'. *Journal of European Economic History*, 26: 105–34.

O'Rourke, K. H. and Williamson, J. G. (1999) *Globalization and History: The Evolution of a Nineteenth-Century Atlantic Economy*. Cambridge, MA: MIT Press.

Parker, G. and Smith, L. M. (eds.) (1997) *The General Crisis of the Seventeenth Century*. New York: Routledge.

Pope, C. L. (1992) 'Adult Mortality in America Before 1900: A View from Family Histories', in C. Goldin and H. Rockoff (eds.), *Strategic Factories in Nineteenth Century American Economic History*. Chicago, IL: University of Chicago Press, pp. 267–96.

Preston, S. H. and Haines, R. (1991) *Fatal Years: Child Mortality in Late Nineteenth-Century America*. Princeton, NJ: Princeton University Press.

Razzell, P. (1993) 'The Growth of Population in Eighteenth-Century England: A Critical Reappraisal'. *Journal of Economic History*, 53: 743–71.

Sandberg, L. G. and Steckel, R. H. (1980) 'Soldier, Soldier, What Made You Grow So Tall? A Study of Height, Health, and Nutrition in Sweden, 1720–188'. *Economy and History*, 23: 91–105.

—— and —— (1987) 'Heights and Economic History: The Swedish Case'. *Annals of Human Biology*, 14: 101–10.

—— and —— (1997) 'Was Industrialization Hazardous to Your Health? Not in Sweden!', in R. H. Steckel and R. Floud (eds.), *Health and Welfare During Industrialization*. Chicago: University of Chicago Press, pp. 127–59.

Schmidt, I. M., Jorgensen, M. H., and Michaelsen, K. F. (1995) 'Height of Conscripts in Europe: Is Postneonatal Mortality a Predictor?', *Annals of Human Biology*, 22: 57–67.

Scrimshaw, N. S., Taylor, C. E., and Gordon, J. E. (1968) *Interactions of Nutrition and Disease*. WHO Monograph Series, No. 52. New York: United Nations.

Shay, T. (1994) 'The Level of Living in Japan, 1885–1938: New Evidence', in J. Komlos (ed.), *Stature, Living Standards, and Economic Development: Essays in Anthropometric History*. Chicago, IL: University of Chicago Press, pp. 173–201.

Steckel, R. H. (1983) 'Height and Per Capita Income'. *Historical Methods*, 16: 1–7.

—— (1995) 'Stature and the Standard of Living'. *Journal of Economic Literature*, 33: 1903–40.

—— (1998) 'Strategic Ideas in the Rise of the New Anthropometric History and Their Implications for Interdisciplinary Research'. *Journal of Economic History*, 58: 803–21.

—— (2001) 'Industrialization and Health in Historical Perspective', in D. Leon and G. Walt (eds.), *Poverty, Inequality and Health*. Oxford: Oxford University Press, pp. 37–57.

—— (2003) 'Research Project: A History of Health in Europe from the Late Paleolithic Era to the Present'. *Economics and Human Biology*, 1: 139–42.

—— (forthcoming 2005) 'Health, Nutrition and Physical Wellbeing', in S. Carter, S. Gartner, M. Haines, A. Olmstead, R. Sutch, and G. Wright (eds.), *Historical Statistics of the United States: Millennial Edition*. New York: Cambridge University Press.

—— and Floud, R. (eds.) (1997) *Health and Welfare During Industrialization*. Chicago, IL: University of Chicago Press.

Steffensen, J. (1958) *Stature as a Criterion of the Nutritional Level of Viking Age Icelanders*. Arbok hins islenzka fornleifafelags, fylgirit.

Szreter, S. (1988) 'The Importance of Social Intervention in Britain's Mortality Decline c. 1850–1914: A Reinterpretation of the Role of Public Health'. *Social History of Medicine*, 1: 1–37.

Tracy, M. (1964) *Agriculture in Western Europe*. New York: Praeger.

Trotter, M. and Gleser, G. C. (1952) 'Estimation of Stature from Long Bones of American Whites and Negroes'. *American Journal of Physical Anthropology*, 10: 463–514.

Trow-Smith, R. (1967) *Life from the Land: The Growth of Farming in Western Europe*. London: Longmans.

Twarog, S. (1997) 'Heights and Living Standards in Germany, 1850–1939: The Case of Württemberg', in R. H. Steckel and R. Floud (eds.), *Health and Welfare During Industrialization*. Chicago, IL: University of Chicago Press, pp. 285–330.

United Nations (1973) *The Determinants and Consequences of Population Trends*, Vol. 1. New York: United Nations.

van Meerten, M. A. (1990) 'Développement économique et Stature en France, XIXe–XXe Siècles'. *Annales*, 755–77.

Waaler, H. T. (1984) 'Height, Weight, and Mortality: The Norwegian Experience'. *Acta Medica Scandinavica* (Supplement 679).

Weir, D. R. (1997) 'Economic Welfare and Physical Well-Being in France, 1750–1990', in R. H. Steckel and R. Floud (eds.), *Health and Welfare During Industrialization*. Chicago, IL: University of Chicago Press, 161–200.

Werdelin, L. (1985) 'The Stature of Some Medieval Swedish Populations'. *Fornvännen*, 80: 133–41.

White, T. D. (1991) *Human Osteology*. San Diego, CA: Academic Press.

Whitwell, G., de Souza, C., and Nicholas, S. (1997) 'Height, Health, and Economic Growth in Australia, 1860–1940', in R. H. Steckel and R. Floud (eds.), *Health and Welfare during Industrialization*. Chicago, IL: University of Chicago Press, pp. 379–422.

10 The Burden of Grandeur: Physical and Economic Well-Being of the Russian Population in the Eighteenth Century

BORIS MIRONOV

1. Introduction

The eighteenth century was one of the most brilliant centuries in the history of Russia. Resounding victories over Sweden and Turkey allowed Russia to strengthen its position on the shores of the Baltic and Black seas, to annex Poland, the Baltic lands, and the Crimea and ensured for itself the rank of a great military power. Russia built up not only a powerful army and navy but also a national industry. The arts, sciences, and education were developing, foreign- and home-trade turnovers were growing, the economy was becoming commercialized, and considerable economic growth was evident. Some scholars even believe that at the turn of the nineteenth century, Russia neared Britain in terms of national income per capita (Blanchard 1989: 281–3). Much has been written about successes. But the issue of the material conditions of the people has been largely neglected. Were these victories accompanied by an increase in the physical and economic well-being of the Russian population in the eighteenth century or, on the contrary, were they achieved at its expense? That is the question to which I am trying to find answers in this chapter.

2. Processing the Data on Stature

The availability of Russian source material relating to the eighteenth and the first half of the nineteenth centuries does not allow us to use traditional indicators of well-being such as national income per capita, incomes of various social classes, and the level of inequality among them, or real wages. But even if such indicators were at our disposal they would be obviously insufficient to characterize the material conditions of the great majority of the people. The peasantry that comprised about 90% of the population had weak ties with the markets for goods and labour. The lion's share of the products consumed by peasants were produced in

I am grateful to Peter Lindert and John Komlos for advice, help, and responses to queries.

their own households, while they sold only a small part of their agricultural produce to get the money required for the payment of taxes and quitrent to the state and landlords. In the early eighteenth century only 13% of the country's population resided in towns, and by the late eighteenth century this figure fell to just 8%.[1] In terms of the way of life, the greater part of this not-numerous urban population was also engaged in agriculture and did not differ much from peasants (Mironov 1990: 281–3). Owing to this fact, to illuminate changes in the living standard we shall use information about variations in the stature of male conscripts. Stature variation is a good proxy for changes in the overall biological status of the population. For Russia in the eighteenth century it is also a fairly reliable indicator of well-being and the standard of living since in pre-industrial Russian society more than half of a peasant's income was spent to maintain biological status. The earliest reliable budget inspections are from 1877 to 1883 by which time the way of life in the countryside appreciably changed towards the diversification of requirements. According to these budgets, peasants engaged mainly in agriculture spent nearly 54% of their income on the maintenance of biological status (40% on nutrition, 14% on clothes/dwelling) and those engaged mainly in home industry spent 78% (60% on nutrition, 18% on clothes/dwelling) (*Materialy* 1903: 132–4).[2]

To assess variations in the biological and material status, we have information on the stature of 57,549 recruits born in 1700–99 and called up between 1731 and 1835. Compulsory military service was introduced in 1699 and was extended to the whole taxable population in 1705. Unfortunately, the military began to measure stature only after the introduction of the minimum height standards in November 1730 (*Stoletie Voennogo ministerstva* 1902, Vol. 3, part 1, book 1, section 1: 61–2, 88). From 1730 to 1799 there were fifty recruitments, and twenty-six more followed in the first third of the nineteenth century. On average there were two recruitments every three years, although sometimes there were two recruitments a year. Not all of the official lists of recruits have been preserved. But owing to the fact that recruits were generally aged between 16 and 35, though sometimes older, the information available allows us to estimate stature variations for each year of the century. The information on stature was related to those who were medically examined and recruited. Their number varied from 14,000 in 1730 to 132,000 in 1796, to about 200,000 in the 1830s (*Stoletie Voennogo ministerstva* 1902, Vol. 3, part 1, book 1, section 1: 92, 271; Vol. 4, part 3, book 1, section 2: 5–6). Before the introduction of universal compulsory military service in 1874, mainly peasants (83–92% of the population) and the lower strata of the urban population, *meshchane* (3–7% of the population), together constituting about 96.5% of the total population, were recruited (Mironov with Eklof 2000: 238–89, 355). For the nobility (2% of the population), military service was compulsory before 1762 and became voluntary thereafter. As a rule, the nobility served as officers. The clergy (1.5% of the population) was exempted from service and the never-numerous bourgeoisie had the right to pay out of military service. Thus, throughout the century the social composition of recruits was stable: 95–97% were peasants of various categories.

Table 10.1 Variations of minimum height requirements (in cm) and age requirements (years) for recruits of the regular Russian army, 1730–1874

	Min. height for recruits, ≥ 20	Min. height for recruits, <20	Age requirement
1730	160.0	160.0	15–30
1731	160.0	155.6	15–30
1736	157.8	155.6	15–35
1741	160.0	142.2	17–35
1757	160.0	—	20–35
1766	160.0	—	17–35
1825	160.0	—	18–35
1840	160.0	—	20–35
1845	157.8	—	20–35
1854	155.6	—	20–35
1874	153.4	—	20

Source: *Polnoe sobranie zakonov 1830*, Vol. 8, no. 5645 (1730); Vol. 9, no. 7046 (1736); Vol. 11, no. 8446 (1741); Vol. 14, no. 10786 (1757); Vol. 17, no. 12748 (1766); Rediger 1892: 88–95.

The basic age and height requirements of 17–35 years and 160 cm varied significantly; this considerably facilitates the comparison of data for various years (see Table 10.1).

During protracted wars, the military relaxed these requirements, calling up recruits aged between 16 and 50 and of stature 1–5 cm below standards, and in exceptional cases recruiting without restrictions. For example, in 1788 during the Russo–Turkish war volunteers were recruited without stature restrictions (*Polnoe sobranie zakonov 1830*, Vol. 22, no. 16681). This creates some difficulties when data for various years are compared, but the difficulties should not be exaggerated. First, information on the stature of recruits called up in the years when requirements were relaxed is relatively insignificant in the overall database. Second, the maximum effect of relaxing the height requirements during the Russo–Turkish war, lowered the average height of recruits by 1.8 cm. Third, reductions in the height requirements were often caused by an actual decrease in the overall stature of the population.

An accurate assessment of stature and age is an important issue. At all enlistment offices recruits were measured with the aid of a stature-measuring device delivered from the Military Board. It was a tin-bound wooden plank with a scale marked in old Russian measures—*arshin* (71.7 cm), *vershok* (4.445 cm), and fourth and eighth parts of *vershok* (0.556 cm). At both ends the scale was sealed up with the seal of the Military Board (*Stoletie Voennogo ministerstva* 1902, Vol. 4, part 1, book 1, section 1: 125–6). During the medical examination the recruit was stripped to the skin, put to the plank, his back against the scale, a ruler was put on the top of his head and his measure was taken. The accuracy of the measurement was not regulated by instructions and depended, probably, on the honesty of the examiners: in some cases they measured to $\frac{1}{2}$ *vershok* (2.3 cm), in others to $\frac{1}{4}$ *vershok* (the most frequent version), and still in others to $\frac{1}{8}$ *vershok* (0.6 cm). The medical examination of recruits was made in daytime; from daybreak until two o'clock in the afternoon. Examination by candle-light was prohibited. On the one hand, the examiners may have had an incentive to exaggerate stature in exchange for a bribe to accept a person who did not meet the requirements. On the other hand, they had an incentive to understate stature in order to insure against an accusation of intentionally exaggerating stature, especially since stature can alter by up to 2 cm from morning till nightfall, due to a slight compression of the vertebrae while standing. On arrival at the place of their service, recruits were measured for a second time and any deliberate distortion in measurement would be revealed. If a recruit's height proved to be lower than the prescribed standard, the recruit could be sent back at the expense of the examiners, however, if a recruit's height turned out to be greater than the one fixed in the official list, there were no consequences for the examiner since the army was interested in tall soldiers. An over-riding wish to avoid problems led examiners to tend to understate actual stature. The repeated measuring showed that the understating was within the range 0.5–2.2 cm, but no claims from recruits of erroneous measuring were ever brought forward to the selection committees.[3]

The data on assessment of age are worse. Official policy demanded verification of age with documents from censuses that had been taken regularly since 1719, or with registers of births, which had been kept more or less regularly by parish priests since the 1730s. Verification of age with documents was, however, somewhat burdensome for officials. The case was aggravated by the fact that in the eighteenth century administrative and territorial divisions were altered several times. Owing to this the materials of the latest census taken in one district were often kept in the archives of another district and it was indeed difficult and sometimes impossible (e.g. because of a fire—rather a frequent occurrence) to find the required documentation. As a result, it was only in dubious cases that documentation was required, while in most cases simple questioning was used. As usually happens when censuses are taken in traditional societies with low literacy levels (in Russia in the eighteenth century literacy among peasants did not exceed 1%), people tended to give ages ending in 0 or 5 (the so-called problem of age heaping). Some were also fond of the figure thirty-three (the age of Christ), and many men exaggerated their age. Being aware of this peculiarity, the selection committee officials apparently were more likely to understate the given age of recruits than to overstate it. In 1790 it was permitted to recruit carpenters from Kostroma province for the Black Sea fleet with no restrictions on their age or stature but with only the requirement that they should be healthy and fit for service. On arrival at the place of service 180 recruits were measured and questioned about their ages. Their remeasured stature turned out to be on average 1 cm higher (generally speaking this is normal since a man's stature varies during the day) but according to further questioning, average age turned out to be 10 years higher than that stated in the official lists. In the course of verification it was found that the ages of thirty-five recruits were indeed distorted. According to official lists the average was 30 years, but according to questioning at the place of service it was 58 years and according to the documents it was 37 years (*Central State Archive of the Navy*: f. 406, op. 8, d. 9, ll. 86, 114, 87–110). This example was an exceptional case of age distortion but one that reveals typical errors made in stature measurement and age assessment. Selection committees understated both stature and age; stature mostly insignificantly as it could be easily verified by the second measuring, but age sometimes significantly since it was more difficult to verify. Age distortion requires special care when using stature annual data and compels us to prefer five-year and ten-year data in which the problem of age heaping is largely eliminated. At the beginning of the nineteenth century the quality of measurement of recruits was largely improved—the accuracy of measurement was improved up to $\frac{1}{8}$ *vershok* (0.6 cm) and age was verified with documents.

Table 10.2 Stature of Russian recruits by birth year, 1700–99, by five-year cohorts (in cm)

Birth year	Recruits of ages 24–27	All recruits	
		N	x
1700–4	164.3	202	164.7
1705–9	164.4	870	164.1
1710–14	163.4	2426	163.5
1715–19	164.2	1790	163.2
1720–4	164.3	1620	162.6
1725–9	163.5	546	163.4
1730–4	164.3	2259	164.3
1735–9	165.0	5176	164.6
1740–4	164.6	1415	164.9
1745–9	165.1	2929	164.7
1750–4	164.9	2295	163.6
1755–9	163.8	3680	163.4
1760–4	162.8	3861	163.5
1765–9	163.8	6230	163.4
1770–4	165.1	6951	163.0
1775–9	163.9	4585	163.6
1780–4	161.8	1914	162.2
1785–9	161.8	2380	160.5
1790–4	160.5	2959	160.3
1795–9	160.0	3161	159.5

Notes: $N =$ Number of observations in the sample. $x =$ Raw mean of the sample.

Source: Central State Archive of the Navy f. 2 (Kantseliaria glavnoi artillerii i fortifikatsii), op. ShGF (Shtab general-fel'dtseikhmeistera); Archive of the Military-Historical Museum of the Artillery, the Engineers and the Intercommunication (Arkhiv Voenno-istoricheskogo muzeia artillerii, inzhenernykh voisk i voisk sviazi, Russia, St. Petersburg), f. 406 (Posluzhnye i formuliarnye spiski morskogo vedomstva), op. 8. (Rekrutskie spiski i rekrutskie nabory).

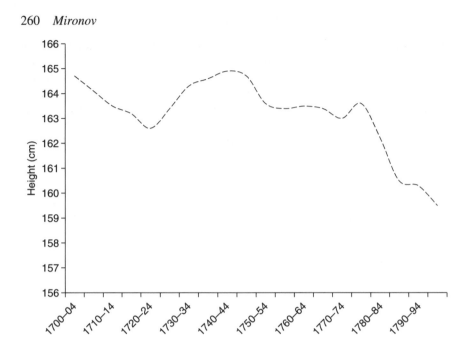

Figure 10.1   Height of Russian recruits by birth year, 1700–99

Correspondingly, the accuracy of data relating to the last third of the eighteenth century is in principle higher than that of the previous period.

A check on the character of the distribution of stature data over five-year and ten-year periods indicates that in most cases the distribution of individual statures is close to normal. This enables us to use the Komlos–Kim method for the assessment of the average stature of the entire population on the basis of the truncated sample (Komlos and Kim 1990: 116–20).

Thus, the accuracy of data on the stature and age of recruits selected by military recruitment committees in the eighteenth century was not ideal; however, it was good enough to allow us to use them for a scientific analysis. Common inaccuracy in stature measurement is within the limits of random sampling errors. Inaccuracy in age assessment is neutralized if average five-year and ten-year data are used and the problem of truncated stature data can be neutralized with the use of the Komlos–Kim method. Now we turn to the analysis of the stature data (Table 10.2 and Figure 10.1).

3. The Resulting Patterns in Stature

These statistical results are of a preliminary character. The work on the formation of the database has not yet been completed. In addition to gaps in the data for some years, several samples have regional biases. As a consequence, the sample Russian mean may be either overestimated or underestimated as compared with the population mean, depending on what regions are represented in the sample. For example, according to our sample data, the mean stature of a 16–19-year-old cohort in 1785–9 was lower by 4.6 cm in comparison with the same age cohort in 1780–4. This improbable result is explained by the fact that the sample for 1780–4 includes recruits from the southern fertile provinces, which had relatively high average heights, while the sample for 1785–9 includes recruits from the northern provinces, which had relatively low average heights.

As seen in Table 10.2, in 1700–24 the sample mean stature consistently decreased and within twenty-five years diminished by 2.1 cm, from 164.7 cm to 162.3 cm. In the twenty years that followed, from 1725 to 1744, there was an opposite trend, so that by 1740–4 the average stature of recruits (164.9 cm) slightly exceeded the level of the early eighteenth century. In the following fifty-five years stature began to decrease again and in 1795–9 it was only 159.5 cm, or 5.2 cm less than the level of 1700–4 and by 5.4 cm less than the level of 1740–4. Hence it follows that the biological standard of living of the population declined in 1700–24 and 1745–99 and rose in 1725–44. Let us consider some factors which could account for such movements.

4. Factors Behind the Development of Stature

4.1 Epidemiological environment

A hypothesis for any serious effect of the epidemiological environment on the observed fluctuations in stature should be rejected, since it was stable during the period under study (Kahan 1968: 353–77). The frequency and intensity of epidemics in the period from 1725 to 1744, when the biological status rose, was not much different than in the two other periods from 1700 to 1724 and from 1745 to 1799 when the status declined. Consequently, it appears that the variation in the stature of recruits was due in the main to an increase in labour costs and a worsening of consumption among the lower social classes which were called up for military service. Direct information on working hours and consumption for the eighteenth century is not, however, available. Instead, let us turn to some indirect indicators—agricultural production, prices, obligations, and taxes.

4.2 Grain output

Between 1696 and 1796, in European Russia (within the boundaries of 1696), nearly 21.4 million hectares of woods were cleared and put to agricultural use. The share of meadows and pastures rose from 20% to 31% of total agricultural land. In European Russia sown area was extended by 2.5 times, while population increased by 2.2 times (taking into account people living in territories annexed during the eighteenth century). Total crop area was extended even more, owing to the transition from a two-field system to a three-field system and from a system of land long disused to a system of regular fallow land. This is clearly seen from the following data: in 1763–96 in European Russia sown area was extended by 1.5 times, while in 1780–1800 total output increased by 1.6 times and according to some estimates even doubled (Rubinshtein 1957: 327–34; Tsvetkov 1957: 110–18, 133; Mironov 1979: 115–17). Since no major technical innovations were introduced into agriculture it is reasonable to assume that this required an increase in labour costs on the part of the peasantry. The increase in crop area resulted in an increase in agricultural produce. Before the 1770s, grain harvests rose also, owing to rising yield capacity. In 1696–1763 crop area was extended by 1.7 times, yield capacity rose by 1.3 times, consequently corn harvests increased by 2.2 times whereas population increased by 1.8 times (see Table 10.3).

However, the intensive cultivation of land without proper application of fertilizers and a decrease in fallow fields, as well as unusually adverse weather conditions throughout most of Europe (Borisenkov and Pasetskii 1988: 62–91, 504; Komlos 1989: 110–11), resulted in a decline in yield capacity by 39.9% in the main agricultural regions in the last three decades of the eighteenth century (see Table 10.4).[4]

Due to this fall in yields, capacity grain output began to lag behind the increase in crops, but remained ahead of population growth. In 1780–1804, although population increased by 19%, total grain output increased by 28%, that is, by 8% per capita. Thus the production of grain, the main foodstuff, outstripped population growth and contributed to the increase in labour costs on the one hand and to the growth of the main foodstuff production on the other hand. However, the total number of cattle decreased (Rubinshtein 1957: 389–401); the decline in fodder supply in particular is indicative of this. In 1696–1763 meadows and pasture areas decreased by 6%, and in 1763–96 they increased only by 21%, while population increased by 63% (see Table 10.3).

Table 10.3 Size (in 1,000 ha) and distribution of land resources in eighteenth-century European Russia, crop capacity, and population (in millions)

Year	Plough-land	Meadows/ pastures	Forest	Total	Crop capacity[a]	Population
1696	31,976	67,068	213,416	405,091	3.4	13.0
1725	41,848	66,296	213,958	418,219	4.0	16.2
1763	53,865	63,308	205,890	423,128	4.4	23.5
1796	81,359	76,650	217,322	485,465	3.2	38.2

[a] Output/Seed ratios for the main grains

Source: Indova 1970: 141–55, Kabuzan 1971: 52, Klochkov 1915: 150, Tsvetkov 1957: 110–14.

Table 10.4 Output/seed ratios for the major grains in central Russia in the eighteenth century, by decades

Grain	1710s	1720s	1730s	1740s	1750s	1760s	1770s	1780s	1790s
Rye	2.9	3.6	3.2	4.3	3.7	4.7	4.2	3.3	3.1
Wheat	3.9	3.7	3.9	3.6	3.3	3.8	4.3	3.2	3.0
Oats	2.7	4.1	3.3	3.8	3.5	4.5	4.8	3.4	3.6
Barley	3.9	4.5	4.0	3.7	4.3	4.7	4.2	3.5	3.1
Average	3.0	3.9	3.4	4.0	3.6	4.6	4.4	3.4	3.3

Source: Indova 1970: 141–55.

In the 1790s net output of food grains per rural capita was approximately 250 kg, excluding oats (100 kg) and excluding seeds (Rubinshtein 1957: 374–80). This is the amount of grain consumed by the peasantry in Russia in 1896–1913 (Mironov 1995: 71). In the eighteenth century they did not produce potatoes, the consumption of which in 1896–1913 had increased the calorie content of nutrition by 10%. On the other hand, the output of meat, dairy produce, vegetables, fish, and game was undoubtedly greater. In 1896–1913 the average stature of recruits (minimum height standard being lesser) was 166.6 cm, while in 1790–9 it was 5.9 cm less! The average height of the men born in 1896–1915 was 166.6 cm (Mironov 2000: 345).

Why was this so? In 1790–9 a peasant had to sell a considerable part of his agricultural produce in order to pay taxes, rent, and to buy other goods that he needed and did not produce himself. The analysis of tax and rent explicitly shows this (see Tables 10.5 and 10.6).

4.3 Taxes and obligations

From Tables 10.5 and 10.6 it is obvious that the burden of taxes and obligations increased for all categories of taxable population, though in varying degrees. Landlord peasants suffered most of all. Even with the grain price rise taken into account the rent they paid to landlords rose almost uninterruptedly up to the 1770s, by which time it had doubled as compared with 1700–9. After the powerful peasant uprising of 1774–5 average quitrents actually decreased but nevertheless in 1790–9 exceeded the level of 1724–9 by 1.44 times. By the 1770s the total amount of payments by corvée peasants, that is, with direct taxes taken into account and with a correction for grain price, had increased by 1.4 times. They decreased thereafter, but even in 1790–9 they were 7% higher than in 1700–9. Per capita payments by other categories of peasants were lower than payments of landlord peasants. Before the 1770s they rose, but then declined and in 1790–9 even fell below the level of 1720s (corresponding information for 1700–19 is not available). Because of the necessity

Table 10.5 Changes in the burden of taxes and dues on seigniorial serfs in eighteenth-century Russia (per capita)

Years	Direct taxes			Quitrent[a]			Total of taxes and quitrent			Corvée[c]		Index of grain prices		Nom. prices of rye/pud,[d] in kopecks
	Kopecks	Index[b]		Kopecks	Index[b]		Kopecks	Index[b]		Desiatin	Index	Nominal	In silver	
		A	B		A	B		A	B					
1700–9	27	100	100	40	100	100	67	100	100	0.60	100	100	100	4.3
1710–19	n.a.	n.a.	n.a.	50	125	69	n.a.	n.a.	n.a.	n.a.	n.a.	180	149	8.3
1720–9	70	259	96	70	175	67	140	209	79	n.a.	n.a.	263	218	12.6
1730–9	70	259	115	90	225	100	160	239	106	n.a.	n.a.	226	190	10.9
1740–9	70	259	94	120	300	108	190	284	103	n.a.	n.a.	277	233	12.3
1750–9	70	259	103	160	400	159	230	343	136	n.a.	n.a.	251	208	9.4
1760–9	70	259	72	200	500	138	270	403	111	0.75	125	362	264	17.6
1770–9	70	259	58	350	875	197	420	627	141	1.20	200	444	320	20.5
1780–9	70	259	37	500	1,250	182	570	851	124	n.a.	n.a.	686	420	34.1
1790–9	96	356	32	700	1,750	158	796	1,188	107	1.50	250	1,110	566	44.1

[a] In money and kind.
[b] Index A does not take into account price changes; index B has been deflated to reflect changes in nominal prices.
[c] Complete cultivation of a certain number of desiatins of land per year; the desiatina was equal to 2.7 acres or 1.09 ha.
[d] Pud = 16.38 kg.

Source: L. V. Milov 1965: 208, 269, Miliukov 1905: 489, Mironov 1985: 54–5, Rubinshtein 1957: 156–7, Semevskii 1903: 52–3, 59, 82–3, 584–5, Chechulin 1906: 122–3, Tikhonov 1974: 294, 298.

Table 10.6 Changes in the burden of taxes and dues from state peasants (I), Appanage peasants (II), church (from 1764 Economicheskie) peasants (III), seigniorial peasants (IV), and burgers (V) in eighteenth-century Russia (per capita)

Period	I			II			III			IV		V		Height (cm)
	Kopecks	Index[a]		Kopecks	Index[a]		Kopecks	Index[a]		Index[a]		Kopecks	Index A	
		A	B		A	B		A	B	A	B			
1724–9	111	100	100	111	100	100	111	100	100	100	100	120	100	163.4
1730–9	110	99	115	110	99	115	110	99	115	114	134	120	100	164.5
1740–9	110	99	94	110	99	94	110	99	94	136	130	120	100	164.8
1750–9	110	99	104	110	99	104	110	99	104	164	172	120	100	163.5
1760–9	174	157	114	126	114	114	203	183	133	264	192	128	115	163.4
1770–9	270	243	144	270	243	144	270	243	143	371	222	200	180	163.2
1780–9	340	306	117	340	306	117	340	306	117	478	185	200	180	161.3
1790–9	388	350	83	388	350	83	388	350	83	604	144	200	180	160.7

[a] Index A does not take into account price changes; index B has been deflated to reflect changes in nominal prices.

Notes: For all categories (I–V), direct taxes and quitrents are shown.

Source: See Table 10.5.

of payments peasants sometimes had to sell produce they needed themselves for their own consumption and this substantially undermined their biological status. To discharge payments in 1700–9, a landlord peasant had to sell 250 kg of rye, while in 1790–9 it was 289 kg and in the 1770s even 325 kg. During this century the payments of burgers rose the least—nominally by 80%. Burgers, however, suffered not only from an increase in taxes and obligations but also from a rise in the prices of foodstuffs. They had to buy a considerable part of their food in the market since their own households could not provide all necessary supplies, as was the case with peasants. The comparison of the stature of recruits from various social groups vividly supports the conclusions made on the basis of the analysis of the tax and rent dynamics (see Table 10.7).

The biological status of burgers suffered most of all: their stature decreased by 2.3 cm from 1700–59 to 1760–99. The stature of Appanage or court peasants (who belonged to the tsar's family) decreased by 2.1 cm, of landlord peasants by 2 cm, of state-owned peasants by 1.9 cm, of clergy by 1.6 cm, of manor serfs (house-serf peasants who were in landlords' service) by 1.1 cm and of church peasants (who were confiscated from the Church in 1764) by 0.7 cm. The biological status of non-Russian peoples of the Volga region (Tatars, Mordovians, Chuvashes, and Bashkirs: the ethnic origin of recruits of other nationalities was not defined in the sources) suffered least of all. By the end of the eighteenth century landlord peasants had the lowest biological status, while non-Russian peoples and clergy had the highest. It is notable that on the scale of stature, social groups are arranged in accordance with their position on the scale of payments that they made to the state and to their masters. Unfortunately, nobility serving in the army were never measured. The procedure was thought to be humiliating for their dignity, and so information on their stature is not available. Undoubtedly they were the tallest people.

Table 10.7   Height by social groups, 1700–99 (in cm)

	1700–9	Rank	1700–59	Rank	1760–99	Rank	Decrease in stature	
							1700–59	1760–99
State peasants	164.2	7	163.6	4	161.7	7	−0.6	−1.9
Church peasants	164.3	6	163.1	7	162.4	3	−1.2	−0.7
Seigniorial peasants	164.7	5	163.1	8	161.1	5/6	−1.6	−2
Appanage peasants	165.0	4	163.2	5/6	161.1	5/6	−1.8	−2.1
Burgers	165.0	3	164.1	2	161.8	6	−0.9	−2.3
Manor serfs	165.2	2	163.2	5/6	162.1	4	−2	−1.1
Clergy	167.0	1	164.1	1	162.5	2	−2.9	−1.6
Non-Russian people of the Volga region	—	—	163.9	3	163.3	1	—	−0.6
Standard deviation	0.934	—	0.444	—	0.743	—	—	—

Source: See Table 10.2

The stature of their manor serfs indirectly testifies to that. Manor serfs were among the tallest in the various categories of peasant and were 1 cm taller than other landlord peasants.

What made the state raise taxes and landlords increase rent? Years when the tendency for a fall in the biological standard of living was replaced by a tendency for its rise are very indicative and suggest an answer to this question. First of all let us note 4 five-year periods when short-term and insignificant rises in biological status set in: 1725–9, 1740–4, 1760–4, and 1775–9. In my opinion, in three cases these rises were connected with the accession to the throne of a new emperor. Each time, the accession was accompanied by the remission of arrears and a temporary weakening of the state machinery pressure on the taxable population. This was a substantial concession, since annual arrears on direct taxes made up 4–5% of the total amount of payment (Chechulin 1906: 143–4; Troitskii 1966: 134–44). The rise of the biological status in 1775–9 can be linked with the peasant uprising in 1774–5, which raged over a vast territory for two years and after which rent payments were decreased for some time.

In 1700–24, when we first observe a decline in the biological status of recruits, Russia was waging a difficult and exhausting war with Sweden for the Baltic lands, which ended in 1721 with Russia's victory and the Nishtadt peace. During intervals in fighting in the West, Russia also fought against Turkey (1700–13) and Persia (1722–3) and simultaneously carried out serious political, economic, social, cultural, and administrative reforms. Formation of a regular army, prolonged wars, building of towns, canals and roads, construction of a fleet, of factories, and reform of management required enormous funds from the state on whose initiative all these were going on. The state obtained these funds through tax increases, the use of state regalia within certain areas (monetary, salt, alcohol drinking, etc.), and the emission of inferior money (the so-called coin spoiling). In 1701–21 state revenue grew by 2.9 times at the expense of direct taxes, regalia, and various kinds of dues and duties (Kafengauz and Pavlenko 1954: 391).[5] Despite this, revenues did not defray state expenses completely. In 1701–21 the share of military expenditure in the budget was at minimum 76% and at maximum 96% (Kafengauz and Pavlenko 1954: 383). Conscription became customary to provide personnel for the newly formed regular army and navy. In 1699–1723 the military called up nearly 365,000 people (15,200 a year) (*Stoletie Voennogo ministerstva* 1902, Vol. 4, part 1, book 1, section 1: 72–3). In 1719 Russia had only 7,570,000 males (Kabuzan 1971: 10) and this represented a significant loss of able-bodied men for the civilian economy. By the end of the northern war, according to the evidence of some contemporaries, people groaned under burden of war, high prices, and impoverishment. A decrease in the stature of recruits by 2.1 cm indeed testifies to the lowering of the physical and perhaps general well-being of the population, but hardly speaks of its disastrous fall. On the whole neither direct nor indirect per capita taxes *collected in cash* (with regard to the grain rise) were increased (Kafengauz and Pavlenko 1954: 391). But with regard to the growth of obligations *in kind* (recruitment, delivery of horses and carts for the transportation of military cargoes, etc.), the total tax burden was increased since conversion of the recruitment obligation to money raised direct tax by 23% (Kahan 1985: 348). If we also take into consideration the devastation of war-struck areas, asynchronies of variations in taxes, rent, and prices, and also the fact that in reality more taxes were collected than were noted on paper (part of them collecting in the hands of officials from the local and central administration), the well-being of the population in the first quarter of the century was generally lowered, and this was reflected in the lowering of the biological status of the taxable population.

With the end of the military operations in 1721 and the death of the tireless emperor in 1725, a certain easing set in. The biological status of the population began to rise gradually and within twenty years exceeded the pre-war level. A second fall in the biological standard of living which went on for fifty-five years (the fall halted only in 1760–4 and 1775–9) began in 1745–9 and was also largely due to wars. During this period Russia fought several wars with: Prussia (1757–62), Turkey (1768–74, 1786–91), Poland (1768–72, 1792, and 1794–5), Sweden (1788–90), Persia (1795–6), and France (1798–9). In 1763–1800 military expenditure on the army and navy absorbed 67% of the state budget revenue (Chechulin 1906: 256–7). The most difficult was the war with Turkey. In expenditure and manpower losses it outstripped even the northern war. Military fatalities alone were 215,000, 2.2 times more than in the northern war (Urlanis 1960: 54–8, 261–70, 340). During the first war against Turkey, in 1769, Catherine II had to turn to foreign loans and the issue of banknotes threw the country's money circulation into confusion. By 1800 the rate of exchange of a banknote rouble had fallen to 66.3 kopecks in silver and in 1796 the state debt, from the issue of banknotes, was 216 million roubles, which exceeded the budget revenue by 3.9 times (Chechulin 1906: 256–7; Liashchenko 1952: 415–18). Finally, the spoils of war in the form of new territories, the northern Black Sea lands in particular, required considerable investments on the part of the state infrastructure, defence, settling, and development.

The second important reason why state taxes increased was the fact that, in the years of the fall in the biological standard of living, the state was carrying out extensive structural reforms in the country. Earlier we mentioned the reforms of Peter I. The reforms of Catherine II were no less significant and intensive and they also absorbed considerable funds. The empress carried out major administrative and legal reforms, and she also encouraged the development of industry, science, literature, education, journalism, book-printing, theatre and art, opened foreign markets for Russian agriculture, extended contacts with West European countries in all spheres of life, and founded hospitals for orphans, among many other things (Riazanovsky 1984: 254–75).

The process of westernization that had begun in Russia in the early eighteenth century was one of the main causes of the nobility's desire to increase their income to the level required for leading a luxurious life in European style. This desire was encouraged by a favourable economic situation, which developed in

Russia as a result of the price revolution. In 1700–99 the general level of prices, in silver, rose by 5 times and grain prices by 5.7 times (including 2.7 times between 1760 and 1999) (Mironov 1985: 169–75, 1986: 228). The phenomenal price rise had no connection either with economic depression or with over-population. It was caused by the fact that Russian prices were denominated in silver, which in the early eighteenth century meant that average prices were approximately seven times lower than those in western Europe. During the eighteenth century, Russian prices caught up with the European prices as a result of Russia's entry into the European market as an important supplier of primary commodities, mainly grain, hemp, flax, furs, and also iron (Mironov 1985: 110–11). As compared to 1690–9, by 1726 foreign-trade turnovers in silver had risen by 2.5 times and by 1791–1800 by 26.5 times. The role of foreign trade in the country's total revenue increased. In 1724 nearly 25% of the country's aggregate commodity output was traded in the foreign market and by 1800, this share increased to 41% (Mironov 1985: 113). The catch-up of Russian prices as well as the rapid growth of Russian exports of agricultural produce that started in the 1760s after the liberalization of grain exports (before that time grain exports were limited and depended upon the price level) created an extremely favourable economic situation most of all for landlords. In pursuit of money by any means, they expanded the area under cultivation, and increased the corvée to meet the growing requirements for manpower. Where it was unprofitable to expand cultivation they increased quitrents for their peasants, forcing peasants to expand crop area or to engage in non-agricultural trades.

The landlord peasantry (7,057,000 of both sexes or 51.5% of total population in 1719 and 19,585,000 or 57.3% of the population in 1795) (Kabuzan 1971: 59–118) was the common source of income for both landlords and the state. Naturally they competed for a greater share of the income. Under Peter I a compromise had been reached—the income was shared equally. Peter I's successors, however, became strongly dependent on the nobility and gradually let them almost completely appropriate the state's share. This was due to the fact that the increase in the landlords' rent, as a rule, outran the rise in grain prices while the increase in taxes lagged behind the rise in prices. The share of income from landlord peasants acquired by the state fell gradually from 50% to 12.1% over the eighteenth century. As a result the state budget lost enormous funds, which were re-appropriated by the landlords and spent on their personal whims (see Table 10.8).

The nobility also laid claim to state-owned and former church peasants. Here too, the empresses made concessions, transferring nearly one million of the state-owned peasants to the possession of the nobility. This brought considerable losses to the treasury as rent slipped away from the treasury and into the pockets of landlords (Semevskii 1882: 153–92; Semevskii 1906: 1–71). The nobility's claim for former church peasants (1,626,000 of both sexes in 1719 and 2,610,000 in 1795) was rejected and income from these allowed the government to patch up holes in the state budget.

Table 10.8 Losses to the state treasury from the gap between the increase in the poll tax (in 1,000 roubles) and grain prices, 1725–1800

Period	Years	Seigniorial serfs (in 1,000s)	Annual poll tax levied	Received by treasury	Index of nominal prices (1701–25 = 100)	Real annual receipt per seigniorial serf (1725–44 = 100)	Losses to state from price rise[a]
1725–44	20	3,193	2,235	44,700	132	100.0	10,836
1745–62	18	3,781	2,647	47,646	126	104.5	9,832
1763–82	20	4,402	3,081	61,620	241	54.8	36,052
1783–94	12	5,105	3,573	42,876	471	28.0	33,773
1795–97	3	5,617	5,617	16,851	620	30.4	14,133
1798–1800	3	5,617	7,077	21,231	505	40.7	17,027
Total	76			243,924			121,653

[a] The direct taxes received by the state treasury are depreciated in proportion to the rise in prices.

Source: See Table 10.5.

5. Conclusion

The eighteenth century is notable for the fall in the average biological standard of living of the majority of the Russian population. Biological status took a turn for the worse twice: in 1700–24, when the stature of recruits decreased by 2.1 cm, and in 1745–99 when it decreased by 5.1 cm. These periods were separated by two relatively favourable decades when the biological standard of living reverted to the initial level of 1700–4. From 1700–4 to 1795–9, the average stature of recruits decreased from 164.7 cm to 159.5 cm or by 5.2 cm. This decrease in the biological status occurred against the backdrop of considerable economic growth and was caused not by economic depression but mainly by the rises in taxes and obligations which deteriorated the material conditions of common people and forced them to work longer hours and more intensively. To some extent it was also caused by adverse weather conditions, increases in the price of food, as in the rest of Europe, and by the increase in Russian grain exports, which must have meant that less was left for the domestic population. This decrease in stature during a time of overall economic growth followed the general European pattern for the eighteenth century (Komlos 1998: 779–802).

Increases in payments to the state were linked with the wars Russia waged to obtain an outlet into the Baltic and Black seas, and the status of a great power and with reforms carried out by the monarchy which were largely aimed at westernization. The increase in obligations to landlords was caused by their desire to have means for a comfortable and wasteful life. Under Peter I the burden of war and modernization was distributed evenly among all social classes and national income met the requirements of the whole society and, owing to this, the decline in average well-being was minimized. Under Elizaveta and Catherine II, however, all expenses were shifted on to the people's shoulders and the people's interests were sacrificed in favour of the nobility, who appropriated the results of the economic growth and modernization. In consequence of this, the well-being of the general population suffered great damage—under the rule of the two empresses the biological standard of living of the broad masses fell by 2.6 times more than under Peter I.

At the end of the seventeenth and the beginning of the eighteenth centuries Russian recruits were approximately of the same height as French or British soldiers (164.7 cm) (Floud and Harris 1997: 100–5) but shorter than American (173 cm) (Sokoloff 1995: 136; Costa and Steckel 1997: 50–2), Austro–Hungarian (171.4 cm) (Komlos 1989: 57), Swedish (168.5 cm) (Sandberg 1980: 91–105; Sandberg and Steckel 1987: 101–10), and German recruits (Komlos 1990: 607–21). In the second half of the eighteenth century everywhere in Europe the stature of recruits decreased, but by variable degrees: in Austro–Hungary by 4.3 cm, in Britain by 2.5 cm, in Sweden by 2 cm; only American soldiers preserved their former high stature (Komlos 1989: 75–6). Thus, in the eighteenth century, in terms of decrease in the biological standard of living, Russia kept pace with Europe, although the causes of this all-European phenomenon were different. While Britain experienced the Industrial Revolution, the rest of the western European countries were getting ready for it, being at the stage of proto-industrialization; all were experiencing economic growth. Russia also grew economically and was being modernized in every respect, but on a different basis. At the cost of a decrease in the well-being of its citizens, Russia became a great military power, Britain tuned into the world's workshop and other western European countries were getting ready to carry out their industrial revolutions. High costs everywhere paid for military or economic grandeur.

These results allow us to draw some general conclusions that are in full conformity with the observations made by Richard Steckel in his chapter: (1) Economic growth can be accompanied with decreasing well-being of populations, or at any rate with decreases in their biological status because of (a) resource-absorbing conflicts of state-building, wars and reforms and (b) because of increasing inequality in the distribution of income. (2) Before the Industrial Revolution, Russia, in terms of biological status and probably in terms of the standard of living, did not appreciably differ from England or the other western European countries, since the average height of men in most European countries in the eighteenth and early nineteenth centuries was approximately 164 or 165 cm (see also Steckel, Table 11.1, in this volume). (3) In pre-industrial Russia, there was no close correlation between income per capita and well-being. Therefore the adequate valuation of standards of living must include several dimensions: biological status, real wage, life expectancy, income per capita, distribution of income, and sensitivity to short-term economic stress.

Notes

1. There were two main causes of a reduction in the urban proportion of actual population: the difference in mortality between town and country (the former had much higher mortality than the latter) and the comparatively slow migration of peasants to towns (Mironov with Ben Eklof 2000: Vol. 1, 464). In 18th century Europe, the percentage of the urban population was increasing. In 1800 agglomerations of 2000 inhabitants or more amounted to 37% in the Netherlands, 33.6 in United Kingdom, 23.3 in Germany, 19 in France, and 9.8 in Sweden. In most other European countries though, and elsewhere in the world, the urban population amounted to no more than 10%; in the USA 6.1% (de Vries 1984: 39, 50, 76; Bairoch 1989: 243–50; see also Steckel, Table 11.2, this volume).
2. In western countries in the pre-industrial era, workers and peasants also spent more than half of their income on the maintenance of the biological status (Braudel 1979: 144–50). In accordance with Engel's law, as a consumer's income decreases, the proportion of income spent on food increases. In 1986, the share of income spent on food and beverage was 55.7% in India, 38% in the Soviet Union, 27.7% in Spain, 20.5% in West Germany and 12.3% in the USA (US Bureau of Census 1990: 842).
3. Central State Archive of the Navy: f. 406, op. 8, d. 9, ll. 87–110; d. 14, ll. 25–50, 111–18; Archive of the Military-Historical Museum of the Artillery, the Corps of Engineers and the Intercommunication: f. 2, op. ShGF, d. 4943, ll. 132, 160.

4. About the influence of changing climate on height, see also Steckel's chapter in this volume.
5. This is not counting considerable state obligations in kind—recruitment, delivery of horses and carts for the transportation of military cargoes, felling of trees for shipbuilding, building of roads, fortresses, towns etc., whose value it is difficult to estimate.

References

Archive of the Military-Historical Museum of the Artillery, the Corps of Engineers, and the Intercommunication, Russia, St. Petersburg (Tsentarl'nyi gosudarstvennyi arkhiv Voenno-morskogo flota).

Bairoch, P. (1989) 'Urbanization and the Economy in Pre-industrial Society: The Findings of Two Decades of Research'. *Journal of European Economic History*, 18(2): 243–50.

Blanchard, I. (1989) *Russia's 'Age of Silver': Precious-metal Production and Economic Growth in the Eighteenth Century*. London and New York: Routledge.

Borisenkov, E. P. and Pasetskii, V. M. (1988) *Tysiacheletniaia letopis' neobychainukh iavlenii prirody*. Moscow: Mysl'.

Braudel, F. (1979) *Les structures du quotidien: le possible et l'impossible*. Paris: Arman Colin, pp. 144–50.

Central State Archive of the Navy, Russia, St. Petersburg (Arkhiv Voenno-istoricheskogo muzeia artillerii, inzhenernykh voisk i voisk sviazi).

Chechulin, N. D. (1906) *Ocherki po istorii russkikh finansov v tsarstvovanie Ekateriny II.* St. Petersburg: Senatskaia tipografiia.

Costa, D. L. and Steckel R. H. (1997) 'Long-Term Trends in Health, Welfare, and Economic Growth in the United States', in R. H. Steckel and R. Floud (eds.), *Health and Welfare during Industrialization*. Chicago and London: University of Chicago Press, pp. 47–90.

Floud, R. and Harris, B. (1997) 'Health, Height, and Welfare: Britain, 1700–1980', in R. H. Steckel and R. Floud (eds.), *Health and Welfare during Industrialization*. Chicago and London: University of Chicago Press, pp. 91–126.

Indova, E. I. (1970) 'Urozhai v Tsentral'noi Rossii za 150 let (Vtoraia polovina XVII–XVIII v.)', in V. K. Iatsunskii (ed.), *Ezhegodnik po agrarnoi istorii Vostochnoi Evropy za 1965 g*. Moscow: Akademiia Nauk SSSR, pp. 141–55.

Kabuzan, V. M. (1971) *Izmeneniia v razmeshchenii naseleniia Rossii v XVIII-pervoi polovine XIX v*. Moscow: Nauka.

Kafengauz, B. B. and Pavlenko, N. I. (eds.) (1954) *Ocherki istorii SSSR. Period feodalizma. Russia v pervoi chetverti XVIII v. Preobrazovaniia Petr*. Moscow: Akademiia Nauk SSSR.

Kahan, A. (1968) 'Natural Calamities and their Effect upon the Food Supply in Russia'. *Jahrbüher der Geschichte Osteuropas*, 16: 353–77.

——(1985) *The Plow, the Hammer, and the Knout: An Economic History of Eighteenth-Century Russia*. Chicago: University of Chicago Press.

Klochkov, M. V. (1915) 'Ocherki podushnoi perepisi pri Petre Velikom'. *Zhurnal Ministerstva narodnogo prosveshcheniia*, 55 (January): 110–50.

Komlos, J. (1989) *Nutrition and Economic Development in the Eighteenth-Century Habsburg Monarchy: An Anthropometric History*. Princeton, NJ: Princeton University Press.

Komlos, J. (1990) 'Height and Social Status in Eighteenth-Century Germany'. *Journal of Interdisciplinary History*, 20 (Spring): 607–21.

—— and Kim, J. H. (1990) 'Estimating Trends in Historical Heights'. *Historical Methods*, 2 (Summer): 116–20.

—— (1998) 'Shrinking in a Growing Economy? The Mystery of Physical Stature during the Industrial Revolution'. *Journal of Economic History*, 58 (September): 779–802.

Liashchenko, P. I. (1952) *Istoriia narodnogo khoziaistva SSSR*, 2 vols. Moscow: Gosudarstvennoe izdatel'stvo politicheskoi literatury.

Materialy vysochaishe uchrezhdennoi 16 noiabria 1901 g. Komissii po issledovaniiu voprosa o dvizhenii s 1861 g. po 1901 g. blagosostoianiia sel'skogo naseleniia srednezemledel'cheskikh gubernii sravnitel'no s drugimi mestnostiami Evropeiskoi Rossii (1903), Vol. 3: 3. St. Petersburg: P. P. Soikin.

Miliukov, P. N. (1905) *Gosudarstvennoe khoziaistvo Rossii v pervoi chetverti XVIII stoletiia i reforma Petra Velikogo*. St. Petersburg: V. S. Balashev.

Milov, L. V. (1965) *Issledovanie ob "ekonomicheskikh primechaniiakh k General'nomu mezhevaniiu": K istorii russkogo krest'ianstva i sel'skogo khoziaistva vtoroi poloviny XVIII v*. Moscow: MGU.

Mironov, B. N. (1979) 'Prichiny rosta khlebnykh tsen v Rossii XVIII v.', in A. M. Anfimov (ed.), *Ezhegodnik po agrarnoi istorii Vostochnoi Evrop*. Kiev: Vishcha shkola, pp. 109–25.

—— (1985) *Khlebnye tseny v Rossii za dva stoletiia (XVIII-XIX vv)*. Leningrad: Nauka.

—— (1986) 'Le mouvement des prix des céréales en Russie du XVIII-e siècle au début du XX-e siècle'. *Annales: Économies. Sociétés. Civilisations*, 41 (Janvier–Février): 217–51.

—— (1990) *Russkii gorod v 1740–1860-e gody: demograficheskoe, sotsial'noe i ekonomicheskoe razvitie*. Leningrad: Nauka.

—— (1995) 'Diet and Health of the Russian Population from the Mid-Nineteenth to the Beginning of the Twentieth Century', in J. Komlos (ed.), *The Biological Standard of Living on Three Continents: Further Explorations in Anthropometric History*. Boulder: Westview Press, pp. 59–80.

—— (2000) *Sotsial'naia istoriia Rossii perioda imperii (XVIII-nachalo XX v.): Genezis lichnosti, demokraticheskoi sem'i, grazhdanskogo obshchestva i pravovogo gosudarstva*, 2 vols, 2nd edn. St. Petersburg: Dm. Bulanin.

—— with Eklof, B. (2000) *The Social History of Imperial Russia, 1700–1917*, 2 vols. Boulder: Westview Press.

Polnoe sobranie zakonov Rossiiskoi imperii (1830), Sobranie pervoe, 45 vols. St. Petersburg: Vtoroe otdelenie Sobstvennoi e. v. kantseliarii.

Rediger, A. F. (1892) *Komplektovanie i ustroistvo vooruzhennoi sily*. St. Petersburg: S. N. Khudekov.

Riazanovsky, N. V. (1984) *A History of Russia*, 4th edn. New York and Oxford: Oxford University Press.

Rubinshtein, N. L. (1957) *Sel'skoe khoziaistvo Rossii vo vo vtoroi polovine XVIII v: Istoriko-ekonomicheskii ocherk*. Moscow: Gospolitizdat.

Sandberg, L. G. (1980) 'Soldier, Soldier, What Made You Grow so Tall? A Study of Height, Health, and Nutrition in Sweden, 1720–1881'. *Economy and History*, 23: 91–105.

—— and Steckel, R. H. (1987) 'Height and Economic History: The Swedish Case'. *Annals of Human Biology*, 14: 101–10.

Semevskii, V. I. (1882) 'Pozhalovanie naselennykh imenii pri imperatore Pavle'. *Russkaia musl'*, 12: 153–92.

——(1903) *Krest'iane v tsarstvovanie imperatritsy Ekateriny II*, 1: 2. St. Petersburg: M. M. Stasiulevich.

——(1906) *Pozhalovanie naselennykh imenii v tsarstvovanie Ekateriny II: ocherk po istorii chastnoi zemel'noi sobstvennosti v Rossii*. St. Petersburg: N. N. Kushnerov.

Sokoloff, K. L. (1995) 'The Heights of Americans in Three Centuries: Some Economic and Demographic Implications', in J. Komlos (ed.), *The Biological Standard of Living on Three Continents: Further Explorations in Anthropometric History*. Boulder: Westview Press, pp. 133–50.

Stoletie Voennogo ministerstva, 1802–1902 (1902), 3–4: 4. St. Petersburg: Berezhlivost.

Tikhonov, I. A. (1974) *Pomeshchich'i krest'iane v Rossii: Feodal'naia renta v XVII-nachale XVIII v*. Moscow: Nauka.

Troitskii, S. M. (1966) *Finansovaia politika russkogo absoliutizma v XVIII veke*. Moscow: Nauka.

Tsvetkov, M. A. (1957) *Izmenenie lesistosti Evropeiskoi Rossii s kontsa XVII stoletiia po 1914 g*. Moscow: Akademiia Nauk SSSR.

Urlanis, B. T. (1960) *Voiny i narodonaselenie Evropy: Liudskie poteri vooruzhennykh sil evropeiskikh stran v voinakh XVII-XX vekov. Istoriko-statisticheskoe issledovanie*. Moscow: Sotsekgiz.

US Bureau of Census, Statistical Abstract of the United States (1990), 110th edn. Washington DC, 842.

Vries, J. de (1984) *European Urbanization, 1500–1800*. London and Cambridge, MA: Methuen, pp. 39, 50, 76.

11 Maternal Mortality as an Indicator of the Standard of Living in Eighteenth- and Nineteenth-Century Slavonia

EUGENE A. HAMMEL AND AARON GULLICKSON

1. Introduction

The task of the social sciences was succinctly put by C. Wright Mills (1959): to show how the lives of little people were shaped by the passage of great events. This chapter is about how the life chances of peasant women, in their most primal experience, childbirth, were shaped by the blind and impersonal forces of institutional and market change.

Insights into the standard of living in the past may rely on different kinds of data. General historical accounts give a broad but often imprecise view. Detailed economic information is often unavailable or difficult to interpret. A third source is information on the plausible impacts of changes in standard of living on the demographic rates and health of populations. Where demographic data are more reliable and more specific than economic or social indicators, we may reverse the indicative arrow and obtain a closer insight into the conditions of life.

In this chapter we seek to combine all forms of evidence. General information on regional economic history is relatively abundant. Detailed economic information is sporadic and inspecific; good time series are especially rare. Demographic information is often reasonably good, indeed quite good if derived from family reconstitution of parish records. Thus our best practical approach to understanding the economic and social history of the region is through examination of the demographic record, a record of the results of levels and changes in the 'standard of living'.

Earlier research on the Croatian data was supported by grants from the National Science Foundation (Early Fertility and Mortality Change in Europe SBR-9120159) and the National Institute of Child Health and Development (Economic and Cultural Factors in Demographic Behavior R01 HD29512). Other support came from grants from the National Institute of Aging (Heritability of Longevity in Historical Peasant Europe (1R03 AG16074) and from the Center for the Economics and Demography of Aging, U.C. Berkeley. Grantors are not responsible for the outcomes of the research. Hammel is indebted to Dr Josip Kolanović and his colleagues at the State Archive of Croatia for access to the data, to Dr Jasna Čapo-Žmegač and her colleagues at the Institute for Ethnology and Folklore, Zagreb, for assembly of the data, to Ruth Deuel, Jasna Čapo-Žmegač, and Marcia Feitel for assistance in family reconstitution work, to Kenneth Wachter for statistical advice, and to participants at the Arild conference for their comments. None of these institutions or persons is responsible for any errors.

We briefly recapitulate and refine earlier analyses of demographic responses to economic and social stress in the population of Slavonia in a period of tumultuous structural change *c*.1750–1900 and then focus on maternal mortality (MM). Our motivation is to contribute to the long-running debate on the costs of industrialization and more broadly on the costs of development in general. Who pays the short-term costs of structural change? Did demographic indicators improve or worsen as feudalism relaxed, monetization increased, and capitalist agriculture struggled to develop? What role did traditional and imposed social structures and arrangements play in the risk of MM?

This chapter will show that:

- The strength of short-term Malthusian responses to food shortage, as proxied by grain prices, was high by contemporary standards and increased in times of crisis and over the long term.
- The physical stature of military recruits in the broader region diminished until about 1850, then rose.
- MM was often higher than that in other regions of the same historical period.
- The expectable physiological patterns appear: MM is most severe at the first birth, usually increases with age for each parity, and is higher for multiple births.
- MM increased episodically in periods of military mobilization when male labour was withdrawn from family farming and replaced by female labour. Military parishes show higher levels of MM than civil parishes.
- MM increased over time, commensurate with monetization, land shortage, general immiseration, diversion of male labour to wage earning, and decay of the joint family system that provided household economies of scale in labour.
- The rate of increase in MM was greater for new brides (primiparous females), who were traditionally at the bottom of the household hierarchy, than for more established wives.
- The infant mortality rate shows some of the same episodic structure and increase over time as MM, confirming the impacts of economic and social change on infants, perhaps through stress on their lactating mothers or declines in surrogate nursing.
- The mortality of mothers after the immediate postpartum period ('background mortality' (BM)) also shows some of these effects, suggesting their influence through maternal depletion, as well as through more rapidly acting disease and obstetrical difficulties (MM).

2. The Study Region

The region (see Map 11.1) is of interest because until 1848 part of it and until 1871 the remainder, were inhabited by a servile peasantry. It exhibited scarcely any modern economic development until after the First World War.

Slavonia is the triangle of land between the Drava and the Sava rivers, with its apex in Srem and its base at the Ilova River. It fell to the Ottomans in 1526, was

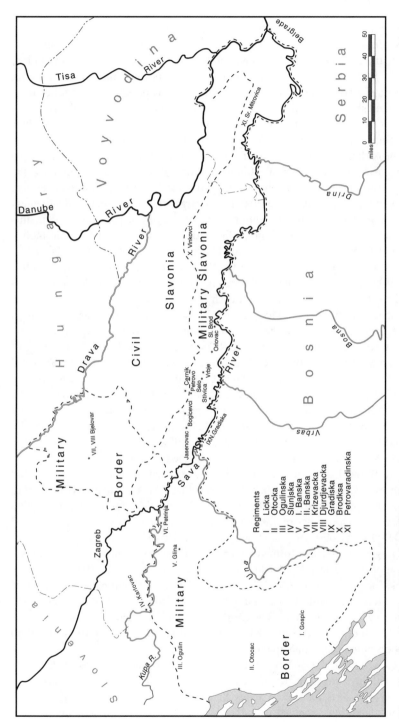

Map 11.1 Croatia, Slavonia, and the Military Border

reconquered by the Habsburgs 1683–90, and repopulated by both Catholic and Orthodox Slavs as well as some Hungarians, Slovaks, and Germans. Population growth on the new frontier was rapid, both by natural increase and migration. Households were relatively autarkic, and tended to become more complex over historical time. Economies of scale in such households provided some relief from emerging land shortage, even though agricultural intensification (other than through increased or more efficient labour inputs) was virtually nil (Hammel and Wachter 1996a,b; Hammel and Kohler 1997; Kohler and Hammel 2001).

From the earliest reoccupation, but formalized in 1745, the region along the Sava River was part of the Austrian Military Border, directly administered by the Habsburg crown, populated by peasants obliged to render perpetual military service. Ultimately, the Border system was abandoned, largely because of its ineffectiveness under late nineteenth-century conditions. Six of the seven parishes used in this analysis were military parishes. The Military Border experienced fourteen mobilizations in the period under consideration (1756, 1763–4, 1778–9, 1788–90, 1792, 1799, 1804–12, 1814–15, 1820–21, 1831, 1846, 1848, 1859, 1866). These mobilizations differed in intensity and duration, but we have virtually no detail on which local regiments were most impacted in each.[1]

The impact of military service on the Bordermen was very great. Even in peacetime, frontier duty could draw off an important fraction of adult manpower, from about 10% (Rothenberg 1966: 92; Roksandić 1988: vol. I, 24) to a third of militarily able men (under the so-called canton system). Although feudal taxes and obligations were less in the military than in the civil zone, there was a head tax, and obligatory labour demands were high. For example, in 1810 the six regiments west of Slavonia furnished additionally about 5 days/year from men who were not invalided (see below) (Roksandić 1988: vol. I, 24, 27, 122). The church imposed a tithe. Conditions were sometimes exacerbated by illegal exaction of labour for the benefit of Austrian officers. The burdens reached critical impact in wartime. In 1792–1801 the Border mustered over 100,000 men, almost double the usual number of about 55,000, and in those wars suffered 38,000 casualties (Rothenberg 1966: 93). During the hostilities with Turkey, 1787–91, the total population of parts of the Slavonian and Banat regions of the Border is reported to have plummeted from 343,000 to 57,000 persons (Vaniček 1875, III: 474). The Third Provisional Croatian Regiment that was formed under French command during the Napoleonic occupation of the western Border lost 80% of its personnel on the Russian front in 1812 (Roksandić 1988: vol. II, 292–3). In 1802, 54% of the adult male population of the six western regiments was classified as invalided; in 1810 it was still 42% (Roksandić 1988: vol. II, 30–1). The Military Border was decommissioned in 1871 and united with civil Croatia in 1881. Unlike civil serfs, military serfs incurred no amortization burden on emancipation.

The region north of the Border was part of civil Croatia, administered by Croatian feudatories of the Hungarian crown. Feudal tenure in civil Croatia was terminated in 1848, but former serfs incurred a heavy financial burden, required to amortize the value of the land they received over the next twenty years. (Implementation was delayed perhaps by a decade or two on account of administrative and legal confusion.) Many civil serfs were landless or almost landless and worked for wages on the latifundia that dominated the civil zone of Slavonia.

Agriculture in both zones was extensive, with an emphasis on stockbreeding, and there was little improvement in agricultural technology. Accommodation to land pressure was achieved by economies of scale in large, complex, joint households, which appear to have become more common after about 1750.[2] These were later undermined by increasing monetization and intra-household rivalry, especially after emancipation, as money taxes replaced feudal labour obligations, and also as the more personalistic elements of the Napoleonic and successor codes began to replace the more communally oriented customary law.

Peasants produced mostly for subsistence. However, as monetization progressed, and debt burdens mounted, peasants in the civil zone increasingly worked for wages to pay debts and taxes. In the military zone, men not on border patrol nor stationed away from home often worked for wages in repairing roads, hauling goods, and so on, in addition to their corvée obligations. In both zones, open range pig herding was a source of money income. Peasant plots were ultimately minuscule and in civil Slavonia coexisted with large estates. Attempts to introduce manufacturing (glass or silk spinning) mostly failed, in part because of the lack of transportation infrastructure. There was some commercial extraction of natural resources (charcoal, lumber, and potash) after 1870, especially in the former military zone. Until the mid-nineteenth century freight transport for export was by wagon over rough mountain roads to Adriatic ports. The Sava River was choked with debris and unsuitable for large-scale water transport. The first railroad reached Zagreb only in 1861; the line serving Slavonia from the Danube along the Sava to Zagreb and ultimately to Rijeka was not built until 1871. All these lines terminated in ports controlled by Austria or Hungary. Commercialization of agriculture on large properties was impeded by lack of transport, by competition from Austrian and Hungarian interests, and by the import of cheap foreign grain to regional markets (Vienna, Budapest) through Adriatic ports and thence via Austrian and Hungarian rail lines (Tomasevich 1955; Karaman 1972).

Both mortality and fertility were sensitive to fluctuations in grain prices (thus plausibly to grain supply), and that sensitivity peaked in the 1840s (Hammel 1985; Hammel and Galloway 2000*a,b*), as social and economic conditions worsened. Fertility control was known and practised from an early date and levels of fertility show evidence of decline perhaps as early as the 1760s–80s, plausibly in response to land shortage and parental desires to provide viable inheritance to their children (Hammel 1993; Hammel and Herrchen 1993; Hammel 1995). Abortion was practised at least from the 1760s, and appears to have increased in response to economic privation (Hammel and Galloway 2000*a*). The region, like neighbouring parts of Hungary, became politically notorious for its low fertility (Andorka and Balazs-Kovacs 1986; Vassary 1989). The military population, although subject to occupational risks until 1871, seems to have been in a more favourable economic position.[3]

3. Measures of Economic and Demographic Stress

We use several measures of stress, against a more general and less measurable historical background. The most direct economic measure is the fluctuation in grain prices in regional markets, reflecting supply-side climatic influences on harvests, since in a largely subsistence economy, little change in demand occurred.[4] This fluctuation is measured as annual (or monthly) differences from a moving average, and analysis focuses on changes in the elasticity of mortality and fertility with respect to grain prices, over time.[5] Increases in elasticity (positive for mortality, negative for fertility) are taken as indicators of increased stress. Information on the stature of persons is another potential measure of stress. Figure 11.1 shows the five-year lag sum elasticities of mortality and fertility with respect to grain prices for twenty-five Croatian parishes (including the seven used for reconstitution), and the heights of Hungarian soldiers, centred on their decade of birth (Komlos 1989: table 2.1).[6]

The sensitivity of mortality and fertility to price shocks rises in the post-Napoleonic period, reaches a peak in the 1840s, and then falls back by the early 1850s. Detailed analysis suggests increased sensitivity of mortality across a broad range of military parishes in times of military mobilization (Hammel and Galloway 2000*b*). The rise in the 1840s suggests increasing crisis for the peasants before civil emancipation in 1848 and liberalization of military tenure in 1850. The fallback suggests some amelioration thereafter when the fruits of the labour of civil serfs became their own with cancellation of feudal obligations, but before the burdens of amortization were felt. Similarly, military serfs may have invested more when they were assured of the heritability of tenure for their children. After 1848 there were fewer mobilizations, and cordon duty was less onerous, since the Bosnian–Serbian frontiers functioned more as customs borders than as military lines or anti-plague barriers.[7] The fallback may also reflect an improved disease environment after

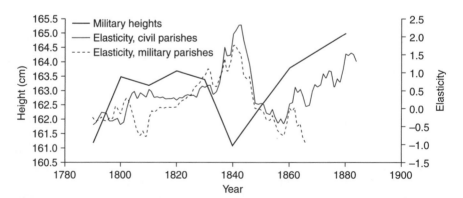

Figure 11.1 Five-year lag sum elasticities of mortality for civil and military Croatian parishes, and Hungarian military heights centred on decade of birth

cessation of the great cholera epidemics or simply a culling of the more vulnerable in the previous peak.

There is also some evidence of increasing crisis in the elasticities beyond the 1850s. After the amelioration of the early 1850s, the elasticity of mortality increases again for civil serfs. This increase may reflect the burden of amortization and pressure to produce or work for cash. There is a spike and then a fallback in the elasticity of mortality for military serfs. The elasticities of fertility ameliorate in the 1850s, and then intensify (negatively) for a time in the 1860s. It is notable that the elasticity of fertility in the same year as a price shock (and indeed with a monthly lag commensurate with the second trimester of pregnancy) comes to dominate the fertility response, suggesting that abortion became more frequent as a means of fertility control. Increased recourse to abortion (for which the region was notorious in medical, legal, and ecclesiastical circles) may indicate increased economic pressure to control births and may have had deleterious health effects.[8]

There are no height data on Croatian military recruits; as an approximation we examine here information from Komlos' study of Hungarian recruits (1989), which we might use as a rough guide to regional conditions. The heights of recruits, shown by the decade of their birth, descend to a low point at about the same time as the peaking of elasticities of mortality and fertility with respect to price shocks. These minimal adult heights may reflect malnutrition in childhood and also retarded development *in utero* and during infancy; that is, they may reflect the nutritional status of the mothers. However, there is no indication in these data (on Hungarians) that this nutritional crisis deepened or even continued much beyond the 1850s. Instead, it may reflect economic and social conditions leading to the Revolution of 1848.

We should also take into account changes in family composition of households. Multiple family households seem relatively rare in the earliest censuses of 1698 and 1702. A large proportion of households at that time was of new in-migrants, and these were predominantly nuclear in structure.[9] Reliable data on household size and composition are rare, and all such data are difficult to interpret. Nevertheless, complex households appear to increase to the mid-nineteenth century and then decline. We conjecture that increases in size and complexity were an adaptation to an increasing scarcity of land that did not allow subdivision of holdings into viable plots for heirs. Economies of scale were generated in larger and more complex households, since adult labour inputs could be specialized. Households could continue to be autarkic and generalist, as they appear to be in the earliest census (Hammel and Kohler 1997).[10] The general social and economic history literature for Croatia is replete with discussions of the collapse of the 'joint household system' or *zadruga* in the last half of the nineteenth century. As noted, firm, consistent, and comparable data, especially in time series are hard to find, and samples are often small. Nevertheless, we cite as an example Čapo-Žmegač's finding (1990) of an increase in the proportion of multiple-family households on the estate of Cernik (one of our seven reconstituted parishes) in the first part of the nineteenth century, and a decline in that proportion in the second half.

Many authors have deplored the decline of the *zadruga*, citing as evidence instances of the division and dissolution of households. In this they ignore the fact that, as epiphenomenona of an agnatic, patrivirilocal residence pattern, such households normally dissolved, only to be reconstituted in later generations.[11] Notwithstanding this criticism, the frequency of occurrence of such households did decline, and their corporacy was diminished. Especially important was the growing frequency of 'secret divisions' (*tajne diobe*), in which peasants divided their holdings without reporting the often prohibited change. Contemporary political debate and legislation focused intensely on mechanisms for preserving the family system, traditional inheritance practices, and a guaranteed minimal size of homestead.[12]

It is important to note the social position of women in these 'patriarchal' households. The senior wife, usually the wife of the eldest competent male, thus in principle the 'father's wife' or 'elder brother's wife', managed the labour of co-resident women, and her domination of them and of her sons was an important dynamic. Women born into the household ordinarily left it on marriage.[13] Women marrying into the household were strangers to it and typically viewed as the sources of conflict and ultimate fission. The relations between mothers-in-law and daughters-in-law, and between brothers' wives, were classically difficult. Women worked hard, often in field labour and especially when men were absent. The most recent brides were at the bottom of the hierarchy. Their husbands were usually junior males who, as younger men, were most likely to be called away for military duties.

4. Data

The core of this analysis uses reconstituted records of baptisms, marriages, and burials from seven contiguous parishes of central Slavonia, in the region of Cernik–Nova Gradiška (see Map 11.1). Cernik was a civil parish, the others, including neighbouring Nova Gradiška, were military. Cernik was a modest market town, Nova Gradiška until 1871 the headquarters of the Gradiška regiment, 3 km from Cernik. This analysis is based only on the Catholic population; suitable records for the Orthodox population, constituting about a quarter of the total, were not recoverable, and the numbers of Jews and Protestants were minimal. No Muslims remained after 1691.[14]

The reconstitutions are based on 23,307 marriages 1717–1864, 112,181 baptisms 1714–1898, and 94,077 burials 1717–1898.[15] The seven parishes enter and leave the dataset at different times, but often only because of the division of large parishes into smaller ones. Data availability ceases for different kinds of records at somewhat different times in different parishes. These characteristics pose problems of potential compositional effects for the analysis. The parish data are of good quality, especially after 1760. Table 11.1 shows the pattern of data availability over time. Other analyses of these and more general demographic data from the region suggest that the parishes were broadly similar.

Table 11.1 Data availability by parish and date

Parish	Marriages		Baptisms		Burial	
	Start	End	Start	End	Start	End
Bogičevci	1790	1857	1789	1897	1789	1897
Cernik	1717	1864	1714	1898	1717	1898
Nova Gradiška	1756	1857	1756	1898	1756	1898
Oriovac	1726	1857	1724	1857	1726	1891
Petrovo Selo	1766	1857	1766	1857	1766	1857
Štivica	1790	1857	1789	1857	1789	1857
Vrbje	1790	1857	1789	1898	1789	1898
Overall	1717	1864	1789	1898	1717	1898

In this analysis we use the subset of data for mothers with extant first marriage records: 13,202 marriages, 56,546 baptisms in those marriages, 8,737 baptisms of the mothers, and 7,119 burials of mothers. The 56,546 birthings in these 13,202 reproductive histories form the units of observation in the analysis. The mean age of mothers at parturition was 30.7. The mean birth interval was 2.6 years. Out of the total parturitions 2.6% were multiple births. The median year of birthing was 1819; the mean was 1817.

Within sixty days of these births 417 mothers died, yielding a crude 'rate' of MM of 0.0074; this is a gross rate, not taking into account estimates of background mortality (BM) unrelated to pregnancy.[16] The age of a woman at each birth was reckoned from the calendrical dates of that birth and her marriage and her age at marriage. Age at marriage was reckoned from the dates of wife's baptism and marriage where available, else calculated from the dates of marriage and death and reported age at death, if known. For the remaining women, age at marriage was imputed from the mean age of women of known age.

5. Maternal Mortality

In western countries until quite recently MM was common and until perhaps the mid-nineteenth century was often at levels similar to those in modern Less Developed Countries (LDCs).[17] While the estimation of MM has serious problems (see below), its use as an indicator of the level of well-being and an insight into family structure and gender relations is generally accepted. Because it is, like other aspects of women's reproductive health, a central topic of intellectual and practical concern, because it is so prominent in the European past and because its diminution occurred only in the latest stages of what might loosely be called modernization, it is an inviting topic for historical analysis, and especially for a volume on the standard of living in the past. Figure 11.2 shows maternal deaths per live birth over varying spans of time from England, Germany, Sweden, and from the Slavonian data.

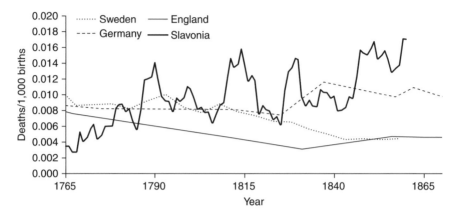

Figure 11.2   Historical maternal mortality rates

The trend is flat or downward overall in England, Sweden, and Germany (with a short increase in Germany after 1825); thus while MM was steady or declining in those countries, it was increasing in Slavonia until after the 1860s. Peak levels of MM in Slavonia equalled or exceeded those in most other locales.

5.1   Definitions of MM

Clinically and broadly defined, maternal death is death that occurs in consequence of pregnancy. In practice and by modern internationally agreed definition, maternal deaths are deaths occurring during pregnancy or within some established span of time after parturition (see the discussion in Andersson *et al.* 2000). Current international definitions use a 42-day time span. Demographic historians have variously used thirty, forty-two, and sixty days (Wrigley *et al.* 1997: 309, n.144).

Definitions of MM based on elapsed time since giving birth of course omit pregnancy-related deaths prior to that point (e.g. from eclampsia, miscarriage, abortion, etc.). Selection of different spans may also have different consequences. The risk of mortality is highest at the termination of pregnancy, then declines rapidly.[18] A summary of the excellent Swedish data (Wrigley *et al.* 1997: table 6.28), following Schofield (1986), shows that 29% of maternal deaths after a live or stillbirth occurred on the day of birth (day 0), 19% in days 1–3, and 11% in days 4–6. Ninety-two per cent of these deaths had occurred by thirty days, 96% by forty-two days, and 98% by sixty days. Recalculated as daily risks, all categories show dramatic decline from birth to day 2, then a slower decline out to day 60 (see Figure 11.3). The risk of death following a stillbirth is much higher than that following a live birth (Wrigley *et al.* 1997: 310) and these deaths occur rapidly. Andersson *et al.* (2000) show that having had a previous stillbirth is an important risk factor in subsequent births; thus women with difficulties in parturition are at special risk.[19] Illegitimate births are initially the next riskiest, perhaps reflecting an

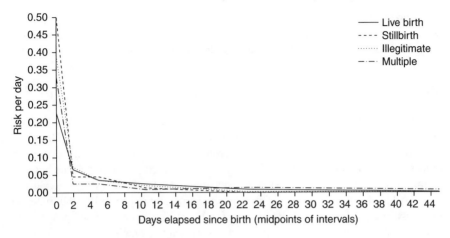

Figure 11.3 Risk per day of maternal death, by category

inferior physical condition of mothers bearing children out of wedlock, or poor care before, during, and after birthing. Maternal deaths associated with multiple births are the next riskiest.

5.2 The two foci of MM analysis

Analyses of historical MM have focused on two issues: (1) estimating the level, and (2) searching for correlates. Since most determinations of MM are based on elapsed time since birth, the accuracy and completeness of baptismal registration are essential, as noted. Some crosschecks are available from other data sources. In the reconstitution data, there were 417 maternal deaths within sixty days of 56,546 parturitions (see above). In 350 burial records, there are notations suggesting childbirth issues.[20] Of these only 311 are the deaths of adults; neonates also die in childbirth.[21] The overall rate of 0.0074 maternal deaths per live birth approaches the high end of the range calculated by Schofield (1986: 238) for Sweden 1756–1860 (maximum 0.011), is higher than any of the analogous rates from thirteen English parishes except in the period 1650–99 (maximum 0.041), approaches the peak German rates given by Imhof (1986: 125) for 1810–99 (maximum 0.010) and the German rates reported by Knodel 1825–99 (0.010–0.012) (1986). The Slavonian peak rates, as noted, are even higher.

In the census of 1910 data given for all of Croatia 1906–10 show MM per live birth closely fluctuating around 0.005 (Croatia 1905: table III, 56). The census distinguishes *babinje* (*Wochenbett*, childbed) at 0.004, *bolesti rodila* (*Geburtskrankheiten*, diseases of birthing) at 0.0007, and *babinja groznica* (*Kindbettfieber*, childbed fever) at 0.0002. The first category accounts for 81% of the sum of these, the second for 14%, and the last for 5%. These categories scale well to our expectations of the timing of MM of different kinds: childbed deaths from direct obstetrical causes occurring rapidly, indirect deaths more slowly, and deaths from infection perhaps slowest. The overall rate estimated for historical Slavonia is about double that reported for Croatia as a whole 1906–10.[22]

5.3 Stillbirths

Since the rate of MM per stillbirth is much greater than that for live births, the true rate of MM cannot be accurately estimated from live births alone. However, available data on stillbirth rates for Slavonia and environs are quite uncertain, reflecting not only differences in obstetrical practice across time and space but also variation in the propensity to baptize (and thus record as live births) neonates *in extremis* (Table 11.2). Because of this, we make no attempt to inflate the maternal mortality rate per live birth on the basis of either stillbirths or assumed proportions of parturients undelivered. In any case, our focus is not so much on estimation of the rate as on the correlates.

5.4 Multiple births

It is clear from the literature that parturients are at greater risk of death in a multiple than in a single birth. We mark confinements as multiple if more than one baptism occurs with the same mother on the same date. In analysis it is the birthing, not the infant, which is the event of interest. Note that parity counts in this analysis are counts of birthings, not of children born.

5.5 Background mortality

While the majority of deaths within a short time of parturition can be expected to be direct obstetric deaths, the proportion that is will vary according to the occurrence of

Table 11.2   Stillbirth rates

Location	
Military Border 1830–47	0.0074
Croatia 1874–80	0.0106
Croatia 1881–90	0.0131
Croatia 1891–1900	0.0188
Croatia 1901–10	0.0222
Croatia 1906–10	0.0222
Požega County 1906–10	0.0179
Nova Gradiška 1910	0.0087
Five Swedish parishes	0.0298

Source: Schofield 1986: table 9.2.

epidemic disease and the efficacy of obstetrical techniques. Our approach in graphical analysis is to subtract the estimated risk of BM from that of mortality within the critical time period, to obtain an estimate of net MM. In regression analysis we use background mortality centred on the year of birth as a predictor of maternal death so that estimates of the effects of other predictors are effectively of their influence on net MM.

There are several ways to estimate BM. Wrigley *et al.* (1997: 312 *ff.*) use the mortality rate of husbands in the same critical period. Indeed, deducing the MM rate by comparing male to female mortality has been a common practice (see for example Henry 1987). However, where there are other correlated components to the gender difference, MM will be mis-estimated. For example, where tuberculosis was an important cause of death, female survivorship in the eighteenth–nineteenth centuries was often markedly worse than that of men. Cortes-Majo *et al.* (1990) have pointed to this specifically; more general discussions of gender differences are found in Ginsberg (1989) and Hammel *et al.* (1983). The numbers of males and females with tuberculosis as the reported cause of death in the Slavonian data are 1,640 and 1,622, respectively, almost equal. By contrast, the numbers of males and females suffering some form of violent death (drowning, kicks by horses, falls from trees, murder, gunshot, etc.) were 190 and 91, respectively. Thus, using males for BM would result in an underestimate of MM.

We have estimated BM, by calendar year and age of mother, with a risk period from 61 to 730 days after giving birth and for nulliparous women, within two years of marriage. Two years is somewhat shorter than the mean birth interval (2.6 years).[23]

6. Analysis

We focus on individual women in order to examine the correlates of individual cases. The unit of analysis is a birthing to a specific mother. 'Mother' means a particular woman in her first marriage, and 'birthing' means one of a series of birthings to that mother, in that marriage. At each such birthing, a mother has a known or estimated age, a known parity, and we know whether either she or her current husband is in a first or later marriage.[24] The parish, date of birth, date of marriage, and other ancillary data are also known. The outcome variable is whether or not the mother died within sixty days of the index birth. The tool employed is logistic regression.[25] We follow a parallel approach in analysing background mortality, that is, deaths to parturient women 61–730 days after birthing.

6.1 Risk factors

Different plausible factors may account for differences in MM risk. We have some expectations from the literature and earlier work on this region.

1. Some factors are presumably biological, namely parity, age, multiple birthing, and prior stillbirths. Generally speaking, the risk of death in childbirth is highest at the first parity, falls, and then climbs at successive parities, although it may fall off

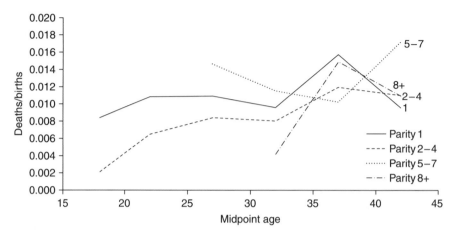

Figure 11.4   Maternal mortality by age and parity, Slavonian data

on account of selection effects, the more robust women surviving to have the higher order births. The risk tends to increase with age at each parity. Figure 11.4 shows data from the Slavonian parishes. Risk in the Slavonian data rises with age at parity 1 except for the rare cases of women having a first birth past age 37 (where numbers are minuscule). Risk also rises with age at parities 2–4. Risk declines with age up to age 37 for parities 5–7, then rises; the decline is anomalous. Risk rises with age for parities over 7, then falls at the end, but the estimates are based on rather small numbers. Thus, the general expectations are more or less confirmed where data are sufficiently dense. At any age, risk is usually highest for parity 1, then lowest at parity 2–4, then increasing with parity except for selection effects. At any parity, risk tends to increase with age, although this trend exhibits some irregularities. These are also the same patterns described by Knodel (1986: table 7) for historical German data.

2. An interesting question is whether the risk of death is increased by short birth intervals. It is difficult to examine it without adequate pregnancy histories. For example, under a maternal depletion hypothesis we might expect a negative relationship between mortality and the length of the previous interval or of the mean interval over all previous births. However, if intervals are lengthened by unknown stillbirths or abortions that may traumatize the mother, or if conception delay is lengthened by ill health, this relationship could be obscured or even reversed. Therefore we expect that risk will be lower where the lifetime average birth interval is long, but higher where the immediately preceding interval is long.[26]

3. Some ecological factors may enter. Some parishes are closer to the Sava River and thus to swamps that were malarial until quite late in the nineteenth century. Six of the seven parishes were military. Earlier work leads us to anticipate that civil parishes became more sensitive to economic fluctuation and were under greater economic stress before emancipation in 1848, with some amelioration thereafter. However, a greater reactivity to economic conditions may have occurred while

general mortality levels were declining. The great cholera epidemics of the 1830s had ceased by then, and by the later decades of the century, swamps were being drained, so that endemic malaria was less of a problem.[27] As noted, these two trends may not be in conflict; that is, it is possible that overall mortality was declining while at the same time mortality was becoming more sensitive to short-term economic changes. The proportion constituted by maternal deaths out of all deaths of married women increased after 1850. It is not attributable to the intrusion of ill-prepared physicians into the birthing process (cf. Högberg and Broström 1986), since we do not have any evidence of the entrance of physicians or of the use of lying-in hospitals in this area.

4. A likely effect of increased labour demands brought about by monetization and pressures to produce cash, could have been increased workloads for women. Female workloads could also have been induced by episodic withdrawal of male labour, especially in the military parishes, during periods of mobilization. Since the organization of female labour in joint households was hierarchical, and the youngest brides traditionally did the hardest work, we might expect that younger women would show the strongest evidence of sensitivity to such labour demands. We will show that mortality at first parity increased faster than mortality at higher parities.

6.2 Compositional problems

There are several kinds of potential compositional problems (see Section 4, Table 11.1).

- Marriages begin at the latest in the seven parishes (B, C, G, O, P, S, V)[28] in 1790, end in six in 1857, and in one in 1864.
- Baptisms are recorded in all seven parishes from before 1790 to 1857 in seven parishes but beyond 1857 only in four (B, C, G, and V).
- Burials are recorded in all seven parishes from before 1790 to 1857 in seven parishes but beyond 1857–1891 in one (O) and to 1898–99 in four (B, C, G, and V).

From this it can be seen that it is all right to start analysis in 1790 (by which time data quality is already excellent), but not clear where to end it. Indeed, a case can be made that it is all right to start analysis in any parish as soon as the data in it seem reliable, since overall results would be affected over time only by inter-parish compositional differences, which could be controlled. After 1857 there are no more marriages, with the result that lower order parities gradually disappear from analysis, since the stock of marriages ages after 1857. Mortality should drop for several years since there were no new first births (which are the riskiest), but gradually mortality might rise, as more and more birth were at successively higher and somewhat riskier parities and as women aged. We solve this problem by truncating graphical analysis in 1860, before compositional change in the parity structure becomes severe, or by controlling for parity in the regression analysis.[29]

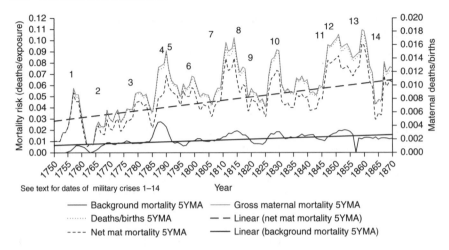

See text for dates of military crises 1–14

—— Background mortality 5YMA   —— Gross maternal mortality 5YMA

········ Deaths/births 5YMA   − − Linear (net mat mortality 5YMA)

‒ ‒ ‒ ‒ Net mat mortality 5YMA   —— Linear (background mortality 5YMA)

Figure 11.5   Gross maternal, background, and net maternal risk and probability of dying in childbirth, by year, five-year moving averages for all parities

6.3   Graphical analysis

Here, as elsewhere, risk is defined as the total number of deaths in a year (maternal or background) divided by person-years of exposure. Figure 11.5 shows five-year moving averages of (gross) MM risk, BM risk, net maternal mortality risk, and the probability of dying in childbirth (for comparison with the standard reporting measure) from the 1750s to the 1860s.[30] The common measure of maternal deaths per birth (or per *n* births) tracks gross MM well. Net MM, that is, gross MM minus BM, also tracks gross MM well, differing only where there are marked fluctuations in the background.

Figure 11.6 shows net MM separately at parity 1 versus higher order births, truncating parity 1 data in 1860 to avoid the results of the cessation of marriage recording in 1857, but continuing higher order parities to 1870. The peaks of mortality for the two parity series are similar but not identical. The long-term increase in net maternal mortality at parity 1 is greater than for higher order births. This difference may offer a critical insight into explanatory scenarios. If MM is increased by increased labour demands on women, especially as economies of scale diminished with the decline of the joint household system, the data suggest that it was the youngest wives that bore the brunt of these demands. They were at the bottom of the household hierarchy, with few political allies. Their husbands were the youngest of a set of brothers, thus themselves political juniors, and would have been the most likely to be called up for military service, thus more likely to be absent. These young wives would have been asked to do most of the work. It is their mortality that increases most sharply over the long-run.

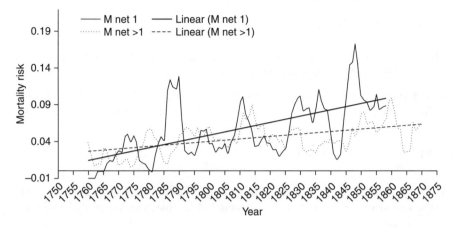

Figure 11.6 Net maternal mortality at parities 1 and > 1, five-year moving averages

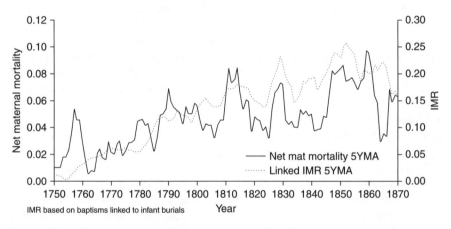

Figure 11.7 Net maternal mortality and infant mortality, five-year moving averages

6.4 Confirmatory evidence in infant mortality

We examine infant mortality in Figure 11.7 to detect any similarities to MM. Infant mortality increases over the time period, at about the same rate as net MM. There is also a rough coincidence of peaks and troughs for net maternal and infant mortality after about 1780. Both of these outcomes suggest that many of the social and economic factors affecting mothers also affected their infants. Indeed, the deaths of mothers may have led directly to the deaths of nursing infants, especially as the joint family system decayed and surrogate nursing became more difficult, but this effect would have been small, since relatively few mothers died, compared to infants.

7. Regression Analysis

The unit of analysis in the logistic regression model[31] is the individual birthing by a mother. We distinguish two kinds of outcome:

- Maternal death, with the outcome scored 1 for death within sixty days, else 0.
- Background death, with the outcome scored 1 for death within 61–730 days, else 0, but women who died within sixty days were excluded.

Independent variables are, depending on the model:

- Age.
- Parity (dummies, grouped with parity group 2–4 omitted since it has expectably the lowest mortality: 1, 5–7, 8+, coded 1 if the parity of the birth falls in any group, else 0).
- Parish (dummies, with Cernik, the civil parish, omitted, coded 1 if the birth was in each parish, else 0).
- The preceding birth interval, or for parity 1, the interval from marriage.
- The mean lifetime birth interval.
- Crisis period (the occurrence of any of the crises described above, thus coded 1 for a crisis period, else 0). Multi-year crises were specified to include all of the relevant years. Single-year crises were coded to include the year of the crisis and the following year, since mobilization late in a year would imply absence of males early in the next.
- Multiple birth (coded 1 if the birth was a multiple birth, else 0).
- Year (calendar year of the birth minus 1815). Effectively, this is the influence of calendar year on higher order births; see below.
- Parity1*year (interaction of Parity 1 and Year, thus the effect of calendar year on parity 1 births only).
- BM (sometimes the variable of interest, also a covariate where MM is the dependent variable). Using this as a predictor effectively turns analysis into that of net MM.[32]

Table 11.3 shows the resulting estimates and corresponding probability values.[33] Because we have prior reason to anticipate the direction of effect of each of the variables, from theory or from broader data, we accept as significant those results for which the two-tailed probability is less than 0.10, thus the one-tailed alpha level is 0.05. We include physiological factors in the model but do not test them separately, given the space constraints for this chapter. We test for the occurrence of any of the military or other crises listed earlier but do not test them separately, for the same reasons.

In Table 11.3 are three sets of columns. The first lists the covariates. The second gives results for MM (0–60 days), and the third for BM (61–730 days). Readers should use Table 11.3 to make their own judgements about the direction and significance of effect of variables.

Table 11.3 Results of logistic regression

Covariates	Death within 60 days of birth		Death between 60 days and 2 years of birth	
	Effect	Standard error	Effect	Standard error
Intercept	−5.046***	0.337	−3.783***	0.194
Age	0.012	0.009	0.022***	0.006
Parity				
Parity 1	0.597**	0.130	0.064	0.087
Parity 2–4 (reference)	—	—	—	—
Parity 5–7	−0.081	0.145	−0.011	0.082
Parity 8+	−0.067	0.224	−0.126	0.129
Previous birth interval	0.226***	0.032	0.200***	0.021
Lifetime mean birth interval	−0.626***	0.081	−0.670***	0.053
Number of births				
Single birth (reference)	—	—	—	—
Multiple	0.709***	0.205	0.076	0.160
Background mortality	0.018*	0.008	—	—
Parish				
Parish B	0.717***	0.211	0.432**	0.155
Parish C (civil, reference)	—	—	—	—
Parish G	−0.021	0.153	0.363***	0.088
Parish O	0.330	0.174†	0.185	0.116
Parish P	0.297*	0.150	0.509***	0.091
Parish S	0.245	0.213	0.180	0.145
Parish V	0.142	0.186	0.323**	0.114
Crisis period				
No crisis (reference)	—	—	—	—
Military crisis	0.314**	0.106	0.005	0.066
Year (origin = 1815)	0.004*	0.002	0.003*	0.001
Parity 1*Year	0.009*	0.004	0.003	0.003
Number of birthings	56,546	56,129		
Number of deaths to mothers	417	1,124		
DF	56,528		56,112	
Deviance	4761.4		10,739	
Model χ^2	163.9		278	
DF χ^2	17		16	

$p < 0.1$; * $p < 0.05$; ** $p < 0.01$; *** $p < 0.001$; p-values based on two-sided tests.

Notes: 1815 is the median year of birthings. The effect of parity 1 is the effect in 1815. The effect of parity 1*Year is the effect of the year difference from 1815 on parity 1 births.

7.1 Discussion

The stability of nominal data linkage results pursued by different methods and different persons in the history of this project, and the richness of redundancy in the records, give us some confidence that the reconstitution is very close to the actual interpersonal and inter-event connections of the time. Potential truncation biases consequent on the 'deathbed migration' of parturient women, whose deaths would escape our notice, are probably small, since alternative analysis taking such bias into account by demanding firm evidence of survival, gave very similar results (not shown here). Potential biases from compositional effects in changes in the parish constitution of the dataset or shifts in the parity distribution as the marriage stock aged after 1857 have been taken into account either by censoring the observations appropriately or by controlling for place and parity.

It is important to note that the graphical presentations distinguish between net and gross MM and BM, the first being the second minus the third. Similarly, the use of BM as a predictor of MM means that the results for other variables pertain directly to net MM, namely to the residual variance in MM after accounting for correlation with BM. The data show that

- Patterns of MM and BM show generally expectable effects of age, parity, and multiple births.
- MM is highest at parity 1, lowest at parities 2–4, sometimes higher at parities 5–7, but falling at parities over 8, with plausible selection effects emerging in the parity 5–7 range.
- MM and BM increase with age, given parity.
- The risk of MM and BM is higher for multiple births.
- The risk of MM and BM is higher if the lifetime mean birth interval for mothers is short.
- The risk of MM and BM is higher if the immediately previous birth interval is long.
- MM and BM increase over time, the former more than the latter.
- MM but not BM increases during episodes of mobilization of male labour for military purposes, taken jointly. If examined singly, not all crises have a significant effect, but all are in the expected direction (not shown here).
- Military parishes usually show higher MM and BM than the civil parish.
- Fluctuations and trends in MM and BM are roughly commensurate with other indicators of demographic stress, such as the elasticity of mortality and fertility with respect to grain prices, and to some extent with stunting in the adult stature of some soldiers of the region.
- MM, BM, and to some extent vulnerability as indicated by elasticities of mortality and fertility, continue to increase after major military mobilizations had ceased but in a period of increasing monetization, amortization burden for civil serfs, and decay of the joint family system.
- MM at parity 1 increases more steeply than MM at other parities over historical time. The episodic increases at parity 1 are proportionally greater than at later parities.
- Infant mortality follows the same trend of long-term increase in MM and BM, and to some extent echoes the episodic peaks.

The use of female mortality beyond the traditionally critical sixty-day period for estimation of BM, rather than the use of male mortality within the sixty-day period, suggests that narrow estimation of MM, 'death in childbirth', far from exhausts the assessment of the burdens of childbirth on women. That we find important physiological and socio-economic correlates of BM as well as of MM is of particular interest.

That the physiological variables of age and parity show generally expectable patterns with respect to MM and BM gives us further confidence in the reliability of the data. Parity effects other than selection effects, however, are seldom significant in BM. Risk is expectably increased by multiple births. The effects of the mean birth interval, negatively associated with MM and BM, suggest that maternal depletion, as well as obstetrical difficulties and post-partum sepsis may have played an important role in MM overall. The positive associations between length of the immediately previous interval and MM or BM suggest that difficulty in bringing a pregnancy to successful termination in a live birth, with unfavourable implications for the following pregnancy, may play a role. The data do not permit us to support this inference directly with information on spontaneous abortions, stillbirths, or the consequences of intentional abortion.

The long-term increase of MM and BM parallels some specific, and some general indicators of social and economic stress. The elasticities of mortality and fertility with respect to grain prices, hence the vulnerability of the population to short-term food crises, show something of the same trend, although it is raggedly interrupted after 1850 and shows differences between civil and military parishes. Evidence of nutritional insufficiency in the declining stature of military recruits in neighbouring Hungary follows a parallel trend but only up to 1850. Infant mortality shows the same increasing trend as MM and BM, possibly independently, but possibly affected directly by the deaths of mothers, inability to lactate, and losses of household economies of scale for surrogate nursing. At a more general level, there were changes in social and economic structures. The feudal system collapsed; whatever its burdens, its customary protections also collapsed, and for civil serfs there was an added burden of amortization. Military obligations lessened after the Napoleonic wars, and there were few significant effects of mobilizations on MM and BM thereafter; nevertheless MM and BM did increase after 1815. The need for cash increased over time, especially as feudal dues were increasingly converted to monetary taxes and as amortization payments had to be met. The joint family system, which afforded some economies of scale, permitted self-sufficiency, and lowered the need for cash decayed rapidly, in the civil zone and in the military zone after decommissioning. All of these trends parallel the long-term increase of MM and BM.

The episodic peaks in MM are of particular interest. Graphical presentation shows a reasonable match between such peaks and periods of military mobilization (see Figure 11.5). The regressions show that MM is positively correlated with such mobilizations in general, although not always with any particular mobilization. That coincidence is not apparent for BM. We would expect that exogenous disease effects would become more important after the sixty-day cut-off for MM, while direct obstetrical deaths would predominate in the first day or so of the sixty-day span, with puerperal disease emerging thereafter, then deaths from other causes but exacerbated by parturition. Since the general crisis effect and many of the individual crises effects are strong for MM but not for BM, we infer that the effect of crisis was felt predominantly on factors directly related to parturition, and that disease introduced by soldiers returning home was of lesser consequence. Since it was the absence of males, rather than their presence that seems operative, our attention focuses on the withdrawal of male labour from the household, on the shift of labour burden to women, some of whom were pregnant, parturient, or nursing, others of whom would otherwise have been able to assume the ordinary labour burdens of the former. Losses of household economies of scale as the joint family system decayed would have exacerbated these matters. The secular trend towards wage labour, drawing men away from the family farm, would have increased these effects over time.[34]

That women at parity 1 were at higher risk may not be entirely a physiological phenomenon but may reflect the inferior position and greater labour demands on new brides, as well as the juniority and probably more frequent absence of their husbands. It is noteworthy that the secular increase in mortality occurs at a higher rate at parity 1 than at later parities. Further, the episodic increase at times of military mobilization is generally greater at parity 1 than at later parities.

8. Conclusion

In this analysis we have applied graphical techniques and logistic regression to try to understand the correlates of MM in eighteenth- and nineteenth-century Slavonia, defining gross MM as death occurring within sixty days of a birth, BM as death occurring 61–730 days after a birth, and net MM as the difference between these. MM was high by the standards of the time and probably higher than MM in the rest of Croatia in the early twentieth century.

Physiological factors such as age, parity, multiple birthing, and birth intervals show expectable results. These results increase our confidence in the reliability of the data derived from family reconstitution. However, our interest is mostly in social and economic factors. The data show that in this region, peripheral to emerging centres of industrialization and political power, competing interests in Austria and Hungary limited economic development. Globalization of world grain markets, competition from cheap foreign grain, and inferior local transportation infrastructure were important constraints on such development. Macro-level social structures were slow to change, the emancipation of civil serfs occurring in 1848 but of military serfs only in 1871.

Maternal mortality as customarily defined, within sixty days of birth, was as high as or higher than that in other, contemporary European countries, indeed higher than most historical levels except those in seventeenth-century England. Rapid changes in socio-economic conditions—the collapse of serfdom and imposition of money taxes and amortization burdens, increasing monetization, and the decay of the joint family system—appear to have exacerbated MM, as well as other indicators of demographic vulnerability such as responses to food supply and the infant mortality rate.

Periods of military mobilization also exacerbated MM. Some of these effects were felt not only within sixty days of birthing but also extend out two years, suggesting that nursing, as well as parturient mothers were made more vulnerable by these changes. Nevertheless, crisis effects are stronger for MM than for BM, suggesting that it was the absence of males that was determinative.

The most plausible general hypothesis to explain these changes is that withdrawal of male labour from family subsistence farming resulted in extra burdens of heavy labour imposed on females, some of whom were pregnant or nursing. Such withdrawal of male labour would have occurred during military mobilizations and would have been worsened by increased participation in wage labour to meet the growing need for cash. Similar exacerbation would have resulted from losses in economies of scale, especially in the availability of labour by non-pregnant or non-parturient females, as the joint household system decayed. These hypotheses are supported at the micro-level by evidence that the most socially vulnerable of women, brides new to the household, had higher levels of mortality and a more rapid increase in that mortality overtime.

In general, no part of this historical borderland between Europe and Asia, between the Habsburgs and the Turks, between Christianity and Islam, between feudalism and capitalism, tells a pretty story. In this account with general sources sharpened by demographic analysis, we see that the burdens of change fell more heavily on the peasant than on the lord, on the poor than on the rich, on women than on men, and on the most vulnerable women in particular. That was the price of progress, in a transformation that indeed ultimately left everyone better off, even if out-migration was until 1945 the safety valve that may have permitted re-balancing of land and labour. It is ironic that the same factors of economic globalization, development of cheap transportation, and the collapse of ancient social systems leading to the difficulties here depicted, also facilitated their solution, as the victims of structural change escaped to the New World.

Some of these conclusions could be reached from a reading of the general economic, social, and ethnographic history of the region. Others could not be. Nowhere in that history would we have seen that MM increased over time, or that it bore more heavily on the youngest wives. Nowhere would we have seen that the episodic and secularly increasing diversion of male labour from family farming impacted wives, or that losses of household economies of scale increased the labour burden of women and diminished their sources of support as mothers. The demographic evidence here presented not only reinforces that from the broad historical sources, it adds a critical and often more penetrating insight into the standard of living and its changes. The ghost of the Reverend Malthus serves us well.

Notes

1. The standard sources (Hietzinger 1817, 1820; Vaniček 1875; Rothenberg 1960, 1966) are often inspecific about which regimental regions of the Border were most directly involved. However, in these major crises, most may have been.

2. Such households are referred to in the ethnographic and historical literature (but not in peasant discourse) by the term *zadruga* (loosely, 'co-operative'). They are typically agnatically defined, with father and married sons, or married brothers, or even cousins. They were perhaps most developed in the Military Border of Croatia, encouraged and codified by the Austrians as a way to ensure household survival while some manpower was drawn off for military purposes; their mean size in the six western regiments was about eleven persons (Roksandić 1988: vol. I, 35). (For a review of issues concerning such households, see Tomasevich 1955: 178 *ff.*; Hammel 1968; Hammel 1972, 1977, 1980*a,b*, 1984; Todorova 1993; Čapo-Žmegač 1996.) Equally important in the present context was the effect of such households or their near analogs in households of closely related agnatic kin that were located in close propinquity, on the presence of multiple females associated with a core of male agnates, either as their wives or sisters. These women provided economies of scale in female labour, reciprocal child care, surrogate nursing, and mutual succour and assistance. While the universality or typicality of such households have been criticized as a facet of the orientalization and essentialization of 'Balkan' populations (Todorova 1993; Čapo-Žmegač 1996), they were frequently attained during the cycle of household development, even when not common in the cross section. Even in medieval times households containing more than one conjugal unit were less than half of all households, in the cross section. The attainment of multiple conjugal units is strongly influenced by demographic conditions. Thus, for example, the number of households containing a married father and a married son is a function of the overlap in the married lives of parents and children and thus strongly dependent on age at marriage and longevity. The number of households containing married brothers is strongly dependent on the net reproduction rate. Indeed, the virtual impossibility of the universality of fraternal joint families can be shown by the fact that for the average married pair to have two sons surviving to marry would require that the population double in each generation. (On these issues, see Halpern and Anderson 1970; Hammel 1990.)

3. This contention is disputed by some Croatian historians as a self-serving claim of Austrian apologists; nevertheless, the peasants of the time apparently evinced a preference for military status because feudal dues were less than in the civil zone, and the military establishment is sometimes reported to have provisioned villages in times of famine. To be sure, such reports are from Austrian sources. Much of our information about economic developments is general and insufficiently specific with respect to region. Regions were diverse. The Austrian sources give little systematic information on the local military border except 1830–47. Hungarian sources often do not differentiate between Hungary proper, Croatia, and Slavonia. There are no wage series, only some price series.

4. The grain prices are regional prices based on the Vienna market and correlate closely with those of the Budapest market and (for a more limited time range) prices on the Zagreb market. Regional grain prices mostly reflect supply, conditioned largely by regional climatic factors. We have no information on local prices or the supply factors driving them. Neither do we have information on shifts in demand, plausibly driven by military provisioning in time of war. Peasants rarely bought or sold grain. They could buy it in time

of need only if they engaged in wage labour to raise cash; they could sell it in time of surplus to raise cash for taxes and amortization payments. Grain was produced commercially on the large estates in the civil zone, but not in the military zone.

5. Elasticity is the proportional change in some quantity induced by a 100% change in another. For example, if the elasticity of mortality with respect to the price of grain were 0.2 (20%), a doubling of the price of grain would increase mortality by 20%. Elastiticies may be positive or negative. Such elasticities may be estimated over several time segments. For example, one may estimate the effect on mortality levels in year *t* of price changes in that and the previous 4 years, that is, at yearly lags 0, 1, 2, 3, and 4. The sum of these lagged elasticities, the 'five-year lag sum', is often used as a summary measure. See Hammel and Galloway (2000*a, b*) for an explication of the method and application to Slavonian data.

6. These are the heights of 'taller Hungarian soldiers', that is, those with heights above the historically highest lower boundary imposed. Komlos gives data for the decade of birth, for example, '1790', thus with a decade centre at 1795. Under the assumption that nutritional deprivation would have its most lasting effects if it occurred during late pregnancy and before weaning, one would choose to centre the height data on the centre of the decade of birth. If, on the other hand, one assumed that the most important effects occurred during the adolescent growth spurt, when some 'catch-up' is possible, one would centre perhaps on age 15. I am obliged to Richard Steckel for his comments on this matter at the Arild conference, giving his preference for centring on the decade of birth.

7. Of course, the exact mechanisms are unknown and differ for civil and military serfs. For civil serfs, feudal dues in the form of corvée labour were relatively light. Additional feudal taxes could be assessed. Church tithes were assessed and may not have changed at all. Only peasants with allodial holdings were subject to strictly feudal dues. Civil serfs also farmed so-called industrial land, land arrogated from the commons, in which the landlord also had rights, and paid a sharecropping portion to the landlord. Such dues would not have changed with emancipation. The levels of these dues varied according to the practices of different estates. Military serfs had obligations as border guards after the Napoleonic wars, as well as in road maintenance, fortification maintenance, and haulage. These would not have changed until 1871. Such obligations also differed in practice between different parts of the Military Border.

8. The ethnographic, historical, and medical accounts suggest that herbal abortifacients were used and also that crude mechanical abortion was employed, often resulting in tetanus.

9. Karl Kaser, personal communication.

10. Theories about the origins and functions of complex family organization abound. The potential for such 'patriarchal' organization has deep roots in Indo-European social structure and kinship systems. The value of such organization to the households themselves in frontier situations has been noted above. There were also advantages to overlords seeking to maximize the availability of labour, especially in periods of peak labour demand, such as military mobilization or mass corvée labour on large estates, since a single adult male from such households could be left to tend the family plots while the rest were drawn off.

11. Agnatic kin are those related by links through males. Patrivirilocal residence is a pattern in which a bride resides with her husband who resides with his father or other agnatic kin.

12. For a useful summary of the economic issues, see Tomasevich (1955) and for information on extant and divided households in 1890, see Zoričić (1894).

13. If a household had no sons, the husband of at least one daughter might move into the household of the wife's parents.

14. In the census of 1857 the Gradiška Regiment had a population of 56,402, of which 76% were Catholic, 24% Orthodox, plus 6 Uniates, 7 Protestants, and 3 Jews.

15. Evidence from scattered libri status animarum and the Chronicle of the Monastery of Cernik indicates that infants were usually baptized at birth by the midwife. We use 'baptism' and 'birth' synonymously.

16. Strictly speaking, this is an estimate of the probability of dying, not a rate. In the body of the analysis we use a mortality rate, defined as the number of deaths divided by exposure time in person-years.

17. Loudon (1992: table 1.1) shows levels between 4.7 and 5.1 per thousand for England and Wales, 1851–1900. Wrigley *et al.* (1997: table 6.29) estimate rates in the range of 12–17 per thousand baptisms (corrected for stillbirths and no births, thus 'per confinement' and corrected for background mortality) for England 1600–1750. Rates for Germany, Sweden, and rural France, adjusted to achieve comparable definitions, were estimated by these authors to be in the range 9–12 per thousand between about 1700 and 1900.

18. However, where rates of abortion and of fatal consequences of abortion are both high, some substantial fraction of maternal deaths may occur earlier, typically 3–6 months earlier. Similarly, deaths from ectopic pregnancy, eclampsia and some from infectious disease exacerbated by immune suppression will occur before parturition, not after. See Högberg (1985: 1–22) for discussion and data.

19. This chapter and others by Prof Ulf Högberg and colleagues at Umeå University are some of the most detailed analyses of the subject in the literature.

20. in partu, in partus, paru, partu, dificilis partus, parus dificilis, puerperium, in puerperio, in puerperium, in puerperis, partu infelico, post-partum, post-partum sanguini, peritonitis puerpera, pleuritis et puerper, sepsis puerperalis, texak porod (Cr. 'difficult birth').

21. Notice that burial records are not written for unbaptized persons, so that there are several hundred cases in which baptism must have been immediate.

22. Tables 57 and 58 of the census give regional breakdowns for the more common causes of death, but there are no data on those related to MM. Thus it is impossible to narrow the comparison to Slavonia or segments thereof.

23. More precisely and for computational convenience, we count deaths and exposure time from birth up to the 61st day, and from birth (or from marriage for nulliparous women) to the 731st day. The two-year window gives a count of deaths from all causes. Subtracting the sixty-day set from the 730-day set gives deaths and exposure within the two-year but beyond the two-month window. The corresponding mortality rates are computed from these deaths and exposures. Note that what we compute is a mortality rate, $m(x)$, not a ratio of deaths to live births or a crude rate of deaths per women in some age range. Note also that using a longer span after sixty days to estimate BM will begin to pick up deaths from pregnancy-related causes, such as abortion, ectopic pregnancy, eclampsia, as the end of the BM span begins to capture women returning to fecundability, that is, pre-parturitional deaths at the next parity.

24. Reconstitution gives many examples of couples with linked children but no record of the marriage itself. Such 'sibsets', as we call them, because they consist of sets of persons with the same parents, could be the children of couples who married outside the parish and subsequently migrated in, or children to a marriage with no surviving record. We do not include such data here, because parity, age, and remarital status of mother are unknown. Similarly, although we can identify higher order marriages from the marriage

records, we have not yet fully automated linkages between successive marriages and thus do not include higher order marriages here.

25. We follow the traditional practice of assuming that a woman who did not demonstrably die within sixty days of giving birth actually survived to the end of the sixty-day period. We were concerned that we might in this way miss some women who might have emigrated and died outside the parish within sixty days, and conducted a parallel analysis in which we demanded evidence of survival in the form of some other event occurring to the mother. If that event were a last birth, we did not admit that birth to the analysis but used it only as a censoring event. The two forms of analysis did not differ importantly in their results. Similarly, we assume that women who did not die in the 61–730 day period following a birth did survive it.

26. Obviously, there is no difference between these intervals for women whose terminal parity is 1, and the expectation suggested will be clearest for women with higher terminal parities.

27. 541 of 31,683 attested causes of death were for smallpox (variola, febris variolanus). Almost all of these were reported after 1850. How much of total adult mortality was smallpox related is not yet clear.

28. Bogičevci, Cernik, Nova Gradiška, Oriovac, Petrovo Selo, Štivica, and Vrbje.

29. Note also that any aggregate analysis of MM may be sensitive to changes in overall fertility. If fertility is controlled by stopping behaviour, depending on the stopping point different proportions of women will bear children at parities of different risk. We do not attempt to take these factors into account but have opted to control for parity level at appropriate points in the analysis.

30. The probability of dying in childbirth, estimated as maternal deaths per birth, is the usual measure employed, sometimes per 1,000, or 10,000, or 100,000 births.

31. Logistic regression is one of several accepted methods for analysing dichotomous outcomes. Here the outcome is whether the mother dies or not. The coefficient for any independent variable is the logarithm of the relative odds ratio, or;

$$ln(P_{x_i}/(1 - P_{x_i})),$$

where P_{x_i} is the probability that the outcome (death to the mother) will occur to a mother with characteristic x_i. Confidence intervals for the coefficients are estimated in the usual way, as some multiple of the standard error of the coefficient.

32. We are indebted to Mike Hout for suggesting this.

33. The collection of birthings analysed here is not a formal random sample, so that the application of the traditional rules of inference can only be approximate.

34. It is important to note that in some degree, the movement of grain prices parallels our narrative of socio-economic change. One could plausibly offer a model in which grain price changes, in the short and long run, were the driving forces, rather than the structural changes in the labour market and in the households of peasant producers. Some changes in grain prices were of course correlated with the structural shifts. Grain prices sometimes increased in time of mobilization, either because of military buying or because of drops in supply as labour was drawn off the farm, or both. As peasants were drawn off the family farm into wage labour to raise cash for taxes and amortization, or to buy food as family farms became smaller through inheritance division, production may have dropped, again raising prices. Simply substituting grain price movements for a broader story of change seems to us to sacrifice historical richness for numerical precision.

References

Andersson, T., Bergström, S., and Högberg, U. (2000) 'Swedish Maternal Mortality in the 19th Century by Different Definitions: Previous Stillbirth but not Multiparity Risk Factor for Maternal Death'. *Acta Obstet Gynecol Scand*, 79: 679–86.

Andorka, R. and Balazs-Kovacs, S. (1986) 'The Social Demography of Hungarian Villages in the Eighteenth and Nineteenth Centuries (with Special Attention to Sárpilis, 1792–1804)'. *Journal of Family History*, 11: 169–92.

Čapo-Žmegač, J. (1990) 'Economic and Demographic History of Peasant Households on a Croatian Estate, 1756–1848'. Doctoral Dissertation, Department of Demography, Berkeley, CA: University of California.

——(1996) 'New Evidence and Old Theories: Multiple Family Households in Northern Croatia'. *Continuity and Change*, 11(3): 375–98.

Cortes-Majo, M., Garcia-Gil, C. *et al.* (1990) 'The Role of the Social Condition of Women in the Decline of Maternal and Female Mortality'. *International Journal of Health Services*, 20(2): 315–28.

Croatia (1905) *Statistički godišnjak Kraljevine Hrvatske i Slavonije*. Zagreb.

Ginsberg, C. A. (1989) *Sex-Specific Mortality and the Economic Value of Children in Nineteenth-Century Massachusetts*. New York: Garland Publishing.

Halpern, J. M. and Anderson, D. (1970) 'The Zadruga, a Century of Change'. *Anthropologica*, 12: 83–97.

Hammel, E. A. (1968) *Alternative Social Structures and Ritual Relations in the Balkans*. Englewood Cliffs, NJ: Prentice-Hall.

——(1972) 'The Zadruga as Process', in P. Laslett (ed.), *Household and Family in Past Time*. Cambridge: Cambridge University Press, pp. 335–73.

——(1977) 'Reflections on the Zadruga'. *Ethnologia Slavica*, 7: 141–51.

——(1980*a*) 'Household Structure in 14th Century Macedonia'. *Journal of Family History*, 5: 242–73.

——(1980*b*) 'Sensitivity Analysis of Household Structure in Medieval Serbian Censuses'. *Historical Methods*, 13: 105–18.

——(1984) 'On the *** of Investigating Household Form and Function', in R. M. Netting and R.Wilk (eds.), *Households: Comparative and Historical Studies of the Domestic Group*. Berkeley, CA: University of California Press, pp. 29–43.

——(1985) 'Short Term Demographic Fluctuations in the Croatian Military Border of Austria, 1830–47'. *European Journal of Population*, 1: 265–90.

——(1990) 'Demographic Constraints on the Formation of Traditional Balkan Households', in A. Laiou (ed.), *Marriage and the Family in Byzantium*, Dumbarton Oaks Papers, no 44. Washington DC: Dumbarton Oaks, pp. 173–80.

——(1993) 'Censored Intervals in Family Reconstitution: A Sensitivity Test of Alternative Strategies with Historical Croatian Data', in D. Reher and R. Schofield (eds.), *Old and New Methods in Historical Demography*. Oxford: Clarendon University Press, pp. 125–44.

——(1995) 'Economics 1: Culture 0. Fertility Change and Differences in the Northwest Balkans 1700–1900', in S. Greenhalgh (ed.), *Situating Fertility: Anthropology and Demographic Inquiry*. Cambridge: Cambridge University Press, pp. 225–58.

——and Galloway, P. R. (2000*a*) 'Structural and Behavioural Changes in the Short-Term Preventive Check in the Northwest Balkans in the 18th and 19th Centuries'. *European Journal of Population*, 16: 67–108.

—— and Galloway, P. R. (2000*b*) 'Structural Factors Affecting the Short-Term Positive Check in Croatia, Slavonia, and Srem in the 18th-19th Century', in T. Bengtsson and O. Saito (eds.), *Population and Economy: From Hunger to Economic Growth*. Oxford: Oxford University Press, pp. 227–48.

—— and Gullickson, A. (2003) 'Maternal Mortality on the Croatian-Bosnian Border 1700–1900'. Population Association of America, Minneapolis, 2 May.

—— and Herrchen, B. (1993) *Statistical Imputation in Family Reconstitution*. Proceedings of the IUSSP XXIInd International Population Conference, Montreal, IUSSP.

—— Johanssen, S. R. *et al.* (1983) 'The Value of Children During Industrialization: Sex Ratios in Childhood in Nineteenth Century America'. *Journal of Family History*, 8: 346–66.

—— and Kohler, H. P. (1997) 'Kinship-Based Resource Sharing in the Agrarian Economy of Frontier Slavonia, 1698: Evidence from an Early Census'. *Journal of the History of the Family*, 1: 407–23.

—— and Wachter, K. W. (1996*a*) 'Evaluating the Slavonian Census of 1698. Part I: Structure and Meaning'. *European Journal of Population*, 12: 145–66.

—— and Wachter, K. W. (1996*b*) 'Evaluating the Slavonian Census of 1698. Part II: A Microsimulation Test and Extension of the Evidence'. *European Journal of Population*, 12: 295–326.

Henry, L. (1987) 'Mortalité des hommes et des femmes dans le passé'. *Annales de Demographie Historique*, pp. 87–118.

Hietzinger, C. (1817) *Statistik der Militaergraenze des Oesterreichischen Kaiserthums*. Vienna: Gerold.

—— (1820) *Statistik der Militaergraenze des Oesterreichischen Kaiserthums*. Vienna: Gerold.

Högberg, U. (1985) *Maternal Mortality in Sweden*, Medical Dissertations New Series No 156. Umeå: Umeå University.

—— and Broström, G. (1986) 'The Impact of Early Medical Technology on Maternal Mortality in Late 19th Century Sweden'. *International Journal of Gynaecology and Obstetrics*, 24(4): 251–61.

Imhof, A. E. (1986) 'Regulation, manipulation und explosion der bevölkerungsdichte—uas der Sicht eines Sozialhistorikers', in O. Kraus (ed.), *Regulation, Manipulation und Explosion der Bevölkerungsdichte: Vortrage gehalten auf der Tagung der Joachim Jungius-Gesellschaft der Wissenschaften Hamburg am 15. und 16. November 1985*. Göttingen: Vandenhoeck und Ruprecht.

Karaman, I. (1972) *Privreda i društvo Hrvatske u 19. Stoljeću*, Zagreb: Školska Knjiga.

Knodel, J. (1986) 'Two Centuries of Infant, Child, and Maternal Mortality in German Village Populations', in A. Brandström and L. G. Tedebrand (eds.), *Society, Health and Population During the Demographic Transition*. Stockholm: Almqvist & Wiksell International, pp. 23–48.

Kohler, H. P. and Hammel, E. A. (2001) 'On the Role of Families and Kinship Networks in Pre-Industrial Agricultural Societies: An Analysis of the 1698 Slavonian Census'. *Journal of Population Economics*, 14(1): 21–49.

Komlos, J. (1989) *Nutrition and Economic Development in the Eighteenth-Century Habsburg Monarchy*. Princeton, NJ: Princeton University Press.

Loudon, I. (1992) *Death in Childbirth: An International Study of Maternal Care and Maternal Mortality, 1800–1950*. Oxford: Clarendon Press.

Mažuran, I. (1988) *Popis naselja stanovništva u Slavoniji 1698. Godine*. Osijek: Jugoslavenska Akademija Znanosti i Umjetnosti.

Mills, C. W. (1959) *The Sociological Imagination*. New York: Oxford University Press.

Roksandić, D. (1988) *Vojna Hrvatska: La Croatie Militaire. Krajiško društvo u francuskom carstvu 1809–1813*. Zagreb: Školska Knjiga.

Rothenberg, G. E. (1960) *The Austrian Military Border in Croatia, 1522–1747*. Urbana, IL: University of Illinois Press.

——(1966) *The Austrian Military Border in Croatia, 1740–1881*. Chicago: University of Chicago Press.

Schofield, R. (1986) 'Did the Mothers Really Die? Three Centuries of Maternal Mortality in "The World We Have Lost"', in L. Bonfield, R. M. Smith, and K. Wrightson (eds.), *The World We Have Gained: Histories of Population and Social Structure*. Oxford: Basil Blackwell, pp. 231–60.

Todorova, M. N. (1993) *Balkan Family Structure and the European Pattern: Demographic Developments in Ottoman Bulgaria*. Washington, DC: American University Press.

Tomasevich, J. (1955) *Peasants, Politics and Economic Change in Yugoslavia*. Stanford: Stanford University Press.

Vaniček, F. (1875) *Specialgeschichte der Militärgrenze*. Vienna: Kaiserlichen-Königlichen Hof u. Staatsdrückerei.

Vassary, I. (1989) 'The Sin of Transdanubia'. *Continuity and Change*, 4: 429–68.

Wrigley, E. A., Davies R. S., Oeppen, J. E., and Schofield, R. S. (1997) *English Population History from Family Reconstitution 1580–1837*. Cambridge: Cambridge University Press.

Zoričić, M. (1894) *Die bäuerlichen Hauscommunionen in den Königreichen Kroatien u. Slavonien*. Internationales Congres für Hygiene und Demographie, Budapest: Pester Buchdrückerei.

12 The Standard of Living in Denmark in the Eighteenth and Early Nineteenth Centuries

HANS CHR. JOHANSEN

1. Introduction

The traditional view among Danish historians is that the standard of living in Denmark was low and fluctuating from year to year up to 1775. In the last quarter of the eighteenth century, a series of agricultural reforms and other measures were introduced which promoted economic growth, and by the middle of the nineteenth century, the situation had changed in such a way that short-term economic stress had largely disappeared and only the poorest inhabitants lived on the margin of existence (see Johansen 1998).

This view has mainly been based on non-quantitative sources, but in the following sections will be tested by means of various quantitative analyses in order to find out what the content of different measures really is and in which way the various measures can be used to evaluate the changes in the standard of living.

2. GNP and Real Wages

Danish figures for GNP have only been calculated back to 1818 and are relatively rough estimates for the earliest years and therefore not suitable for analysis.

Sources for calculation of real wage indices are, on the other hand, available, but the use of such indices in analyses gives rise to at least two important questions. The first is for how large a proportion of the population the indices are relevant as measures of the standard of living, and the second is what they really measure with regard to the standard of living.

Wage earners were, until the second half of the nineteenth century, a small proportion of the total Danish population and the monetary economy was, on the whole, little developed until the late eighteenth century. Between 1700 and 1850 nearly 80% of the population were living in rural districts, mainly from agriculture. For most of the eighteenth century those living from the land they tilled were mainly tenants, from whom the estate owners were responsible for collecting taxes. Most of these payments and other transactions between the tenants and the estate owners and the public authorities took place in kind, and as well most of the servants and day-labourers working on farms and estates were given food and accommodation where they worked and were paid little, if any, of their incomes in money wages. This situation changed during the period of agricultural reforms, as many of the farmers became freeholders and started selling their surplus products on the open

Table 12.1 Occupational distribution of the Danish population in 1801

	No. of inhabitants (1,000s)	Total population (%)	Income from wages
Rural areas			
Civil servants	15	1.6	+
Estate owners	4	0.5	—
Farmers	261	28.1	—
Cottagers with land[a]	143	15.4	—
Artisans and tradesmen	32	3.5	—
Living-in servants	123	13.3	(+)
Day-labourers	34	3.6	(+)
Cottagers without land, etc.	100	10.7	(+)
Pensioners, poor people, etc.	23	2.5	—
Provincial towns			
Civil servants	7	0.8	+
Military personnel	6	0.6	+
Merchants	5	0.5	—
Artisans	22	2.4	—
Other businessmen	12	1.3	—
Journeymen, apprentices, etc.	7	0.8	(+)
Living-in servants	13	1.5	(+)
Day-labourers	10	1.1	+
Pensioners, poor people, etc.	7	0.8	—
Copenhagen			
Civil servants	8	0.8	+
Military personnel	18	2.0	+
Merchants	3	0.3	—
Artisans	13	1.4	—
Other businessmen	13	1.4	—
Journeymen, apprentices, etc	15	1.6	(+)
Living-in servants	14	1.5	(+)
Day-labourers	7	0.8	+
Pensioners, poor people, etc.	11	1.2	—
Total	926	100.0	—

[a] The division line between a farmer and a cottager with land was one barrel of 'Hartford', a measure of land value and therefore different in size from the most fertile to the poorer soils. On average land the cottager would have up to *c*.10 acres and at least the cottagers with the smallest fields would have to supplement their income by day-labour work.

Note: (+) indicates that the group may have got part of their income in money, but most of it in kind.

market, and an increasing number of day-labourers came to receive most of their incomes from money wages.

In the towns, a majority of the population consisted of artisans and traders and the people employed by them. The latter group lived to a large extent in the houses of their masters, which means that among journeymen and urban day-labourers, few—mainly in Copenhagen—had a household of their own and received money wages.

The result of this is demonstrated in a schematic form in Table 12.1 with figures based on the 1801 census. Less than 10% of the population were living solely from money incomes and among those most were salaried civil servants, who were covered in a less satisfactory way by a real wage index based on workers' wages. Among the groups which may have received a certain part of their income in money, the largest one is that of the servants, who no doubt were still paid mostly in kind while living with their employers. The second largest group were cottagers without land, comprising old people, some day-labourers, single women, and others. Some of them were probably day-labourers who, to an increasing extent, received money wages but there were also some who were former farmers receiving food and other necessities from the new tenant or owner who had taken over their tenancy or bought their farm.

The conclusion of the survey in Table 12.1 is, therefore, that before the agricultural reforms and even to some extent in the first decades after the reforms had been introduced, a real wage index based on wages paid to unskilled workers only indicates the level of the standard of living for a minority of the population.

For the rest of the population, there is no guarantee that the fluctuations in a real wage index reflected the same effect on their standards of living. Some may have been almost unaffected by wage and price changes because of the subsistence economy they were living in and others may have benefited in some cases from a decline in the index and suffered from a rise, as the following sections will indicate.

3. The Content of a Danish Real Wage Index

The types of wages that can be found in eighteenth-century Danish sources are primarily daily wages for day-labourers in the larger towns and on some estates, and also some series for building workers in Copenhagen. All such series are characterized by being unchanged over very long periods (Falbe-Hansen 1869; Thestrup 1991). The scattered evidence points to almost the same rates for the same type of work between 1660 and the late eighteenth century, and after that a rise due to the inflation during the Napoleonic wars. The daily rate was higher in summer months than in winter months because of longer working days.

This means that unless there had been great changes in the number of days employed from year to year—and we do not know that—then the decisive factor for the development of the standard of living throughout most of the eighteenth century must have been the price fluctuations and the long-term development in prices, primarily those of the most important foodstuffs, out of which rye was the staple food for most of the population.

The most complete price series are the so-called *kapitelstakster*, that is, the yearly official prices for rye and several other foodstuffs. They exist for each diocese and for a few smaller areas from the early seventeenth century until the late twentieth century. They were determined by the authorities late in each year and used for conversions between payments in kind and payments in money. Later research has shown that they reflect the actual price levels although on the low end and also yearly fluctuations in a satisfactory way (Warming 1913: 115 *f.*).

An evaluation of the value of a real wage index for measuring changes in the standard of living must therefore be based on an analysis of the effect that changes in the *kapitelstakster* had on the incomes of various segments of the population.

4. The Long Run Development in the Eighteenth Century

Two price series are shown in Figure 12.1. One is the Sealand official price series for rye in the eighteenth century; the other is based upon a somewhat broader basket of foodstuffs (Statistiske Meddelelser 4, 15, 1; Thestrup 1991).

The trend in both price series is clearly rising after 1740 and with an unchanged wage rate; this would mean a declining real wage index, which is in sharp contrast to the traditional view of a rise in the standard of living of the Danish population at least after the mid-1770s. The price series during the Napoleonic wars are less informative because of hyper inflation in the years up to 1814. In order to solve this puzzle, it is necessary to have a closer look at the background of the long-run changes in rye prices.

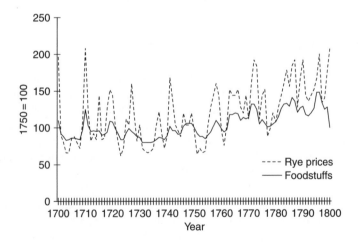

Figure 12.1   Price indices, 1700–1800

The rise in grain prices in the second half of the eighteenth century was not just a Danish experience. The most likely explanation is that, in spite of increasing food production due to agricultural reforms, the total European population was growing still more rapidly and created a heavy demand for basic foodstuffs, but this explanation need not necessarily be valid for every corner of Europe. There may have been areas with slower growth in population which nevertheless experienced increasing prices because their grain markets were integrated into the larger European market.

This was the case in Denmark. Estimates of the development in production and population during the reform years indicate an increasing surplus of rye not used on the farm for own consumption and fodder. This surplus could be sold at more and more profitable prices, which would clearly have improved the standard of living of the new group of owner-occupiers selling their surplus products on the open market. This group of surplus producers became at the same time an ever-increasing proportion of the population because this development acted as a strong incentive for the remaining tenants to buy their farms, freeing them from several payments in kind which were substituted by fixed monetary payments of interest and instalments on loans. Taxes paid directly by the farmers to the revenue officers were also now gradually coming to be paid in money and were not rising with the price level until after 1800.

Among the tradesmen in the towns, the merchants were no doubt also gaining from this development. They were normally middlemen in the expanding market for grain exports; also many master artisans profited from the increasing purchasing power of the farmers.

The servants, journeymen, and others who lived in the households of their employers continued receiving most of their income in kind and were therefore only marginally influenced by the price rise. Perhaps employers with rising production and income may have even given their servants a better diet than in earlier years when their economic situations had been less satisfactory.

It is consequently most likely that any decline in the standard of living due to stagnant wages and rising prices was limited to a small minority of money wage earners, and that the majority of the population followed the path expected by non-quantitative historians of a rising standard of living.

5. Short-Run Fluctuations in the Eighteenth Century

According to Figure 12.1 rye prices were fluctuating more than the other prices, and are thus an important factor in analysing short-term changes in a real wage index. Recent research has shown that already in the eighteenth century these frequent price changes were almost identical from one diocese to another, indicating that the Danish grain market was already a national market at that time. Furthermore, comparisons with fluctuations in the markets at Königsberg and Amsterdam indicate that price changes followed 'world market prices', which was also natural since

Copenhagen, the largest Danish net importer in the whole of the kingdom, was situated on the Sound through which the major supplies to western Europe passed on their way from the Baltic surplus areas to the importing nations in the West (Johansen 1988). The Danish market was protected by the prohibition of imports in years with sufficient supplies and exports in years with a bad harvest. Since Norway normally got a large part of its rye imports from Denmark, shortage situations were more likely to influence the situation in the northern part of the monarchy, because Danish producers could secure sufficient domestic supplies by reducing shipments to Norway—and perhaps also to the Danish towns—and in poor harvest years the ban on imports was lifted.

This means that Danish prices reflected not only Danish harvest results, but were part of a larger supply/demand situation. Although the main relationship was that poor Danish harvests resulted in high prices, it was also possible that a bad harvest in western Europe and a better situation in the Baltic area, including Denmark, might result in large supplies from eastern Europe to the deficit areas, but at high prices because of the inelastic demand in the West. The tendency towards such equilibrating trade was probably rising during the eighteenth century. It is therefore necessary to analyse several different situations, taking into consideration both price and quantity effects when trying to find out how the various parts of the population were influenced by changes in the rye prices (cf. Table 12.2).

Situation no. 4 in Table 12.2 is probably the most unlikely since this would only occur if there was easy access to ample imports in years with a poor Danish harvest. Among the other situations, it is only no. 5 which would be very detrimental to the whole of the society—in the other situations the majority would benefit from movements away from the normal because the inelastic supply and demand conditions would compensate for quantity changes by the price change. Situation no. 5 was, however, one that occurred rarely after the late eighteenth century because of the agricultural reforms.

In the analysis of short-term fluctuations, it also appears that a real wage index with the price of rye as the most important factor is unable to reflect the situation of the majority of the population.

Table 12.2　Influence of harvest results on the living standards of various segments of the population

Harvest	Prices	Change in living standard			
		Producers	Servants	Tradesmen	Workers
1. Abundant	Low	(+)	+	+	+
2. Abundant	High	+	+	(+)	—
3. Bad	High	(+)	(−)	—	—
4. Bad	Low	—	(−)	(+)	+
5. Very bad	High	—	—	—	—

6. The Evidence of Mortality Statistics

The number of deaths in the eighteenth and early nineteenth centuries is shown in Figure 12.2. The development from 1735 onwards is based on contemporary national statistics, while the pre-1735 figures are partly reconstructed by inflating figures from the counts of a sample of parish registers in each diocese.

There are large fluctuations in the numbers from year to year until the late 1770s, followed by a significant diminution of the movements. Also, from the 1770s the gross mortality rates started to decline. This is in good agreement with the expectations of a rise in the general standard of living from the 1770s.

In order to test whether there is a relationship between the mortality fluctuations and the rye prices, correlation coefficients have been calculated for each diocese for the pre- and post-1775 periods. The coefficients are shown in Table 12.3.

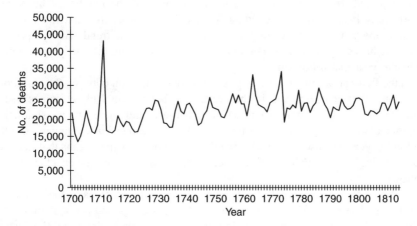

Figure 12.2 Number of deaths in Denmark, 1700–1814

Table 12.3 Correlation coefficients between changes in rye prices, $(p_t - p_{t-1})/p_{t-1}$, and changes in mortality, $(m_t - m_{t-1})/m_{t-1}$

	1736–74	1775–1814
Diocese		
Sealand	0.47	0.07
Funen	0.13	− 0.08
Ribe	0.45	− 0.03
Århus	0.42	0.10
Viborg	0.34	0.02
Ålborg	0.27	− 0.14

Note: The prices used are those determined in December the previous year in order to reflect harvest year prices.

After the mid-1770s the coefficients are very low and sometimes show a negative correlation, but even before 1775 the coefficients are low and explain only about one-fifth of the fluctuations, and the differences between the dioceses do not reflect any special patterns with regard to the size of land holdings, quality of land, or ownership. These results could be interpreted in various ways. One is that the agricultural reforms had the expected effects. There were, after 1775, very few years with situation no. 5 in Table 12.2 and therefore the majority of the population benefited from the rising price level, which resulted in only few years with undernourishment and high mortality. Another explanation could be that prices, to an increasing extent, did not reflect the harvest situation in Denmark, but the situation on the European grain market as a whole. A third might be that diseases that were not dependent on the general nourishment situation of the population caused several of the epidemics during the large mortality years.

For the country as a whole the change over time has been investigated for a still longer period. In Table 12.4, series for rye prices and the number of births and deaths have been used in a lagged model. The variables are the relative deviations from a nine-year moving average in order to eliminate the trend. The rye price is from the harvest year and the demographic events are from the partly overlapping calendar year that follows it.

In the first period, there is a highly significant covariation between the variations in the number of deaths and in the rye prices, but the total effect comes in the calendar year immediately after the poor harvest, and there are no significant coefficients in later years. For births, the effect is weaker but continues over the following year because the effect is via the conceptions, which means that many of the 'missing' births under normal circumstances would have taken place in the following year.

In the second period after 1775, the impact of price fluctuations on the number of deaths has disappeared—the parameter has the wrong sign and is not significant—which can be taken as a sign of the improvement of harvest yields and the general nourishment situation in the country. The impact on births is weaker and of shorter duration than before 1775. Also, the influence on the variation in the number of marriages for which statistics are now available is relatively weak. Finally, in the third period after 1840 all effects have disappeared.

In a somewhat similar study, Patrick R. Galloway has analysed the period 1756–1870, and for the period as a whole found a relation between the short-term variations in the demographic event rates and grain prices—although the effect is smaller for Denmark than for most other European countries. However, he does not divide this period into sub-periods and it is consequently not possible in his calculations to see to what extent the effect changes over time (Galloway 1988).

For those years after 1775 for which mortality statistics distributed according to the age of the deceased persons are available, some calculations have also been made for specific age groups (children and adults) in order to see if some of these were more vulnerable to changes in grain prices than the population at large. The worst inflation years between 1807 and 1814 have been left out because they may

Table 12.4 Covariation between fluctuations in demographic events and rye prices, 1669–1890

Dependent variable	Parameter estimates of rye price		R^2	DW
	Harvest year	Previous year		
1669–1775				
Births	−0.05772	−0.05824	0.32	2.00
(*t*-value)	(−3.59)	(−3.35)	—	—
Deaths[a]	0.27367	—	0.61	2.03
(*t*-value)	(6.32)	—	—	—
1775–1840				
Births	−0.04112	−0.00784	—	—
(*t*-value)	(−3.51)	(−0.61)	0.31	2.11
Deaths	−0.02344	—	—	—
(*t*-value)	(−0.77)	—	0.08	2.02
Marriages	−0.03012	—	0.21	2.09
(*t*-value)	(−1.35)	—	—	—
1840–90				
Births	−0.00112	−0.02302	0.09	1.87
(*t*-value)	(−0.08)	(−1.69)	—	—
Deaths	−0.08380	—	0.19	2.14
(*t*-value)	(−1.89)	—	—	—
Marriages	−0.02637	—	0.05	2.11
(*t*-value)	(−0.55)	—	—	—

[a] For 1711 (a plague year with an extremely high mortality), a dummy variable has been used.

have diverged from the pattern in the remaining years. None of these calculations do, however, give significant results indicating a close relationship between changes in mortality and rye prices and in most cases the correlations are, if anything, negative.

7. Human Stature

Several investigations from the second half of the twentieth century have used human height as a measure of material well-being, but this measure is of relatively little value in the Danish case until late in the period dealt with in this chapter.

Before 1789, the estate owners oversaw conscription for the national service and it was not normal practice for them to measure their soldiers. In this early period it is only for mercenaries that we have statistics of heights, and they indicate that only relatively tall people were recruited, so that they provide a biased sample of the total population.

In 1789 a new conscription system was introduced—from that time the total male rural population was measured at a draft board, but the urban youth were not included until after 1849.

National statistics based on this material were not published until the 1850s, but a few regional samples have been collected by contemporaries and later researchers. These samples show relatively constant average heights from 1789 to the 1850s ranging between 165 and 167 cm; a growth process is not evident until the second half of the nineteenth century, and then with a growth rate of *c*.1 cm per decade. This development is therefore of little value in trying to estimate changes in the standard of living in the eighteenth and early nineteenth centuries. Also, none of the samples has information from the 1830s, which was a period of high mortality and one in which some other European studies have shown a decline in physical height.

8. Future Research

The various quantitative measures demonstrated above do not, in a convincing way, refute the traditional idea of a substantial improvement in the standard of living for most inhabitants after 1775, but neither can they be used to confirm this assertion, since several of the measures are either ill-suited for the purpose or are taken from imperfect sources.

If further quantitative research is to be made, it will be necessary to include other variables and to use more direct measures of the harvest result than the rye prices provided.

Only preliminary results of such analyses are at present available, but they indicate that the years with serious undernourishment of large parts of the population, which were frequent among the years with high mortality rates early in the eighteenth century, gradually became more rare. After 1775, it was only in 1786 and to some extent in 1787 that, for the last time in Danish history, there seems to be a clear connection between two consecutive bad harvests in 1785 and 1786 and a corresponding peak on the mortality curve (Johansen 2002).

If further and more penetrating research can confirm these results, then the traditional understanding of the development of the Danish standard of living seems to be the right one. Living standards were improving from 1775 onwards, and to such an extent that the frequently occurring crises of the previous centuries no longer prevailed.

References

Falbe-Hansen, V. (1869) *Hvilke forandringer er der siden Amerikas opdagelse foregaaet i priserne på Danmarks væsentligste frembringelser og i arbejdslønnen her i landet.* København: Thanning & Appel.

Galloway, P. R. (1988) 'Basic Patterns in Annual Variations in Fertility, Nuptiality, Mortality, and Prices in Pre-Industrial Europe'. *Population Studies*, 42(2): 275–302.

Johansen, H. C. (1988) 'Demand and Supply Factors in Late Eighteenth Century Grain Trade', in W. G. Heeres *et al.* (eds.), *From Dunkirk to Danzig, Shipping and Trade in the North Sea and the Baltic 1350–1850*. Hilversum: Verloren Publishers, pp. 281–98.

——(1998) 'Food Consumption in the Pre-Industrial Nordic Societies'. *Scandinavian Economic History Review*, 1: 11–23.

——(2002) *Danish Population History 1600–1939*. Odense: University Press of Southern Denmark.

Statistiske Meddelelser 4, 15, 1 (1904) *Oversigt over kapitelstakster 1600–1902*. København: Statens Statistiske Bureau.

Thestrup, P. (1991) *Mark og skilling, kroner og øre. Pengeenheder, priser og lønninger i Danmark i 350 år (1640–1989)*, Arkivernes Informationsserie. København: G. E. C. Gad.

Warming, J. (1913) *Håndbog i Danmarks Statistik*. København: G. E. C. Gad.

13 Short-Term Demographic Changes in Relation to Economic Fluctuations: The Case of Tuscany During the Pre-Transitional Period

MARCO BRESCHI, ALESSIO FORNASIN, AND
GIOVANNA GONANO

1. Introduction

Economic, social, and demographic quantitative analysis has paid much attention to the short-term relationship between economic (the prices of consumer goods in particular) and demographic time series. In the last few years, research in this field has further developed thanks to new and stimulating methodological approaches. With reference to the numerous studies on demographic and economic short-term variations in England, carried out after Lee (1981), Bengtsson and Reher have recently suggested the existence of a school which we may call 'the economic history school of short-term analysis'. This school is not only characterized by its choice of problems and its sampling method but also its choice of statistical techniques (Bengtsson and Reher 1998: 100–1). The work presented here might not necessarily be included in this 'new' school, but it follows the same method of research in terms of the analytical techniques adopted.

The area considered in this research is the Grand Duchy of Tuscany, over the time period from 1823 to 1854. Although the general picture was in constant evolution during this period, population trends in Tuscany still reflect the crisis of the old regime. Depending on the context being considered—whether urban or rural, whether mostly composed of paid workers or of owners working their land, and so on—a bad harvest or a sudden rise in prices had a negative influence on the consumption of indispensable goods and therefore on the living standards of a significant part of the population. Since levels of consumption can have a relationship with some demographic variables, mortality in particular, the assumption made is that variations in the latter during this short period can be used as a reliable indicator of living standards.

More precisely, the aim of this chapter is to identify how different 'territories', each with their own economic, social, and demographic characteristics, experienced different demographic outcomes when faced with fluctuations in wheat prices. Once the close relationship between fluctuations in wheat prices and mortality has been established, we indicate how such a link became particularly strong only in the case of specific age groups. The correspondence between prices and mortality fluctuations was not necessarily direct and was linked to economic and social factors. To disentangle this complicated 'knot', we first contrast the demographic reactions of the urban population with those of the rural population, and then undertake a deeper analysis of the reactions of the rural population. The rich and detailed statistical documentation produced by the Tuscan Public Records Office permits us to consider the mortality reactions of infants, children, youths, adults, and the elderly to fluctuating wheat prices in forty-three different agrarian regions.

2. Territory, Wealth, and Population

The characteristic features of Tuscany in the 1800s are the close association of land rent, the predominance of agriculture, and the high density of population (Pazzagli 1992). The three maps thus traced give a brief outline of the situation.[1] The first one (Figure 13.1)

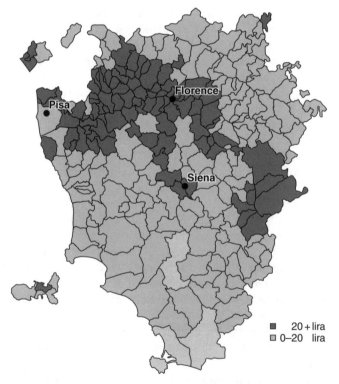

Figure 13.1   Taxable land rent for hectare, Grand Duchy of Tuscany (1834)
Source: Archivio di Stato di Firenze, *Catasto della Toscana*, b. 934.

shows the value of the taxable land rent for each community. The area with higher levels of taxable income coincides almost precisely with the mixed cultivation territories hinged on the traditional Tuscan plot (Figure 13.2). This is also the land where most of the population of the region is concentrated (Figure 13.3). The central and bearing axis of this compact territory is the path of the River Arno, which horizontally connects Pisa and Florence and, after a sharp curve slightly north of Florence, traces the outline of a wide arc reaching the plain of Arezzo. Its basin becomes particularly wide along its horizontal stretch due to the ramifications of its tributaries towards both the north and the south.

Because of the central position of the Arno, this territory was called the *Toscana del fiume* (Tuscany of the river). It opposed the 'other Tuscany', which consists of the mountainous territory of the Apennines further north, the area south-east of Siena—*la terra senza dolcezza d'albero* ('the land without the harmony of trees')—mainly fit for seed and, on the south-west, the Maremma marshes, where the massive work of drainage undertaken during the first half of the nineteenth century had not ameliorated its desolate landscape (Table 13.1).

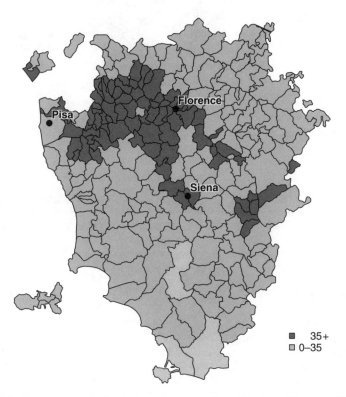

Figure 13.2 Percentages of mixed crop cultivation, Grand Duchy of Tuscany (1834)
Source: Biagioli 1975.

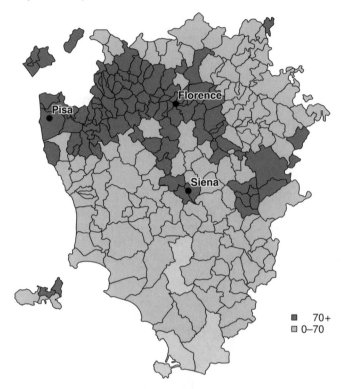

Figure 13.3   Population density in km², Grand Duchy of Tuscany (1823–54)
Source: Archivio di Stato di Firenze, *Stato civile di Toscana. Statistica decennale* bb. 12182–3.

Table 13.1   Grand Duchy of Tuscany. Principal socio-economic indicators (1832–4)

	Tuscany of the river	Other Tuscany	Grand Duchy
Area (%)	32	68	100
Inhabitants (in %)	66	34	100
Inhabitants per km²	133	33	64
Taxable land rent (in %)	72	28	100
Value (lira) per ha	50	9	21
Land for mixed cultivation (in %)	72	28	100
Real rent (in %)	85	15	100
Number of weekly markets (in %)	66	34	100
Amount of trade in weekly markets (in %)	85	15	100

Note: The markets data refer to the year 1854.

Source: Pazzagli 1992: 41, 46.

The 'Tuscany of the river' region covers an area of about 7,000 km^2, one third of the whole of Grand Duchy, and includes 66% of the total population (around 1.4 million) with a density of 133 inhabitants per km^2, against 33 inhabitants per km^2 present in the 'other Tuscany'. The difference is even more striking when considering the rent values. Three quarters of the whole land income, that is, the main source of wealth in an agrarian area such as the Grand Duchy, is concentrated in the river countryside. This gap is also reflected in the average value per land unit (fifty lira against nine lira per ha) and therefore in the value of the plots, which was 5–6 times higher in the 'Tuscany of the river' region. The data reported in Table 13.1 also highlight the close relation between the number of inhabitants, the land rent, and the use of the land. The 'Tuscany of the river' region represented in the nineteenth century a third of the Grand Duchy territory, 72% of which was characterized by mixed cultivation and it contained 66% of the entire population and produced 72% of the income.

The three elements illustrated so far (inhabitants, rent, and land usage) and the close relationship that united them makes us clearly understand the great differences between the region of Tuscany hinged on the Arno river and the so-called 'other Tuscany'. The gap becomes more evident when other indicators are explained. In fact, the data about the real rent (Table 13.1) indicate 85% of taxable rent coming only from the 'Tuscany of the river' region, proof of the wide and dense network of towns, villages, and castles that made the region a particularly populous and active rural centre. In the central-southern part of the region, near Siena, only two towns— Volterra and Montalcino—out of the fourteen bishop-ruled towns contained more than 2,500 inhabitants. Here, as in the mountains, the populated centres were far apart and looked over an empty and large territory, characterized by scattered sharecropper settlements, as in the *Senese*.

The urban centres represent the nodal points of the territory not only because of their administrative and jurisdictional functions, but also thanks to their role as food-centres and as markets for the countryside produce. Even here the data are clear in giving the same percentage; 66% of Tuscan weekly markets and 66% of Tuscan inhabitants are located in the 'Tuscany of the river'. The amount of trade in the river area was even higher, reaching 85%, which is equivalent to the real rent level, indicating that the richest part of the region is hinged on the Arno river. If the gap between the 'Tuscany of the river' and the 'other Tuscany' looks rather clear at the level of macro indicators, it becomes less clear when the size and characteristics of the rural population are taken into consideration. The economy in the region was based on agriculture: according to different estimates, however close, 55% of the active population worked on the land. The figure rises to 68% when considering only the rural area land (Bandettini 1956; Pazzagli 1992). It can be assumed that in the countryside and in the smaller districts about three of every four inhabitants lived in rural families. The degree of rurality appears to have been higher in the *Senese* countryside, where 75% of the workers were employed on the land, while in the countryside around the Arno river the percentage falls to well below 70%. The various occupations of the people in the mountainous region, as well as the instability and mobility of the inhabitants of the Maremma region, make the estimates of the size of the agricultural population even more uncertain. However, even in these two areas the land, as well as the complementary and integrative activities of breeding, forestry, and vegetal coal production, remained pivotal to the local economy.

However, in an agricultural world universally hinged upon sharecropping and—excluding the mountainous areas—characterized by large landed properties,[2] important differences seem evident at the territorial level.

Some of the research carried out at the micro-level allows us to outline a few differentiating features of the rural populations in the south and the north of Tuscany (Torti 1979, 1982; Pazzagli 1980, 1992; Doveri 1990). The first one, as indicated by Table 13.1, concerns the different number of inhabitants for each cultivated hectare of land. In the 'Tuscany of the river' region, such an indicator takes values that are around 1.5 inhabitants rising to above 2.5 inhabitants in the more intensively cultivated areas. In the *Senese* countryside, in spite of the predominance of rural population, the ratio takes very low values (just over 0.5 inhabitants). This relatively low value is the effect of extensive allotment, of a low degree of agricultural intensity and the widespread use of letting a third or a fourth of the arable land to lie fallow every year.

In other words, the small, rich, and much exploited plots found in the 'Tuscany of the river' region called for more workers than those necessary to manage the large, less specialized, and only partially exploited plots in the south. It is in fact with greater land availability that the *Senese* worker can reduce (and maybe overcome) the apparent gap separating him from the farmers of the more intensively cultivated lands in the 'Tuscany of the river' region. Moreover, although the evidence is thin, it appears that both farm labourers and wage earners were becoming more numerous in the river area. Where it is possible to identify the different rural categories of the population, the proportions of these agricultural wage earners reach one-fifth and one-third respectively.[3] The proportions found in the southern area are significantly smaller.

Finally, if we consider that the wage earners and the daily workers were joined by a good part of those indicated as 'destitutes' in the 1841 census, the 'Tuscany of the river' region—being more wealthy than the other one—could possibly have had proportionally many more poor people. The greater presence of urban centres, where the outcasts and the destitutes were more numerous, could also explain this.

3. Sources

To set up a wealthy 'Tuscany of the river' region against a poor 'other Tuscany' region is a schematic device, but one that helps with understanding the complexity and importance of the differences that become broader as we look deeper into the matter. The simplification proposed above is due to the lack of effective quantitative indicators of the wealth of small population segments or individuals. It is in fact the fringe segments—including those without income (at the time called the 'necessary' destitutes) as well as some categories with a fixed income, such as farm labourers, casual workers, wage earners, and so on—that are more sensitive to recession and react, from a demographic standpoint, with greater evidence.

Even without a more substantial quantitative correlation to describe the population according to their wealth, we can assert that the tight bond that linked together the rent, the land usage, and the typology of the land workers allows for a division of Tuscany into different territories. Each one of these has a certain explanatory potential, especially with regard to variables that highlight the socio-economic traits of its inhabitants. Therefore, given the characteristics inherent to the separate territories, an approach that takes them as the starting point for the analysis should permit greater insight into the link between price fluctuation and mortality.

This approach fits Tuscany well thanks to the numerous and detailed sources of information available on cereal prices, mortality rates, and the features and usage of the land prevailing in each of the agrarian regions. In order to comprehend this aspect of the research, and better understand the work done so far, a short description of the data is essential.

As far as prices are concerned, only wheat, being the most common cereal, has been considered. The data relate to the Florence market, which can be considered representative of the whole of Tuscany for the following reasons. From the eighteenth century onwards, the cereal market in Tuscany was one of the most integrated of all Europe (Persson 1999). Already in 1768, in fact, the Grand Duchy had enacted a legislation inspired by the principles of free exchange for the commerce of cereals, a first in Europe (Mirri 1972). Also, of all the regions in the peninsula, Tuscany had the best system of transportation and the most extensive road network (Mori 1986). Finally, when comparing the Florence time series to others relating to the Grand Duchy, where possible, simultaneous price movements can be detected, although the former are slightly higher.[4]

With regard to the information on demography, we relied on documentation which is in some ways unique, kept by the State Archives in Florence; namely, the *decennial statistics*. These statistics cover the period from the years immediately after the French Restoration in the Grand Duchy government (1815) until the formation of the new Italian State (1861). They recorded the total number of marriages, births differentiated by sex and legitimacy, deaths according to sex, and the total number of deaths (without distinction by sex) according to age group, for each community of the Grand Duchy.[5] Despite some limitations, the series are detailed and reliable (Breschi 1990).

The temporal unit used to rebuild both the demographic and economic time series is based on the solar year, since the demographic data were only available on an annual basis. We adapted the wheat prices[6] which could instead be gathered every month, to these data. This procedure does not alter the direction of the various price fluctuations; in fact it makes the price series less volatile, since the most striking variations are in proximity of the harvest—immediately before or after—between June and July. This discontinuity is alleviated in our series because it is distributed over two years instead of one.

The statistical model used for the short- and medium-term relationship between the economic and demographic time series is based on a distributed lag model (DLM).[7] In order to apply this statistical method some comments are necessary. The first-order autoregressive process provides the most parsimonious description of the data. The estimation technique, taking into account the problem of autocorrelation, is based on the iterative maximum likelihood method (Harvey 1981: 191–5). With regard to the lagged independent variables, we include values for lags of 0–2 years in the regressions of total deaths, early childhood mortality (q_{1-4}), and age-classed deaths, 6–20, 20–60, and beyond 60 years. For the analysis of infant mortality (q_0), we instead used two lags (lag 0 and 1). Finally, to obtain de-trended values for all demographic and economic series used, we applied a least-squares regression, a simple technique that provides a good fit to the data without loss of observations. We then calculated the ratio between observed and predicted values. These became the transformed values for all the economic and demographic series.[8]

A further clarification is needed regarding the scale of our investigation. In recent years, efforts have been made to overcome some initial limitations due to an overly aggregated approach. Almost all investigations of European pre-industrial societies looked at national entities (England, France, and Switzerland) or large regional areas (almost always corresponding to administrative entities). More recently, attention has moved towards the consideration of populations with specific socio-economic traits, or those characterized by clear social differences (Reher 1990; Galloway 1993). In this work, although the analysis centres on a whole state body, the scale of the investigation has been adapted to the minimum territorial unit allowed by the method employed.

The pattern of land allotment within the Grand Duchy in the first half of the nineteenth century is well known. Many studies on the subject have been carried out for the years 1832–5 and in particular on the land cadastre (Biagioli 1975). For the purpose of this work, the partitions made by previous authors were not judged to be entirely satisfactory. We were therefore compelled to develop a new set on the basis of uniformity criteria, taking into account an outline of already-existing area divisions in the region (Zuccagni-Orlandini 1832; Biagioli 1975; Pazzagli 1979).

Consequently, although we have data available for single communities, we decided to use a slightly larger scale. We have divided the Grand Duchy of Tuscany into agrarian areas, each representing a territory as uniform as possible and at the same time distinct from the neighbouring areas. We have also taken into account that in each area the number of inhabitants should satisfy the minimum prerequisites requested by the econometric method adopted. To summarize, the following are the uniformity criteria taken into account: geo-morphological characteristics, predominant cultivation methods, type of agricultural management, and number of inhabitants.

To avoid distorted results, we decided to exclude from the agrarian regions those communities with a town population that was either too numerous or which clearly exceeded the rural population. Thus the towns of Florence, Pistoia, and Siena were excluded, since their borough territories did not go beyond the town-walls, and so were Pisa, Livorno, Prato, Arezzo, and Grosseto.[9] In conclusion, after this process of aggregation and exclusion, we considered forty-three agrarian regions and eight 'urban' areas.

4. Economic Fluctuations and Mortality—the Regional Picture

The issues arising from the data analysis suggest many different research possibilities at various levels. As regards the short-term interaction between mortality and economic fluctuations, we can state that the correlation between price variation and mortality is always significant, even in such a short time span (1823–54) that is characterized by little variability in prices,[10] low levels of mortality, and the absence of virulent, widespread epidemics (Breschi 1990). In fact, the relation between price fluctuation and deaths (total adjusted deaths) was both immediate and delayed. The same year that witnesses a price increase (lag 0) shows a positive correlation with mortality; the year after (lag 1) a negative correlation, the following year (lag 2) we again notice a positive correlation. A similar pattern has been found in Tuscany over longer periods. By contrast, the demographic response was not so immediate in some areas of northern Italy (Table 13.2). These initial empirical analyses show a variability of reactions within central-northern Italy similar to that already observed in the European countries (Galloway 1988).

The picture is even clearer when the Tuscan population is considered according to age groups (Table 13.3). The probability of dying during the first year of life (q_0) is completely independent of short-term price fluctuations, while for other age groups the mortality response (q_{1-4}) to a price oscillation is significant and distributed over some years. The differences in reaction may be caused by food intake habits. During the time period in question, weaning took place around the end of the first year; throughout the nineteenth century this was the age indicated even for foundlings as the time limit for wet nursing (Corsini 1991). Breastfeeding not only allowed infants independence from the market situation, but it also protected them from epidemics, which were, however, not particularly widespread during the period under investigation (Del Panta 1980). As the protection received through breastfeeding came to an end, babies paid a heavy toll, however delayed. The possible explanation for the delay (more on this later) can be inferred—especially in the *Senese* countryside—from the working calendar of the parents.

The price increase—taken as a wide indicator of worsening living conditions—immediately affected (lag 0) adults from the ages 20 to 60, and in a lesser way, the elderly (ages 60 and beyond). If, on the one hand, the latter could be considered weaker due to their physical decline, on the other hand, it must be noted that this group experienced high mortality levels even during 'normal' years. Moreover, the importance of the role of the elderly within the family should not be underestimated, especially in the more traditional rural areas (Barbagli 1984). In the year immediately after the increase (lag 1), as indicated by the coefficient sign, we notice a decrease of deaths. We can say that after the initial effect on mortality, there is no

Table 13.2 Estimated elasticity of wheat price fluctuations on total adjusted deaths[a], Italy

Country	Period	Adj. R^2	Constant	Lag 0	Lag 1	Lag 2	Lag 3	Lag 4	Sum Lag	D-epid.
Tuscany	1823–54	0.32	0.503***	0.191***	-0.108	0.430***	—	—	0.513***	—
	1823–1934	0.13	0.481***	0.278***	0.118	0.121	—	—	0.517***	—
	1823–1934	0.73	0.651***	0.145***	0.042	0.146***	—	—	0.333***	0.719***
Friuli	1800–76	0.40	0.653***	-0.053	0.185**	0.295***	-0.069	-0.023	0.335***	0.269**
Bologna										
Urban	1699–1779	0.36	0.496***	0.112	0.459***	-0.232**	0.112	0.038	0.509	0.157***
Rural	1699–1779	0.38	0.999***	0.073	0.188***	-0.175***	0.063	-0.171**	-0.022	0.294***
Ravenna										
Urban	1711–85	0.28	1.047***	0.023	0.249*	-0.121	0.067	-0.302**	-0.084	0.450***
Rural	1711–85	0.52	1.312***	-0.167	0.071	0.034	-0.113	-0.185	-0.360	0.707***

[a] Total adjusted deaths to eliminate the demographic effect of fluctuations in births.

Note: Level of significance: ***1%, **5%, *10%.

Sources: Bologne and Ravenna: Scalone 2002; Friuli and Tuscany 1823–1934: Breschi and Gonano 2000.

Table 13.3 Estimated elasticity of wheat price fluctuations on different mortality indicators by age, Tuscany 1823–54

	Adj. R^2	Constant	Lag 0	Lag 1	Lag 2	Total lag
Total adj. deaths[a]	0.32	0.503***	0.191***	− 0.108	0.430***	0.513***
q_0	− 0.04	1.052***	− 0.088	0.035	—	− 0.053
$_4q_1$	0.11	0.612***	0.064	− 0.187	0.517***	0.394***
d_{5-20}	0.24	0.265	0.205	0.048	0.500***	0.753***
d_{20-60}	0.34	0.366**	0.280**	0.018	0.355**	0.654***
d_{60+}	0.26	0.479***	0.307***	− 0.056	0.286*	0.537***

[a] Total adjusted deaths to eliminate the demographic effect of fluctuations in births.

Note: Level of significance: ***1%, **5%, *10%.

second round. The following year (lag 2) the mortality rate rises again. The effects seem to be diluted in time, but the efforts to fight off the crisis continue to undermine even those who, for many reasons, might be expected to have been better equipped to face a recession.

Breschi and Gonano (2000) have found broadly similar results, again at the regional level, during the entire nineteenth century and at the beginning of the twentieth century (Table 13.2). The living conditions of large parts of the Tuscan population remained anchored to a rural form of economy and society. Demographic indicators show the beginning of a full demographic transition around the end of the 1880s. The persistence of a tight link between economic fluctuation and demographic mortality fluctuation should not therefore come as a surprise. A variety of empirical tests have been made to measure the reaction of the population of Tuscany to economic fluctuations (Breschi, Derosas, and Manfredini 1999; Livi Bacci 1998; Livi Bacci and Breschi 1990). The rich and detailed documentary material available from about the beginning of the nineteenth century allows us to investigate the 'geography' of the short-term link between economy and demography: a crucial investigative perspective for one of the most complex and rich regions on the Italian peninsula.

5. Economic Fluctuations and Mortality—Analogies and Territorial Differences

A desegregated approach is of particular importance when using panel data for the forty-three agrarian regions and the eight urban areas. Using a cross-sectional time-series model with random effects,[11] we found (for the total population and each age group) results largely consistent (in terms of lag effects and statistical significance) with those obtained with the DLM (Table 13.3).[12] Moreover, we can now appreciate the significant effect of the panel-level (region/area) standard deviation: the fraction of variance due to regional heterogeneity is equal to 93%. This was to be expected, given not only the large difference between urban areas and rural regions, but also in particular the high heterogeneity observed within the same rural territory. Indeed, the variance rate due to regional heterogeneity is still high (89%) even if we drop the eight urban areas from the analysis.

Before passing on to a detailed analysis of the results for the forty-three agrarian regions under examination, a consideration of the short-term relationship between economic variables and mortality in the urban and rural populations is of great interest. The results of this analysis, conducted using a method entirely analogous to that used for the whole population, are summarized in Table 13.4. For the urban population, the values obtained by introducing a dummy into the model to signal the epidemic of 1835 are also reported. Some urban centres, Livorno in particular, were affected by a localized, though acute, cholera epidemic, which, as is well known, especially affected the adult population (Betti 1857).

The values for the rural population do not differ greatly from those observed for the whole region (Table 13.3). Furthermore, the population of the forty-three agrarian regions represents three-fourths of that of the whole of Grand Duchy. The oscillations in economic variables seem to have had a heightened effect on population mortality among the rural population, both adults and the elderly. This confirms, once more, the absence of any influence of prices on infant mortality (q_0) while, as we have already seen, there seems to be a delayed effect on children (q_{1-4}).

The picture is less clear for the urban population. The adult and elderly populations were the sole groups to feel the consequences of the time-limited economic downward period once the epidemic of 1835 (which occurred, among other things, during a period of falling prices) was brought under control. As with the rural population, an immediate increase (lag 0) is evident in relative death rates. The mortality of the younger population seems entirely indifferent to the oscillations in economic variables. We must, however, bear in mind that the measurement of infant mortality in the urban context is problematic due to the presence of institutions for the care of abandoned babies. In the capital, the number of births was swollen by more than a fifth due to the presence of abandoned infants, mostly belonging to families from the countryside. At the same time, more than a few Florentine children died outside the city, due to the contemporary practice of sending babies and those still breastfeeding to a wet nurse in the countryside.[13]

Over this brief period at least, the population of the principal cities and the rural population of Tuscany would seem, therefore, to react in similar ways.

This result was also observed when limited to total adjusted deaths, throughout the entire period 1823–1934 (Breschi and Gonano 1998). Furthermore, preliminary analyses conducted by Scalone (2002) on the urban centres of Bologna and Ravenna and the surrounding rural regions seem to confirm certain homogeneity in the reactive behaviour of these two population groups (Table 13.2). This relative homogeneity with regard to demographic behaviour seems to diminish as soon as the investigation on the forty-three agrarian regions is carried out. The presentation of the results is limited to those age groups demonstrating a greater reactivity and variability in reaction at the territorial level.

Table 13.4 Estimated elasticity of wheat price fluctuations on different mortality indicators by age, rural and urban Tuscany 1823–54

	Adj. R^2	Constant	Lag 0	Lag 1	Lag 2	Total lag	D. epid.
Rural Tuscany							
Total adj. deaths[a]	0.29	0.530***	0.248**	−0.210	0.438***	0.476***	—
q_0	−0.01	1.119***	−0.123	0.001	—	−0.121	—
$4q_1$	0.19	0.633***	0.103	−0.350	0.618***	0.371*	—
d_{5-20}	0.14	0.403	0.231	−0.138	0.508**	0.601*	—
d_{20-60}	0.43	0.283**	0.370***	−0.003	0.365**	0.731***	—
d_{60+}	0.38	0.438**	0.377***	−0.025	0.220	0.572***	—
Urban Tuscany							
Total adj. deaths[a]	0.05	0.642***	0.181	0.044	0.138	0.364*	—
q_0	0.27	0.888***	0.057	0.057	—	0.114	—
$4q_1$	0.01	0.812***	−0.06	0.220	0.035	0.193	—
d_{5-20}	0.09	0.438	0.133	0.413	0.030	0.576**	—
d_{20-60}	0.02	0.728***	0.131	0.055	0.091	0.277	—
d_{60+}	0.09	0.663***	0.214	−0.125	0.252	0.341*	—
Urban Tuscany (with dummy epidemic)							
Total adj. deaths[a]	0.28	0.524***	0.265**	0.010	0.199	0.475***	0.283***
q_0	0.39	0.870***	0.082	0.047	—	0.127	0.130*
$4q_1$	0.02	0.716***	0.007	0.188	0.088	0.283	0.229
d_{5-20}	0.27	0.309	0.221	0.365	0.109	0.696**	0.333***
d_{20-60}	0.47	0.567***	0.243**	−0.012	0.195	0.426**	0.431***
d_{60+}	0.29	0.544***	0.302**	−0.157	0.307*	0.452***	0.266***

[a] Total adjusted deaths to eliminate the demographic effect of fluctuations in births.

Note: Level of significance: ***1%, **5%, *10%.

Figures 13.4–13.6, depicting the significance level of the estimated coefficients,[14] support our view with regard to the territorial distribution of the mortality response to wheat price fluctuations. The relationship is significant in the 'Tuscany of the river' region and in the *Senese* area, while it is very low, or almost absent, in the other areas. On the other hand, the inhabitants of the mountains or the Maremma marshes were less dependent on cereals, due to both alimentary consumption and access to the market. These two territories, although largely opposite in terms of their characteristics, shared certain forms of cultivation, since both had large areas of meadow and pasture. There were more animals for breeding and diary produce than in the territories of intensive cultivation, where cattle were used to work the land (Pazzagli 1992).

If we focus our analysis solely on the area of the river basin and the *Senese* area, the results suggest that we are faced with three dichotomies. First, a demographic one, showing different behaviour according to the age groups of adults and children (q_{1-4}); second, a chronological one, which contemplates the reactions at lag 0 and lag 2; and finally, a less evident, territorial one, setting the area of mixed cultivation against single-crop cultivation.

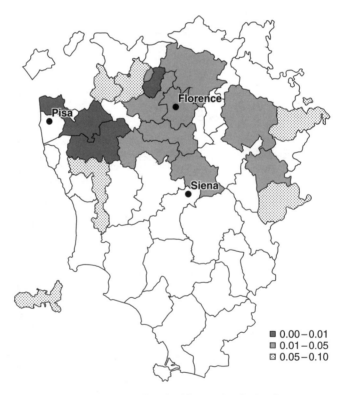

Figure 13.4   Adult deaths (d_{20-60}). DLM, significance level—lag 0

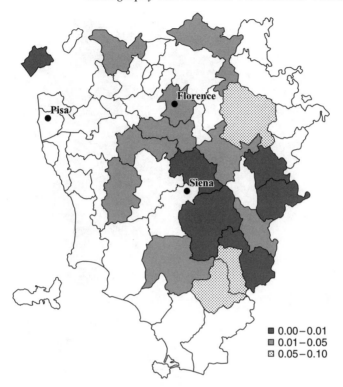

Figure 13.5   Adult deaths (d_{20-60}). DLM significance level—lag 2

We will now try to explain how the events took place, following a chronological order.

As the wheat prices rose, the immediate reaction in terms of mortality (lag 0) is most evident in the territory of mixed cultivation; that is, in the richest area of Tuscany. In this case, the people mostly at risk were the adults, followed by the elderly.

This is a well-known mechanism. The price rise corresponded to the decrease of the immediate availability of grain and, at the same time, access to the market became more difficult. The most seriously affected areas were those with a high population density, with olive trees and vineyards. These areas had a very low surplus of grain, if not a negative one, and a relatively high number of people had to rely on the market to acquire the cereals they needed (Biagioli 1991; Pazzagli 1992).

It should be pointed out that in some territories of mixed cultivation, such as the pasture regions, sharecroppers had diversified their incomes and therefore had access to a wider variety and choice of alimentary goods. Frequently, however, this was not the case. The sharecroppers' families were often in debt to the landowner; if they could use part of their best produce—olives and grapes—it was only to reduce the debt, certainly not to better their diet (Giorgetti 1974). The greater market

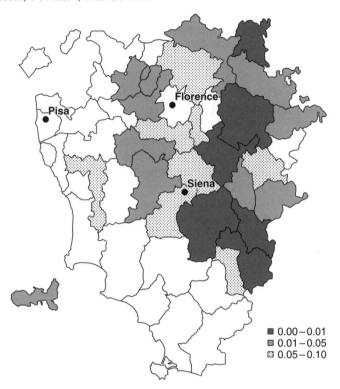

Figure 13.6   Child mortality rates (q_{1-4}). DLM, significance level—lag 2

dependence of the population from the 'Tuscany of the river' basin is explained, as we have often mentioned, by the more consistent presence of the poor, the farm labourers, and the wage earners in the countryside, and the high number of people residing in the urban centres.

The solar year following an increase in prices displays an evident negative correlation between wheat price and mortality, although with low intensity, in various agrarian regions and across all age groups (except infants). Such results can be explained by the fact that, after a period of time marked with an increase, mortality generally decreased since the weakest tended to be the most vulnerable initially.

We observe another increase in mortality during the following year (lag 2), although this time the consequences weigh more heavily upon children aged from one to five than upon adults. The agrarian areas most affected are not the same as those at lag 0. At lag 2, in fact, the areas of mixed cultivation are largely saved, while the effect of a price oscillation on death rates in the age group 1–4 (q_{1-4}) is particularly evident in the area of single-crop cultivation, 'the land without the harmony of trees'.

How can we explain such an apparent anomaly? In the *Senese* area and more widely over the whole of the south-eastern part of Tuscany, agriculture was poorer than in the north. However, the production of cereals was sufficient for a small population, even in times of scarcity (Pazzagli 1992: 210). As the volume of produce decreased, subsistence appears to have been still guaranteed, since we do not notice an increase in mortality.

In this area, however, traditional sharecropping regulated production relations in the countryside, and the economy as a whole was less developed. The portion of produce that was consumed by the farmers' families was usually higher, and relations with the market were consequently rare. Therefore, as the price increase diminished incomes, it also made the rural population more dependent on the market for the diversification of their diet. It thus is likely to have worsened quality of life, although in a limited way.

It should be added that, because of either the price increase or the need to overcome the poor summer produce, the sharecropper was inclined to intensify cereal production. This possibility existed in the geographical area of single-crop cultivation where a system of agrarian rotation allowed for a quarter, or even a third of the land to be left fallow. It might be that in the most difficult years fallow lands were cultivated, or that a second harvest was attempted with a consequent production of a spring cereal after a winter one. Moreover, the same crop was sometimes cultivated in the same field for two consecutive years, meaning that the rhythm of rotations could be intensified, and causing an impoverishment of the land. A reaction of this type would have merely delayed the negative consequences of a bad harvest, inducing a cycle of poor harvests rather than avoiding them altogether.

A rise in mortality among adults has the effect of increasing the number of orphans, the group most at risk (Breschi and Manfredini 2002). This factor probably condemned many youngsters, but it was not the only one: children could remain alone for other reasons as well. As the land for cultivation increased in the years immediately following the crisis, so did the demand for workers. The consequence was a longer absence of women—and mothers—from their homes. The situation was made worse when another child was born in the family. In this case, a period of economic difficulty started a form of competition among the children, causing an increase in mortality of younger children (Breschi and Derosas 2000; Breschi, Derosas, and Manfredini 2000).

Of course we are still making hypotheses but, for certain, the price of lower mortality incurred during the year zero had to be paid eventually. Adults did pay their toll, but those who paid mostly dearly were the children; that is, the ones who initially seemed to have gained most.

6. Conclusion

By applying the distributed lag model we have been able to explore the relationship between fluctuations in wheat prices and mortality, with reference to Tuscany in the first half of the nineteenth century. Some of the results partly reflect what was already known, but others raise new questions regarding the reaction mechanisms of a population to an agrarian crisis.

In particular, the effects on mortality of fluctuations in wheat prices are positive and almost always concentrated in lag 0. This model is representative of both the urban and rural populations, when the latter is considered as a whole. Town and countryside present more similarities than differences, as with regard to the various age groups. The adults and the elderly largely paid the consequences of an agrarian crisis. Infants—the weakest age group by far, and the one subject to highest overall mortality rates—were largely indifferent to wheat price oscillations. Slightly older children seem to have felt the consequences after a short delay.

The analysis of the forty-three rural regions permitted a specification of what some of the important links are in the complex relationship between economy and demography.

The evidence provided by travellers in the 1800s has provided a traditional picture of a wealthy country with a high standard of living—the 'Tuscany of the river'—as opposed to the desolate view of miserable areas—the Maremma marshes—or to the poor ones as the *Senese* countryside. At times, the bucolic images associated to the wealthiest part of the Grand Duchy have been matched to the difficult life conditions in the countryside (Giorgetti 1974), but its economic supremacy was never in doubt, nor was the fact that the inhabitants of the 'Tuscany of the river' region lived, on average, better than the others.

Some of the results emerging from our research appear almost in contrast with the images described—their very wealth itself might have been one of the weak points of the rich territories. Next to the well-off population also lived the poor, or at least the most fragile, in a higher proportion than elsewhere. We have noticed how under particular conditions, as during the times of price increase, it is not the general degree of wealth that warrants a good standard of living but the social composition of the population.

We are dealing, as we have already mentioned, with results that require some further verification, and therefore they must be treated with a certain caution. One initial step, albeit limited to the population of one village, would appear to reinforce what has already been stated.

We have a database at our disposal relating to the village of Casalguidi, located in the heart of the mixed agriculture region, which permits us to follow the life stories of individuals and families. Therefore, it is possible to study 'close up' the relationship between economic variables and mortality over a slightly longer period (1819–59) than the one covered in this chapter.

In some preliminary analyses, the effects of the economic crises on the mortality rates among the population of Casalguidi have been investigated, with particular reference to infants and children (Breschi, Derosas, and Manfredini 1999, 2000; Breschi *et al.* 1999). The analysis of these life stories allows us to keep multiple 'variables' at hand: those relating to the individual (sex, age, etc.), household (structure, profession of the head of the household, etc.), and context (the presence of epidemics, wars, etc.). The results observed in the microcosm of Casalguidi point, nevertheless, in the same direction as those encountered in agrarian regions where mixed agriculture was prevalent.

As in the whole region, the infants of Casalguidi were completely indifferent to price oscillations. Their death rates were, if anything, more sensitive to the changing of the seasons, with the added risks brought about by the summer and winter months. Another factor inducing greater mortality was modest socio-economic position of the parents, and, in particular, the age at which the child was weaned. At an individual level too, the death rate among children (younger than ten years old) does not seem to be connected to price oscillations, once factors which clearly play a far more direct role (such as, for example, the economic condition and viability of the parents) have been taken into account.

Once more, it is the parents, generally without any difference, who pay the highest price in the same year of a price increase. However, the added risk does not affect all adults but is mainly concentrated among wage earners, farmers, and small artisans. Among the elderly, the economic crisis affected only those who lived alone or in a nuclear family.[15]

If the investigation of these forty-three agrarian regions at the macro-level has opened up broad questions, the exploration at a micro-level (of a community, its families, and individuals) has provided some answers. It is, therefore, possible that this method might lead us to achieve greater clarity as to the reasons why the mountainous and marsh regions appear more impervious to economic stress, or why the countryside, 'the land without the harmony of trees', should instead react in such a complex and rich fashion.

Notes

1. All the maps used in this work had been drawn on the basis of a digital chart in the *Laboratorio informatico di Archeologia medievale* of the *Dipartimento di Archeologia dell'Università di Siena* within the project 'Demografia, economia e società nella Toscana dell'Ottocento'. We would like to thank Professor Tommaso Detti who has kindly allowed us to use it.

2. All over Tuscany the small land property was around 10%, coming in the first position in some communities of the mountainous areas (Detti and Pazzagli 2000).

3. The results are based on a detailed analysis of the nominative data of the 1841 census, and from their integration with data from a fiscal source.

4. What is considered here is a price variation, not its level. Therefore the Florence time series is perfectly compatible with the aim of this study.

5. '1 day–1 year', '2–5 years', '6–10 years', '11–20 years', '21–30 years', ..., '81–90 years', '100-years', and finally 'age unknown'. The age groups, sufficiently detailed from the first synthesis picture (year 1818), are even more abundant from the year 1855: 'from day 1 to 6 months', 'from 6 to 12 months', and then in yearly groups until year four; finally, in five-year groups (5–10, 10–15, ..., 95–99, 100-years, age unknown).

6. An annual price is published based on an average of monthly wheat prices (Bandettini 1957).

7. For a recent review of this method and results, see Bengtsson and Reher (1998).
8. Alternative de-trending techniques are, of course, possible. We considered two other possibilities for differentiating the natural logarithms of the original data and calculating ratios of observed values to a eleven-year centred moving average. However, we opted for least squares regression since the first method is not appropriate for our data (we analyse a thirty-year period) and in the second case we overly reduce the number of observations.
9. This last borough presents a low absolute value for the number of inhabitants in such a large territory, but they are all concentrated in a single small area. Moreover, the borough's extension formed a separate territorial unit, which could not be assimilated by any of the neighbouring agrarian areas.
10. Prices show relatively low fluctuations compared, for example, to the Napoleonic years and the crisis of 1816–17 when they increased by about 300–400%. However, during the poor harvests from 1845 to 1847, wheat prices rose by about 40% in the Florence market. The magnitude of this increase does not reflect the scarcity of local wheat production. The government, also under the pressure of popular demonstrations, abolished all duty on grains and promoted special wheat imports (Bandettini 1960: 17–18). A less favourable series of harvests commenced towards the end of the analysed period, with price increases of around 30–40%.
11. The estimates of the model were obtained using the *Xtregar* procedure in the STATA7 package. This procedure estimates cross-sectional time-series regression models when the disturbance term is first-order regressive. *Xtregar* offers the Baltagi-Wu GLS estimator of random effects.
12. The values of the coefficients are, of course, different from those of Table 13.3. In order to avoid redundancy and not to mislead, we have decided not to tabulate the results obtained with the *Xtregar* procedure.
13. In reality, the decennial statistics on deaths refer to the resident population, and therefore ought to contain those deaths of residents, which occurred outside the community. This is virtually 'certain' at least up until 1847. Childhood deaths were, however, 'elusive' (also due to their elevated numbers) over the course of the complex 'counting' operation conducted in the central offices of the Tuscan Civic State (Del Panta 1985; Breschi and Del Panta 1993).
14. The maps drawn using the coefficient values result are very similar to the ones presented. This is also the reason why we preferred to give more emphasis to the degree of statistical significance rather than to the size of the coefficients (elasticities).
15. These results are the outcome of new and preliminary analysis we carried out after having inserted two new data sets into the demographic database. One of these deals with house ownership and the other with the level of taxes paid by each household. These initial observations would appear to indicate that a higher degree of fragility in adults and the elderly could be linked in particular to household typologies and to the 'wealth' variable.

References

Bandettini, P. (1956) *La popolazione della Toscana alla metà dell'Ottocento*. Turin: Industria Libraria Tipografica Editrice.
——(1957) *I prezzi sul mercato di Firenze dal 1800 al 1890*. Turin: Industria Libraria Tipografica Editrice.

——(1960) *L'evoluzione demografica della Toscana dal 1810 al 1889*. Turin: Industria Libraria Tipografica Editrice.

Barbagli, M. (1984) *Sotto lo stesso tetto. Mutamenti della famiglia in Italia dal XV al XX secolo*. Bologna: Il Mulino.

Bengtsson, T. and Reher, D. (1998) 'Short and Medium Term Relations between Population and Economy', in C.-E. Núñez (ed.), *Debates and Controversies in Economic History. Proceedings of the Twelfth International Economic History Congress*. Madrid: Fundación Ramón Areces e Fundación Fomento de la Historia Económica, pp. 99–115.

Betti, P. (1857) *Considerazioni mediche sul colera asiatico che contristò la Toscana negli anni 1835–36–37–49*. Florence: Tipografia delle Murate.

Biagioli, G. (1975) *L'agricoltura e la popolazione in Toscana all'inizio dell'Ottocento: un'indagine sul catasto particellare*. Pisa: Pacini.

——(1991) 'Il podere e la piazza. Gli spazi del mercato agricolo nell'Italia centro-settentrionale', in P. Bevilacqua (ed.), *Storia dell'agricoltura italiana in età contemporanea*, III, *Mercati e istituzioni*. Venice: Marsilio, pp. 30–63.

Breschi, M. (1990) *La popolazione della Toscana dal 1640 al 1940. Un'ipotesi di ricostruzione*. Florence: Università degli studi di Firenze, Dipartimento Statistico.

——and Del Panta, L. (1993) 'I *passaggi*: una fonte particolare dello stato civile toscano'. *Bollettino di demografia storica*, 19: 71–92.

——and Derosas, R. (2000) 'The Contribution of the Eurasian Project to the Demographic History of Italy: Results and Perspectives on Infant and Child Mortality', in M. Neven and C. Capron (eds.), *Family Structures, Demography and Population. A Comparison of Societies in Asia and Europe*. Liège: Laboratoire de Démographie de l'Université de Liège, pp. 211–34.

——Derosas, R., Lagazio, C., and Manfredini, M. (1999) 'L'influenza del contesto familiare sulla sopravvivenza dei bambini. Risultati di indagini microdemografiche sull'Italia dell'Ottocento'. *Bollettino di Demografia Storica*, 30/31: 187–211.

——Derosas, R., and Manfredini, M. (1999) 'Family, Economy and Environment. Three Case-Studies on Mortality in 19th Century Italy', in M. Breschi, R. Derosas, and M. Manfredini (eds.), *New Perspectives in Demographic Micro-Studies Italy 19th Century*. Udine: Dipartimento di Scienze Statistiche, pp. 9–47.

——Derosas, R., and Manfredini, M. (2000) 'Infant Mortality in Historical Italy: Interactions Between Ecology and Society', in T. Bengtsson and O. Saito (eds.), *Population and the Economy: From Hunger to Modern Economic Growth*. Oxford: Oxford University Press, pp. 457–89.

——and Gonano, G. (1998) *Oscillazioni di breve periodo nei decessi per età, nei prezzi e nel clima, Toscana 1818–1939. Primi esperimenti*. Note di Ricerca, 17. Udine: Università degli studi di Udine, Dipartimento di Scienze Statistiche.

——and Gonano, G. (2000) 'Relazioni di breve periodo tra decessi per età, prezzi e clima. Toscana 1818–1939', in L. Pozzi and E. Tognotti (eds.), *Salute e malattia fra '800 e '900 in Sardegna e nei paesi dell'Europa Mediterranea*. Sassari: EDES, pp. 81–119.

——and Manfredini, M. (2002) 'Parental Loss and Kin Repercussions in a Rural Italian Village', in R. Derosas and M. Oris (eds.), *When Dad Died: Individuals and Families Coping with Family Stress in Past Societies*. Bern: Peter Lang, pp. 369–87.

Corsini, C. A. (1991) 'Breastfeeding, Fertility and Infant Mortality: Lessons from the Archives of the Florence Spedale degli Innocenti', in *Historical Perspectives on Breastfeeding*. Florence: UNICEF, Istituto degli Innocenti.

Del Panta, L. (1980) *Le epidemie nella storia demografica italiana (secoli XIV–XIX)*. Turin: Loescher.

Del Panta, L. (1985) 'Lo Stato Civile Toscano: una fonte per lo studio della mobilità temporanea'. *Bollettino di demografia storica*, 2: 51–7.

Detti, L. and Pazzagli, C. (2000) 'La struttura fondiaria del Granducato di Toscana alla fine dell'ancien régime. Un quadro d'insieme'. *Popolazione e storia*, numero unico: 15–47.

Doveri, A. (1990) *Territorio, popolazione e forme di organizzazione domestica nella provincia pisana alla metà dell'Ottocento*. Florence: Dipartimento Statistico, Università degli Studi di Firenze.

Galloway, P. R. (1988) 'Basic Patterns in Annual Variations in Fertility, Nuptiality, Mortality, and Prices in Pre-Industrial Europe'. *Population Studies*, 42: 275–303.

——(1993) 'Short-Run Population Dynamics Among the Rich and Poor in European Countries, Rural Jutland, and Urban Rouen', in D. S. Reher and R. S. Schofield (eds.), *Old and New Methods in Historical Demography*. Oxford: Oxford University Press, pp. 84–108.

Giorgetti, G. (1974) *Contadini e proprietari nell'Italia moderna. Rapporti di produzionee contratti agrari dal sec. XVI ad oggi*. Turin: Einaudi.

Harvey, A. (1981) *The Econometrics Analysis of Time Series*. London: Philip Allan.

Lee, R. D. (1981) 'Short-Term Variation: Vital Rates, Prices and Weather', in E. A. Wrigley and R. S. Schofield (eds.), *The Population History of England 1541–1871: A Reconstruction*. London: Edward Arnold, pp. 356–401.

Livi Bacci, M. (1998) *La popolazione nella storia d'Europa*. Bari-Rome: Laterza.

——and Breschi, M. (1990) 'Italian Fertility: An Historical Account'. *Journal of Family History*, 15(4): 385–408.

Mirri, M. (1972) *La lotta politica in Toscana intorno alle 'riforme annonarie' (1764–1775)*. Pisa: Pacini.

Mori, G. (1986) 'Dall'unità alla guerra: aggregazione e disgregazione di un'area regionale', in G. Mori (ed.), *Storia d'Italia Einaudi. Le regioni dall'Unità ad oggi. La Toscana*. Turin: Einaudi, pp. 3–44.

Pazzagli, C. (1979) *Per la storia dell'agricoltura toscana nei secoli XIX e XX, dal catasto particellare lorenese al catasto agrario del 1929*. Turin: Fondazione Luigi Einaudi.

——(1980) 'L'agricoltura montana della zona amiatina nella seconda metà del XIX secolo'. *Rivista di storia dell'agricoltura*, 2: 57–78.

——(1992) *La terra delle città. Le campagne toscane dell'Ottocento*. Florence: Ponte alle Grazie.

Persson, K. G. (1999) *Grain Markets in Europe 1500–1900. Integration and Deregulation*. Cambridge: Cambridge University Press.

Reher, D. S. (1990) 'Economic Fluctuations and Demographic Behavior in Urban Spain', in D. S. Reher (ed.), *Town and Country in Pre-Industrial Spain. Cuenca, 1550–1870*. Cambridge: Cambridge University Press, pp. 123–49.

Scalone, F. (2002) 'Confronto tra serie demografiche e dei prezzi in Emilia-Romagna durante i secoli XVII-XVIII', in M. Breschi and P. Malanima (eds.), *Prezzi, redditi, popolazioni in Italia: 600 anni (dal secolo XIV al secolo XX)*. Udine: Forum, pp. 73–95.

Torti, C. (1979) 'Struttura e caratteri della famiglia contadina: Cascina 1841', in *Contadini e proprietari nella Toscana moderna. Studi in onore di G. Giorgetti*, Vol. II. Florence: Olshki, pp. 173–201.

——(1982) 'Attività economiche e strutture familiari: prime ricerche su Pontedera fra '700 e '800', in *La demografia storica delle città italiane*. Bologna: CLEUB, pp. 467–93.

Zuccagni-Orlandini, A. (1832) *Atlante geografico, fisico e storico del Granducato di Toscana*. Florence: Stamperia Granducale.

14 New Evidence on the Standard of Living in Sweden During the Eighteenth and Nineteenth Centuries: Long-Term Development of the Demographic Response to Short-Term Economic Stress

TOMMY BENGTSSON AND MARTIN DRIBE

1. Introduction

One of the longest lasting economic-historical debates concerns the development of standard of living in the pre-industrial and early industrial periods. Whether or not the standard of living increased during the Industrial Revolution has been fiercely debated since the time of Marx, Engels, and the classical economists (e.g. Taylor 1975). In the early 1980s new evidence and estimations further fuelled this debate regarding the English case (Crafts 1982; Lindert and Williamson 1983). More recently there has also been a growing interest in the differences in standard of living between the East and the West, and what may have caused these differences (e.g. Goody 1996; Frank 1998; Lal 1998; Landes 1998; Pomeranz 2000; see also O'Brien 2001). This debate is also intimately connected to the broader question of why the West, rather than the East, was first to experience modern economic growth. In this debate a multitude of factors have been stressed, among them are differences in natural resources, technological development, institutional setting, access to colonial markets, cultural and religious factors, and so on.

This work has been done within the project *From Hunger to Modern Economic Growth. Demography and Family Behaviour in Sweden, 1650–1900*, with financial support from the Bank of Sweden Tercentenary Foundation and the Swedish Council for Social Research. Tommy Bengtsson gratefully acknowledges the opportunity to carry out this study while guest professor at the Danish Center for Demographic Research in Odense in 1999/2000. Previous versions of the paper have been presented at the ESF conference 'New Evidence of Standard of Living in Europe and Asia', in Arild, Sweden; the Department of Economic History, Lund University; the Department of Economics at Northwestern University; the Sound Economic History Conference, University of Copenhagen; the Fourth European Historical Economics Society Conference, Merton College, Oxford; and the annual meeting of the Social Science History Association in Chicago 2001. We are grateful to participants at these seminars for most valuable comments and suggestions.

While some authors have approached the issue by constructing various macro-economic indicators on production, wages, or productivity, others have focused on indicators of 'quality of life', such as housing conditions, working conditions, and the like. There have also been attempts to measure living standards by the health status of the population. One of the most straightforward ways of doing this is to study the development of life expectancy and mortality, where increased longevity could be seen as the ultimate indicator of a higher standard of living. In the last decades we have also seen a rapidly growing attention to various anthropometric measures (heights, body mass index, etc.) as indicators of standard of living (e.g. Engerman 1976; Steckel 1979, 1995; Komlos 1985; Steckel and Floud 1997; Floud, Wachter, and Gregory 1990; Fogel 1993).

In this chapter we propose a rather different measure of standard of living, which has been developed within the Eurasia Project on Population and Family History (EAP)[1] as a complement to the more traditional measures. It focuses on the way individuals and families in pre-industrial society responded to short-term economic stress, by which is meant short-term changes in income, employment opportunities, or food availability. We have made a long-term study of the mortality and fertility response to short-term economic stress, as measured by grain price fluctuations, for a rural area of western Scandia, Sweden, during the period 1766–1895, taking into account the structural changes this economy underwent. Our analysis focuses on the landless—the social group whose members lived closest to the margin. They were the group most vulnerable to economic stress and the least able to counteract its negative effects, the group that had the fewest options for ameliorating their lot in hard times (see Bengtsson and Dribe 2000). We include in this category all families whose land holdings were below subsistence level, that is, the semi-landless smallholders and crofters as well as completely landless labourers, soldiers, and artisans.[2] By studying how the landless responded to economic stress over time, we are able to give a new dimension to their standard of living. Higher mortality in response to short-term economic stress must be regarded as a clear indicator of a low standard of living, and a development towards a weaker mortality response should be interpreted as a positive development of living standards. Similarly, we argue that a fertility response to economic stress—whether intentional or not—could be interpreted as indicating a high degree of vulnerability to economic fluctuations, and thus of a rather low level of standard of living. Before turning to these issues, however, we shall review previous research on the standard of living development in Sweden. That will allow us to make more explicit comparisons of the results obtained by various methods and approaches.

2. The Standard of Living Development in Sweden—Where Do We Stand?

There can be little disagreement on the long-term development of standard of living in Sweden between, say, 1750 and 1914. As a result of the agricultural and industrial revolutions, living standards over much of the nineteenth and the early twentieth centuries increased tremendously by whatever indicators one chooses. Real wages, gross domestic product (GDP), educational levels, urbanization, and life expectancy all increased, while fertility declined, as did mortality in most age groups. However, when it comes to the development of the standard of living *within* this period there is much more uncertainty as to when, more precisely, the improvements occurred in various social groups.

2.1 Agricultural production

Most scholars seem to agree that per capita production of vegetable products (mostly grain) increased rapidly during the first half of the nineteenth century. As early as the second half of the eighteenth century there were several indications of a new and positive development of Swedish agriculture, the most notable being the beginning of the enclosure movement. However, it was not until the first decades of the nineteenth century that the process of agricultural transformation gained speed with more rapid and universal enclosures, new crops, crop rotations, improved tools, and land reclamation (e.g. Heckscher 1949; Utterström 1957; Martinius 1982; Magnusson 1996; Gadd 2000; Schön 2000). Most scholars also seem to agree that both agricultural production and productivity, at least in terms of increased production per worker employed in agriculture, increased as a result of these changes. Judging mainly from various indirect evidence on consumption and foreign trade, Utterström believed production of vegetable products to have doubled between 1815 and 1860, while population increased by only 60% (Utterström 1957: 700). Also using information on exports of agricultural products, and making assumptions regarding the development of domestic consumption, Martinius estimated that labour productivity in agriculture increased by 0.6–0.9% annually between the 1830s and 1860 (Martinius 1970: 168–74). One important novelty in this regard was the increased cultivation of potatoes in Sweden, as well as in other parts of Europe, during this period. Potato cultivation together with increased usage of iron tools were important factors in overcoming diminishing returns on the newly reclaimed land (Gadd 1983; see also Schön 2000). In the Historical National Accounts of Sweden, Schön (1995) also presents a similar picture: starting in the 1820s production per capita of both vegetable and animal products increased rapidly, but it stagnated during the 1830s and the 1840s. In the late 1840s, agricultural production per capita showed a rising trend, and the increase was rapid in the 1850s. In Scandia in particular, this agricultural development was paralleled by increased exports of grain (e.g. Fridlizius 1981) and urbanization (Bengtsson 1990: 186–7), two indicators of economic growth.

Thus, there seems to have been a pronounced positive economic development in the agricultural sector at least from the first decade of the nineteenth century. This, however, does not tell us very much about the development of standard of living in various social groups. To do that, we need more information on the distribution of the increased product among the various social groups.

2.2   Real wages for agricultural workers

It is difficult to detect a continuous increase before the second half of the nineteenth century (Jörberg 1972: vol. II, 337). Figure 14.1 shows real wages (measured as day-wages for agricultural workers deflated by the prices of rye).[3] In Sweden as a whole, real wages seem to have declined between the late 1770s and the early 1800s. They then increased until the early 1820s, after which a slight decline took place until around 1850. After 1850 real wages increased continuously, indicating a steady improvement in the standard of living of the agricultural labourers. The development in Malmöhus County (locus of the four parishes of this study) deviates somewhat from this picture, by not showing any decline in real wages in the final decades of the eighteenth century. Instead, the real wage level stayed rather constant, albeit with marked short-term fluctuations, until the 1860s, thereafter it increased for the rest of the century. However, as was pointed out above, the rate of growth towards the end of the century is exaggerated due to the use of rye price as the deflator (see note 3). Nonetheless, there can be little doubt that real wages increased steadily from the 1860s onwards. Thus, to the extent that real wages for day-labourers give an accurate picture of the standard of living for landless labourers, it does not seem as if they gained very much from the agricultural transformation that occurred during the first half of the nineteenth century. However, the agricultural transformation may also have led to a higher, and seasonally more even, employment for agricultural workers, which means that stagnating real day-wages do not necessarily imply declining real income

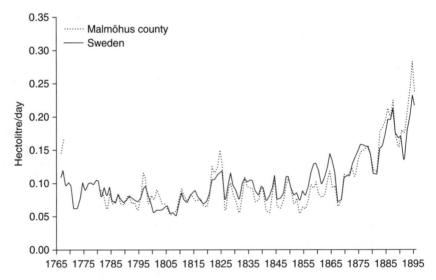

Figure 14.1   Real wages (day-wage/rye price) in Malmöhus County and Sweden, 1766–1895

Source: Jörberg 1972.

(e.g. Schön 2000). For England it has been estimated that the number of hours worked per year in agriculture increased by around 30% between 1760 and 1830 (Voth 2001: 129), which supports the idea that labour input increased considerably during the agricultural revolution. While it seems indisputable that the standard of living for labourers increased after the 1860s, it is more difficult to draw firm conclusions regarding the development during the first half of the nineteenth century.

It is likely that commercialization of agriculture and increased production and productivity raised the incomes of the market-producing peasants, leading to an increased stratification of the peasant group (Winberg 1975). One indication of such stratification is the pattern of increasing textile consumption from the 1830s onwards. Initially the demand for high quality textiles grew fastest, which may be interpreted as indicating rising incomes in the wealthier social groups. But in the late 1840s the demand for everyday textiles also started to increase, which reflects the rising incomes of the larger peasant groups (Schön 1979).

2.3 Investment in human capital

The level of investment in human capital has often been seen as an important dimension of standard of living, and some measure of educational level is usually included in the indices of standard of living, such as the Human Development Index. The level of literacy in Sweden in 1800, as measured by writing ability, was 10–30%; by 1900 it was over 90%. The increase was rather modest in the beginning, but it accelerated considerably after 1850 (see Johansson 1977), partly as a result of the introduction of compulsory education in 1842. A more detailed study of Scandia, however, has shown marked discontinuities in the development of literacy in the early nineteenth century, when the level of writing ability varied with economic cycles (Nilsson and Svärd 1994). This study also clearly demonstrates the marked social differences in writing ability in this period. About half of the male freeholders could write; only 10% of the landless could. Moreover, there were also considerable regional differences between peasants in the commercialized areas of southwestern Scandia and the more peripheral regions of the northeast. Thus, in the late eighteenth century freeholders were demanding writing skills and mustering the necessary resources to make the investment, while it was not until the second half of the nineteenth century that most landless labourers learned to write. This seems to indicate that the development of literacy corresponds fairly well with the development of real incomes in the different groups.

2.4 Demographic indicators of standard of living

Figure 14.2 reports the period life expectancy at birth (e_0) in Sweden from 1766/70 to 1891/95. The second half of the eighteenth century shows no clear trend. In the

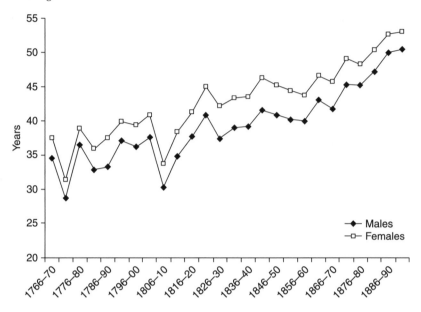

Figure 14.2   Life expectancy at birth (e_0) in Sweden, 1766/70–1891/95

Source: Berkeley Mortality Database, Department of Demography, University of California, Berkeley.
http:/demog.berkeley.edu/wilmoth/mortality

years 1772–3 and 1808–9 life expectancy dropped quite dramatically due to widespread famine following severe harvest failures (1771–2) and epidemics (e.g. typhus) during the Finnish War (1808–9) (Hofsten and Lundström 1976: 47). After 1810 life expectancy increased until the early 1820s, followed by a stagnation or very weak increase, between the late 1820s and the late 1850s. After 1860 life expectancy increased steadily for the rest of the nineteenth century. Broadly speaking, this development seems to agree fairly well with the real wage development pictured in Figure 14.1. Until around 1810 real wages declined slightly followed by an increase until the mid-1820s, after which comes a period of stagnation before the continuous increase starts in the mid-1860s. Thus, it appears as if both the economic and demographic indicators show a similar development: some improvement in the beginning of the nineteenth century, stagnation during the period of agricultural transformation and steady increase after the 1860s. For Malmöhus County the development seems to deviate slightly from the early nineteenth-century real wage improvements, otherwise it looks quite similar.

The increased life expectancy can to a large extent be accounted for by the dramatic decline in infant and child mortality from the late eighteenth century onwards. Adult mortality shows an increasing tendency during the late eighteenth century but then starts to decline in the first decades of the nineteenth century and after about 1850 declines more rapidly (e.g. Statistics Sweden 1999: 116). In the late 1840s and the early 1850s child mortality (ages 1–14) turned upwards again, quite substantially

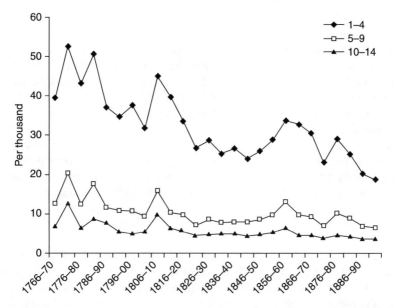

Figure 14.3a Age-specific death rates for male children (1–14 years) in Sweden, 1766/70–1891/95

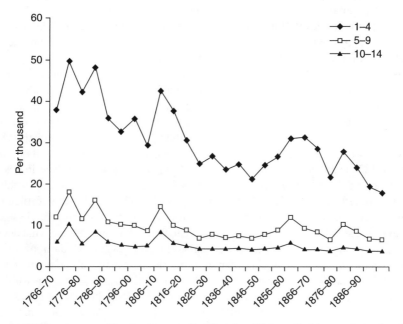

Figure 14.3b Age-specific death rates for female children (1–14 years) in Sweden, 1766/70–1891/95

but only temporarily, as shown in Figure 14.3(a) and (b). Sandberg and Steckel (1988) have argued that this increase was largely caused by typical 'children's diseases,' whose causes are known to be related to nutrition, for instance, measles, whooping cough, and dysentery (see also Hofsten and Lundström 1976: 47–9; Rotberg and Rabb 1985: 305–8). This led them to conclude that the nutritional status of children probably declined during this period (Sandberg and Steckel 1988). Fridlizius, however, questioned this conclusion, arguing that most of the *increase* in child mortality during this period was caused by diseases related only weakly to nutrition, or not at all: scarlet fever, diphtheria, and croup, while measles and whooping cough show roughly the same frequency as before (Fridlizius 1989). Thus, although child mortality unquestionably increased during the late 1840s and the 1850s, it still remains unclear to what extent this was related to changes in nutrition.

2.5   *Anthropometric measures of standard of living*

In more recent years increasing attention has been devoted to various anthropometric measures of standard of living, most notably heights and body mass index (see Steckel 1995 for a review). Here we will limit our attention to heights, since this is the only measure available for Sweden in this period. Human final height serves as a measure of net-nutrition, that is, actual food intake minus claims on nutrition made by body maintenance functions, work, and disease. Even if genetic factors have an impact on individual height, the differences in average heights between different populations can largely be accounted for by environmental rather than genetic factors (Steckel 1995). In particular the nutritional intake and disease load during infancy and adolescence—the two most pronounced growth phases of humans—are important determinants of final height.

Sandberg and Steckel have in several articles studied the development of heights in Sweden using data for soldiers (Sandberg and Steckel 1980, 1987, 1988, 1997). They found soldiers born in the early nineteenth century to have been about 1 cm taller than their counterparts born in the second half of the eighteenth century, indicating an improvement in standard of living (Sandberg and Steckel 1980). However, what is perhaps more interesting is their finding that the cohorts born in the late 1830s and the 1840s experienced declining heights, which would indicate a worsening of the situation, at least for the social groups from which the soldiers were recruited, during this period (Sandberg and Steckel 1988). It is difficult to immediately connect the declining stature for cohorts born during the 1840s to lower living standards, since, as was made clear above, it is uncertain to what degree the increase in child mortality was related to changes in standard of living. Since heights measure net- rather than gross-nutrition, it may well be the increased disease load facing these cohorts that accounts for the decline in stature, which in turn might be only weakly related to nutrition and standard of living. Thus, also in the case of heights, it turns out to be difficult to draw any firm conclusions concerning the standard of living development for the landless in the phase of agricultural transformation. After this temporary decline in stature, a continuous increase begins, showing no adverse effects of the more rapid industrialization in the final decades of the nineteenth century (Sandberg and Steckel 1997).

2.6 Proletarianization and standard of living

The period of agricultural transformation from the late eighteenth century onwards also witnessed a dramatic change in the social structure of the Swedish population during what has been termed the proletarianization of the countryside. While the number of peasants increased by 10% between 1750 and 1850, the number of landless quadrupled (Wohlin 1909: 197, 257; see also Winberg 1975: 17). This increase of the landless population came mostly as a result of increased household formation in the landless groups, and not from social differences in fertility. It became increasingly common that the children of landed peasants could not maintain the social status of their parents. The development of agriculture, in particular the increased demand for labour that development gave rise to, made it possible to establish an independent household without having access to land; something that was much more difficult before the agricultural transformation. Malmöhus County was proletarianized earlier than the country as a whole, and the proportion of the landless there was already considerable in the second half of the eighteenth century (Lundh 1999).

The question is whether this proletarianization process also implied a pauperization of the population, thereby increasing the number of poor and destitute. In a pioneering study of nineteenth-century middle Sweden, Lundsjö used taxation data to measure poverty ratios, in which the poor were defined as those who could not pay even the lowest tax. The poverty ratios varied closely with the harvest outcome indicating that the number of poor according to this definition was highly dependent on the economic circumstances. However, it is difficult to find a clear pattern linking proletarianization with increased poverty. Quite the contrary, the region with the most pronounced agricultural development and proletarianization (the western parts of the country) showed declining poverty, while the eastern part, with a much slower economic and demographic development, experienced rising poverty rates (Lundsjö 1975). Similarly, Söderberg, using the same measure for southern Sweden in the nineteenth century, found declining poverty rates in the areas that were changing most rapidly, while the areas of slower growth saw their poverty ratios increase (Söderberg 1978).

It appears that a more pronounced increase in the standard of living for the lower social strata did not take place until the second half of the nineteenth century. From then onwards agricultural production and real wages for agricultural workers grew, and the literacy rate increased as did heights. Life expectancy at birth increased due to a decline in mortality rates in all age-groups, and while proletarianization increased, pauperization decreased. The earlier pattern of development is less clear. The agricultural transformation during the first half of the nineteenth century raised the incomes of market-producing peasants, widening the gap between landed peasants on the one hand and the landless and semi-landless groups on the other. However, to what extent the standard of living of the landless and semi-landless declined or remained unchanged during this process remains unclear from the evidence presented here. Several indicators point to stagnation rather than a decline, while the development of stature, and possibly also mortality, could indicate a worsening of the situation at least among children. Moreover, since the demographic data presented above refer to the whole population and it seems likely that the landed groups saw an improvement in their situation, the standard of living of the landless could actually have been even worse than the aggregate figures indicate.

In the remainder of this chapter we try to shed new light on this issue of the standard of living of the landless groups during the agricultural transformation and early industrialization. Our approach to the study of standard of living focuses on the vulnerability of landless groups to economic fluctuations. Our empirical analysis examines three phases of the period 1766–1895: the pre-transformation phase (1766–1815), the transformation phase (1815–65), and the post-transformation, or industrialization, phase (1865–95).

3. A New Approach to Standard of Living

We measure the standard of living by the ability to overcome short-term economic stress. If one cannot fulfil one's long-term plans—to survive, to marry, and to have children—in the face of acute short-term changes in the environment, one can be said to have a rather low standard of living. Thus, sensitivity to short-term economic stress reveals a low level of standard of living. By short-term economic stress, we mean variations in income or the cost of living, particularly in food prices, from one year to the next or even within short time spans. Variations in food prices were often substantial and possibilities to compensate by increasing income were few. Temperature data could also be used as an alternative indicator of short-term economic stress. Because poorer households often could not afford to heat their houses in winter, the members were consequently more susceptible to disease, and were in frailer health than members of wealthier households. But short-term economic stress could stem from other sources as well, such as highly virulent epidemics, changes in taxation, wars, etc. There is no doubt however, that the changes in harvests and food prices were of great concern for a majority of the population up to the twentieth century, which is the reason for choosing food prices as the indicator of short-term economic stress.[4] Most people spent a major share of their income on food, and bread dominated the diet.[5]

To justify the choice of grain price as an indicator of short-term economic stress, it is necessary to establish a link between food prices and consumption. Generally, it is believed that the change in production is smaller than in price (Wrigley 1987: 93; Livi-Bacci 1991: 61; see also Bengtsson 2004). Even though large price changes—30% or more from one year to the next—were common, changes in production were somewhat smaller. How much then did the calorie intake change with such changes in grain production? While we do not have any calorie calculations for southern Sweden, we have it for nearby Copenhagen. The yearly decline in calorie intake per head in Copenhagen could be as much as 14% during the worst years of the eighteenth century (Thestrup 1971: 258–9). This figure is based on the assumption that the quantity and quality of other food items, like pork and beef, were not influenced by the bad harvest, which is optimistic. Not all people had to lower their consumption in bad years, however some inhabitants had to lower it more. A qualified guess is that a decline in the calorie intake for the poorer parts of the population by about 10 to 20% was a likely outcome of quite normal price increases during the pre-industrial period. In years of very high prices, the effects are bound to have been much bigger for these groups while other groups certainly benefited from high prices.

Since people in the past were well aware of the short-term variation in harvests and demand for labour, they planned for it. The most obvious measure taken would be to store food, but storage was very costly in the past, since a large part of the stored grain was lost while in storage. As much as 20% per year might be lost when storing grain; for potatoes the figure would be even bigger. Moreover, the nutritional content of the stored food was degraded. Consequently, the quantities of food stored in the past were only very limited (e.g. Persson 1999: ch. 3). Saving money to buy food could be costly as well, since prices went up in years of bad harvests. Diversification of production was therefore necessary. When harvests failed, efforts were made to find additional sources of consumption in other vegetables and meat. It is, however, unlikely that it was possible to fully compensate the gap in consumption this way. Another potential way of smoothing per capita consumption was to send some family members away to seek food and/or employment elsewhere. That way what food there was lasted longer for the remaining family members, and hopefully the migrating family member could bring something back as well.

If these measures failed, the family could borrow food or money to maintain consumption. Kin, neighbours, employers, and churches gave loans for consumption. Borrowing from the church or a bank depended, however, to a large extent on access to land or other assets that could be used as collateral, or security, for loans (Svensson 2001). Relatives and employers were more likely sources of help. Employers had a legal responsibility to take care of their workers, as had parents to take care of their children and vice versa when the parents became old.

If all the measures taken by employers, family, and kin failed, the local community or state might provide help. The poor law system, which was a local responsibility, became more regulated all over Sweden during the 1830s and the 1840s (Skoglund 1992). However, it was intended for only a few categories of the needy, amounting to a very small percentage of the population: the utterly destitute, often elderly and/or handicapped persons with no resources at all.[6] Other social welfare measures, such as extra social spending on roads and other public works in years of high unemployment, were modest. The spending on creating new jobs averaged around 1% of the annual governmental expenditures with a peak of 2.6% in 1846 (Olofsson 1996: 121).

Naturally, measures to smooth consumption are likely to have differed between different groups in society. Therefore, one important question is how different individual and household characteristics, such as land-ownership, social status, position in the household, etc., influenced the demographic response to economic and demographic stress. For example, households that farmed their own land and employed servants or labourers, were probably in a better position to avoid the most serious effects of economic stress, while those totally lacking resources had much smaller opportunities to undertake such measures, which made them highly vulnerable to stress.

The idea of analysing the demographic response to short-term economic stress in different social groups by combining longitudinal micro-demographic data with macro-economic data was first developed by Bengtsson (1989, 1993) and has been refined within the EAP project, in particular when it comes to the importance of household characteristics and transfers within the household in conditioning the response to stress (Bengtsson 2004). Although this standard of living concept can also be used in modern welfare societies (after suitable modification), it has been developed for situations where data are sparse and where living standards are low. The ideas originate from analyses of the effects of economic stress, measured by food price variation, on mortality, fertility, and nuptiality carried out at macro level and bear some similarities to Amartya Sen's concepts 'functionings' and 'capabilities', as shown in the introduction of this volume.

4. Area, Data, and Statistical Model

The dataset is based on family reconstitutions carried out within the Scandian Demographic Database[7] for nine parishes in western Scandia in southern Sweden. The sample used in this paper consists of four of these nine parishes: Hög, Kävlinge, Halmstad, and Sireköpinge. The social structures of the parishes varied somewhat. Hög and Kävlinge were dominated by freeholders and tenants on crown land, a group rather similar to the freeholders regarding its social characteristics, while Halmstad and Sireköpinge were totally dominated by tenants on noble land (see Bengtsson and Dribe 1997; Dribe 2000). In addition to the peasant group, the parishes also hosted various landless and semi-landless groups, dependent on working for others to cover the subsistence needs of the family. In this chapter we will focus our attention on the landless and the semi-landless. Table 14.1 shows the social status of family heads in the four parishes. The peasant group has been subdivided according to type of land (freehold/crown land and noble land) and the productive potential of the landholding measured in *mantal*.[8] The dividing line chosen—1/16 of a *mantal*—was the minimal amount of land required in the beginning of the nineteenth century to be considered as a landed peasant (*besuttenhetsgräns*) and it corresponded roughly to 15 acres in Scandia at that time (Sommarin 1939: 23, 29). As Table 14.1 clearly shows, the number of smallholders increased over the nineteenth century especially on freehold and crown land, implying that the proportion of peasants having landholdings below the minimum requirement increased, which serves to indicate the increased social differentiation

Table 14.1 Social structure of family heads in the four parishes, 1766–1895 (in %)

Social group	1766–1815	1815–65	1865–95
Higher occupations/nobility	1	1	1
Landed peasant			
Freeholders/crown tenants > 1/16	13	13	13
Noble tenants > 1/16	25	12	2
Semi-landless groups			
Freeholders/crown tenants < 1/16	0	6	13
Noble tenants < 1/16	0	2	2
Cottagers/crofters	28	26	8
Landless groups			
Agricultural labourers	18	25	40
Artisans/qualified labourers	2	4	11
Soldiers	4	5	4
Lodgers	1	4	3
Others/n.a.	8	1	2
Total	100	100	100
Person-years	16,235	26,307	15,597

Source: Parish records (vital events), poll-tax registers.

and stratification of the peasant group we discussed in Section 2. Viewed as a single group, however, the proportion of peasants with land taxed in *mantal* declined from 38% in the first period to 30% in the last period.

The semi-landless includes crofters and cottagers as well as peasants with land below subsistence level. These groups were dependent on working for others to earn supplementary income. The exact status of the crofter group is somewhat unclear, even though there is much to indicate that they should be considered as a semi-landless group, perhaps more like smallholders than like the completely landless labourers (e.g. Jonsson 1980; see also Dribe 2000). However, there also appears to have been changes over time in the way these groups were classified. People listed as cottagers at one point in time were later called crofters, and it is not clear whether any real change in their circumstances had taken place (cf. Lundh 2002; Persson 2002). This made it necessary to merge the two groups together in the analysis. In any case, we can safely assume that crofters, cottagers, and smallholders did not belong to the group of market-producing peasants that we believe gained most from the agricultural transformation, which makes it reasonable, at least for our purposes in this chapter, to merge them with the landless group.[9]

The landless group, as defined in Table 14.1, increased from 33% in the first period to 60% in the final one. Despite increasing productivity in agriculture, the vulnerability of this group of non-landholders may have increased over the nineteenth century as a result of the increasing market penetration of rural society and a greater dependency on wage labour. This process is also connected to a more general social differentiation of rural society in the nineteenth century, where not only did new landless groups emerge, but the differences within the peasant group grew larger, as is clear from the increasing number of smallholders in Table 14.1 (see also Winberg 1975: 55–6). Thus, according to this view, eighteenth-century Scandia may have been more egalitarian, although all groups were in general at a lower level of standard of living, than it was during the first half of the nineteenth century, which may in turn have also increased the vulnerability of these groups in times of economic hardship.

In 1766 the four parishes had a population of 1,310 inhabitants, which had increased to 3,866 by 1894: an annual increase of 0.8% over this 128-year period. The growth rate was lower in the second half of the eighteenth century (0.8% between 1766 and 1800) than in the first half of the nineteenth century (1.0% between 1800 and 1850). Then in the second half of the nineteenth century the rate of growth fell back to the same level as in the late eighteenth century (0.7% 1850–1894), primarily due to considerable out-migration following the urbanization process of this period (Bengtsson and Dribe 1997).

The family reconstitutions were carried out using data on births, marriages, and deaths, from the late seventeenth century up till 1894. The material is of high quality, with only a few years missing, even though a certain degree of under-recording has been discovered (Bengtsson and Dribe 1997). The reconstitutions were carried out automatically using a computer program. The method used has been described in a previously published work in great detail, which will not be reproduced here. The method has been carefully evaluated, and it seems satisfactory overall (Bengtsson and Lundh 1991). Additional manual linking and corrections have considerably increased the number of linked events (see Dribe 2000: 26). The database contains all individuals who were born in, or migrated into, any of the parishes. Instead of sampling a certain stock of individuals, for example, a birth cohort, each individual is followed from birth, or time of in-migration, to death, or out-migration.

We have used the annual poll-tax registers (*mantalslängder*) to determine where the families lived and whether they had access to land. The registers, set up for tax collecting purposes, give the size of each landholding, the type of ownership (i.e. noble, crown, church, or freehold), and the number of servants and lodgers. Information from these registers has been linked to the reconstituted families, whereby information has been obtained, not only on the demographic events, but also on the economic realities of these families.

4.1   Measurement of economic stress

Information on grain prices and wages at different administrative levels are available in the market price scales (*markegångssättningen*). In a previous study we presented this material for these parishes and analysed the price development of different crops (Bengtsson and Dribe 1997). We will not reproduce that analysis here, but we will point out some of its more important findings that are relevant to the present analysis. First, the prices and wages in the market price scales seem to reflect the market prices in the towns and the regions in a satisfactory way. We analysed the prices at town, county, and *härad* level (*härad* is an administrative level between the county and the parish) in our previous analysis and found a very high degree of correspondence.

Second, the price developments of different crops (rye, barley, and oats) show a very similar development over time. We will use the price of rye in the analysis below as an indicator of economic fluctuations, but it can probably be seen as a more general indicator, which is not highly dependent on the actual mix of different crops in consumption and production. However, we lack data for long periods of time for some commodities of increasing importance, such as potatoes, animal products, housing, clothing, etc. Although we can expect that they became more important in the family budgets over time, even in the later part of the nineteenth century a large proportion of the food budget was spent on grain (Myrdal 1933). Thus, we believe that the fluctuations in grain prices were of great importance to rural families throughout all three phases of the whole period, and that they will therefore serve as rather good indicators of the economic situation of families, in particular of the landless.

We also lack data on nominal wages at, or below, county level for the first period. Until the 1850s and the 1860s nominal wages were constant for long periods of time, implying that real wages, in the short term, mainly reflected grain price fluctuations. As was discussed previously, real wages, as measured by nominal wages deflated by the price of rye, stayed quite constant in Malmöhus County until the mid-1860s and then increased steadily for the rest of the century (see Figure 14.1 above). In the short-run real wages show considerable variation, mostly due to variation in the rye price. Since our prime concern in this chapter is with the demographic response to short-term economic fluctuations, it makes sense to use the rye price as an indicator of economic stress.

Figure 14.4 shows the logarithms of rye prices (actual values and Hodrick–Prescott trend) at the local level in the area under study.[10] Clearly, there is a long-term trend in the price development, as well as medium-term cycles. It is not within the scope of the present study to analyse these trends and cycles. In order to picture the short-term fluctuations, we need to de-trend the series by subtracting the Hodrick–Prescott trend[11] from the logged actual values. These de-trended series are used in estimating the multivariate models below.

Traditionally, particularly in aggregate studies, grain prices have often been used as proxies for harvest outcome, so that high grain prices reflect a bad harvest and low food supply, leading to increased mortality, delayed marriages, etc. However, when doing micro studies on small communities, the relationship between local harvest outcome and grain prices can be expected to have been rather weak, since a number of other factors become more important, such as trade, different external factors, the harvest outcome outside the region, etc. A comparison of grain prices and harvest outcome in western Scandia also corroborates this expectation;

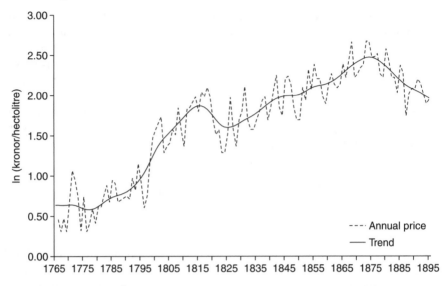

Figure 14.4   Natural log local rye prices (actual values and HP-trend), 1766/70–1891/95
Source: Bengtsson and Dribe 1997.

there is only a very weak relationship between local harvest outcome and grain prices in the region.[12] In times of a local harvest failure, grain could be bought from other regions, thereby smoothing prices. Similarly, severe harvest failures in other regions or other exogenous events could drive up local grain prices, without changes in the local harvest outcome. This implies that the grain price can only serve as a very poor indicator of the local harvest outcome. Instead, local grain prices must be seen as determined mainly exogenously. Ideally, we should include both the local harvest outcome and grain price in the analysis. For shorter periods of time this is also possible and has shown to be fruitful in the analysis of migration (Dribe 2000, 2003a). For the long period of time analysed here, however, this has not been possible, so we have limited the analysis to grain prices.

For the landless and the semi-landless groups studied here, rising grain prices can be expected to have lowered the real wages, provided that they were paid money wages and that they were dependent on the market for their consumption. We know that they were often paid partly in money and partly in kind (e.g. Granlund 1944), but even in cases where they were paid in kind, the wage could be denoted in money and then converted into grain using the market price sales which implies that also payments in kind were negatively affected by high prices of grain. Hence, it is probably safe to assume that completely landless labourers were negatively affected by high grain prices.

In estimating the models in the empirical analysis we use combined time-series and event-history analysis, which makes it possible to run regressions on the change of life status, that is, dying or giving birth to a child, measuring the effects of different explanatory variables (or covariates) on the hazard of the event. More specifically, we use the Cox proportional hazards model, which is distinguished from other proportional hazards models by not requiring any specification of the underlying hazard function with time varying external (community) covariates (Cox 1972; see also Collett 1994). The main interest in this case is to estimate the impact of different covariates on the hazard of the event.[13] The model applied to mortality can be written as:

$$\ln h_i(a) = \ln h_0(a) + \beta X_i + \gamma Z(t),$$

where $h_i(a)$ is the hazard of the event for the ith individual at age a; $h_0(a)$ is the 'baseline hazard', that is, the hazard function for an individual having the value zero on all covariates; β is the vector of parameters for the individual covariates X_i that are estimated; and γ is the parameter for the external time varying covariate $Z(t)$.

In the fertility analysis, we use time since last birth as the duration time (a) instead of age. In discussing the results below, relative hazards (or hazard ratios) are used as measures of the difference between groups with different values on the covariates. The relative hazards are the difference in the hazard of the event for the group under consideration, relative to the reference category. A value of 1.50 implies that the hazard of the event of interest in the group is 50% higher than in the reference category, while a figure of 0.50 implies that the hazard is 50% (or half) of the hazard in the reference category.

The aggregated economic indicator (de-trended values of natural log rye price) is included in the regressions as a communal or external covariate (e.g. Bengtsson 1993), which means that the aggregate economic information is used as a time-varying covariate common to all individuals in the risk set at each point in calendar time. We show the mortality response to a 10% increase in prices in the tables, which was a modest price change during this period. The increase was higher than 120% in no fewer than fourteen years during this period.

5. Mortality Response to Economic Stress

From our previous discussion of what we know about the development of standard of living using traditional measures, we would assume that the mortality response to economic fluctuations among the landless was much the same until after about 1850, when we expect it to become weaker. We also expect the mortality response to be pronounced for children above age 1 and for adults in the working age group. The reason why we do not believe that infants and the elderly, that is, the groups normally considered to be the most vulnerable, to gain most from increasing standards of living is that both these groups seem more responsive to factors other than external economic stress. Infants seem to be more dependent on breast-feeding practices, and the elderly on their investments earlier in life in sustaining arrangements and relationships, both financial and personal.[14] We also expect the change in mortality response to economic stress in the second half of the nineteenth century to be much the same for males and females, since opportunities to work outside the home increased for both sexes.

The reason why we do not expect the response to short-term economic stress to decline during the transformation of the agricultural sector in the beginning of the nineteenth century is that this development seems to have favoured the landed groups rather than the landless, as was previously discussed. Contemporary evidence also indicates that the landless had problems finding jobs in bad harvest years in the beginning of the nineteenth century. Furthermore, the poor relief system was reorganized by the end of this period, indicating previous incapability to take care of the poor (Skoglund 1992; Banggaard 2002).

With regard to the social welfare system, we expect the conditions in all four parishes to be much the same, since such a small percentage of the population was taken care of by the poor law system. If there were to be any difference, we would expect Hög and Kävlinge, which were dominated by freeholders and crown tenants, to be somehow different from Halmstad and Sireköpinge, which were dominated by estate owners, since the different social groups might well have different economic and social motivations, as well as different opportunities.

Table 14.2 shows the Cox regression estimates for mortality among adults in working ages, 25–55 years. The reason why we start at age 25 and not 15 is that we have a lot of migration among young servants (e.g. Dribe and Lundh 2002), for which we have no data before 1829. In model 1 the covariates are parish, sex, birth year, and rye prices. In model 2 we also estimate the effects of short-term economic stress on females and males individually, by including an interaction term. All estimations are made for all three periods: 1766–1815, 1815–65, and 1865–95. The number of events is between 129 and 323, with the lowest number for the last period. Somewhat surprisingly we only find a strong mortality response during the second period, while we are unable to detect any evidence for a mortality response among the landless in the working age group during the pre-transformation phase (1766–1815) and the industrialization phase (1865–95). The response during the transformation phase is quite strong; a 10% increase in food prices is followed by a 10% increase in mortality within a year (12% for males and 8% for females). There are no statistically significant differences between adult males and females in any of the periods, which indicate a rather uniform response between the sexes.

The mortality differentials between the parishes change over time. It is highest in Sireköpinge in the first period, Halmstad in the second period, and Kävlinge in the third period. We also estimated a model in which the effect of living in a freeholder/ crown tenant parish or a noble tenant parish on the vulnerability of short-term economic stress on landless was accounted for by including an interaction term, without finding any consistent pattern (not presented here). Thus, the landless are equally vulnerable in the parishes regardless of social structure and potential differences in poor law systems.

Table 14.2 Effects of food prices on mortality in ages 25–55 for landless and semi-landless in the four parishes, 1766–1895

Covariate	1766–1815			1815–65			1865–95		
	Average	Model 1	Model 2	Average	Model 1	Model 2	Average	Model 1	Model 2
Parish									
Hög	14.0%	1.00	1.00	13.4%	1.00	1.00	8.4%	1.00	1.00
Kävlinge	12.6%	1.68*	1.68*	19.2%	1.64**	1.64**	19.0%	1.70	1.71
Halmstad	36.0%	1.80**	1.80**	32.1%	2.21***	2.21***	31.5%	1.47	1.47
Sireköpinge	37.3%	2.61***	2.61***	35.3%	1.35	1.36	41.2%	1.15	1.15
Sex									
Males	51.6%	1.00	1.00	48.3%	1.00	1.00	49.1%	1.00	1.00
Females	48.4%	1.02	1.03	51.7%	0.97	0.99	50.9%	1.77	1.76***
Birth year	1753.4	0.99	0.99	1799.7	1.01**	1.01**	1842.1	1.00	1.00
10% increase in rye prices	−0.01	1.67%	—	0.01	10.12%***	—	0.01	1.89%	—
10% increase in rye prices on									
Males	—	—	−0.79%	—	—	12.37%	—	—	−4.60%
Females	—	—	4.18%	—	—	8.01%	—	—	5.73%
Events	—	258	258	—	323	323	—	129	129
Total time	—	48,529	48,529	—	41,537	41,537	—	17,162	17,162
Max. log. Likelihood	—	−1,891.8	−1,891.5	—	−2,296.3	−2,296	—	−799.3	−798.93
Chi-square test	—	23.8	24.5	—	40	40.5	—	14.0	14.7
Overall p-value	—	0.000	0.000	—	0.000	0.000	—	0.030	0.040
Parameters	—	6	7	—	6	7	—	6	7

*p < 0.10, **p < 0.05, ***p < 0.01.

Table 14.3 Effects of food prices on mortality in ages 1–15 for landless and semi-landless in the four parishes, 1766–1895

Covariate	1766–1815			1815–65			1865–95		
	Average	Model 1	Model 2	Average	Model 1	Model 2	Average	Model 1	Model 2
Parish									
Hög	10.2%	1.00	1.00	10.7%	1.00	1.00	6.7%	1.00	1.00
Kävlinge	10.6%	1.53	1.52	18.8%	1.27	1.27	16.7%	1.82**	1.83**
Halmstad	37.4%	1.06	1.06	35.6%	1.02	1.02	36.5%	1.08	1.08
Sireköpinge	41.8%	1.37	1.37	34.8%	0.88	0.87	40.0%	1.37	1.37
Sex									
Males	51.6%	1.00	1.00	50.8%	1.00	1.00	51.1%	1.00	1.00
Females	48.4%	1.20	1.20	49.2%	0.78**	0.76***	48.9%	0.92	0.92
Birth year	1783.9	1.00	1.00	1833.5	1.00	1.00	1874.5	0.98***	0.98***
10% increase in rye prices	−0.01	4.95%	—	0.00	5.93%**	—	0.00	−5.54%	—
10% increase in rye prices on									
Males	—	—	3.67%	—	—	0.04%	—	—	−2.34%
Females	—	—	6.06%	—	—	14.34%***	—	—	−8.70%
Events	—	275	275	—	418	418	—	318	318
Total time	—	20,493	20,493	—	31,739	31,739	—	17,301	17,301
Max. log. Likelihood	—	−2,017	−2,017	—	−3,251.2	−3,247.6	—	−2,302.1	−2,301.7
Chi-square test	—	11.5	11.7	—	20.5	27.6	—	23.1	24.0
Overall p-value	—	0.074	0.112	—	0.002	0.000	—	0.001	0.001
Parameters	—	6	7	—	6	7	—	6	7

$*p < 0.10$, $**p < 0.05$, $***p < 0.01$.

As Table 14.3 shows, we find a rather strong response to short-term economic stress among children aged 1 to 14 during the second period, though not as strong as for their parents. In this case, we find that it is only the girls that suffer. The response is somewhat stronger than for adults. They have a 14% mortality increase in response to a 10% increase in prices, compared to an 8–12% increase for adults. During the first period, there is a somewhat weaker response (not statistically significant) than in the second period, and it does not differ between boys and girls. Again there is no response in the final period, and in that case, the number of events is quite large (318 deaths).

The level of differences between the parishes is small except for the final period when mortality was far higher in Kävlinge; the same result as for their parents. The effects of economic stress during the industrialization phase are stronger in the noble tenant parishes than in the freeholder/crown tenants parishes, that is, the opposite of the case for their parents (not presented here). Among children the total number of deaths in all three periods were larger than for adults: during the final period more than twice as large. Still, we find no influence of short-term economic stress on children for the last period.

To summarize, we find very strong effects of short-term economic stress on the mortality among the landless during the period of agricultural transformation. The impact was strong on both parents in their working ages and their children, in particular their daughters. Even with a more complex model taking household composition and the individual's position within the household into account, the main result is the same (Bengtsson 2000; Bengtsson and Dribe 2000). From previous research on cause-specific mortality, we know that excess mortality in both the adults and the children resulted from infectious diseases, airborne and waterborne, though not always from the same disease (Bengtsson 2000). Thus, we find no evidence that a single disease was spread in bad years but rather that they died of any common disease due to low resistance, which implies that they were malnourished. Mortality typically increased in the spring after a fall with increasing food prices. The rapid response implies that their resistance was low. Another indication of low resistance is that not just very high prices but also moderately high prices affected mortality, while mortality did not decline much in years of low prices (Bengtsson 2000). Evidently, many among the landless lived close to the margin. Remedial measures taken at individual, household, or societal level failed for this group.

Perhaps the most important finding is that the price effects on mortality among children and adults belonging to the landless group are stronger in the middle period than either before or after. We certainly expected the effects to disappear or at least be weaker in the last period, since we believe that the standard of living increased. But why was it weaker during the first period, before the agricultural transformation? One might argue that the ties between employer and employee were stronger before the agricultural transformation (Bengtsson 2000; Solar 1995) and that the social distances between and within various groups were smaller. The enclosure movement broke up the villages, and that destroyed social networks and alliances. New landless and semi-landless groups were created by the movement and the commercialization of agriculture increased the market dependency of both landless and semi-landless.

6. Fertility Response to Economic Stress

The existence of a fertility response to economic stress can also be seen as an indicator of standard of living, although the mechanisms are not as straightforward as they are with mortality. In times of economic stress, fertility may be affected both intentionally through deliberate fertility control (i.e. postponement of births or abortions), and unintentionally, through effects of short-term economic stress: lower fecundity, foetal loss, or separation between spouses. The problem is how to separate these different effects, or in other words, how to decide whether an observed response results from intentional acts or unintentional effects. It is not within the scope of this chapter to deal with this question in detail.[15] Instead, we will argue that a fertility response to short-term economic stress can be viewed as an indicator of standard of living, regardless of whether that response is intentional or not. That an unintentional fertility response to economic hardship can be viewed as an indication of a low level of standard of living is probably not so controversial. A deliberate postponement of births in a year of economic stress must also indicate that the family is experiencing difficult times. Hence, we argue that our measure of the fertility response to economic stress, together with the results on the mortality response presented above, can serve as an indicator of the vulnerability of these families to economic fluctuations, and thus of their standard of living.

The model estimated is very similar to the mortality models presented above; the chief difference being the inclusion of several age covariates to control for differences in fertility between women of different ages. Observation time is measured as the time since last birth and not age as in the mortality models. The results of model estimations are displayed in Table 14.4. For all three periods, we find the expected age pattern of fertility. Fertility is highest in the age groups below 30 and then drops off gradually at higher ages. In the two later periods, fertility seems to be lower in Hög, while there are no corresponding differences between the parishes in the first period. The year of birth is used to control for potential average cohort effects on fertility.

Table 14.4 shows some noteworthy differences between the three periods in the response to short-term economic stress. In the period 1766–1815, we find a weak, but not significant, effect of prices on negative fertility; fertility drops 1.5% after a 10% increase in prices. In the second period 1815–65, there is a stronger, and statistically significant effect and also find an almost equally strong effect up to two years after the price change. The total fertility decline during a two-year period, from a 10% increase in food prices, is about 7%. During the final period, there is no significant effect, neither in year one nor in year two. Apparently the pattern in the previous two periods of fertility fluctuations being sensitive to economic fluctuations, as measured by rye prices, had been broken.

Table 14.4 Effects of food prices on fertility for landless and semi-landless in the four parishes, 1766–1895

Covariate	1766–1815			1815–65			1865–95		
	Average	Model 1	Model 2	Average	Model 1	Model 2	Average	Model 1	Model 2
Age									
15–25	3.6%	1.00	1.00	3.6%	1.16	1.15	5.3%	0.80*	0.80*
25–30	11.6%	1.00	1.00	13.7%	1.00	1.00	15.8%	1.00	1.00
30–35	18.6%	0.85	0.85	20.8%	0.83***	0.83***	20.8%	0.78***	0.78***
35–40	22.5%	0.60***	0.60***	22.9%	0.64***	0.64***	21.6%	0.63***	0.63***
40–45	22.2%	0.31***	0.30***	21.4%	0.34***	0.34***	20.5%	0.31***	0.31***
45–50	21.4%	0.10***	0.10***	17.6%	0.06***	0.06***	16.0%	0.06***	0.06***
Parish									
Hög	15.6%	1.00	1.00	19.3%	1.00	1.00	13.8%	1.00	1.00
Kävlinge	22.0%	0.96	0.96	24.8%	1.29***	1.29***	16.8%	1.10	1.10
Halmstad	29.0%	1.07	1.07	30.0%	1.37***	1.37***	24.9%	1.32***	1.32***
Sireköpinge	33.4%	1.02	1.01	25.9%	1.23***	1.23***	44.5%	1.28**	1.28**
Birth year	1758.5	0.99**	0.99**	1805.2	1.01***	1.01***	1843.9	1.01	1.01
10% increase in rye prices	0.00	−1.54%	−1.21%	0.00	−4.75%***	−4.16%***	0.00	2.23%	2.23%
10% increase in rye prices, lagged one year	−0.01	—	−1.00%	0.00	—	−2.58%**	0.00	—	0.59%
Events	—	618	618	—	1,730	1,730	—	1,168	1,168
Total time	—	2,823.1	2,823.1	—	7,553.6	7,553.6	—	4,646.8	4,646.8
Max. log. likelihood	—	−3,708.5	−3,708.4	—	−11,957	−11,955	—	−7,572.6	−7,572.6
Chi-square test	—	169	169	—	580	584	—	368	368
Overall p-value	—	0.000	0.000	—	0.000	0.000	—	0.000	0.000
Parameters	—	10	11	—	10	11	—	10	11

*$p < 0.10$, **$p < 0.05$, ***$p < 0.01$.

What do these results tell us about the standard of living development in the four parishes? The rather strong fertility response, especially in the second period, serves to indicate that landless families lived rather close to the margin. The mortality results also pointed in the same direction, showing a clear effect of short-term economic stress on adult mortality for both men and women. The hardship brought by increasing food prices forced landless families to adapt their behaviour, for example, by postponing childbirth. It may also be that during times of economic stress their nutritional status deteriorated to such an extent that their fecundity was negatively affected, thereby lowering their fertility. It is, however, unlikely that temporal migration was of major importance for the variations in fertility, simply because it was too low and because the response was too rapid. As the analysis of mortality clearly demonstrated, the period of increasing commercialization and agricultural transformation, with its resulting increases in production and productivity, did not imply any immediate increase in the standard of living for the landless. The fertility response shows much the same thing. If anything, the fertility response to economic stress grew stronger during the second period, indicating the marginalization of the landless. In the final period, however, the improvements in agriculture also affected the landless. The previously strong connection between fertility and food prices was broken, which must be seen as a strong indicator of an increased living standard in this social group.

7. Conclusion: The Long-term Development of Standard of Living

We began with a review of earlier investigations of the development of standard of living in Sweden, and it now seems appropriate to place the results of our investigation in the context of that development. While agricultural production increased in the beginning of the nineteenth century, real wages for agricultural labourers did not start a secular increase until the 1860s, which does not completely rule out the possibility that real income could have increased before that time, had the number of days worked increased or the mix of consumption changed in favour of cheaper goods. However, the patterns in consumption of textiles indicate that the standard of living did not rise for the lowest strata of society until the second half of the nineteenth century. Similarly, both the heights of adults and the demographic indicators (life expectancy and age-specific mortality) indicate that it was not until after the 1850s that a sustained improvement in standard of living was realised.

Our results show a similar picture. It is not until the final period (1865–95) of the 128 years we have considered that the close connection between fluctuations in food prices and mortality and fertility was completely broken. Especially during the first half of the nineteenth century births were postponed, intentionally or unintentionally, in times of economic stress. Furthermore, in this second period (1815–65) adult mortality of both males and females, as well as female child mortality, increased in times of high prices. This clearly shows that landless people were highly vulnerable to economic fluctuations, which as we have argued in this paper, can be seen as an indicator of the level of well-being.

In previous analyses, we have also argued that the landless group had very few resources to fall back on in difficult times. Postponement of marriage of their children was an option that became available only very late in the family life cycle and thus was of less importance. Even when that option was feasible, it made little difference since they did not spend much on this event in any case (Bengtsson and Dribe 2000). Resorting to migration was seldom a sensible option before the final decades of the nineteenth century. Before the spread of industrialization or urbanization, moving the entire family to a similar parish nearby would do nothing to improve their situation (Dribe 2003*b*). Since the children of the landless normally left home just as soon as they were old enough to work as servants, it was seldom possible to send them away even earlier when times were bad (Dribe 2000). Borrowing money was difficult because the landless lacked collateral. Finally, as has already been mentioned, the poor relief system was designed to take care of only the very neediest (the sick, the handicapped, and the elderly); a tiny percentage of the population, not large numbers. This near-total lack of recourse in hard times affected both the mortality and the fertility of the landless in such times.

Our results also shed some new light on the situation of the landless groups during the period of agricultural transformation in the first half of the nineteenth century. Earlier work has found that despite increasing agricultural productivity, the living standards of those on the bottom stayed low in this period. Our results not only support this view but also show that there are clear indications that the standard of living of the landless actually deteriorated during this transformation phase. Adult mortality of both males and females became highly responsive to economic stress, as did female child mortality. Similarly, the fertility response seems to have strengthened and lasted longer, compared to the previous period. The agricultural transformation initially increased the ranks of the landless. Rural society became more differentiated. The standard of living of a great many individuals actually declined, while it rose for some of the new groups (cf. Winberg 1975). The salience of this development is highlighted by the increasing attention paid to the question of the poor from the 1830s onwards (see, for example, Olofsson 1996).

Part of the explanation behind the increased vulnerability during the first decades of the nineteenth century might have been the enclosure reforms which dramatically transformed the countryside. Villages were broken up, and that made the situation for the landless more precarious in several respects. The immediate economic effect on the landless was often severe. They lost common land on which they had previously been able to raise livestock which they could either eat or sell. According to nineteenth-century observers, they were made much more dependent on wage labour (see Utterström 1957: 574–8). The enclosures made the landless more dependent on the market for employment as well as for consumption. In the long run the commercialization of agriculture led to a higher standard of living for the landless. In the short run, however, they were less able to feed themselves when they had no cash and wage labour was hard to find. Later on, in the second half of the nineteenth century, when real wages started to increase substantially, the standard of living of the landless group also increased.

In addition, it is also possible that the breaking-up of the village communities following the enclosures, which increased the geographic isolation of many landless people, had some negative implications for the assistance given to the landless in times of economic stress. This too may have contributed to an increasing vulnerability to economic fluctuations for these people.

To conclude, our results show that this way of approaching the issue of the long-term standard of living development is a useful complement to other measures and provides an important additional dimension to the standard of living in the past. Our results corroborate previous findings on the increase in standard of living for broad groups in society during the second half of the nineteenth century, but also support a more negative view of the standard of living development of the landless during the agricultural transformation in the first half of the nineteenth century.

Notes

1. The EAP is a comparative project dealing with historical demography from a household perspective in five European and Asian populations: Belgium, China, Italy, Japan, and Sweden. For a description of the basic ideas, see, for example, Bengtsson and Campbell (1998) and Bengtsson (2004).
2. For a more detailed definition, see Section 4 below.
3. As Jörberg points out, using the rye price instead of a cost of living index (containing a more realistic bundle of consumption goods) will give a reasonably good approximation until the final decades of the nineteenth century when the real wage gain will be somewhat overestimated (Jörberg 1972: vol. II, 335).
4. See Section 4 for a discussion of the relationship between harvest outcome and grain prices at the local level, and how grain prices can be assumed to have affected the landless.
5. For example, in nineteenth-century Sweden, spending on food was 83% of the typical household budget (Myrdal 1933: 115), and of that sum, 59% was spent on grain (Jörberg 1972: vol. II, 182).
6. The proportion of the population that got poor relief in Sweden in 1829 was only 2.1%. It was even smaller in Scandia (Skoglund 1992). For a more detailed discussion, see Bengtsson (2004).
7. The Scandian Demographic Database is a collaborative project between the Regional Archives in Lund and the Research Group in Population Economics at the Department of Economic History, Lund University. The source material is described in Reuterswärd and Olsson (1993).
8. *Mantal* is an old tax unit used to measure the productive potential of the farm and as a basis for the taxes to be paid to the crown (see for example Dribe 2000: 26–7).
9. We also tried analysing the truly landless group separately, which yielded practically identical results.
10. See Bengtsson and Dribe (1997) for details on the construction of the series.

11. With a Hodrick–Prescott (HP) filter a smooth curve is fitted through a time series, rather than a deterministic trend (e.g. linear or polynomial) or a moving average, which have been shown to have undesirable effects on the data (e.g. Harvey and Jaeger 1993). It is also a less crude way of de-trending than the use of first differences, leaving more of the medium-term cycles. However, Harvey and Jaeger (1993) argue that the HP filter might create spurious cyclical patterns (medium-term), which could imply that observed correlations between series, de-trended by a HP filter, could be overestimated. However, despite these problems the HP filter is used in this study to de-trend the aggregate series to be used as communal covariates in Cox regressions, since the same and even larger problems are associated with the alternative approaches available to us. The smoothing parameter was set to 100, which is the value normally used for annual data.

12. For a more detailed discussion and analysis of this problem, see Dribe (2000: ch. 7).

13. For the basic concepts of event-history analysis, see any standard textbook on the topic, for example, Collett (1994).

14. Estimations of models for infants and the elderly not reported here also support this conclusion.

15. For a deeper analysis of the fertility response to economic stress in the same area, see Bengtsson and Dribe (2002). That paper discusses in more detail social differences in the response, seasonal patterns, linearity, and threshold effects, as well as whether the response is intentional or not.

References

Banggaard, G. (2002) 'Sygdom og Sundhet: Offentlige ingreb og deres virkninger i Sydsverige, *c*.1750–1894'. *Lund Papers in Economic History* 76, Lund.

Bengtsson, T. (1989) 'Reallön och vuxendödlighet. Livsförlopp i Västanfors 1750–1849'. *Meddelande från Ekonomisk-historiska institutionen, Lunds universitet* 60, Lund.

——(1990) 'Migration, Wages and Urbanization in Sweden in the Nineteenth Century', in A. van der Woude, A. Hayami, and J. de Vries (eds.), *Urbanization in History: A Process of Dynamic Interactions*. Oxford: Clarendon Press.

——(1993) 'Combined Time-Series and Life-Event Analysis. The Impact of Economic Fluctuations and Air Temperature on Adult Mortality by Sex and Occupation in a Swedish Mining Parish, 1757–1850', in D. Reher and R. Schofield (eds.), *Old and New Methods in Historical Demography*. Oxford: Oxford University Press.

——(2000) 'Inequality in Death. Effects of the Agrarian Revolution in Southern Sweden 1765–1865', in T. Bengtsson and O. Saito (eds.), *Population and Economy: From Hunger to Modern Economic Growth*. Oxford: Oxford University Press.

——(2004) 'Living Standard and Economic Stress', in T. Bengtsson, C. Campbell, J. Z. Lee *et al.*(eds.), *Life under Pressure: Mortality and Living Standards in Europe and Asia, 1700–1900*. Cambridge, MA: MIT Press.

——and Campbell, C. (1998) 'Microanalysis of Effects of Short-Term Economic Stress on Mortality', in C.-E. Núñes (ed.), *Debates and Controversies in Economic History. Proceedings of the Twelfth International Economic History Congress*. Madrid: Fundación Ramón Areces e Fundación Fomento de la Historia Económica.

——and Dribe, M. (1997) 'Economy and Demography in Western Scandia, Sweden, 1650–1900'. *EAP Working Paper* No. 10. Kyoto: International Research Center for Japanese Studies.

——and ——(2000) 'Risk Management in the Family. Demographic Responses to Short-Term Economic Stress in Southern Sweden during the Agricultural Transformation, 1829–1865', in M. Neven and C. Capron (eds.), *Family Structures, Demography and Population. A Comparison of Societies in Asia and Europe.* Liège: Laboratory of Demography.

Bengtsson, T. and Dribe, M. (2002) 'Fertility Response to Short-Term Economic Stress. Deliberate Control or Reduced Fecundability?'. *Lund Papers in Economic History* 78, Lund.

——and Lundh, C. (1991) 'Evaluation of a Swedish Computer Program for Automatic Family Reconstitution'. *Lund Papers in Economic History* 8, Lund.

Carlsson, G. (1970) 'Nineteenth Century Fertility Oscillations'. *Population Studies*, 24: 413–22.

Collett, D. (1994) *Modelling Survival Data in Medical Research.* London: Chapman & Hall.

Cox, D. R. (1972) 'Regression Models and Life Tables'. *Journal of the Royal Statistical Society B*, 74: 187–220.

Crafts, N. F. R. (1982) 'Regional Price Variations in England in 1843: An Aspect of the Standard-of-Living Debate'. *Explorations in Economic History*, 19: 51–70.

Dribe, M. (2000) *Leaving Home in a Peasant Society. Economic Fluctuations, Household Dynamics and Youth Migration in Southern Sweden, 1829–1866.* Södertälje: Almqvist & Wiksell International.

——(2003a) 'Migration of Rural Families in Nineteenth Century Southern Sweden. A Longitudinal Analysis of Local Migration Patterns'. *History of the Family*, 8: 247–65.

——(2003b) 'Dealing with Economic Stress through Migration. Lessons from Nineteenth Century Rural Sweden'. *European Review of Economic History*, 7: 271–99.

——and Lundh, C. (2002) 'People on the Move. Determinants of Servant Migration in Nineteenth Century Sweden'. *Lund Papers in Economic History* 80, Lund.

Engerman, S. (1976) 'The Height of U.S. Slaves'. *Local Population Studies*, 16: 45–50.

Floud, R., Wachter, K., and Gregory, A. (1990) *Height, Health and History. Nutritional Status in the United Kingdom, 1750–1980.* Cambridge: Cambridge University Press.

Fogel, R. W. (1993) 'New Sources and Techniques for the Study of Secular Trends in Nutritional Status, Health, Mortality and the Process of Aging'. *Historical Methods*, 26: 5–43.

Frank, A. G. (1998) *ReOrient. Global Economy in the Asian Age.* Berkeley: University of California Press.

Fridlizius, G. (1981) 'Handel och sjöfart—förändringens tid', in O. Bjurling, (ed.), *Malmö stads historia, del 3.* Malmö: Allhems förlag.

——(1989) 'The Deformation of Cohorts. Nineteenth Century Mortality Decline in a Generational Perspective'. *Scandinavian Economic History Review*, 37: 3–17.

Gadd, C.-J. (1983) *Järn och Potatis. Jordbruk, teknik och social omvandling i Skaraborgs län 1750–1860.* Göteborg: Department of Economic History, Göteborg University.

——(2000) *Den agrara revolutionen 1700–1870.* Stockholm: Natur & Kultur.

Goody, J. (1996) *The East in the West.* Cambridge: Cambridge University Press.

Granlund, J. (1944) 'Avlöningsformer', in A. Lindblom (ed.), *Arbetaren i helg och söcken. Kulturhistoriska studier. Del 2 Vardag och fest.* Stockholm: Tidens förlag.

Harvey, A. C. and Jaeger, A. (1993) 'Detrending, Stylized Facts and the Business Cycle'. *Journal of Applied Econometrics*, 8: 231–47.

Heckscher, E. F. (1949) *Sveriges ekonomiska historia, del 2*. Stockholm: Albert Bonniers förlag.

Hofsten, E. and Lundström, H. (1976) *Swedish Population History. Main Trends from 1700 to 1970*. Stockholm: SCB.

Johansson, E. (1977) *The History of Literacy in Sweden*, Educational Reports 12. Umeå: Department of Education, University of Umeå.

Jonsson, U. (1980) *Jordmagnater landbönder och torpare i sydöstra Södermanland 1800–1880*. Stockholm: Almqvist & Wiksell International.

Jörberg, L. (1972) *A History of Prices in Sweden 1732–1914*, Vol. II. Lund: Gleerups.

Komlos, J. (1985) 'Stature and Nutrition in the Habsburg Monarchy: The Standard of Living and Economic Development in the Eighteenth Century'. *American Historical Review*, 90: 1149–61.

Lal, D. (1998) *Unintended Consequences. The Impact of Factor Endowments, Culture and Politics on Long-Run Economic Performance*. Cambridge, MA: MIT Press.

Landes, D. S. (1998) *The Wealth and Poverty of Nations*. New York: W. W. Norton and Co.

Lee, R. D. (1993) 'Inverse Projection and Demographic Fluctuations: A Critical Assessment', in D. S. Reher and R. S. Schofield (eds.), *Old and New Methods in Historical Demography*. Oxford: Oxford University Press.

Lindert, P. H. and Williamson, J. G. (1983) 'English Workers' Living Standards during the Industrial Revolution: A New Look'. *Economic History Review*, 36: 1–25.

Livi-Bacci, M. (1991) *Population and Nutrition. An Essay on European Demographic History*. Cambridge: Cambridge University Press.

Lundh, C. (1999) 'The Social Mobility of Servants in Rural Sweden, 1740–1894'. *Continuity and Change*, 14: 57–89.

——(2002) 'Husmän och torpare under Duveke gods 1765–1894', in C. Lundh and K. Sundberg (eds.), *Gatehus och gatehusfolk i skånska godsmiljöer*. Lund: Nordic Academic Press.

Lundsjö, O. (1975) *Fattigdomen på den svenska landsbygden under 1800–talet*. Stockholm: Stockholm Studies in Economic History.

Magnusson, L. (1996) *Sveriges ekonomiska historia*. Stockholm: Rabén Prisma.

Martinius, S. (1970) *Agrar kapitalbildning och finansiering 1833–1892*. Göteborg: Department of Economic History, Göteborg University.

Martinius, S. (1982) *Jordbrukets omvandling på 1700- och 1800-talen*. Lund: Liber.

Myrdal, G. (1933) *The Cost of Living in Sweden 1830–1930*. London: P. S. King and Sons.

Nilsson, A. and Svärd, B. (1994) 'Writing Ability and Agrarian Change in Early 19th-Century Rural Scandia'. *Scandinavian Journal of History*, 19: 251–74.

O'Brien, P. K. (2001). 'Metanarratives in Global Histories of Material Progress'. *International History Review*, 23: 253–304.

Olofsson, J. (1996) *Arbetslöshetsfrågan i historisk belysning. En diskussion om arbetslöshet och social politik i Sverige 1830–1920*. Lund: Lund University Press.

Persson, C. (2002) 'Torp- och backstugesittargrupperna i några olika näringsgeografiska miljöer enligt Tabellverket', in C. Lundh, and K. Sundberg (eds.), *Gatehus och gatehusfolk i skånska godsmiljöer*. Lund: Nordic Academic Press.

Persson, K. G. (1999) *Grain Markets in Europe 1500–1900. Integration and Regulation*. Cambridge: Cambridge University Press.

Pomeranz, K. (2000) *The Great Divergence. China, Europe and the Making of the Modern World Economy.* Princeton, NJ: Princeton University Press.

Reuterswärd, E. and Olsson, F. (1993) 'Skånes demografiska databas 1646–1894. En källbeskrivning'. *Lund Papers in Economic History* 33, Lund.

Rotberg, R. I. and Rabb, T. K. (eds.) (1985) *Hunger and History. The Impact of Changing Food Production and Consumption Patterns on Society.* Cambridge: Cambridge University Press.

Sandberg, L. G. and Steckel, R. H. (1980) 'Soldier, Soldier, What Made You Grow so Tall?'. *Economy and History*, 23: 91–105.

——and——(1987) 'Heights and Economic History: The Swedish Case'. *Annals of Human Biology*, 14: 101–10.

——and——(1988) 'Overpopulation and Malnutrition Rediscovered: Hard Times in 19th-Century Sweden'. *Explorations in Economic History*, 25: 1–19.

——and——(1997) 'Was Industrialization Hazardous to Your Health? Not in Sweden!', in R. H. Steckel and R. Floud (eds.), *Health and Welfare During Industrialization.* Chicago: University of Chicago Press.

Statistics Sweden (1999) *Befolkningsutvecklingen under 250 år. Historisk statistik för Sverige.* Demografiska rapporter 1999: 2. Stockholm: Statistics Sweden.

Schön, L. (1979) *Från hantverk till fabriksindustri.* Kristianstad: Arkiv.

——(1995) *Historiska nationalräkenskaper för Sverige: Jordbruk med binäringar 1800–1980.* Lund: Department of Economic History, Lund University.

——(2000) *En modern svensk ekonomisk historia. Tillväxt och omvandling under två sekel.* Stockholm: SNS.

Sen, A. (1992) *Inequality Reexamined.* Cambridge, MA: Harvard University Press.

Skoglund, A.-M. (1992) *Fattigvården på den svenska landsbygden år 1929.* Stockholm: School of Social Work.

Solar, P. (1995) 'Poor Relief and English Development Before the Industrial Revolution'. *Economic History Review*, 48: 1–22.

Sommarin, E. (1939) *Det skånska jordbrukets ekonomiska utveckling 1801–1914, del 2–3.* Lund: Skrifter utgivna av de skånska hushållningssällskapen.

Steckel, R. H. (1979) 'Slave Heights Profiles from the Coastwise Manifests'. *Explorations in Economic History*, 16: 363–80.

——(1995) 'Stature and the Standard of Living'. *Journal of Economic Literature*, 33: 1903–40.

——and Floud, R. (eds.) (1997) *Health and Welfare During Industrialization.* Chicago: University of Chicago Press.

Svensson, P. (2001) *Agrara entreprenörer. Böndernas roll i omvandlingen av jordbruket i Skåne ca 1800–1870.* Stockholm: Almqvist & Wiksell International.

Söderberg, J. (1978) *Agrar fattigdom i Sydsverige under 1800-talet.* Stockholm: Almqvist & Wiksell International.

Taylor, A. J. (1975) 'Editor's Introduction', in A. J. Taylor (ed.), *The Standard of Living in Britain in the Industrial Revolution.* London: Methuen & Co.

Thestrup, P. (1971) *The Standard of Living in Copenhagen 1730–1800. Some Methods of Measurement.* Copenhagen: G. E. C. Gads Forlag.

Utterström, G. (1957) *Jordbrukets arbetare.* Stockholm: Tidens förlag.

Voth, H.-J. (2001) *Time and Work in England 1750–1830.* Oxford: Oxford University Press.

Winberg, C. (1975) *Folkökning och proletarisering. Kring den sociala strukturomvandlingen på Sveriges landsbygd under den agrara revolutionen.* Göteborg: Department of Economic History, Göteborg University.

Wohlin, N. (1909) *Den jordbruksidkande befolkningen i Sverige 1751–1900*. Stockholm: P. A. Norstedt & söner.
Wrigley, E. A. (1987) *People, Cities and Wealth. The Transformation of Traditional Societies*. Oxford: Basil Blackwell.

15 Individuals and Communities Facing Economic Stress: A Comparison of Two Rural Areas in Nineteenth-Century Belgium

MICHEL ORIS, MURIEL NEVEN, AND GEORGE ALTER

1. Introduction

This chapter is located at a crossroad. On one side, it is a partial synthesis of research done within the framework of the *Eurasian Project for the Comparative History of Population and Family*, where we explored the influence of the economic structure and conjuncture on demographic behaviour (Bengtsson and Campbell 1998; Bengtsson and Saito 2000: 12–16 for first presentations). On the other side, it addresses the classic 'standard of living debate' about the first phase of economic modernization that emerged in England during the late 1950s.[1] These vigorous discussions expanded to include more and more countries (with an emerging debate about the comparison between East and West), an increasing number of dimensions (regional disparities, differentials by gender, social status, ethnicity, etc.), new data (especially family budgets and the study of heights and handicaps through military records), as well as new methodological approaches. This volume is an illustration of this dynamic and an attempt to advance the debate.

This chapter examines the impact of the Industrial Revolution on the standard of living of rural areas in a region experiencing rapid economic development. In Section 2 we start with a discussion about the standard of living debate in Belgium, we then present two neighbouring but very different rural areas of eastern Belgium: the East Ardennes and the Land of Herve. Our objective is to understand how inhabitants of the countryside facing different local conditions coped with such a fundamental and rapid modernization of the regional economy. We use the technical and intellectual tools of our discipline, historical demography, to measure their successes and failures. Section 3 develops a structural approach emphasizing progressive adaptations over the medium term, 10–40 years. Our inspiration comes

This research is a part of the *Eurasia Project for the Comparative History of Population and the Family*. We have benefited from support from the Belgian National Funds for Scientific Research (Crédits d'Aide aux Chercheurs) and from the University of Liège (Fonds spéciaux de Recherche). We would like to thank Tommy Bengtsson and Martin Dribe for their detailed comments, as well as David Reher, Frans Van Poppel, and Peter Lindert who discussed a previous version.

from the study of demographic regimes. Since the discovery of the homeostasis of pre-industrial populations, research in this field has shown the complexity and the variety of interactions between demographic behaviours, as well as between demographic and economic structures. More recently, historical demography and the history of the family, which developed as largely independent disciplines, have engaged in a new dialogue (see issue 2000–2 of the *Annales de Démographie historique*), and the family system has emerged as the decisive cultural determinant of demographic responses to economic insecurity (Alter 1988; Lee and Campbell 1997; Reher 1997; Neven 2000, etc.).

We consider how the Industrial Revolution changed the rural economy, family system, and demographic regime. This interdisciplinary approach to rural society reveals a paradox observed by present-day demographers in numerous Third World countries: high life expectancy in a context of poverty and even pauperization (Preston 1996: 533–4). To understand this paradox, Section 4 adopts the analytical approach developed in the Eurasia Project for dealing with the complex problem of the sensitivity of the demographic behaviours to economic stress. We observe the effects of short-term variations in the cost of living on life course transitions (death, childbirth, marriage, migration). By integrating longitudinal individual data and economic series, we can compare the vulnerability of the inhabitants of our two study areas, the Land of Herve and East Ardennes. This analysis highlights the difference between 'voluntary' (marriage and migration) and 'involuntary' (fertility and mortality) demographic responses. Although much in this study is peculiar to the Belgian context, we believe that these results are also relevant for a broader discussion of the transition from uncertainty to economic and demographic security.

2. Background

2.1   The standard of living debate in Belgium

The conventional view about the standard of living in nineteenth-century Belgium is the product of three traditions. The first one is the closest to our own approach, since it focuses on demographic responses. Following Goubert and Meuvret's footsteps, Belgian researchers have observed the classic process in which mortality crises became progressively less frequent and less severe. Much attention was devoted to the last major crisis between 1845 and 1847. The combination of potato blight, bad weather that reduced cereal harvests, a typhus epidemic, and the decline of proto-industrial textile production caused a crisis in Flanders, which is often compared with the Great Irish Famine.[2]

At the national level, correlations have been calculated between demographic rates and food prices. André and Pereira-Roque (1974: 52–8) noted that the crude birth rate was negatively associated with prices. They concluded that Belgian women were able to control their reproduction in poor economic conditions well before the decisive fertility decline began in 1873. Such an interpretation is debatable, however. First, from a statistical point of view, most of the correlation between food prices and birth rates is due to common trends: increase between 1850 and 1872, decrease since 1873. When the series are de-trended, the relationship becomes unclear or disappears. (See Bruneel *et al.* 1987: 314, for the same observation about the eighteenth century.) Second, variations in fertility can be due to other factors, like the physiological impact of hunger on fecundability or the psychological consequences of stress (less frequent sexual relations), that do not imply intentional birth control. Overall, the conventional view is that Belgian mortality became independent from economic fluctuations after 1847/50, but nothing is really clear as far as fertility is concerned.

Franklin Mendels based his famous theory of proto-industrialization on the case of Flanders. His views of the link between marriage and labour market stimulated a rich flow of excellent research, but little work has been done on the nineteenth century (for a recent synthesis, see Devos 1999). Yoo (1996) demonstrated that even during the twentieth century marriage remained extremely sensitive to economic fluctuations. Research has also established that the definitive break with the Malthusian system of late marriage and high proportions remaining unmarried occurred around 1860, starting in the centres of the Industrial Revolution, especially coal and iron districts (Lesthaege 1977; Devos 1999). Recently, Patricia van den Eeckhout and Peter Scholliers (1997: 160) were surprised to note the lack of research about links between labour markets, real wages, and migration, except two case studies about the coal and iron town of Seraing (De Saint-Moulin 1969; Oris 1997).

A second research tradition pays more attention to tensions between population and resources, stressing the importance of structural constraints and their transformation during the formation of an international, then global economy. Bruneel *et al.* (1987) offer a good synthesis of the debate between Malthusian and Boserupian interpretations of the relationships between demography and economy. Belgian experience since 1700 clearly demonstrates a predominance of population growth over increasing agricultural production. Martine Goosens (1992: 180) has shown that the demographic expansion of Belgium was 30% faster than the growth of agricultural production from 1806 to 1846. During the eighteenth century, the substitution of potatoes for cereals offered a partial solution, but food prices rose until 1873. In that year, the massive arrival of American cereals produced a sudden drop in prices and a new era for the rural population (Bruneel *et al.* 1987: 313).

Two things prevented this rising Malthusian pressure from resulting in major demographic disasters, other than the crisis in Flanders. First, Belgium was the first country in continental Europe to follow the British example. The Belgian Industrial Revolution was rapid, intense, and successful, and it resulted in a continuous increase in the wages of workers in factories and mines during the 1850s and 1860s (Gadisseur 1981). These higher incomes covered the cost of rising food prices, which was profitable for the peasantry and induced food imports from neighbouring countries (Deprez 1948; Degrève 1982). Second, improvements in roads and the early development of a dense railway network led to a unification of prices by the middle of the century (Oris 1998: 12–17). In this context the classic question of the English debate—was the standard of living decreasing or increasing during the Industrial Revolution—remains open. It was an immediate concern for officials and intellectuals during the nineteenth century, and dozens of workers' family budgets were collected and published in 1855 and 1891.

Time series or 'serial' analyses were conducted during the interwar years in the Department of Economics at the Catholic University of Leuven. This tradition—the third one in Belgian historiography—has been carried on almost continuously by the Flemish historians in Ghent and the Free University of Brussels, who use a variety of sources to explore (usually annual) fluctuations of food prices, wages, real wages, and consumption. In the most recent synthesis, Peter Scholliers concluded that the standard of living declined between 1800 and 1850, and then rose (Scholliers 1996).

There is no agreement among historians about the interpretation of this rise. An optimistic view stresses the impressive progress of real wages between 1850 and 1873. By the end of the depression, the labour force participation of married women had fallen according to a comparison of the 1853 and 1891 budgets, which was a sign of improvement in the family wage economy (Alter 1984). Leboutte (1987) has suggested that the shock of depression in 1873 initiated fertility decline. A pessimistic view, based on wage and price data, pays less attention to the progress observed during the third quarter of the century. Scholliers (1991, 1996) argues that the contribution of adult married women to the household economy remained vital in 1891, and that the situation in 1900 was merely a return to conditions of 1800.

Such differences of interpretation show that many questions remain open in spite of the quality, quantity, and diversity of the studies. First, research focused on the modern proletariat is mainly concentrated on the Walloon industrial cities, while the peasantry and rural populations have only been well explored in the Flemish part of Belgium (see Vandenbroeke 1984 for a valuable synthesis, and more recently Vanhaute 1992 and Scholliers 1996). This two-sided historiography reflects the widening gap between 'poor Flanders' and industrializing Wallonia during the nineteenth century. But almost nothing is known about the rural Walloon populations who lived in close proximity to the Industrial Revolution. The standard explanation is a stereotype: a rural exodus towards growing towns. However, Vandermotten and Vandewattyne (1985) have clearly shown that the number of inhabitants in the Walloon countryside did not decline before the very end of the nineteenth century. Questions about the structural adaptations of the rural populations of Wallonia and the evolution of their standard of living have been completely untouched.

A second set of questions revolves around chronology and transitions. Was 1850 a turning point, the decisive transition 'from hunger to modern economic growth' (Bengtsson and Saito 2000)? What about the economic depression between 1873 and 1890? At a micro level, we need to translate these problems into questions about individuals and their families: When did people stop dying in years of high prices? Was the family able to cope with medium- or short-term stress? How did they choose among household members when there was too little food for everyone?

In particular, when did the situation of married women improve? Between the micro and the macro views, a regional perspective is also important. At this level, we can consider differences and changes in agrarian structures, various ties to urban areas, and the nature and intensity of pressures from the industrial world on rural society. For this reason, our analysis compares two distinctive rural communities.

2.2 A comparison of two rural areas in an industrializing region

The present analysis is focused on a comparison between two adjacent but very different rural areas, the East Ardennes and the Land of Herve. These areas are separated by the River Vesdre, on which the city of Verviers is located, and their comparison can be seen as a contrast between the archaic and the modern countryside. Much of the territory of Sart is located in an area called the 'Hautes Fagnes', a high plateau of peat bogs and forests. The population is concentrated in half a dozen hamlets, which form islands in the woods. The inhabitants of Sart preserved a complex economy of multiple activities. Most of them were smallholders who supplemented their incomes with forest products and proto-industrial wool spinning. Recognized members of the community also had a variety of rights on the extensive lands held in common. Many households had one or two animals in a common herd foraging in the forests. 'Slash and burn' agriculture was still being practised, and community elders chose a piece of forest to burn, which was then divided among families for cultivation (Vliebergh and Ulens 1912; Hoyois 1981).

The Land of Herve, especially the heart of the plateau, was a very different environment. Since the sixteenth century, proto-industry in woollen textiles developed in association with a precocious transition from subsistence to commercial agriculture. Raising cattle required less labour and allowed the inhabitants to devote themselves to craft production. In the late eighteenth to early nineteenth century more than 20,000 people were engaged in spinning or weaving, either part or full time (Haesenne-Peremans 1981: 59, 74–5; Servais 1982b; Gutmann 1988). Grassland enclosed by hedges made up more than 85% of the cultivated area. Production was highly specialized in dairy products (especially a famous cheese), fruit, and to a less extent, meat. With this structure and its international markets, the Herve plateau has been called 'the most modern countryside of Europe' (Gutmann 1988). From a social point of view, the situation was more ambiguous. Proto-industrial workers were proletarianized through a putting-out system dominated by merchant-clothiers in the city of Verviers. Paul Servais (1982a,b) has shown, however, that rural families accumulated savings, generation after generation, to gradually acquire land. In the late eighteenth century, between 68% and 75% of agricultural land belonged to local peasants. The region had three outstanding characteristics: the proliferation of small properties, the local origin of the landowners, and their fundamentally peasant status.

Eastern Belgium was at the heart of the economic transformation of continental Europe. In 1798, William Cockerill constructed the first spinning machines on the continent for two rich families of clothiers in Verviers, the Biolley and the Simonis. In 1817, his son John Cockerill moved the family factory to Seraing where he established a coal and iron empire, which was soon followed by local competitors (Van der Herten *et al.* 1995). During the nineteenth century, the East Ardennes and the Land of Herve were profoundly influenced by the expanding Industrial Revolution in textiles in Verviers, only 20 km away, and the coal and iron centre of Liège 40/50 km away. Together, the industrial agglomerations centred on these cities grew from 65,000 inhabitants to more than 500,000 between 1800 and 1900. The urban population of the province of Liège increased from 20% to more than 60%. This huge external force affected the countryside and its population in many ways.

Although this volume is primarily devoted to rural societies, the two areas studied here were fundamentally affected by these external forces, and we cannot understand changes in the East Ardennes and the Land of Herve without referring to the Industrial Revolution.

2.3   Data

Our analysis is based on individual life histories observed in population registers. Population registers are exceptionally good sources for individual, longitudinal, and contextual analyses. In addition to cross-sectional snapshots of the population from periodic censuses, they include continuous registration of births, deaths, and marriages and recording of in- and out-migration as well. The data are individual but grouped into households, which we observe evolving over time (Alter 1988; Neven 2000: ch.1). In the East Ardennes, our sample is the population of Sart, a large municipality (56.9 km^2) located between the towns of Spa and Verviers. This commune is unusual because the administration opened and updated two population registers between 1811 and 1846, while the population register system in the rest of Belgium was only instituted on 16 October 1846. Between 1812 and 1900, the population of Sart varied between 1,800 and 2,500 inhabitants. Our database includes 11,402 complete and incomplete biographies, which represent 199,196 person-years. The second sample is a cluster of three Hervian municipalities situated between Verviers and the Dutch border: Charneux, Clermont, and Neufchâteau. Here observation starts on 16 October 1846 and ends in 1900. We observe 21,435 individual biographies and 254,409 person-years during these 54 years. The average population was 4,683, but it was slowly decreasing over time.

3. A Macro (Regional) Comparison of the Influences of Socio-Economic Changes on Family and Demographic Systems

In the early nineteenth century, the Land of Herve, the East Ardennes, and territories that are now parts of Germany belonged to a single industrial region, where 'around 30,000 spinners and some thousands of weavers worked at home for the merchant-clothiers of the Vesdre valley' (Hélin 1993: 127). However, the impact of industrial activity was different in our two study areas. Censuses of the French period indicate that 48% of the male and 66% of the female labour force in the Land of Herve identified themselves with the textile sector (Servais 1982*a*: 238), compared to only 5% of people working in Sart in 1811. These statistics do not reflect a simple reality because of the multiple economic activities in each region, but they do indicate quite different orientations. While communal lands were an important resource for inhabitants of the East Ardennes, they had already disappeared in the Land of Herve. Many spinners were landless and totally dependent on proto-industrial activity (Patriarca 1986: 15–23). Moreover, if dairy farming made small farms viable in the Land of Herve (Servais 1982*c*: 306), the additional income from proto-industry was decisive for many families.

The first spinning machines reached Verviers in 1798, and diffusion was very rapid until 1810/11. By 1831, rural domestic spinning production had disappeared. The population response was immediate: between 1805 and 1850 Charneux and Clermont lost respectively 26% and 16% of their inhabitants, with the most important losses between 1805 and 1831 (16% and 11%). Moreover, the proportion of agricultural land owned by peasants decreased sharply from about 70% in 1806 to only 30% in 1862. The work of generations, who struggled for three centuries to maintain landownership at a time when peasant property was declining all over western Europe, was destroyed in 50 years (Servais 1982*b*: 190–1). The Land of Herve experienced a cruel introduction to the nineteenth century.

During the same period, Sart in the East Ardennes achieved an impressive growth from 1,800 to 2,400 inhabitants between 1812 and 1851/52, entirely due to a surplus of births over deaths. Table 15.1 below offers a synthesis of the demographic regimes in our two rural regions over the century. Between 1811 and 1845, the average crude death rate was 23.5 per thousand but it reached 41.5 in 1816 and approached 30 from 1815 to 1821. In addition to war and fevers in 1814–15, there were bad harvests and high prices in 1811–12 and 1816–17 and the second misfortune was followed by the appearance and diffusion of typhus (Desama 1985: 104). In East Belgium, this was the last major traditional crisis, the last time that the great killers of the Old Regime—war, hunger, and epidemic—acted together (Alter and Oris 2000: 339). The relatively high level of I_m ($= 0.44$), an index of the proportion married, was perhaps compensation for marriages postponed during the Napoleonic wars and the bad years that followed it. Around 1820, I_m reached 0.49, the average age at first marriage declined from one to two years, and the proportion married in the age group 25–34 was above 60% among females, 55% among males (Alter and Oris 1999*a*: 137–40). With a total marital fertility rate (for ages 20 +) of 8.7 children per woman, the relaxation of Malthus' prevent restraint (access to marriage) produced a crude birth rate of almost 32 births per thousand inhabitants, significantly above the level of mortality. Positive natural increase exceeded net out-migration, producing an average population growth of 0.5% per year.

In the outmoded agricultural system of the East Ardennes this resulted in population pressure, because resources did not expand. Apart from the practice of

Table 15.1 Demographic regimes and family systems in the Land of Herve and East Ardennes. A set of indicators, 1811–1900

	1811–45	1846–72	1873–90	1891–1900	Total
Part 1: Land of Herve					
Marriage					
Mean age at 1st marriage, males	—	30.10	30.30	—	30.20
Mean age at 1st marriage, females	—	28.40	28.00	—	28.20
Mean age at 1st marriage, both sexes	—	29.00	28.90	—	29.00
Proportions marrying (I_m)	—	0.33	0.34	0.30	0.33
Age gap between spouses at 1st marriage	—	2.20	2.50	—	2.30
Proportion of wives older than husbands	—	31.90	27.90	—	30.40
Proportion of widows remarrying	—	3.50	4.20	—	3.80
Hammel–typology					
Proportion of solitaries	—	9.40	12.90	8.60	10.50
Proportion of no-family households	—	6.00	6.80	9.90	6.30
Proportion of simple-family households	—	72.20	73.00	74.80	72.40
Proportion of extended-family households	—	7.70	3.80	5.50	6.40
Proportion of multiple-family households	—	4.70	3.60	1.30	4.30
Socio-economy of the household					
Addition to household of kin as workers	—	2.70	2.30	4.60	2.80
Addition to household of life-cycle servants	—	2.30	1.20	1.00	1.90
Married servants	—	0.20	0.10	0.10	0.20
Mean number of adults (15–54) per household	—	2.40	2.30	2.60	2.40
Proportion of households of < 4 persons	—	37.70	40.50	38.40	38.60
Demographic regime					
TMFR 20 +	—	8.60	9.00	8.00	8.70
Life expectancy at birth	—	47.81	49.69	52.26	49.18
Proportions marrying (I_m)	—	0.33	0.34	0.30	0.33
Crude natality rates	—	26.77	27.85	21.65	26.24
Crude mortality rates	—	19.18	18.32	15.74	18.30
Natural balance	—	7.59	9.53	5.92	7.94
In-migration rates	—	36.35	43.98	41.34	39.73
Out-migration rates	—	48.52	53.40	56.87	51.57
Migratory balance	—	−12.16	−9.42	−15.53	−11.84
Migratory intensity	—	84.87	97.38	98.21	91.31
Population movement (annual, in %)	—	−0.46	0.01	−0.96	−0.39

Table 15.1 *(Continued)*

	1811–45	1846–72	1873–90	1891–1900	Total
Part 2: Sart					
Marriage					
Mean age at 1st marriage, males	28.79	30.28	29.43	—	29.43
Mean age at 1st marriage, females	26.96	26.24	25.89	—	26.51
Mean age at 1st marriage, both sexes	27.44	27.98	27.55	—	27.65
Proportions marrying (I_m)	0.44	0.40	0.39	0.39	0.41
Age gap between spouses at 1st marriage	1.83	4.04	3.54	—	2.92
Proportion of wives older than husbands	28.67	19.19	21.85		24.19
Proportion of widows remarrying	—	—	—	—	5.13
Hammel–Laslett typology					
Proportion of solitaries	7.57	7.01	8.13	8.44	6.89
Proportion of no-family households	7.09	5.61	6.04	3.90	5.25
Proportion of simple-family households	74.47	80.76	76.46	78.79	75.69
Proportion of extended-family households	3.78	5.61	6.88	5.63	8.56
Proportion of multiple-family households	7.09	1.00	2.50	3.25	3.61
Socio-economy of the household					
Addition to household of kin as workers	—	—	—	—	2.69
Addition to household of life-cycle servants	—	—	—	—	0.57
Married servants	—	—	—	—	0.10
Mean number of adults (15–54) per household	—	—	—	—	2.37
Proportion of households of < 4 persons	—	—	—	—	36.66
Demographic regime					
TMFR 20 +	8.70	10.80	9.60	7.20	9.20
Life expectancy at birth	39.38	41.08	47.15	52.77	42.83
Proportions marrying (I_m)	0.44	0.40	0.39	0.39	0.41
Crude natality rates	31.68	27.86	27.78	21.36	28.65
Crude mortality rates	23.50	22.29	18.80	14.71	21.27
Natural balance	8.18	5.57	8.98	6.65	7.39
In-migration rates	0.99	25.20	26.09	33.20	16.85
Out-migration rates	3.74	36.25	35.87	40.84	24.08
Migratory balance	−2.75	−11.05	−9.77	−7.64	−7.23
Migratory intensity	4.74	61.45	61.96	74.03	40.93
Population movement (annual, in %)	0.54	−0.55	−0.08	−0.10	0.02

slash and burn, no additional land clearing can be observed. The size of farms stayed small: in 1846, 41% had less than 1 ha, and 36% had 1–4 ha. However, peasants benefited from high prices on the urban market until at least 1843, when the railroad reached Verviers. We noted above that the population of Belgium grew 30% faster than agricultural production between 1806 and 1846, but in the district of Verviers the gap was 69% (Goosens 1992: 180–5). Prices in Verviers and the Land of Herve were consequently 5–10% higher than in the rest of Belgium (Oris 1998: 12–17). It was a situation with both opportunities and risks for peasants in the Ardennes.

The Malthusian contest between population and subsistence reached a climax in 1845–7 with the potato blight and typhus epidemic. The crisis was not as dramatic in East Belgium as in Flanders, where there were thousands of deaths among the rural flax spinners. Nevertheless, the East Ardennes could not sustain its recent population growth, and the socio-economic system imploded as it had 50 years earlier in the Land of Herve. When children born in the 1820s reached adulthood in the 1850s, they found few opportunities to establish their own households. As we can see in Table 15.1, the population of Sart fell by 0.55% each year between 1846 and 1872. I_m decreased to 0.40, which offset rising marital fertility and reduced the birth rate by 4 points.

But the real motor of demographic decline was out-migration, and an attractive destination was nearby. In the textile centre of Verviers, entrepreneurs sought labour first in the town and among unemployed rural spinners, and then began to attract surplus rural population (Desama 1985). Although there are some obvious problems in the registration of migration in our sources, especially in the late 1830s and early 1840s, it is clear that a largely immobile society discovered mobility in the middle of the century. Sart lost 1% of its population each year through net out-migration between 1846 and 1872, but the turn-over involved 6% of the inhabitants each year! This is less than the 8.5% observed in the Land of Herve at the same time. The difference between the two areas increased between 1873 and 1890 when 10% of the Hervian population changed residence each year. More striking is the qualitative difference: in the Land of Herve the age- and marital status-specific rates indicate that the married were even more mobile than the single (Neven 2000: 478). This pattern can be related to the increasing number of renters among the farmers, who moved from tenancy to tenancy: 'family migration has accordingly been described as a form typical of agricultural populations' (Langewiesche and Lenger 1987: 93). In Sart, as late as 1878, around 66% of the land belonged to native peasants. The poor soils of the East Ardennes were much less attractive for the urban bourgeoisie and for the nobility who invested extensively in the rich commercial agriculture of the Land of Herve.

The disappearance of proto-industry and progressive 'ruralization' of large areas of East Belgium can be measured in demographic indicators. Life expectancy in the Land of Herve was close to 48 years in the middle of the nineteenth century. This is a level that the whole province of Liège only reached in 1890 after almost 20 years of mortality decline. Sart had a lower value, 41.1 years, but paradoxically while it was becoming poorer and even depopulated after 1851, life expectancy improved throughout the nineteenth century. This is just one facet of a more general 'paradox of growth'. Between 1846 and 1872, the booming industrial towns experienced a serious epidemiological depression. Expectation of life in these urbanizing areas fell to 35 years and even dropped below 30 years during years of cholera or smallpox. A part of the explanation is that both the Land of Herve and the East Ardennes escaped the murderous cholera invasions of 1848–9 and 1866 and suffered much less than urban inhabitants from tuberculosis and digestive diseases in spite of increasing rural–urban migration (see Neven 1997 for an examination of the mortality crises and causes of death).

In 1873–4 the massive arrival of cheap American cereals started a long agricultural depression in northwest European markets. The price of 100 kg of rye fell from 24.55 francs in 1874 to 13.25 in 1889 (Oris 1998). The rural population suffered almost everywhere from a drastic decline in their incomes. Within about twenty years, the crisis forced the transition from subsistence to commercial agriculture serving the urban markets. The East Ardennes endured this transition, and by 1890–1900 the slopes of the Hautes–Fagnes had fully adopted the Hervian model of livestock breeding. A community like Sart also relied upon the sale of products from its extensive forests, which became more valuable in the nineteenth century because the coal-mines required timber. The Land of Herve is one of the rare places that did not suffer so much from the depression of 1873–1890; it had become 'modern' a century earlier. Continued high prices of butter, milk, and cheese supported its rural economy (Neven 2000: 81–7).

However, cattle breeding and agro-forestry required a smaller workforce than traditional agriculture or the proto-industry-agriculture combination, and the arrival of mechanization in the countryside in the late nineteenth century reinforced this tendency. Pressure from marital fertility remained high and neo-Malthusianism had still not replaced the traditional Malthusian check of late marriage and high proportions never-married. This form of control was particularly impressive in the Land of Herve where I_m stayed around 0.33/0.34 between 1846 and 1890 before it fell to 0.30 between 1890 and 1900; 0.05 to 0.09 lower than in Sart. The demographic health of the 'stayers', a mixture of modern mortality and traditional fertility and nuptiality, was paid for by the many 'leavers' who went to the towns. The Industrial Revolution and the consequent urbanization offered an escape for excess population and prevented the countryside from becoming rural slums. In spite of their differences, the experiences of both the Land of Herve and East Ardennes appear very similar to that of Ireland after the Great Famine. The Irish population survived and even improved its living standards thanks to massive out-migration to England and North America (Ó Grada 1993; Guinanne 1997: 4–6 and *passim*). However, in eastern Belgium the outlet was a few dozen and not hundreds or thousands of kilometres away.

This demographic regime was both determined by the family system and determinant of it. Low values of the proportions married (I_m) reflect difficulties in getting married. The average age at first marriage was around 30 for men, 28 for the Hervian women, and 26–27 for women in Sart. The difference between women in

Herve and Sart are related to the sex composition of the marriage market. Among unmarried people aged 18–44 the number of males per hundred females was below 100 from 1852 to 1891 in the Land of Herve and above 130 in East Ardennes after the 1840s (Alter and Oris 1999*a*: 139; Neven 2000: 457). Selective migration by gender is the explanation. Factories in Verviers recruited married men from the proto-industrial workers in the Land of Herve. Moreover, dairying was traditionally a female task. Economic change in Sart left less and less opportunity for employment of women, especially after the disappearance of spinning. Instead, they found positions in Verviers, not in the textile factories as often assumed, but in domestic and commercial services (Desama 1985; Alter 1988).

It was very difficult to establish a household in a nuclear family system where neolocalism was the rule. The old Walloon adage is 'marriage requires a household'. Moreover, as in some French regions studied by Martine Ségalen (1987) and unlike the English or Swedish experiences, lifecycle servant-hood was marginal among the rural populations of East Belgium (see Table 15.1, Section 3). Children stayed at home and often did not leave before age 29 or 30. These are among the highest ages at leaving home ever observed in historical populations, not only because marriage was late but also because an important group never left (Capron and Oris 2000; Neven 2000: 428–35).[3] George Alter (1996) has stressed the importance of the European pattern of late marriage and high proportions of never married as a source of support for the elderly. The timing of marriage and fertility meant that married people aged 60–65 normally lived with one of their younger children. Those 'stayers' who remained when parents reached age 70 had passed the normal age for marriage, and in the Land of Herve more than 80% of them never married. Staying at home to take care of old parents was an additional cause of a permanent celibacy for 20–25% of children. The extent of their 'sacrifice' was not clear until they reached old age themselves. Between ages 55 and 90 less than 1% of the married lived alone, compared to 15% of widowers, 19% of widows, and 22% of the never-married (Neven 2000: 547). The difference is large but even among the unmarried 78% avoided isolation, sometimes moving to escape it.

These results modify the nuclear-hardship hypothesis. Falling into isolation was not the normal destiny of old people in the nuclear family system of nineteenth-century East Belgium. The massive migratory flows affected the number of kin available to help, but distance did not break family ties, although gender selection existed (see Alter 1999). The situation was a bit different in the East Ardennes because peasant ownership held families on the land. In Sart one-third of the old men or women lived with a married child.

Although their starting points were different and the roads that they followed during the nineteenth century diverged, the Ardennes and the Land of Herve both demonstrate continuity in family systems and demographic regimes. Economic modernization was not followed by clear changes in marriage and fertility. Until the end of the century, people from the Ardennes and Herve continued to marry and leave home late (or never). Out-migration to the booming industrial towns did increase dramatically, but migration helped to relax tensions in the countryside.

These were clearly societies under pressure and on the defensive, but their high and rising life expectancies indicate success on that important demographic dimension.

4. Individual Transitions and Short-Term Economic Stress

4.1 From macro to micro

4.1.1 Standard of living and demographic sensitivity in East Belgium. Our discussion of the macro regional context raised an apparent contradiction since poor areas, where the need for labour was decreasing, benefited from higher life expectancy. To understand this paradox, we must opt for a micro-demographic approach. Indeed, the standard of living—a notion that is both social and economic— provides an interface that might allow us to explain the apparent gap between the regional economy and individual demographic behaviour. However, this concept is problematic in a rural context, where it is difficult to measure production and consumption not passing through the market: 'many agricultural workers received not only money, but food, clothes, lodging, a portion of the harvest, etc., depending on the local customs. Part of rural family incomes, very difficult to evaluate but obviously not trivial, completely escaped from the monetary economy' (Oris 1998: 5; Gadisseur 1990: 830–41). In contrast, data collected on wages for nineteenth-century Belgium come exclusively from industrial and urban sectors (at least as far as continuous annual series are concerned, see Scholliers 1996). Thus, our approach to the standard of living must go beyond the study of real wages.

  We adopt here an indirect and dynamic concept of the standard of living designed for longitudinal microanalysis in the Eurasia Project, that is, vulnerability to short-term economic stress. As Bengtsson (2004) explains, 'from a modern perspective, one would believe that family heads would do everything to smooth consumption in the short run in order to secure the survival of all the members of the family'. Among the demographic behaviours, he distinguishes between voluntary and involuntary responses. Migration and postponed marriage belong to the first category. In the same way, sending young children to live with relatives, or sending older children to work elsewhere and remit their incomes can be considered as solutions to overcome bad times. On the other hand, in a 'natural fertility' regime, mortality and fertility may both be considered involuntary behaviours. Both are closely linked together, especially as far as infant and child mortality is concerned. That is why fertility and mortality analyses must be undertaken together. In this context, age and sex must also be considered carefully since 'the weaker a person's position is within the household, the more vulnerable he or she is to short-term economic stress' (Bengtsson 2004). The young and the elderly, being dependent on other people, were a priori the most vulnerable.

  Overall and without even considering some particular sub-populations, the Land of Herve and the East Ardennes were both potentially vulnerable to economic fluctuations embodied in price movements. In the pastoral Herve area, scarcely 10%

of the land was not devoted to meadows and orchards; 88% of the arable lands were devoted to pasture (agricultural census 1846). Milk and butter, the main local products, were produced for the market. Thus, the inhabitants of the Land of Herve could not resort to subsistence farming. They bought foodstuffs on the neighbouring markets of Aubel and Verviers, which were imported from Germany or the rest of Belgium (Deprez 1948: 46–7), and they were at the mercy of price fluctuations in these markets. From this point of view, Hervian rural society was more urban than rural, in contrast to the East Ardennes where the inhabitants produced a large part of what they consumed. However, the East Ardennes was so poor that it could not produce enough to sustain its population without imports of additional food (Hoyois 1981; Oris 1998: 10–11). In Sart, this situation existed in the eighteenth century, but the problem worsened between 1800 and 1850, when the population grew from 2,000 to 2,400 inhabitants. In the middle of the nineteenth century, a third of the exploitable land was devoted to basic crops, which benefited from the industrial and demographic growth of the Verviers market. Consequently, the Ardennes peasant was in an ambiguous situation. An increase in the price of cereals might be positive as well as negative, because he was both a producer and a consumer. Much depended on the extent of the crisis, its duration, and, also, the possibility of substitution among different foods.

Due to their deeply different agrarian structures, it was obviously impossible to use common economic series for both areas. For East Ardennes prices for the main crops of the area, rye and oats, are used. For the Land of Herve we prefer an approximation of the cost of living and a rough estimate of incomes.

4.1.2   Sart in eastern Ardennes: oats and rye. By all accounts, Sart, our study area in the Belgian Ardennes, was a poor community. Elsewhere, we have analysed heights from military conscription lists, which show that men in Sart were very short, a sign of poor nutrition during childhood (Alter and Oris 2000). Poverty made the demographic system of Sart highly sensitive to economic stress, but we find a complex interaction between a relatively primitive local agricultural system and a highly dynamic regional economy. As described in the preceding section, the ambivalent position of Sart in the emerging urban industrial economy is indeed reflected in differing demographic responses to its two main crops, oats and rye. During the nineteenth century, rye was the main cereal used for bread in eastern Belgium. Although bread from whitened wheat flour was preferred, it was still too expensive for most families (Scholliers 1994). Potatoes also played an important role in the diets of urban workers, but they were probably not a significant factor in Sart until the second half of the century (Hoyois 1981: 786–91). During the 'Potato Famine' of 1846 urban mortality rose, but Sart was unaffected (Alter and Oris 2000: 339–40). In the rural Ardennes, the poor supplemented their diet with a *bouillie* (porridge) of oats, which could not be made into bread. Thus, oats and rye played different roles in the urban and rural markets. In urban markets, rye was a substitute for both more (wheat) and less expensive (potatoes) alternatives. Oats were less important in cities but an essential component of the rural diet.

Both rye and oats were grown for home consumption in Sart (census of 1846), and surpluses could be sold in nearby urban markets. The long-run evolution of their prices appears in Figure 15.1. The prices of both grains, but especially rye, decreased in the 1820s, as conditions normalized after the great crisis of 1816–17 (Deprez 1948). From the end of the 1820s, an upward trend was observed, slow and progressive for oats, quicker for rye. At the beginning of the 1860s, oats prices stagnated, while rye, once more, decreased more clearly. Then, the trend turned up again and prices reached their peak in 1873–4, before dropping sharply in a context of economic depression and the invasion of American cereals. Prices only rose again in the last decade of the nineteenth century (Oris 1998: 4).

Apart from these common trends, the short-term dynamics of these grain prices differed. Although the prices of oats and rye were moderately correlated with each other, the price of rye was much more volatile than the price of oats. Rye prices reached higher highs and lower lows. Furthermore, rye prices tended to rise about a year before oats prices at least until 1850. That year marks a major turning point, because price fluctuations were more pronounced and more numerous during the first half of the nineteenth century. From 1811 to 1849, the average difference between the annual price and the price trend was 2.20 francs for oats and 3.50 francs for rye.[4] Those differences fell to 1.22 francs and 2.44 francs respectively between 1850 and 1900. Increased price stability is also evident in the decrease in the number of years with high prices, especially for oats: from 1811 to 1849 the annual price was 10% above the trend in 21 years, while there were only 12 similar peaks during the fifty following years. Since rye was a better substitute for other parts of the urban

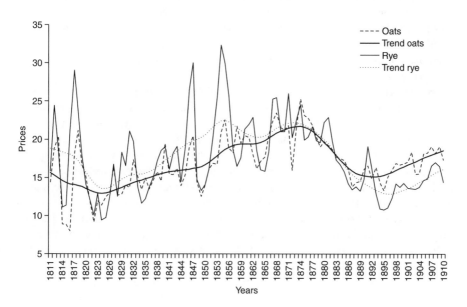

Figure 15.1 Prices and trends in Sart, 1811–1910

diet (wheat and potatoes), we believe that rye prices are a better indicator of real wages (or incomes) for Sart peasants. On the other hand, oats played a special role during hard times as the last resort of the poor in rural areas. One must also notice that in the last quarter of the nineteenth century, the balance between these cereals reversed: the collapse of prices in the 1870s affected rye more deeply. From then on, rye was cheaper than oats, which had previously been the lower price grain.

4.1.3   Land of Herve: cost of living and butter prices. Due to lack of information concerning real wages, we chose to use the cost of living index created by Scholliers (1993) for the whole of Belgium. This index is based on the accounts of the charity institutions of Ghent and of the socialist cooperative *Vooruit* as well as the average rents of 332 buildings. Information in the family budgets collected during the 1850s and the beginning of the 1890s is used to weight the commodities included in the index. These two sets of family budgets take into account changing consumption patterns over this half century, resulting in two different weighting scales (see Scholliers 1993: 231). This cost of living index considers about 85% of the total expenses of a worker's family, and it can be considered very representative of expenses at the time. Although it is not perfect, it is the best index currently available in Belgium, especially because there are no similar data specifically for rural areas. Since it is based on numbers collected in northern Belgium, however, it might not reflect local trends in other places. This weakness primarily concerns the first decades of the nineteenth century, when 'east Belgium suffered from its extreme position, near the borders with Prussia and the Netherlands, far away from major rivers that permitted much cheaper supplies (half as expensive)' (Oris 1998: 13). From 1830, differences within Belgium diminished and prices standardized (Deprez 1948: 47–57; Oris 1998: 12–17). The period under observation for the Land of Herve only covers the second half of the nineteenth century, but it remains true that the Scholliers index was closer to the situation of the urban working class than the peasantry, even in the Land of Herve.

Butter prices in the Verviers market from 1851 to 1910 provide information on potential incomes for the Land of Herve.[5] A large proportion of land was devoted to dairy farming, and even during the proto-industrial period, the value of dairy products clearly exceeded the value of textile production. All Hervians did not sell butter, but the Land of Herve was so highly specialized in dairy production that overall incomes almost certainly rose when the price of butter increased.

Both series used for the Land of Herve are smoother than the cereal prices used for the Ardennes (Figure 15.2). Major peaks were less numerous: between 1846 and 1900, only six or seven years were more than 10% higher than the trend. The last significant increase in the cost of living index and the price of butter occurred in 1867, when times were good for the whole country. A major turning point in 1873–4 is not apparent in the two indexes used here. On the contrary, prices continued increasing until 1880, which can easily be explained in the Hervian context. The agricultural crisis of 1873 first affected farming based on cereals. The Land of Herve, which had already made the transition to a new agricultural system, based on

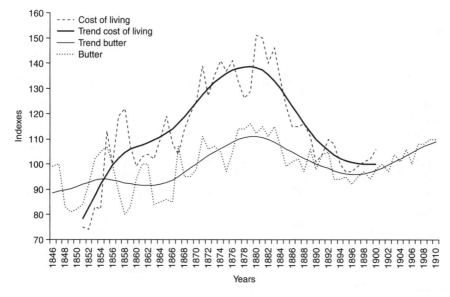

Figure 15.2   Prices and trends in Land of Herve, 1846–1910

pasture and dairy production as explained above, was not affected by competition with the American products. The price of butter only began to decrease seven or eight years later, when other rural regions of Belgium moved towards the Hervian mode of production and became direct competitors.

4.2   Involuntary answers: mortality and fertility

Demographic responses to oats and rye in Sart appear to differentiate between voluntary and involuntary effects. Mortality and the fertility of the poor follow the price of oats. The relationship between mortality and prices is the most complex by far. In another study (Alter, Oris, and Servais 1999) we have examined a number of methodological problems that make it difficult to discern the underlying effect of food prices on mortality in a rural community. For example, we show that epidemics, most of which were not related to economic conditions, can either exaggerate or conceal the statistical association between prices and mortality. For this reason our estimate of the effect of grain prices on the relative risk of mortality (Table 15.2) does not include the years 1812–19, 1858, and 1871.

Our most surprising finding is that the prices of oats and rye were associated with mortality in opposite ways. An increase in the price of oats (with a lag of one year) was followed by a rise in mortality; while mortality went down when the price of rye went up. These relationships appear to result from the dual nature of the family economy in an agricultural society embedded in an industrializing region. As we noted peasants are both consumers and producers. To the extent that high prices

Table 15.2 Effects of grain prices on relative risks of demographic events by sex and period, in Sart, Belgium

	Oats		Rye	
	Relative risk	*p*-value	Relative risk	*p*-value
Part 1				
Mortality[a], 1820–46				
Female				
0	0.95	0.52	0.96	0.39
1–14	0.99	0.86	**0.90**	0.01
15–54	**1.12**	0.05	**0.90**	0.00
55 +	0.99	0.88	**1.06**	0.08
Male				
0	**0.86**	0.02	1.04	0.27
1–14	1.01	0.84	**0.91**	0.03
15–54	1.10	0.10	0.98	0.57
55 +	**1.10**	0.06	**0.94**	0.05
Mortality[a], 1847–99				
Female				
0	0.98	0.69	0.98	0.59
1–14	0.93	0.24	0.99	0.71
15–54	**1.11**	0.04	**0.96**	0.06
55 +	1.04	0.37	0.99	0.68
Male				
0	0.96	0.31	1.01	0.71
1–14	0.91	0.13	1.04	0.16
15–54	0.99	0.75	1.00	0.97
55 +	1.02	0.55	0.99	0.52
Fertility[b], 1812–46				
All	**1.02**	0.05	**0.98**	0.01
Cultivators	1.02	0.20	**0.98**	0.05
Labourers	**0.93**	0.11	1.03	0.42
Fertility[b], 1847–99				
All	1.00	0.98	1.01	0.39
Cultivators	1.03	0.17	1.00	0.99
Labourers	0.96	0.40	1.01	0.57
Part 2				
Migration[c]				
Female				
1812–46	0.95	0.43	1.02	0.66
1847–99	0.97	0.46	0.99	0.65
Male				
1812–46	1.02	0.77	1.02	0.37
1847–99	0.98	0.51	1.00	0.94

Table 15.2 *(Continued)*

	Oats		Rye	
	Relative risk	*p*-value	Relative risk	*p*-value
Marriage[c]				
Female				
1812–46	**1.09**	0.00	**0.95**	0.00
1847–99	1.01	0.72	**0.96**	0.02
Male				
1812–46	**1.05**	0.09	**0.97**	0.08
1847–99	0.97	0.31	1.00	0.98

[a] Models also include occupation of head of household and year. We eliminate 1812–19, 1858, and 1871 from the mortality analysis to remove the effects of epidemics. Price variables are differences from trend lagged by one year.

[b] Married women with at least one child. Models also include occupation of head of household and survival of preceding child. Price variables are differences from trend lagged by one year.

[c] Unmarried persons aged 18–34. Models also include occupation of head of household and relationship to head of household. Price variables are differences from trend.

Note: Bold figures are significant at the 10% level.

indicate a harvest failure and insufficient resources, they imply hard times and reduced nutrition. In an international market economy, however, high prices can also result from external conditions that are unrelated to the local harvest, such as the potato blight. When price increases are caused by conditions somewhere else, peasants benefit as producers. Thus, the positive correlation between mortality and oats prices reflects the hardship caused by a shortage of the peasants' food of last resort. The negative correlation between mortality and the price of rye implies that high prices in urban markets were a profitable opportunity.

It is also instructive to see who suffered when prices went up (see Table 15.2). In Sart between 1820 and 1846, the groups most vulnerable to short-term variations in the price of oats were married adults of both sexes and old men. The positive effects of an increase in rye prices appear in all age groups except old women and male infants.

The relationship between oats prices and mortality disappeared after 1850 with only one exception: married women. This falls in the period of greatest industrial expansion in eastern Belgium. Improvements in the transportation system created a homogeneous national market, characterized by less volatile prices. At a local level, this is also the period in which out-migration began to reduce the total population of Sart. Although there was almost no industrial activity in Sart, the community may have benefited from industrial expansion in a number of ways. On the one hand, there were new opportunities to profit from the expanding urban market, such as the increased demand for timbers to be used in the coal-mines (Hoyois 1981: 517–18). On the other hand, rural–urban migration reduced population pressure, and out-migrants probably sent remittances to their families in Sart (on the familial context of out-migration and the family ties of out-migrants, see Alter and Oris 1999*a*).

We also find a complex association between short-term fluctuations in fertility and grain prices (Alter and Oris 1999*b*). When all women are considered, fertility appears to be positively associated with oats prices and negatively associated with rye prices. However, when we separate women in households headed by a day-labourer, we see the opposite pattern. These poor women were less likely to give birth in years following a rise in oats prices. As noted above, the mortality of married women was also very sensitive to oats prices. In addition, we found that prices had a stronger effect on the mortality of the wives of day-labourers than on other married women (Alter, Oris, and Servais 1999). Thus, it seems likely that food shortages had a disproportionate effect on the poorest women, who were most dependent on oats, the cheapest grain. These effects are greatly attenuated after 1847, but the fertility of labourers' wives still shows a tendency to decrease when the price of oats rose.

While it is difficult to determine why fertility was sensitive to grain prices, this pattern suggests that variations in fertility were primarily involuntary rather than voluntary. Our evidence does not distinguish between physiological effects (such as reduced fecundity due to malnutrition) and behavioural effects (such as less frequent coitus during a crisis), but it does imply that short-term variations in fertility were due to extreme poverty, not to family planning (Alter and Oris 1999*b*, for the detailed demonstration).

Since the effects of prices on mortality almost disappeared in the East Ardennes after 1850, it is not surprising to find no effect of the cost of living in the more advanced Land of Herve during the period 1846–1900 (see Table 15.3). We also looked for differences among socio-economic groups, but the results were negative: after the mid-nineteenth century there was no demographic response to prices in Hervian society. This contrasts with studies of the seventeenth and eighteenth centuries, which show that some sub-populations, especially weavers, were very vulnerable to hardship and dependent on markets (Haesenne-Peremans 1981: 169; Gutmann 1988: 173).

From 1846 to 1900 there is one exception to this rule. The mortality of married Hervian women rose when the price index increased, and this effect was more pronounced than the one observed in Sart. In fact, while the socio-economic status of the household head, the size and the composition of the household, the relationship to the head, etc. reveal differential mortality among unmarried adults and married men, married women were indifferent to everything but prices (for a detailed analysis of adults' differential mortality in the Land of Herve, see Neven 2000: 504–8). This group includes fertile women, and fertility was also significantly affected by economic changes. The probability of the next birth declined and birth intervals were longer when the cost of living increased. Mothers were exhausted by repeated pregnancies on top of their domestic tasks and other contributions to the household economy, especially in dairy production.[6] Furthermore, mothers have been known to reduce their own portions in times of scarcity. Clearly, married women in the Land of Herve, as well as in Sart, were still vulnerable in the second half of the nineteenth century; they were the last group whose life depended on prices!

Table 15.3 Demographic responses to price fluctuations in the Land of Herve, 1846–1900. Estimated relative risks for a 10% deviation from the trend

	Cost of living[a]				Prices of butter[a]			
	Men		Women		Men		Women	
	Rel. risk	p-value	Rel. risk	p-value	Rel. risk	p-value	Rel. risk	p-value
Fertility[b]								
Marriage to first birth	—	—	1.02	0.75	—	—	0.96	0.39
Intervals following a birth	—	—	**0.96**	0.05	—	—	0.98	0.28
Mortality[c]								
Ages 0–1	**0.92**	0.05	0.97	0.66	0.97	0.57	**0.92**	0.06
Ages 2–14	—	—	—	—	—	—	—	—
Married and widowed, 15–54	0.92	0.17	**1.49**	0.03	0.95	0.59	1.24	0.37
Never married, 15–54	0.93	0.22	0.93	0.25	1.18	0.54	**1.76**	0.04
Ages 55–90	1.18	0.24	1.15	0.43	1.15	0.36	0.97	0.53
Out-migration								
Singles 18–44[d]	0.97	0.31	**0.94**	0.01	0.99	0.79	0.98	0.48
Leaving home[d]	0.95	0.32	**0.93**	0.08	0.98	0.72	0.94	0.13
Married 20–54	0.98	0.69	1.10	0.97	1.14	0.40	1.12	0.61
55–90	0.95	0.40	0.96	0.51	0.95	0.30	1.12	0.78
First marriage[d] Unmarried, ages 18–44	1.14	0.53	1.12	0.77	1.15	0.48	1.13	0.56

[a] Difference between logarithm of annual series and logarithm of trend.
[b] Model includes age of mother and occupation of head of household.
[c] Model includes occupation of head of household and time period.
[d] Model includes occupation of head of household, parents' presence or time of death, persons in household by age, siblings in household, time period, sex ratio in community, and cohort ratio in community.

Note: Bold figures are significant at the 10% level.

The lengthening of birth intervals may also explain the surprising decrease in mortality for the youngest children when the cost of living increased. We have shown elsewhere that Hervians less than two years old were much more likely to die when they had a sibling born less than 24 months before them (Neven 2000: 388). By reducing fertility, an increase in the cost of living increased the spacing between births and reduced infant mortality. This is another demonstration that biological factors, largely associated with the fertility history of the mother, were more important for an infant's survival than socio-economic factors (see Oris, Derosas, and Breschi, 2004, for a detailed discussion).

The price of butter, our indicator of short-term changes in income, is the smoothest series among the four used in our analyses. We do not find clear associations between butter prices and Hervian mortality or fertility. Changes in butter prices did not affect the mortality pattern, especially when prices were included in general models with family variables, such as household composition or relation to the household head (Neven 2000: 506).

4.3.   *Voluntary answers: marriage and out-migration*

During the nineteenth century the inhabitants of both the Ardennes and the Land of Herve experienced rising pressure due to both population growth and the changing regional economy. In this context, late marriage and out-migration were the main safety valves for these populations. Both marriage and migrations were voluntary responses, but they took place within the limits of strict demographic and family systems.

In the first half of the nineteenth century, out-migration was still a marginal behaviour in Sart, and marriage was the main check on population growth. Short-term variations in nuptiality were negatively associated with changes in the price of rye and positively with changes in the price of oats. We saw the opposite above: an increase in the price of rye was a good sign for the inhabitants of Sart, lowering their mortality and increasing their fertility. Evidently, young, unmarried adults had a different perspective. We hypothesize that they viewed the world as wage earners and consumers, not as producers or subsistence farmers. For wage earners, an increase in the price of rye signalled a decrease in the real wage. Rye prices clearly mattered to workers in Verviers, the most frequent urban destination from Sart, and variations in the migration stream would have conveyed this effect to real wages in rural areas as well.

The attenuation of links between short-term fluctuations in prices and demographic responses after 1847 also applies to the marriage and out-migration of young single adults. In the Land of Herve the demographic system was continuously under pressure, and throughout the second half of the nineteenth century, it remained very difficult for young couples to start a family. We cannot find traces of any specific marriage behaviour consistent with responses to annual price fluctuations (see Table 15.3).[7] A rise in butter prices (an increase of Hervian potential incomes) did tend to reduce migration but not to a statistically significant extent. The strongest response was for unmarried people, especially women who were 7% less likely to move when the cost of living rose 10% above the trend.

Unlike the migration pattern of the unmarried, married adults were indifferent to short-term price fluctuations. When they out-migrated, 78% stayed within the borders of the Land of Herve; only 18–19% left for the industrial agglomerations of Verviers and Liège or for the adjacent Dutch (Maastricht) and German (Aachen, Köln) towns. In contrast, urban and industrial destinations attracted 50% of young adults leaving the parental home. For married adults, moving was not changing their economic roles, and their mobility was determined by socio-economic and familial characteristics—like moving from farm to farm in a society of tenants—not by short-term stress, which did not vary within the rural environment. The same was true for old people (55–90) whose out-migration depended on their age, sex, marital status, position in their household, presence of children, etc., but not on variations in prices (for a specific study about the determinants of old age migrations, see Neven 2003).

5. Contrasting Verdicts: Structural Adaptations and Short-Term Stress

For hundreds of years the rural population of East Belgium lived in a Malthusian system and responded to population growth in multiple ways. In the eighteenth and early nineteenth centuries, commercial and industrial revolutions, accompanied by the integration of national and international markets, ended long-established patterns and profoundly changed the regional economy of both the Land of Herve and the East Ardennes. At a macro level, two main patterns emerged, and we can say that both the modern and the traditional countryside lost quantity and gained quality. First, one can consider their adaptations to economic change a success, because they achieved high and increasing life expectancies, even at the cost of gradual depopulation. Second, except for an increase in out-migration, neither the family system nor the demographic regime were modified in spite of the deep economic and social changes of the nineteenth century.

Population pressure strained the family system which was already characterized by late marriage and high proportions never-marrying. Restricted access to marriage was reinforced, especially in the Land of Herve. The booming industrial towns offered a new outlet to the 'losers' who could not be accommodated in rural areas, but the increasing flows from rural areas to the towns did not relax the Malthusian system. All those who could establish a household in the village did so, but they were few and becoming fewer. In the East Ardennes as well as in the Land of Herve, children who reached adulthood while continually living with their parents had to accept constraints that restricted their choices and chances. Among other things, their departures were more affected by parental and family needs than their own individual choices. Other studies tell us that the children who were able to establish themselves in the village were not selected by gender or birth rank (Neven 2000: 318–23). From this point of view, the inheritance rules in the Napoleonic code continued old egalitarian regional customs. The small number of court cases disputing inheritances suggests that ties within the sibling group were usually good enough to divide inheritances informally (Servais forthcoming).

Another indicator of the efficient management of the tensions inherent in a family system under pressure is that married people could rely on their children. Consistent with older theories of modernization, mortality in the Land of Herve and East Ardennes declined before marital fertility, which was uncontrolled for most of the nineteenth century. While urban populations started to control their reproduction in the 1850s or 1860s, the inhabitants of the countryside continued to see children as a source of wealth and support in old age. The Malthusian system, especially the high proportion never-married, made this 'strategy' efficient, because few old people finished their life isolated. If necessary, parents, especially widowed mothers, could rely on children who had out-migrated to the industrial towns years earlier (Alter 1999: 20; Neven 2003). Parents' success in retaining their adult sons and daughters at home strained family ties. With average ages at leaving home of 25 years for women and 27–28 for men tensions between the generations were obvious (Capron and Oris 2000). Stress was apparently higher in a society where renters were predominant, like the Land of Herve, than in an area of small properties like East Ardennes.

The ties of children with their fathers and mothers were of different natures, based largely on the dichotomy of authority versus devotion (Alter 1999: 24). Since their domestic role placed adult married women in a good position to retain food resources for themselves, maternal devotion can be seen as the underlying cause of their excess-mortality and hyper-sensitivity to prices, which continued to affect married women even after the rest of the population stopped responding to economic fluctuations. Clearly, the family system in nineteenth-century East Ardennes and the Land of Herve distributed an excessive part of the burden of hard times on married women and unmarried adults, while infants and to some extent the *pater familias*, were spared.

A systematic study of the demographic consequences of short-term economic stress informs this general perspective. The experience of the East Belgian countryside shows how difficult it is to link behaviour to economic data. In the poor community of Sart during the period 1820–46, mortality and fertility were strongly affected by variations in the price of oats, the most basic sustenance of the poor. When oats were in short supply, the poor went hungry, and this hunger resulted in more deaths and fewer births. Marriage, however, responded to the price of rye not oats. This shows the difference between the physiological effects of food shortage and the psychological perceptions that govern a voluntary response. These responses also reveal the ambivalent position of an economically backward area in a rapidly advancing region.

After 1850, economic crises were rarely fatal, except for childbearing women, whose fecundity was also affected. This pattern is very clear and quite similar in two areas with completely different social, economic, and agrarian structures. Both the East Ardennes and the Land of Herve made a decisive step on the road from uncertainty to security after 1850.

This transition also put more emphasis on voluntary demographic responses. In the second half of the nineteenth century marriage and out-migration were dominated by family needs and the structural constraints of rural communities. Both responses became increasingly independent of short-term economic stress. In the Land of Herve, married adults were indifferent to price fluctuations. Only the out-migration of unmarried adults showed the effects of short-term economic stress. In fact, a more detailed study has shown that in periods of high prices the household tended to push out unrelated workers (day-labourer, domestics, etc.), but to hold kin, especially children, more tightly (Neven 2000: 466). Hervians adopted a 'defensive logic', keeping everybody at home in bad times. Of course, this did not prevent them from leaving, since out-migration rates increased continuously from 1850 until 1900 (see Table 15.1). But a part of this increase, particularly as far as family migrations are concerned, is due to changing land tenure. Decreasing landownership among the peasants resulted in a growing class of renters, who were obliged to move from farm to farm within the same region.

Another aspect of rising mobility was the departure of young adults from their parental homes. Their out-migration constituted an 'offensive logic' of departures in good times. Recent research has challenged the traditional association between crisis and migration. Working on migrations between Ghent in Belgium and the French city of Armentières during the nineteenth century, K. Dillen (2001: 446) noted: 'migration was not in the first place an escape, but a fairly natural phenomenon.... Subsistence migration was rather an exception and not the other way around. As a result, this means that migration was a positive choice most of the time.' The same could be said for mobility in Sart and the Land of Herve, which challenges the idea that 'in the short run, particularly in the period between 1850 and First World War, crises in rural economy promoted mobility'(Moch 1992: 111). In the Land of Herve at least, structural adaptations provoked 'crises' (as shown in Section 3), but short-term term variations followed a different logic.

In this chapter, we asked: how did demographic and family systems distribute the burdens of hard times? The answers offered here contribute to the Belgian debate on the standard of living (see Section 2.1). We also believe that our results show the general value of a demographic approach based on longitudinal data. The standard of living, much less the quality of life, cannot be understood without considering individual aspirations and trajectories in the context of families and households.

Notes

1. In his 1989 introduction to a collective volume, Peter Scholliers shows how British historians E. Hobsbawm and R. Hartwell took up the debate of inter-war economists Keynes and Kuczynski, starting a continuous flow of research (cf. Scholliers 1989: especially 6–8).
2. We do not want to impose numerous references, some of them very local, on an international audience. One of us has published an exhaustive bibliography of the studies about the population history of Belgium, and we take the liberty to refer to this publication. For the research on demographic crises, look in Oris (1994: notices 2028 to 2149, 178–88).
3. In the Land of Herve, cohabitation between an old parent and the last children staying at home was ended by death or occasionally by the out-migration of the elder in 77% of the cases. Only 33% of these living arrangements ended because of the departure of the children. The large majority of the 'stayers' did their 'duty' until the end.
4. Trends for all series (see Figure 15.1 as well as Figure 15.2) have been estimated using the Hodrick–Prescott method. For a critique, see Harvey and Jaeger (1993).

5. Prices in Verviers have been built from the *Prix moyen des grains et des autres produits alimentaires vendus à Verviers,* a series which was annually published in the *Exposé de la situation de la Ville de Verviers, 1851–1910.* For the years 1879 and 1889, they have been completed by the *Moniteur belge.*
6. As we noted above, dairy production, which was the essential component of the Hervian economy in the second half of the nineteenth century, was traditionally a female task (Segalen 1980: 87–104). Consequently, we can suspect a greater pressure on adult women in the Land of Herve, than in more traditional rural areas like Ardennes.
7. In this context, even the evolution of the matrimonial market analysed through the sex ratio of unmarried people aged 18–44 had no clear influence on marriage levels (Neven 2000: 457).

References

Alter, G. (1984) 'Work and Income in the Family Economy: Belgium, 1853 and 1891'. *Journal of Interdisciplinary History,* 15(2): 255–76.

——(1988) *Family and the Female Life Course. The Women of Verviers, Belgium, 1849–1880.* Madison: University of Wisconsin Press.

——(1996) 'The European Marriage Pattern as Solution and Problem: Household of the Elderly in Verviers, Belgium, 1831', in A. Bideau, A. Perrenoud, K. A. Lynch, and G. Brunet (eds.), *Les systèmes démographiques du passé.* Lyon: Programme Rhône-Alpes de Recherches en Sciences sociales, pp. 4–19.

——(1999) 'Vieillir dans les ménages d'une ville industrielle: l'impact de l'âge de migration (Verviers, début du XIXe siècle)'. *Annales de Démographie Historique,* 2: 9–29.

——Capron, C., Neven, M., and Oris, M. (2002) 'When Dad Died: Household Economy and Family Culture in 19th Century East Belgium', in R. Derosas and M. Oris (eds.), *When Dad Died. Individuals and Families Coping with Family Stress.* Bern: Peter Lang, pp. 401–32.

——and Oris, M. (1999a). 'Access to Marriage in the East Ardennes During the 19th Century', in I. Devos and L. Kennedy (eds.), *Marriage and Rural Economy. Western Europe Since 1400.* Turnhout: Brepols, pp. 133–51.

——and——(1999b) 'Fertility and Fecundity in 19th Century Ardennes'. Social Science History Association Meeting, Fort Worth, 11–15 November.

——and——(2000) 'Mortality and Economic Stress. Individual and Household Responses in a Nineteenth-Century Belgian Village', in T. Bengtsson and O. Saito (eds.), *Population and Economy: From Hunger to Modern Economic Growth.* Oxford: Oxford University Press, pp. 335–70.

——, ——, and Servais, P. (1999) 'Prices, Crises, and Mortality in the Belgian Ardennes'. Unpublished paper, PIRT, Indiana University.

André, R. and Pereira–Roque, J. (1974) *La démographie de la Belgique au 19ᵉ siècle.* Brussels: Université de Bruxelles.

Bengtsson, T. (2004) 'Living Standards and Economic Stress', in T. Bengtsson, C. Campbell, J. Z. Lee *et al., Life Under Pressure. Mortality and Living Standards in Europe and Asia, 1700–1900.* Cambridge, MA: MIT Press

——and Campbell, C. (1998) 'Microanalysis of Effects of Short-term Economic Stress on Mortality', in Núñes, C. E. (ed.), *Debates and Controversies in Economic History. Proceedings of the Twelfth International Economic History Congress.* Madrid: Fundación Ramón Areces e Fundación Fomento de la Historia Económica, pp. 115–31.

—— and Saito, O. (2000) 'Introduction', in T. Bengtsson and O. Saito (eds.), *Population and Economy: From Hunger to Modern Economic Growth.* Oxford: Oxford University Press, pp. 1–20.

Bruneel, C., Daelemans, F., Dorban, M., and Vandenbroeke, C. (1987) 'Population et subsistances dans l'espace belge, XVIe–XIXe siècles', in A. Fauve-Chamoux (ed.), *Evolution agraire et croissance démographique.* Liège: Ordina, pp. 293–324.

Capron, C. and Oris, M. (2000) 'Ruptures de cohabitation entre parents et enfants dans les villes et les campagnes du Pays de Liège au 19ᵉ siècle', in A. Bideau, P. Bourdelais, and J. Légaré (eds.), *De l'usage des seuils. Structures par âge et âges de la vie.* Paris: Société de Démographie historique, pp. 229–69.

Degrève, D. (1982) *Le commerce extérieur de la Belgique 1830–1913–1939. Présentation critique des données statistiques.* Brussel: Académie royale de Belgique.

Deprez, M. (1948) 'Essai sur le mouvement des prix et des revenus en Belgique au début du 19ᵉ siècle'. Ph.D. Thesis in History, University of Liège.

De Saint-Moulin, L. (1969) *La construction et la propriété des maisons expressions des structures sociales. Seraing depuis le début du XIXe siècle.* Brussels: Crédit communal.

Desama, C. (1985) *Population et révolution industrielle. Evolution des structures démographiques à Verviers dans la première moitié du 19ᵉ siècle.* Paris: Les Belles Lettres.

Devos, I. (1999) 'Marriage and Economic Conditions Since 1700: The Belgian case', in I. Devos and L. Kennedy (eds.), *Marriage and Rural Economy. Western Europe since 1400.* Turnhout: Brepols, pp. 101–32.

Dillen, K. (2001) 'From One Textile Centre to Another: Migrations from the District of Ghent to the City of Armentières During the Second Half of the 19th Century. A Closer Look at the Underlying Mechanisms of 19th Century Migration'. *Revue Belge d'Histoire Contemporaine*, 31: 3–4, 431–52.

Gadisseur, J. (1981) 'Le triomphe industriel', in *L'industrie en Belgique. Deux siècles d'évolution, 1780–1980.* Ghent: Crédit Communal de Belgique & Société Nationale de Crédit à l'Industrie, pp. 75–84.

—— (1990) *Le produit physique de la Belgique 1830–1913. Présentation critique des données statistiques. Introduction générale. Agriculture.* Brussels: Palais des Académies.

Goosens, M. (1992) *The Economic Development of Belgian Agriculture: A Regional Perspective, 1812–1846.* Brussels: Académie royale de Belgique.

Guinanne, T. W. (1997) *The Vanishing Irish. Households, Migration, and the Rural Economy in Ireland, 1850–1914.* Princeton, NJ: Princeton University Press.

Gutmann, M. P. (1988) *Towards the Modern Economy. Early Industry in Europe, 1500–1800.* Philadelphia, PA: Temple University Press.

Harvey, A. C. and Jaeger, A. (1993) 'Detrending, Stylized Facts and the Business Cycle'. *Journal of Applied Econometrics*, 8: 231–47.

Haesenne-Peremans, N. (1981) *La pauvreté dans la région liégeoise à l'aube de la révolution industrielle. Un siècle de tension sociale (1730–1830).* Paris: Les Belles-Lettres.

Hélin, E. (1993) 'Vie et mort des bassins industriels', in E. Hélin, *Recherches et essais (1947–1990).* Liège: C.I.P.L, pp. 121–48.

Hoyois, G. (1981) *L'Ardenne et l'Ardennais. L'évolution économique et sociale d'une région.* Brussels: Editions culture et civilisations.

Langewiesche, D. and Lenger, F. (1987) 'Internal Migration: Persistence and Mobility', in K. J. Bade (ed.), *Population, Labor and Migration in 19th and 20th Century Germany.* New York, NY: St. Martin's Press, pp. 87–100.

Leboutte, R. (1987) 'Au carrfour des transitions: fécondité, niveau de vie et culture populaire'. *Annales de Démographie historique*, pp. 175–211.

Lee, J. Z. and Campbell, C. (1997) *Fate and Fortune in Rural China. Social Organization and Population Behavior in Liaoning 1774–1873*. Cambridge: Cambridge University Press.

Lesthaeghe, R. (1977) *The Decline of Belgium Fertility, 1800–1970*. Princeton, NJ: Princeton University Press.

Moch, L. P. (1992) *Moving Europeans. Migrations in Western Europe since 1650*. Bloomington-Indianapolis: Indiana University Press.

Neven, M. (1997) 'Epidemiology of Town and Countryside. Mortality and Causes of Death in East Belgium, 1850–1910'. *Revue Belge d'Histoire Contemporaine*, 27(1–2): 39–82.

—— (2000) 'Dynamique individuelle et reproduction familiale au sein d'une société rurale. Le Pays de Herve dans la seconde moitié du XIXe siècle'. Ph.D. Thesis in History, University of Liège, 3 vols.

—— (2003) '*Terra Incognita*: Migration of the Elderly and the Nuclear Hardship Hypothesis'. *The History of the Family. An International Quarterly*, 8(2): 267–95.

Ó Gráda, C. (1993) *Ireland Before and After the Famine: Explorations in Economic History, 1808–1925*, 2nd edn. Manchester: Manchester University Press.

Oris, M. (1994) *Bibliographie de l'histoire des populations belges. Bilan des travaux des origines à nos jours*, Liège: Derouaux Ordina.

—— (1997) 'Le champ migratoire de Seraing entre 1857 et 1900. L'impact de la dépression économique sur l'attraction d'une grande ville industrielle'. *Revue du Nord*, 79 (April/September): 531–47.

—— (1998) 'A Brief Discussion on the Economic Series in 19th Century Belgium'. *Eurasia Project on Population and Family History. Working Paper Series* 19.

—— Derosas, R., and Breschi, M. (2004), 'Infant and Child Mortality', in T. Bengtsson, C. Campbell, J. Z. Lee et al., *Life Under Pressure. Mortality and Living Standards in Europe and Asia, 1700–1900*. Cambridge. MA: MIT Press, pp. 359–98.

Patriarca, S. (1986) 'Farmers, Spinners, Weavers and their Families: Protoindustry and the Factory System in Charneux, Belgium, 1770–1870'. Masters Thesis in History, Austin, TX: University of Texas.

Preston, S. H. (1996) 'Population Studies of Mortality'. *Population Studies*, 50(3): 525–36.

Reher, D. S. (1997) *Perspectives on the Family in Spain. Past and Present*. Oxford: Clarendon Press.

Scholliers, P. (1989) 'Introduction', in P. Scholliers (ed.), *Real Wages in 19th and 20th Century Europe: Historical and Comparative Perspectives*. New York/Oxford: Berg, pp. 3–12.

—— (1991) 'Le travail des femmes mariées et le niveau de vie en Belgique au 19ᵉ siècle à travers les budgets de familles ouvrières', in Société Belge de Démographie (ed.), *Historiens et populations. Liber Amicorum Etienne Hélin*. Louvain la Neuve: Académia, pp. 729–45.

—— (1993) 'The Cost of Living in Nineteenth Century Belgium'. *Studia Historica Oeconomica. Liber Amicorum Herman Van der Wee*. Leuven: Universitaire Pers, pp. 221–38.

—— (1994) 'Pain et inégalités sociales aux XIXe et XXe siècles', in *Une vie de pain. Faire, penser et dire le pain en Europe*. Brussel: Crédit Communal, pp. 111–23.

—— (1996) 'Real Wages and the Standard of Living in the Nineteenth and Early Twentieth Centuries'. *Vierteljahrschrift fur Sozial- und Wirtschaftesgeschichte*, 83(3): 307–33.

Ségalen, M. (1980) *Mari et femme dans la société paysanne*. Paris: Flammarion.

—— (1987) 'Life-course Patterns and Peasant Culture in France: A Critical Assessment'. *Journal of Family History*, 12(1–3): 215–23.

Servais, P. (1982*a*) *La rente constituée dans le ban de Herve au 18ᵉ siècle*. Brussels: Crédit communal de Belgique.

—— (1982*b*) 'Industries rurales et structures agraires: le cas de l'Entre-Vesdre-et-Meuse aux 18ᵉ et 19ᵉ siècles'. *Revue belge d'Histoire contemporaine*, 13: 179–206.

—— (1982*c*) 'Les structures agraires du Limbourg et des Pays d'Outre-Meuse du 17ᵉ au 19ᵉ siècle'. *Annales E.S.C.*, 37(2): 303–19.

—— (forthcoming) 'Transmissions patrimoniales en période de transitions industrielles: les campagnes liégeoises au XIXe siècle', in P. Bertrand and A. Amalric (eds.), *Actes du Colloque 'Pouvoir de familles et familles de pouvoir'*. Toulouse: Université de Toulouse.

Vandenbroeke, C. (1984) *Vlaamse koopkracht gisteren, vandaag en morgen*. Leuven: Kritak.

van den Eeckhout, P. and Scholliers, P. (1997) 'Social History in Belgium: Old Habits and New Perspectives'. *Tijdschrift voor Sociale Geschiedenis*, 23(2): 147–81.

Van der Herten, B., Oris, M., and Rogiers, J. (eds.) (1995) *La Belgique industrielle en 1850*. Brussels: Crédit Communal.

Vandermotten, C. and Vandewattyne, P. (1985) 'Les étapes de la croissance et de la formation des armatures urbaines en Belgique'. *La Cité belge d'aujourd'hui: quel avenir? Bulletin trimestriel du Crédit Communal de Belgique*, 39(154): 41–62.

Vanhaute, E. (1992) *Heiboeren: bevolking, arbeid en inkomen in de 19de eeuwse Kempen*. Brussels: Free University of Brussels Press.

Vliebergh, E. and Ulens, R. (1912) *L'Ardenne. La population agricole au* xıxe *siècle*. Brussels: A.Dewit.

Yoo, Tae-Ho (1996) 'L'effet de la conjoncture économique sur la nuptialité en Belgique'. *Recherches économiques de Louvain*, 32: 469–86.

16 Living Standards in Liaoning, 1749–1909: Evidence from Demographic Outcomes

JAMES Z. LEE AND CAMERON D. CAMPBELL

1. Introduction

There has been considerable debate about levels and trends in the standard of living in China during the Qing (1644–1911) dynasty. The consensus used to be that living standards were lower in China than in Europe. Influenced by Malthus' portrait of China during the late eighteenth century as a land of misery and poverty where the desire to maintain high fertility triggered the incessant operation of the positive check, a long line of observers argued that the nineteenth century was a time of rising population pressure in China and stagnant or declining living standards.[1] Scholars who have detected evidence of rising mortality during the nineteenth century in data from lineage genealogies from selected regions of China have attributed such trends to increasing population pressure and worsening conditions during the late Qing period (Liu 1985; Harrell 1995b).

Recent scholarship has called into question this received wisdom. Based on estimates of per capita production and consumption, Kenneth Pomeranz argues that living standards in China were probably comparable to those in Europe at least until the middle of the eighteenth century, though they may have declined during the nineteenth century (Pomeranz 2000; Chapter 1, this volume). Similarly, Bozhong Li has argued that at least in some parts of China, per capita production and consumption were stable or rose until the middle of the nineteenth century (Li 1998; Chapter 2, this volume). James Lee and Wang Feng, meanwhile, have argued that the Malthusian understanding of the Chinese demographic system was fundamentally incorrect, especially when it came to the relationship between living standards and demographic behaviour (Lee and Wang 1999). They suggest that the preventive check played a more important role in China than Malthus and his intellectual heirs realized because couples deliberately adjusted their fertility behaviour according to their economic circumstances.[2] From their perspective, the sustained rise in China's population during the Qing period was a response to improving

A previous version of this manuscript was presented at the conference 'New Evidence on the Standard of Living in Preindustrial Europe and Asia', August 1–5, 2000, Arild, Sweden. We are grateful to conference participants for their comments and suggestions.

living standards, not an unfortunate side-effect of couples' desire to maintain high fertility at any cost.

In this chapter, we assess changes in living standards of rural residents of Liaoning in northeast China during the eighteenth and nineteenth centuries. Rather than estimate per capita production or consumption, we use demographic rates as indices of the standard of living. We focus on trends in demographic rates and the sensitivity of rates to short-term economic fluctuations. In international comparisons, high death rates are commonly treated as evidence of low living standards, and rising death rates as evidence of declining standards.[3] For historical China, levels of male marriage should also have reflected the standard of living. One of the most important determinants of the chances that a man would marry was the supply of females, which in turn depended on the prevalence of female infanticide. This, of course, was affected by economic conditions (Lee and Campbell 1997). Marital fertility should also have been sensitive to the standard of living, since couples calibrated their numbers of surviving children according to their economic circumstances (Lee and Wang 1999).

In drawing inferences about living standards from the sensitivity of demographic rates to economic conditions, we make use of a concept of the standard of living advanced in Bengtsson, Campbell, Lee *et al.* (2004) and applied by participants in the Eurasia Project. Building on the literature on associations between real incomes and demographic rates (Lee 1981; Bengtsson and Ohlsson 1985; Galloway 1988; Lee 1990; Bengtsson 1993), Bengtsson, Campbell, Lee *et al.* (2004) argue that comparisons of demographic responses to short-term economic stress by region, period, household composition, individual context, and socio-economic status yield insight into differences between and within populations in the standard of living. The sensitivity of demographic rates to economic conditions reflect the ability, or inability, of households and their members to maintain minimum consumption levels during times of economic hardship. A response of demographic rates to short-term economic stress, in other words, reflects a failure to smooth consumption, and indicates a low standard of living.

From this framework, we specify how we will interpret possible outcomes. If living standards declined during the nineteenth century, we expect it to be reflected in rising rates of mortality, falling rates of fertility and male marriage, and increases in the sensitivity of demographic rates to short-term economic stress, as reflected in the prices of key grains. If living standards improved, we expect the reverse. Mortality should have fallen, and fertility and male marriage rates should have risen, and all rates should have become less sensitive to economic conditions. If living standards were stable, rates and their sensitivity to economic conditions should not have changed over time.

Our primary substantive interest is in the response of demographic behaviour and living standards to the rise in population density in Liaoning during the eighteenth and nineteenth centuries. For some time after the founding of the Qing dynasty in 1644, northeast China was a sparsely populated frontier region. The state actively encouraged migration into the area during the seventeenth and eighteenth centuries.

A previous analysis of a smaller sample revealed that by the middle of the nineteenth century, the densely settled areas closest to what is now Shenyang, the provincial capital and at the time the prefectural capital, showed signs of rising population pressure on land (Lee and Campbell 1997). In the analysis, we will examine whether the rise in population density was accompanied by signs of decreasing living standards, including rising mortality, delayed marriage, reduced fertility, and increased sensitivity to short-term economic stress.

We also examine whether and how commercialization in southern Liaoning during the nineteenth century affected demographic behaviour and living standards there. A substantial portion of the population for which we have data lived near the coast of the Bohai Gulf on the Liaodong peninsula in southern Liaoning. Many of the villages were in the hinterland of Yingkou, a port that was heavily involved in coastal trade in the early nineteenth century, and became a treaty port involved in international trade in 1858. Customs records suggest that in the last decades of the nineteenth century, the volume of maritime trade, both domestic and international, through Yingkou was enormous. We will investigate whether or not commercialization affected living standards in southern Liaoning by comparing its demographic rates and their sensitivity to short-term economic stress to those of other Liaoning regions. We will also assess the impact of the opening of Yingkou as a treaty port by making comparisons between the first and second halves of the nineteenth century for southern Liaoning.

This study's focus on Liaoning distinguishes it from other attempts to analyse living standards in China before 1949. Most studies of levels and trends in living standards, productivity, consumption, and related issues in historical China have focused heavily on the Jiangnan region (Perkins 1969; Elvin 1973; Huang 1990; Li 1998; Chapter 2, this volume; Pomeranz 2000; Chapter 1, this volume). The Jiangnan region was one of the wealthiest and most densely populated areas in China, and accordingly very different from the rest of China. While there have also been some relevant studies of the economic history of north China (Huang 1985; Pomeranz 1993) and the southeast (Faure 1989), there have been very few analyses of the northeast. Levels and trends in regions other than Jiangnan, of course, merit far more attention than they have received because they accounted for an increasing share of China's population through the Qing period. Through empirical study of regions like the northeast, it will be possible to evaluate the suggestion by Pomeranz (2000) that living standards for China as a whole may have fallen during the Qing period not because they fell in any one region, but rather because a rising share of the population lived in regions where living standards were lower than in Jiangnan.

This study is also distinguished by its coverage on a continuous basis of the period from the late eighteenth century to the beginning of the twentieth century. Most other assessments of levels and trends in productivity, living standards, and related issues in China have focused either on the end of the nineteenth century or the beginning of the twentieth century (Brandt 1989; Faure 1989; Rawski 1989; Pomeranz 1993), or else on the eighteenth century (Li 1998; Chapter 2, this volume; Pomeranz 2000; Chapter 1, this volume). Direct measurements of trends from the end of the eighteenth century to the beginning of the twentieth remain very rare, so that inferences about changes in conditions in China during the nineteenth century, for example, the one by Pomeranz in this volume, have been based on the interpolation of estimates from the late eighteenth and early twentieth centuries.[4]

We organize the remainder of this chapter into four parts. First, we provide background on the population we study and introduce the longitudinal, nominative household register data that describe it. We focus discussion on the strengths and limitations of the household registers as a source for the study of mortality, fertility, and nuptiality. We also discuss the grain price data we use to analyse the sensitivity of rates to economic conditions in the short term. Second, we describe the event-history methods we use to measure trends in demographic rates and the sensitivity of rates to economic conditions. We introduce the regression methods for limited dependent variables that we use and summarize the right-hand side variables in our model. Third, we present descriptive results on time trends in rates as well as regression results on secular trends in rates and their sensitivity to economic conditions. We conclude with some remarks on the implications of our results for our understanding of late Imperial China.

2. Background

We use the household register data from the 'Household and Population Registers of the Eight Banner Han Chinese Army' (*Hanjun baqi rending hukou ce*).[5] These were compiled on a triennial basis for a number of Han Chinese banner populations living on state farms in the northeast and certain other locations from the early eighteenth century until 1909. The Qing relied heavily on these registers for civilian and military administration of these populations. They accordingly devised a remarkable system of internal cross-checks to ensure consistency and accuracy. First, they assigned every person in the banner population to a residential household (*linghu*) and registered them on a household certificate (*menpai*). Then they organized households into clans (*zu*), and compiled annually updated clan genealogies (*zupu*). Finally, every three years they compared these genealogies and household certificates with the previous register to compile a new register. They deleted and added people who had exited or entered in the last three years and updated the ages, relationships, and occupations of those people who remained. Each register, in other words, completely superseded its predecessor.

The registers recorded at three-year intervals for each person in the target population the following information in order of appearance: relationship to their household head; name(s); adult banner status; age in *sui*[6]; animal birth year; lunar birth month, birth day, and birth hour; marriage, death, or emigration, if any during the intercensal period; physical disabilities, if any and if the person is an adult male; name of their kin-group head; banner affiliation; and village of residence. Individuals were listed one to a column in order of their relationship to the head, with his children and grandchildren listed first, his co-resident siblings and their descendants listed next, and then uncles, aunts, and cousins. Wives were always listed immediately after their husbands.

The banner registers provide far more comprehensive and accurate demographic and sociological data than the *baojia* household registers and lineage genealogies common elsewhere in China (Harrell 1987; Skinner 1987; Telford 1990; Jiang 1993). This is true for the entire northeast, which was the Qing homeland and was under special state jurisdiction, distinct from the provincial administration elsewhere. Regimentation of the population actually began as early as 1625, when the Manchus made Shenyang their capital and incorporated the surrounding communities into the banner system (Crossley 1997; Ding 1992; Elliott 2001). By the late eighteenth century, not only was the population registered in remarkable precision and detail, migration was strictly controlled, not just between northeast China and China proper, but between communities within northeast China as well. Government control over the population was tighter than in almost any other part of China. Indeed, individuals who departed from the area without permission were actually identified in the registers as 'escapees' (*taoding*). As a result, the Eight Banner household registers are the most extensive and detailed records of a rural Chinese population in the late Imperial period (Lee and Campbell 1997: 223–37).

Our data are a subset from a sample of registers that provide more than 750,000 observations of over 100,000 individuals who lived on fifteen state farms in Liaoning from the middle of the eighteenth century to the beginning of the twentieth century. Table 16.1 summarizes the numbers of observations from each of the eleven state

Table 16.1 Available data

	Observations[a]	Distinct individuals
North	179,684	34,177
Dami	22,615	3,962
Feicheng Yimiancheng	60,266	9,206
Dadianzi	60,580	13,727
Bakeshu	36,223	7,282
Central	82,334	15,497
Guosantun	32,742	4,912
Daxingtun	49,592	10,585
Daoyi	104,568	15,846
South	148,960	32,909
Gaizhou Rending	38,235	7,104
Gaizhou Mianding	21,286	4,104
Niuzhuang Liuerbao	47,044	9,269
Gaizhou Manhan	42,395	12,432
Total	515,546	98,429

[a] These figures exclude observations where individuals have died, married out, become *taoding*, or are otherwise recorded as having exited since the last register.

farm systems we use here. We excluded four of the fifteen state farms because one, Chengnei, was urban, while another three had not yet been coded when this chapter was first written.

The population of the eleven state farms grew dramatically over the century and a half for which we have data, providing an excellent opportunity to survey the impact of rising population density on demographic behaviour and living standards. According to Figure 16.1, growth occurred in two distinct phases. The population grew steadily from 1749 to 1888 at an annual rate of approximately 0.5%. This was a respectable rate for a pre-industrial population, especially in light of the fact that most of it was attributable to natural increase. In-migration played a role only in the late eighteenth century and the beginning of the nineteenth century. From 1888 to 1909, the state farm populations exploded, growing at a rate of nearly 2% a year. In-migration, or more likely absorption into the state farms of already present residents of the region, appears to have accounted for much of the increase. Natural increase appears to have played only a minor role.[7]

As Table 16.1 indicates, the state farms were distributed among three very different regions. The northern state farms were located in a hilly and isolated region in the northeast of the province. We expect living standards there to have been poor. The central state farm systems, including Daoyi, were located just to the north of what is now Shenyang, currently the capital of Liaoning and the prefectural capital during the Qing period.[8] While these populations would have benefited materially from their proximity to a major administrative centre, their death rates are likely to have reflected a 'suburban penalty'. The southern state farm systems were all located in or near what is now Gaiping county on the Liaodong Peninsula. They were

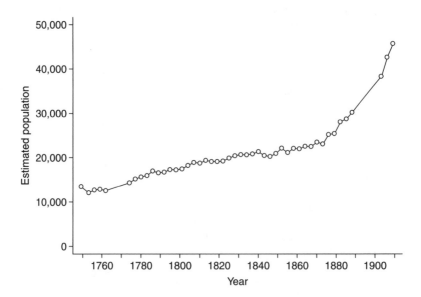

Figure 16.1   Estimated population size, 11 Liaoning state farm systems

either on or close to the coast of the Bohai Gulf. They were close to Yingkou, which became a treaty port open to international trade in 1858. Accordingly, the region was heavily involved in coastal trade, and during the last half of the nineteenth century, in international trade as well. As a result, the economy in this region was much more commercialized than in the central or northern region, at least during the last half of the nineteenth century.

We apply a number of restrictions to the observations included in the analysis. We have excluded all observations where an individual is recorded as having exited since the last register, whether by death, out-marriage, out-migration, or illegal departure. Depending on the demographic outcome we study, there are additional restrictions on the observations that we use. Because the registration of daughters was incomplete, we only consider male births when we examine reproduction. As discussed later, for methodological reasons we exclude, from the event-history analyses of mortality and nuptiality, observations from the registers where both the immediately succeeding one and the one after it were missing.

The major limitation of the registers for demographic analysis is that they omit most sons who died in infancy and early childhood, as well as most daughters. Sons typically first appeared not in the register immediately following their birth, but in the one after it. If they died before the compilation of that register, there would be no record of their existence. As for daughters, in most of the state farm systems they never appeared in the registers as long as they lived as daughters in their natal families. Women only appeared in the registers once they were married. When they appeared, they did so as a member of their husband's household. As a result of these limitations, we cannot analyse infant mortality. We can only analyse the child mortality of males. Finally, our estimates of fertility are based solely on surviving male births, and need to be adjusted to yield estimates for all births of both sexes.[9]

Overall, the registers are an excellent source for the study of mortality. Deaths since the last register are annotated, so that by record linkage we can create a dichotomous indicator of whether or not an individual dies in the next three years. Other exits from the registers are almost all annotated, whether by out-marriage, out-migration, or illegal departure, thus individuals who have left the population can be censored from the time of their departure. Unannotated disappearances are rare.

The major limitation of the data is that we do not know dates of death, only the three-year period in which they occur. In examining price effects, therefore, we are limited to looking at how average prices in the three years between two registers affected the probability of dying in that three-year period. There are also a small number of individuals who survive to absurdly advanced ages that we exclude from consideration on the assumption that their entries in the register were being carried forward even after they had died.

The registers are also an exceptional source for the study of male first marriage. Because marital status is recorded for individuals in every register, and individuals can be linked across registers, we infer whether or not a male has married by examining whether his status has changed from being unmarried to being married or widowed between one register and the next. The major limitation is that once again, as was the case with deaths, we do not have precise dates of marriage. We only know that marriages took place in the three years between two successive registers. In examining price effects, therefore, we are limited to looking at how average prices in the three years between two registers affected the probability of marrying in that three-year period. An additional, though minor, shortcoming is that in the rare cases where a man married but his new wife died before the next available register, there would be no evidence of his marriage, because he would appear single in both registers.[10]

In spite of the limitations noted earlier, the registers are also an excellent source for the study of reproduction. Because children are listed immediately after their parents in the registers, establishing paternity and maternity is straightforward. From the age reported for the child in their first appearance, we can also calculate their year of birth. For the analysis of fertility we generated a file of person-year observations for married women that included variables describing their characteristics at the time of the most recent available register along with a count of the number of births attributed to them for that year. In contrast with the analyses of mortality and nuptiality, therefore, we can examine how prices in a year affected the chances that a married woman would have a surviving birth in that year.

To study the influence of economic conditions on the probability of demographic events, we supplement the household register data with grain price series from an empire-wide system to monitor food conditions that began elsewhere in China as early as the late seventeenth century and was extended to Liaoning into the late eighteenth century (Wu 1996). In this system, county magistrates reported the price of five major food grains (rice, wheat, husked and unhusked millet, soybean, and sorghum) each week to the provincial government. The governor, in turn, prepared each month a brief summary for the central government of the lowest and highest county prices by prefecture. These monthly prefectural summaries of the highest and lowest reported prices provide the bulk of our price data.

We use monthly price reports from Fengtian prefecture in Liaoning. To date we have collected 1,500 of these lunar monthly summary reports.[11] Our previous analysis suggests that the fluctuations in grain prices in this area reflect changes in climate and harvest yields more than changes in market demand or state intervention, thus prices should be a proxy for peasants' grain production (Lee and Campbell 1997: 31–5). Since the peasants in our populations produced primarily for themselves, and are likely to have bought or sold only a small portion of their grain on the market, prices should be a proxy for their food consumption. Even if peasants were heavily involved in the market, results on historical Europe suggest that they would not have benefited from high prices, because the inverse correlation between production and prices was strong enough that for small producers the benefits of being able to sell at a higher price, were typically offset by the drawbacks of having less to sell (Galloway 1988). Thus we expect high prices to have been associated with poor harvests and reduced consumption, and low prices associated with good harvests and increased consumption.

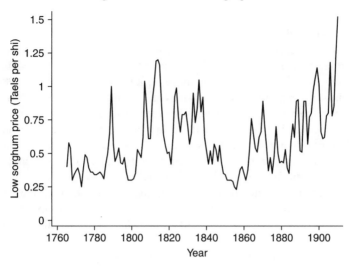

Figure 16.2   Annual average of low sorghum prices

Sorghum was a key crop in the region, thus we use its price as an indicator of conditions. We use the low sorghum price series because we believe it was more reflective of the situation in rural areas than the high price series, which are most likely to have been from urban areas. Figure 16.2 summarizes low sorghum prices during the period under consideration. Since the sustained increase that began in the 1880s may have been an artefact of inflation, and may not have reflected actual reductions in consumption or real income, we excluded the period after 1888 from the analysis of price effects. Prices before 1888 were clearly volatile, in some cases doubling or tripling from one year to the next and then remaining high for several consecutive years.[12] Since there was no secular trend in prices before 1888, and regressions using detrended prices series yielded broadly similar results, in our analysis we made use of logged raw prices.

3. Methods

To detect long-term trends in demographic rates and measure their sensitivity to sorghum prices, we make use of discrete-time event-history analysis. Specifically, we use regression methods for limited dependent variables. As described below, the type of regression depended on the dependent variable. To detect trends and sensitivity to prices, we included as right-hand side variables interactions between year and region, as well as between logged low sorghum prices and region.[13] The logged prices are base 1.1, so that coefficients represent the effects of a 10% change in prices. We do not include main effects of year and price, so for each there are a total of four interactions, one for each region. Coefficients on these terms are accordingly specific to each region, and do not measure slopes relative to the slope for an omitted reference category.

For each of three demographic events, mortality, fertility, and nuptiality, we estimate three models. We estimate one model over the entire period for which demographic data are available and price results are interpretable: 1780–1888. We also divide this period into two halves and estimate separate models for each to examine whether there were changes between periods in trends in rates and their sensitivity to price. We expect that if the last half of the nineteenth century was one of declining living standards, especially in the less commercial northern and central regions, rising mortality or falling fertility and nuptiality would be more apparent there than for the period as a whole. We also expect that if increasing commercialization in southern Liaoning during the last half of the nineteenth century led to improvements in living standards, mortality there may have fallen, nuptiality or fertility may have increased, or rates in general may have become less sensitive to prices.

In the case of nuptiality, the dependent variable is a dichotomous indicator of whether or not a man marries for the first time in the next three years. We only include observations of men who have not yet married. Instead of logistic regression, we use complementary log–log regression.[14] In this case, the coefficient for an interaction between year and region measures the average annual change in the chances of marrying in the next three years for men in the specified region. Similarly, the coefficient for an interaction between logged price and region measures the effect of a 10% increase in low sorghum prices in the region. Because we expect the men who married early, at the modal ages, and late to have differed in terms of what affected whether or not they would marry in a particular time interval, we carry out separate analyses for the age ranges 6–15 *sui*, 16–25 *sui*, and 26–40 *sui*.[15]

For mortality, the dependent variable is a dichotomous indicator of whether or not an individual dies in the next three years. Again, we use complementary log–log regression. We carry out separate analyses for the age ranges 2–15, 16–55, and 56–75 *sui* because the determinants of mortality differed between childhood, adulthood, and old age. For the youngest age group, we only analyse male mortality because only a few of the state farm systems had appreciable numbers of daughters recorded. For adulthood and old age, we carried out analyses by each sex.[16]

For fertility, the dependent variable is a count of the number of births attributed to a married woman in a year. Since the dependent variable is a count, we use Poisson regression. Whereas the analyses of mortality and nuptiality made use of triennial observations, the analysis of fertility makes use of a specially constructed file of annual observations described in the section on data. We accounted for variation by age in the probability of having a birth by inclusion of a fifth-order orthogonal polynomial and interactions between its terms and the region indicators, though to save space we do not present the estimated coefficients.

4. Results

We organize our presentation of results by demographic outcome. We begin with fertility, proceed to nuptiality, and end with mortality. In each case, we begin by presenting relevant indices of levels for regions and state farms. Because differences in levels between regions and state farm systems probably had many causes beyond differences in living standards, we present this information largely as background material and avoid drawing conclusions about living standards from it. We proceed to visual inspection of time trends in the demographic outcome of interest. We conclude with results on time trends and sensitivity to prices from the event-history analysis.

4.1 Fertility

In spite of differences in economic context, variation in fertility levels between regions was less pronounced than variation within regions. Table 16.2 presents indices of fertility, male nuptiality, and mortality for the eleven state farm systems, along with totals for each region. The total marital fertility rate (TMFR) in the

Table 16.2 Levels of fertility, nuptiality, and mortality

	TMFR[a] 16–50	Percentage of men ever married				Life expectancy		
		6–15 *sui*	16–25 *sui*	26–35 *sui*	36–50 *sui*	males 1 *sui*	males 16 *sui*	females 16 *sui*
North	1.86	4.4	47.1	80.3	88.6	45.9	43.0	41.2
Dami	1.35	5.1	39.9	70.5	80.0	46.7	40.5	38.8
Feicheng Yimiancheng	1.81	3.0	41.1	78.9	88.9	43.1	44.3	40.7
Dadianzi	1.97	6.4	56.9	85.3	92.1	51.1	44.2	47.4
Bakeshu	1.89	2.9	44.6	80.4	88.5	44.7	40.4	36.0
Central	1.99	2.2	41.3	74.4	84.1	41.2	43.0	38.5
Guosantun	2.14	2.6	40.9	74.4	84.4	42.8	43.9	37.1
Daxingtun	1.91	2.0	41.6	74.5	84.0	39.5	42.2	40.2
Daoyi	1.94	2.8	42.2	75.0	83.3	38.3	41.8	38.3
South	1.89	3.8	42.2	75.0	86.5	49.9	44.6	43.9
Gaizhou Rending	1.89	4.9	46.9	76.6	87.1	52.0	44.6	45.6
Gaizhou Mianding	2.02	3.1	49.2	81.0	89.5	48.7	41.8	40.8
Niuzhuang Liuerbao	1.96	3.5	47.1	78.6	86.0	48.1	45.4	43.2
Gaizhou Manhan	1.72	5.0	46.9	76.6	87.1	49.0	47.1	43.4
Total	1.90	3.5	45.3	77.7	86.5	44.1	43.0	41.7

[a] The calculation of marital fertility is based on male births to married women that survive to be recorded in a register. Adjustments for the omission of female births and births that die in infancy and childhood without being registered would yield a higher figure. As explained in note 9 in previous work we have used an adjustment factor of 2.91.

highest fertility region, the central, was only 0.13 higher than in the lowest fertility region, the north. Fertility levels in the south lay in between. In contrast, the difference between the adjacent and to some extent overlapping Gaizhou Mianding and Gaizhou Manhan state farms was 0.3. The most extreme within-region difference, of course, was between Dami and the other northern populations. As we collect additional auxiliary data on the organization of specific state farm systems, we hope to understand the reasons behind such intense local variation.

Living standards may actually have been improving. Fertility appears to have been on the increase during the last half of the nineteenth century. Figure 16.3 presents cohort total marital fertility rates. The horizontal axis identifies the year in which the women of a cohort reached age 50. According to the figure, the completed fertility of women reaching age 50 fluctuated without exhibiting a trend until the 1850s. On average, married women reaching age 50 had roughly 1.75 registered sons. After a spike in the 1860s, there was a steady upward drift, so that married women reaching the end of their reproductive years in the first decade of the twentieth century had an average of nearly two sons.

Improvements were limited to the north and south. Results from event-history analysis confirm that fertility rose in the south and especially in the north between 1780 and 1888, but remained stable in the central region. Table 16.3 presents coefficients for year and logged low sorghum prices for each region from a model for the entire time period and models for the two sub-periods. According to the results for the entire time period, fertility in the north increased by about 0.3% a year. The implication is that over a 100-year period, rates there increased by about 35.4%. Over the same period, the coefficient for the south implies that rates in that region

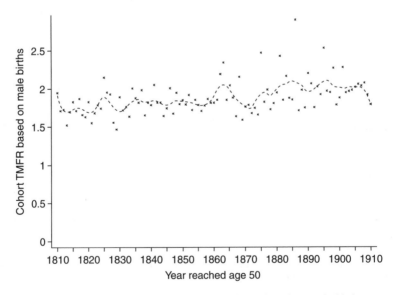

Figure 16.3   Cohort total marital fertility rate (16–50 *sui*) based on male births

Table 16.3 Coefficients for year and logged low sorghum price from Poisson regression of number of male births in the next year for married females

	Model 1: 1780–1888		Model 2: 1780–1834		Model 3: 1834–88	
	Coefficient	*p*-value	Coefficient	*p*-value	Coefficient	*p*-value
Year						
North	0.0030	0.00	0.0050	0.00	0.0087	0.00
Central	0.0004	0.49	0.0064	0.00	0.0051	0.00
Daoyi	−0.0007	0.18	−0.0004	0.82	0.0031	0.02
South	0.0008	0.04	−0.0007	0.67	0.0006	0.54
Logged low sorghum price						
North	−0.0121	0.00	−0.0394	0.00	−0.0016	0.72
Central	0.0001	0.99	−0.0244	0.00	0.0011	0.86
Daoyi	−0.0147	0.00	−0.0173	0.01	−0.0204	0.00
South	−0.0011	0.73	−0.0179	0.00	0.0158	0.00
N	315,862		141,394		174,468	

Note: The models did not include main effects of year or low sorghum price, only the interactions between them and the four dichotomous indicators of region. To save space, coefficients for the region indicators and their interactions with the terms of the fourth-degree orthogonal age polynomial are not presented in this table. We restricted analysis to observations where the immediately succeeding observation was also available.

rose by about 8%. Examination of the coefficients for the sub-periods reveal that the overall increase in the south was the result of a jump from one time period to the next, since there were no trends within time periods, while the rise in the north stemmed from a sustained increase over both periods. There were trends within periods in the central region, but these were overwhelmed by differences between the periods.

Examination of sensitivity of fertility to grain prices yields broadly similar results, suggesting improvements in living standards everywhere but Daoyi. According to Table 16.3, between 1780 and 1834 fertility rates in all regions were sensitive to grain prices. The north was the most sensitive: a 10% increase in low sorghum prices lowered fertility rates there by 3.9% in the north. A similar price increase reduced fertility in Daoyi by 1.73% and in the south by 1.79%. In the later period, 1834–88, rates in the north were no longer affected by low sorghum prices, and rates in the south actually exhibited a positive association with prices. Rates in Daoyi, meanwhile, were as sensitive to prices as ever, if not more so.

4.2 Nuptiality

Marriage markets appear to have been integrated within regions but not between them. Variation between regions was more apparent for male marriage than for fertility. Whereas 88.6% of men between the ages of 36 and 50 *sui* in the north were or had been married, only 83.3% in Daoyi and 84.1% in the other central farm systems had been married. Once again, the south was in the middle. Variation within regions was far less pronounced than was the case with marital fertility, Dami aside. Proportions married in the central state farm systems were almost identical and varied little in the northern and southern systems. We are hesitant to draw any conclusions from a comparison of levels of male marriage because they may be affected by conditions outside the farm systems. For example, low proportions married in Daoyi may simply reflect the effects of proximity to a large city, Shenyang.

Long-term stability in the proportions of men in late middle age who had ever married suggests that the overall supply of females changed little. According to Figure 16.4, between 1760 and 1910, the percentage of men aged 36–45 who had ever married hovered between 80 and 90. Since the major source of variation over time in the supply of marriageable females was female infanticide and neglect, the implication is that there was no secular trend in their incidence. To the extent that female infanticide and neglect was a response to economic stress, there is little evidence here of a long-term decline in living standards.

Inequality in male access to marriage, however, increased over time: according to Figure 16.4 the range of ages over which men first married widened substantially. In other words, a progressively largely proportion of families found it within their wherewithal to acquire brides for their sons while they were still young. Thus the proportion of men marrying at young ages increased steadily, even though the proportion of men who ever married by the time they reached late middle age remained

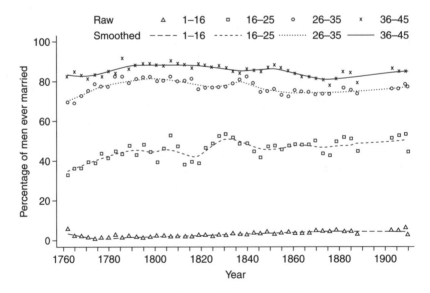

Figure 16.4   Percentage of men married at different ages in Liaoning

stable or perhaps even fell slightly. The proportion of men aged 16–25 who had ever married doubled from one-quarter to one-half between 1760 and 1910.

Event-history analysis confirms the increase in inequality in male access to marriage. Coefficients in Table 16.4 indicate that while those who would marry did so at younger and younger ages, those who had not married by the time they reached adulthood were steadily less likely to never marry. The chances that a man aged 6–15 would marry in the next three years increased in every region from 1774 and 1888. The smallest increase was in the central region, where chances rose by 0.38% a year, and highest in the south, where they rose by 1.33% a year. Over 100 years, in other words, the chances of marrying in the next three years increased by 46% in the north and 278% in the south. Coefficients for the age ranges 16–25 and 26–40, meanwhile, indicate that in every region the chances that a man who was still unmarried after age 15 would marry in the next three years declined.

Male marriage does not appear to have responded in a consistent fashion to current grain prices.[17] Only in the central region between 1774 and 1834 was the

Table 16.4 Coefficients for year from the complementary log–log regression of marriage in the next three years for never-married males

	Model 1: 1744–1888		Model 2: 1774–1834		Model 3: 1834–88	
	Coefficient	p-value	Coefficient	p-value	Coefficient	p-value
Age 6–15						
North	0.0114	0.00	0.0124	0.03	0.0120	0.00
Central	0.0038	0.08	0.0310	0.00	−0.0031	0.49
Daoyi	0.0099	0.00	0.0343	0.00	0.0204	0.00
South	0.0133	0.00	0.0113	0.10	0.0174	0.00
N	33,276		14,536		18,740	
Age 16–25						
North	−0.0060	0.00	−0.0098	0.00	−0.0056	0.03
Central	−0.0036	0.01	0.0105	0.06	−0.0034	0.36
Daoyi	−0.0020	0.06	−0.0061	0.19	0.0065	0.04
South	−0.0013	0.20	−0.0123	0.01	−0.0007	0.79
N	17,277		8,416		8,861	
Age 26–40						
North	−0.0015	0.39	−0.0156	0.67	0.0087	0.03
Central	−0.0045	0.12	0.0050	0.43	−0.0076	0.25
Daoyi	−0.0086	0.00	−0.0066	0.17	0.0012	0.87
South	−0.0059	0.00	0.0664	0.02	−0.0076	0.12
N	8,229		3,534		4,695	

Notes: The models did not include main effects of year or low sorghum price, only the interactions between them and the four dichotomous indicators of region. To save space, coefficients for the region indicators and their interactions with the terms of the orthogonal age polynomial are omitted from this table. We restricted analysis to observations where the immediately succeeding observation was also available.

effect of low sorghum prices in the expected direction. A 10% increase in grain prices lowered the chances of marriage in the next three years by 10.9% for males age 6–15, and by 6.1% for males aged 16–25. In the other regions and time periods, increases in sorghum prices either had no effect, or else increased the chances of marriage. Previously, we have argued that such results may indicate that reductions during bad times in the financial capacity of households to secure brides for their sons may have been offset by increased desperation by households with daughters to reduce expenses or raise funds by marrying them off (Campbell and Lee 1998).

4.3   Mortality

Pronounced differences in mortality levels were apparent between the central region, including Daoyi, and the north and south. According to Table 16.1, male life expectancy at age 1 in the south exceeded that in Daoyi by 11.6 years. Similarly, female life expectancy at age 16 in the south exceeded that in Daoyi by 5.6 years. We attribute low life expectancy in the central region, including Daoyi, not to lower living standards but rather to their close proximity to densely populated Shenyang and to their own higher population density. We suspect, in other words, that there was a 'suburban penalty' associated with living in a rural area immediately adjacent to a major city.

At least in the north and south, substantial differences within regions were also apparent. Once again, in many cases the state farm systems that differed the most were adjacent or even overlapping. Female life expectancy at age 16 was 8.4 years higher in Dadianzi than in Dami. Male life expectancy at age 16 was 5.3 years higher in Gaizhou Manhan than in Gaizhou Mianding. Female life expectancy at age 16 was 3.1 years higher in Daxingtun than in Guosantun. As was the case with fertility, an understanding of the source of these pronounced local variations will have to await additional details on the organization of specific state farm systems.

Child mortality declined remarkably over time, raising the possibility of an improvement in living standards. According to Figure 16.5, until the 1840s it was typical for roughly one-third of boys aged 1–15 to die within the next three years. After that, it was more common for only one-tenth to one-fifth of such boys to die within three years. Child mortality tends to be caused by acute infectious diseases. The lethality of many of these diseases is conditioned by the nutritional status of the child, and thus a sustained reduction in child mortality in the absence of improvements in public health and medicine may reflect improvements in living standards.

Pronounced gender differences were apparent in the evolution of adult mortality over time. Figure 16.6 presents male and female period life expectancies at age 16 from the middle of the eighteenth century to the beginning of the twentieth century. There is some suggestion that male life expectancy was rising especially during the

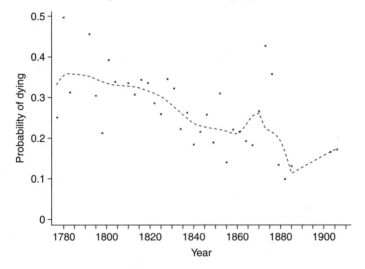

Figure 16.5   Probability that a male aged 1 *sui* will die before reaching age 16 *sui* in Liaoning

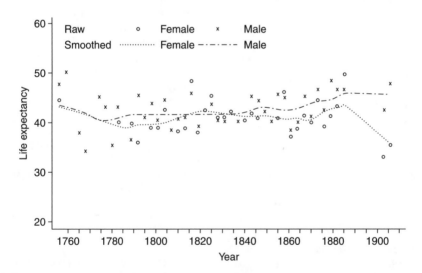

Figure 16.6   Male and female period life expectancy at age 16 *sui* in Liaoning

last half of the nineteenth century. Female life expectancy exhibited little trend. Short-term fluctuations in mortality levels were if anything more pronounced than long-term trends. Increases or decreases of several years from one three-year period to the next were not uncommon. The early 1880s appear to have been especially favourable to adult males, while the first decade of the twentieth century was extremely unfavorable to adult females.

Event-history analysis reveals that the reduction in male child mortality took place in all regions and in both time periods.[18] The most pronounced decline was in the south, where the chances of dying in the next three years fell by 1.28% every year. The mildest decline was in the central state farm systems, where chances fell

Table 16.5 Coefficients for logged low sorghum price from the complementary log–log regression of death in the next three years

	Model 1: 1734–1888		Model 2: 1774–1834		Model 3: 1834–88	
	Coefficient	*p*-value	Coefficient	*p*-value	Coefficient	*p*-value
Males, age 1–15 *sui*						
North	0.0064	0.58	0.0102	0.68	−0.0124	0.53
Central	−0.0234	0.11	−0.0786	0.08	−0.0106	0.62
Daoyi	0.0246	0.03	0.0378	0.03	−0.0022	0.94
South	0.0092	0.46	0.0164	0.45	0.0198	0.33
N	45,595		19,767		25,828	
Males, age 16–55 *sui*						
North	−0.0013	0.87	0.0106	0.53	−0.0099	0.42
Central	−0.0201	0.06	−0.0340	0.36	−0.0222	0.10
Daoyi	0.0364	0.00	0.0247	0.09	0.0291	0.11
South	−0.0116	0.18	0.0044	0.79	−0.0233	0.06
N	103,900		48,184		55,716	
Females, age 16–55 *sui*						
North	−0.0231	0.01	−0.0093	0.61	−0.0150	0.23
Central	−0.0436	0.00	−0.1022	0.01	−0.0393	0.01
Daoyi	0.0158	0.10	−0.0004	0.98	0.0448	0.02
South	0.0030	0.74	0.0114	0.51	0.0159	0.23
N	79,790		37,308		42,482	
Males, age 56–75 *sui*						
North	0.0186	0.03	−0.0060	0.75	0.0089	0.50
Central	−0.0168	0.14	0.0128	0.75	−0.0207	0.16
Daoyi	0.0399	0.00	−0.0040	0.81	0.0754	0.00
South	0.0050	0.60	0.0111	0.55	0.0034	0.79
N	20,118		8,856		11,262	
Females, age 56–75 *sui*						
North	−0.0215	0.01	−0.0445	0.02	0.0004	0.97
Central	−0.0002	0.99	−0.0540	0.23	0.0063	0.70
Daoyi	0.0183	0.10	−0.0132	0.48	0.0323	0.13
South	0.0037	0.72	0.0172	0.38	0.0057	0.70
N	21,665		9,860		11,805	

Notes: The models did not include main effects of year or low sorghum price, only the interactions between them and the four dichotomous indicators of region. To save space, coefficients for the region indicators and their interactions with the terms of the fourth-degree orthogonal age polynomial are omitted from this table. We restricted analysis to observations where the immediately succeeding observation was also available.

by only 0.64% a year. The cumulative effect of such declines would have been dramatic. The 1.06% annual reduction in the north would have translated into a two-thirds reduction in the chances of dying over the course of a century.

Trends in adult mortality were less consistent. They differed by region, age, and sex. In the north there was evidence of a widespread reduction in the chances of dying. Mortality appears to have fallen for adult males and for elderly males and females. In the centre and south, few trends were apparent. The exceptions were that adult female mortality rose in the south and elderly female mortality rose in the central regions.

The residents of Daoyi appear to have lived closest to the margin, and conditions there worsened over time. According to the coefficients in Table 16.5, mortality there appears to have been the most sensitive to grain price variations. Increases in low sorghum prices raised mortality at all ages and for both sexes in Daoyi, but had no effect or contradictory effects in the remaining regions. Males were more sensitive than females, and the elderly more sensitive than adults. Accordingly, the most extreme response in Daoyi was among elderly males: a 10% increase in prices raised their mortality by 3.99%. Moreover, comparison of coefficients between periods suggests that for everyone except male children, mortality rates were more sensitive to prices between 1834 and 1888 than they were between 1774 and 1834.

5. Conclusion

Overall, we find little evidence that living standards in the northern and southern state farm systems declined during the nineteenth century. If anything, they appear to have improved. Marital fertility rates rose in the north and south. Fertility rates also ceased being sensitive to economic conditions in the last half of the nineteenth century in every region except Daoyi. Couples, apparently, no longer needed to delay births when grain prices were high to maintain minimum consumption levels. As for marriage, some men married at progressively earlier ages, though the proportion of men who eventually married changed little. Mortality rates every-where except Daoyi, moreover, were insensitive to grain fluctuations.

One of the most intriguing pieces of evidence of improving living standards in northern and southern Liaoning was the decline in male child mortality. This decline is highly unexpected, and additional investigations are clearly necessary. Since there are no other direct measurements of trends in child mortality in nineteenth-century China other than for the members of the Qing Imperial lineage (Lee, Wang, and Campbell 1994), it is impossible to determine whether or not this is anomalous. The implications of the decline also need to be examined. If mortality fell at the same pace in very early childhood, or infancy, then the apparent rise in fertility may reflect increases in the numbers of children who survive to an age when their parents register them, and not actual increases in the number of births.

The residents of the central region were not as fortunate as the residents of the north and south. In the centre, especially in Daoyi, the standard of living appears to have stagnated or declined. Marital fertility in Daoyi and the other central state farm systems did not change between 1780 and 1888. In Daoyi, fertility rates remained as sensitive to prices between 1834 and 1888 as they had been between 1780 and 1834, if not more so. Early marriage increased the least in Daoyi and in the remaining central state farm systems, and marriage rates of men aged 26–40 fell the fastest in Daoyi. The central state farms other than Daoyi had the slowest reduction in male child mortality and a sustained increase in elderly female mortality. Finally, only in Daoyi were mortality rates sensitive to grain prices at all ages and for both sexes.

The differences between north and south on the one hand and the centre on the other are linked to their economic contexts. The central state farm systems were in densely settled areas close to Shenyang. The city was a key administrative centre, and its fortunes were tied to those of the Qing state, which faced numerous and increasing difficulties through the nineteenth century. Dependent on such a city and living in a densely populated area with few economic opportunities, the residents of the central state farm systems had to adjust. They kept their fertility in check, adjusting it according to economic conditions. They were unable to indulge in early marriage for their sons in the same way that families in other regions could. Finally, in Daoyi especially, families appear not to have been able to maintain consumption at minimum levels during times of economic stress. Across the entire age range, death rates rose when prices did.

The north and south were more sparsely populated, so that through the entire period there was ample room for growth. The south especially benefited from proximity to the coast and to the port at Yingkou in particular. Married couples increased their fertility throughout the period, and eventually reached the point where they no longer adjusted it in response to short-term economic stress. More so than the residents of the central region, they indulged in early marriage for their sons. Finally, they could ride out periods of high prices without any consequences for their mortality rates.

The overall picture of Liaoning that emerges is very different from the one commonly painted for China as a whole from the late eighteenth century to the beginning of the twentieth century, which emphasizes stagnation or decline. With the exception of the densely settled area immediately around Shenyang conditions seem to have been improving. This reflected the likely availability of open land and in the south, proximity to a port that was initially involved in the coastal trade and later involved in international trade. While these results cannot be generalized to other regions in China, and do not shed much light on Pomeranz's (2000) suggestion that living standards for the country as a whole may have declined during the nineteenth century because a rising share of the population lived in regions where living standards were low, they are nevertheless one piece of the puzzle. They do suggest that there may have been a diversity of trends, not only between regions, but within them as well. They confirm that a proper assessment of changes in China during the nineteenth century will require examination of empirical results from all of the regions.

More generally, the results confirm the utility of examining demographic outcomes to help reconstruct trends in living standards in the past, especially in situations where more direct measures are absent. A classic approach consisting of an examination of time trends in three different rates, mortality, fertility, and nuptiality, yielded broadly consistent results. In the north and south, when mortality fell, fertility increased, and for some men, marriage became earlier. In the centre, when mortality rose, fertility decreased, and marriage remained unchanged or became less common. More importantly, a new approach applied in the Eurasia project that treats the sensitivity of rates as an indicator of low living standards (Bengtsson, Campbell, Lee *et al.* 2004) yielded results consistent with those from the classic approach. Fertility and mortality were most sensitive to economic conditions in the central state farms, which according to the results form the classic approach, had been the worst off. We expect that additional refinements of this approach are likely to be even more fruitful.

Notes

1. See Lee and Wang (1999) for an extended discussion of Malthus' continuing influence on analyses of Chinese population and society.
2. The positive check also played a role, but not in the way that Malthus thought. Whereas Malthus and others emphasized the adverse effects of misery and poverty on death rates across the age range, Lee and Wang argue that the calculated use of infanticide by couples to adjust family size and sex composition to their circumstances predominated.
3. As discussed in Bengtsson, Campbell, Lee *et al.* (2004, ch. 2), composite indices of standard of living constructed for countries by the United Nations, the World Bank, and other organizations almost always include a measurement of the level of mortality, often the infant mortality rate but sometimes life expectancy.
4. Though historical studies of long-term trends in mortality in China based on lineage genealogies such as Liu (1985) and Harrell (1995a) have remarkable time depth, in some cases extending back into the Ming dynasty (1368–1644), the limitations of retrospectively compiled lineage genealogies as a source have also prevented such studies from examining death rates in the late nineteenth century and early twentieth century.
5. See Appendix A of Lee and Campbell (1997) for a detailed introduction to these data.
6. According to the traditional Chinese procedure for calculating age, individuals were 1 *sui* at birth, and aged by 1 *sui* every Lunar New Year. As a result, ages reckoned in *sui* are on average 1.5 years higher than western ages.
7. Unfortunately none of the registers from between 1888 and 1903 has been located, thus a precise accounting of this increase is not yet possible.
8. Note that even though Daoyi is in the central region, and very close to Guosantun and Daxingtun, we treat it separately here since we have studied it previously and already have empirical results for it.
9. See Lee and Campbell (1997: 66–8) for an adjustment of fertility estimates for Daoyi that made use of indirect methods. We concluded that multiplying the TMFR based on surviving male births by 2.91 yields a reasonable estimate of the level of fertility based on all births. This adjustment is the product of two factors: 1.5 to account for boys who died without ever being registered, and 206/106 to account for female births.

10. Another limitation of the registers is that they do not allow married women to be traced back to their natal families; thus we do not know whether families obtained brides for their sons from within the same register population, or from other populations in the area. In other words, we cannot study intermarriage.
11. See Lee and Campbell (1997: 31–5) for additional details on the grain price series.
12. Many of the most prominent spikes were associated with extended spells of unfavourable weather such as cold summers (Lee and Campbell 1997: 34).
13. We also included main effects of region, operationalized as a set of three dichotomous indicator variables for central, Daoyi, and south. North was the omitted category. To save space, we do not present the coefficients for these terms.
14. Complementary log–log regression is more appropriate for event history than logistic regression because it yields coefficients that are comparable to those from continuous-time proportional hazards models (Long 1997).
15. Because marriage rates varied substantially by age within each interval, we included a fourth-order orthogonal polynomial in age, along with interactions between the terms of the polynomial and region. To save space, we do not present the coefficients for these terms.
16. To account for variation in age-specific probabilities of dying within these age ranges, we include a quadratic orthogonal for age, interacted with the region indicators. Once again, to save space we do not present the coefficients for these terms.
17. To save space, we do not present the estimated coefficients here.
18. To save space, we do not present the estimated coefficients here.

References

Bengtsson, T. (1993) 'Combined Time-Series and Life-Event Analysis: The Impact of Economic Fluctuations and Air Temperature on Adult Mortality by Sex and Occupation in a Swedish Mining Parish, 1757–1850', in D. Reher and R. Schofield (eds.), *Old and New Methods in Historical Demography*. Oxford: Clarendon Press, pp. 239–53.
——Campbell, C., Lee, J. Z. *et al.* (2004) *Life Under Pressure: Mortality and Living Standards in Europe and Asia, 1700–1900*. Cambridge, MA: MIT Press.
—— and Ohlsson, R. (1985) 'Age-Specific Mortality and Short-Term Changes in the Standard of Living: Sweden, 1751–1859'. *European Journal of Population*, 1: 309–26.
Brandt, L. (1989) *Commercialization and Agricultural Development: Central and Eastern China, 1870–1937*. Cambridge: Cambridge University Press.
Campbell, C. and Lee, J. (1998) 'Economic and Household Constraints on Male First Marriage in Northeast China, 1789–1909'. Unpublished manuscript.
Crossley, P. (1997) *The Manchus*. Cambridge, MA: Blackwell.
Ding, Y. (1992) *Qingdai baqi zhufang zhidu yanjiu* (Research on the eight banner garrison system during the Qing). Tianjin: Guji chubanshe.
Elliott, M. (2001) *The Manchu Way*. Stanford: Stanford University Press.
Elvin, M. (1973) *The Pattern of the Chinese Past*. Stanford: Stanford University Press.
Faure, D. (1989) *The Rural Economy of Pre-Liberation China: Trade Expansion and Peasant Livelihood in Jiangsu and Guangdong, 1870–1937*. Hong Kong, New York: Oxford University Press.
Galloway, P. R. (1988) 'Basic Patterns in Annual Variation in Fertility, Nuptiality, Mortality, and Prices in Pre-Industrial Europe'. *Population Studies*, 42: 275–303.

Harrell, S. (1987) 'On the Holes in Chinese Genealogies'. *Late Imperial China*, 8(2): 53–79.

——(ed.) (1995*a*), *Chinese Historical Microdemography*. Berkeley, CA: University of California Press.

——(1995*b*) 'Introduction: Microdemography and the Modeling of Population Process in Late Imperial China', in idem (ed.), *Chinese Historical Microdemography*. Berkeley, CA: University of California Press, pp. 1–20.

Huang, P. (1985) *The Peasant Economy and Social Change in North China*. Stanford: Stanford University Press.

——(1990) *The Peasant Family and Rural Development in the Yangzi Delta, 1350–1988*. Stanford: Stanford University Press.

Jiang, T. (1993) *Zhongguo jindai renkou shi* (Modern Chinese Population History). Hangzhou: Zhejiang renmin chuban she.

Lee, J. and Campbell, C. (1997) *Fate and Fortune in Rural China: Social Organization and Population Behavior in Liaoning, 1774–1873*. Cambridge: Cambridge University Press.

——and Wang, F. (1999) *One-Quarter of Humanity: Malthusian Mythology and Chinese Realities*. Cambridge, MA: Harvard University Press.

——, ——, and Campbell, C. (1994) 'Infant and Child Mortality Among the Late Imperial Chinese Nobility: Implications for Two Kinds of Positive Check'. *Population Studies*, 48(3): 395–411.

Lee, R. (1981) 'Short-Term Variation: Vital Rates, Prices, and Weather', in E. A. Wrigley and R. S. Schofield (eds.), *The Population History of England 1854–1871: A Recon-struction*. Cambridge: Cambridge University Press, pp. 356–401.

——(1990) 'The Demographic Response to Economic Crisis in Historical and Contemporary Populations', *Population Bulletin of the United Nations*, 29: 1–15.

Li, B. (1998) *Agricultural Development in Jiangnan, 1620–1850*. New York: St. Martin's Press.

——(2005) 'Farm Labour Productivity in Jiangnan, 1620–1850', in this volume chap. 2.

Liu, T.-J. (1985) 'The Demography of Two Chinese Clans in Hsiao-shan, Chekiang, 1650–1850', in S. B. Hanley and A. P. Wolf (eds.), *Family and Population in East Asian History*. Stanford: Stanford University Press, pp. 13–61.

Long, J. S. (1997) *Regression Models for Categorical and Limited Dependent Variables*. Thousand Oaks, Beverley Hills, CA: Sage Publications.

Perkins, Dwight (1969) *Agricultural Development in China, 1368–1968*. Chicago, IL: Aldine Publishing.

Pomeranz, K. (1993) *The Making of a Hinterland: State, Society, and Economy in Inland North China, 1853–1937*. Berkeley, CA: University of California Press.

——(2000) *The Great Divergence: Europe, China, and the Making of the Modern World Economy*. Princeton, NJ: Princeton University Press.

Rawski, T. (1989) *Economic Growth in Pre-War China*, Berkeley, CA: University of California Press.

Skinner, W. G. (1987) 'Sichuan's Population in the Nineteenth Century: Lessons from Disaggregated Data'. *Late Imperial China*, 8(1): 1–79.

Telford, T. A. (1990) 'Patching the Holes in Chinese Genealogies: Mortality in the Lineage Populations of Tongcheng County, 1300–1880'. *Late Imperial China*, 11: 116–36.

Wu, C. (1996) 'Liyong liangjia biandong yanjiu Qingdai de shichang zhenghe' (Grain price studies of market integration during the Qing). *Zhongguo jingji shi yanjiu*, 2: 88–94.

17 Demographic Responses to Short-Term Economic Stress in Eighteenth- and Nineteenth-Century Rural Japan: Evidence from Two Northeastern Villages

NORIKO O. TSUYA AND SATOMI KUROSU

1. Introduction

This study examines the patterns and trends of demographic responses to changes in living standards in two farming villages in northeastern Japan from 1716–1870, using the local population registers called *ninbetsu-aratame-cho*. Focusing on four types of demographic outcome—mortality, fertility, first marriage, and migration— we analyse the impact of short-term economic stress on individual behaviour. Adopting the concept developed by Bengtsson (2004), we define short-term economic stress not at the individual level but at the community level, as measured by annual changes in local rice price with various time lags. Given that the setting of this study—two agrarian villages in pre-industrial Japan—depended primarily on rice farming, the use of annual variations in local rice price is appropriate to measure short-term economic stress in the communities.

In pre-industrial rural communities in which households were the primary unit of production as well as of consumption, demographic responses to short-term economic stress would also have been influenced by the resources and wealth available within households. We therefore account for the effects of the amount of land owned by each household on the four types of individual demographic behaviours. Since the households in the two villages were almost entirely agricultural, the use of household landholding is appropriate to measure household resources and wealth.

Using the discrete-time event-history analysis model, this study seeks to answer three specific questions. First, among the four demographic behaviours under consideration, how did the nature of their responses to short-term economic stress caused by fluctuations in agricultural output differ? Second, whether these demographic responses to short-term economic stress were affected by household resources, and if so, how? Third, did the patterns of demographic responses to short-term economic stress change over time?

In the next section, we briefly explain the general population trends in Tokugawa Japan,[1] the villages examined in this study and changes in their population sizes, and temporal changes in local socio-economic conditions and policy contexts. We also discuss the nature of rice prices and household landholding in the contexts of agrarian economy and family farming in Tokugawa Japan. We then explain the data and variables used in the model in this study, and finally examine the patterns and trends of demographic responses to short-term economic stress caused by fluctuations in local rice price, by conducting a series of discrete-time event-history analyses of: (1) mortality by sex and life stage; (2) marital fertility; (3) first marriage by sex and marriage type; and (4) out-migration by sex and reasons of migration. The chapter concludes with a summary of the findings and a discussion of their implications.

Because Tokugawa Japan was a society with enormous local variations in demographic patterns, family systems, and economic development, evidence from a study based on data from two farming villages is clearly not sufficient to provide a general picture of living standards as measured by demographic responses to short-term economic stress in pre-industrial Japan. Nevertheless, by examining an array of demographic responses to fluctuations in local rice price and household landholding, this study is expected to shed light on the nature of the relationships among demographic behaviour, local economy, and household resources in the Japanese past.

2. Background

2.1   *Population changes and economic conditions in Tokugawa Japan*

Changes in population size in Tokugawa Japan (1603–1868) can be characterized by three phases: rapid growth in the seventeenth century, stabilization in the eighteenth century, and moderate increase in the nineteenth century. The rapid growth of the seventeenth century is argued to have been due to sharp increases in population in all regions of the country, whereas the stabilization of the eighteenth century was a consequence of two contrasting changes: population decline in the northeast and population growth in the southwest.[2] Japan's population again started to increase gradually in the early nineteenth century and picked up speed after the 1850s, and was accompanied by economic development throughout the country (Hayami 1986: 316–17).

Little direct evidence exists concerning economic conditions in seventeenth-century Japan. However, existing studies suggest that, as judged from real wages in farming villages, economic conditions in some parts of rural Tokugawa Japan seem to have been improving from the early eighteenth to the early nineteenth centuries. For example, according to Saito (1998: 25–31), the average real wages of agricultural day-labourers in eastern and central Japan increased throughout the eighteenth century until they started to decline in the 1820s. Hayami and Kito (2004) also point out that the real wages of servants in farming households in central Japan rose in the eighteenth century.[3] Further, Hayami (1985: 91–2) has argued that the northeast experienced the beginnings of the commercialization of agriculture in the latter half of the eighteenth century.

On the other hand, Japan experienced a number of widespread crop failures and famines in the eighteenth and early nineteeth centuries, of which the largest were the Kyoho famine (1732–3), the Tenmei famine (1782–7), and the Tempo famine (1833–8). In the mid-1750s, the Horeki famine also caused widespread damage to rice crops in the northeastern region (Hayami 2001: 47–9). Before recovering from the damages caused by the Horeki famine, the region was devastated by the Tenmei famine in the 1780s, which according to historical evidence was by far the most serious famine recorded in early modern Japan (Narimatsu 1985: 199–200). Half a century later, in the 1830s, the region was again hit by another large-scale famine known as the Tempo famine, which was the last major famine in the Tokugawa period.

In summary, the evidence on economic conditions in eighteenth- and nineteenth-century rural Japan is somewhat contradictory. As seen from changes in average real wages in farming villages, the economy appears to have developed and economic conditions to have improved in the eighteenth and the early part of the nineteenth centuries. On the other hand, however, a series of widespread famines must have had a negative effect on the standard of living in the agrarian villages. For north-eastern Japan in particular there is no clear evidence suggesting that real wages in agriculture increased, while a great deal of evidence exists to indicate that the region was affected seriously by the series of large-scale famines. Overall, unlike the central and eastern regions, economic conditions in northeastern Japan in the eighteenth and early nineteenth centuries do not seem to have improved dramatically, and this economic 'stagnation' may have been responsible in part for the population decline in the region.

2.2   The setting and local population changes

The settings of this study are Shimomoriya and Niita, two farming villages in the present Fukushima prefecture in northeastern Japan (see Maps 17.1 and 17.2). During the Tokugawa period, both belonged to the Nihonmatsu domain that governed the central part of the prefecture. Located at the foot of the Ou mountain range, Shimomoriya was susceptible to cold summers and poor harvests resulting from chilly gusts off the mountains (Narimatsu 1985: 1–3). Because the village was located in a hilly area with severe winter weather, most of its agricultural land was not fertile and unfit to grow cash crops such as mulberry trees.[4] Located in a plain between the capital town of Nihonmatsu and the market town of Koriyama, two major population centres in the domain at that time, Niita enjoyed a better climate for agriculture (Narimatsu 1992: 4–6). Though situated north of Shimomoriya, Niita had more fertile agricultural land fit to be cultivated as rice paddies and as mulberry fields.[5] Nonetheless, lying on the banks of the Gohyaku river, the village was vulnerable to frequent floods.

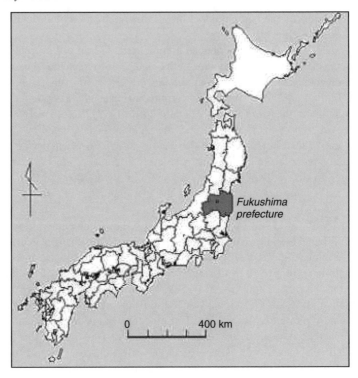

Map 17.1   Japan with Fukushima prefecture marked

Though somewhat different in their geographical conditions, both villages were almost entirely agricultural (inhabited almost entirely by peasants) and depended mostly on rice agriculture, supplemented by a number of dry crops (Narimatsu 1985: 152–80, 1992: 6; Nagata, Kurosu, and Hayami 1998). Given the under-developed and under-mechanized agricultural technologies of the time, the north-eastern region, in which the two villages were located, was the northernmost boundary of rice farming in Tokugawa Japan. These circumstances often put the villagers at the mercy of fluctuations in harvest yields, driving their living standards to near or below subsistence levels.

As mentioned, northeastern Japan experienced a number of famines and crop failures in the eighteenth and nineteenth centuries (Saito 2002).[6] Let us see how the populations in the villages of Shimomoriya and Niita were affected by these famines and crop failures. As illustrated in Figure 17.1, according to the local population registers (*ninbestu-aratame-cho*, NAC), Shimomoriya was a relatively small village with a population of 419 in 1716. The village population was relatively stable in the first thirty-five years for which the records are available, until it started to decline at around the time of Horeki famine in 1755–6. Devastated by the great

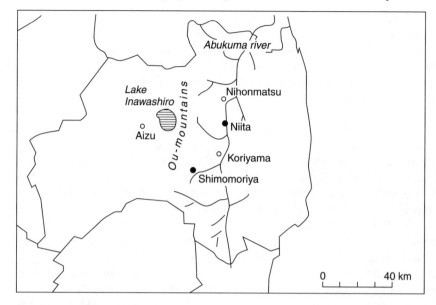

Map 17.2   Fukushima prefecture

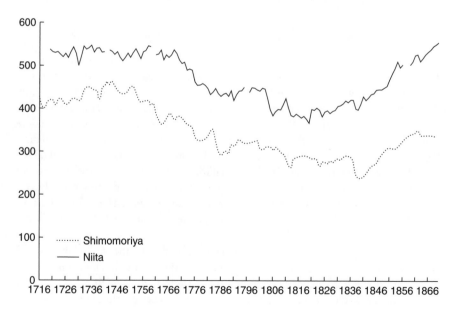

Figure 17.1   Population size of the villages of Shimomoriya and Niita, 1716–1870

Tenmei famine in 1782–7, the village population further declined to 286 in 1786—a decline of 32% in the seventy years from 1716. Though the population was restored somewhat during the 1790s–1820s, it again took a dramatic downturn during the Tempo famine in 1833–8, reaching a nadir of 238 in 1840. Although the population recovered gradually afterwards, to 328 by 1869, it did not recover the 1716 level during this period.

Niita was a larger village with a population of 538 in 1720 (see Figure 17.1). The village population was also stable, as in the case of Shimomoriya, for about fifty years, until it began to decline in 1770. Owing mainly to the Tenmei famine in the mid-1780s and a long spell of bad weather preceding it (Koriyama-shi 1981*a*: 340–1, *b*: 176–80), Niita's population plunged from 530 in 1770 to 430 in 1786—a decline of 19% in a mere fifteen years. After the population fluctuated at the level of around 420–450 from 1786 to 1800, it decreased again in the early 1800s. Reaching a nadir of 367 in 1820, the village population then started a gradual increase. The population size of Niita was not as seriously affected as Shimomoriya by the Tempo famine; it recovered, and even surpassed, the 1720 level by the late 1860s.

In summary, except in the first few decades of the records, when they were stable, and in the last few decades, when they showed an upturn, the population sizes in the two villages were in overall decline. Especially large net population losses occurred at the times of the two major famines in the mid-1780s and the late 1830s. Hence, although the evidence is by no means definitive, these findings seem to suggest that the village populations were affected negatively by the acute decline in agricultural output caused by widespread famine and crop failures.

2.3   Rice price and agrarian economy in Tokugawa Japan

As we just saw above, the population sizes of the two villages declined at the times of known major famines. How did local grain prices fluctuate under these economic hardships? Were there any trends in grain price variations? The only available series of grain prices in Tokugawa Japan with sufficiently long duration are rice prices. This study uses rice price series in the local market of Aizu to measure annual fluctuations in agricultural output, which in turn serves as a measure of short-term economic stress.[7] Unlike grain prices in pre-industrial Europe, rice prices in Tokugawa Japan were not always determined by market factors such as harvests and the demand for consumption, trades, and storage, but were often influenced by the political and policy-related decisions of domain governments. Here, a brief explanation of the nature of the rice price and the agrarian economy in Tokugawa Japan is in order.

A major characteristic of the Tokugawa economy is the *kokudaka* system (Hayami 1985: 75–107). Under the increasing prevalence of a money economy, the central and domain governments adopted this system under which all agricultural output was measured, taxes on peasants were assessed (not individually but on villages as a whole), and the incomes of domain lords and their warriors (*samurai*) were determined in terms of the value of one unit (*koku*) of rice yield.[8] The system was facilitated by the separation, both physically and socially, between *samurai* and peasants (Hayami 1985: 75–8). Whereas *samurai* all lived in the castle town of their domain lord, villages were inhabited almost exclusively by peasants; thus in Tokugawa Japan the so-called 'landed warriors' ceased to exist and *samurai* essentially became salaried officials of domain governments. Meanwhile, peasants were required to pay taxes: in some domains they were required to pay solely in rice; while in others they were required to pay in money—it was thus necessary to have a sort of exchange rate between rice and money.

For example, if the domain government required their peasants to pay 500-*koku*-worth of taxes half in rice and half in money, peasants would have had to sell rice in the market to pay for the 250-*koku*-worth of taxes in money. If crops failed and there was not enough yield to pay for the 250-*koku* of taxes in rice, they would have had to buy rice in the market. The government then sold the rice collected as taxes in the market to obtain necessary funds. Putting it differently, harvested rice could have three uses: to be consumed directly by peasants, to be sold by peasants directly to merchants (commercial rice), and to be paid as taxes to domain governments or to the central government if peasants lived in areas governed directly by the Tokugawa shogunate (tax rice).

Evidence indicates that in the Nihonmatsu domain peasants were required to pay taxes with a combination of rice and money (Koriyama-shi 1981*b*: 320–4). Therefore, if the local rice price took an abrupt upturn due to a crop failure, the domain government had a strong incentive to curb the increase since if the rice price became too high too quickly, peasants would not have been able to buy the rice needed to pay for taxes. On the other hand, if the rice price became too low, it pressed hard on the livelihood of the *samurai* and put the domain government in a financial predicament, since the income of the domain government and the salaries of its *samurai* were obtained by selling tax rice in the market. In this sense, the rice price in the local market is not only an indicator of harvest variations, but also served as an exchange rate between rice and money. Given that there are no data on local rice prices based solely on the market conditions in the Nihonmatsu domain (nor northeastern Japan in general), we use the 'exchange-rate' based rice price data from the local market of Aizu.

Despite the government-controlled nature of rice prices, annual variations in rice prices in the market of Aizu seem to reflect fairly well local crop failures at the time of major famines. As shown in Figure 17.2, the local rice price shows an upsurge at around the times of the three major famines of Kyoho (in 1730s), Tenmei (in 1780s), and Tempo (in 1830s), although increases are by no means limited to the years of known famines.

2.4 Family farming and household landholding

In pre-industrial rural Japan, households were not only the unit of consumption but also that of production. Small-scale family farming became increasingly prevalent during the Tokugawa period and came to be the dominant type of agriculture by the

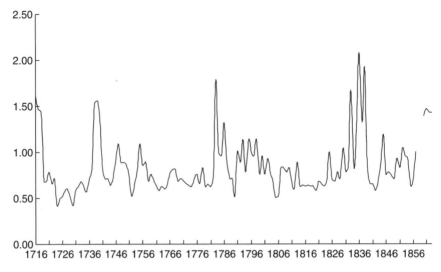

Figure 17.2   Raw rice prices (*ryo* per *koku*) in the market of Aizu, 1716–1863

first half of the eighteenth century (Smith 1977: 105–17; Hayami 1985: 92–3). As explained above, in the Tokugawa agrarian economy peasants paid taxes on the expected yields of the land they owned. Taxes were imposed not on individual households but on villages, and when some households were unable to fulfil their tax burden, other households (in particular, households of other titled peasants) had to make up the balance.

In the Nihonmatsu domain, the land used to produce rice was divided by lottery among all households in a village (*nawabiki*). The main purpose of the lottery was to equalize landholding among the households within a village. Shimomoriya appears to have held this lottery every ten years (Nagata, Kurosu, and Hayami 1998). Niita held a new lottery only once, in 1794, after the peasants petitioned for a lottery to correct the inequalities that they perceived (Narimatsu 1992: 138–9). In between lotteries peasants could obtain more land by borrowing it from other peasants who needed to loan or pawn their land because of economic difficulties. Actual land-holding among households in farming villages in the domain was therefore adjusted by borrowing, loaning, and pawning land (Koriyama-shi 1981*b*: 276–9).

Villagers of agrarian villages were divided between titled peasants (called *honbyakusho*) who held land and landless peasants (called *mizunomi*) who owned no land (and thus were free from tax responsibilities). These landless peasants mostly served as tenant peasants to titled peasants. Though efforts were made to keep peasants (and their households) more or less equal and to equalize their tax burdens, inequalities clearly existed, not only between titled and landless peasants, but also among titled peasants according to their households' landholding. The amount of land held by each household (called *mochidaka*) is the best available indicator of the socio-economic status of households in our two almost totally agricultural villages.[9]

Examining temporal changes in household landholding in the two villages, our preliminary analysis found that the size of the average landholding increased from around 8–10 *koku* per household in the eighteenth century to around 11–12 *koku* in the nineteenth century. Later in the chapter, we will examine differences in the nature of demographic responses to changes in household landholding in the eighteenth and in the nineteenth centuries, separately.

2.5 *Trends of regional and local socio-economic changes*

Periodization of history is always somewhat arbitrary. However, looking at temporal changes in local development, domain policy contexts, and environmental conditions in the Nihonmatsu domain and in northeastern Japan as a whole, we can discern, to some extent, the trends of socio-economic changes during the entire 154-year period under consideration (1716–1870).[10] The Nihonmatsu domain government was in debt from the late seventeenth century (Nagata, Kurosu, and Hayami 1998). In an attempt to achieve financial solvency, the government thus implemented several extraordinary taxes during 1728–49. The combination of these extra taxes and a series of poor harvests contributed to a major peasant uprising in 1749, after which taxes were reduced and delayed payment was allowed (Koriyama-shi 1981*b*: 351–60; Nihonmatsu-shi 1982: 79–81).

The commercialization of agriculture based on family farming also began on a large scale in the 1750s (Hayami 1985: 91–2). Due to the continuing agricultural commercialization and also because of an intensified need to increase rice production after the Tenmei famine in the 1780s, the Nihonmatsu domain government reversed its official economic policy at around the end of the eighteenth century. Once having discouraged the development of proto-industries, the domain government began to encourage locally specialized production of cash crops such as mulberry and lacquer trees (Nagata, Kurosu, and Hayami 1998). This resulted in the proto-industrialization of villages in the domain, as seen in the growth of the silk textile and lacquer industries.

The region was again seriously affected by the great Tempo famine in the 1830s. After the Tempo famine, the rigid social structure and hierarchy of Tokugawa Japan that had been sustained for almost two and half centuries became increasingly slack, leading to the period called *bakumatsu*, the last years of the Tokugawa political regime.

3. Data and Methods

3.1 *Data*

This study draws the data from the local population registers called *ninbetsu-aratame-cho* (NAC) in the villages of Shimomoriya and Niita.[11] In both villages, the

NAC was enumerated annually at the beginning of the third lunar month. Surviving NAC registers in Shimomoriya cover the 154 years from 1716 to 1869 with only 9 years missing (1720, 1729, 1846, 1850, 1858, and 1864–7). In Niita, the surviving NAC registers cover the 151-year period from 1720 to 1870, during which there are only 5 years missing (1742, 1758, 1796, and 1857–8). Thus, in the two villages there exist virtually undisrupted records spanning the latter half of the Tokugawa era. Because the format and contents of the NAC registers are almost identical for the two villages, and also because our preliminary analysis indicated that the patterns and causal structure of demographic responses to rice price fluctuations and household contextual variables were not substantially different between them, this study pools together the records from the two villages.

In addition to the continuity of the existing records, the NAC registers in the two villages have other advantages as demographic data. First, the registers were compiled using the principle of current domicile; thus, the NAC data are all *de facto*.[12] Registers compiled this way give far more exact demographic information than those based on the principle of legal residence although the latter *de jure* principle seems to have been much more prevalent (Cornell and Hayami 1986).

Second, in the NAC registers of the two villages, the dates (month and year) of births and deaths were annotated as far as these events occurred during the period of observation. The dates of occurrence of these events were not normally given in local population registers in Tokugawa Japan (Smith 1977: 19; Saito 1997), so this is additional evidence of the high quality of the population registers in Shimomoriya and Niita. One exception is infants who died before the first registration after birth. As was the case elsewhere in pre-industrial East Asia, local population registers of pre-industrial Japanese communities enumerated only those infants who survived from birth to the subsequent registration. Consequently, infants who died before the first registration after birth were excluded and thus never come under observation. This under-registration of infant deaths is probably the most serious shortcoming of our data source, and we have to keep this in mind when we interpret the results of the analysis of infant mortality and marital fertility.

Third, exits from the records for unknown reasons are extremely rare in the NAC registers of the two villages. Such 'mysterious disappearances' consisted of merely 0.6% (19 cases) of all exits during the 154 years covered by Shimomoriya's NAC, and only 0.3% (13 cases) of all exits during the 151 years recorded by Niita's register.[13] Therefore, we can determine, in most cases, the timing of entrance to the 'universe' of observation (due to birth or in-migration) as well as the timing of death or other exit, even though the two villages experienced considerable in- and out-migration (Tsuya 2000).

The original annual NAC records (which were organized into one sheet per year for each household) were first linked into time-series data sheets called 'Basic Data Sheets (BDS)' for all households. The BDS were then entered into machine-readable form, from which a relational database was created (for specifics, see Hayami 1979; Ono 1993). Using this database containing all information available in the NAC, it is not only possible to derive for each individual (and for each household) indices of demographic and life course events, but also to link all individuals (present in the village) to the records of other household members.

From the relational database, we constructed a rectangular file for our multi-variate analyses, using a person-year recorded in the population register as the unit of observation. Although it is possible to compute chronological age for residents whose births were recorded in the NAC registers, the majority of individuals appearing in the registers were either present at the beginning of the records or had migrated into the villages some time after their birth. Moreover, the NAC information used to construct the covariates of our analyses is organized in terms of the timing of NAC registration. Hence, for the purposes of our analysis, it is necessary and appropriate to use as our measure of individual age the variable indicating the number of NAC registrations each individual went through after birth until his or her exit from the universe of observation due to death or emigration. Therefore, in this chapter, the word 'age' refers to the age measured in terms of the timing of the NAC registration (NAC age).[14] Measured in this way, the youngest possible NAC age of individuals included in our analysis is one.

3.2 Methods

This study conducts a series of discrete-time event-history analyses of demographic responses to changes in local rice price and household landholding. Using a series of logistic regression models, the model relates an individual's probability of experiencing a given demographic event—death, marital birth, first marriage, or out-migration—in the interval of the next one year following the beginning of the interval.

Because the data for our analyses are constructed with a *person-year* as the unit of observation, individuals are likely to contribute more than one observation. This built-in interdependence among observations can affect the standard errors in multivariate analyses.[15] Thus, to take the effects of inter-correlation among observations obtained from the same individuals into account, we estimate the logistic regression with robust standard errors based on Huber's formula (Huber 1967).[16]

4. Variables

4.1 Dependent variables

This study has four general dependent variables: mortality, marital fertility, first marriage, and out-migration. In the analysis of mortality, the dependent variable is a dichotomous variable measuring whether an individual died or not within the next one year from an NAC registration to the immediately succeeding registration.[17] Out of the 6,543 individuals appearing in the population registers in the two villages, there were 2,839 deaths (1,479 male and 1,360 female deaths) recorded in the NAC registers. Dividing the life cycle into four segments—infancy at age 1, childhood from ages 2 to 14, adulthood from ages 15 to 54, and old age covering ages 55 to 74—we estimate the logistic regression model for males and females separately.

In the analysis of marital fertility, a 'birth' is a birth *recorded* in the NAC register, rather than an actual birth. Hence, we analyse, strictly speaking, not marital fertility but marital reproduction. Our dependent variable is a dichotomous variable indicating whether a married woman of reproductive age (15–49) records a birth within the next one year (until the subsequent NAC registration).[18] To 2,127 women aged 15–49 appearing in the population registers in the two villages, there were 2,620 births (1,346 male births and 1,274 female births) recorded and matched. Given the possibility of sex differentials in infant mortality as well as of sex-selective infanticide, our analysis of marital fertility also differentiates births by their sex.

Providing that the focus of our analysis is on marital fertility/reproduction, we need to clarify the definition of a woman 'at risk' of having a (recorded) birth within marriage. We restrict the analysis to married women who were alive and present in the village throughout a 'current' year (one year until next registration), and had their husbands residing in the village at the beginning of the current or previous year.[19] Put differently, we exclude women who died during a current year and those who did not have their husbands living in the village from the beginning of the previous year.

Turning to the analysis of first marriage, our dependent variable is a dichotomous variable measuring whether or not a never-married individual experiences first marriage within the next one year. Being influenced by local customs, marriage and its registration in pre-industrial Japan were largely contextual; the timing (year) of first marriage therefore had to be inferred from an entry of a new household member between two consecutive registrations and concomitant changes in relationships among household members. Hence, we measured the timing of first marriage by comparing household members between two consecutive registrations and, if changes occurred, taking the difference between the year of birth and the year of marriage as defined above.

Measurement of the timing of first marriage is straightforward for individuals who were under constant observation from birth. However, a problem arises for those who had already been present when the records began, or for those who first appeared in the records some time after birth. Many women especially moved into or out of the villages due to marriage and marital disruption whereas only a small proportion of them remained in their native villages throughout their lifetimes (Tsuya 2000). Given the high geographical mobility of women associated with marriage, it is unwise to limit the analysis of first marriage to women who lived in the villages throughout their adult years, for doing so renders the data too small and selective. Thus, we used a less conservative definition of 'first marriage' than the usual: if marriages were observed for the first time for individuals who were under age 50 and had neither a spouse nor a child listed when they first appeared in the registers, those marriages were regarded as 'first marriages'.

Our analysis of first marriage looks at ages 10–49 for males and 5–49 for females.[20] Our multivariate analysis is also confined to individuals who were residing in the villages *prior to* their 'first marriage' as defined above.[21] The data for our analysis of first marriage consists of 1,169 single males and 1,072 single females who were at risk of experiencing first marriage, with 805 recorded male first marriages and 814 female first marriages.

Furthermore, our analysis of first marriage distinguishes three types of marriages based on individual movements annotated in the NAC records: intra-village virilocal marriages (called 'virilocal marriages' hereafter); intra-village uxorilocal marriages (called 'uxorilocal marriages'); and marriages accompanying out-migration from the villages (called 'marry-out' marriages). Specifically, based on the annotations of the names of the originating village and the head of household of origin, we identified individuals who married within the village and those who married out of the village (i.e. emigrated upon marriage). Intra-village marriages were further differentiated in terms of post-nuptial residential patterns into virilocal and uxorilocal marriages.

Finally, with regard to the analysis of out-migration, our dependent variable is a dichotomous variable indicating whether or not a resident of Shimomoriya or Niita moved out of the village within the next one year.[22] In our analysis, out-migration refers to the observed movement of any persons (both legal and other residents) out of the villages to other communities. Thus, 'out-migration' includes both the movements of individuals whose legal domicile was in one of the two villages and the return migration of persons whose legal domicile was elsewhere. To 6,543 individuals who appeared in the population registers in the two villages, 4,230 out-migrations (2,489 male and 1,741 female) were recorded.

The NAC registers in Shimomoriya and Niita annotated in detail information on people's movements across the village boundaries, including: (1) the name of destining village and the name of the household head of destination for out-migrants and those of origin for in-migrants; and (2) the reasons for migration. Based on the first piece of information, we can differentiate the out-migration of 'natives', individuals whose legal domicile was in one of the two villages, from the migration of 'non-natives' whose legal domicile was elsewhere. We therefore examine migration of natives and non-natives separately.

Using the information on reasons for migration, out-migration of natives can be further differentiated into movements due to: marriage, adoption, service, change of legal domicile, absconding (i.e. illegal disappearance from the village), and other.[23] Among these, service (*hoko*) is by far the most common reason for male out-migration with 68% of such movements being service-related. Service (*hoko*) refers to all forms of contract labour lasting any duration of time longer than six months (thus, shorter-term employment or daily wage labour is not included in service). The second most common reason for male out-migration is due to absconding (*kakeochi*), which constituted 16% of the out-migration of native males from the two villages. Absconding refers to leaving the village of legal domicile without notifying the local authority of the move. Since the remaining reasons comprise only small proportions, we focus on migration due to service or absconding in our analysis of out-migration of native males. As for out-migration of native females, their reasons were mostly marriage (41%) or service (35%), with absconding constituting the third-largest category (12%). Our analysis of out-migration of native females therefore is divided into these three types of movements. To avoid the estimation bias caused by increasingly selective populations who survived to very old age, we restrict our analysis of out-migration to individuals under age 75.

4.2   Covariates

Our event-history analysis model has four general groups of covariates: (1) local rice prices; (2) household landholding net of number of kin household members; (3) time periods; and (4) the current age and residing village of each index individual, which are always included in the model as control variables. In the analyses of adult and old-age mortality as well as in the analyses of out-migration of native males and females, marital status of each index individual is also controlled for.

As mentioned at the outset of the chapter, we use annual rice prices in the local market of Aizu to measure short-term economic stress. In our earlier study of mortality in the two villages (Tsuya and Kurosu 2000*a*), we examined the effects of different rice price series—prices in Aizu and in the central market of Osaka—using different specifications: raw prices, de-trended prices based on moving averages, and prices de-trended using the Hodrick–Prescott filter.[24] We found that fluctuations in agricultural output in the two northeastern villages were best measured by raw prices (with or without logarithm), rather than de-trended prices. This study therefore uses the log of raw rice price. To further examine the nature of effects of rice price variations, we also test the effects of prices time-lagged by up to five years. Because of strong auto-correlation among annual rice prices, our model includes rice price for only one year at a time.

Household landholding (*mochidaka* in *koku*) is a continuous variable measuring the total productive capacity of the land held by the household. This variable is introduced primarily to measure the amount of household economic resources, though this variable may also be a proxy for the wealth and socio-economic status of household.[25] The demographic effects of landholding are estimated, net of number of kin household members. Total household size, including servants and non-kin, was found in one of our earlier studies to be highly multicolinear with landholding since, given the under-mechanized agricultural technologies of the time, large landholding often required several helping hands (Tsuya, Kurosu, and Nakazato 1997). Theoretically, it is also appropriate to control for the number of co-resident kin, rather than total household size, as non-kin and servants are thought to have had much less access, if any, to the resources and wealth of the households they served.

Our model also takes into account the demographic effects of different time periods within the entire 154-year period (1716–1870) under consideration. As explained in the previous section, there are considerable temporal differences in local economic development, policy contexts, and environmental conditions in the domain and in northeastern Japan as a whole during the eighteenth and nineteenth centuries. First, the commercialization of agriculture based on small-scale family farming with high labour intensity began on a large scale in the middle of the eighteenth century (Hayami 1985: 91–2). At around the turn of the century, the domain government reversed its official policy and began encouraging production of cash crops, resulting in proto-industrialization in many agrarian villages in the domain (Nagata, Kurosu, and Hayami 1998). Finally, in the late 1830s (after the Tempo famine), the rigid social structure and stratification of the Tokugawa regime started to crumble, leading to the period called *bakumatsu*, the last years of the Tokugawa period. Therefore, we divide the 154-year period into four sub-periods: before 1760, 1760–99, 1800–39, and 1840–70.

Current age of an index individual is a covariate the effect of which we need to control, because demographic behaviour is a function of age. This variable consists of 5-year age groups, except for ages 1–4, at which mortality is thought to be high. Because the data from the two different villages are pooled, a dichotomous variable indicating whether index individuals were residing in Shimomoriya or not is also included in the model. Marital status is included in our models for adult and old-age mortality as well as in the models for out-migration of native males and females. This covariate consists of five categories: never married, currently married, widowed, divorced, and marital status unknown.

5. Results of the Discrete-Time Event-History Analyses

In this section, we examine, in a multivariate context, demographic responses to short-term economic stress and household resources, focusing on each of the four demographic behaviours: mortality, marital fertility, first marriage, and out-migration. For each of these four behaviours, we estimate two sets of models. The first model includes only the rice price and time periods, in addition to the two control variables of age and village of residence. In the second model, household landholding (net of number of kin household members) is added to the first model. We also estimated the models with interactions between rice price and landholding, as well as between time periods and price or landholding. We report the results of the models with interactions only when such interactions are statistically significant without over-specifying the model. Table 17.1 presents the means of the covariates used in the analysis of mortality, and Table 17.2 presents the corresponding descriptive statistics for the covariates used in the analyses of marital fertility, first marriage, and out-migration.

5.1 Mortality

Using different time lags (current year up to five years before), we first examine the effects of logged rice price in the local market of Aizu on the mortality of males and females at different life stages. We find considerable differences in the magnitude and significance of mortality responses to fluctuations in rice price by gender and life stage (table not shown).[26] Rice prices are in general associated significantly and

Table 17.1 Means of the covariates used for the discrete-time event-history analysis of mortality responses to short-term economic stress: the villages of Shimomoriya and Niita, 1716–1870

Covariates	Infant	Child	Adult	Old age
Male				
Logged rice price in Aizu, current year	−0.236	−0.229	−0.240	−0.252
Landholding (in *koku*)	12.447	12.102	12.673	10.492
Time period (1716–59)				
1760–99	0.247	0.253	0.287	0.321
1800–39	0.239	0.254	0.234	0.233
1840–70	0.172	0.162	0.139	0.081
Female				
Logged rice price in Aizu, current year	−0.218	−0.228	−0.235	−0.247
Landholding (in *koku*)	12.340	12.554	12.566	11.266
Time period (1716–59):				
1760–99	0.242	0.247	0.295	0.327
1800–39	0.244	0.258	0.245	0.266
1840–70	0.194	0.173	0.148	0.090

Notes: In the analysis of mortality, infant refers to age 1, childhood to ages 2–14, adult to ages 15–54, and old age to ages 55–74. For the definition and measurement of age, see the text.

Table 17.2 Means of the covariates used for the discrete-time event-history analysis of responses of marital fertility, first marriage, and out-migration to short-term economic stress: the villages of Shimomoriya and Niita, 1716–1870

Covariates	Marital fertility	First marriage		Out-migration	
		Male	Female	Male	Female
Logged rice price in Aizu, current year	—	—	—	−0.240	—
Time lag by 1 year	−0.245	—	—	—	−0.244
Time lag by 3 years	—	−0.244	−0.229	—	—
Landholding (in *koku*)	12.469	11.359	12.668	12.166	12.348
Time period (1716–59)					
1760–99	0.287	0.281	0.256	0.285	0.288
1800–39	0.229	0.259	0.289	0.2380	0.251
1840–70	0.149	0.159	0.197	0.135	0.145

Notes: The analysis of marital fertility looks at married women aged 15–49; the analysis of first marriage looks at never-married males aged 10–49 and never-married females aged 5–49; and the analysis of out-migration looks at males and females (of all marital statuses) under age 75. For the definition and measurement of age, see the text.

positively with female infant and child mortality, while the association with male childhood mortality is, though mostly positive, statistically insignificant. This suggests that female infants and children were more highly responsive to short-term economic stress caused by annual fluctuations in agricultural output, but that the chances of survival for males were largely unaffected by such variations.

By contrast, we find that local rice price variations had a significant positive effect on the mortality of adult and elderly men, and their mortality responses to these local economic fluctuations were immediate and short-lived. On the other hand, the mortality effects of rice price variations on adult and elderly women were mostly insignificant, with the possible exception of elderly women, whose mortality increased significantly with increases in rice prices with a one-year time lag. This suggests that, in contrast to mortality at earlier years of life, the mortality of men in adulthood and old age responded immediately to short-term economic stress, while the mortality of women in adult and elderly years was largely unaffected by such stress.

Table 17.3 presents the results of discrete-time event-history analysis of male and female mortality rates at different life stages, including not only local rice prices but also household landholding as the covariates. As shown in the table, the nature of the mortality effects of local rice price fluctuations does not change when household landholding is added to the model. With regard to the effects of household land-holding (per kin household member), three things stand out in the table. First, there are significant and negative interactions between rice price and landholding, as well as between landholding and time periods in female infant mortality. This suggests that, while infant girls were highly vulnerable to short-term economic stress caused by changes in local economic conditions, their likelihood of death was much lower if they lived in households with resources and wealth. This tendency was especially strong in the period from 1760–99 and, though to a lesser extent, in the period from 1800–30. These two sub-periods include the decades of the two most serious and prolonged famines (1780s and 1830s). Thus, it may have been the case that the health benefits that infant girls enjoyed by living in a wealthy household were especially important when the economic condition in the community deteriorated seriously due to large-scale famines. Putting it differently, the survival chances of infant girls in economically deprived households were much worse when local economic conditions deteriorated, and this was especially the case in the times of acute economic difficulty.

Second, household landholding significantly reduced the mortality of adult and elderly men as well as the mortality of elderly women, while adult female mortality was unaffected. In the case of elderly men, the mortality-reducing effect of land-holding is also curvilinear. This suggests that, except for adult women, adults and the elderly were likely to benefit from the resources and wealth of their households in countering health risks. Such protective health effects of household resources were especially strong for elderly men.

Third, there are clear but opposite time trends in female child mortality and old-age mortality. Female child mortality decreased over time. By contrast, the

Table 17.3 Estimated effects of logged rice prices and household landholding on the probability of dying in the next one year by sex: Shimomoriya and Niita, 1716–1870

Covariates	Infant		Child		Adult		Old age	
	Male	Female	Male	Female	Male	Female	Male	Female
Logged rice price, in current year	−0.201	2.416**	0.057	0.317#	0.392*	−0.006	0.730**	0.076
Landholding	0.014	0.018	0.007	−0.001	−0.022**	0.006	−0.545**	−0.015*
Landholding, squared	—	—	—	—	—	—	0.001*	—
Time period								
1760–99 (P2)	−0.544#	1.575**	−0.207	−0.285	−0.151	−0.388**	0.117	0.025
1800–39 (P3)	−0.103	0.441	−0.333*	−0.336#	0.573**	−0.264#	0.163	0.191
1840–70 (P4)	−0.574	0.398	−0.276	−0.525**	0.166	−0.554**	0.430*	0.506**
Price*landholding	—	−0.104**	—	—	—	—	—	—
P2*landholding	—	−0.145**	—	—	—	—	—	—
P3*landholding	—	−0.079#	—	—	—	—	—	—
P4*landholding	—	−0.031	—	—	—	—	—	—
Log-likelihood	−305.8	−276.0	−1,171.6	−964.1	−1,474.7	−1,680.5	−1,524.4	−1,414.0
χ^2	6.48	35.94	177.12	176.49	94.31	50.46	158.55	171.33
(d.f.)	(7)	(11)	(11)	(11)	(18)	(18)	(15)	(14)
$p > \chi^2$	0.000	0.000	0.000	0.000	0.000	0.000	0.000	0.000
No. of observations	1,129	1,062	11,592	10,904	28,142	26,800	8,952	8,107
No. of events	88	83	266	216	270	313	389	366
No. of individuals	1,129	1,062	1,487	1,481	2,148	2,041	849	746

** Significant at 0.01 level. * Significant at 0.05 level. # Significant at 0.10 level.

Notes: The analysis above controls for current age, residing village, and the number of kin members in household. For adult and old-age mortality, the effect of marital status of index individual is also controlled. The coefficients were estimated by using person-year recorded in local population registers as a unit of observation; estimation of standard errors takes into account the effects of contribution of more than one observation from the same individuals by using Huber's formula.

mortality of elderly men and women increased as time passed. We speculate that the loosening of rigid social (and intra-household) hierarchies by age and gender during the last years of the Tokugawa regime might have worked in favour of the health of female children, who were the most powerless members of the family and household, while it worked against the elderly, who had enjoyed respect and esteem under the traditional family system.

5.2   Marital fertility

We next examine the effects of rice prices, using different time lags, on the prob-ability of having a recorded marital birth among women aged 15–49 in the two villages (table not shown). We find that marital fertility (to be more precise, the likelihood of having a recorded marital birth) was mostly unaffected by annual fluctuations in local rice price, although the effects were always negative, as expected. We also do not see any notable differences in the effects of logged rice price by sex of birth. Our earlier study on marital fertility in the two villages found the widespread use of sex-selective and parity-specific infanticide to achieve a relatively small family size with sex-balanced offspring set (Tsuya and Kurosu 1999). In this earlier study, we also found that the fertility effects of rice prices remain insignificant, even after controlling for many family-related characteristics including the number and sex-composition of surviving children. Altogether, we interpret the lack of response of marital fertility to local economic fluctuations to imply that, in these villages, strong family control was not limited to times of economic hardships, but was practised regularly.[27]

As shown in Table 17.4, the effects of local rice price variations on marital fertility remain insignificant after introducing household landholding (and other covariates) into the model. However, household landholding significantly increases the likelihood of having a recorded marital birth, especially a female birth. This suggests that women in better-off households were more likely to have a recorded female birth than were women in poor households. This in turn implies that living in wealthier households with more resources, women could afford to keep a baby, especially a female baby, without resorting to infanticide.

Finally, we can see that there are significant temporal differentials in marital fertility. The likelihood of a recorded marital birth became significantly higher in the nineteenth century, especially during the last three decades of the Tokugawa era (1840–70). As explained before, the rigid social stratification became increasingly unstable during the last decades of the era, and the gender hierarchy accordingly became more flexible which in turn may have enabled wives/couples to keep female babies.

5.3   First marriage

We next examine the effects of logged raw rice prices on the probability of first marriage of single men and women by type of marriage, using different time lags.

Table 17.4 Estimated effects of logged rice price and household landholding on the probability of having recorded marital birth in the next one year: women aged 15–49 in Shimomoriya and Niita, 1716–1870

Covariates	All births	Male births	Female births
Logged rice price, time-lag by 1 year	−0.019	0.065	0.267
Landholding	0.006[#]	0.007	0.022*
Landholding squared	—	—	−0.005
Time period			
1760–99 (P2)	−0.049	0.000	−0.155
1800–39 (P3)	0.199**	0.184*	0.014
1840–70 (P4)	0.338**	0.185[#]	0.354**
P2*rice price	—	—	−0.315
P3*rice price	—	—	−0.725*
P4*rice price	—	—	−0.331
Log-likelihood	−5952.80	−3790.44	−3626.86
χ^2	494.02	261.89	243.64
(d.f.)	(13)	(13)	(17)
$p > \chi^2$	0.0000	0.0000	0.0000
No. of observations	18,900	18,900	18,900
No. of events	2,023	1,039	984
No. of individuals	1,600	1,600	1,600

** Significant at 0.01 level. * Significant at 0.05 level. [#] Significant at 0.10 level.

Notes: Estimated with person-year recorded in local population registers as a unit of observation. Estimation of standard errors takes into account the effects of contribution of more than one observation from the same individuals by using Huber's formula. The analysis above controls for the effects of age, residing village, and the number of kin members in household.

For both men and women, the effects of rice price variations are almost entirely negative (i.e. in the theoretically expected direction), indicating that the likelihood of first marriage declined at times of economic downturn (table not shown). We also find that, for both sexes, rice prices with a three-year lag have the strongest effect. Therefore, we use logged raw prices with a three-year time lag in our extended model.

Female first marriages responded more quickly to price fluctuations than did male first marriages. This suggests that female marriages were more vulnerable to changes in local economic conditions than were male marriages. This in turn implies that as economic conditions in the community deteriorated, daughters' marriages were forgone or delayed before those of sons. Given the small offspring size prevalent in the two villages (Tsuya and Kurosu 1999), it is likely that a considerable proportion of men were the primary family heir.[28] It may therefore be the case that male first marriages were more resilient to local economic downturn than were female first marriages because families would have put a higher priority on their male heirs' marriages than on their daughters'.

We also note the different effects of rice price variations on first marriages by marriage type. Male virilocal marriages and female intra-village (especially virilocal) marriages were most responsive to rice price fluctuations with 2–4 year time lags whereas male uxorilocal marriages and female marry-out marriages were largely unaffected. This suggests that local economic conditions influenced the probability of first marriage occurring within the villages, except for marriages in which a man moved into his bride's household. Such uxorilocal marriages were relatively small in number and different social and economic factors are thought to have operated in those marriages.

Table 17.5 presents the results of discrete-time event-history analysis of first marriage by sex that includes not only price variations but also household land-holding in the model. As shown in the left panel of the table, even after landholding is introduced into the model, the effects of rice price fluctuations remain significant and strongly negative for male marriages, especially male virilocal marriages.

We can also see that household landholding (net of number of kin members) significantly increased the likelihood of male first marriages. Since a large majority of male first marriages were virilocal (i.e. men brought their bride into their household), this suggests that household economic resources enhanced the chances of first marriage among inheriting sons. Furthermore, the effect of household landholding on male virilocal marriages was not only positive but also curvilinear. This means that, whereas landholding did not make much difference between male heirs of landless peasants and male heirs of peasants with only a small landholding, differences were larger between inheriting sons in households with a medium landholding and inheriting sons in households with a large landholding.

There are clear temporal differentials in the likelihood of male first marriage regardless of marriage type. The probability of male first marriage became significantly lower in 1800–70, relative to 1716–59 (see the left panel of Table 17.5). Given the nearly universal male marriage in the two villages, this finding indicates a delay in the timing of male first marriage in the nineteenth century.

Turning to the probability of female first marriage by marriage type (see the right panel of Table 17.5), three things stand out. First, a downturn in economic conditions in the community as measured by local rice prices significantly reduced the likelihood of female intra-village virilocal marriage, that is, marriage of a woman with a man residing in the same village. This mirrors the negative effect of prices on male virilocal marriage. These findings suggest that the deterioration of local economic conditions reduced the likelihood of first marriages within the villages for men and women alike.

Second, household landholding is positively associated with the likelihood of female uxorilocal marriage. This again mirrors the positive effect of landholding on male uxorilocal marriage. We interpret these findings together to mean that the chances of obtaining a marriage partner for inheriting sons and daughters were enhanced by household wealth and resources in pre-industrial Japanese agrarian villages.

Third, there is a very strong and clear trend of decline in the age-specific probability of female first marriages of all types. The likelihood of female first marriage declined significantly and linearly as the time passed. Our earlier study found the

Table 17.5 Estimated effects of logged rice prices and household landholding on the probability of first marriage in the next one year by sex and type of marriage: never-married males aged 10–49 and never-married females aged 5–49 in Shimomoriya and Niita, 1716–1870

Covariates	Male first marriages			Female first marriages			
	All	Virilocal	Uxorilocal	All	Virilocal	Uxorilocal	Marry-out
Logged rice price, time lag by 3 years	−0.369**	−0.349*	−0.255	−0.312*	−1.369**	−0.176	−0.149
Landholding	0.028*	0.059**	0.069#	0.0004	0.013	0.053*	−0.000
Landholding squared	—	−0.001**	−0.003*	—	—	−0.002	—
Time period							
1760–99	−0.147	−0.185	−0.359	−1.033**	−0.868**	−0.745**	−0.810**
1800–39	−0.375**	−0.410**	−0.556*	−1.375**	−1.274**	−0.779**	−1.215**
1840–70	−0.352**	−0.365*	−0.665*	−1.585**	−1.872**	−0.897**	−1.252**
Log-likelihood	−2146.41	−1765.08	−502.85	−1784.48	−780.84	−913.76	−905.00
χ^2	494.12	414.21	102.84	838.09	353.27	325.80	417.91
(d.f.)	(13)	(14)	(14)	(12)	(14)	(14)	(13)
$p > \chi^2$	0.0000	0.0000	0.0000	0.0000	0.0000	0.0000	0.0000
No. of observations	8,530	8,530	8,530	8,384	8,384	8,384	8,384
No. of events	698	529	102	709	205	240	264
No. of individuals	1,169	1,169	1,169	1,072	1,072	1,072	1,072

** Significant at 0.01 level. * Significant at 0.05 level. # Significant at 0.10 level.

Notes: Estimated with person year recorded in local population registers as a unit of observation. Estimation of standard errors takes into account the effects of contribution of more than one observation from same individuals by using Huber's formula. The analysis above controls for the effects of age, residing village, and the number of kin members in household. The results for 75 males who married out of the villages are not shown because the results are statistically unstable due to a small number of events.

increasing delay of first marriage among women in these two villages (Tsuya and Kurosu 2000*b*), and this result confirms that finding.

5.4 Out-migration

We now turn to the results of the event-history analysis of out-migration. We first estimated the effects of logged raw rice prices on the probability of out-migration of both native and non-native individuals and also on the reason for migration of native persons, using different time lags (table not shown). We found that there were clear and contrasting gender differences in migration responses to rice price fluctuations. The likelihood of male out-migration decreased when local economic conditions deteriorated. Male migration responses were immediate and, though they became weaker as time passed, lasted for a few years. By contrast, female out-migration was in general unaffected by economic variations in the community. This suggests that male out-migration in the two villages, compared to female out-migration, was more sensitive to changes in local economic conditions.

We also found that the migration responses of native men to price fluctuations tended to be more immediate, while those of non-native men were less immediate but lasted longer. Furthermore, although the patterns of migration responses present a contrast between the sexes when we look at out-migration as a whole, the responses of males and females are similar when we focus on natives by reasons of migration. Local economic downturn reduced the likelihood of service-related out-migration of native males and females, while it significantly raised the likelihood of absconding by both sexes. In addition, changes in local economic conditions affected male service migration more quickly than they did female service migration, though the effect on female service migration lasted much longer.

In summary, male out-migration was in general much more responsive to changes in local economic conditions than was female out-migration, and this was due primarily to the fact that a large part of male migration was service-related. On the other hand, female out-migration was much less responsive to local economic changes, owing in part to the fact that the proportion of female labour-related migration was small, and also to the fact that out-migration due to marriage, which represented the largest proportion of female migration, was little affected by annual changes in local economic conditions. Nonetheless, for both native males and native females, the likelihood of service out-migration declined when local economic conditions worsened, because the deterioration of economic conditions was not limited to their own villages but affected the entire Nihonmatsu domain or even the whole north-eastern region. Because the destinations of service migration were mostly villages within the domain (Narimatsu 1985: 103–4; Takahashi 1999), a downturn in local economic conditions negatively affected the local labour market, therefore reducing the opportunities of service outside the villages. By contrast, for both males and females, absconding increased significantly at the times of economic hardship, as expected.

Table 17.6 presents the results of the event-history analyses of out-migration of native men and women, based on the models that include not only price variations

Table 17.6 Estimated effects of logged rice prices and household landholding on the probability of out-migration in the next one year by sex and reason of migration: native males and females aged under 75 in Shimomoriya and Niita, 1716–1870

Covariates	Migration of native males				Migration of native females			
	All migration	Migration			All migration	Migration		
		Marriage	Service	Absconding		Marriage	Service	Absconding
Logged rice price, in current year time-lag by 1 year	−0.375**	−0.071	−0.672**	0.488**	—	—	−0.484*	1.483**
Landholding	−0.055**	−0.146**	−0.024**	−0.018*	−0.066**	−0.020**	−0.020#	−0.122**
Landholding squared	0.001**	0.003**	0.001**	—	0.001**	—	0.001*	0.002**
Time period								
1760–99	0.144#	0.686**	−0.250**	1.684**	0.291**	−0.308#	0.247#	2.087**
1800–39	0.002	0.560*	−0.425**	1.795**	0.017	−0.591**	−0.032	2.134**
1840–70	−0.811**	0.690*	−1.462**	0.532	−0.541**	−0.857**	−1.935**	1.559**
Log–likelihood	−5,642.98	−749.19	−3,895.87	−1,341.47	−4,252.08	−1,765.37	−1,785.79	−838.73
χ^2	632.14	250.08	451.92	358.78	797.89	747.47	258.22	213.59
(d.f.)	(23)	(21)	(23)	(22)	(23)	(22)	(22)	(23)
$P > \chi^2$	0.0000	0.0000	0.0000	0.0000	0.0000	0.0000	0.0000	0.0000
No. of observations	48,807	45,500	48,807	48,807	45,485	45,485	45,241	45,485
No. of events	1,309	131	834	237	959	413	334	138
No. of individuals	2,789	2,690	2,789	2,789	2,789	2,789	2,741	2,789

** Significant at 0.01 level. * Significant at 0.05 level. # Significant at 0.10 level.

Notes: Estimated with person-year recorded in local population registers as a unit of observation. Estimation of standard errors takes into account the effects of contribution of more than one observation from the same individuals by using Huber's formula. The analysis above controls for the effects of age, residing village, number of kin household members, and marital status. In the model for male migration due to marriage, 3,307 observations were dropped because men whose marital status were unknown or those at age 45–49 did not at all experience the event in question. In the model for female migration due to service, 244 observations were dropped because none of the women whose marital status were unknown experienced the event in question.

but also household landholding. As shown in the table, household landholding significantly and uniformly lowers the probability of all types of out-migration for both sexes, and the negative effects are often not linear. This suggests that both men and women were less likely to migrate out of their villages if they lived in households with greater resources and wealth. Although a one-unit (*koku*) increase in landholding does not always have the same effect, there is a large difference in the likelihood of out-migration between individuals living in households with zero or only a small landholding and those in households with large landholding.

Finally, as shown in Table 17.6, similar temporal differences are observed for both sexes in the overall probability of out-migration. Relative to the earliest sub-period (1716–59), the likelihood of out-migration in 1760–99 was significantly higher (this being the case especially for female out-migration), while the likelihood of out-migration became significantly lower in 1840–70. Increases in the probability of out-migration in 1760–99 were due primarily to dramatic increases in absconding at the time of acute and prolonged economic hardship caused by the Tenmei famine in the 1780s (Tsuya 2000). The propensity of absconding was also high in the following sub-period of 1800–40, being propelled by hardships caused by the Tempo famine in the 1830s and a series of years of bad weather preceding it. On the other hand, the probability of out-migration in 1840–70 declined, solely due to a large reduction in service migration, and this was especially the case for male out-migration because a large proportion of male out-migration consisted of labour migration. For females, in addition to declines in service migration, decreases in marriage-related migration contributed to lowering the overall probability of female migration since the out-migration of native women for marriage declined sharply over time.

6. Temporal Changes in the Causal Mechanism of Demographic Responses

In the previous sub-sections, we found that there were significant temporal differentials in demographic responses to short-term economic stress. In order to directly examine whether there were any changes over time in the causal mechanisms of these demographic responses, we further conducted the discrete-time event-history analyses of the effects of rice price fluctuations on mortality, marital fertility, first marriage, and out-migration by dividing the entire period under consideration (1716–1870) into two sub-periods: the eighteenth century (1716–99) and the nineteenth century (1800–70). The choice of the cut-off point for this division is based on our preliminary analysis of changes in the average household landholding by decades and also in part to patterns in the fluctuations of local rice prices.

In short, these separate analyses, divided into sub-periods, showed significant changes in the nature of the effects of rice price variations and household landholding only on first marriage, while there were no notable changes in their effects on the remaining three demographic outcomes, that is, mortality, marital fertility, and out-migration (data not shown). Specifically, the responses of mortality by sex and life stage as well as those of marital fertility to price variations and landholding were largely unchanged even after we divided the entire period into the two sub-periods. The effects of rice price and landholding on out-migration also did not change much, except that the size of the negative effect of rice price variations on male out-migration more than doubled in the nineteenth century, compared to that in the eighteenth century.

By contrast, the nature of nuptiality responses to price fluctuations and land-holding differed substantially between the sub-periods of 1716–99 and 1800–70.[29] Examining the responses of all first marriages by sex for the two sub-periods, we found that it was only in the nineteenth century (1800–70) that the probability of first marriage for both sexes declined significantly when local economic conditions deteriorated, whereas the probability of first marriages was not influenced by variations in local economic conditions in the eighteenth century (table not shown).[30] On the other hand, the probability of male first marriage was significantly higher for those who belonged to wealthier households in the eighteenth century, but the effects of landholding became insignificant for male marriage in the nine-teenth century. The likelihood of female first marriage was largely unaffected by landholding throughout the two sub-periods.

Comparing these results with those on the pooled analysis shown in Table 17.5, we can conclude that the significant responses of male and female first marriages to local rice price fluctuations were due largely to the significant nuptiality responses of both sexes concentrated in the nineteenth century (1800–70). The significant effect of household landholding on the probability of male first marriage found by the pooled analysis was due primarily to significant differentials in the probability of male first marriage by household landholding concentrated in the eighteenth century (1716–99).

7. Conclusions and Discussion

There exists an extensive literature on the effects of short-term economic stress, usually measured by fluctuations in grain prices, on vital rates in pre-industrial Europe. According to Galloway (1988), the strength of the link between grain price fluctuations and mortality seems to vary across societies and periods, whereas fertility tended to be highly sensitive to grain price variations throughout most of pre-industrial Europe. The high sensitivity of overall fertility to local economic fluctuations is thought to be due primarily to the sensitivity of the probability and timing of first marriage. Though there are not enough studies on migration responses to grain price fluctuations to form a consensus, migration is also thought to have been sensitive to changes in local economic conditions.

Our study of two agrarian villages in the northeast of Japan based on micro-level multivariate analysis offers new insights on demographic responses to short-term economic stress in pre-industrial rural Japan. We found that first marriage and out-migration were most responsive to short-term economic stress, though the magnitude and nature as well as the type and reason of the responses varied between these two demographic behaviours.

The probability of first marriage for both men and women decreased significantly in times of economic stress, and this was especially the case in the nineteenth century. Further, the nuptiality response to short-term economic stress was not immediate, but had a time lag of 2–4 years. Among different types of first marriages, virilocal marriages were most sensitive to economic stress, with some time lag. This suggests that virilocal marriages, in which a man brought the bride into his household, were sensitive to local economic conditions. This also implies that in virilocal marriages, local economic conditions a few years prior to the marriage mattered most, probably because the decision-making power regarding inheriting sons' marriages in pre-industrial Japanese agrarian households was in the hands of their parents/families and planning for such a family matter was long term, starting a few years prior to actual marriage. Clearly, inheriting sons and their families were reluctant to make a decision to take a bride when the economic prospects were unfavourable.

Migration was also highly sensitive to changes in local economic conditions, and this was especially true for male out-migration. The probability of male out-migration declined significantly when local economic conditions deteriorated. The response of male out-migration to short-term economic stress was immediate and lasted for a few years. Male out-migration declined under economic stress primarily because a large proportion of it was labour migration. Since a large part of labour migration was destined to other localities within the Nihonmatsu domain, the deterioration of the local economic conditions meant reduced labour opportunities in the domain as a whole, thus decreasing opportunities for out-migration for employment. Looking at out-migration by motivation, service migration and absconding both appear to have been highly sensitive to short-term economic stress, but the directions of the effects were opposite: when local economic conditions worsened, service migration decreased but absconding increased, and this was true for both sexes.

Mortality responses to short-term economic stress were limited mostly to two gendered-life-stage groups: females during infancy and childhood, and men in adult and elderly years. The responsiveness of mortality of baby girls was especially high and immediate. Moreover, at times of economic hardship, the survival of baby girls also depended on the resources and wealth of their households. When local economic conditions deteriorated, the mortality of female infants was significantly reduced if they lived in wealthy households. The mortality of adult and elderly men was also sensitive to economic stress, and this was especially true for elderly men.

As to why mortality responses were largely limited to opposite sexes at the two ends of the life cycle—female infants and elderly men—we speculate that the economic and social sensitivity of their mortality in the context of physiological robustness may constitute part of the explanation. Being physiologically more robust than male infants, female infants were nonetheless socially and economically the most vulnerable sub-population in pre-industrial rural Japan. On the other hand, having survived until the age of 55 or above, elderly men generally held a high status within their households and community. When economic conditions in the community deteriorated, these elderly men suffered a high degree of relative deprivation, thus making them highly vulnerable to short-term economic stress. To a lesser extent, this interpretation may also be applicable to adult men and elderly women.

We have also found that household resources and wealth influenced all four demographic behaviours under consideration, although the nature, direction, and magnitude of the demographic effects differ by sex, life stage, and type of behaviour. Migration was strongly influenced by household landholding, while the responses of first marriage, mortality, and marital fertility to landholding were more limited. Household landholding significantly and consistently lowered the likelihood of out-migration of both sexes, and this was the case regarding migration for all reasons: labour migration, migration due to marriage, and absconding.

The probability of first marriage among inheriting sons and daughters increased significantly with their households' landholding, although the degree of increase was not always linear. As virilocal marriages constituted a large majority of all male marriages, male first marriages were generally sensitive to household landholding. On the other hand, uxorilocal marriages being only a minority, female first marriages as a whole were not as responsive to landholding. Because marriages in pre-industrial Japan were largely family and household enterprises (Tsuya and Kurosu 2000*b*), it is understandable that household resources and wealth, as measured by landholding, increased the likelihood of the first marriages of inheriting sons and daughters.

Household landholding also increased the probability for a married woman to have a recorded female birth (but not a male birth). This implies that those women living in households with more resources and wealth could afford to keep a baby girl without resorting to infanticide. Landholding also reduced the likelihood of death among adult men and elderly men and women. This suggests that adult men and elders held enough power and status within the household to enjoy their households' resources, while infants, children, and adult women (who spent a majority of their years as daughters-in-law) had less control over household resources.

This study also discerned temporal trends and differentials in some of the four demographic behaviours under consideration. Especially notable were changes that occurred during the last sub-period of 1840–70 in female demographic behaviours. During this sub-period, female child mortality declined sharply, the likelihood of a recorded female birth increased precipitously, and female age at first marriage, while increasing steadily, went up especially notably. As a result, women's mean age at first marriage increased from 12.5 years in 1716–59 to 16.5 years in 1840–70. Altogether, these findings provide yet another piece of demographic evidence to support the general discussion of the improvements in female socio-demographic status that occurred during the last decades of Tokugawa Japan (Hayami and Kito 2004).

The relationships between short-term economic stress and demographic behaviours in pre-industrial societies are complex, dynamic, and situational. Clearly, more studies are needed to account for the dynamic mechanisms underlying these relationships. Our study on two agrarian villages in northeastern Tokugawa Japan offers some observations that might help to clarify some of this complexity. Our next agenda is to analyse these relationships in comparative perspective, by taking individual demographic, household, and life-course characteristics into account.

Notes

1. Tokugawa era, in which Japan was under the control of the Tokugawa shogunate in Edo (present Tokyo), begins in 1603 and ends in 1868.
2. According to Hayami (2001: 46), the rapid population increase in the seventeenth century was mainly due to large-scale cultivation of new land that took place across different regions of Tokugawa Japan. Hence, the seventeenth century is called the 'period of great land reclamation'.
3. Examining data on the physical well-being and nutritional status of residents in large cities such as Tokyo and Kyoto, Hanley (1983) argued that the standard of living in mid-nineteenth-century urban Japan was not only higher than that in the einghteenth century, but relatively high in comparison to the industrializing West. However, her arguments do not seem to be applicable to living standards in rural villages, especially those in the northeast.
4. Sericulture became popular in the region at that time, and mulberry leaves were major cash crops. Existing historical records show that several neighbouring villages located in flat land had much higher proportions of fields used for growing mulberry trees (Narimatsu 1985: 53–4).
5. According to a survey by the domain government in 1828 on the use of agricultural land, around 30% of the dry field in Niita was cultivated as mulberry field whereas only 5–10% of the dry field in Shimomoriya was used to grow mulberry trees (Nihonmatsu-shi 1982: 581).
6. Saito (2002) reports that according to one source (Ogashima 1894) there were twenty-eight major famines recorded in the Tokugawa period, and according to another (R. Saito 1966) there were sixty-one estimated famines from 1600 to 1900.
7. Being only around 40 km to the west, Aizu is the neighbouring domain of Nihonmatsu. Unfortunately, rice price series of the Nihonmatsu market are not available, being lost some time in the history. Thus, this study uses rice prices in the Aizu market. Given the geographical proximity of Nihonmatsu to Aizu, the use of Aizu price series is thought to be appropriate. Further, the Niwa family which was the domain lord of Nihonmatsu was in debt to Aizu merchants from the late sixteenth century and the debt was never paid off (Nagata, Kurosu, and Hayami 1998). For this reason, the Aizu rice prices probably had strong influences on the tax rates and finances of the Nihonmatsu domain government and may reflect changes in the tax rates imposed upon peasants in the domain.
8. One *koku* is equivalent to approximately 5 bushels.
9. According to Hamano (2000) who examined different measures of household economic status, household landholding is the most appropriate and most widely used indicator of household economic status in pre-industrial Japanese villages.

10. Among the major regions of Tokugawa Japan, the northeast was in general the one with the least economic development and lowest proto-industrialization. Compared to central and southwestern Japan, the overall level of proto-industrialization in the northeast is considered to have been much more limited.

11. The population registers in Shimomoriya and Niita, like all other communities in the Nihonmatsu domain, were *ninbetsu-aratame-cho* (NAC), rather than *shumon-aratame-cho* (SAC). Though similar in terms of information collected by these two types of registers, SAC was carried out, in its original purpose, to hunt hidden Christians whereas NAC was, as the name indicates, primarily for population registration and investigation (Narimatsu 1985: 11–14, 1992: 10–12).

12. The size of *de jure* population can also be computed for both villages because records were kept as far as one's permanent (legal) domicile was in the villages. However, for persons whose legal domicile was in the village but were not present (residing) there, information on individual circumstances, including demographic events occurring while away from the villages, are generally unavailable.

13. Eighteen out of the nineteen disappearances from Shimomoriya's NAC and seven out of the thirteen disappearances from Niita's registers occurred during 1851–70, the last years of the Tokugawa period.

14. In addition to chronological age (i.e. age according to the Gregorian calendar) and NAC age, there is also the traditional Japanese method of counting age. As in the rest of East Asia, it regards a child as age 1 at birth and adds an additional year on each New Year's Day thereafter. Consequently, if counted by the traditional Japanese method, most newborns, if they survived, appear in population registers at the age of 2 *sai* although in extreme cases they could be on the second day of life. If population registration was conducted on each New Year's Day (which was rarely the case), traditional Japanese age (in *sai*) minus one is equivalent to NAC age.

15. According to Guilkey and Murphy (1993), when records are repeated over five times, the problem of intercorrelation among observations becomes serious and affects the estimation results.

16. The formula was independently discovered by White (1980) and is also known in the econometrics literature as White's method. A summary discussion of the method is given in the STATA Reference Manual (Stata Corporation 1995: 457–65).

17. As mentioned earlier, nine registers for Shimomoriya and five registers for Niita are missing. Thus, for certain two-year periods (and the five-year period from 1863–7 for Shimomoriya and the three-year period from 1856–8 for Niita) it is impossible to determine in which one-year interval an event or right censoring occurred. Accordingly, we restricted our analysis to the years for which an immediately succeeding register is available.

18. Though some women gave birth before age 15 in the two villages, the number was very small. Out-of-wedlock childbearing was also minimal. Only 0.9% of recorded births (i.e. twenty-three births) were out of wedlock. For details, see Tsuya and Kurosu (1998).

19. The one-year lag for husband is due to the assumption that given the gestation period of approximately nine months, a woman could be at risk of giving birth as long as her husband was present in the village at the previous enumeration.

20. Though the youngest recorded age at marriage was 6 for males and 3 for females, such cases were very rare and seem to require a separate explanation. We therefore exclude these outliers from the analysis.

21. Though substantial numbers (304 men and 728 women) migrated into the villages *upon* first marriage during the 154 years of observation, these individuals had to be excluded from the multivariate analysis.
22. When migration consisted of more than one individual (i.e. migrants did not move alone), we counted the event pertaining to each individual as one. For example, when a household of three members moved out of the village, we counted three events; and all the three were used in the analysis. This multiple counting of events in the case of migration of a whole (or part of) household would not seriously affect the results of our analysis because a large majority (90%) of out-migration was by a lone individual.
23. A large majority (82%) of out-migration of male non-natives was mostly due to end of service. As for out-migration of female non-natives, two most common reasons were end of service (54%) and marital disruption (38%).
24. For details on various rice price series in early modern Japan, see Iwahashi (1981), and for the relationship between local rice markets and the Osaka central market in Tokugawa Japan, see Miyamoto (1988: 386–430).
25. Since the two villages under consideration almost exclusively consisted of peasants, we cannot use occupation of household head as an indicator of household socio-economic status as occupation of household head would be a constant, rather than a variable.
26. For the table showing the estimated coefficients of logged rice prices with different time lags on the probability of dying by sex and life stage as well as the tables on marital fertility, first marriage, and out-migration, contact N. Tsuya (tsuya@econ.keio.ac.jp).
27. Previous studies on pre-industrial Japanese villages also found that family control was not limited to the times of economic and environmental hardships. See Saito (1992), Skinner (1987), and Smith (1977: 59–85).
28. The mean number of children ever-observed was 2.8 for a woman whose first marriage was completed.
29. We also conducted the analyses of first marriages by type of marriage for males and females in these two sub-periods separately. The analyses of male first marriages by type of marriage showed that the temporal patterns of responses of all male marriages were virtually the same as those of responses of male virilocal marriages, as expected from the fact that a large majority of male first marriages were virilocal. As for female first marriages, we could not find any clear and discernible temporal patterns by type of marriage because the number of events for each of the three types of marriages became too small by slicing the data many times. Given these findings, we decided to discuss in the text only the results of the analyses on all first marriages by two sub-periods for males and females, respectively.
30. For the tables showing the results of the event history analyses of the four demographic responses to rice price fluctuations and household landholding by the two sub-periods, contact N. Tsuya (tsuya@econ.keio.ac.jp).

References

Bengtsson, T. (2004) 'Living Standards and Economic Stress', in T. Bengtsson, C. Campbell, J. Z. Lee *et al., Life Under Pressure: Mortality and Living Standards in Europe and Asia, 1700–1900.* Cambridge, MA: MIT Press, pp. 27–59.

Cornell, L. L. and Hayami, A. (1986) 'The *Shumon-Aratame-Cho*: Japan's Population Registers'. *Journal of Family History*, 11(4): 311–28.

Galloway, P. R. (1988) 'Basic Patterns in Annual Variations in Fertility, Nuptiality, Mortality, and Prices in Pre-industrial Europe'. *Population Studies*, 42: 275–303.

Guilkey, D. and Murphy, J. (1993) 'Estimation and Testing in the Random Effects Probit Model'. *Journal of Econometrics*, 59: 301–17.

Hamano, K. (2000) 'Meiji-shonen Noka-betsu Bussan Tokei ni tuite: Tama-gun, Shinmachi-mura Shiofuna-mura no Sanbetsu-torishirabe-cho' (Statistics on Agricultural Products in Early Meiji Japan: Registers of Products in the Villages of Shinmachi and Shiofuna in Tama County). *Komonjo Kenkyu*, 52: 22–32.

Hanley, S. B. (1983) 'A High Standard of Living in Nineteenth-century Japan: Fact or Fantasy?' *Journal of Economic History*, 43(1): 183–92.

Hayami, A. (1979) 'Thank You Francisco Xavier: An Essay in the Use of Micro-Data for Historical Demography of Tokugawa Japan'. *Keio Economics Studies*, 6(1–2): 65–81.

——(1985) *Nihon ni okeru Keizai-Shakai no Tenkai* (*Socioeconomic Development in Japan*), 6th edn. Tokyo: Keio Tsushin.

——(1986) 'Population Changes', in M. B. Jansen and G. Rozman (eds.), *Japan in Transition: From Tokugawa to Meiji*. Princeton, NJ: Princeton University Press, pp. 280–317.

——(2001) *The Historical Demography of Pre-modern Japan*. Tokyo: University of Tokyo Press.

—— and Kito, H. (2004) 'Demography and Living Standards', in A. Hayami, O. Saito, and R. P. Toby (eds.), *Economic History of Japan: 1600–1990, Volume 1: Emergence of Economic Society in Japan, 1600–1859*. Oxford: Oxford University Press, pp. 213–46.

Huber, P. J. (1967) 'The Behavior of Maximum Likelihood Estimates under Non-standard Conditions'. *Proceedings of the Fifth Berkeley Symposium on Mathematical Statistics and Probability*, 1: 221–3.

Iwahashi, M. (1981) *Kinsei Nippon Bukka-shi no Kenkyu* (*A Study of the History of Price in Early Modern Japan*). Tokyo: Ohara Shinseisha.

Koriyama-shi (1981*a*) *Koriyama-shi Shi 2: Kinsei, Jyo* (*The History of Koriyama City 2: Early Modern Period, Volume 1*), 2nd edn. Tokyo: Kokusho Kanko Kai.

——(1981*b*) *Koriyama-shi Shi 2: Kinsei, Ge* (*The History of Koriyama City 2: Early Modern Period, Volume 2*), 2nd edn. Tokyo: Kokusho Kanko Kai.

Miyamoto, M. (1988) *Kinsei Nippon no Shijo-Keizai: Osaka Kome-shijo Bunseki* (*Market Economy in Early Modern Japan: An Analysis of the Osaka Rice Market*). Tokyo: Yuhikaku.

Nagata, M. L, Kurosu, S., and Hayami, A. (1998) 'Niita and Shimomoriya of the Nihonmatsu Domain in the Northeastern Region of Tokugawa Japan'. EAP Working Paper Series, No. 20. Kyoto: EurAsian Project on Population and Family History, International Research Center for Japanese Studies.

Narimatsu, S. (1985) *Kinsei Tohoku Noson no Hitobito: Oshu Asaka-gun Shimomoriya-mura* (*People in a Northeastern Agricultural Village in Early Modern Japan: The Village of Shimomoriya, Asaka County, Ou Region*). Kyoto: Mineruva Shobo.

——(1992) *Edo-jidai no Tohoku Noson: Nihonmatsu-han Niita-mura* (*Agricultural Villages in Northeastern Tokugawa Japan: The Village of Niita in Nihonmatsu Domain*). Tokyo: Dobunkan.

Nihonmatsu-shi (1982) *Nihonmatsu-shi Shi, Dai-6-kan: Kinsei III* (*The History of the City of Nihonmatsu, Volume 6: Early Modern Period, No.3*). Nihonmatsu-shi: Nihonmatsu-shi.

Ogashima, M. (ed.) (1894) *Nihon Saii-shi* (*The History of Natural Disasters in Japan*). Tokyo: Nihon Kogyokai.

Ono, Y. (1993) 'Bunka-kei no Keisanki Riyo II: Deta-nyuryoku no Yuzaa Intaafeisu (Rekishi Jinkogaku no Baai)' (Computer Utilization for Humanities II: User Interface for Data Entry, The Case of Historical Demography). *Nihon Kenkyu (Bulletin of International Research Center for Japanese Studies)*, 8: 165–82.

Saito, O. (1992) 'Infanticide, Fertility and "Population Stagnation"': The State of Tokugawa Historical Demography'. *Japan Forum*, 4(2): 248–67.

—— (1997) 'Infant Mortality in Pre-transition Japan: Levels and Trends', in A. Bideau, B. Desjardins, and H. Perez-Brignoli (eds.), *Infant and Child Mortality in the Past*. Oxford: Oxford University Press, pp. 135–53.

—— (1998) *Chingin to Rodo to Seikatsu-suijun: Nihon Keizai ni okeru 18–20-seiki* (*Wage, Labour, and Living Standards: The Japanese Economy in the 18th to 20th Centuries*). Tokyo: Iwanami Shoten.

—— (2002) 'The Frequency of Famines as Demographic Correctives in the Japanese Past', in T. Dyson and C. Ó Gráda (eds.), *Famine Demography: Perspectives from the Past and Present*. Oxford: Oxford University Press, pp. 218–39.

Saito, R. (ed.) (1966) *Fukenbetsu Nenbetsu Kisho Saigai Hyo* (*Tables of Climatic and Natural Disasters by Year and Prefecture*). Tokyo: Chijin Shokan.

Skinner, G. W. (1987) 'Infanticide and Reproductive Strategies in Two Nobi Plain Villages, 1717–1869'. Paper presented at the Workshop on Population Change and Socioeconomic Development in the Nobi Region, Stanford, CA, 15–18 March.

Smith, T. C. (1977) *Nakahara: Family Farming and Population in a Japanese Village*. Stanford, CA: Stanford University Press.

Stata Corporation (1995) *STATA Reference Manual Release 4*, Vol.2. College Station, Texas: Stata Press.

Takahashi, M. (1999) 'Kinsei Ichi-chiiki no Rodo-ido to Rodo-shijo: Keizai-teki ni Hatten-shita Mutsu-koku Asaka-gun Koriyama-kamimachi wo Chushin-to-shite' (Regional Labour Migration and Labour Market in Early Modern Japan: The Case of the Upper Town of Koriyama in Asaka County of Mutsu Province). Paper presented at the annual meeting of Shakai-keizaishi Gakkai, May.

Tsuya, N. O. (2000) 'The Patterns and Covariates of Migration in Eighteenth and Nineteenth Century Rural Japan: Evidence from Two Northeastern Villages'. Paper presented at the 2000 annual meeting of Social Science History Association, Pittsburgh, 26–29 October.

—— and Kurosu, S. (1998) 'Patterns and Covariates of Fertility in 18th and 19th Century Rural Japan: Evidence from Two Northeastern Villages'. EAP Working Paper Series, No. 16. Kyoto: Eurasia Project on Population and Family History, International Research Center for Japanese Studies.

———— (1999) 'Reproduction and Family Building Strategies in 18th and 19th Century Rural Japan: Evidence from Two Northeastern Villages'. Paper presented at the 1999 Annual Meeting of the Population Association of America, New York, 25–28 March.

———— (2000*a*) 'Mortality Responses to Short-Term Economic Stress and Household Context in Early Modern Japan: Evidence from Two Northeastern Villages', in T. Bengtsson, and O. Saito (eds.), *Population and Economy: From Hunger to Modern Economic Growth*. Oxford: Oxford University Press, pp. 422–55.

———— (2000*b*) 'Economic and Household Factors of First Marriage in Early Modern Japan: Evidence from Two Northeastern Villages, 1716–1870', in M. Neven and C. Capron, (eds.), *Family Structures, Demography and Population: A Comparison of*

Societies in Asia and Europe. Liege: Laboratoire de Demographie de l'Universite de Liege, pp. 131–57.

——— and Nakazato, H. (1997) 'Mortality in Early Modern Japan: Patterns and Correlates'. EAP Conference Paper Series, No. 20. Kyoto: Eurasia Project on Population and Family History, International Research Center for Japanese Studies.

White, H. (1980) 'A Heteroskedasticity-consistent Covariance Matrix Estimator and a Direct Test for Heteroskedasticity'. *Econometrica*, 48: 817–30.

Index

Abel, W. 166 n.1, 175
  recommended daily allowance 27
Adachi, K. 50 n.46
adimai 101
adult mortality 303 n.27, 346, 364–5,
  418, 421
Agra 105, 119
agricultural revolution 16, 345
agricultural transformation 15, 343–4, 346,
  349–50, 353, 361, 364–6
agriculture 11, 35, 61
  capital intensification 61
  commercialization 59, 345, 362, 365, 377,
    382–3, 429, 435, 440
  labour productivity 11
  Malthusian views 3
  mixed agriculture 136–7
  slash and burn 377, 382
Ain-i Akbari 119
Aizu market 432–3, 440–1, 455 n.7
Allen, R. C. ix, 11, 13, 79, 88, 115, 145,
  167 nn.7, 12, 174, 198–9
Alsace 210
Alter, G. ix, 16, 384
Amalric, J. P. 219 n.20
Amsterdam 113, 119–20, 132, 176–7,
  187–8, 197, 205–6, 210, 212, 219 nn.19,
  25–6, 311
Amuktamalyada 105
ancestor worship 3
Ancien Régime 197, 200–1, 299
Andersson, T. 286
André, R. 374
annicut 103
anthropometric history xii, xiii, 218 n.8,
  229–30, 244, 248 n.2, 249 n.8
anthropometric measures for standard of
  living 342
Antwerp 113, 175, 197
Ardennes 382, 384, 386, 388, 394, 398 n.6
Arezzo 321, 327
Argentina 247
Arno River 321, 323
artha 105
Asia 1, 4, 112, 138, 173, 299
  agriculture 3–5
  east and west gaps 17–19
  Europe and 1, 6, 8, 10, 12, 17–19,
    132, 299
  population growth 138

prices and wages 112
real wage data 77, 99–100
rice prices 115
standard of living 6–12, *121*
wages 123–4
Attman, A. 129 n.6
Aubel 386
Australia 230, 233–6, 238–9, 247
  heights and health *231*, 233, 236, 238–9
  industrialization 234–5
Austria 244, 281, 298
Austrian Military Border 280
Austrian provisioned villages 300 n.3
Aymard, M. 47 nn.5, 15

Bao, S. 67
bakumatsu 435
Baltic Lands 255, 267
Barrow, J. 67
Basic Need Index 6–7
Baulant, M. 218 n.6
Baxian 33
Bayley, W. H. 107 n.6
bean cakes as fertilizers 29–30, 41, 47 n.10,
  58, 69 n.13
Beijing 36, 43, 124, 133
Belgium 366 n.1, 373–4, 385
  child mortality 385
  Industrial Revolution 375
  migration and postponed marriage 385
  mortality 375
  standard of living debate 374–7
Bellary 101, 104
Benassar, B. 218 n.14, 219 n.24
Bengal 11, 17, 99–100, 102, 105–6
Bengtsson, T. ix, 7, 15, 19 n.3, 166 n.4,
  319, 338 n.7, 366 n.10, 367 n.15, 385,
  404, 423 n.3, 427
Bernard, R. J. 25, 30
Beveridge, W. H. 191 n.3
biological standard of living 267
biological status of the population 268
biological value (BV) 47 n.8
Birmingham 215
Black Death 124
Black Sea 255, 258, 268, 271
Blayo, Y. 48 n.19
blue book business 213
Boehler, J. M. 218 n.6
Bohai Gulf 405, 409

Bologna 330
book publishing 211
Bosnian–Serbian frontiers 282
Bourguignon, F. 166 n.8
Bourguinat, N. 248 n.5
Boxer, C. 49 n.37
Braida, L. 220 n.32
Brandt, L. 123
Braudel, F. P. 30, 50 n.47, 166 n.7
Bray, F. 50 n.49
Breschi, M. x, 15
Brewer, J. 218 n.6
Britain 2, 11–12, 18, 26, 31, 106, 167 n.11,
    173–4, 235, 239, 255, 271
  food shares 139
  Industrial Revolution 272
  life expectancy *136*
  pre-industrial heights 239, *241*
  prices of commodities 102
  real wages 11, 99–100
  weavers in 100
broodzetting 188
bubonic plague 244 *see also* plague
Buchanan, F. 100
Buck, J. L. 26–9, 31–2, 39, 42, 47 n.9,
    48 n.18, 49 n.39, 57, 123
Budapest 281, 300 n.4
Buikstra, J. E. 248 n.6
building labourers 183, 191 n.11
  in Japan 116–17
  in Oxford 118
  real wages 183
Bult, E. J. 191 n.15
burgers *265–6*, 266

Cambridge Group for the History of
    Population and Social Structure 133
Campbell, C. D. x, 16, 48 n.19, 404,
    423 n.3
Canada 247
capitalism 5, 68 n.6, 69 n.10, 299
Čapo-Žmegač, J. 283
Casalguidi 336–7
cash-crop production 49 n.38
Catasto de Ensenada 207
catechism 219 n.16
Catherine II 268–71
Cauvery River 103
Cernik–Nova Gradiška 284, 303 n.28
chain index 176–7
Chang, C-L. 33
Charneux 378–9
Chartier, R. 215, 218 n.13
Chaudhuri, K. N. 129 n.6
Chaudhuri, S. 129 n.6
Chen, B. 50 n.50
Chen, H. 48 n.23
Chennai (Madras) 106

childbirth 14, 277, 287, 289, 292, 297,
    303 n.30, 364, 374
China 2–3, 5, 10, 16, 18, 23–5, 30, 31–2, 33,
    36, 38–41, 43, 46, 55–6, 68 n.4, 69 n.13,
    72 n.46, 115, 121, *126*, 138, 173, 366 n.1,
    403–4, 406, 408, 410, 414, 417–18
  ancestors 5
  cooking methods 31, 38
  daily ration of vegetables 31
  demographic system 403
  droughts 46
  familial agricultural income 33–5
  female infanticide 404
  food 24
  grain price data 406
  gruel as cheap food 115
  Han banner populations 406
  income and consumption 32
  inland navigation 2
  life expectancy 414, 418
  male childhood mortality 412, 420–2
  male marriage 417
  meat and dairy consumption 26–32
  mortality rates 418–21
  nuptiality 415–18
  overpopulation 41
  population growth 138
  poverty 10
  price revolution 66
  real wages 18, 121–3
  restriction on foreign trade 3
  ship-building 43
  smoking habits 36
  spinning and weaving 41, 59, 62, 65
  state farm systems 408
  tax burden 72 n.48, 268
  travelling and pilgrimage 39
Chinese agriculture 28, 32, 34, 55
  average annual grain supply 34
  hog-derived fertilizer 29
  income distribution 33–5
  labourer income and expenditure 31–2
  protein intake 26–8
  Shenshi nongshu 26–7
  xiao shimin 34
Chinese capitalism 68 n.4, 69 n.10
Chinese gentry 33
cholera epidemics 283, 291, 330, 383
Choshi 79, 83–5, 87, *94–5*
Chōshū 89
Christianity 299
Chronicle of the Monastery of Cernik 302 n.15
Ch'uan, H.-S. 50 n.48
Cipolla, C. M. 218 n.13
Clark, G. 24, 160, 167 n.16, 218 n.5
Claverías, B. M. 219 n.21
Clermont 378
Coimbatore 104

Coleman, D. C. 124
Collett, D. 367 n.13
Colquhoun, P. 164
Columbus, C. 132, 245
commercialization 40, 48 n.28, 59, 79, 89, 212,
    281, 345, 362, 364–5, 405, 412, 429,
    435, 440
communicable diseases 232, 236, 244–6, 282
Compère, M. M. 218 n.15
complementary log–log regression 423 n.14
concubine 40
consumer durables and human capital 214, 216
consumer price index (CPI) 11–12, 80, 82, 113,
    115, 129 nn.3–4, 174–6
consuming goods 59
consumption revolution in Europe 199, 210
Copenhagen 309, 312, 341, 350
copper coins 59, 96 n.2
corvée labour 301 nn.7, 10
cost-of-living 6, 11, 146, 158–63, 166 n.1, 187
Cox proportional hazards model 357, 358
Craig, A. M. 49 n.44, 71 n.29
Crawcour, E. S. 129 n.4
Cressy, D. 219 nn.24, 27, 29
Crimea 255
Croatia 280, 283, 287–8, 298, 300 n.2–3
Croatian military recruits 283
crop area 57, 62, 71 n.24, 262, 269
Cunningham, H. 215

DaCruz 36, 49 n.37
Daoyi *407*, 408, 414, 416, 421–2, 423 nn.8–9,
    424 n.13
  central state farm systems 408
  marital fertility *413*, *415*, 422, 423 n.9
  mortality 418, *420*, 421
  nuptiality 415–17
Dasgupta, P. 19 n.1
Davis, M. 50 n.56, *143*
Daxingtun 418, 423 n.8
de Magalhães, J. P. 218 n.14, 219 nn.23–4
Denmark 307, 313–4
  GNP and real wages 307–9
  grain market 311–12
  harvest situation 314
  human stature 315–16
  mortality statistics 313–15
  population 308, 310
  real wage index (Copenhagen) 309–10
  standard of living of 310, 316
Dermigny, L. 49 n.36
Desai, A. V. 121, 129 n.5
de Vries, J. 39, 174, 179, 183–4, 191 nn.11, 17,
    199, 205, 218 n.3, 219 n.19
dharma 105
Diewert, E. 163
Dillen, K. 397
distributed lag model (DLM) 326, 335

dou 48 n.30, 64–6, 71 n.35
double-cropping 57–8, 60–2, 70 nn.17–20,
    22, 41
  crop *mu* 57, 60
  for one year 60–1
  new system 58, 69 n.11
  of rice 58, 69 nn.9, 11, 70 nn.17–20, 22
downward percolation effect of reading 213
Drava River 278
Dribe, M. x, 15, 366 n.10, 367 n.12
Durance River 203

early modern era 139
  decline of the real wage 185
  divergence of 164–5
  intra-national income inequality 132, 138–9
  life expectancy 133
  literacy and book ownership 210–11
  price history of 139
early modern Europe 181–2, 206
  consumption data 49 n.5
  decline in meat consumption 181
  decline in per capita GDP and real wages 77
  demand for industrial products 181
  introduction of the potato 182
  mincerian approach for human capital
    distribution 208
  price protection 160
East and West gaps 17–19
East Ardennes 373–4, 377–80, 382–4, 395–6
  demographic regimes and family
    systems 380–1
East Asia 5, 436, 456 n.14
East Belgium 379, 382, 384–5, 388, 395
East India Company 2, 101, 105, 107 n.5
Eastman, L. 49 n.44
economic stress 15–19, 362–4
Eden, F. M. *143*
Edo 78–9, 82–5, 88, *94–5*, 116
Eichholtz, P. M. A. 176–7, *191*
Elizaveta 271
El Niños 46, 50 n.56
Elsas, M. J. 175, 191 n.3
Elvin, M. 56, 68 n.5, 69 n.12
Engels, F. 341
Engel's law 37–8, 132, 139, 272 n.2
England 17–18, 24, 26, 32, 114, 128, 138, 160–1,
    163–5, 179, 187, 198, 201–2, 206, 210,
    212–13, 215–16, 218 n.14, 220 n.33, 227,
    229, 244, 285–6, 302 n.17, 319, 373
  Civil War 246
  falling-price goods 165
  food expenditures 32
  GDP per capita 198
  household expenditure data *140*, *143*
  housing rents 167 n.16
  inegalitarian era 165
  Industrial Revolution 175

England (*cont.*)
  literacy rates 202
  price index 180
  real income 118, 164
equilibrium trap 56, 61, 68 n.5
Eurasia Project on Population and Family
    History (EAP) 19 n.3, 342, 366 n.1, 373–4,
    385, 404, 423
Europe 1–2, 6, 10–13, 17–19, 23–7, 30–2, 36–41,
    111, 115, 138, 147, 165, 173, 175, 182, 184,
    199–201, 203, 210, 234, 240, 247, 249 n.7,
    299, 325
  Asia and *see under* Asia
  book revolution 210
  bread as chief food 115
  child labour 215
  consumer price index 115
  divergence in early modern prices 165
  educational revolution (1800) 201
  effects of declining real wages 199
  expansion and colonization 228, 243
  food consumption 10
  grain market 314
  illiteracy 203
  introduction of the potato 182
  literacy map 201, *202*
  mass education 201
  population growth 138
  pre-industrial 196–200, 203, 215
  product pattern of price movements 147
  reading and book publishing 211
  real wages *125–8*
  Revolt of 1572 184
  trickle down effect 210
European market 269, 311, 383
European Russia 261, *262*
event-history analysis 356, 411, 414, 417,
    420, 437, 440
  discrete-time 428, 437, 441, 443, 447
  of mortality and nuptiality (China) 409
  of out-migration 449

Faber, J. A. 186, 187
Fairbank, J. K. 49 n.44
Fairchilds, C. 218 n.6
falling-real-price products 158
Fan, S. 39
Fang, X. 31, 32, 59, 67, 68 n.2
Fang, Z. 70 n.18
farm labour productivity 55, 61, 63–6, 70 n.23
  double-cropping system 57–8, 60, 62
  female labour productivity 64–5
  multi-cropping system 61
  optimal farm size 61
  output per worker 64
Feenstra, R. C. 167 n.10
Feinstein, C. H. 173, 175
Feng, W. 18, 68 n.2

Fengtian prefecture 410
fertility response to economic stress 16, 283,
    342, 362–5, 367 n.5
fertilizer revolution 59, 69 n.13
feudal exploitation 72 n.46
feudal society 71 n.26
feudalism 299
Feuerwerker, A. 72 n.45
Finnish War (1808–9) 346
first marriage 285, 289, 409, 438–9, *442*,
    445–9, *446*, 451–2, 454, 457 n.29
First World War 77, 113, 116, 119, 138,
    247, 278, 397
Flanders 4, 374–5, 382
Florence 321, 325–6, 337 n.4, 338 n.10
Floud, R. 230, 248 n.4
Fogel, R. W. 247
food scarcity 133, 149, 166 n.3
Fornasin, A. x, 15
Fortune, R, 73 n.50
Fraga, V. 218 n.14
France 11–12, 25, 30, 161, 163–5, 198, 202, 204,
    206, 213, 215–16, 218 n.14, 220 n.33, 236,
    247, 248 n.5, 268, 272 n.1, 302 n.17
  education 204, 206
  educational expenses data 215
  height trends *231*, 236, 239, 247, 248 n.5
  household total expenditure *141*, *143*
  inegalitarian era 165
  life expectancy *134*
  literacy rates 202
  per capita food intake 24–5, 30
  price movements 164
  schooling for children 204
François, É. 201, 219 n.29
French Revolution 133
French War Era 166 n.2
Fujian 43, 49 n.38, 67
Fukushima prefecture 429
Furet, F. 212, 218 n.14, 220 n.34

Gaizhou 414, 418
Galloway, P. R. 187, 301 n.5, 314, 452
Gawthorp, R. 219 n.29
GDP *see* gross domestic product (GDP)
Gelabert, J. E. 218 n.14
Geng, W. 403
gentry class 33, 44
Germany 37, 206, 236, 238–9, 272 n.1, 280,
    285–6, 378, 386
  book publishing 220 n.31
  heights and health *231*, 236, 238–9
  literacy rates *202*
  meat consumption 30
Gernet, J. 67, 73 n.50
Ghent 244, 376, 388, 397
ghi 115
Gleser, G. C. 240

global colonization 246
global disease spread 243
global divergence in living standards 132
global divergence of real incomes 145–58
globalization 77, 133, 165, 236, 245, 299
Gohyaku River 429
gold coins 96 n.2
Golden Age 174, 178, 184, 187
Gonano, G. x, 15
Gouveia, A. C. 218 n.14
Gradiška Regiment 284, 302 n.14
grain prices 102, 149, 187, 269, 282,
    303 n.34
Grand Canal 45
Granet–Abisset, A-M. 219 n.17
Grantham, G. 47 n.6
Great Irish Famine 374
Gregory, A. S. 248 n.4
Grevet, R. 218 n.11, 219 n.20, 220 n.35
Gribble, J. D. B. 107 n.9
gross domestic product (GDP) 7–9, 12, 68 n.1,
    77, 86, 88–9, 111, 114, 173–4, 187, 196–7,
    199, 218 n.8, 228, 236–7, 245, 343
Grosseto 327
Guangdong 43, 49 n.38, 73 n.49
Guilkey, D. 456 n.15
Gullickson, A. x, 13–4
Guo, S. 46 n.3
Guosantun 423 n.8
Guthrie, H. 47 n.8

Habib, I. 106, 129 n.6
Habsburg 280, 299
Hagen, W. 160
Hajnal hypothesis 186
Halmstad 352, 358
Hamano, K. 455
Hamilton, E. J. 175, 191 n.3
Hammel, E. A. x, 13–14, 301 n.5
Han River 5, 42
Hanley, S. B. 455
härad 355
Harrell, S. 423 n.4
Hart, S. 218 n.14
Hartwell, R. 397 n.1
Harvey, A. C. 367 n.11, 397 n.4
Hasan, A. 129 n.6
Hau, M. 248 n.5
Hausman, J. 167 n.10
Hautes Fagnes 377, 383
Hayami, A. 428, 455
He, L. 72 n.41
health and height *see* height
health and welfare during
    industrialization 229, 239
health decline, possible 244–6
height 13–15, 233–4, 236, 238–9, 242
    and economic depression 236

and economic growth 230
and life expectancy 230
and public health policies 238
and urbanization 232–4
development of stature 261–70
male trends *241–2*, 248 n.4
pre-industrial 236
recovery 246–7
skeletal data 240
temporal patterns 234–7
herring 186, 188–9
Heston, A. W. 129 n.5
Ho, P. 67, 73 n.50
Hobsbawm, E. 397 n.1
Hodrick–Prescott (HP) filter 355, 367 n.11,
    397 n.4, 440
Hoffman, P. T. xi, 11–12, 46, *143*, 160
Hög 352, 358
Högberg, U. 302 n.19
hoku 439
Holland 12, 163–5, 167 n.16, 174–7,
    179–80, 186
    falling-price goods 165
    housing rents 167 n.16
    inegalitarian price movements 164–5
    price index 180
honbyakusho 434
Hong, H. 72 n.46
Hopkins, S. V. 32, 129 n.2, 166 n.7, 175,
    179, 181
Horeki famine 429–30
Horrell, S. 49 n.33, 215
Hoszowski, S. 191 n.3
Houdaille, J. 218 n.14
Household and Population Registers of
    the Eight Banner Han Chinese Army
    (*Hanjun baqi rending hukou ce*) 406
household landholding (*mochidaka* in *koku*) 434,
    440, 447, 454
housing rents 160, 163, 167 n.16
Houston, R. A. 205, 212, 218 n.10, 219 n.20,
    220 n.35
Huang, P. 56, 71 n.28, 72 n.46
Huberman, M. 24
Huddleston, W. 107 n.6
human capital 195, 200, 207, 213
    in early modern Europe 208
    mincerian approach 208
Human Development Index (HDI) 7–8,
    19 n.1, 200
human growth and biological deprivation 230
human welfare measurement 228–9
Humphries, J. 49 n.33, 215, 280
Hungary 202, 207, 244, 281, 297–8, 300 n.3

Iceland 243–4
illicit cohabitation 40
Ilova River 278

Imhof, A. E.　287
income–class differences in spending patterns 146
India 2, 4–5, 11, 17, 111–13, 115, 119–23, *125*, 173, 272 n.2
　agriculture 101–7
　early marriages 4
　modern capitalism 5
　real wages 17–18, 119–21
　rice as staple food 115
　wage comparisons *100*
industrialization 173–4, 195–6, 227–9, 233–7
　agricultural transformation 350
　effect on socio-economic performance 228
　health issues and exposure to diseases 227, 242, 242
　Lewisian model (Japanese) 90
　proto-industrialization 77, 124, 272, 375, 435, 441, 456 n.10
　rural industrialization 57, 59
　stages and heights *231*
　standard of living 173
　temporal patterns 234–7
Industrial Revolution 1, 12, 17, 113–14, 119, 123–4, 132, 165, 175, 195, 199, 227, 272, 373–6, 378, 383
　effect on GDP 114
　growth model 197
　health policies and well-being 238
　impact on rural economy 373–4
　in textiles 378
　living standards before 17, 111, 113, 123, 272
　proto-industrialization 77, 124, 272, 375, 435, 441, 456 n.10
infanticide 3, 18, 404, 416, 438, 445, 454
infant mortality 293, 296–7, 326, 330, 393, 409, 438, 443
International Scientific Committee on Price History 124, 146, 175
intra-village uxorilocal marriages *see* uxorilocal marriages
intra-village virilocal marriages *see* virilocal marriages
irrigation 4, 11, 43, 103, 105–6
Islam 105, 299
Italian State 325
Italy 18, 116, 120, 128, 218 n.4, 220 n.32, 327, 366 n.1
　agricultural almanacs 220 n.32
　literacy rates *202*
　overall mortality rate 18
　real wages 116, *120, 122*
　wheat price fluctuations *328*

Jacks, D. S. xi, 11
Jaeger, A. 367 n.11, 397 n.4

Japan 11–13, 16–19, 68, 73 n.50, 77–9, 82, 84–90, 96 n.1, 112–13, 115–16, 118–19, 124, *127*, 230, 232, 234, 237, 238–9, 366 n.1, 427–33, 435, 439, 445–6, 452–4
　cost of living 80, 85
　family farming and household landholding 433–5
　first marriage 439, 445, 446, 454
　heights and health 238
　land-improvement projects 86
　male childhood mortality 443
　male marriages 446–7, 447, 451, 457 n.29
　marital fertility 445
　marriage and migration 16, 453
　pre-industrial 436, 438
　real wages 18, 79, 85, 116–19
　regional and local socio-economic changes 435
　seclusion policy 96 n.1
　short-term economic stress 452
　status of women 17
　taxation data 433
　wage data 82
　wage labour 78
jenever 178
Jiangnan Region 30, 36, 55–73, 405
　agriculture/farming 30, 56–63, 69 n.12, 71 n.30
　centre of the industry 62
　increased labour productivity 63–6
　peasant standard of living 66–8
　population explosion 56
　quality of the peasants' diet 67
　regional specialization of agriculture 58
Jiaxing prefecture 29
Johansen, H. C. xi, 13–14
Jones, R. 48 n.21
Jörberg, L. 366 n.3
Jorgenson, D. 163

kalawedi 101, 106
Kamermans, J. A. 218 n.6
Kami-Kawarabayashi 80–1, 84, 87, 118, 129 n.4
Kanto 83–4, *94*
Kakeochi 439
kapitelstakster 310
kashira 83
Kävlinge 352, 358, 361
Kilmarnock 220 n.36
Kimpenerwaard 210
Kinai 78–83, 87, *90–3*, 96 n.3
King, G. *143*, 161, 164
Kitada, H. 69 n.11
Kito, H. 428
Knodel, J. 48 n.19, 287, 290
koku 86, 96 n.4, 432–3, 435, 440, 451, 455
kokudaka 86, 88, 432

Komlos, J. 191 n.2, 246, 248 nn.3, 5, 282, 301 n.6
Komlos–Kim method 260
Königsberg 311
Koriyama 429
Kostroma province 258
Kraus, R. 50 n.48
Krishnadeva Raya (1509–29) 105
Kuhn, P. 49 n.40
Kuijpers, E. 218 n.14
Kula, W. 160, 165 n.1
Kunitz, S. 248 n.1
Kurosu, S. xi, 16, 456
Kuznet's curve 77
Kyoho famine (1732–3) 429, 433
Kyoto 78, 80, 116, 118, 129 n.4, 455 n.3

labour productivity 11, 70 n.23, 71 n.30
  definition 63
  four methods for increasing 70 n.23
  modern industrial labour 71 n.30
  see also farm labour productivity
Land of Herve 373–4, 377–8, 382–4, 386, 388, 392–6, 398 n.6, 382
  demographic regimes and family systems 380–1
  demographic responses to price fluctuations 393
  economy, dairy production 398 n.6
  model of livestock breeding 383
  mortality 394
  municipalities 378
  population 382–3, 386, 392–4, 397, 398 n.6
Landes, D. 5, 102
land-intensive imports 41, 44
La Niñas 46
Larquié, C. 219 n.20
Laslett, P. *143*
latifundia 281
Lavely, W. 5, 18, 48 n.19
Lee, J. Z. 16–19, 48 n.19, 50 n.45, 68 n.2, 403–4
Lee, R. D. 319, 423 n.1
Leeuwenhorst 176, 188
Leiden 186, 188–9
Lesger, C. 176, 177, *177*
Levin, P.A. xi, 11
Li, B. xi, 10–11, 16, 30, 42, 50 n.45, 69 n.11, 70 nn.17, 71 n.24, 72 n.38, 121, 403
Li, L. 43
Li, W. 69 n.10
Li, Z. 48 n.20
Liaodong Peninsula 405, 408
Liaoning 403, 405, 410, 412, 421
  economic stress 19
  Fengtian prefecture 410

food price jumps 16
mortality and fertility response to rice price change 16–17, 19
Liège 378, 382
life expectancy 9, 15, 18, 133–6, 230–2, *231*, 345–6, *380*
Lindert, P. H. xi, 11, 24, 32–3, 48 n.25, 167 nn.14–15, 175, 191 n.9, 373 fn.
Lis, H. 30, 47 n.14
literacy 9, 201–3, 206–7, 216
  and access to credit 219
  and book ownership 211
  and social status 204
  historical regions 218 n.13
Little Ice Age 246–7
Liu, T.-J. 423 n.4
Livi-Bacci, M. 247
Livorno 327, 330
livre tournois 215, 220 n.37
logistic regression 289, 294, 298, 412, 424 n.14, 437–8
log–log regression 412, 424 n.14
London 17, 113–14, 116–20, 124, 160, 167 n.13, 191 n.6, 197, 206, 211, 244
Loudon, I. 302 n.17
Lundsjö, O. 349

Maat, G. J. R. 185, 191 n.15
Mackenzie General 107 n.8
Maddison, A. 8, 68 n.1, 69 n.7, 86–7, 166 n.2, 191 n.1, 217 n.1
Madurai 104
mahanadu 103
Malanima, P. 218 n.6
Malmöhus County 344, 346, 349, 355
Malthus, T. R. 3–5, 10, 18, 299, 379, 403, 423 nn.1–2
Malthusian responses 14, 57, 246, 278
Malthusian system 41, 44, 375, 382–3, 395–6
Manchuria 42–3, 73 n.49
Manchus 33, 407
man–land ratio 61–2
Mann, S. 49 n.43
manor serfs 266–7
mantal 352–4, 366 n.8
Marchesini, D. 218 n.14
Maremma 321, 324, 332, 336
marital fertility/reproduction 421, 438
market price scales (*markegångssättningen*) 354–6
market-producing peasants 345, 349, 353
Marks, R. 43, 46 n.3, 49 n.38
Markussen, I. 218 n.11
Marquilhas, R. 218 n.14
Marx, K. 4–6, 18, 341
Massie, J. 164
McEvedy, C. 48 n.21

McKeown, T. 247
Meere, J. M. M de 191 n.16
Meiji 77, 82, 85, 89
Mendels, F. 375
Menzies, N. 50 n.50
Merrill, A. L. 48 n.16
Meuvret, J. 374
Middle Ages 12–13, 186, 218 n.5, 241–3, 244–7
Mills, C.W. 277
Milt-Ward, D. J. 47 n.8
Ming dynasty 25, 29–30, 58–9, 62–4, 66, 69 n.10,
    71 n.24, 72 n.48
minimum subsistence level 66–8
Mironov, B. xi, 13, 15
miso 87
Mitch, D. F. 213, 215
Miyamoto, M. 457 n.24
mizunomi 434
mochidaka 434, 440
modernization 45, 174, 229–30, 234, 236, 271,
    285, 373, 384, 395
Mokyr, J. 48 n.22
monme 79–80
Moor, T. de 188–190
Moosvi, S. 129 n.5
Moreland, W. H. 107 n.1
Morineau, M. 219 n.19
Morrisson, C. 164, 166 n.2
mu 57–8, 61, 63, 69 n.6, 71 n.24
Muellbauer, J. 7
Mukerjee, R. 129 n.5
multi-cropping 61, 63
Munro, T. 104, n.15 106, 107 n.9
Murphy, J. 456 n.15
Mysore 102, 105

nadu 103
Nakamura, S. 86
nan geng nu zhi (man ploughs, woman weaves
    division of labour) 42, 60, 62–3, 71 n.26
Napoleonic Wars 30, 247
Nawab of Arcot 106
nawabiki 434
Nederlandsche Prijsgeschiendenis 176
the Netherlands 12, 17, 25,30, 39, 174–6,
    179, 185–8, 196–9, 201–3, 206, 210,
    218 n.14, 219 n.19, 220 n.33, 230,
    236, 239, 272 n.1,388
  book-holding 210
  city development 198
  economic stagnation 186
  household expenditure data *142, 144*
  meat consumption 186
  price data 188–9
net nutrition 243–4
Neufchâteau 378
Neven, M. xi, 16
Nicolas, J. M. 219 n.30, 220 n.35

Nicolas, S. J. 219 n.30, 220 n.35
Nihonmatsu 429, 433–5, 455
Niita 429–30, 432, 435–6, 439, 455–6
Nilsson, A. 205, 219 n.20
ninbetsu-aratame-cho (NAC) 427, 430,
    435–7, 456
non-essential consumption 36–40
Noordegraaf, L. 182–4, 191 n.19
North America 1, 234, 383
northern Europe 12–13, 187, 240,
    241–2, 244–5, 247
Norway 312

Oddy, D. J. 31, 48 n.17
Oeppen, J. E. 166 n.4
Ohkawa, K. 116, 129 n.4
Onisto, N. 191 n.15
Opium War 44
oriental agriculture 4
oriental despotism 5, 102
Oriental Mode of Production 4
Oris, M. xi, 16
O'Rourke, K. H. 166 n.2
Osaka 78–81, 88–9, 96 n.2, 116, 440, 457 n.24
Osborne, A. 50 n.50
over-investment 12
Oxford wages 116–118
Ouzouf, M. 212, 218 n.14, 220 n.34

Pan, M.-T. 24, 26, 31, 43, 46 n.1, 50 n.53
Paris 25, 113, 160, 163, 197, 204, 210, 212, 244
Parker, G. 218 n.10, 219 n.29
Parthasarathi, P. xiii, 6, 11, 107 n.11, 111–12,
    121, 173
Pengelly, R. *143*
Pereira-Roque, J. 374
Perkins, D. 28–9, 46 n.4, 47 n.13, 50 n.48, 69
    n.13, 71 n.29
Persia 267
Persson, K. G. 191 n.14
Peter I 268, 271
Pettersson, L. 205
Phelps Brown, E. A. 23, 32, 129 n.2, 166 n.7,
    175, 179, 181
Phelps Brown and Hopkins (PBH)
    indices 23, 175
physiological variables of age and parity 297
Pietist movement 218 n.16
Pisa 321, 327
Pistoia 326
Place, L. 101, 103, 106
plebeian comsumption 39
Poisson regression 412
Poland 145, 149, 191 n.3, 196, 198, 255, 268
poll-tax registers (*mantalslängder*) 354
Pomeranz, K. xiii, 6, 10, 16, 48
    n.25, 49 n.33, 50 n.54, 99, 111,
    129 n.1, 137, 403, 405, 422

population growth 56, 69 n.8, 72 n.46, 138
  controlling 69 n.8
  pauperisation of peasants 72 n.46
population pressure 72 n.46
porragoodies 101
Porter, R. 218 n.6
Portugal 124, 202, 212, 218 n.4
Post, J. 47 n.7
Posthumus, N. W. 176, 188–9, 191 n.3
Pot, G. P. M. 177
potato cultivation 237
Prakash, G. 101, 129 n.6
Prato 327
pre-industrial heights 236
pre-modern economic growth 90
Pribram, A. F. 175, 191 n.3
productive goods 59
proletarianization 77, 89, 349
proletarians 212
protein intake 26–8, 30
protein portion 27, 30–1
proto-industrialization 77, 124
Provence 203, 212, 219 n.21
Prussia 73 n.15, 218 n.16, 268, 388
Pumao nongzi 71 n.34
purchasing power parity (PPP) 197, 217 n.2
pycarries 101–2

Qianlong 73 n.50
Qing 26, 30, 45, 48 n.28, n.31,
    49 n.34, 58–9, 62–6, 69 n.12,
    72 n.48
Qing dynasty 44, 403–5, 408
Qing Imperial lineage 421
Qi, Y. 72 n.49
Quan, H. 72 n.46
quasi-hedonic price index 182
Quéniart, J. 218 n.10
quzhong fa 69 n.9

Rappaport, S. 191 n.6
Ravenna 330
Rawski, T. 43
Rayavacakamu 105
Razzell, P. 48 n.19, 133, 247
Read, A. 101
real-income inequality, 163–4
real incomes 11, 132–3, 145–58, 161
real wage 9, 11–15, 17–18, 79–88, 113–14,
    117–18, 121
  agricultural and non-agricultural
    occupations *85*
  and output growth 85–8
  farm labourers *117*
  farm workers, CPI deflator *122–3*
  skilled and unskilled occupations *84*
real wage–GDP gap 89
Reed, B. 33–4, 48 n.26

Reher, D. S. 319, 338 n.7
Reis, J. xiii, 12, 218 n.4
Reischauer, E. O. 49 n.44
relative-price trends 148
repeated-rent index 176, 177, *191*
residence–ownership effect 167 n.18
Rijeka 281
Rostow's stages of economic growth 229
Rotterdam 187
Rowe, W. 49 n.43
rural industrialization 59
  and labour supply 57
  see also industrialization
Russia 13–15, 138
  assessment of stature 256–7
  literacy rates 258
  major grains and exports *263*, 269, 271
  output/seed ratios 263
  per capita national income 255
  population growth 138
  pre-industrial 256, 272
  price revolution 269
  process of westernization 268
  taxes and obligations 13, 263–4, *264*, 266, 280
  well-being of population 256, 272
Russian army 257, 259
  height requirements *257*, *259*, 271
  nineteenth century recruits 259
  wars 267–8, 271
ryo 79, 80, 84

Saito, O. xiii, 12, 84, 129 n.4
Saito, R. 428, 457
saké 87
samurai 86, 88, 433
Sandberg, L. G. 247, 348
Sanderson, M. 218 n.14
Sano, Y. 82
Sart 377–9, 382–4, 386–7, 389, 391–2, 394, 396
  demographic responses to oats and rye 389
  peasants 388
  rural–urban migration 391
Saugnieux, J. 218 n.10
Sava River 278, 280–1, 290
Scalone, F. 330
Scania 15, 342–3, 345, 352, 354–5
Scanian Demographic Database 352, 366 n.7
Schaïk, R. van 191 n.7
Schoenmakers, J. T. 183
Schofield, R. S. 48 n.19, 207, 218 n.14, 286–7
Schollier, P. 375–6, 388, 397 n.1
Scholliers, E. 191 n.20
Second World War 69 n.7, 119, 232
Ségalen, M. 384
Sen, A. 7, 19 n.2, 191 n.13, 352
Senese area 332, 334, 336
Seraing 375, 378
serfs 267, 280–3, 296–7, 301 n.7

sericulture 72 n.46, 455 n.4
Servais, P. 377
Shaanxi 45
Shammas, C. 24, 32, 48 n.22, 179, 220 n.38
Shanghai 72–3 n.49, 124
Shenshi nongshu 26–8, 31
Shenyang 16, 405, 407–8, 416, 418, 422
shi 59, 63–6, 70 n.16
Shimbo, H. 80
Shimomoriya 429–30, 432, 434–6, 439,
    455 n.5, 456 nn.11, 13, 17
ship-building 43
Shiue, C. 47 n.6
shumon-aratame-cho (SAC) 456
Sichuan 33–4, 42
Siena 321, 323, 326
silkworm raising 59, 63
silver coins 79, 112–13
Simonis 378
Sireköpinge 352, 358
Skinner, G. W. 50 n.48, 457
Slavonia 13–14, 278, 284, 300 n.3
    background mortality (BM) 278, 285,
        288–9, 302 n.17
    data 285, 289–90, 301 n.5
    economic and social stress 278, 282–4
    maternal mortality (MM) 278, 285–92
    reconstituted records 284
    stillbirths 286, 288–90
Slesnick, D. 163
Slicher van Bath, B.H. 175
Smith, A. 2–3, 6, 18, 102
Smith, T. C. 457 n.27
Smithian dynamics 42
Smithian growth 77, 90, 124
Snyder, W. 164, 166 n.2
Söderberg, J. 349
sol 220 nn.33, 37
Soltow, L. 191 n.12
Soly, C. 30, 47 n.14
Sommer, M. 48 n.28, 49 nn.40, 43
Songjiang Prefecture 62–6, 72 n.42
Songyi, G. 24, 70 n.20
sorghum 410–12, 414–15, 418
sous 220 n.37
Southern Europe 17, 117, 124, 203,
    242, 244
    loss of dynamism 203
    real wage gap 17, 117
    stagnation 17
    standard of living in urban workers 124
South India 11
    cattle and dairy income 100
    cotton cultivation 103–4
    cotton textile manufacturing 99
    labour market and the standard of
        living 100–2
    mobility of products 101

price of grain 102
wage comparison data *100*
Soviet Union 272 n.2 *see also* Russia
soybean cake *see* bean cakes as fertilizers
Spain 175, 199, 202, 272 n.2
Spooner, F. 166 n.7
Spufford, M. 218 n.9, 219 n.24, n.29
Srem 278
stagnationist approach to GDP
    per capita 197–8
standard of living 3–4, 6–12, 14–16,
    18–19, 23, 27, 40–2, 45–6, 55, 66–8,
    72 n.46, 112, 185, 196, 214
    and long-term growth in Europe 196–200
    conceptualizing and measuring 6–10
    development of 185
    divergence in Europe 113–14
    durable goods 214, 216
    economic indicators of 10
    material consumption approach 199, 200,
        218 n.8
    nineteenth-century decline 40–6
    Malthusian conception 68
state farm systems 408–9, 412–14, 418, 421–2
stature variation *see* height
Steckel, R. H. xiii, 13–14, 230, 247, 248 n.2,
    272, 348
Stephens, W. B. 218 n.10, 219 n.24
    286, 288–90
Stone, R. 143
Strauss, G. 219 n.29
Suzhou Prefecture 67
Suzuki, Y. 84
Svärd, B. 219 n.20
Svensson, P. 205
Sweden 15, 18, 205, 218 n.16, 230, 237, 239,
    244, 247, 255, 267–8, 272 n.1, 285–7, 302
    n.17, 341–5, 348–51, 366 n.1
    agriculture 343–5, 349, 353, 362, 364
    child mortality 286, 348
    data 286
    Human Development Index 345
    level of literacy 345
    mortality response 357–62
    real wages for agricultural workers 344

taccavi 104–6
tael 33, 112
Taiping Rebellion 25, 62
Taiwan 25, 49 n.38, 67
Tambraparni River 104
Tanjore 102–3, 105
Tao, X. 71 n.25
Tempo famine 81, 429, 435, 451
Tenmei famine 429, 432, 435, 451
Thames River 244
Theebe, M. A. J. 176–7, *191*
Thirty Years War 246

Tilly, C. 47 n.6
Tirunelveli 104
tōji 83
Tokugawa Japan 77–9, 86, 88, 112,
  118–19, 427–8, 430, 432–3, 436, 445,
  454–7
  agrarian economy and family farming 428, 434
  population changes and economic
    conditions 428–9
  shogunate (tax rice) 433
Tokyo 78, 455 *see also* Edo
Tomasevich, J. 301 n.12
Torras, J. 218 n.6, 218 n.7
Toutain, J. C. 25, 30, 48 n.16
transactions technology 205
trinity pattern 60, 63
Trotter, M. 240
Tsuya, N. O. xiv, 16, 456–7
Turkey 255, 267–8, 299
Tuscan Civic State 338 n.13
Tuscan Public Records Office 320
Tuscany 15, 18, 319–20, 326–7, 329, 335
  characteristic features 320–4
  early childhood mortality 326
  Grand Duchy 319, *322*, 323, 325–6, 330, 336
  living conditions 329
  population 327, 329
  traditional sharecropping 335
Tuscany of the river (*Toscana del fiume*) 321,
  323–4, 334, 336

Ubelaker, D. H. 248 n.6
Umemura, M. 80
United Kingdom 166 n.2, 272 n.1, 230,
  234, 238
  adverse effects of trade 238
  benchmark estimates of inequality 66 n.2
  cloth output and consumption *37*
United Nations 232, 423 n.3
United States 230, 234, 235, 238–40, 244, 247,
  249 n.8, 272 n.1
urbanization 57, 198, 237, 239, 245
Utrecht 188

Valk, G. 191 n.19
van den Eeckhout, P. 375
Vandermotten, C. 376
Van Der Werf, Y. 218 n.5
van der Woude, A. 179, 183, 191 n.11,
  205, 219 n.19
van Deursen, A. T. 219 n.20, n.29
Vandewattyne, P. 376
van Riel, A. 179
van Santen, H. 129 n.6
van Zanden, J. L. xiv, 145, 164–5, 166 n.7,
  167 n.12, n.14, 187, 191 n.3, n.5, n.21,
  198, 199, 218 n.4
Vasco da Gama 99, 132, 245

Verlinden, C. 167 n.16, 191 n.3
Vermeer, E. 50 n.55
Verviers 377–9, 382, 384, 386
  merchant clothiers 377–8
  price information 388, 398 n.5
  railroads 382
  spinning machines and textile industries 379,
    382, 384
  urban markets 382
Vesdre River 377
Vesdre valley 379
Vikings 243–4
Vooruit 388
Vovelle, M. 219 n.17, n.21

Wachter, K. W. 248 n.4
wage–GDP ratio 77
wage–rent ratio 88
wages 2, 8, 10, 17, 34, 66, 80, *100*, 217 n.2
  see also real wages
wakamono 83
Wales 164, 302 n.17
  real income 164
  house hold expenditure data *140*, 143
  housing rents 167, 7.16
Walker, K. 70 n.22
Wallonia 376
Wang, F. 5, 423 n.1
Wang, J. 68 n.2
Wang, Y.-C. 50 n.46
War of the Roses 246
Washbrook, D. 107 n.4
Watt, B. K. 48 n.16
Weale, M. 19 n.1
Weatherill, L. 143, 218 n.6
Wei, J. 66
weighting schemes and new
    products 179–83
Weir, D. R. 247
West Germany 272 n.2
Western Europe 1, 10, 195, 217 n.1
White, T. D. 248 n.6
Will, P.-E. 24, 47 n.6
Williamson, J. 33, 48 n.25, 79, 82, 88,
    129 n.4, 166 n.1, 166 n.2,
    167 n.14, 175
Wittfogel, K. A. 5
Wong, R. B. 5, 18, 24, 47 n.6, 48 n.19,
    73 n.50, 103
the World Bank 423 n.3
Wrigley, E. A. 48 n.19, 66
Wu, C. 48 n.29, 50 n.50

xiao suiuin 34
Xingshi yinyuan zhuan 49 n.35
Xu, D. 48 n.29, 50 n.50
Xu, X. 71 n.27, 72 n.38
Xtregar procedure 338 n.11

Yamamura, K. 129 n.4
yamen 33–4
Yan, Y. 49 n.42
Yangtze Valley 115, 121, 123
Yangzi Delta 23–9, 31, 39–42,
    44, 55
  corn-planting 44
  land-intensive imports 44
  living standards 42
  spinning an weaving 41
  timber exports 41–2
Yasuba, Y. 96 n.3
Yellow River 44–5
yen 80

Yingkou 405, 409, 422
Yun, B. 218 nn.6–7

zadruga 284
Zagreb 281, 300 n.4
Zeeland 186
Zhang, H. 72 n.42
Zhang, L. 70 n.18, 71 n.25
Zhejiang 36, 44, 67, 70 nn.18, 19
  cropping systems 70 nn.18, 19
  deforestation 44
  silk wear 67
  smoking 36
Zoričič, M. 301 n.12